THE AMERICAN CONSTITUTION

THE AMERICAN CONSTITUTION

Third Edition

C. Herman Pritchett
University of California, Santa Barbara

McGraw-Hill Book Company
New York   St. Louis   San Francisco   Auckland   Bogotá   Düsseldorf
Johannesburg   London   Madrid   Mexico   Montreal   New Delhi
Panama   Paris   São Paulo   Singapore   Sydney   Tokyo   Toronto

THE AMERICAN CONSTITUTION

234567890MAMM783210987

This book was set in Times Roman by National ShareGraphics, Inc.
The editors were Lyle Linder and Barry Benjamin; the cover was
designed by Joseph Gillians; the production supervisor was Charles Hess.
The Maple Press Company was printer and binder.

Library of Congress Cataloging in Publication Data

Pritchett, Charles Herman, date
  The American Constitution.

  Includes indexes.
  1. United States—Constitutional law. I. Title.
KF4550.P7   1977   342'.73'03   76-16102
ISBN 0-07-050877-1

For Jeanie and Philip

CONTENTS

PREFACE

Charles Evans Hughes once observed that the Constitution means what the Supreme Court says it means. This book is an analytical examination of what the Supreme Court has said the American Constitution means. All American judges, both state and federal, have the power to interpret and apply constitutional provisions when relevant to the controversies before them. Only a minute fraction of these rulings rise to the level of the Supreme Court for final decision, but in that number are decisions of the most profound significance for the American nation. The great prestige of the Court is largely due to its accepted position as ultimate interpreter of the Constitution. The judgments of the Court are set forth in reasoned opinions which vary greatly in quality but which at their best may be gems of forensic skill and occasionally even noble literature. With only fifteen chief justices and eighty-six associate justices on the Court since 1789, the impact of individual judicial minds upon constitutional development becomes interestingly visible.

The proper use of this great judicial power has been one of the continuing controversies in American political life. Beginning with Jefferson's attack on Chief Justice Marshall's decisions supporting the authority of the new federal system, there has been a "Court fight" about once every generation, in which the right of nine life-tenured judges to declare basic public policies has been reconsidered. This work, which was first published in 1959, appears in its third edition at a time when the Court is in a period of transition from the activism and inventive assertiveness of the Warren Court to the more restrained and limited conception of the judicial role characteristic of the Burger Court. While some significant changes in constitutional doctrine occur during such periods of reorientation, experience has demonstrated that the pressure for constitutional continuity is very persuasive. The Court emerges as a major rationalizing and stabilizing force, with the awesome responsibility of preserving the great structural and liberating principles of the Constitution as a guide for political actors and citizens in the American republic.

C. Herman Pritchett

THE
AMERICAN
CONSTITUTION

The Making of the Constitution

"By constitution," wrote Lord Bolingbroke in 1733, "we mean, whenever we speak with propriety and exactness, that assemblage of laws, institutions and customs, derived from certain fixed principles of reason, directed to certain fixed objects of public good, that compose the general system, according to which the community hath agreed to be governed." In making this definition, Bolingbroke was naturally thinking mainly of the English constitution, but in fact his statement accorded with the traditional understanding which, as McIlwain says, applied the term "constitution" to the "substantive principles to be deduced from a nation's actual institutions and their development." [1]

The latter part of the eighteenth century, however, brought a new concept of "constitution" into existence. The French and American Revolutions introduced as an essential governmental instrument the written constitution. The general system under which the community agreed to be governed was not, under the new regime, to be left to evolution and deduction. The "laws, institutions and customs" were not to be a heterogeneous assemblage. The fixed principles of reason, the fixed objects

---

[1] Charles H. McIlwain, *Constitutionalism Ancient and Modern* (Ithaca, N.Y.: Cornell University Press, 1940), p. 3.

of the public good, were to be stated specifically in a formal basic document.

To one accustomed to the older view of constitutions, this was a disturbing departure. The Englishman Arthur Young, writing in 1792, spoke with contempt of the French idea of a constitution—"a new term they have adopted; and which they use as if a constitution was a pudding to be made by a recipe." To an Englishman it was obvious that a constitution could not be made; it had to grow.

Actually, of course, constitutions can combine both qualities. The American Constitution was made in the summer of 1787 and has been growing ever since.[2] While many influences went into its making, the Constitution was shaped most directly by the political experience of the Revolutionary period and the painful lessons learned in attempting to operate a government under the Articles of Confederation from 1781 to 1789.

THE POLITICAL THEORY OF THE REVOLUTIONARY PERIOD

The Declaration of Independence has been generally regarded as the cornerstone of American ideas about government and the preeminent statement of American political theory.[3] The basic conceptions had obviously come from Locke, but the doctrines were sharpened and intensified by the experience of resistance to British rule. These principles were so much a part of American thinking that the Declaration referred to them as "self-evident." In addition to the Declaration, the state constitutions adopted between 1776 and 1780 abound in statements of the current political theory.

The first principle of the political thought of the time was that men are by nature endowed with certain inalienable rights. This conception posited the existence of a state of nature antedating the establishment of civil government. In this primeval condition all men were free, in the sense that they were subject to no one, and equal in the right to rule themselves. A body of natural rights belonged to them as men, including the right to "life, liberty, and the pursuit of happiness." These rights not only antedated the existence of government; they were superior to it in authority. As John Dickinson expressed it, "Our liberties do not come from charters; for these are only the declaration of preexisting rights. They do not depend on parchments or seals; but come from the King of Kings and Lord of all the earth."

The exercise of coercive power by governments over men born free and equal could be justified only by the consent of the governed. The process as hypothesized by the Massachusetts Bill of Rights was that "the body politic is formed by a voluntary association of individuals: it is a social compact by which the whole people covenants with each citizen, and each citizen with the whole people, that all shall be governed by certain laws for the common good." The exact nature of the contract on which government was based or the circumstances under which it was entered into were little discussed, but the concept was given a sense of reality by the

[2] The principal constitutional history is Alfred H. Kelly and Winfred A. Harbison, *The American Constitution* (New York: W. W. Norton & Company, Inc., 4th ed., 1970).
[3] See Carl L. Becker, *The Declaration of Independence: A Study in the History of Political Ideas* (New York: Alfred A. Knopf, Inc., 1942).

numerous written compacts which had figured in American development, especially the Mayflower Compact of 1620 and the colonial charters. The slogan "no taxation without representation" was a particular application of the consent theory, with deep roots in English constitutional history.

Government is created by contract to serve the welfare of the people. To quote again the Massachusetts document, the end of government is "to secure the existence of the body politic, to protect it, and to furnish the individuals who compose it with the power of enjoying in safety and tranquility their natural rights, and the blessings of life." A government which fails to serve the ends for which it was set up has breached the contract under which it was established and forfeited the loyalty of its citizens. Thus the right of revolution, obviously fundamental to legitimizing the American action, was defended. The Declaration of Independence stated the case as follows: "Whenever any form of government becomes destructive of these ends, it is the right of the people to alter or to abolish it, and to institute new government, laying its foundation on such principles and organizing its powers in such form, as to them shall seem most likely to effect their safety and happiness."

The consequences of these basic political ideas quickly became visible in the constitutions adopted by the new states. Because of the contract theory, there was a widespread insistence that the constitutions be adopted by conventions especially charged with that duty, instead of by the regular legislatures, and that the draft constitutions be submitted to the voters for approval. Nine of the twelve constitutions adopted by 1778 were drawn up by this method.

Governmental power was limited in several ways. The royal governors had been the symbol of tyranny, and so the executive office in the new constitutions was deliberately weakened, while the legislature, symbol of resistance to foreign rule, was strengthened. In eight states the governor was chosen by the legislature, he had only a one-year term in ten states, his appointing power was generally limited, and he had the veto power in only three states. The one-year rule was common for all officials, not only for governors; as John Adams said, "Where annual elections end, there tyranny begins."

The separation of powers doctrine was also vigorously professed, though the imbalance between the legislature and executive was rather inconsistent with this theory. The Massachusetts formulation earned fame by its doctrinaire quality: "In the government of this commonwealth, the legislative department shall never exercise the executive and judicial powers, or either of them: the executive shall never exercise the legislative and judicial powers, or either of them: the judicial shall never exercise the legislative and executive powers, or either of them: to the end it may be a government of laws and not of men." Other restrictions were sought to be achieved by clear subordination of the military to the civil power, by decentralization of governmental functions, and by bills of rights which forbade governmental interference in certain fields of individual activity. Eight states had such bills of rights, their principles derived largely from the English common law as expounded by Blackstone.

The democratic theory professed in the new constitutions was not consistently practiced, however. Under the colonial government the lower classes had been rather generally excluded from political life. The Revolutionary movement for a time gave promise of bringing the back-country folk and the unfranchised workers into the stream of politics, but actually the circle of power-holders was little changed in the new state governments.[4] Property and religious qualifications for officeholding were general. Indeed, property, religious, and racial limitations were seemingly not regarded as inconsistent with the rights of man or the principles of political philosophy so eloquently stated in the Declaration of Independence, and the exclusion of women was taken for granted.

THE POST-REVOLUTIONARY EXPERIENCE

The American Revolution was conducted by the Continental Congress, composed of delegates from the various states, which met in session after session from 1774 to 1781. It performed the functions of a *de facto* government—raising, directing, and financing armies, sending and receiving diplomatic agents, entering into treaties with foreign countries. But the people of the states did not conceive that they had surrendered any of their rights to the Congress, and no state government felt bound by its decisions.

It was generally agreed that something more effective in the way of intercolonial organization was required. On June 7, 1776, after Richard Henry Lee had moved his resolution in favor of a declaration of independence, he offered a second one proposing a permanent confederation. A committee was appointed on June 12 with John Dickinson as chairman. The committee's major difficulties had to do with whether the states would be represented equally or in proportion to population, how contributions to the general treasury would be apportioned, and what disposition would be made of the claims several states were making to lands stretching back into the interior of the country. The Articles were not adopted and sent to the states until November, 1777. Ratification by every state was required to make them binding. The twelfth state signed in February, 1779, but Maryland was adamant, and did not agree until March 1, 1781, at which time the Articles came into effect.

The framework of government set up by the Articles was quite unlike that of the states. Virtually all functions were concentrated in a single legislative chamber, called a Congress. There was no second branch of the legislature and no separation of executive from legislative powers. Congress was to appoint such committees and civil officers as might be needed to carry on executive work, and it could provide courts only for the limited purposes of dealing with disputes between states and captures and felonies on the high seas.

The authority of Congress did not rest on the people, but on the state legislatures which had created it. Each state legislature chose and paid its delegates to Congress, and each state had one vote. A two-thirds vote of the state delegations was required for the adoption of important measures, and amendments to the Articles required the unanimous consent of the states.

---

[4] Charles A. Beard, *An Economic Interpretation of the Constitution of the United States* (New York: The Macmillan Company, 1913, 1935); Forrest McDonald, *We the People: The Economic Origins of the Constitution* (Chicago: University of Chicago Press, 1958).

The Articles did specify certain rules of interstate comity to which the states were pledged. But the essential powers necessary to an effective central government were denied to the Confederation. Congress could not levy taxes; it could only make a "requisition" on each state for its share of the estimated monetary needs of the union. Congress could not regulate interstate commerce; and although it could make commercial treaties with foreign nations, the states felt free to retaliate against countries which discriminated against their trade. Finally, Congress could not act directly on the citizens; it had to depend on the state governments for the execution of its measures. The Confederation could scarcely be called a government. As the Articles truthfully stated, it was a league of friendship entered into by sovereign states.

As for organizational arrangements, certain executive officers were immediately established. In fact, a secretary for foreign affairs, responsible to the Congress, had been created before the Articles were finally ratified, and also the offices of superintendent of finance and secretary at war. Congress chose a presiding officer with the title of president. A federal prize court had been created in 1780, and it was continued and regularized after the adoption of the Articles. The provision of the Articles for adjudicating disputes between states involved a much more cumbersome arrangement. States in dispute might by joint consent, through the Congress as intermediary, choose commissioners to decide the dispute.

In spite of its limited authority over internal affairs, the Confederation did achieve some successes. The Bank of North America was chartered by Congress in 1781, though the fact that the Articles gave no authority to grant charters of incorporation led the bank to secure a new charter from Pennsylvania. Preparations for the government of the new lands to the west led to adoption of the famous Northwest Ordinance of 1787, applying to the area between the Ohio and the Mississippi. The ordinance provided for the eventual division of this land into from three to five states. In the meantime the territory was to be governed directly by officials chosen by Congress.

In other areas Congress was less successful at temporizing solutions for the problems of the Confederation. Attempts to negotiate commercial treaties with England, France, and Spain failed, in part at least because of doubt whether the states would feel bound by any such treaties. As for internal trade, the rivalries of the states led to various forms of discriminatory taxation. The situation of New Jersey, whose goods came in through New York on one side and Philadelphia on the other, led to Madison's famous comparison of the state to a cask tapped at both ends.

The public finances were very nearly hopeless. During the first two years under the Articles, Congress requisitioned 10 million dollars from the states and received less than 1.5 million dollars. There were no funds to pay interest on the debt, which actually rose after the war was over. Redemption of the worthless Continental currency was impossible. Speculators bought at a heavy discount the certificates of indebtedness issued during hostilities to pay for necessary supplies. Robert Morris, superintendent of finance, resigned in 1786, not wishing, he said, to be a "minister of injustice."

With Congress incapable of dealing with the economic ills of the country, pressure fell on the state legislatures. The most widespread demand was for relief from the burden of debts incurred during the Revolutionary inflation, by state issuance of legal tender paper and by various forms of moratoria on payment of debts. The paper money forces got a majority for their inflationary program in seven state legislatures. When these forces were defeated in Massachusetts, farmers under the lead of Daniel Shays resorted to violence, breaking up court sessions trying debt cases and attempting to seize arms from the government arsenal at Springfield.

Shays' Rebellion was most effective in convincing the conservative and the propertied that there were serious defects in the government both of the states and the Confederation. The Revolutionary enthusiasm for the legislature as the dominant branch of the government had diminished. Now responsible citizens were looking for some way of checking legislatures which, as Madison said, were drawing all power into their "impetuous vortex." In most states the governor was still too weak for this purpose. Here and there were the beginnings of a system of judicial review of legislation. But the only effective control over state radicalism appeared to be a strengthening of the central government. In a paper written in the spring of 1787, Madison, concerned about the absence of any "guarantee to the States of their constitutions and laws against internal violence," thought that establishing central government control over "the internal vicissitudes of State policy, and the aggressions of interested majorities on the rights of minorities and of individuals" would have a "happy effect."

THE MOVEMENT FOR A NEW CONSTITUTION

There were stirrings toward improvement of the Articles before they were even officially in force. The three main weaknesses—lack of authority to raise revenue, to regulate commerce, or to exercise general coercive powers—were obvious to all. Article 13 provided that "Every State shall abide by the determinations of the United States in Congress assembled, on all questions which by this Confederation are submitted to them." Some argued that this article implied powers of enforcement against the states, and Congress studied the problem interminably through committees but characteristically never reached any decision.

If Congress was to have no coercive power over the states with respect to revenues, an alternative was to permit Congress to levy taxes directly. A month before the Articles became effective, Congress sent to the states an amendment permitting it to levy a duty of 5 per cent ad valorem on all imports. Amendment of the Articles required unanimous vote, and this proposal failed when Rhode Island rejected it in 1782. A revised revenue amendment which sought to meet Rhode Island's objection got the approval of only two states in three years. When a committee of Congress reported in 1786 that the lack of a general revenue was placing the very existence of the union in jeopardy, and that the states must permit the establishment of a revenue system, New York wrecked agreement by its lone veto.

As for the commerce power, vulnerable New Jersey pressed for central regulatory power from the beginning, but unsuccessfully. Foreign discrimination against

American commerce led Congress to submit a commerce amendment to the states in 1784, which failed, as did later proposals to the same end.

This continuing demonstration of what a Virginia delegate to Congress called the "imbecillity" of the Confederation could lead only to the breaking up of the union or its reconstitution under a stronger government. There was considerable speculation about and support for the first alternative from 1783 on. The conflicting interests and conditions of the different sections were stressed. The advantages of a connection with the Southern states were widely questioned in the North. Dr. Benjamin Rush of Philadelphia reported that "some of our enlightened men . . . have secretly proposed an Eastern, Middle and Southern Confederacy, to be united by an alliance offensive and defensive. These Confederacies, they say, will be united by nature, by interests, and by manners, and consequently they will be safe, agreeable, and durable."

It was the other alternative which won out, however. In 1782 Hamilton had prevailed on the New York legislature to request that Congress call a general convention, and Massachusetts took similar action in 1785. These efforts failed. What did happen in 1785 was a meeting of representatives from Virginia and Maryland at Washington's home at Mount Vernon, for the purpose of discussing joint problems of navigation on Chesapeake Bay and the Potomac. Ignoring a provision in the Articles which required congressional consent to all agreements between states, they developed a plan for uniform import duties, regulations of commerce, and currency in the two states.

When the Maryland legislature accepted these proposals in December, 1785, it suggested that Pennsylvania and Delaware be invited to join in the plan. In Virginia, Madison saw the possibility of using this initiative to get a general meeting on commercial problems, which the Virginia assembly proposed should meet at Annapolis in September, 1786. Nine states appointed delegates to go to Annapolis, but only five were present at the opening session. They waited three weeks for more delegates and then adjourned. But a report was drafted and sent to every state legislature and to Congress, suggesting that the states designate commissioners to meet in Philadelphia in May, 1787, "to take into consideration the situation of the United States, to devise such further provisions as shall appear to them necessary to render the Constitution of the Federal Government adequate to the exigencies of the Union."

All the states complied except Rhode Island, though New Hampshire delayed until June, after the Convention had assembled. Congress at first ignored the project but in February, 1787, recommended a convention at the time and place already set, to meet for the "sole and express purpose of revising the Articles of Confederation."[5]

[5] Although this "call for a convention" has been regarded as the source of the Convention's authority, in fact eight states had already decided to appoint delegates before the resolution was adopted. The state legislative instruments appointing delegates were the true source of authority for the Convention. See Julius Goebel, Jr., *History of the Supreme Court of the United States: Antecedents and Beginnings to 1801* (New York: The Macmillan Company, 1971), p. 202.

THE CONVENTION: MEMBERSHIP AND PROCEDURE

The Convention was scheduled to meet at the State House in Philadelphia on May 14, 1787, but on that day representatives from only two states, Virginia and Pennsylvania, were present. On succeeding days additional delegates appeared, but it was not until May 25 that a majority of the states were represented. The Convention then organized, with Washington the unanimous choice as presiding officer. The Convention met in its first regular session on Monday, May 28, and continued its deliberations until the completed document was ready for signature on September 17.[6]

The session of May 28 was attended by twenty-nine delegates from seven states. Some seventy-four delegates were appointed, but only fifty-five of them ever attended the sessions. Every state except Rhode Island was eventually represented, New Hampshire's delegates being the last to arrive, on July 23. By any standards, in any country, these men would have been judged a notable assemblage. The French chargé wrote that "if all the delegates named for this Philadelphia Convention are present, one will never have seen, even in Europe, an assembly more respectable for talents, knowledge, disinterestedness and patriotism than those who will compose it"

The fifty-five delegates were comparatively young men, only twelve being over fifty-four years of age, while six were under thirty-one. About half were college graduates. They were almost without exception men of substance and status in the new country—lawyers, physicians, planters, merchants. Most of them had risked their necks in prominent military or civilian posts during the Revolution. But the fact that only eight of the fifty-six signers of the Declaration of Independence were in the Constitutional Convention is evidence that making a constitution enlisted different talents than making a revolution. Of course Jefferson and Paine were in Europe, but Patrick Henry "smelled a rat" and stayed at home, and such Revolutionary figures as Richard Henry Lee, Sam Adams, and John Hancock were also missing.

Among the Convention's leaders, some few stand out and deserve brief mention here. The two figures with greatest prestige were Washington and Franklin. When Washington resigned his commission in December, 1783, he told Congress he was taking his leave "of all the employments of public life." Though the difficulties of the new nation affected him deeply and he was firmly convinced that a stronger government was required, he resisted efforts to enlist his services in the political arena. In August, 1786, he wrote to John Jay: "Having happily assisted in bringing the ship into port, and having been fairly discharged; it is not my business to embark again on a sea of troubles." But in March, 1787, the call of duty overrode all other considerations, and he accepted designation as a delegate from Virginia. He feared that if he did not attend, it would be taken as an indication that he had lost

---

[6] For accounts of the Convention, see Catherine Drinker Bowen, *Miracle at Philadelphia* (Boston: Little, Brown and Company, 1966); Clinton Rossiter, *1787: The Grand Convention* (New York: The Macmillan Company, 1966); Carl Van Doren, *The Great Rehearsal* (New York: The Viking Press, Inc., 1948); Charles Warren, *The Making of the Constitution* (Boston: Little, Brown and Company, 1928).

faith in a republican form of government. He participated seldom in debates, but there can be no doubt that his influence and endorsement were essential to the adoption of the Constitution.

Franklin, by then eighty-one years old and suffering from the gout, was nearing the end of his glorious career and was unable to take an active part in debate. But he was, after Washington, the most influential American of his time, and his talents as a peacemaker helped the Convention ease past several danger points.

The men generally ranked as exercising the greatest influence in the decisions of the Convention are Gouverneur Morris and James Wilson of Pennsylvania, James Madison of Virginia, and Roger Sherman of Connecticut. Morris made 173 speeches, Wilson 168, Madison 161, and Sherman 138. Virginia was also ably represented by George Mason and Edmund Randolph, as was Massachusetts with Elbridge Gerry and Rufus King, and South Carolina with John Rutledge and Charles Pinckney. Oliver Ellsworth of Connecticut, Alexander Hamilton from New York, John Dickinson of Delaware, and William Paterson of New Jersey must also be ranked among the leaders.

Under the Convention's rules as adopted on May 28 and 29, the deliberations were to be completely secret, and they were kept so for thirty years afterward. The official journal was confined to the formal motions made and the ayes and noes. But Madison throughout the proceeding sat with his back to Washington, facing the other members, and writing down what went on in his own version of shorthand. He did this with the silent approval of the Convention. The members trusted him and helped him fill out his reports from their own notes or memories. Madison's notes provide the principal information as to the proceedings of the Convention.[7]

Edmund Randolph started off the work of the body by presenting for the Virginia delegation a series of resolutions, largely drafted by Madison, providing for a new national government. The Convention turned itself into a committee of the whole and for three weeks mulled over the Virginia proposals, as well as a more limited plan placed before the committee by New Jersey. The New Jersey proposal was defeated on June 19. The members then reverted from committee status and, as a convention, began to go over again the various features of the Virginia Plan. One month of discussion produced agreement on a substantial number of points, so that on July 23 the Convention voted to set up a committee of detail which would draft a constitution embodying the principles agreed upon. The members of this committee were Gorham of Massachusetts, Ellsworth, Wilson, Randolph, and Rutledge. This group, however, did more than redraft the Convention's resolutions into documentary form. It expanded some of the resolutions and developed some entirely new provisions. The resulting document was presented to the Convention on August 6 and was the subject of further extended discussion. On September 8 a committee was appointed "to revise the stile of and arrange the articles which had been agreed to by the House"; it consisted of Johnson of Connecticut, Hamilton, Gouverneur

---

[7] All the statements at the Convention quoted in this chapter come from Madison's notes, as printed in Max Farrand (ed.), *The Records of the Federal Convention of 1787* (New Haven, Conn.: Yale University Press, 1937).

Morris, Madison, and King. Morris actually did the bulk of the work for the committee of style, and was responsible for much of the phrasing of the final document.

On September 17, when the Constitution was ready for signing, forty-two delegates were present. Some had departed because they disagreed with the Convention's work. Yates and Lansing of New York had left in the midst of the proceedings, and for the last two months of the Convention Hamilton was thus the sole representative from New York. Although he spoke often, he declined to take the responsibility of casting New York's vote, which was consequently never recorded during the latter part of the proceedings. Others had departed, not because they disagreed with the Convention's results, but because of pressure of other business or because they felt all the important issues had been decided.

Of the forty-two delegates present on September 17, three declined to sign—Mason, Gerry, and Randolph, all of whom had played important parts in the drafting process. Madison records that while the last of the other thirty-nine delegates were still signing the document,

> . . . Doctr. Franklin looking towards the Presidents Chair, at the back of which a rising sun happened to be painted, observed to a few members near him, that Painters had found it difficult to distinguish in their art a rising from a setting sun. I have, said he, often and often in the course of the Session, and the vicissitudes of my hopes and fears as to its issue, looked at that behind the President without being able to tell whether it was rising or setting: But now at length I have the happiness to know that it is a rising and not a setting Sun.

THE MAJOR DECISIONS

The various provisions of the Constitution on which the sun had thus arisen will be the subject of examination and comment at appropriate points throughout this volume. Here an attempt will be made only to place the major decisions of the Convention in their setting, outlining the considerations that were effective in the adoption of these provisions and the alternatives which were discussed and discarded.

A New Constitution

The Convention almost immediately on assembling proceeded to disregard the instructions it had received from Congress to confine its efforts to revising the Articles of Confederation. Because of the suspicions of the state legislatures, which tended to represent the small farmers and debtors, toward the proposal to hold a convention, the supporters of the movement had felt it necessary to play down the real purposes of the call. They had seen the Annapolis meeting of 1786 break up in failure when all but five states were frightened off by talk of strengthening the central government. Consequently, Alexander Hamilton drafted the call for the 1787 meeting in terms merely of revising the Articles, with any changes proposed having to go back to the states for decision as to their adoption.

But once the delegates met, it was obvious that the goals they had in mind required scrapping the Articles. It was too apparent to them that the Confederation, with its powerless Congress, could not provide what they felt the country needed—

security for business development, protection against competitive state taxation, the assurance of a sound currency, encouragement and protection of foreign trade, safety against foreign countries and Indians on the frontier. Thus the Virginia resolutions, which ignored the Articles, were accepted unanimously as the basis for the initial discussions. It was only after the demand of the small states for equal representation in the Senate had been defeated that some delegates began to suggest that the Convention was contravening its instructions. Lansing of New York said his state "would never have concurred in sending deputies to the convention, if she had supposed the deliberations were to turn on a consolidation of the States, and a National Government." Paterson, presenting the New Jersey Plan, limited to revision of the Articles, added: "If the confederacy was radically wrong, let us return to our States, and obtain larger powers, not assume them of ourselves." But when only three states supported the New Jersey Plan, the die was irrevocably cast for a new Constitution.[8]

A National Government

The decision to set up a national government and the decision to draft a new Constitution were two sides of the same coin. It was because the delegates believed a strong central government essential that they could not be content with a patching job on the Articles. The two most eloquent defenses of a national government in the Convention were those of Hamilton and Madison on June 18 and June 19. Hamilton objected to both the Paterson and the Randolph plans. Believing that the British government was the best in the world, he wanted to go as far in that direction as possible, with an executive and an upper chamber both serving for life. "It seemed to be admitted," he said, "that no good [Executive] could be established on Republican principles."

Madison's was a more moderate exposition of the differences between a federal and a national plan. The New Jersey Plan, he said, would correct none of the evils which had brought the delegates together. Would it prevent state violations of the laws of nations and of treaties? Would it prevent encroachments on federal authority? Would it prevent trespass of the states on each other? Would it secure the internal tranquillity of the states (mentioning particularly Shays' Rebellion)? Would it secure the Union against the influence of foreign powers over its members?

Acceptance of the national principle was settled by the vote of June 19. This meant that the government would operate directly upon the people, in contrast with the Confederation, which operated only on the states. It meant that the central government would have power to collect its own taxes, to make laws and enforce them in its own courts. Over each citizen there would be two governments, national and state, both derived from the people, to both of which their citizens would owe obedience.

---

[8] See John D. Lewis (ed.), *Anti-Federalists versus Federalists: Selected Documents* (San Francisco: Chandler Publishing Comaompany, 1967); Herbert J. Storing, *The Complete Anti-Federalist* (Chicago: University of Chicago Press, 1976).

A Separation of Powers

Under the Articles the only governmental institution was Congress, but with a national government there was a necessity of adding executive and judicial instruments, and of relating them all to each other. Montesquieu's work on the separation of powers was known in America at that time and was occasionally quoted by Madison and others, but it probably was not too influential on the decisions of the delegates. The allocation of powers to three separate branches and the division of authority so that each could impose some limits on actions of the other two were established not to fit any theoretical models but to handle the very practical problems the Convention faced.

The Founding Fathers were still so close to George III that dread of a strong executive was very real. Their experience with state legislatures had led them to fear the domination of an overweening Congress. Their experience with paper money democracy as practiced in some states left them wary of putting too much power in the hands of the people. The system of checks and balances, then, was to blunt the drive of popular emotions—to provide, in Madison's words, by a "distribution and organization" of governmental powers "better guards than are found in any other popular government against interested combinations of a majority against the rights of a minority."

A Bicameral Legislature

There was little doubt in the minds of the delegates that if a national government were to be established, it must have a two-house legislature. This was the practice in England and in almost all of the states. The New Jersey Plan for revising the Articles retained a Congress of a single house, but after it was defeated there was no further consideration of a unicameral plan. The two-house legislature of course made possible the compromise between large and small states without which probably no Constitution could have been adopted.

It was generally accepted from the beginning that the House of Representatives would be elected by the people, and that membership would be proportionate to population. Much more difficult was the composition and basis of selection of the Senate. The Randolph plan contemplated that the Senate would be elected by the House from persons nominated by the state legislatures, and that the basis of representation should be the same in both houses. The first feature of this proposal, which would have made the Senate subservient to the House, never got much support. The general sentiment was for election of the Senate by the state legislatures.

The basis of representation in the Senate was the rock on which the Convention almost foundered. The big states wanted representation by population. But in the Congress under the Confederation, and in the Convention itself, each state had one vote, and the small states would not agree to a plan which did not preserve their status in some way. On June 9 Paterson said of the proportional proposal that New Jersey "will never confederate on the plan before the Committee. She would be swallowed up. He had rather submit to a monarch, to a despot, than to such a fate." Wilson was quickly on his feet to reply that if the small states would not confederate on the proportional plan, Pennsylvania would not confederate on any other. On

June 11, just after adopting proportional representation for the House by a vote of nine to two, the committee of the whole accepted the same rule for the Senate by a vote of six to five. It was this defeat for the small states which triggered the presentation of the New Jersey Plan.

The committee's decision was reconsidered by the Convention, and on June 29 proportional representation in the House was reaffirmed, but only by a vote of six to four, with Maryland divided. Ellsworth then proposed that each state have one vote in the Senate, saying that such a variation in the representation of the two houses would be an appropriate recognition of the fact that we were "partly national; partly federal." On July 2 the Convention split five to five on this issue, with Georgia divided. A committee was set up to work over the July 4 holiday for a solution to this impasse. At Franklin's suggestion they proposed equal state representation in the Senate, but the House was to have the sole right to originate all money bills, which the Senate could accept or reject, but not modify.

This compromise was bitterly attacked by some members from the large states, including Madison, Wilson, and Gouverneur Morris. The success of the Convention seemed again in grave danger, and it was at this point that Yates and Lansing of New York went home. However, the crisis passed and the Convention held together. The big states made alternative suggestions—that the Senate representation be on the basis of state wealth, or that the states be divided into three classes on the basis of population, giving the classes one, two, and three senators respectively. But these were futile. On July 16 equal representation in the Senate was adopted by a five to four vote, with Massachusetts divided and New York not voting. Madison records that the next morning the large states held an indignation meeting to discuss what could be done, but that "the time was wasted in vague conversation." And so the issue was settled.

Powers of Congress

The original Virginia Plan proposed to grant Congress its powers under four heads: (1) the same legislative rights vested in Congress by the Confederation; (2) the right "to legislate in all cases to which the separate States are incompetent, or in which the harmony of the United States may be interrupted by the exercise of individual Legislation;" (3) "to negative all laws passed by the several States, contravening in the opinion of the National Legislature the articles of Union;" and (4) "to call forth the force of the Union agst. any member of the Union failing to fulfill its duty under the articles thereof."

This last heading was dropped on May 31 at Madison's suggestion; he was afraid that "the use of force agst. a State, would look more like a declaration of war, than an infliction of punishment, and would probably be considered by the party attacked as a dissolution of all previous compacts by which it might be bound."

The power to negative state laws was eliminated by the Convention on July 17, in spite of the strong protests of Madison, who thought "the propensity of the States to pursue their particular interests in opposition to the general interest . . . will continue to disturb the system, unless effectually controuled." But Gouverneur Morris believed that such a power would "disgust all the States." Besides, "a law that ought to be negatived will be set aside in the Judiciary Departmt." Following the defeat of this plan for a legislative veto of state laws, Luther Martin proposed what ultimately became the supremacy clause of Article VI, which the delegates adopted unanimously as a preferable method of asserting national control over state action.

The second heading of Randolph's proposal was subjected to considerable revision on July 17. Several delegates had earlier objected to the vagueness of the term "incompetent," and wished a more "exact enumeration" of powers, but this was not attempted by the committee of the whole. On July 17 Sherman tried to sharpen up the language by provisions which would give Congress power "to make laws binding on the people of the United States in all cases which may concern the common interests of the Union; but not to interfere with the Government of the individual States in any matters of internal police which respect the Govt. of such States only, and wherein the General welfare of the U. States is not concerned."

Gouverneur Morris thought this left too much power with the states; "the internal police . . . ought to be infringed in many cases, as in the case of paper money & other tricks by which Citizens of other States may be affected." Finally the following language was adopted by a vote of eight to two: "to legislate in all cases for the general interests of the Union, and also in those to which the States are separately incompetent, or in which the harmony of the U. States may be interrupted by the exercise of individual Legislation."

The committee of detail eliminated this provision entirely, in favor of a long list of specific powers which it felt Congress might want to exercise. The list started out with the power to tax and to regulate commerce, included fifteen other grants, and wound up with the sweeping authority "to make all laws that shall be necessary and proper for carrying into execution the foregoing powers, and all other powers vested, by this Constitution, in the government of the United States." The Convention accepted the enumeration approach and went to work on this list, adding or revising some powers, and dropping others. The result was to spell out in detail, rather than to grant by broad generalizations, those powers the absence of which in the Confederation had made the movement for a new Constitution necessary.

Limitations on the Powers of Congress

The general emphasis of the Convention was on assuring that Congress had enough powers to remedy the defects of the Confederation. But conflicting sectional interests led the delegates to insist on inserting certain prohibitions on national power. The slave interest was the one which most feared discriminatory action by the new government. A majority of the Convention was opposed to "this infernal traffic," as Mason called it, but North Carolina, South Carolina, and Georgia would have refused to join the Union if the slave trade had been prohibited. The committee of detail reported a provision that no tax or duty should be laid "on the migration or importation of such persons as the several States shall think proper to admit; nor shall such migration or importation be prohibited." Opposition to this formula was intense. Apart from the moral issue, the fact that other imports would be taxed whereas slaves would not amounted, as Wilson charged, to a bounty on slaves.

Ultimately, on August 25 agreement was reached on a provision that the importation of slaves would not be prohibited before 1808, and permitting a limited power of taxation on imports of slaves.

The prohibition on the power of Congress to levy direct taxes except on an apportionment basis also represented the efforts of the slavery supporters to assure that internal taxes based specifically on slaves could not be adopted. The prohibition of taxes on exports derived not from the slave interest as such, but from the different character of the economy of the eight Northern and five Southern states. The latter, being engaged primarily in the production of agricultural commodities for which the principal market was foreign, feared that a Northern-dominated Congress would adopt export taxes falling most heavily on their trade.

Limitations on the Powers of the States

The supremacy clause was relied on to prevent state legislation contrary to the national Constitution, laws, or treaties, but there were certain specific subjects on which the delegates felt so strongly that they banned state legislation in forthright language. The sharpest feeling was against state paper money and debtor relief laws. Mercer was the only delegate who ever confessed that he was "a friend to paper money," and he warned it was impolitic "to excite the opposition of all those who were friends to paper money." Gorham likewise wondered how wise it was to line up all the paper money addicts against the Constitution. But Ellsworth replied that this was a "favorable moment to shut and bar the door against paper money."

So the Convention voted to forbid the states to coin money, to print money, or to require anything but gold and silver coin to be accepted in the payment of debts. Then, taking account of the state laws which had been passed to relieve debtors of their business obligations, language forbidding the states to pass any law impairing the obligation of contracts was added with little discussion. Gerry's effort to extend the same prohibition to Congress failed.

The Presidential Office

The Virginia Plan contemplated a national executive to be named by electors chosen by Congress. In the debate which began on June 1, Randolph proposed an executive council of three men, contending that "unity in the Executive magistracy" would be "the foetus of monarchy." Wilson replied that unity in the executive would be "the best safeguard against tyranny." Gerry thought that in military matters a plural executive would be "a general with three heads." The inconvenience and impracticability of Randolph's proposal was plain, and a single executive was approved on June 4 by a vote of seven to three.

Although this issue was decided early, the method of election and term of the executive were not. These two problems were closely related. If the executive was to be chosen by Congress, then a fairly long term with no reeligibility was favored, in order to reduce the possibility of intrigue with Congress for a second term. If the President was to be chosen in some other fashion, then reeligibility was not objectionable and a shorter term became possible. The Convention considered many proposals, changed its mind repeatedly, and did not finally resolve the issue until almost the end of its sessions. Wilson said that the question of how to elect the President was "the most difficult of all on which we have had to decide."

The discussions are too complex to follow closely. The committee of the whole left Randolph's plan for election by Congress unchanged. Wilson's alternate proposal that the people elect electors who in turn would elect the President was defeated eight to two on June 2. The Convention was not too comfortable with its decision for congressional election, however, and on July 17 Gouverneur Morris again proposed popular election of presidential electors. The people would not fail to elect a man of "continental reputation," he thought, whereas legislative choice would be "the work of intrigue, of cabal, and of faction." But Pinckney thought the people would be led "by a few active & designing men," and Mason added that "it would be as unnatural to refer the choice of a proper character for chief Magistrate to the people, as it would, to refer a trial of colours to a blind man."

The elector plan failed, and the Convention then reaffirmed legislative election unanimously. Yet two days later Morris was again preaching the need "that the Executive Magistrate should be the guardian of the people, even of the lower classes, agst. Legislative tyranny, against the Great & the wealthy who in the course of things will necessarily compose—the Legislative body." This time Madison joined in urging that the executive should be independent of the legislature, and supported the elector plan. The Convention then switched to electors, but contrary to Wilson's proposal, provided for their choice by the state legislatures, and shortened the term to six years.

This decision led to some dispute over the number of electors to be allotted to the respective states. Then on July 24 Houston from Georgia complained that capable men would be unwilling to come in from the more distant states just to ballot for President, and so the Convention flopped back to the original scheme of legislative election. This change, it was argued, made it necessary to reinstate the ban on re-eligibility, which had been dropped in the meantime, or to lengthen the term to protect the President against congressional domination. The Convention was heckled by suggestions for increasing the tenure to eight, eleven, or fifteen years. King, with tongue in cheek, suggested twenty years—"the medium life of princes." Gerry ejaculated, "We seem to be entirely at a loss on this head," and then added to the confusion by suggesting that the governors of the states select the President, or that the state legislatures do the electing. Dickinson capped this by proposing that the people of each state elect "its best citizen," and that Congress then choose among the thirteen candidates.

Afraid of election by Congress, but unable to agree on a plan of election by the people, the Convention sent to the committee of detail its decision for congressional election for a seven-year term, with no reeligibility. But how would Congress vote for President? If the two houses voted separately, they might never agree on a candidate. If they voted jointly, the big states could name the President. Joint election was adopted on August 24 by a seven to four vote, and an effort to provide that the votes would be cast by states, each state having one vote, failed by six to five. At this point Morris again urged popular election of electors, and lost by only one vote, six to five. The matter was so completely in dispute that it was turned over to a committee of eleven members, one of whom was Morris.

At long last Morris succeeded. The report of the committee proposed that the states appoint electors equaling in number the senators and representatives from the state. These electors were to meet in the respective states and ballot for two persons, one of whom could not be an inhabitant of the same state with themselves. The ballots would be sent to the capital and counted in the Senate. If one candidate received the votes of a majority of the electors, he was elected President. The runner-up was Vice President, an office which this committee invented. If no candidate received a majority, or if two candidates were tied, then the Senate would choose the President from among the five highest candidates. The term was reduced to four years.

This complicated electoral plan, it was generally believed, would enable the large states in effect to "nominate" the leading candidates, none of whom would normally have a majority. Then the small states with their equal votes in the Senate would have a considerable voice in the final selection. This feature was a calculated bid to win the votes of the small states, though Morris sought to rationalize Senate election by arguing that "fewer could then say to the President, you owe your appointment to us." But Wilson pointed out in rebuttal that the Senate had to approve presidential appointments, and that a President named by the Senate would feel obligated to that body, to the point that the Senate would actually take over the appointing power. The plan would have "a dangerous tendency to aristocracy." And so in a final flurry of voting on September 6 the Convention adopted Sherman's suggestion of choice by the House, but with the members from each state having one vote, thus preserving the principle of state equality that election by the Senate would have provided. Only Delaware voted no.

The Vice-Presidency

As just noted, the committee of eleven invented the vice-presidency at a late stage in the Convention. The report of the committee of detail on August 6 had provided for the president of the Senate to exercise the powers and duties of the President in case of removal, death, resignation, or disability. The committee of eleven proposed that the Vice President be available for this purpose, and also made him ex officio president of the Senate. This latter arrangement caused a debate on September 7. Gerry and Mason thought this was an improper mixture of legislative and executive. But Sherman pointed out that "if the Vice President were not to be President of the Senate, he would be without employment."

The Judiciary

There was universal agreement on the need for a national judiciary, the absence of which was one of the weaknesses of the Confederation. Even the New Jersey Plan of revising the Articles called for the creation of a federal supreme tribunal. The Virginia Plan, however, provided for inferior tribunals as well as for a Supreme Court. On June 5 the proposal for inferior courts was attacked by Rutledge, who contended that the state courts should hear all cases in the first instance; the right of appeal to the Supreme Court would be sufficient to protect national rights and provide uniformity of judgments. But Madison argued that there should be "an effective Judiciary establishment commensurate to the legislative authority. . . . A Government without a proper Executive & Judiciary would be the mere trunk of a body without arms or legs to act or move." A compromise was then voted under which the national legislature was empowered to institute inferior tribunals, and this was adopted by a vote of eight to two.

The Randolph proposal that judges, like the President, be elected by Congress was soon eliminated. On June 5 Wilson argued for appointment by the President. "A principal reason for unity in the Executive was that officers might be appointed by a single, responsible person." Madison inclined toward appointment by the Senate, as the more stable and independent branch of the legislature. Franklin entertained the gathering with a Scotch plan "in which the nomination proceeded from the Lawyers, who always selected the ablest of the profession in order to get rid of him, and share his practice among themselves."

On July 18 Gorham's proposal for executive appointment, by and with the advice and consent of the Senate, was rejected by a tie vote. Senate appointment was reaffirmed on July 21, and the matter went to the committee of detail in this posture. In its report, the general appointing power was given to the President, but the appointment of justices and ambassadors remained with the Senate. It was the committee of eleven, reporting on September 4, which gave the appointment of Supreme Court justices to the President, with Senate advice and consent. This formula was accepted by the Convention on September 7, though Wilson objected that blending a branch of the legislature with the executive in appointments would destroy executive responsibility. Gouverneur Morris replied "that as the President was to nominate, there would be responsibility, and as the Senate was to concur, there would be security." There was never any disagreement that judicial tenure should be during good behavior.

The Failure to Include a Bill of Rights

The Convention adopted several provisions aimed to protect individuals against unjust punishment or government reprisal. The committe of detail worked out the treason provision, and it was subjected to intensive discussion on August 20. The Convention also adopted a prohibition on bills of attainder and ex post facto laws, guaranteed a jury trial on criminal charges, and provided that the privilege of the writ of habeas corpus could not be suspended except in cases of rebellion or invasion.

These provisions were not thought sufficient by some delegates. On September 12 Mason expressed his disappointment that the constitutional plan had not "been prefaced with a Bill of Rights," but the attempt which he and Gerry made to get a committee appointed to prepare such a document was defeated ten to zero. Sherman's reason was that "the State Declarations of Rights are not repealed by this Constitution; and being in force are sufficient." Perhaps a more pressing reason was that the delegates had been at the job for three and a half months and wanted to get home.

RATIFICATION OF THE CONSTITUTION

The Virginia Plan called for ratification of the new Constitution by special conventions popularly elected for that purpose. The Convention agreed on July 23 by a vote of nine to one, and on August 31 added the provision bringing the Constitution into operation by the favorable vote of nine state conventions. Madison thought from the beginning that ratification by conventions rather than by state legislatures was essential. The theoretical reasons were that the new government must derive its authority directly from the people. There were also some practical considerations which were frankly stated. Thus on July 23 Randolph warned of "the local demagogues who will be degraded by [the Constitution] from the importance they now hold," and who would spare no effort to defeat the proposal. "It is of great importance therefore that the consideration of this subject should be transferred from the Legislatures where this class of men, have their full influence to a field in which their efforts can be less mischievous." Others were more diplomatic in referring to the conventions as "more likely to be composed of the ablest men in the States."

Abandonment of the rule of unanimity in adoption of the Constitution was obviously necessitated by Rhode Island's refusal even to attend the Convention. The delegates also contemplated that resistance might be expected from other states. Gorham said that "the present advantage which N. York seems to be so much attached to, of taxing her neighbours [by the regulation of her trade], makes it very probable, that she will be of the number." On August 30 Carroll argued that unanimity was "necessary to dissolve the existing confederacy which had been unanimously established," but Butler "revolted at the idea, that one or two States should restrain the rest from consulting their safety." Nine was finally fixed as the number of states necessary for ratification because, as Mason said, this "had been required in all great cases under the Confederation" and was therefore "familiar to the people."

The forces favorable to adoption of the Constitution sought to get the conventions elected as promptly as possible, before the opposition had a chance to organize. Unquestionably many farmers and backwoodsmen, who would have tended to oppose the Constitution, were neutralized in this way. About three-fourths of the male white citizens over twenty-one failed to vote in the elections for convention delegates, Charles A. Beard contends, either on account of their indifference or their disfranchisement by property qualifications. He thinks it is probable that a majority of the voters in at least six states opposed ratification. His thesis that the Constitution was adopted primarily by the manufacturing, trade, shipping, and creditor interests in the country, and that the small farming and debtor interests were largely opposed to the Constitution, has been vigorously challenged by more recent studies. It now appears quite probable that class distinctions at the time were much less significant, that property qualifications for voting excluded few from the polls, and that the Constitution was adopted by people who were primarily middle-class property owners, including farmers.

Whatever the bases of the alignments, the political campaign over ratification was intense and bitter. One of its legacies was the most famous commentary on

American government, *The Federalist*. These essays were newspaper articles written to influence the vote in the doubtful state of New York by Madison, Hamilton, and John Jay. Although their discussions of the proposed Constitution may not have had great influence at the time, they have been widely accepted as authoritative guides to constitutional interpretation.

The first state convention to ratify the Constitution was that of Delaware on December 7, 1787, which was less than three months after the document was signed. Pennsylvania ratified five days later. New Jersey (December 19), Georgia (January 2), Connecticut (January 9), Massachusetts (February 6), Maryland (April 23), and South Carolina (May 23) followed. New Hampshire was the ninth state, and its ratification on June 21, 1788, brought the Constitution into effect. However, without New York and Virginia the union could not have succeeded. Virginia came in by a narrow margin on June 25, and New York followed on July 26, though an attempt to attach conditions to its ratification almost succeeded. North Carolina finally ratified on November 21, 1789, and Rhode Island held out until May 29, 1790.[9]

The absence of a bill of rights provoked the most widespread criticism in the ratifying conventions, and in Massachusetts, New York, and Virginia the promise that a bill of rights would be added was instrumental in securing the votes needed for ratification. Several of the state conventions submitted lists of proposed amendments to the new Constitution at the time they ratified, and there was a general agreement that addition of a bill of rights to the Constitution through the amending process would be a first order of business.

The motive force for putting the new government in operation was supplied by the Confederation Congress. On September 13, 1788, it adopted a resolution designating "the present seat of Congress," which was New York, as the site of the new government. The resolution also fixed the first Wednesday of January, 1789, as the day for choosing presidential electors, the first Wednesday of February for the meeting of electors, and the first Wednesday of March, which fell on March 4, for the opening session of the new Congress. Various delays kept Congress from convening on that day, however, and it was not until April 30, 1789, that George Washington was inaugurated as the first President of the United States.

The framing of the American Constitution has been the subject of never-ending controversy. Some have seen the Founders as little short of demigods; for others they were a "reform caucus" of practical politicians. Was the Constitution a democratic or an aristocratic instrument? Were its drafters conservatives or liberals? Was the document more concerned with establishing the powers of the new government or the limitations on those powers?

There is room for such disagreement, because the basic truth about the Constitution is that it was the product of compromise. The men who met in Philadelphia in the summer of 1787 were generally of the opinion that government is a "necessary evil"; they were jealous of individual rights and had strong loyalties to their states.

---

[9] Jonathan Elliot (ed.), *The Debates in the Several State Conventions in the Adoption of the Federal Constitution,* 5 vols. (Washington, D.C.: Taylor & Maury, 1854).

But experience with the Articles had demonstrated that a weak government could not provide the security and prosperity they wanted, and the amazing thing is how unanimous the Convention was in seeing the need for a central "government of powers." As Martin Diamond has said: "This was the great and novel idea which came from the Convention: a large, powerful republic with a competent national government regulated under a wise Constitution."[10]

[10] "What the Framers Meant by Federalism," in Robert A. Goldwin (ed.), *A Nation of States* (Chicago: Rand McNally & Company, 1963), p. 37.

Chapter 2

Amendment of the Constitution

The United States thus launched its experiment in building a federal government on the basis of a written document which has conditioned the entire development of American governmental experience since 1789. Public policy has been continuously subject to the test of constitutionality. Much of the rhetoric of public debate has been in terms of invoking the support of the document for proposals favored, and throwing doubt on the constitutional legitimacy of actions opposed.

A perennial problem of American politics has been the meaning of the American Constitution. As years and decades have passed, changes have occurred in the physical world. Technical discoveries or inventions have affected the life of the country. Population has multiplied. The political party has undergone a transformation from a despised source of faction to an indispensable instrument of representative government. Public agencies have taken over responsibilites undreamed of in the eighteenth century. Standards of public morality have changed. How is a government of continental proportions and world-wide responsibilities, with a peacetime budget of well over 350 billion dollars, to be accommodated within the confines of a document drafted almost two centuries earlier for a handful of people in thirteen isolated states along the Atlantic seaboard?

One answer is that the framers of the Constitution were wise enough to avoid the evil of too great specificity in drafting key provisions of the document. Their general intent was to stick to fundamentals and leave implementation to subsequent legislative decision. Thus no departmental organization of the executive branch was written into the Constitution. The question of a system of lower courts was left to Congress, as was the matter of presidential succession beyond the Vice President, and the time, place, and manner of electing representatives and senators. The powers given to the President and to Congress were typically stated in fairly broad language. Although there was a spelling out in Article I, section 8, of congressional authority in a number of areas, the section wound up with what was called "the sweeping clause," conferring on Congress the power "to make all laws which shall be necessary and proper for carrying into execution the foregoing powers, and all other powers vested by this Constitution in the government of the United States, or in any department or officer thereof."

Nevertheless, no amount of drafting skill could be expected to eliminate the necessity of revision and development to adapt the Constitution to the unforeseen and the unforeseeable. This adaptation has taken two forms—constitutional amendment and constitutional interpretation.

THE DEVELOPMENT OF ARTICLE V

Formal provision for revision of the Constitution through amendment was made by Article V. The original Virginia Plan had provided for amendments, and added that "the assent of the National Legislature ought not to be required thereto." On June 11 Mason urged the necessity of an amending clause, saying: "The plan now to be formed will certainly be defective, as the Confederation has been found on trial to be. Amendments therefore will be necessary, and it will be better to provide for them, in an easy, regular and Constitutional way than to trust to chance and violence." The reason for excluding Congress from the process as he saw it was that "they may abuse their power, and refuse their consent on that very account."

The committee of detail later produced a revised plan for amendments which also eliminated Congress. On the application of the legislatures of two-thirds of the states, Congress would be required to call a convention for amendment of the Constitution. This plan was adopted on August 30, but by September 10 the Convention was quite unhappy about it. Madison said the language was too vague. Hamilton said there must be an easier way of securing amendments. The states would never "apply for alterations but with a view to increase their own powers." Congress would be "most sensible to the necessity of amendments," Hamilton thought, and should be able to initiate the process.

The Convention then began to rewrite the amending provision on the floor, with Madison putting the various suggestions into the form finally adopted. Legislatures of two-thirds of the states could still request Congress to call a convention, but Congress itself by a two-thirds vote in each house could propose amendments to the states. Amendments initiated in either fashion would have to be ratified either by the legislatures or special conventions in three-fourths of the states, according to the mode of ratification specified by Congress.

Rutledge then objected that "he never could agree to give a power by which the articles relating to slaves might be altered by the States not interested in that property and prejudiced against it." Consequently a proviso was added protecting the clauses pertaining to slavery from amendment until the year 1808. Then on September 15 Sherman had a last-minute fear "that three fourths of the States might be brought to do things fatal to particular States, as abolishing them altogether or depriving them of their equality in the Senate." He wanted another proviso that no state should by amendment "be affected in its internal police, or deprived of its equal suffrage in the Senate." Madison warned that if the Convention once began with these "special provisos," every state would insist on some for its boundaries or exports. However, "the circulating murmurs of the small States" led Gouverneur Morris to propose adding the proviso protecting equality in the Senate, and it was agreed to unanimously. Thus Article V was completed.

USE OF THE AMENDING POWER

The presence of the amending clause was one of the factors which led Jefferson, originally inclined to oppose the Constitution, to decide in its favor. Since 1789 the procedures of Article V have been utilized to add twenty-six amendments to the Constitution. The first ten of these amendments were drafted to meet the widespread protests against the absence of a bill of rights in the original Constitution. To fill this gap, twelve amendments were proposed by the First Congress on September 25, 1789. The first two failed of ratification, but acceptance of the remaining ten was completed on December 15, 1791. The substance of these and subsequent amendments will be discussed at appropriate points throughout this volume. Here we are interested only in the chronology and general circumstances of adoption.

The Eleventh Amendment was adopted in 1795, its purpose being to override the Supreme Court's holding in *Chisholm* v. *Georgia* (1793) which allowed federal courts to accept jurisdiction of a suit against a state by a citizen of another state. The Twelfth Amendment, ratified in 1804, was intended to prevent a repetition of the confusion attendant on the presidential election of 1800, when Jefferson and Burr received an equal number of electoral votes. As the candidates for President and Vice President of the same party, they were supported by all the party's electors, but under the original language of Article II, there was no separate designation of votes for these two offices. Thus the election had to be decided by the House, where the Federalists were tempted to vote for Burr to spite Jefferson. The Twelfth Amendment requires electors to vote for the two offices separately.

The Thirteenth, Fourteenth, and Fifteenth Amendments were adopted as a result of the Civil War. The Thirteenth Amendment, which abolished slavery, was ratified in 1865. The Fourteenth, the longest of the lot and too complex to summarize at this point, aimed to protect the rights of the newly freed Negroes. It also dealt with certain political problems which were an aftermath of the war. When it appeared that the Fourteenth Amendment would not secure the right to vote for Negroes, the Fifteenth Amendment, ratified in 1870, was adopted specifically guaranteeing the right to vote against denial or abridgement on the basis of race or color.

The next two amendments reflected the progressive political philosophy of the first part of the twentieth century. The Sixteenth, ratified in 1913, reversed another Supreme Court decision, *Pollock* v. *Farmers' Loan & Trust Co.* (1895), and authorized the federal government to levy taxes on incomes. The Seventeenth Amendment, ratified two months later, provided for direct popular election of senators.

The Eighteenth Amendment, which became effective in 1919, was the controversial prohibition amendment. Suffrage for women was guaranteed in 1920 by the Nineteenth Amendment. The Twentieth Amendment, ratified in 1933, fixed the date for convening the regular annual session of Congress on January 3 and the beginning of presidential terms on January 20. In addition, it sought to clarify certain points with respect to presidential succession. The Twenty-first Amendment, also adopted in 1933, repealed the Eighteenth, but did give the states full powers to prohibit the transportation, importation, or use of intoxicating liquor.

The Twenty-second Amendment, ratified in 1951, limits a President to two terms in office. The Twenty-third (1961) permits residents of the District of Columbia to vote for President and gives the District three electoral votes. The Twenty-fourth (1964) forbids the states to use the poll tax as a voting requirement in federal elections. The Twenty-fifth (1967) provides for the appointment of a new Vice President when the office of the Vice President becomes vacant for any reason, and also authorizes the Vice President to act as President if the President is incapacitated. The Twenty-sixth (1971) gives the vote to eighteen-year-olds in both state and federal elections. The potential Twenty-seventh Amendment guaranteeing equal legal rights for women was adopted by Congress in 1972, but by 1976 it required the votes of four more states for ratification.

THE "POLITICAL" CHARACTER OF THE AMENDING PROCESS

The Supreme Court has generally regarded the amending process as almost entirely a concern of Congress, subject to very little in the way of judicial supervision or control. For example, after the Civil War the states which had attempted to secede and which had not been readmitted to the full enjoyment of the privileges of states were required by Congress to ratify the Fourteenth and Fifteenth Amendments as a condition to their readmission. The Supreme Court refused to question this requirement.[1]

Until 1939, however, the Court was willing to pass on procedural problems pertaining to the adoption of amendments. In the *National Prohibition Cases* (1920), it ruled that the two-thirds vote in each house required to propose an amendment means two-thirds of the members present—assuming the presence of a quorum—and not a vote of two-thirds of the entire membership. In *Leser* v. *Garnett* (1922), the validity of the Nineteenth Amendment was attacked on the ground that the ratifying resolutions in two states were adopted in violation of those states' rules of legislative procedure. But the Court regarded official notice of ratification from the states to the United States Secretary of State as conclusive upon him, and held that his certification was conclusive on the courts.

The Eighteenth Amendment was the first to specify a period of years—in this

[1] *White* v. *Hart* (1872).

case, seven—within which ratification had to be effected. In *Dillon* v. *Gloss* (1921) the Court ruled that there was no doubt about the power of Congress to fix a definite period for ratification, "within reasonable limits," and it agreed seven years was reasonable. The implication of this ruling seemed to be that an amendment could not be ratified when it had been before the country for more than a "reasonable" time. Consequently, when the child labor amendment, which Congress had proposed in 1924, with no time limit specified, was ratified by Kansas and Kentucky in 1937, efforts were made to get a judicial ruling that because of the lapse of time the amendment was no longer open for ratification.

In *Coleman* v. *Miller* (1939), however, the Court refused to take responsibility for deciding what was a "reasonable" period for ratification. That was an essentially political question, which Congress would have to determine. Four members of the Court went further to hold that the Court's assertion in *Dillon* v. *Gloss* that amendments must be ratified within a reasonable period was entirely unauthorized, and nothing more than an "admonition to the Congress in the nature of an advisory opinion." Their view was that the entire process of amendment was political and "not subject to judicial guidance, control or interference at any point." Even the majority decision, it should be noted, left open the possibility of only a bare minimum of judicial control over the amending process, and it is significant to note that the Court has not dealt with an amending clause problem since *Coleman* v. *Miller*.

THE PROPOSING OF AMENDMENTS

Of the two methods which Article V provides for proposing amendments—by a two-thirds majority of each house of Congress, or by a convention summoned by Congress at the request of the legislatures of two-thirds of the states—only the former has been employed. On numerous occasions state legislatures have petitioned Congress to call a convention, but always unsuccessfully. In the early part of this century some thirty-one states, meeting the two-thirds requirement at that time, submitted petitions for an amendment to provide for direct election of senators. Congress failed to call a convention, but eventually proposed the amendment itself.

In 1962 the Council of State Governments asked state legislatures to petition for a convention to adopt a package of three "states' rights" amendments, but the number responding fell far short of the required two-thirds. After the Supreme Court ruling in *Reynolds* v. *Sims* (1964), that members of both houses in the state legislatures must be elected from equal population districts, Senator Everett M. Dirksen spearheaded an effort to persuade two-thirds of the state legislatures to petition for a convention which would propose an amendment overriding that decision. He almost succeeded, securing petitions from thirty-three of the required thirty-four legislatures.

This campaign concentrated new attention on the many uncertainties surrounding the convention device. If two-thirds of the legislatures submit petitions, must they be in identical language, and must they be received within a limited time period? May Congress refuse to act on the petitions? If Congress does refuse, can the courts force Congress to act? If a convention is called, how are the delegates chosen, and what are the voting rules in the convention? Can a convention be prevented from going beyond the subject for which it was convened, as the Constitutional Convention did in 1787?

These unknowns are so serious that it would be well for Congress to adopt general implementing legislation before it is faced with a valid convention call.[2] However, it would be preferable not to use the convention method at all. The principal support for the convention device has come from interests sponsoring proposals which could not gain congressional approval. It is an alternative attractive to manipulators of opinion who find it more congenial to work in the recesses of fifty state legislatures than in the glare of the congressional spotlight. The national interest in the amending process is best protected by leaving the responsibility for proposing amendments in the halls of Congress.

It is settled that the President plays no official role in the proposing of amendments, in spite of the provision in Article I, section 7, that "every order, resolution, or vote to which the concurrence of the Senate and House of Representatives may be necessary. . . shall be presented to the President." Presumably the reason is that proposing an amendment is not an exercise of ordinary legislative power.[3] Another factor is that, since proposed amendments must be passed by a two-thirds vote of each house and since that is the margin necessary to override a presidential veto, no purpose would normally be served by presidential participation in proposing amendments. The fact that the President does not pass on proposals for amendment of course constitutes no reason why he should not interest himself in proposed amendments.

THE RATIFICATION OF AMENDMENTS

The ratification of all amendments to the Constitution except one has been by vote of three-fourths of the state legislatures. Only in the case of the Twenty-first Amendment, which repealed the Eighteenth, did Congress require the use of state conventions. The reason for this exception was the fear in Congress that the overrepresentation in the state legislatures of rural areas, which tended to be "dry," might imperil adoption of the amendment, whereas conventions would more equitably represent the views of the urban areas. The 1962 Council of State Governments' proposal would have deprived Congress of its authority to select the state convention mode of ratification.[4]

A state which has refused to ratify a proposed amendment may later change its mind and vote favorably. In *Coleman* v. *Miller* the Supreme Court said such action

---

[2] Legislation for this purpose proposed by Senator Sam Ervin was passed by the Senate in 1971 and 1973. A special committee of the American Bar Association made similar proposals in a 1974 report, "Amendment of the Constitution by the Convention Method Under Article V" (Chicago: American Bar Association, 1974). See also "Proposed Legislation on the Convention Method of Amending the United States Constitution," 85 HARVARD LAW REVIEW 1612 (1972); Charles L. Black, Jr., "Amending the Constitution: A Letter to a Congressman," 82 YALE LAW JOURNAL 189 (1972).

[3] See *Hollingsworth* v. *Virginia* (1798); *Hawke* v. *Smith* (1920).

[4] States cannot make ratification depend upon a popular referendum vote; *Hawke* v. *Smith* (1920). But in 1975 the Illinois legislature required a 60 percent vote in each house for ratification of proposed amendments, a device adopted to insure defeat of the Equal Rights Amendment.

should be regarded as a political matter with the ultimate authority of decision in Congress. However, it has been thought that an affirmative vote on ratification cannot be subsequently withdrawn, even though the amendment has not been proclaimed in effect. Ohio and New Jersey attempted to withdraw their approval of the Fourteenth Amendment before its ratification had been announced. After some uncertainty, the Secretary of State disregarded the withdrawal votes and proclaimed the amendment in effect. Congress supported this decision by adopting a concurrent resolution to the same effect.

This issue seemed likely to be raised again in connection with the proposed Twenty-seventh Amendment, for by 1976 two of the thirty-four states that had initially ratified the amendment (Tennessee and Nebraska) had voted to rescind their action.

APPRAISAL OF THE AMENDING PROCESS

Perhaps the most striking fact about the amending process is the infrequency with which it has been used. Excluding the initial ten amendments, which must be considered practically part of the original Constitution, amendments have been adopted at a rate of less than one per decade. Following the Civil War amendments, there was a period of over forty years during which the Constitution appeared unamendable. This was an era of agrarian discontent, industrial unrest, and growing interest in political and economic reforms. The conservatism of the Supreme Court, symbolized by its invalidation of the income tax in 1895, made constitutional amendment seem a necessary step toward achieving liberal legislative goals.

Under these circumstances there was much talk about the necessity of easing the amending process. In 1913, however, the long liberal campaign for the income tax and direct election of senators succeeded, and the women's suffrage amendment followed shortly thereafter. Also, adoption of the Eighteenth Amendment revealed the possibility of a small but dedicated pressure group exploiting the amending machinery successfully. With six amendments added to the Constitution between 1913 and 1933, the amending process no longer seemed so formidable. Moreover, the liberalization of the Supreme Court's views by President Franklin Roosevelt's appointments substantially eliminated liberal interest in further amendments.[5]

After the 1930s, pressure for amendments came principally from conservative political quarters. The increase in executive power and congressional expenditures, the acceptance of new welfare functions domestically and new responsibilities internationally by the federal government, the reduced role of the states, and liberal tendencies in the Supreme Court were all factors stimulating conservative recourse to the amending process. During the 1950s, the Bricker Amendment to limit the federal government's power to enter into international agreements as well as a proposal to place a ceiling on federal income taxation were conservative measures that failed of adoption. In the 1960s, efforts to override the Supreme Court's decisions on

[5] See Clement E. Vose, *Constitutional Change: Amendment Politics and Supreme Court Litigation since 1900* (Boston, Mass.: D. C. Heath and Company, 1972).

"one person, one vote" and Bible reading in the public schools were defeated. The 1970s saw an organized effort to reverse the Court's abortion decision. Thus far the only amendment secured by conservative forces was the Twenty-second, limiting the President to two terms. In contrast, the four amendments adopted since 1961 have had a generally liberal character; three of the four extend the franchise, while the potential Twenty-seventh guarantees equal rights for women.

The adoption of four, possibly five, amendments since 1961 is evidence that the amending machinery is not hard to operate if there is a genuine consensus on the need, and may even lead to some concern that amendments are too easy to achieve. The Twenty-fourth Amendment has been criticized because the same goal could almost certainly have been secured by statute. It is of prime importance that the Constitution retain its brevity and be limited to basic structural arrangements and the protection of individual liberties. It would be disastrous if it became, through the amending power, a vehicle by which pressure groups and crackpots could impose their nostrums on the nation.

Interpretation of the Constitution

More gradual but more continuous than the amending process in adapting the Constitution to changing conditions is the device of constitutional interpretation. In fact, it has been the possibility of modification of constitutional meanings over the years to meet new times and new necessities which has permitted resort to formal amendment to be relatively infrequent.

The process of constitutional adaptation is one which goes on at many levels and in many contexts. There are adaptations which develop on an entirely unplanned basis in the form of usages or customs or methods of procedure or institutions. Perhaps the most striking example in American history is the prompt development after 1789 of a party system, for which the framers had not planned and which in fact they had taken some pains to try to prevent. The development of committees in Congress, the tradition against a third term, the use of executive agreements instead of treaties, the rule that representatives must be residents of the districts they represent in Congress—these and many other customs and usages represented evolutionary adjustments of the constitutional system to practical problems with which it was confronted.

A much more intentional and sophisticated type of constitutional interpretation goes on in the decision making of the executive and legislative branches. President Truman's decision to seize the steel mills in 1952, or President Roosevelt's destroyers-for-bases deal with Britain in 1940, were consciously based on theories of executive power under the Constitution. Likewise when Congress is considering legislation of a novel character, it is sure to hear many speeches defending or attacking the constitutionality of the proposal.

The most highly rationalized type of constitutional interpretation is no doubt that engaged in by judges, and particularly by the Supreme Court of the United States, which is the focus of this volume.[1] Wherever the process of constitutional interpretation goes on, it is guided by some more or less articulate theory of the meaning of the Constitution. But in the 190 years during which the American nation has sought to relate the words of the written document to the diversity of its economic interests, political strivings, and moral goals, every conceivable rationalization has been developed for demonstrating that the policy preferences of the interpreter are in accord with the "true meaning" of the Constitution. The major theories of constitutional interpretation deserve brief consideration.

APPROACHES TO CONSTITUTIONAL MEANING

The Intention of the Framers

One widely supported proposition is that the meaning of the Constitution should be determined by reference to the intention of the men who made it. It seems natural and logical that in the famous case of *Marbury* v. *Madison* (1803), where the issue was whether the judiciary had authority to invalidate acts of Congress, Chief Justice Marshall should have asked about "the intention of those who gave this power." But it is significant that, 175 years later, scholars are still disputing as to whether Marshall's conclusions about the intent of the framers on this important issue were supported by the evidence.

There are more difficulties than one might imagine in determining the intent of the framers. Fifty-five delegates were present at one or more sessions of the Convention, but some took little or no part in the proceedings. Some propositions on which they voted were carried by narrow majorities. What was said, and the reasons given for votes cast, is known almost entirely through James Madison's incomplete notes. On no issues did all members speak; on few did a majority speak. Many decisions must have been compromises that fully pleased no one.

If the intention of the fifty-five men at Philadelphia cannot be discovered with assurance, what chance is there of determining the intention of the delegates to the state ratifying conventions whose votes put the Constitution into operation? The ultimate in uncertainty is reached if we seek to discover the intention of the people who elected the delegates to the state conventions.

The same problems are presented by amendments to the Constitution. What

---

[1] For general discussions of the Supreme Court's role in constitutional interpretation, see Alexander M. Bickel, *The Least Dangerous Branch* (Indianapolis: The Bobbs-Merrill Company, Inc., 1962); Paul L. Murphy, *The Constitution in Crisis Times, 1918–1969* (New York: Harper & Row, Publishers, Incorporated, 1972); William F. Swindler, *Court and Constitution in the Twentieth Century: The New Legality, 1932–1968* (Indianapolis: The Bobbs-Merrill Company, Inc., 1970).

did the members of Congress who drafted the First Amendment in 1789 or the Fourteenth Amendment in 1866 intend by such broad phrases as "freedom of speech" or "equal protection of the laws"? Historical data can throw some light on the purposes behind such language, but all too often "intention of the framers" has been a rhetorical device employed by partisans to read their own policy preferences into the Constitution.

Justice Brennan had something useful to say about intentions of the framers in *School District of Abington Township* v. *Schempp* (1963), where the Court had to decide whether the saying of prayers and reading of the Bible in public schools constituted an establishment of religion contrary to the First Amendment. Justice Brennan thought "a too literal quest for the advice of the Founding Fathers" on this issue would be "futile and misdirected." The history was "ambiguous," the structure of American education has greatly changed since 1791, and we are a vastly more diverse people religiously than were our forefathers. Consequently, Brennan believed that, instead of looking for the intent of the framers, it would be more fruitful to inquire whether the practices challenged in the *Schempp* case threatened those consequences of interdependence between religion and the state "which the Framers deeply feared."

Where the Supreme Court has used history to support its conclusions, it has often been very bad history. Historian Alfred H. Kelly has noted two techniques used by the Court. One is the "creation of history a priori by . . . 'judicial fiat' or 'authoritative revelation.' " He suggests that several of Marshall's most notable opinions involve the creation of history by judicial fiat, with little if any inquiry into "actual history."

A second method is what Kelly calls "law-office history," that is, extended essays in constitutional history usually written for the purpose of justifying the reversal of precedent by proving that the precedent itself was contrary to the original intention of the Constitution. Nineteenth-century illustrations of law-office history are Chief Justice Taney's essay in the *Dred Scott* case on the Negro's role in early America, designed to prove that the Constitution was a "white man's document," and Chief Justice Fuller's essays in the *Income Tax Cases,* designed to break down the established precedents that income taxes were not direct taxes. The activist Court of the 1950s and 1960s also used the historical essay to justify departures from established doctrines in several fields.[2]

The Meaning of the Words

There is a second theory of constitutional interpretation which also employs the historical approach but for a different purpose. This is the method of interpretation on the basis of the meaning of the words at the time they were used. W. W. Crosskey's reinterpretation of the Constitution is based on this method.[3] On the

[2] Alfred H. Kelly, "Clio and the Court: An Illicit Love Affair," in Philip B. Kurland (ed.), *The Supreme Court Review: 1965* (Chicago: The University of Chicago Press, 1965), pp. 119–158. See also Charles A. Miller, *The Supreme Court and the Uses of History* (Cambridge, Mass.: The Belknap Press, Harvard University Press, 1969).

[3] W. W. Crosskey, *Politics and the Constitution in the History of the United States* (Chicago: The

flyleaf of his first volume he offers as his touchstone this quotation from Justice Holmes: "We ask, not what this man meant, but what those words would mean in the mouth of a normal speaker of English, using them in the circumstances in which they were used." As employed by Crosskey, this method of research in word usage during the era of constitutional formulation yielded a "specialized dictionary," on the basis of which he radically revised the meaning of many of the key provisions in the Constitution.

The search for original word meanings, like that for intent of the framers, assumes the binding nature of the obligations imposed by the decisions of 1787 on subsequent generations. Both approaches have the value, necessary to all law, of seeking to preserve some sense of stability and continuity in the agreements and understandings on which legitimate governmental power is based. In searching for the original meaning of the words, however, the second approach employs somewhat narrower lexicographic skills as opposed to the social history on which the first method relies. It is more closely confined by the document itself and is more closely related to the processes by which the written instruments of private law are construed.

The objections to these two methods of constitutional interpretation are likewise somewhat similar. Original meaning may be as difficult to establish as original intent. Crosskey's work is sufficient confirmation of this point. The original word meanings which his laborious research in the written materials of the time purports to establish can perhaps legitimately be challenged only on the basis of equally laborious research which reaches other conclusions. But certainly observers who have not done this research are entitled to express reservations about the validity of conclusions attributing original meaning to words, which differ so markedly from the meanings accepted for those words only a few years after adoption of the Constitution by responsible jurists and statesmen, many of whom had themselves been active in the drafting and adoption of the Constitution.

Perhaps the most serious objection to both methods, however, is the extent to which they propose to make a nation the prisoner of its past, and reject any method of constitutional development save constitutional amendment. Both reject the legitimacy of change by consensus or usage. Both deny the possibility that evolution in moral standards or political ideology can be given effect in the Constitution without changing its language.[4]

Logical Reasoning

Logical analysis is an alternative to the historical methods of determining constitutional meaning, and is particularly worthy of note because of the extensive use made of it by Chief Justice Marshall in his great decisions. The method is most aptly demonstrated by reference again to *Marbury* v. *Madison*. There Marshall cites no judicial decisions to support his arguments. While referring to "original intention,"

University of Chicago Press, 1953).

    [4] As alternative to the textual method of constitutional interpretation, Charles L. Black, Jr., proposes that constitutional law should use "the method of reasoning from structure and relation." *Structure and Relationship in Constitutional Law* (Baton Rouge, La.: Louisiana State University Press, 1969).

he makes no effort to quote contemporaneous evidence or opinion. His argument is primarily an exercise in logic. "It seems only necessary to recognize certain principles," he says, "supposed to have been long and well established, to decide it." The major principle is that the Constitution is the supreme law of the land. The Supreme Court has taken an oath to uphold the Constitution. The conclusion logically follows that when an act of Congress conflicts with the superior law, the Supreme Court cannot enforce it but must declare it null and void.

This position has been so long accepted that the logic supporting it may seem unassailable. Yet is it not equally logical to argue that, since the Constitution is the supreme law of the land, and since the President has taken an oath to support the Constitution, he cannot enforce a decision of the Supreme Court which conflicts with the Constitution, but must declare it null and void?

The problem is simply not one to which logic can guarantee a correct answer. The fallacy of the logical form may be made clearer by stating a part of Marshall's argument as a syllogism.

> Major premise: A law repugnant to the Constitution is void.
> Minor premise: This law is repugnant to the Constitution.
> Conclusion: This law is void.

Assuming the validity of the major premise, the soundness of the conclusion depends upon whether the minor premise is *factually* true. But logic cannot tell us whether a particular law is repugnant to the Constitution. That is a matter of informed opinion and judgment. This explains why Justice Holmes said, in one of the most famous passages in his lectures on *The Common Law:* "The life of the law has not been logic: it has been experience. The felt necessities of the time, the prevalent moral and political theories, intuitions of public policy, avowed or unconscious, even the prejudices which judges share with their fellow-men, have had a good deal more to do than the syllogism in determining the rules by which men should be governed."[5]

Another device often employed in Supreme Court decisions is to test a constitutional argument "by pushing it to its logical conclusion." Obviously there is some utility in examining the soundness of a proposed decision by considering its logically possible implications, so long as these implications are not treated as inevitable consequents of the ruling. But all too often the purpose of this technique is to demonstrate that if the Court accepts the constitutionality of a particular legislative or executive action, which may seem comparatively mild and reasonable, there will be no logical stopping place at which the Court could forbid extensions of the same principle until a clearly unconstitutional result had been reached. Consequently it is claimed that the Court must forbid even the initial steps down the road toward an unconstitutional terminus. Thomas Reed Powell called this method "the parade of the imaginary horribles."

    [5] Mark DeWolfe Howe (ed.), *The Common Law* (Cambridge, Mass.: The Belknap Press, Harvard University Press, 1963), p. 5.

The Experiential Approach

Historical evidence as to the intent of the framers, textual analysis of the language of the Constitution, and application of the rules of logical thinking all have a useful place, but neither alone nor in combination can they supply the key to constitutional interpretation. There is a further factor, which Holmes designated as "experience." The experiential approach is one which treats the Constitution more as a political than a legal document. It considers current understandings as relevant as the debates of the Constitutional Convention. It frankly recognizes that interpretation of the Constitution will and must be influenced by present-day values and by the sum total of American experience.

The intention of the framers is surely part of that experience, but so are the breadlines of 1933 and the sit-ins of the 1960s. The meaning of the words as originally used is a relevant datum, but so also is the language of each presidential message to Congress. One may invoke logic and technical rules of construction, but one may also invoke such intangibles as "the spirit of the Constitution." The goal of constitutional interpretation, it may be suggested, is the achieving of consensus as to the *current meaning* of the document framed in 1787, a meaning which makes it possible to deal rationally with current necessities and acknowledge the lessons of experience while still recognizing guidelines derived from the written document and the philosophy of limited governmental power which it sought to express.

This approach recognizes the right of each generation to adapt the Constitution to its own needs, to the extent that such adaptations are reconcilable with the language of the Constitution. Naturally, the provision that the President shall have a four-year term cannot be reinterpreted to justify a five-year term. But the meaning of the clause giving Congress the authority to regulate commerce among the states or forbidding cruel and unusual punishment may legitimately change over a period of time. Marshall was defending this notion of a flexible Constitution when he said in *McCulloch* v. *Maryland:* "We must never forget, that it is a constitution we are expounding," one which is "intended to endure for ages to come, and consequently, to be adapted to the various crises of human affairs." Holmes put the conception of the "living" Constitution into eloquent language when he wrote, in the case of *Missouri* v. *Holland* (1920):

> When we are dealing with words that also are a constituent act, like the Constitution of the United States, we must realize that they have called into life a being the development of which could not have been foreseen completely by the most gifted of its begetters. It was enough for them to realize or to hope that they had created an organism; it has taken a century and has cost their successors much sweat and blood to prove that they created a nation. The case before us must be considered in the light of our whole experience and not merely in that of what was said a hundred years ago.

The experiential approach is profoundly disturbing to those who demand of the Constitution that it supply the certainty of absolutes and rigid guarantees against change. Instead of providing a single right answer, it permits a number of right answers, from among which choices must be made by the political process. It is a profound mistake, however, to think that the range of choice is left unlimited by this freedom. Not everything that the public may currently want to do is necessarily constitutional. The distinctive feature of the experiential approach is that decisions on constitutional allowability are made with full recognition of the need for the adjustments and expansions inevitable in a dynamic society. The constitutional system is not regarded as separate from the political system, but a necessary part of it, performing the vital function of giving order and structure to the inevitable processes of change.

THE PERSONAL FACTOR IN JUDICIAL INTERPRETATION

When we say that the Supreme Court has made a decision, we actually mean that the nine justices who compose the Court at a particular point in history have made the decision. Often, in fact, it is a decision made by only five members of the Court, with which the remaining four disagree. These justices are men—men of varying abilities, backgrounds, and political preferences—who have been fortuitously elevated to the highest judicial body by the process of presidential selection. How the Constitution will be interpreted by these men depends in part upon what kind of men they are and how the world looks to them.[6]

This has not always been understood. During considerable periods of American history there has been a popular impression that when men were appointed to the Supreme Court, they somehow became depersonalized and disembodied of all ordinary prejudices and passions. In the rarefied atmosphere of their chambers they were presumed to be at work discovering the law by the exercise of pure reason. This myth has typically been strongest during periods when the Court was under conservative domination, and it served the purpose of convincing the public that judicial protection of property or the thwarting of regulatory legislation was not an expression of the personal preferences of the justices but a voicing of the authentic commands of the Constitution. This myth, however, was finally and irretrievably destroyed in the years from 1935 to 1937, when it became all too apparent that the doctrine which the Supreme Court majority was expounding was their personal laissez-faire economic beliefs. As Max Lerner said, the public learned then "that judicial decisions are not babies brought by constitutional storks."

It is an equally grave error, however, to jump to the conclusion that Supreme Court justices typically determine the meaning of the Constitution merely by consulting their personal preferences. There is an institutional ethos about the Court which cannot fail to have a restraining effect upon the most opinionated justice. One of these institutional factors, for example, is *stare decisis,* the rule of precedent. The individual judge may think that a particular precedent is wrong or outmoded. If so, he may follow his personal preference and state his reasons for voting to overrule the earlier holding. He is free to do that. But he is not free to ignore the precedents, to act as though they did not exist. He has free choice, but only among limited

6 See Leon Friedman and Fred L. Israel (eds.), *The Justices of the United States Supreme Court, 1789–1969: Their Lives and Major Opinions,* 4 vols. (New York: Chelsea House and R. R. Bowker Company, 1969).

alternatives and after he has satisfied himself that he has met the obligations of consistency and respect for settled principles which his responsibility to the Court imposes upon him. His private views as an individual help to form and may be incorporated into his public views as a justice, but they are not the same thing.

From 1789 to 1976 the Supreme Court had fifteen Chief Justices and ninety associate justices.[7] Biographies of the more important of these men provide excellent insights into the characteristic processes of judicial review as well as their own particular problems and contributions. Here it is possible to note only the principal judicial personalities and the major historical influences associated with the Court's power to interpret the American Constitution.[8]

The Pre-Marshall Court

The first decade of the Court's history was singularly unimpressive. President Washington's appointees were uniformly Federalists, and the entire judiciary quickly developed a definite partisan tone. John Jay, the first Chief Justice, spent one year in England on a diplomatic mission and ran twice for Governor of New York while on the bench. After he succeeded the second time, he resigned the chief justiceship in 1795. John Rutledge, another original appointee, failed to attend a session of the Court during its first two years. Appointed Chief Justice to succeed Jay, he served for four months before the Senate refused him confirmation, and then went insane.

Oliver Ellsworth, the next Chief Justice, resigned in 1800. James Wilson, also a member of the original Court, was an able lawyer but also a land speculator who narrowly avoided imprisonment for debt. Samuel Chase, appointed in 1795, dominated the Court in the latter part of this period. He was blatant in giving effect to his Federalist views from the bench, and in 1800 a term of the Court could not be held because he was absent electioneering for Adams. When the Jeffersonians came into power, he was impeached, but escaped conviction.

Though the Court had comparatively little business during these years, it did make some significant decisions. For one thing, it declined to advise President Washington on some legal questions in the field of foreign relations which he submitted to the Court and thereby established a precedent against giving "advisory opinions." Also the Court strongly supported federal authority against the states in two important decisions. *Ware* v. *Hylton* (1796) held the treaty of peace with Britain to override a Virginia law on the sensitive issue of debts owed by Americans to British subjects. The decision in *Chisholm* v. *Georgia* (1793) asserted that states could be sued in federal courts by citizens of other states, a holding so bitterly resented by the states that the Eleventh Amendment was quickly adopted to void it.[9]

---

[7] Three Associate Justices were promoted to the post of Chief Justice.

[8] See Charles Warren, *The Supreme Court in United States History* (Boston: Little, Brown and Company, rev. ed., 1947); Robert G. McCloskey, *The American Supreme Court* (Chicago: University of Chicago Press, 1960).

[9] See Julius Goebel, Jr., *History of the Supreme Court of the United States: Antecedents and Beginnings to 1801* (New York: The Macmillan Company, 1971).

The Marshall Court

One month before Thomas Jefferson's inauguration in 1801, John Marshall was appointed Chief Justice by the outgoing Federalist administration. For the next thirty-five years he dominated the Court and did more than any other man in Supreme Court history to determine the character of the federal constitutional system. It was Marshall who in *Marbury* v. *Madison* (1803) successfully asserted the Court's power to declare acts of Congress unconstitutional. It was Marshall who in *McCulloch* v. *Maryland* (1819) established the broad authority of Congress to achieve national purposes under the "necessary and proper" clause and other broad grants of constitutional power. It was Marshall who in *Gibbons* v. *Ogden* (1824) first construed the commerce clause and struck down state regulation of commerce. It was Marshall who in *Dartmouth College* v. *Woodward* (1819) expanded the coverage of the contract clause and encouraged the judicial protection of vested rights which was to be a theme of great significance throughout much of the Court's history. It was Marshall who by his courage, his convictions, and his intellectual vigor raised the Supreme Court from a third-rate status to a position of constitutional equality with President and Congress.[10]

The Federalist dominance in membership was soon lost on the Marshall Court as new appointments were made by Republican Presidents, but with few exceptions these colleagues were no match for Marshall. One exception was the able and much underrated William Johnson, whose disagreements with Marshall made him the first great dissenter. Another was the scholarly Joseph Story, nominally a Republican but actually closely attuned to Marshall's views. Thus Marshall was able to direct the Court for more than three decades toward his twin goals—strengthening the powers of the federal government and protecting the rights of private property.

The Taney Court

Roger B. Taney, Democrat from Maryland, was appointed Chief Justice by President Jackson in 1836. Taney's Jacksonian democracy was in marked contrast with Marshall's federalism. States' rights and state police powers were emphasized more on the Court and central authority less. Property rights retained their influence with the Court, but it was agrarian property—land and slaves—rather than the commercial-creditor classes which now won judicial favor.

During his first twenty years on the Court, Taney's attachment to the economic interests of the South and West made him look like an economic liberal. But this same attachment led to the fatal *Dred Scott* decision in 1857, which permanently blackened Taney's reputation. No less intent than Marshall in his determination to preserve the prerogatives of judicial review and control, Taney's great talents were spent in his latter years in a lost and unworthy cause. He died in 1864, an embittered man who had lived too long.[11]

---

[10] See Albert J. Beveridge, *The Life of John Marshall,* 4 vols. (Boston: Houghton Mifflin Company, 1916); Leonard Baker, *John Marshall: A Life in the Law* (New York: The Macmillan Company, 1974); Robert K. Faulkner, *The Jurisprudence of John Marshall* (Princeton, N.J.: Princeton University Press, 1968).

[11] See in particular Carl B. Swisher, *History of the Supreme Court of the United States: The Taney Period, 1836–64* (New York: The Macmillan Company, 1974).

The Post-Civil War Court

The next three Chief Justices—Salmon P. Chase, Morrison R. Waite, and Melville W. Fuller—fell far short of the stature of Marshall and Taney, and failed to mold the Court in their own image. The *Dred Scott* decision had plunged the Court to its lowest depths. Congress revealed its contempt for the Court by changing its size three times in seven years for obvious political purposes. When the Court showed signs of declaring some of the Reconstruction legislation unconstitutional in 1868, Congress brusquely withdrew the Court's jurisdiction to decide the case.[12]

With no strong leadership, the intellectual quality of the Court for the first time was to be found in its associate justices—men like Samuel Miller of Iowa (1862–1890), Stephen J. Field of California (1863–1897), Joseph P. Bradley of New Jersey (1870–1892), and John M. Harlan of Kentucky (1877–1911). Gradually the Court regained its prestige by reestablishing contact with the dominant trends of the times. The postwar period was one of raw and rapid industrial expansion. A continent was being harnessed with railroads, resources were being exploited, great fortunes built. At first the Court was reluctant to legitimize the economic freedom which the burgeoning corporations demanded. In the *Slaughter-House Cases* (1873) and in *Munn v. Illinois* (1877) it declined to use the newly adopted Fourteenth Amendment to strike down state regulatory legislation.

But eventually the pressures were too strong to resist. The due process clause, interpreted by the Court as valueless to protect the civil rights of Negroes, was readily adapted to protect the property rights of corporations. The high point in the Court's dedication to the new capitalism came in 1895, with no less than three significant decisions. One declared the income tax unconstitutional. Another held that the sugar trust did not violate the Sherman Act. The third upheld the jailing of the Socialist leader, Eugene V. Debs, for violating a federal court injunction against a strike by the railway workers' union.

The Holmes Decades

Fuller was Chief Justice until his death in 1910, and was succeeded by Edward D. White of Louisiana. In 1921 former President William Howard Taft took the post and held it until 1930. The most influential and distinguished member of the Court during these years, however, was Associate Justice Oliver Wendell Holmes. Appointed by President Theodore Roosevelt in 1902 from the highest court of Massachusetts, he steadily grew in stature and reputation until his resignation in 1932 at the age of ninety-one.

His character and intellectual alignments defy any brief summary. The public knew him as the great dissenter, and thought of him as a liberal because his dissents were often protests against the denial of civil liberties or the judicial invalidation of liberal legislation. But these protests were less an expression of political liberalism than of a philosophy of limited judicial review which insisted that judges should not

---

[12] See Charles Fairman, *History of the Supreme Court of the United States: Reconstruction and Reunion, 1864–88* (New York: The Macmillan Company, 1971).

substitute their views for those of legislators so long as the legislative policy remained within the bounds of reason.

Holmes's colleagues were generally reluctant to accept such limitations on judicial power. In *Lochner* v. *New York* (1905) the Court struck down a ten-hour law for bakers against Holmes's warning that "the Fourteenth Amendment does not enact Mr. Herbert Spencer's Social Statics." But his position was gradually strengthened in the country and on the Court, as by the appointment of Charles Evans Hughes in 1910, fresh from his work as a reform governor of New York. Hughes left the Court in 1916 to run for President, but that same year President Wilson named to the Court an ardent progressive, Louis D. Brandeis, and got him confirmed in spite of the opposition of the organized bar and big business.

The phrase, "Holmes and Brandeis dissenting," quickly became a part of American folklore as these two men, though proceeding from differing premises, joined in case after case to protest the Court's policies. In 1925 the duo became a trio as President Coolidge named his liberal Attorney General, Harlan F. Stone, to the Court. In their dissenting opinions they mapped out an alternative to the doctrinaire conservatism of the Court majority which, if adopted in time, would have averted the crisis into which the Court was heading.

The Hughes Court and the New Deal

Hughes returned to the Court in 1931 as Chief Justice. A much more flexible man than Taft, he had the responsibility of guiding the Court in its review of the constitutional aspects of the new and experimental legislation enacted by the New Deal to combat the Great Depression. On the Court he headed, Brandeis and Stone had been joined by Benjamin N. Cardozo, appointed in 1932 to fill the Holmes vacancy. These three justices could generally be counted on to uphold the New Deal, but they were offset by four conservative justices—Willis Van Devanter, appointed by Taft in 1910; James C. McReynolds, named by Wilson in 1914; and two Harding appointees of 1922, George Sutherland and Pierce Butler. The balance of power on the Court thus rested with the Chief Justice himself and with the ninth member, Owen J. Roberts, appointed by Hoover in 1930.

The initial tests of 1934 seemed to suggest that the Court would accept the new legislative trends by a vote of five to four, but this forecast soon proved mistaken. In 1935 and 1936 the Court invalidated a series of important federal and state regulatory laws, usually by a vote of five to four or six or three, depending upon whether Roberts alone, or Roberts and Hughes, voted with the conservative bloc. After his electoral triumph in 1936 President Roosevelt, who had had no Court vacancies to fill during his first term, undertook to eliminate this judicial barrier to reform by a proposal to increase the Court's size to fifteen justices.

Juggling the size of the Court was no longer so acceptable as it had been in the 1860s, however, and the Court-packing plan was defeated in Congress. However, in several key cases in the spring of 1937 Roberts swung over to the liberal side, giving the administration some five to four victories. At the end of the term Van Devanter retired, and President Roosevelt had his opportunity to begin remaking the Court.

The Recent Court

Between 1937 and 1943 President Roosevelt appointed eight members to the Court (one position being filled twice) and elevated Harlan Stone to the chief justiceship.[13] All these appointees were economic liberals, and there ceased to be any danger of judicial invalidation of regulatory legislation affecting property. The characteristic problem of the Roosevelt Court dealt rather with civil liberty, and the justices, in spite of their basic libertarian leanings, quickly found themselves more divided than ever, but now over the nature of their judicial responsibility for the protection of libertarian goals. Justices Hugo Black, William O. Douglas, Frank Murphy, and Wiley Rutledge were a cohesive group as firmly committed to the use of judicial power to protect civil liberties from legislative infringement as the anti-New Deal conservatives had been in the protection of economic freedom a decade earlier. Justice Felix Frankfurter, on the other hand, argued that the Holmes tradition called for judicial restraint in both areas.[14]

The libertarian temper of the Roosevelt Court was substantially diluted by President Truman's four appointments. Chief Justice Fred Vinson replaced Stone on the latter's death in 1946. Both Rutlege and Murphy died in the summer of 1949, thus leaving only Black and Douglas in the Court's activist bloc. The most difficult problems of the Vinson Court were those generated by the cold war against communism. In its most celebrated decision, it upheld the Smith Act convictions of the leaders of the American Communist Party in *Dennis* v. *United States* (1951), with Black and Douglas dissenting, and it was careful to refrain from interfering with the "Red" hunts of congressional investigating committees.[15]

On Vinson's death in 1953, President Eisenhower named Earl Warren of California to be Chief Justice. In the first term under his leadership the Court unanimously declared unconstitutional racial segregation in the public schools, boldly overturning the doctrine of "separate but equal" which had been used to justify segregation for almost sixty years.

President Eisenhower had the opportunity to make four additional appointments—John M. Harlan, grandson of the earlier Harlan, replacing Jackson; William J. Brennan, Jr., replacing Minton; Charles E. Whittaker, replacing Reed; and Potter Stewart, replacing Burton. With the appointment of Brennan, a liberal Catholic Democrat, a new four-judge activist bloc developed on the Court, as Brennan voted rather consistently with Warren, Black and Douglas. The other new members of the Court, however, tended to look to Justice Frankfurter for intellectual leadership, and particularly after 1957 there were a series of five to four defeats for the activist bloc.

President Kennedy made two appointments to the Court in 1962. Whittaker's place was taken by Byron R. White, forty-four-year-old ex-Rhodes scholar and

[13] Alpheus T. Mason, *Harlan Fiske Stone: Pillar of the Law* (New York: The Viking Press, Inc., 1956).

[14] C. Herman Pritchett, *The Roosevelt Court: A Study in Judicial Politics and Values, 1937–1947* (Chicago: Quadrangle Books, 1969).

[15] C. Herman Pritchett, *Civil Liberties and the Vinson Court* (Chicago: University of Chicago Press, 1954).

famous football player who had been Deputy Attorney General in the Kennedy administration. When Justice Frankfurter retired because of illness, his seat was filled by Arthur J. Goldberg, dynamic general counsel for the AFL–CIO. The Court's balance was swung sharply toward the liberal side by these appointments, as was immediately evidenced by dramatic decisions dealing with such controversial matters as legislative reapportionment, prayer and Bible reading in public schools, and increased procedural protections in criminal prosecutions.

In 1965 President Johnson asked Justice Goldberg to become United States Ambassador to the United Nations, and to fill the vacancy the President named one of his close advisers, Abe Fortas, member of a prominent Washington law firm who in 1963 had argued the famous case of *Gideon* v. *Wainwright* before the Court. Justice Clark retired in 1967 to avoid any conflict of interest after his son, Ramsey, was named Attorney General. To his place President Johnson appointed Solicitor General and former court of appeals judge Thurgood Marshall, the Court's first black and the man who as chief counsel for the NAACP had argued the school desegregation case, *Brown* v. *Board of Education* (1954), before the Court.

The Warren Court was one of the most controversial in Supreme Court history.[16] Its decisions defending minority rights and civil liberties made the impeachment of Earl Warren a favorite demand of the radical right. The attacks on the Warren Court came from three principal quarters—from Southern opponents of the desegregation decision; from those who contended that the Court had handicapped the fight against Communist subversion by its limitations on congressional investigatory power and insistence on the procedural rights of "political offenders"; and from those who maintained that the Court had infringed state authority over a wide range of activities, including economic regulation, procedure in criminal cases, religious observances in the public schools, and legislative apportionment.

In Congress the assault on the Court reached a climax in the closing days of the 1958 session, when a series of measures intended to curb or reverse the Court were narrowly defeated.[17] The Court soon thereafter withdrew from some of the positions which had led to congressional anger, particularly with respect to judicial control over congressional investigating committees.

Then in 1962 the Court again stirred up a storm by declaring unconstitutional religious observances in the public schools *(Engel* v. *Vitale)* and opening up state legislative-apportionment practices to judicial review and control *(Baker* v. *Carr).* However, efforts to reverse the Court's rulings by constitutional amendments failed, and in the legislative-apportionment field the Court proceeded to carry through a political revolution by requiring the long underrepresented urban and suburban areas to be given their proper weight in state legislatures.

Warren notified President Johnson of his intention to resign in 1968, effective upon confirmation of his successor; but Justice Fortas, nominated to the post by

16 For a somewhat critical account, see Philip B. Kurland, *Politics, the Constitution, and the Warren Court* (Chicago: The University of Chicago Press, 1970).
17 See C. Herman Pritchett, *Congress versus the Supreme Court, 1957–1960* (Minneapolis: The University of Minnesota Press, 1961); Walter F. Murphy, *Congress and the Court* (Chicago: University of Chicago Press, 1962).

Johnson, was unable to secure confirmation by the Senate. Warren then continued to serve for another term until replaced by Nixon appointee Warren Earl Burger. Nixon's announced goal was to return the Court to the control of conservative "strict constructionists," and he made three more appointments of men meeting this test: Harry A. Blackmun, replacing Fortas who resigned in 1969, and Lewis F. Powell Jr. and William H. Rehnquist, on the retirement of Hugo Black and John M. Harlan.

On the Burger Court, the four Nixon appointees tended to form a conservative bloc which could generally count on the support of White or Stewart or both, leaving the liberal trio of Douglas, Black, and Marshall in a minority role. However, there was no wholesale reversal of Warren Court holdings. Rather, the Burger Court acted in a mixed or ambiguous fashion, leaving many Warren era rulings intact. While retreating moderately in the area of criminal procedures, it maintained a generally strong commitment to First Amendment rights and took activist positions on such issues as abortion, sex discrimination, capital punishment, and the rights of prisoners and inmates of mental institutions.[18] The retirement of Justice Douglas in late 1975, and his replacement by John Paul Stevens, a moderately conservative member of the Court of Appeals for the Seventh Circuit, appeared to confirm the Court's trend toward a less active policy role, and an accelerated tendency toward limitation or reversal of Warren Court precedents became evident in the mid-1970s.

In summary, the American constitutional system is one in which important policy questions are frequently cast in the form of a lawsuit and brought to the Supreme Court for decision. The Court is basically a public law court, and its highest public law function is to determine the current meaning of the Constitution when that is necessary to settle a judicial controversy that comes before it. In the search for current meanings the justices inevitably consult their own policy preferences, but the institutional setting is one which forces responsibility upon them and requires them to meet high standards of consistency and logic. Theirs is the difficult task of moving with the times, yet without departing from constitutional fundamentals or impairing that popular expectation of judicial stability which is so necessary an asset to the moral authority of the Court.

---

[18] Critical accounts of the Nixon Court are found in James F. Simon, *In His Own Image: The Supreme Court in Richard Nixon's America* (New York: David McKay Company, Inc., 1973); Leonard W. Levy, *Against the Law: The Nixon Court and Criminal Justice* (New York: Harper & Row, Publishers, Incorporated, 1974). See also Stephen L. Wasby, *Continuity and Change: From the Warren Court to the Burger Court* (Pacific Palisades, Calif.: Goodyear Publishing Company, Inc., 1976).

Chapter 4

Nation and State

One of the serious reservations which the framers had in setting up a new Constitution was whether a large country would be a threat to the freedom of its citizens. The delegates who opposed the Virginia Plan for a strong central government had a picture in their minds, drawn in part at least from the experience of the Greek city-states, of the "small republic" as the ideal form of government. Roger Sherman put it this way: "The people are more happy in small than large States."

The problem was that small republics were too weak, standing alone, to protect their independence and their economies, and so they had to associate in some common organization for mutual protection. But Sherman and other supporters of the New Jersey Plan believed that a confederation limited to the functions of keeping the peace among the states and defending them against foreign enemies was all that was needed.

It was James Madison's role to answer the small republic argument. He contended that, from antiquity to the current American states, small republics had been beset by conflicts between classes which were fatal to liberty. A large republic would be preferable, for there, he argued, liberty would be protected by "the great variety of interests, parties, and sects which it embraces." An "extended republic of the United States" would be divided into many groups, no single one amounting to a majority. Only as smaller groups voluntarily associated could majorities be formed, a process which would force each group to moderate its position and protect the liberties of all.

The Convention was persuaded by Madison's argument and even more by realization that their goals of security, peace, and economic development could be achieved only through a strong central government. But the Founders' insistence on also preserving the states as strong organs of local government forced them to invent a federal system.

We now think of the threefold distinction among the confederal, federal, and unitary forms of government as self-evident. But in 1787 only two forms, the confederal and the national (unitary), were recognized. The opening words of the resolution proposing the Virginia Plan stated these two alternatives: a "merely federal" union or "a National Government." "Merely federal" meant a confederation such as was then in existence. It was because this "merely federal" plan had failed that the Virginia delegation proposed a truly "national" government. But what actually emerged from the Convention was the blueprint for a large republic intended to achieve both liberty and security by a division of responsibilities and functions which has come to be considered the true form of federalism.

The Constitution, it should be noted, does not use the term "federalism." Because of the vague theoretical origins of American federalism, disagreement over the nature of the Union was almost inevitable. The existence of sharply divisive sectional interests led to the exploitation of these disagreements for intensely practical purposes. Regional differences were compounded by localistic patriotism and hope of economic gain. Where such animus is present in constitutional issues, judicial decisions are not likely to be accepted as final. During the first half of the nineteenth century these controversies were fostered by all the resources of the political process, and ultimately had to be resolved by a bitter civil war. Only after the nature of the Union had been determined by the arbitrament of arms was it possible for the courts to continue with adjudication of the lesser but continuing problems of adjustment in the federal system.

THE NATURE OF THE UNION

A Compact of States or of People?

The prevailing political philosophy of the eighteenth century, as we have seen, stressed contract as the basis of governmental authority. The Constitution was such a contract, but who were the parties to it—the states or the people of the United States? The language of the Constitution could be cited to support both views. Article VII provides that approval by conventions in nine states "shall be sufficient for the establishment of this Constitution *between the states* so ratifying the same."[1] On the other hand, the Preamble to the Constitution declares that it is "the people of the United States" who "do ordain and establish this Constitution," and conventions rather than state legislatures were chosen as the instruments of ratification

---

[1] Italics supplied.

precisely to emphasize the popular base of the contract. Again, it could be pointed out that, although the Articles of Confederation had specifically provided that the states were sovereign, the Constitution was discreetly silent on the location of sovereignty.

Interposition

After the establishment of the new government, the first significant theoretical attack on the authority of the national government came in the form of the famous Kentucky and Virginia Resolutions against the Alien and Sedition Acts. The first paragraph of the Kentucky Resolutions, which Jefferson drafted, reads:

> *Resolved,* That the several states composing the United States of America are not united on the principle of unlimited submission to their general government; but that, by compact, under the style and title of a Constitution for the United States, and of amendments thereto, they constituted a general government for special purposes, delegated to that government certain definite powers, reserving, each state to itself, the residuary mass of right to their own self-government; and that whensoever the general government assumed undelegated powers, its acts are unauthoritative, void, and of no force; that to this compact each state acceded as a state, and is an integral party; that this government, created by this compact, was not made the exclusive or final judge of the extent of the powers delegated to itself, since that would have made its discretion, and not the Constitution, the measure of its powers; but that, as in all other cases of compact among parties having no common Judge, *each party has an equal right to judge for itself, as well of infractions as of the mode and measure of redress.*

In a second set of resolutions passed in 1799, the Kentucky legislature proclaimed: "That a Nullification, by those sovereignties, of all unauthorized acts done under color of that instrument, is the rightful remedy." Madison, who drafted the Virginia Resolutions, contributed the concept of "interposition" to American constitutional history in the third paragraph of those resolutions, when he concluded "that, in case of a deliberate, palpable, and dangerous exercise of other powers, not granted by the said compact, the states, who are parties thereto, have the right, and are in duty bound, to interpose, for arresting the progress of the evil, and for maintaining within their respective limits, the authorities, rights, and liberties, appertaining to them."

Did Madison and Jefferson mean to claim that the Union was a system of fully sovereign states, a confederation from which each state could retire at any time? Did they mean that refusal to be bound by any objectionable act of Congress was within the rights of the states, and that an attempt to enforce the act on a state would justify its secession? It seems highly unlikely. While they referred to the states as sovereign, they also conceded that the national government was sovereign. Acceptance of the divisibility of sovereignty was common at that time.

The Kentucky and Virginia Resolutions were circulated among the other states, and they elicited responses from at least seven, mostly in the Federalist Northeast, upholding the concept of federal supremacy and denying the right of a state to nullify federal law. Jefferson's victory over the Federalists in the election of 1800, due in no small part to popular resentment over the Alien and Sedition Acts, terminated this episode. But within a decade the New England states were themselves to enunciate extreme states' rights doctrine, under the pressure of the severe economic hardships they experienced as a result of President Jefferson's embargo policy. This sectional disaffection was increased by the strains of the War of 1812, during which the New England states sometimes refused to cooperate with American military operations and continued considerable trade with Britain. The Hartford Convention of 1814–1815, in which this movement culminated, recommended to the legislatures of the states represented that they pass measures to protect their citizens from the operation of unconstitutional national acts. But before the resolutions even got to Washington, the war was over, the complaints were forgotten, and the only result of the Convention was to annihilate the Federalist party.

Nullification

The theory of nullification originated with Jefferson's statement in the Kentucky Resolutions that "where powers are assumed which have not been delegated, a nullification of the act is the rightful remedy." This idea was later developed as a rationalization for Southern opposition to the increase in tariff rates between 1816 and 1828. John C. Calhoun, alarmed at the open talk of secession in the South, offered the doctrine of nullification as a substitute, contending that it was a logical extension of the Virginia and Kentucky Resolutions.

In 1832 a South Carolina convention passed an "Ordinance of Nullification" declaring the federal tariff acts null and void and forbidding federal agents to collect them in the state. President Jackson immediately challenged this action, saying that the power of nullification was "incompatible with the existence of the Union," and sent gunboats into Charleston harbor to enforce the tariff. The nullification statute was eventually repealed by the state after Congress had worked out a compromise measure on the tariff rates.

Secession

In the years preceding the Civil War, with the controversies over slavery and the tariff going on around them, Southern statesmen shifted their ground from the right of nullification to secession as the means to preserve their economic life and social institutions. Jefferson Davis pointed to the reservations which Virginia, New York, and Rhode Island had made in ratifying the Constitution, wherein they asserted that the powers granted to the federal government might be reassumed by the people in case of oppression, and concluded: "The right of the people of the several States to resume the powers delegated by them to the common agency, was not left without positive and ample assertion, even at a period when it had never been denied."[2]

For Calhoun, secession was justified as a final remedy to preserve a state's rights. According to his theory, after a state had interposed its authority to prevent federal action, the federal government could appeal to the amending process. If three-fourths of the states upheld the federal claim, the matter was settled as far as

---

[2] Jefferson Davis, *The Rise and Fall of the Confederate Government* (New York: D. Appleton & Company, Inc., 1881), vol. 1, p. 173.

those states were concerned. But the dissenting state was not obliged to acquiesce in all instances.

Lincoln's decision to use force to keep the Southern states in the Union and the victory of the North in the Civil War closed the debate over the legality of secession. The final decision was rendered at Appomattox Courthouse. After the war, the Supreme Court tidied up a bit in *Texas* v. *White* (1869). The case hinged on the question whether or not Texas had ever left the Union, and the Court held:

> When, therefore, Texas became one of the United States, she entered into an indissoluble relation. . . . The act which consummated her admission into the Union was something more than a compact; it was the incorporation of a new member into the political body. And it was final. The union between Texas and the other States was as complete, as perpetual, and as indissoluble as the union between the original States.

Chief Justice Chase summed up the principle involved: "The Constitution, in all its provisions, looks to an indestructible Union, composed of indestructible States."

NATIONAL SUPREMACY

Division of Powers

In essence, American federalism is a form of political organization in which the exercise of power is divided between two levels of government, each having the use of those powers as a matter of right, and each acting on the same citizen body. The appropriate division of powers between these two levels was one of the major concerns of the Constitutional Convention, and the pattern of allocation which emerged was fairly complex, as the following summary indicates:

1. Exclusively national powers   Since a nation obviously must speak with one voice in foreign relations, the power to declare war and make treaties was allocated to the national government. For different but equally obvious reasons, a uniform monetary system was essential, which necessitated central control of the power to coin money.

2. Exclusively state powers   Since the federal government was one of delegated powers, obviously any powers not delegated to it remained with the states. Rather than leave this matter to inference, however, the Tenth Amendment spelled it out: "The powers not delegated to the United States by the Constitution, nor prohibited by it to the States, are reserved to the States respectively, or to the people." There has been much misunderstanding about this amendment, and it has often been viewed as the principal guarantor of the rights of the states. Actually it adds nothing new to the Constitution, being simply declaratory of the relation between the national government and the states.[3]

[3] Walter Berns, "The Meaning of the Tenth Amendment," in Robert A. Goldwin (ed.), *A Nation of States* (Chicago: Rand McNally & Company, 1963), pp. 126–148.

3. Concurrent powers   The Constitution expressly gives to the national government such important powers as levying taxes and regulating commerce, but it makes no effort to prohibit the states from also exercising such authority within their own borders.

4. Powers prohibited to the national government   According to the principle that the national government is one of delegated powers, which was accepted by the framers though not spelled out until the Tenth Amendment was added, the national government has no authority to exercise powers not authorized by the Constitution. It was this argument, we have seen, which was used at the Convention to deny the necessity for a protective bill of rights. However, the framers did include in the original Constitution a few express prohibitions on federal power, such as those against the levying of direct taxes or suspending the writ of habeas corpus. When the Bill of Rights was added, the extensive prohibitions of the first eight amendments were incorporated in this group.

5. Powers prohibited to the states   In Article I, section 10, a group of activities is forbidden to the States. The purpose of these prohibitions is primarily to enforce the exclusive nature of national control over foreign relations, the monetary system, and foreign commerce. A further prohibition, which does not fall into any of these three categories, is on any law impairing the obligation of contracts.

6. Powers prohibited to both the nation and the states   Certain prohibitions on the states in Article I, section 10, are also imposed on the national government by the preceding section. These include the ban on passing bills of attainder and ex post facto laws, and granting titles of nobility.

Legislative Supremacy

With this rather elaborate division of functions and powers between the two levels of government, disputes are bound to occur. The Constitution supplies a principle for settling them in the "supremacy clause" of Article VI: "This Constitution, and the laws of the United States which shall be made in pursuance thereof; and all treaties made, or which shall be made, under the authority of the United States, shall be the supreme law of the land; and the judges in every state shall be bound thereby, any thing in the Constitution or laws of any state to the contrary notwithstanding."

The effectiveness of this section was early demonstrated in the case of *McCulloch* v. *Maryland* (1819). In 1818 the Maryland Legislature levied a tax on the politically unpopular Bank of the United States, which had been chartered by the federal government. The cashier of the Baltimore branch of the Bank refused to pay the tax and was convicted of violating the law by the state courts. The Supreme Court unanimously upheld the Bank's position, Chief Justice Marshall basing his opinion squarely on the supremacy clause. "If any one proposition could command the universal assent of mankind," he wrote, "we might expect it would be this: that the government of the Union, though limited in its powers, is supreme within its sphere of action." Consequently, no state had any power "to retard, impede, burden, or in any manner control, the operations of the constitutional laws enacted by congress."

When Congress enters a field in which it is authorized to act, then, its legislation supersedes all incompatible state regulations. In practical terms, however, the question whether Congress has preempted a given area is a difficult one, since federal statutes seldom state whether all local rules on the matter are suspended. It falls ultimately to the Supreme Court to determine the relation of federal and state statutes. In *Pennsylvania* v. *Nelson* (1956), Chief Justice Warren attempted to codify the tests which the Court has used to guide such decisions. First, is the scheme of federal regulations so pervasive as to make it a reasonable inference that Congress has left no room for the states? Second, do the federal statutes touch a field in which the interest of the national government is so dominant that it must be assumed to preclude state action on the same subject? Third, does enforcement of the state act present a serious danger of conflict with the administration of the federal program?

In the *Nelson* case, a conviction for violation of the Pennsylvania sedition act had been reversed by the state supreme court on the ground that a federal sedition act (the Smith Act of 1940) had occupied the field and superseded the state law. The United States Supreme Court agreed. Using the three criteria just suggested, Warren concluded that Congress had taken over the entire task of protecting the country from seditious conduct when it passed the Smith Act, even though no express intention to exclude the states was stated in that statute.

Dual Federalism

Congressional supremacy, thus established under Marshall, had to face a different kind of challenge from the Taney Court, grounded on the Tenth Amendment. Under the influence of Taney's states' rights constitutional theories, the Supreme Court on many occasions took its legal bearings more from this amendment than from the national supremacy clause. Espousing a doctrine called "dual federalism," the Court assumed that the two levels of government were coequal sovereignties, each supreme within its own sphere. Thus the fact that certain powers had been reserved to the states constituted a limit on the authority specifically delegated to the national government.

From 1890 to 1937 the Court with its laissez-faire philosophy found it convenient to use the Taney doctrine. On the one hand the federal government was restricted from enacting economic regulation by "invisible radiations" from the Tenth Amendment, and on the other hand the states were barred from interference with the workings of the economic system by the due process clause of the Fourteenth Amendment.

The theory of dual federalism received its clearest statement in *Hammer* v. *Dagenhart* (1918). By a five to four vote, the Court here invalidated a congressional statute restricting the transportation in interstate commerce of goods produced by child labor. For the majority, Justice Day wrote: "The grant of authority over a purely federal matter was not intended to destroy the local power always existing and carefully reserved to the States in the Tenth Amendment." He went on to say that in interpreting the Constitution it should never be forgotten that "the powers not expressly delegated to the National Government are reserved" to the states and the people by the Tenth Amendment.

To arrive at this conclusion Justice Day had to misquote the amendment; the term "expressly" does not appear in its text. He had to ignore judicial precedent; Marshall in *McCulloch* v. *Maryland* had held that the omission of the word "expressly" had left the question whether a particular power had been delegated to the national government to be answered by a "fair construction of the whole instrument." Justice Day had also to assume a position which was historically inaccurate; when the Tenth Amendment was under consideration in the First Congress the anti-Federalists had tried to insert the word "expressly," but had been voted down. In any case, the commerce power had been expressly delegated to Congress. These errors did not go unchallenged. Speaking for the four dissenters Justice Holmes declared: "I should have thought that the most conspicuous decisions of this Court had made it clear that the power to regulate commerce and other constitutional powers could not be cut down or qualified by the fact that it might interfere with the carrying out of the domestic policy of any State."

Much of the struggle in the middle 1930s between the conservative members of the Supreme Court and President Roosevelt may be seen as a clash between Taney's dual federalism and the older national supremacy of Marshall. In the end it was the interpretation of Marshall and Roosevelt which prevailed. In a series of cases culminating in *United States* v. *Darby Lumber Co.* (1941), the reconstituted and rejuvenated Supreme Court upheld a number of federal laws which directly affected local policies. In the *Darby* opinion Justice Stone wrote that the Tenth Amendment "states but a truism that all is retained which has not been surrendered. There is nothing in the history of its adoption to suggest that it was more than declaratory of the relationship between the national and state governments as it had been established by the Constitution before the amendment." The *Darby* decision specifically overruled *Hammer* v. *Dagenhart.*

More recent state efforts to question congressional supremacy have given the Court little trouble. *Maryland* v. *Wirtz* (1968) upheld an amendment to the Fair Labor Standards Act which extended minimum wage coverage to nonprofessional and nonadministrative employees of state public schools, hospitals, and related institutions. In *Fry* v. *United States* (1975), the federal wage and salary controls imposed under the Economic Stabilization Act of 1970 were held applicable to state employees. But a 1974 wages and overtime law was held to violate state sovereignty in *National League of Cities* v. *Usery* (1976), and *Wirtz* was overruled.

Judicial Supremacy

Implementing the principle of national supremacy requires that the Supreme Court have authority to review the decisions of state courts. The Judiciary Act of 1789, in section 25, provided for such review of final judgments or decrees "in the highest court of law or equity of a State in which a decision in the suit could be had," in three classes of cases: (1) where the validity of a federal law or treaty was "drawn in question," and the decision was against its validity; (2) where a state statute was questioned as "repugnant to the constitution, treaties or laws of the United States," and the decision was in favor of its validity; and (3) where the construction of the federal Constitution, treaty, or statute was drawn in question, and the decision was against the title, right, privilege, or exemption claimed. These categories were all based on the principle that if the Constitution and laws of the United States were to be observed, the Supreme Court would have to have an opportunity to review decisions of state courts which ruled adversely on asserted federal rights.

The Supreme Court's power of review over state supreme court decisions was not established without incident. In *Fairfax's Devisee* v. *Hunter's Lessee* (1813) the Supreme Court (John Marshall not sitting because his brother was involved in the litigation) reversed a decision of the Virginia high court regarding the land rights of British subjects who were protected under the Jay Treaty. Virginia refused to acquiesce in the decision; the state court argued that although a state was bound to respect the Constitution, laws, and treaties of the United States as supreme, it was obliged to follow only its own interpretations, not those of a federal court. Because the courts of the United States represented one sovereignty, they could not review decisions of state courts, which belonged to another sovereignty.

Consequently the Supreme Court's order was returned unobeyed. The Court in *Martin* v. *Hunter's Lessee* (1816) strongly reaffirmed its right to review state decisions. Justice Story answered Virginia's argument with the statement that the Constitution was not ordained by the states, but by the "people of the United States," and these people could invest the national government with whatever powers they thought proper. "The courts of the United States can, without question, revise the proceedings of the executive and legislative authorities of the States. . . . Surely, the exercise of the same right over judicial tribunals is not a higher or more dangerous act of sovereign power."

The second Supreme Court order bypassed the Virginia supreme court and was directed to the court in which the case had originated. There the mandate was obeyed. Charles Warren, the historian of the Court, has termed Story's opinion in this case as having been ever since "the keystone of the whole arch of Federal judicial power."[4] However, the states' rights forces were not easily daunted, and they returned to the attack in *Cohens* v. *Virginia* (1821). Congress had passed an act authorizing the District of Columbia to conduct lotteries to finance civic improvements. The state of Virginia, which had a law forbidding lotteries, arrested and convicted two persons for selling the Washington tickets within its domain. After conviction, the defendants appealed to the Supreme Court. The Virginia Legislature was highly incensed at this reiteration of federal appellate jurisdiction over state courts, and denied the existence of any such authority. The argument for the state was that the Supreme Court could not exercise appellate powers over a state court decision to which a state was a party, since the Constitution placed all cases in which a state was a party within the Supreme Court's *original* jurisdiction. Counsel argued that the power of the federal judiciary was either exclusive or concurrent, but not paramount. Where it was concurrent, "whichsoever judiciary gets possession

[4] Charles Warren, *The Supreme Court in United States History* (Boston: Little, Brown and Company, rev. ed., 1947), vol. 1, p. 449.

of the case [first], should proceed to final judgment, from which there should be no appeal."

Again the Supreme Court rejected the anarchic principles of this contention. Marshall held that where a state had obtained a judgment against an individual and in so doing had overruled a defense set up under the Constitution or laws of the United States, it was the undeniable right of the Supreme Court to review the decision. Then the Court examined the merits of the case and decided against the defendants on the ground that Congress had not intended the lottery tickets to be sold outside the District of Columbia. Many Virginia officials and newspapers were enraged at the assertion of federal jurisdiction, but because of the decision on the merits they were left with no order to disobey or resist.

Nullification and the Courts

The right to review and reverse judgments of state courts and to review state legislative or executive action through Supreme Court reexamination of state or lower federal court orders has been challenged from time to time by the theory of nullification. Rather surprisingly, the principal episodes of this kind occurred in the Northern states. The first controversy, *United States* v. *Peters* (1809), concerned the decision of a lower federal court in Pennsylvania on a claim growing out of a prize case from the Revolutionary War. The state Legislature defied the court's judgment and declared it to be in violation of the Eleventh Amendment. In the Supreme Court's decision Marshall made short shrift of the state's claim to interfere with the actions of a federal court, saying: "If the legislatures of the several States may, at will, annul the judgments of the courts of the United States, and destroy the rights acquired under those judgments, the constitution itself becomes a solemn mockery; and the nation is deprived of the means of enforcing its laws by the instrumentality of its own tribunals."

Shortly before the Civil War, nullification reappeared in the North. In Wisconsin, Sherman M. Booth, a Milwaukee newspaper editor, helped rescue an escaped slave from a deputy federal marshal. Booth was arrested by federal authorities, and since there were no federal prisons in the area, he was placed in a local jail to await trial. A judge of the Wisconsin supreme court issued a writ of habeas corpus and declared the federal Fugitive Slave Law unconstitutional. The federal marshal appealed to the entire state supreme court against the obvious irregularity of a state judge issuing orders to federal officials. But the Wisconsin supreme court upheld the judge both on the issuance of the writ and the unconstitutionality of the law. The marshal then appealed to the United States Supreme Court. But before that Court could hear the case, Booth was convicted in federal district court and sentenced to a fine of $1,000 and a month in prison. Once again Booth applied to the Wisconsin supreme court for habeas corpus and once again that court issued the writ, freeing Booth.

In *Ableman* v. *Booth* (1859) Chief Justice Taney voiced the unanimous opinion of the Supreme Court that Wisconsin "has reversed and annulled the provisions of the Constitution itself, and the [Judiciary] act of Congress of 1789, and made the superior and appellant tribunal the inferior and subordinate." If Wisconsin could so control the actions of federal agencies within that state, so could every other state. The language of Article VI was "too plain to admit of doubt or to need comment." The decisions of federal courts were "as far beyond the reach of the judicial process issued by a State judge or a State Court, as if the line of division was traced by landmarks and monuments visible to the eye." In closing his opinion, Taney, himself a firm believer in states' rights, affirmed that "no power is more clearly conferred by the Constitution and laws of the United States, than the power of this court to decide, ultimately and finally, all cases arising under such Constitution and laws."

In 1956 the dust was blown off the doctrines of interposition and nullification, as they were invoked by several Southern states in protest against the Supreme Court's decision invalidating racial segregation in the schools. In its act of nullification the state of Alabama laid down the basic premise of its action:

> WHEREAS the states, being the parties to the constitutional compact, it follows of necessity that there can be no tribunal above their authority to decide, in the last resort, whether the compact made by them be violated; and, consequently, they must decide themselves, in the last resort, such questions as may be of sufficient magnitude to require their interposition.

On these grounds the Legislature of Alabama declared, "The decisions and orders of the Supreme Court of the United States relating to the separation of races in the public schools are, as a matter of right, null, void, and of no effect; and . . . as a matter of right, this State is not bound to abide thereby."[5]

All such actions and arguments are condemned by their opposition to the mainstream of American history and constitutional development. In the 1958 Little Rock case, *Cooper* v. *Aaron,* the Supreme Court disposed sharply and decisively of the contention that the Governor and Legislature of Arkansas were not bound by the Court's 1954 decision declaring segregated schools unconstitutional. Later, in *Bush* v. *Orleans School Board* (1960) the Court quoted with approval the terse comment of a federal district court: "The conclusion is clear that interposition is not a *constitutional* doctrine. If taken seriously, it is illegal defiance of constitutional authority."

ADMISSION OF NEW STATES

With the migration to the territory between the Appalachians and the Mississippi, it was apparent even before the Constitutional Convention that new states might well be formed in the area. The claims of certain states to western territory had been ceded to the general government when the Articles of Confederation were adopted, with the understanding that Congress would eventually organize the territory into states and admit them to the Union. By the Northwest Ordinance of 1787, the Confederation Congress provided that the Northwest Territory was to be divided

---

[5] Act no. 42, Special Session 1956, Alabama, reprinted in 1 RACE RELATIONS LAW REPORTER 437 (1956).

into not less than three nor more than five states, and that 60,000 inhabitants would be requisite for admission of a state.

Article IV, section 3, provides for the admission of new states into the Union by Congress. The only stated limitations on congressional discretion are that "no new state shall be formed or erected within the jurisdiction of any other state; nor any state be formed by the junction of two or more states, or parts of states, without the consent of the legislatures of the states concerned as well as of the Congress."

Thirty-five new states were admitted to the Union between 1791 and 1912. Five were carved out of the territory of older states—Vermont, Kentucky, Tennessee, Maine, and West Virginia. In the first four cases the legislature of the older state gave its consent. But West Virginia was formed from the western counties of Virginia during the Civil War when Virginia was in military opposition to the Union. In this situation consent was given by a rump legislature from the area convened especially for this purpose. After the war, Virginia formally consented to the dismemberment.

Of the remaining thirty states, all but two went through a probationary status as organized territories before they were admitted as states. The exceptions were Texas, which upon its admission in 1845 was an independent republic, and California, which was formed out of a region ceded by Mexico in 1848.[6]

The normal procedure by which a territory becomes a state calls for Congress to pass an enabling act allowing the territorial government to convene a popular convention to propose a state constitution. If the voters ratify this constitution, it is submitted to Congress for approval. Congress then may pass a resolution admitting the new state. A statehood resolution, like other legislation, is subject to presidential veto, but unlike other statutes, once adopted it is irrepealable.

Congress may grant or withhold statehood for any reasons it chooses. Before the Civil War the primary motive in admission was to maintain a balance between slave and free states. Nevada was admitted, in spite of its sparse population, to provide a necessary ratifying vote for the Thirteenth Amendment. Hawaii and Alaska were strong candidates for admission from at least 1944, when the platforms of both political parties recommended statehood, but various political considerations delayed favorable action by Congress. Alaska finally won admission in 1958, and Hawaii in 1959.

Under the Northwest Ordinance of 1787 new states were to be admitted "on an equal footing with the original states, in all respects whatever." Consequently it is surprising that the Constitutional Convention of the same year voted, nine states to two, against placing a similar equal status provision in Article IV. However, this omission has had no practical effect, for the principle of equality is a fundamental part of American constitutional law. Thus the joint resolution admitting Texas in 1845 specified that Texas "shall be admitted unto the Union . . . on an equal footing with the existing States."

---

[6] The joint resolution admitting Texas to the Union provided that four additional states could be formed from its territory and be entitled to admission. Some Texans have expressed interest in this possibility as a way of getting eight additional Senate seats for Texas. But in spite of the 1845 law, Congress would have to give consent for admission of the new states, which seems unlikely.

The Supreme Court has on many occasions recognized equality of status as an inherent attribute of the federal Union. *Coyle* v. *Smith* (1911) supplies the best illustration of its position. Under the enabling act admitting Oklahoma as a state, Congress had specified that the capital should be located at Guthrie for at least seven years. After four years, the Oklahoma Legislature ordered the capital moved to Oklahoma City. The Supreme Court held that the state was not bound by the congressional limitation, reasoning as follows:

> The power is to admit "new States into *this* Union." "This Union" was and is a union of States, equal in power, dignity and authority, each competent to exert that residuum of sovereignty not delegated to the United States by the Constitution itself. To maintain otherwise would be to say that the Union, through the power of Congress to admit new States, might come to be a union of States unequal in power, as including States whose powers were restricted only by the Constitution, with others whose powers had been further restricted by an act of Congress accepted as a condition of admission.

Another illustration of the ineffectiveness of preadmission restrictions after admission was supplied by the experience of Arizona, which proposed a state constitution providing for the recall of elected officials, including judges. President Taft objected to this feature, and vetoed the resolution of admission. Arizona then amended her constitution to eliminate this provision, and was then admitted. Shortly thereafter Arizona, secure in her statehood, put recall of judges back into her constitution.

An exception to the "equal footing" doctrine arose under the Submerged Lands Act of 1953, which ceded to the coastal states ownership of land and resources under adjoining seas to a distance of 3 miles from shore or to the state's "historic boundaries."[7] The Supreme Court interpreted this statute to grant Florida and Texas jurisdiction 10 miles into the Gulf of Mexico, since their "historic boundaries" were 3 marine leagues, whereas all other states have only 3 miles.[8] That the Atlantic seaboard states have jurisdiction only to the 3-mile limit was confirmed in *United States* v. *Maine* (1975).

OBLIGATIONS OF THE NATIONAL GOVERNMENT TO THE STATES

There are several obligations which the Constitution imposes upon the national government with respect to the states. Under Article V no state may be denied equal representation in the Senate without its consent. Again, the government must respect the territorial integrity of the existing states in the formation of new states, as noted in the preceding section. In addition there are three other obligations, all appearing in Article IV, section 4, which deserve more extended treatment.

---

[7] This statute reversed the Supreme Court decision in *United States* v. *California* (1947), which had denied states ownership rights in coastal waters.

[8] *United States* v. *States of Louisiana, Texas, Mississippi, Alabama, and Florida* (1960).

Guarantee against Invasion and Domestic Violence

The protection against foreign invasion is simply a corollary of national self-defense. Article IV, section 4, goes on to provide that, on application of a state legislature, or of the governor if the legislature cannot be convened, the United States shall guarantee a state against "domestic violence." A statute adopted by Congress in 1795 spelling out this obligation uses the term "insurrection" rather than domestic violence. On at least sixteen occasions states have sought federal assistance in suppressing domestic violence. A recent instance was the Detroit riots in the summer of 1967, in connection with which Governor Romney charged President Johnson with delaying the dispatch of troops for political reasons. Afterward Attorney General Clark sought to clarify the situation for the future by specifying what the states must do before the President can act. First, the governor must make a finding that "serious domestic violence" exists, which cannot be brought under control by law enforcement resources available to him. The legislature or governor must then request the President to employ the armed forces to bring the violence under control.

A request from the state legislature or governor is not necessary, however, where domestic violence threatens the enforcement of national laws. Article I, section 8, authorizes Congress to provide for calling forth the militia to execute the laws of the Union, suppress insurrections, and repel invasions. In 1792 Congress adopted legislation which, as revised in 1795, provided:

> That whenever the laws of the United States shall be opposed, or the execution thereof obstructed, in any state, by combinations too powerful to be suppressed by the ordinary course of judicial proceedings, or by the powers vested in the marshals by this act, it shall be lawful for the President of the United States, to call forth the militia of such state, or of any other state or states, as may be necessary to suppress such combinations, and to cause the laws to be duly executed.[9]

An important presidential use of troops to enforce national laws occurred in Chicago in 1894. A strike by the railwaymen's union against the Pullman Company had spread to trains using Pullman equipment, causing an almost complete stoppage on the railroads operating out of Chicago. The federal district attorney in Chicago obtained an injunction against Eugene Debs, the leader of the union, and other labor officials, forbidding them to hinder the mails or interstate commerce in any way. When the injunction went unheeded and violence increased, the federal marshal informed the United States Attorney General that an emergency existed with which he was unable to cope. President Cleveland then ordered federal troops into the city to restore order and assist in getting the trains running. This action was not taken in pursuance of a request by the state executive. In fact, Governor Altgeld strongly protested Cleveland's order.

Debs and the other leaders were arrested for contempt of court in disobeying the injunction and received sentences of from three to six months. The Supreme

[9] 1 Stat. 424 (1795).

Court refused to issue a writ of habeas corpus, upholding the presidential action in a unanimous opinion with these words:

> The entire strength of the nation may be used to enforce in any part of the land the full and free exercise of all national powers and the security of all rights entrusted by the Constitution to its care. The strong arm of the national Government may be put forth to brush away all obstructions to the freedom of interstate commerce or the transportation of the mails. If the emergency arises, the army of the Nation, and all its militia, are at the service of the Nation to compel obedience to its laws.[10]

In 1957 President Eisenhower found it necessary to use federal troops to control violence in Little Rock, Arkansas, and enforce court orders seeking to accomplish gradual desegregation of the local high school. Again in 1962 federal troops had to be used to quell violence arising out of a school integration controversy at the University of Mississippi, which had been ordered by the federal courts to admit James H. Meredith as its first black student.[11]

In March, 1965, Alabama state troops on the order of Governor George Wallace halted a voting rights march which Martin Luther King was attempting to lead from Selma to Montgomery. A federal district judge enjoined state officials from interfering with the march. Governor Wallace then sent a telegram to President Johnson requesting that he provide "sufficient federal civil authorities or officers" to guarantee the safety of the marchers and citizens along the route, alleging that his state could not afford the cost of mobilizing the National Guard. President Johnson complied, but expressed regret that "the Governor and the legislature of a sovereign state [should] decline to exercise their responsibility and . . . request that duty be assumed by the Federal Government."[12]

Guarantee of a Republican Form of Government

Article IV, section 4, provides that "The United States shall guarantee to every State in this Union a republican form of government." This is the only limitation in the Constitution on the internal governmental organization of a state. No definition is provided of a republican form of government, but the language may be interpreted as requiring a form somewhere between a monarchy or oligarchy on the one hand, and a pure or direct democracy on the other.[13]

In designating the "United States" as responsible for this guarantee, the Constitution does not specify which branch has the responsibility for its enforcement. The Supreme Court, however, has ruled on several occasions against judicial enforcement of the clause. The first occasion was in the case of *Luther* v. *Borden* (1849). In 1841 Rhode Island was still operating largely under the system of government established by a charter from Charles II which made no provision for amendment. Dissident groups, protesting mainly against the limits on suffrage, combined to form a

---

[10] *In re Debs* (1895).

[11] On the general subject of civil disorder, see "Riot Control and the Use of Federal Troops," 81 HARVARD LAW REVIEW 638–652 (1968).

[12] *The New York Times*, March 26, 1965.

[13] See William M. Wiecek, *The Guarantee Clause of the U. S. Constitution* (Ithaca, N.Y.: Cornell University Press, 1972).

popular convention which drafted a new constitution. Elections were held the following year, and Thomas Dorr was elected Governor. All the while the old charter government continued to operate and was attempting to put down what it regarded as a rebellion. When one of its agents tried to arrest a Dorr supporter, he was sued for trespass, and one of the issues at the trial was whether the charter government was "republican" under the terms of the Constitution.

Chief Justice Taney for the Supreme Court denied that a court possessed the machinery either to hold a plebiscite or to interrogate enough witnesses to determine which government had the support of a majority of the people. This was a purely political decision which had to be made by Congress. Taney wrote:

> Under this article of the constitution it rests with Congress to decide what government is the established one in a State. For as the United States guarantee to each State a republican government, Congress must necessarily decide what government is established in the State before it can determine whether it is republican or not. And when the senators and representatives of a State are admitted into the councils of the Union, the authority of the government under which they are appointed, as well as its republican character, is recognized by the proper constitutional authority. And its decision is binding on every other department of the government, and could not be questioned in a judicial tribunal.

In this case no representatives had been elected from Rhode Island while the dispute was in progress, so there had been no congressional contest over seating. But the constitutional guarantee against domestic violence had been invoked. The President had recognized one of the contending governors as the legitimate executive authority of the state, and had taken steps to call out the militia to support his authority, should that be necessary. The announcement of this presidential determination had in fact been responsible for terminating Dorr's rebellion against the charter government. After the President had made such a decision, Taney continued,

> . . . is a circuit court of the United States authorized to inquire whether his decision was right? Could the court, while the parties were actually contending in arms for the possession of the government, call witnesses before it, and inquire which party represented a majority of the people? . . . If the judicial power extends so far, the guarantee contained in the constitution of the United States is a guarantee of anarchy, and not of order.

The Supreme Court had occasion to reiterate that the republican form of government guarantee is judicially nonenforceable in a 1912 case where it was alleged that the insertion in the Oregon constitution of a provision for direct legislation by way of the initiative and referendum deprived the state of a republican form of government. The Court's reply was that, in the absence of any determination on this point by the political departments of the federal government, it would refuse to consider such charges.[14] More recently, the Court dealt with the republican form of government provision in connection with the problem of apportionment and representation in state legislatures, to which we now turn.

[14] *Pacific States Telephone & Telegraph Co.* v. *Oregon* (1912).

REPRESENTATION IN STATE LEGISLATURES

Until 1962 the states were free from any federal constitutional controls over apportionment and districting in their legislatures, and they followed a great variety of representation practices. David and Eisenberg divided the states into four general classes on the basis of their representation arrangements:[15]

1   Sixteen states had an equivalent of the "federal" plan, in which one house (like the United States Senate) had a fixed apportionment of representation among fixed districts with no regard for population, while the other house was apportioned more or less on the basis of population. In seven of these states, counties were treated exactly like states in the federal union, each county having at least one representative in the lower house and equal representation with other counties in the upper house. Towns were represented in the lower houses of Vermont and Connecticut.

2   In nine states, the constitution provided for a straight population basis of representation in one house and some kind of qualified population standard in the other house. Some of these states were close to the federal pattern. In California, the requirement that no county have more than one state senator limited Los Angeles County, with a population of over six million, to a single member in the state Senate.

3   In sixteen states, population was the principal criterion for both houses, but was qualified in one way or another for both.

4   In the final group of nine states, population was the constitutional criterion for representation in the entire legislature.

In the nineteenth century these provisions for representation of each county or town and the various departures from population representation did not result in great inequalities of election districts. But as large urban centers developed in the present century, they were increasingly underrepresented. Moreover, in rurally controlled legislatures the power-holders took steps to protect their position, either by writing new restrictions on population representation into the constitution or by failing to redistrict when such action would have given additional representatives to urban areas.

It was a situation of this latter sort with which the Supreme Court was confronted in the famous 1962 case of *Baker* v. *Carr*.[16] The constitution of Tennessee provided for ninety-nine members of the House and thirty-three members of the Senate, and directed the Legislature to allocate, at least every ten years, the senators and representatives among the several counties or districts "according to the num-

---

[15] Paul T. David and Ralph Eisenberg, *State Legislative Redistricting* (Chicago: Public Administration Service, 1962), pp. 8–10.

[16] There is an extensive literature on the consequences of *Baker* v. *Carr*. See particularly Robert G. Dixon, Jr., *Democratic Representation: Reapportionment in Law and Politics* (New York: Oxford University Press, 1968); Gordon E. Baker, *The Reapportionment Revolution* (New York: Random House, Inc., 1966); Nelson W. Polsby (ed.), *Reapportionment in the 1970s* (Berkeley: University of California Press, 1971); Ward E. Y. Elliott, *The Rise of Guardian Democracy* (Cambridge, Mass.: Harvard University Press, 1974).

ber of qualified voters in each." Despite these mandatory requirements, no reapportionment had been made since 1901. During the period between 1901 and 1950, the population grew from 2,021,000 to 3,292,000, but the growth was very uneven among counties. Thus 37 percent of the voting population could control twenty of the thirty-three members of the Senate, while 40 percent of the voters could control sixty-three of the ninety-nine members of the House.

In 1959 suit was brought in federal district court by certain citizens of Tennessee against state election officials under the Civil Rights Act of 1871, alleging deprivation of federal constitutional rights. The principal obstacle to success in their suit was that in *Colegrove* v. *Green* (1946) the Supreme Court had declined to rule on a similar claim made against congressional districts in Illinois, where likewise a failure since 1901 to obey the constitutional mandate to redistrict every ten years had resulted in population inequalities as great as nine to one. The Court, speaking through Justice Frankfurter, had held in a four to three decision that these election controversies constituted a political thicket which judges must avoid.

In *Baker* v. *Carr,* however, the Court reversed the *Colegrove* rule and held the Tennessee complaint to be justiciable. Justice Brennan asserted two main grounds for refusing to follow *Colegrove.* First, Frankfurter's position on justiciability had been supported by only three of the seven participating justices. Justice Rutledge, who supplied the fourth vote, actually agreed with the three dissenters that the issue was justiciable, and only voted as he did because he felt that it would be unwise to upset the Illinois arrangements so soon before the congressional elections of 1946.

Second, Brennan traced the "political question" doctrine, on which Frankfurter had relied, all the way back to *Luther* v. *Borden* to demonstrate that it did not cover the Tennessee type of election controversy. A true political question, from his view, was presented only where there was a separation of powers issue at stake. A political question was one that the courts should avoid out of deference to the President or Congress, as in *Luther* v. *Bordon.* Since there was no such conflict here, the question was justiciable.

Justice Frankfurter, dissenting along with Harlan, argued on the contrary that the significant factors in past judicial refusals to get involved in political questions were these:

> . . . the caution not to undertake decision where standards meet for judicial judgment are lacking, the reluctance to interfere with matters of state government in the absence of an unquestionable and effectively enforceable mandate, the unwillingness to make courts arbiters of the broad issues of political organization historically committed to other institutions and for whose adjustment the judicial process is ill-adapted.

The Tennessee case, Frankfurther felt, fell squarely in this tradition of controversies that do not lend themselves to judicial standards or judicial remedies.

Justice Frankfurther made specific use of the republican guarantee clause in his argument, saying: "The present case involves all of the elements that have made the Guarantee Clause cases nonjusticiable. It is, in effect, a Guarantee Clause claim masquerading under a different label."

Legislative apportionment, Frankfurther continued, was a political problem bound to prove vastly embarrassing to courts if they got involved in it. There are no standards for decision except political preferences and competing political philosophies, while "in every strand of this complicated, intricate web of values meet the contending forces of partisan politics." This was the political thicket which the Court majority would require the federal district courts to enter, he warned, with no standards or constitutional principles to guide them, no indication of what kind of remedies they could formulate to correct legislative apportionments.

Justice Brennan, however, assumed that the Court would be equal to developing remedies when the need arose. None were required here, since the Court merely held that the complaint against Tennessee's legislative districts should not have been dismissed. This ruling opened the gates to a flood of suits.

The first one to reach the Court was *Gray* v. *Sanders* (1963), involving not a state legislature but rather the Georgia county-unit system of primary elections to statewide offices, a system deliberately designed to give control of the electoral process to rural minorities. The Supreme Court, with only Justice Harlan dissenting, invalidated the county-unit plan on the ground that no preferred class of voters is permissible under the Constitution and by American traditions. Every voter is equal to every other voter in his state: "The conception of political equality from the Declaration of Independence, to Lincoln's Gettysburg address, to the Fifteenth, Seventeenth, and Nineteenth Amendments can mean only one thing—one person, one vote." Applying this conception to the present case, Douglas concluded:

> Once the geographical unit for which a representative is to be chosen is designated, all who participate in the election are to have an equal vote—whatever their race, whatever their sex, whatever their occupation, whatever their income, and wherever their home may be in that geographical unit. This is required by the Equal Protection Clause of the Fourteenth Amendment.

While *Gray* v. *Sanders* was a voting case, not an apportionment case, the standard of "one person, one vote" had obvious relevance for legislative districting. However, there were many who expected that the court would apply this rule to only one house of bicameral state legislatures, leaving room for other principles in the makeup of the second house. But in *Reynolds* v. *Sims* (1964) and fourteen companion cases the Supreme Court confounded these expectations and made "one man, one vote" the constitutional rule for both houses. The legislatures of all fifteen states under review were declared unconstitutional by the Court, with varying majorities of from six to eight justices, because of substantial violations of the one-man, one-vote standard.

Chief Justice Warren wrote the opinion of the Court in all of these cases. He started with "the basic standard of equality among voters," as established in *Gray* v. *Sanders* and supported by general principles of representative government, majority rule, and equal protection of the laws. Representative government, the Chief Justice said, "is in essence self-government through the medium of elected representatives of the people, and each and every citizen has an inalienable right to full and effective participation in the political processes of his State's legislative bodies." He rejected any sophisticated notions about representation. "Legislators represent people, not trees or acres. Legislators are elected by voters, not farms or cities or economic interests."

The principle of representative government is majority rule, Warren went on. It is logical and reasonable "that a majority of the people of a State could elect a majority of that State's legislature. To conclude differently, and to sanction minority control of state legislative bodies, would appear to deny majority rights in a way that far surpasses any possible denial of minority rights that might otherwise be thought to result." The Chief Justice was of course not insensitive to minority rights, but he thought that "our constitutional system amply provides for the protection of minorities by means other than giving them majority control of state legislatures."

The principle of equality Warren believed to be essential to both representative government and majority rule. No one would argue that some voters could vote two, five, or ten times for state legislators, or that votes of certain citizens should be given a weight of two, five, or ten times that of voters in other areas. But this is what happens when legislative districting schemes "give the same number of representatives to unequal numbers of constituents. . . . To the extent that a citizen's right to vote is debased, he is that much less a citizen."

The Supreme Court firmly rejected the idea that the rule of equality might be applied to only one house of a bicameral legislature. The right to equal representation in one house, Warren said, "would amount to little if States could effectively submerge the equal-population principle in the apportionment of seats in the other house." The two houses might compromise on some issues, but "in all too many cases the more probable result would be frustration of the majority will through minority veto in the house not apportioned on a population basis."

The Court rejected any analogy between state legislatures and the Congress, where the Senate represents states and the House population. The system of representation in the federal Congress, the Chief Justice noted, was the fruit of a compromise between the larger and smaller states which averted a deadlock in the Constitutional Convention. It arose from "unique historical circumstances . . . based on the consideration that in establishing our type of federalism a group of formerly independent states bound themselves together under one national government." At the heart of the federal system remains the concept of "separate and distinct entities which have delegated some, but not all, of their formerly held powers to the single national government." In contrast, "political subdivisions of states—counties, cities, or whatever—never were and never have been considered as sovereign entities," but only as "subordinate governmental instrumentalities created by the State to assist in the carrying out of state governmental functions."

The Court made it clear that it did not mean to impose impractically strict requirements. What was required of each state was that it make "an honest and good faith effort to construct districts, in both houses of its legislature, as nearly of equal population as is practicable." Mathematical exactness was not intended. Further, the states might use political subdivision lines in drawing districts, "so long as the resulting apportionment was one based substantially on population and the equal-population principle was not diluted in any significant way." In fact, "a State can rationally consider according political subdivisions some independent representation in at least one body of the state legislature, as long as the basic standard of equality of population among districts is maintained." In general, "so long as the divergences from a strict population standard are based on legitimate considerations incident to the effectuation of a rational state policy, some deviations from the equal-population principle are constitutionally permissible." But "neither history alone, nor economic or other sorts of group interests," nor considerations of area alone, "are permissible factors in attempting to justify disparities from population-based representation."

Justices Stewart and Clark, who had been part of the majorities in *Baker* and *Gray,* dissented. For Justice Stewart the holding that both houses of a bicameral state legislature must be apportioned on a population basis represented "the uncritical, simplistic, and heavy-handed application of sixth-grade arithmetic." The true view of representative theory was that it must accommodate "the interests and aspirations of diverse groups of people, without subjecting any group or class to absolute domination by a geographically concentrated or highly organized majority. Representative government is a process of accommodating group interests through democratic institutional arrangements." Toward this end population factors have often been "to some degree . . . subordinated . . . to achieve the important goal of ensuring a fair, effective, and balanced representation of the regional, social, and economic interests within a State."

Justice Stewart believed that any plan which "reasonably achieves" such balanced representation of interests "without sacrificing the principle of effective majority rule" could not be considered unconstitutional. He concluded:

> I think that the Equal Protection Clause demands but two basic attributes of any plan of state legislative apportionment. First, it demands that, in the light of the state's own characteristics and needs, the plan must be a rational one. Secondly, it demands that a plan must be such as not to permit the systematic frustration of the will of a majority of the electorate of the State.

Application of this twofold test led Stewart and Clark to uphold the legislative apportionments of New York, Colorado, Illinois, and Michigan, all of which were condemned by the Court majority as violative of one man, one vote. In addition, Stewart alone would have approved the Ohio apportionment. The Stewart-Clark standard gave the same result as one man, one vote in the ten other states which the Court considered in the spring of 1964.[17]

The other dissenter, Justice Harlan, continued the vehement opposition he had expressed in *Baker* and *Gray.* The bulk of his opinion was devoted to two points. The first was the inapplicability of the equal protection clause to representation matters. He contended that section 2 of the Fourteenth Amendment, authorizing

---

[17] In four of these cases, however, Justice Stewart voted to remand for further proceedings.

Congress to reduce the representation in the House of states which deny or abridge the right to vote, was the sole remedy intended for representation errors, and that there was no thought when the amendment was adopted of controlling the elective franchise by section 1.[18] Second, he contended that giving courts "blanket authority and the constitutional duty to supervise apportionment" was an "intolerable and inappropriate interference . . . with the independent legislatures of the States."

The decisions in *Baker* v. *Carr* and subsequent cases were surprisingly popular, considering the drastic remedies they imposed. Within a few years after *Reynolds,* the great majority of state legislatures had been reapportioned on something close to a one-man, one-vote basis, sometimes by uncoerced legislative action, sometimes by legislatures acting under court orders, and sometimes by direct court action.

Effforts to organize opposition in Congress to the Court's mandate were unsuccessful. The principal effort was the Dirksen Amendment, offered in 1965 and 1966. It would have required one house of a bicameral state legislature to be apportioned on the basis of population but would have permitted the other house to be apportioned "among the people on the bases of population, geography, and political subdivisions in order to insure effective representation in the State's legislature of the various groups and interests making up the electorate." The Dirksen Amendment was defeated in the Senate in 1965, when it failed by seven votes to get the two-thirds majority needed, and it lost again in 1966 by the same margin.

Subsequent developments in the interpretation and enforcement of the *Reynolds* ruling can be considered under six headings. First, how rigid would the Court be in applying its equal population rule? The gross variations in *Swann* v. *Adams* (1967) were clearly unacceptable, with ranges of 30 percent among Florida senate district populations and 40 percent among house districts. But in *Kirkpatrick* v. *Preisler* (1969) and *Wells* v. *Rockefeller* (1969), where the variations were minimal, the apportionment plans were still invalidated because of failure to show that "a good-faith effort to achieve precise mathematical equality" had been made. Even many friends of the one-man, one-vote rule felt that this was an unrealistic standard, and the Court subsequently modified its stand.

In *Abate* v. *Mundt* (1971), a districting plan for a New York county board of supervisors with a total deviation from equality of 11.9 percent was approved, the Court noting that the plan did not contain any built-in bias favoring particular political interests or geographic areas. Then *Mahan* v. *Howell* (1973) held that reapportionment of the Virginia legislature resulting in a variation of 16.4 percent from the ideal district was acceptable because required to maintain the integrity of traditional county or city boundaries. Similarly, *Gaffney* v. *Cummings* (1973) upheld a Connecticut reapportionment plan where the maximum deviation between districts totaled 7.83 percent.[19] The Court added that an otherwise acceptable plan was not

---

[18] Justice Harlan's position on this issue is rebutted by William W. Van Alstyne, "The Fourteenth Amendment, the 'Right' to Vote, and the Understanding of the Thirty-ninth Congress," in Philip B. Kurland (ed.), *The Supreme Court Review: 1965* (Chicago: The University of Chicago Press, 1965), pp. 33–86.

[19] But *Chapman* v. *Meier* (1975) invalidated a Court-ordered plan with a 20 percent deviation, saying that a Court-ordered plan "must be held to higher standards than a State's own plan."

made constitutionally vulnerable because its purpose was to provide districts that would achieve "political fairness" between major political parties.

A second issue was raised by the occasional use of multimember districts. Such districts are suspect because they may have the effect, and may in fact be adopted for the purpose, of denying representation to minorities within the expanded district. In *Fortson* v. *Dorsey* (1965) and *Burns* v. *Richardson* (1966), the Court held that multimember districts were not illegal per se and that any invidious effect must be demonstrated in the record. While there was substantial evidence of dilution of the votes of blacks and poor people by a multimember district in Indiana, it was not sufficient to convince the Court in *Whitcomb* v. *Chavis* (1971) that this was invidious underrepresentation. However, *Connor* v. *Johnson* (1971) held that, where a federal court was called upon to fashion an apportionment plan, it should not make any use of multimember districts because "single-member districts are preferable . . . as a general matter."[20] And in *White* v. *Regester* (1973), the Court agreed that two multimember districts must be disestablished because of the history of discrimination against blacks and Mexican-Americans residing in them.

A third problem concerns the relation of the one-man, one-vote rule to gerrymandering of election districts. Equality of population is no guarantee against gerrymandering. In fact, to the degree that the achievement of population equality requires the disregarding of local government boundaries, it makes gerrymandering easier. While recognizing this fact, the Supreme Court has been reluctant to undertake the task of controlling gerrymanders unless there is an obvious racial motive involved. Even in *Wright* v. *Rockefeller* (1964), where there was a strong prima facie case that congressional district lines had been drawn with racial considerations in mind, the Court held that the evidence was not compelling.

A fourth development concerns the extension of the one-man, one-vote rule to local government. *Sailors* v. *Board of Education of Kent County* (1967) ruled that the functions of a county board of education were essentially administrative rather than legislative and that consequently there was no constitutional objection to a system whereby each local school board, regardless of population in its area, had one vote on the county board. But in *Avery* v. *Midland County* (1968), the Court did apply the rule to local government, holding that where county, city, or town governments elect their representatives from single-member districts, the districts must be substantially equal in population. The same requirement was applied to public college trustees in *Hadley* v. *Junior College District* (1970).[21]

Fifth, there has been a spillover of the one-man, one-vote rule from legislative elections to other voting situations. *Kramer* v. *Union Free School District* (1969) struck down a New York State law limiting the right to vote in school district elections to owners of real property in the district or parents of children enrolled in

---

[20] This position was repeated in *Chapman* v. *Meier* (1975) and *East Carroll Parish School Board* v. *Marshall* (1976).

[21] But it is constitutional for city council members or county commissioners to be elected at large, with the requirement that each member come from a separate election district the population of which varies widely; *Dusch* v. *Davis* (1967), and *Dallas County, Alabama* v. *Reese* (1975).

the local public schools. Similarly, *Cipriano* v. *City of Houma* (1969) held unconstitutional as a denial of equal protection a Louisiana law giving only property taxpayers the right to vote in elections called to approve issuance of revenue bonds by municipal utilities. *City of Phoenix* v. *Kolodziejski* (1971) extended this principle to elections for the approval of general obligation bonds.[22]

By contrast, *Salyer Land Co.* v. *Tulare Water Storage District* (1973) approved a plan for electing a water district's board of directors which limited the right to vote to landowners in the district and weighted their votes according to the assessed valuation of their land. Also relevant is *Gordon* v. *Lance* (1971), which upheld a state constitutional requirement that 60 percent of the voters in referendum elections must approve bonded indebtedness or tax increases.

Finally, the Court in *Fortson* v. *Morris* (1966) declined to interpret the one-man, one-vote rule as invalidating the provision of the Georgia constitution allowing the state legislature to select the governor from between the two top candidates in an election where no candidate secured a majority. The one-man, one-vote rule applied only to "voting cases," said Justice Black; it had no relation to how a state should elect its governors.

CONTROL OVER TERRITORIES

Jefferson's doubts about the authority of the federal government to acquire new territory are well known. In making the Louisiana Purchase he felt he had been justified in seizing the opportunity to protect American rights to the Mississippi waterway, but for future defense of the Constitution he requested Congress to propose a formal amendment. No such action has ever been taken, and few have thought this course necessary. John Marshall supplied the constitutional justification for the acquisition of new domain when he held in 1828: "The Constitution confers absolutely upon the government of the Union, the powers of making war, and of making treaties; consequently, that government possesses the power of acquiring territory, either by conquest or by treaty."[23]

Marshall might reasonably have construed at least two other provisions of the Constitution as conferring the right to increase the territory of the United States: the power of Congress to admit new states and to govern territory. There is also the fact that the United States as a sovereign nation has the same rights under international law to obtain new land as any other nation.[24] The Supreme Court has long treated the matter as completely closed.

In contrast, the power of Congress to "dispose" of territory is explicitly written into the Constitution.[25] With the possible exception of the Webster-Ashburton

---

[22] *Hill* v. *Stone* (1975) struck down an ordinance which divided voters in city bond elections into two categories—(1) those owning taxable property and (2) all other registered voters; bond issues had to be approved by majority vote of both groups.

[23] *American Insurance Co.* v. *Canter* (1828).

[24] See *Jones* v. *United States* (1890).

[25] Art. IV, sec. 3.

Treaty, this power has been exercised only in the granting of independence to the Philippine Islands and in minor leasing alterations with Panama in the Canal Zone area.

Article IV, section 3, gives Congress power to "make all needful rules and regulations" respecting territories of the United States. This is a plenary grant of authority, and in its exercise Congress may act with full national and local sovereignty.[26] Congressional power is not wholly unlimited, however. In *The Insular Cases* (1901)[27] a badly divided Supreme Court made a distinction between territories which were "incorporated" and those which were "unincorporated." In the former, which are supposedly destined for statehood, Congress must accord all the rights and privileges of the Constitution except those clearly applicable only to state citizens, such as participation in a national election. In the "unincorporated" areas, however, it is mandatory only that "fundamental" rights be guaranteed. Since the admission of Alaska and Hawaii as states, there are no longer any "incorporated" territories.

The District of Columbia has a distinctive and unique status. By Article I, section 8, Congress has power of "exclusive legislation" in the District. Though the District was allowed home rule prior to 1874, it was thereafter completely deprived of any right to control its own affairs. To all intents and purposes it was governed by the House and Senate committees on the District of Columbia, with three presidentially appointed commissioners administering the local government.

A long succession of efforts to restore to the District's residents, the great majority of whom are black, the right to elect their own governmental officials failed in Congress. The Twenty-third Amendment, adopted in 1961, did grant District voters the right to vote in presidential elections, and the District has an elected nonvoting delegate in the House of Representatives. In 1973 Congress finally passed compromise legislation giving partial home rule to the District. The act provides for an elected mayor and thirteen-member city council. The District government has the power to tax, but its budget must be submitted to Congress, which continues to make annual appropriations for the District. Congress reserves the right to legislate for the District at any time, and acts passed by the District council must lie before Congress for thirty days and can be vetoed by concurrent resolution.

Puerto Rico is in a category by itself. In 1950 Congress proposed through Public Law 600 a "compact" between Puerto Rico and the United States whereby Puerto Rico would adopt a constitution acceptable to Congress, and would then assume a "Commonwealth" status. Only two advance restrictions were placed on this constitution: that it provide for a republican form of government and that it contain a bill of rights. This compact arrangement was approved by referendum vote, and a constitution was subsequently drafted. With only minor changes Congress gave its consent to this document as the fundamental law of Puerto Rico.

The constitution is much like that of the United States, providing for popular elections, separation of powers, a bicameral legislature, judicial review, and an enu-

---

[26] *First National Bank* v. *Yankton County* (1880); *Simms* v. *Simms* (1899).
[27] *DeLima* v. *Bidwell* (1901); *Downes* v. *Bidwell* (1901).

meration of certain guaranteed rights, including a maximum working day of no more than eight hours unless overtime pay is given.

Most federal laws do not apply in Puerto Rico, but Congress can pass legislation specifically applicable there. Puerto Ricans do not pay federal income tax, and Congress has given the island certain tax advantages. Puerto Ricans are of course American citizens and can move freely between Puerto Rico and the United States.

Under this Commonwealth status, control over Puerto Rico's foreign policy remains with the United States. In addition to conforming to the Puerto Rican constitution, local legislation must also conform to the terms of Public Law 600, the law approving the Puerto Rican constitution, and the applicable provisions of the United States Constitution. Appellate jurisdiction over the decisions of the Puerto Rican supreme court is exercised by the Court of Appeals for the First Circuit in cases involving the writ of habeas corpus or questions of federal law. It is very probable that island court determinations of local law will be treated as final.

Theoretically, Congress could at any time revoke the compact entered into with Puerto Rico and resume direct rule over the island, but such action is most unlikely. There is some sentiment for statehood, but in the 1972 elections the candidate favoring continuance of commonwealth status handily defeated both the statehood and the independence candidates. In 1975 a presidential commission approved a proposal to make Puerto Rico an "associated state," akin to the quasi-independent states that exist in the British Commonwealth.

There are certain other territories in the possession of the United States. The Virgin Islands and Guam have a large measure of self-government, though their governors are appointed from Washington. Their residents have full rights of American citizenship. The residents of Samoa, however, are classed as American "nationals," a condition less than full citizenship but involving allegiance to the United States and the obligation of protection by the American government. Certain former Japanese islands in the Pacific—the Marianas, Marshalls, and Carolines—are held by the United States as trust territories under the supervision of the United Nations. In 1976 Congress approved commonwealth status, involving United States citizenship and sovereignty, for the northern Mariana Islands. The Panama Canal Zone is a strip of land on either side of the Panama Canal which the United States controls under treaty with Panama. In 1976 the State Department was engaged in treaty negotiations with Panama looking toward eventually yielding American control of the Canal Zone, negotiations which had become the subject of intense controversy.

Interstate Relations

Federalism is characterized not only by the vertical relationships between nation and state examined in the preceding chapter, but also by horizontal contacts between state and state. The Constitution foresaw five kinds of interstate problems and adopted language for handling them.

INTERSTATE PRIVILEGES AND IMMUNITIES

Article IV, section 2, provides: "The citizens of each state shall be entitled to all privileges and immunities of citizens in the several states." There is no definition of the privileges and immunities to which citizens in the several states are entitled. Neither is it made clear whether the citizen is entitled to these privileges in his own state, or when he is temporarily in other states, or both. Nor is any test of state citizenship suggested.

The earliest effort at interpretation of this language was that of Justice Bushrod Washington, sitting in federal circuit court in the case of *Corfield* v. *Coryell* (1823). A New Jersey statute prohibited any person who was not an actual inhabitant or resident of New Jersey from gathering oysters in the state. Was this statute in conflict with Article IV, section 2? Washington decided that it was not. The privileges and immunities which the Constitution protects, said Washington, are those "which are, in their nature, fundamental; which belong, of right, to the citizens of all free governments." The justice thought it would "be more tedious than difficult" to enumerate these rights, but then risked tedium by suggesting quite a list, including the right of a citizen of one state to pass through, or reside in, other states for purposes of trade or profession; the right to institute and maintain court actions; exemption from higher taxes than are paid by other citizens of the state; and the elective franchise, as regulated by the laws of the state in which it is exercised.

The effect of the privileges and immunities clause, then, is to forbid any state to discriminate against citizens of other states in favor of its own citizens with respect to these "fundamental" rights. As Justice Miller said in the *Slaughter-House Cases* (1873), the purpose of the clause was "to declare to the several States, that whatever these rights, as you grant or establish them to your own citizens, or as you limit or qualify, or impose restrictions on their exercise, the same, neither more nor less, shall be the measure of the rights of citizens of other States within your jurisdiction."

However, Article IV, section 2, does not preclude a state from treating out-of-state citizens differently when there are acceptable reasons why the two groups should be placed on different footings. Technical requirements for access to the courts may be somewhat different for out-of-state than for local citizens.[1] The right to engage in normal businesses is protected, but the practice of certain professions connected with the public interest, such as medicine or law, can be restricted by individual states, and persons who pursue these professions must prove to the state government competence in their fields.

In addition, some public rights do not accrue to a citizen who moves across a state line. The privilege of sharing in the use of public property may be denied to nonresidents, as in *Corfield* v. *Coryell*, or offered at a higher rate than that charged local citizens. Thus tuition in state universities is usually lower for state citizens than for outsiders.[2] Wildlife was once considered to be part of the public trust administered by the state for all of its citizens,[3] but more recently the ownership doctrine has been labeled as a mere "fiction expressive in legal shorthand of the importance to its people that a State have power to preserve and regulate the exploitation of an important resource."[4] This power of regulation must not be exercised unfairly where the differentiation rests solely on out-of-state citizenship. Higher fees for hunting or fishing in the case of outsiders can be justified on the ground that local citizens pay additional taxes which are used in part for the upkeep of the public domain, or the state may show that there is an added cost in enforcing its police regulations against people who live outside the state. But grossly discriminatory

---

[1] *Ward* v. *Maryland* (1871); *Miles* v. *Illinois Central Rr.* (1942).

[2] But in *Vlandis* v. *Kline* (1973), the Supreme Court ruled that a Connecticut statute which required students admitted to state universities as nonresidents to pay nonresident tuition for their entire four years was unconstitutional as a denial of due process. A Washington law requiring one year of residence in the state to qualify as a resident for tuition purposes was upheld in *Sturgis* v. *Washington* (1973). In *Spatt* v. *New York* (1973), the Court upheld a state law denying state scholarships to award winners who chose to go to a college outside the state.

[3] *Geer* v. *Connecticut* (1896).

[4] *Toomer* v. *Witsell* (1948).

licensing fees for out-of-state commercial fishermen were invalidated in *Toomer* v. *Witsell* (1948) and *Mullaney* v. *Anderson* (1952).

INTERSTATE TRAVEL

Originally, protection of the right to travel from state to state was derived from general principles of federalism. *Crandall* v. *Nevada* (1868) held that a tax of $1 per passenger on commercial vehicles leaving the state interfered with the government's need to call citizens to cross state lines in order to fill offices and wage wars and with citizens' rights to carry on business among the states and to seek redress of grievances from the government. In *Ward* v. *Maryland* (1871), the privileges and immunities clause was used to strike down a state license tax on out-of-state drummers; and in *Edwards* v. *California* (1941), a statute making it a misdemeanor to bring indigents into the state was invalidated on the basis of the commerce clause.

More recently the right to travel has been related to individual freedoms. The right to travel abroad, which does not involve considerations of federalism, was upheld in *Kent* v. *Dulles* (1958) as an element of the liberty protected by the due process clause of the Fifth Amendment. In *United States* v. *Guest* (1966), the right to travel was characterized as "fundamental" without reference to any particular provision of the Constitution, and interference with that right was the basis for a civil rights action charging criminal conspiracy.

The equal protection clause was invoked in *Shapiro* v. *Thompson* (1969) to strike down state and District of Columbia laws which denied welfare assistance to persons who had not been resident in the state or District for one year. The right of interstate travel was called so fundamental that there was no need "to ascribe the sources of this right to travel interstate to a particular constitutional provision." The one-year residency requirement was a limitation on that right which was not justified by any compelling state interest and so was an invidious classification denying equal protection. In like fashion, *Dunn* v. *Blumstein* (1972) held residency requirements for voting an unconstitutional limitation on the "fundamental personal right . . . to travel." And *Memorial Hospital* v. *Maricopa County* (1974) ruled that an Arizona durational residency requirement for free medical care "penalizes indigents for exercising their right to migrate to and settle in that State."

On the other hand, *Vlandis* v. *Kline* (1973) and *Sturgis* v. *Washington* (1973) rather inconsistently upheld residence requirements of one year before out-of-state students would become eligible for resident tuition rates in state universities; these decisions failed to mention the right to travel. Obviously the equal protection rationale for interstate travel is subject to restrictions which impress the Court as furthering legitimate state interests.

FULL FAITH AND CREDIT

Article IV, section 1, commands that each state accord full faith and credit to three types of official acts of sister states: public records, statutes, and court decisions.[5]

[5] See Robert H. Jackson, *Full Faith and Credit: The Lawyer's Clause of the Constitution* (New York: Columbia University Press, 1945).

Congress is given power to issue uniform regulations for authentication of the legal papers which deserve such recognition, and to determine the precise effect to be given such documents. Even without this explicit requirement some obligation of the sort would have existed under the doctrine of comity in international law. As a demonstration of friendship, nations customarily recognize as valid the public proceedings of other countries, provided there is no contrary local policy. The Constitution, however, removes the matter of faith and credit from considerations of mutual courtesy and amity and makes it a legal duty enforceable in federal courts.

Judicial Proceedings

Under authority of the full faith and credit clause Congress passed legislation in 1790 and 1804, providing a simple method of authentication and commanding that judicial proceedings and public records be given the same effect in every court that they had in the court which issued them. Because of these explicit provisions the matter of according full faith and credit to judicial acts is relatively uncomplicated, except in divorce cases, which are considered below. In 1813 a young attorney named Francis Scott Key argued before the Supreme Court that the obligation imposed by Article IV had been met when a state merely received a sister-state judgment as evidence and weighed it with the other evidence in the case. The Court, however, rejected this contention and held that a judgment conclusive in one state must be recognized as final in all others.[6]

This conclusiveness is not automatic. A person who has secured a court order in one state and wishes to have it enforced against a person who has since gone to another state must bring a new legal action in the latter state. In this action the court will accept the original decree, examine it, and if it finds the order to be properly authenticated, will issue an enforcement order of its own. This must be done even if the public policy of the second state would not have permitted such a decision had the case originated there. The defendant may appear in court and contest the order. He may not, however, reargue the merits of the case. The only valid line of attack open to him is the claim that the court where the original decree was handed down did not have proper jurisdiction over either the parties or the subject matter involved in the dispute.[7]

A second situation in which the full faith and credit clause applies to judicial proceedings occurs where a judgment of a court in one state is offered *in defense* against a new proceeding in another state growing out of the same facts that were involved in the original suit. An illustration would be supplied where a decree of divorce granted in one state was offered as a bar to a divorce suit by the other party to the marriage in a second state. Because of the lenient divorce laws in some states, particularly Nevada and Florida, a major problem has arisen as to whether other states are required to give full faith and credit to these "quickie" divorces.

Historically a divorce suit has been treated as an action *in rem*, that is, a proceeding against the marriage status. A court must have jurisdiction over the marriage status in order to grant a divorce decree, and the test of jurisdiction has

[6] *Mills* v. *Duryee* (1813).
[7] *M'Elmoyle* v. *Cohen* (1839).

been domicile. Where both parties were domiciled in the same state, there could of course be no question about the jurisdiction of courts in that state. The full faith and credit problem arose where the husband and wife were domiciled in different states, and where the plaintiff brought the divorce suit in the state of his or her domicile. What is the obligation of courts in the state of the defendant's domicile, or courts in states other than the two states of domicile, to recognize the validity of such a divorce?

The rule prevailing up to 1906 is illustrated by the case of *Atherton* v. *Atherton* (1901), which held that, where husband and wife are domiciled in different states, a decree granted in either state is to be given full faith and credit. The virtue of the *Atherton* doctrine was its certainty. A divorce granted in a state where the plaintiff was domiciled was valid in all states, even if the defendant had no personal service (i.e., notice of the suit) and was not represented in court. The objection to the *Atherton* doctrine was that it permitted ex parte divorces, that is, divorces in which only one party to the marriage was in court. Justice Jackson once said that to him the notion of an ex parte divorce was as perverse and unrealistic as ex parte marriage.[8]

In *Haddock* v. *Haddock* (1906) the Supreme Court upset the certainty of *Atherton*. A husband, having transferred his residence from New York to Connecticut, brought suit for divorce there against his wife who had remained in New York. The Supreme Court held this suit to be one *in personam,* i.e., against the wife rather than against the marriage status, and consequently personal service or her voluntary appearance in court was required. Since neither had been had, the decree was ineffective as to the wife in the state of her domicile. Nevertheless, the Court held that a state had the inherent power to determine the marital status of its own citizens and consequently ruled that the husband's divorce was effective in his home state. The result of this holding was that the Haddocks, when both were in Connecticut, were divorced; when both were in New York, were married; and when the husband was in Connecticut and the wife in New York, he was legally single and she was still married. A later comment by Justice Jackson also seems appropriate to this situation: "If there is one thing that the people are entitled to expect from their lawmakers, it is rules of law that will enable individuals to tell whether they are married and, if so, to whom."[9]

Fortunately much of the confusion inherent in this situation was eliminated by the sensible action of most of the states in recognizing out-of-state divorces as a matter of comity. Moreover, for a considerable period there appeared to be no disposition to question the power of each state to determine for itself what should constitute domicile for divorce purposes. In 1942, however, the lax Nevada domicile requirement of only six weeks was responsible for the case of *Williams* v. *North Carolina.* Two residents of North Carolina, which has relatively rigid divorce laws, went to Nevada, lived in a tourist court for six weeks, shed their respective spouses,

[8] *Rice* v. *Rice* (1949).
[9] *Estin* v. *Estin* (1948).

married each other, and then returned to North Carolina. That state refused to recognize the validity of the Nevada divorce, and brought bigamy charges against the couple. They were convicted on the ground that the Nevada divorce had no effect in North Carolina because adequate notice of the proceedings had not been given to the North Carolina spouses, under the *Haddock* doctrine.

A divided Supreme Court reversed this finding by overruling *Haddock* v. *Haddock*. The majority was disturbed about the possibility that a person could be "a bigamist for living in one state with the only one with whom the other state would permit him lawfully to live." The *Williams* decision held that the "substituted service" here employed met the requirements of due process. The divorce decree was thus "wholly effective" in Nevada to change the marital status of the two couples, and the full faith and credit clause required other states to recognize this change, even though it might conflict with their public policy. "Such is part of the price of our federal system," said Justice Douglas.

The state court conviction had not been based on a contention that there was no bona fide domicile in Nevada, and consequently the Supreme Court had no occasion to examine this issue in the first *Williams* decision. However, North Carolina, rebuffed in its first attempt, brought another bigamy prosecution (in spite of the fact that one of the home-staying spouses had died and the other had remarried), this time alleging that the Nevada domicile was a sham, and consequently that North Carolina was under no obligation to recognize the decrees. In this second proceeding, *Williams* v. *North Carolina* (1945), the Supreme Court, still divided, upheld the right of North Carolina courts to decide for themselves, before recognizing the validity of an out-of-state divorce, whether residents of the state had established a bona fide domicile outside the state.

Subsequent to the second *Williams* decision, the Court sought to restore some measure of stability to the situation by holding that if the question of bona fide residence was specifically argued in a court of one state, in a case where both parties to the marriage were before the court or represented by counsel, an assertion of jurisdiction by that court would not be reexamined in any court of another state [10]

The net result of the *Williams* decisions is a recognition of the right of any actual domiciliary state to grant ex parte divorces to which other states must accord full faith and credit. The Court, however, in its post-*Williams* phase, drew back from some of the consequences of ex parte divorces. In *Estin* v. *Estin* (1948), the Court created the concept of a "divisible" divorce, effective as to termination of the marital status but ineffective to determine property rights of the parties, alimony payments, or custody of children. In the *Estin* case, a New York court's spouse support order was held to have survived a valid Nevada divorce. Justice Jackson, protesting this "Solomon-like conclusion," did not see how it could be *full* faith and credit to hold the Nevada decree half good and half bad. "It is good to free the husband from the marriage; it is not good to free him from its incidental obligations." But the Court has found the concept of divisible divorce decrees to be a useful one, and has

[10] *Sherrer* v. *Sherrer* (1948); *Coe* v. *Coe* (1948).

continued to employ it for the purpose of achieving what it regards as desirable public policies.[11]

The recent relaxation of divorce laws in most states has reduced the problems, since fewer persons feel obliged to resort to out-of-state divorces. In *Sosna* v. *Iowa* (1975), the Court held that a one-year residency requirement for divorce was justified on grounds of the state's interest in requiring those seeking a divorce from its courts to be genuinely attached to the state as well as by the state's desire to insulate its divorce decrees from the likelihood of successful collateral attack.

State Legislation

The matter of the extrastate effect of state statutes has been less satisfactorily resolved than that of judgments or records. Not until 1948 did Congress legislate with respect to the full faith and credit to be given to state statutes, and this legislation has as yet had little impact. In general, no state is obliged to enforce the criminal laws of another state.[12] For other types of statutes, the general principle is that the full faith and credit clause does not abolish the dominance of local policy over the rules of comity. Thus the effect of the *Dred Scott* decision was that Scott, though he had become a free man during his residence in Illinois, where slavery did not exist, on his return to Missouri became subject to its local policy as stated in its laws and judicial decisions, and so reverted to slave status.[13]

Problems as to the extrastate effect of a state statute customarily arise when a statute of one state is set up as a defense to a suit brought under the statute of another state, or where a foreign statute is set up as a defense to a suit or proceeding under a local statute. The Supreme Court's practice in handling such conflicts was well summed up by Justice Stone in *Alaska Packers Association* v. *Industrial Accident Commission* (1935): "The conflict is to be resolved, not by giving automatic effect to the full faith and credit clause, compelling the courts of each state to subordinate its own statutes to those of the other, but by appraising the governmental interests of each jurisdiction, and turning the scale of decision according to their weight." Cases involving the full faith and credit to be accorded statutes have arisen in three principal fields: commercial law, insurance, and workmen's compensation.

RENDITION

The obvious gap in federalism caused by the fact that full faith and credit is never given by one state to another state's criminal laws is to a great extent closed by the obligation imposed by the command of Article IV, section 2, that: "A person charged in any state with treason, felony, or other crime, who shall flee from justice, and be found in another state, shall on demand of the executive authority of the state from which he fled, be delivered up, to be removed to the state having jurisdiction of the crime." Edmund Randolph, the first Attorney General of the United

---

[11] See *Rice* v. *Rice* (1949); *Vanderbilt* v. *Vanderbilt* (1957); *Simons* v. *Miami Beach First National Bank* (1965).

[12] *Huntington* v. *Attrill* (1892).

[13] *Dred Scott* v. *Sandford* (1857).

States, offered the opinion that this part of the Constitution was not self-executing. Accordingly, Congress in 1793 passed a statute affirming the obligation of a governor to surrender a fugitive from another state.

Under international law there is no right on the part of one nation to demand the return of a fugitive unless there is a treaty between the two countries providing for extradition. It is usual in such treaties for the crimes for which extradition can be requested to be specifically listed. Political offenses (that is, those against a particular government or governing group rather than against the state itself) are almost universally nonextraditable; nor will a nation usually extradite its own citizens. Moreover, a person extradited under a treaty arrangement can be tried only for the crime which was alleged in the request for surrender. If other charges are to be pressed against the prisoner, he must first be allowed to return to the country to which he had fled.

The Constitution states no such restrictions. It simply specifies that "fugitives" from justice shall be turned over to the demanding executive authority. The question whether certain crimes were excluded from rendition was raised on the very eve of the Civil War in *Kentucky* v. *Dennison* (1861). William Lago, a free Negro, had been indicted in Kentucky for assisting a slave to escape. To avoid trial Lago fled across the border to Ohio, and the Governor of Kentucky presented a request for Lago's return. Dennison, the Governor of Ohio, refused to comply on the ground that the crime in question was one which the Constitution had not meant to include.

Kentucky brought suit in the Supreme Court for a writ of mandamus to compel Dennison to perform his duty. The Court was aware of the political situation in March, 1861, and realized that a direct order to the Governor of Ohio would probably be disobeyed. The tactics adopted by Chief Justice Taney were, first, to reject absolutely the contention that certain crimes were outside the purview of Article IV. Neither could Taney see any doubt that it was the duty of the Governor of Ohio to return the fugitive.

Then, having firmly established what was the law in the case, Taney began to extricate the Court from the position of having to issue an order which would be ignored. Whether the Court, Taney hedged, could command Governor Dennison to perform this function was an entirely different question. The statute of 1793 had not provided any means to compel the execution of the duty of rendition; nor could the federal government constitutionally coerce a state official. "Indeed, such a power would place every State under the control and dominion of the General Government." Although this is dubious doctrine so far as general nation-state relations are concerned, the rule of the *Dennison* case has been respected subsequently in rendition matters.

It should be emphasized that although governors occasionally refuse to return a fugitive, orderly rendition is the normal course of events. To eliminate serious breaches of justice, Congress in 1934 exercised its power under the commerce clause to make it a federal offense for anyone to cross a state line fleeing from justice or for anyone to help another to do so. Since this act provides that the fugitive must be tried in the federal district court in the state from which he fled, the prisoner is readily available to local officials if the federal government does not complete its prosecution. Moreover, since 1936, most states have adopted a uniform criminal extradition act.

INTERSTATE COMPACTS

In recent years there have been numerous protests against the centralizing tendencies of the federal government. One means to avoid concentration of power in Washington and to permit state handling of problems which extend beyond the borders of a single state has been the interstate compact. Initially this method was used to solve relatively minor issues, such as marking disputed land or water boundaries. In the twentieth century, however, the device has been more fully exploited. Compacts between states have regulated such diverse matters as conservation of natural resources in gas, oil, water, and timber; civil defense coordination for possible emergencies; mutual sharing of water power of large rivers; water and air pollution control; development of interstate metropolitan areas and interstate facilities such as bridges and harbors; regulation of ocean fisheries; and interstate programs of graduate and professional education.

Perhaps the most famous interstate compact has been that between New York and New Jersey which established the Port of New York Authority to develop and operate harbor and transportation facilities in the bistate area. In 1953 the same states signed another important compact regulating labor practices in the New York port area. Because of the evidence of crime and racketeering along the waterfront, the states agreed on a comprehensive set of regulations for licensing and employment on the docks. To enforce the terms of the agreement, the compact set up a two-man waterfront commission, with one member from each state. No person can work as a stevedore or longshoreman in the port area without securing a license from the commission.

Truly sovereign states would be at liberty to make treaties at will, but the Constitution imposes definite limitations on the states in this respect. Article I, section 10, clause 1, provides: "No state shall enter into any treaty, alliance, or confederation . . ." while the third clause of the same section stipulates that: "No state shall, without the consent of Congress . . . enter into any agreement or compact with another state, or with a foreign power." Obviously the justification for the interstate compact must be found in the uncertain distinction between "treaty" and "agreement or compact." Presumably this distinction is a political question for Congress to determine in giving its consent.

Although congressional consent to interstate compacts is required, there is no set formula as to when and how that approval should be registered. The assent may be given before or after the agreement; it may be explicit, implicit, or tacit.[14] Nor is there any form in which Congress must cast its approval. It may be done by specific statute, by a joint resolution, by ratification of a state constitution which contains such a compact, or by means of a compact between Congress and the states involved.[15] Congress may even extend blanket approval to future agreements in certain specified areas.

[14] *Virginia* v. *Tennessee* (1893).
[15] *Burton's Lessee* v. *Williams* (1818).

No case has arisen in which a compact has been held unconstitutional by the Supreme Court. Still, there can be no doubt that interstate agreements must conform to the Constitution; otherwise the combined action of two states and a congressional majority could amend the Constitution. The presidential veto is an added safety device to that supplied by the courts.

Once a state has formally ratified a compact and the approval of Congress has been obtained, the agreement is binding on the state and all its officers—executive, legislative, and judicial. A state cannot unilaterally declare that a compact is in violation of its constitution and use this as a basis for withdrawal.[16]

DISPUTES BETWEEN STATES

There are, in general, three methods open to a nation in settling disputes with its neighbors: war, diplomacy, or submission of the controversy to some form of judicial determination. Under the Constitution only the last two methods are open to American states. Interstate diplomacy might terminate in an informal agreement between governors or in a full-fledged compact requiring the consent of Congress. Litigation between states is handled exclusively by the Supreme Court under its original jurisdiction, according to Article III, section 2, of the Constitution.

The Articles of Confederation made Congress the tribunal of last resort for interstate disputes and laid down elaborate provisions for the selection of a panel of impartial arbiters to hear the controversies. The Constitutional Convention discussed a similar proposal which would have given jurisdiction over territorial and jurisdictional disputes to the Senate, but finally decided that the scope of the federal judicial power would render this grant unnecessary.

The first question which the Supreme Court must answer in hearing a dispute between states is whether or not the matter is properly a controversy between states. This matter is not always so simple as it might appear at first glance. After the Civil War, Louisiana defaulted on certain state bonds and under the Eleventh Amendment she could not be sued without her consent by citizens of other states. A group of bondholders from New Hampshire tried to evade this provision by nominally transferring their holdings to New Hampshire and having that state bring suit against Louisiana for payment. The Court viewed this as a mere subterfuge and refused to decide the case.[17] However, some twenty years later South Dakota bondholders gave their state government full title to some North Carolina securities on which that state had defaulted. In this case the Supreme Court by a five to four vote held that there was an actual controversy between states and that its jurisdiction had been properly invoked. Judgment was given in favor of South Dakota.[18]

On the whole, in controversies between states the Supreme Court has strictly applied its usual standards of what constitutes sufficient injury to bring about a real "case or controversy."[19] It has refused to entertain suits where a state has sought to enjoin other states from forbidding the importation of prison-made goods or levying

---

[16] *West Virginia ex rel. Dyer* v. *Sims* (1951).
[17] *New Hampshire* v. *Louisiana* (1883).
[18] *South Dakota* v. *North Carolina* (1904).
[19] See discussion of the "case or controversy" requirement in Chap. 6.

inheritance taxes on intangibles held by its citizens in another state.[20] On several occasions, the Court has gone out of its judicial way to discourage litigation and to suggest that the disputing states settle their controversies by negotiation or compact.[21] On the other hand, the Court has accepted cases where serious and irreparable injury was allegedly threatened by such hazards as sewage pollution of large rivers or by the diversion of vitally necessary water from interstate streams. The Court has extended its jurisdiction to disputes such as those involving state boundaries, where it might have claimed that the issue was "political" rather than legal.[22]

Once a case between two states has been accepted by the Court, the next problems which arise are what law should be applied and what procedure the Court should follow. Generally the law of the case is decided on principles of international law modified by the exigencies of a federal system. In *Kansas* v. *Colorado* (1907) Justice Brewer noted that federal law, state law, and international law would be employed as the situation might demand. He also suggested that in judging interstate conflicts the Court had been in effect "building up what may not improperly be called interstate common law."

Where the factual issues involved in these disputes are complicated, the Court frequently appoints a "special master," usually a member of the Supreme Court bar, to act as a fact finder. He may have the right to summon witnesses and take depositions. After the findings of the master are filed, the Court will allow the parties to the case to submit exceptions and will hear argument on the objections. It is not unusual, however, for the master's report as filed to be adopted by the Court in its final decree.

There always exists, potentially at least, the problem of what the Supreme Court might do if one of the states chose to ignore or disobey the judgment. The nearest this question came to a practical answer was in the historic Virginia-West Virginia dispute. As part of the terms of its becoming a separate state during the Civil War, West Virginia had agreed to assume its just share of the Virginia state debt and the compact had been duly ratified by Congress. In 1907, after four decades of negotiation had yielded no monetary results, Virginia brought suit for collection. The litigation continued to 1915, when the Supreme Court affirmed the report of its special master and fixed the amount of West Virginia's liability. However, West Virginia still made no motion to pay.

The matter came to a head in 1918. Chief Justice White spoke for a unanimous Court and warned West Virginia:

> That judicial power essentially involves the right to enforce the results of its exertion is elementary. . . . And that this applies to the exertion of such power in controversies between States as the result of the exercise of original jurisdiction conferred upon this court by the Constitution is therefore certain.[23]

---

[20] *Alabama* v. *Arizona* (1934); *Massachusetts* v. *Missouri* (1939).
[21] *Washington* v. *Oregon* (1909); *Minnesota* v. *Wisconsin* (1920); *New York* v. *New Jersey* (1921).
[22] See discussion of the "political question" doctrine in Chap. 8.
[23] *Virginia* v. *West Virginia* (1918).

The Chief Justice asserted that it was patent from the wording of the legislative and judicial articles in the Constitution and from the limitations placed thereby on the states, that the federal government had the power to enforce a court decision against a recalcitrant state. There were two general remedies available. First, Congress could legislate. Second, further court action was possible. Precisely what course of compulsion could or would be pursued was not indicated. The case was postponed for reargument on the judicial remedies which should be invoked and to allow time for congressional action or further opportunity for peaceful settlement. Before the case was reopened, the West Virginia Legislature appropriated the money to meet the obligation.

In a different type of problem, but one also involving West Virginia, that state tried to withdraw from a compact which had been approved by Congress. The state supreme court had ruled that the compact violated the state constitution and was therefore void. In *West Virginia ex rel. Dyer* v. *Sims* (1951), the Supreme Court reversed, Justice Frankfurter writing:

> It requires no elaborate argument to reject the suggestion that an agreement solemnly entered into between States by those who alone have political authority to speak for a State can be unilaterally nullified, or given final meaning by an organ of one of the contracting States. A State cannot be its own judge in a controversy with a sister State.

Chapter 6

Judicial Power and Organization

The federal judiciary, asserted Alexander Hamilton in No. 78 of *The Federalist,* is "beyond comparison the weakest of the three departments of power." He went on:

> The judiciary, from the nature of its functions, will always be the least dangerous to the political rights of the Constitution, because it will be least in a capacity to annoy or injure them. The Executive not only dispenses the honours, but holds the sword of the community. The legislature not only commands the purse, but prescribes the rules by which the duties and rights of every citizen are to be regulated. The judiciary, on the contrary, has no influence over either the sword or the purse; no direction either of the strength or of the wealth of the society; and can take no active resolution whatever. It may truly be said to have neither force nor will, but merely judgment.

This appraisal of the comparative power positions of the three branches seems accurate enough 190 years later. Nevertheless, for present purposes it is "judgment" rather than "force" or "will" that is most important. Since this is a study of the meaning of the American Constitution as judicially determined, it is appropriate that a survey of the three departments of government begin, not with Article I, which creates and empowers the Congress, nor with Article II, which establishes the executive, but with Article III, which pertains to the judiciary. An understanding of judicial power and organization and the conditions under which constitutional controversies are decided by the federal courts, which it is the purpose of this section to supply, is required both for itself and for the background it provides to the discussions in the subsequent sections of this volume.

FEDERAL JUDICIAL POWER

Article III begins with this sentence: "The judicial power of the United States shall be vested in one supreme court, and in such inferior courts as the Congress may, from time to time, ordain and establish." This language tells who is to exercise the federal judicial power, but it does not define that power. In practice, the judicial power exercised by the federal courts is an amalgam of constitutional authority, legislative authorization and interpretation, traditional forms, and prudential practice. The federal courts behave as they do partly under the directives of the Constitution and Congress, and partly because they stand in the time-honored tradition of the English common-law and equity courts. In addition, their development has been shaped by the overriding necessity of accommodation to a federal system with a dual structure of courts, which continually creates problems of adjustment and division of responsibilities.

Power to Decide Cases and Controversies

The basic power of the federal courts, as indicated in Article III, section 2, is to decide "cases" and "controversies." This authorization has been interpreted to foreclose the handling of any case by the federal courts unless it meets four tests: (1) it must involve *adverse parties* (2) who have a substantial *legal interest* (3) in a controversy growing out of a *real set of facts* (4) which admits of an *enforceable determination* of the legal rights of the parties. As Chief Justice Hughes said in *Aetna Life Insurance Co.* v. *Haworth* (1937): "A justiciable controversy is . . . distinguished from a difference or dispute of a hypothetical or abstract character . . . The controversy must be definite and concrete, touching the legal relations of parties having adverse legal interests. . . . It must be a real and substantial controversy admitting of specific relief through a decree of conclusive character." These conditions are so well understood that they customarily raise no difficulties, but we shall see in Chapter 8 that they do impose limitations of real importance on judicial review.

The power of the federal courts to enforce their decisions is likewise normally taken for granted, but in fact the courts have no enforcement machinery at their direct disposal except for a few marshals. The judiciary must look to the executive and Congress for help in case of any real resistance to its orders. Whether apocryphal or not, Andrew Jackson's comment, "John Marshall has made his decision, now let him enforce it," reveals the hollowness of the Supreme Court's authority unless it is sustained by the support of its governmental colleagues and the backing of public opinion.

The matter of the enforceability of judicial decisions was most strikingly raised by the Supreme Court's 1954 ruling on the constitutionality of racial segregation in the public schools.[1] Recognizing the bitterness of the resistance which this ruling would evoke, the Court authorized a pattern of compliance which could be varied in character and speed to meet local conditions. When in 1957, in spite of these ameliorative efforts, mob violence and official state obstruction frustrated enforcement of the court order in Little Rock, Arkansas, President Eisenhower promptly made it clear that the entire compulsive power of the government was available to enforce the judicial decree, stating: "Failure to act in such a case would be tantamount to acquiescence in anarchy and the dissolution of the Union."

The Contempt Power

In order to carry out their primary function of making binding decisions in cases or controversies, the federal courts possess certain auxiliary sanctions. First is the power to punish for contempt of their authority. The origin of the contempt power was in England, where disobedience of court orders was regarded as contempt of the king himself. Presumably the courts of the United States would have enjoyed similar power without specific legislation, but in fact the Judiciary Act of 1789 did confer power "to punish by fine or imprisonment, at the discretion of said courts, all contempts of authority in any cause or hearing before the same."

Contempts may be either civil or criminal. A civil contempt consists in the refusal of a person to obey a court order, and the purpose of the sanction is to preserve and enforce the rights of the parties in the proceeding. Civil contempt may be purged by obedience to the court order. In a criminal contempt, however, the purpose of the punishment is to vindicate the authority of the court. The act of contempt has been completed, and the guilty person cannot purge himself of contempt by subsequent action. The same conduct may amount to both civil and criminal contempt, and the court may impose both coercive and punitive measures in the same proceeding.[2]

The judicial power to punish for contempt has often been a source of serious concern. It was historically a summary power, i.e., exercised by the judge without jury or other procedural protections. Moreover, as developed in England it applied to contempts committed out of court as well as those in the presence of the court. American experience has resulted in limiting the contempt power in both respects.[3] A congressional act of 1831 confined its exercise to misbehavior in the presence of the court "or so near thereto as to obstruct the administration of justice," and to disobedience to lawful writs or orders of the court.

As for summary punishment for contempt, it is now authorized by Section 42(a) of the federal rules of criminal procedure only when the judge certifies that he saw or heard the conduct constituting the contempt. The discretion which a judge exercises in summarily punishing contempts occurring in his presence is seldom challenged successfully on appeal, but it did happen in *In re McConnell* (1962), where counsel for one of the parties had been held in contempt for insisting on

---

[1] *Brown* v. *Board of Education* (1954).
[2] *United States* v. *United Mine Workers* (1947).
[3] On the problem of out-of-court contempt by newspapers in commenting on judicial proceedings, see Chap. 21.

asking questions which the judge had barred. The Supreme Court, observing that "a vigorous, independent bar" was as necessary in our system of justice as an independent judiciary, reversed the conviction.[4]

A novel problem was presented by *Sacher* v. *United States* (1952), which involved the contempt of court sentences passed on the lawyers for the defendants in the 1949 Smith Act prosecution of eleven Communist Party leaders.[5] The nine months' trial of the case was among the most turbulent and hectic in American court annals. The five principal defense lawyers carried on a running battle with Judge Medina which appeared "wilfully obstructive" of the conduct of the trial. The trial judge was convinced that the lawyers had deliberately badgered and insulted him throughout the long months of the trial. On many occasions he warned counsel that their conduct was contemptuous, but in order not to delay the trial or deprive defendants of counsel, he did not cite them for contempt until after the jury had brought in its verdict and been discharged. Immediately thereafter he asked the lawyers to stand up, read them a small portion of a lengthy "contempt certificate" he had prepared, found them all guilty of contempt, and sentenced them to prison.

The Supreme Court majority upheld Medina's procedure, on the ground that he himself had heard and seen the contempt. But Justice Frankfurter, dissenting along with Black and Douglas, contended that this rule "merely permits summary punishment" of contempts committed in the presence of the court; it does not command it. He argued that even though the contempt had occurred in the presence of the court,

> no judge should sit in a case in which he is personally involved and that no criminal punishment should be meted out except upon notice and due hearing, unless overriding necessity precludes such indispensable safeguards for assuring fairness and affording the feeling that fairness has been done.

While *Sacher* has not been overruled, the similar procedure followed by a trial judge who had been scandalously reviled by a defendant was invalidated in *Mayberry* v. *Pennsylvania* (1971). The Court held there that no judge who had been "cruelly slandered" in his own court could maintain "that calm detachment necessary for fair adjudication" and that therefore the fact of contempt should have been tried before another judge. Judge Julius Hoffman likewise followed the Medina procedure in the tumultuous 1969 trial of the Chicago Seven. His contempt judgments, delayed until the end of the trial, were reversed by the court of appeals, which directed a new trial before a different judge. In that trial, only one of the two lawyers and three of the seven defendants were convicted of contempt.[6]

All contempts occurring outside the court, according to Rule 42(b), must be prosecuted only after notice; there must be representation by counsel, trial by jury

---

[4] *Holt* v. *Virginia* (1965) held that a lawyer who moved for a change of venue on the ground that the judge was biased was not in contempt. Similarly *Maness* v. *Meyers* (1975) ruled that a lawyer may not be cited for contempt for advising a client to refuse on Fifth Amendment grounds to produce subpoenaed material. See also *Eaton* v. *City of Tulsa* (1974) and *In re Little* (1972).

[5] *Dennis* v. *United States* (1951). See Chap. 23.

[6] *In re Dellinger* (1972); *United States* v. *Seale* (1972). See also *Taylor* v. *Hayes* (1974).

if provided for by act of Congress, and—where the contempt involved disrespect to or criticism of the judge—trial before a different judge.

Though criminal contempt proceedings are so similar to ordinary criminal trials, they have not been covered by the constitutional requirements of grand jury indictment and trial by jury. The objection to jury trial has been that a judge's authority would be seriously compromised if that judge had to depend upon a jury verdict for defense of his or her position against contemptuous assaults. However, Congress can, if it wishes, require trial by jury in the federal courts for contempts, and it has done so in several statutes.[7]

One reason why the unfettered judicial contempt power was accepted was because criminal contempt sentences were generally for a relatively short period. But in *Green* v. *United States* (1958), contempt sentences of three years were imposed on two of the eleven Communist Party leaders who had been convicted of violating the Smith Act in 1951 but had failed to appear in court for sentencing. Contempt sentences of such severity were unprecedented, and three members of the Court—Black, Warren, and Douglas—protested that severe punishment under summary conditions, where the same "functionary" lays down the law, prosecutes, sits in judgment on his own charges, and punishes as he sees fit, amounted to "autocratic omnipotence." Justice Black thought that "there is no justification in history, in necessity, or most important in the Constitution for trying those charged with violating a court's decree in a manner wholly different from those accused of disobeying any other mandate of the state."

There was an indication in *United States* v. *Barnett* (1964) that a majority of the Court was willing to accept absence of jury trial in criminal contempts only when the punishment was "minor" or "trivial." This hint was confirmed in *Cheff* v. *Schnackenberg* (1966). Though the Court still denied that a criminal contempt proceeding was a criminal prosecution within the meaning of the Bill of Rights guarantee of trial by jury, it held, in an exercise of its supervisory power over the federal courts, that sentences exceeding six months for criminal contempt could not be imposed without jury trial.

Two years later, in *Bloom* v. *Illinois* (1968), the Court held the six-month rule applicable to the states as well, and in its opinion accepted the position that "convictions for criminal contempt are indistinguishable from ordinary criminal convictions."[8]

In the aftermath of the Chicago Seven trial, Judge Hoffman sought to avoid the six-month limit by assessing contempt sentences of six months or less for a number

---

[7] The Civil Rights Acts of 1957 and 1964 require jury trial for contempt if the penalty imposed on conviction is a fine in excess of $300 or imprisonment for more than forty-five days. The Clayton Act of 1914 requires a jury trial in contempt proceedings arising out of disobedience to federal court orders provided the conduct complained of also constitutes a criminal offense under federal or state laws. A provision of the 1932 Norris-LaGuardia Act which provided jury trial in cases of contempt arising under that act was replaced in 1948 by a statute (U.S. Code Title 18, sec. 3692) providing a broader guarantee of jury trial "in all cases of contempt arising under the laws of the United States governing the issuance of injunctions . . . in any case involving or growing out of a labor dispute." Nevertheless, in *Muniz* v. *Hoffman* (1975), the Supreme Court held this provision inapplicable and denied jury trial in an action for criminal contempt for violation of the Labor Management Relations Act.

[8] In *Duncan* v. *Louisiana* (1968), the Court had ruled that jury trial must be provided in state courts for all serious crimes, i.e., those for which the statutory penalty is more than six months.

of individual acts by defendants and their counsel and cumulating them for total sentences of up to four years. This strategem was predictably voided on appeal. In the *Mayberry* case, the trial judge had by a similar method calculated sentences of eleven to twenty-two years, which were vacated by the Supreme Court ruling.[9]

Refusal to testify before a grand jury may be punished as civil or criminal contempt after a judicial order requiring the testimony has been secured. However, *Harris* v. *United States* (1965) held that such a proceeding is governed by Rule 42(b), requiring notice and hearing. *Shillitani* v. *United States* (1966) and *Pappadio* v. *United States* (1966) likewise involved refusal to testify before a grand jury. A federal court imposed two-year sentences of contempt but gave the witnesses the unqualified right to be released if and when they obeyed the order to testify. The Court held that the conditional nature of the sentences rendered each of the actions a civil contempt proceeding for which indictment and jury trial were not constitutionally required. However, since the term of the grand jury which had demanded the testimony had expired, imprisonment would no longer serve any useful coercive purpose, and so the Court vacated the contempt judgments.

Power to Issue Writs

The Judiciary Act of 1789, in section 14, gave all courts of the United States power "to issue writs of *scire facias, habeas corpus,* and all other writs not specially provided for by statute, which may be necessary for the exercise of their respective jurisdictions, and agreeable to the principles and usages of law." In addition, the Supreme Court was authorized to issue writs of mandamus "in cases warranted by the principles and usages of law, to any courts appointed, or persons holding office, under the authority of the United States." It was this provision which was to be held unconstitutional in *Marbury* v. *Madison* (1803).

The writ of habeas corpus, though mentioned in Article I, section 9, is issued only in accordance with statutory authorization. The historic purpose of the writ had been to challenge detention by executive authorities without judicial trial, and up to 1867 it was not available against any sentence imposed by a court of competent jurisdiction. But in that year Congress gave federal courts a broad authorization to issue writs of habeas corpus to prisoners in custody "in violation of the constitution or of any treaty or law of the United States."

Similarly the equity power to issue writs of injunction is dependent upon congressional authorization and subject to congressional limitation. In the original act of 1789, Congress provided that no equity suit should be maintained where there was an adequate remedy at law. In 1793 it passed the first of a long series of statutes limiting the power of federal courts to issue injunctions against state courts or state officers. In 1867 the federal courts were forbidden to enjoin the collection of federal taxes.[10] The Norris-LaGuardia Act of 1932 restrained the use of injunctions in labor disputes.[11] Under the Emergency Price Control Act of 1942, the Emergency Court

[9] See also *Codispoti* v. *Pennsylvania* (1974). In this case, however, the Court made clear that punishment meted out during a trial for acts of contempt in the presence of the Court could exceed six months, since each contempt was "a discrete and separate matter at a different point during the trial."

[10] See *Bob Jones University* v. *Simon* (1974); *Alexander* v. *Americans United Inc.* (1974).

[11] The act was held constitutional in *Lauf* v. *E. G. Shinner & Co.* (1938). See also *Boys Markets* v. *Retail Clerks Union, Local 770* (1970).

of Appeals was the only court permitted to enjoin price control orders or regulations, and it was limited to permanent injunctions. It could not issue temporary
restraining orders or interlocutory decrees. Chief Justice Stone, in upholding this
limitation, said that there "is nothing in the Constitution which requires Congress to
confer equity jurisdiction on any particular inferior federal court."[12]

Other Judicial Powers

Federal courts possess the power of making rules governing their process and practice, but this too is derived from statutes.[13] The process acts of 1789 and 1792 were
upheld by Chief Justice Marshall in *Wayman* v. *Southard* (1825). Although he regarded the rule-making power as essentially legislative in nature, he thought that
Congress could delegate to courts the power to "fill up the details."

The federal courts have full authority to appoint special aides required for the
performance of their duties, such as masters in chancery, referees, or auditors. Insol-
vent enterprises which come under judicial control are normally administered by
court-appointed officers. In particularly complex cases a court may appoint aides to
take testimony and to make findings and recommendations.

Attorneys are officers of the courts, which have inherent power over their admission to practice and disbarment, subject to any general statutory qualifications
that may be imposed. These powers, however, cannot be used, in Chief Justice
Taney's words, in an "arbitrary and despotic" manner.[14] The Test Oath Act of 1862
sought to exclude former Confederates from the practice of law in the federal
courts, but the Supreme Court in *Ex parte Garland* (1867) held it unconstitutional as
a bill of attainder.[15]

LEGISLATIVE STRUCTURING OF THE COURT SYSTEM

It took congressional action to turn the bare outlines of Article III into a functioning judicial establishment.[16] The First Congress set up the organization and defined
the jurisdiction of the federal judicial system by the famous Judiciary Act of 1789.

---

[12] *Lockerty* v. *Phillips* (1943). On injunctions generally, see "Developments in the Law: Injunctions," 78 HARVARD LAW REVIEW 994–1082 (1965); Owen M. Fiss, *Injunctions* (Mineola, N.Y.: The
Foundation Press, Inc., 1972).

[13] Rules proposed by the Supreme Court are submitted to Congress and go into effect automatically
if Congress does not act on them within ninety days. In 1972 the Court, with Douglas dissenting,
promulgated new Federal Rules of Evidence which the judiciary had been fourteen years in the process
of developing. Congress, alarmed that the rules involved some substantive legislation and not merely a
recasting of procedure, postponed the effective date and worked for two years on revisions in the Court
proposals before adopting the new rules in 1974. See James W. Moore and Helen I. Bendix, "Congress,
Evidence, and Rulemaking," 84 YALE LAW JOURNAL 9 (1974). Federal Rules of Criminal Procedure,
submitted by the Court to Congress in 1974, were likewise delayed and revised before Congress gave
approval in 1975.

[14] *Ex parte Secombe* (1857).

[15] The more recent experience with limitations on admission to the bar is discussed in Chap. 23.

[16] See Felix Frankfurter and James M. Landis, *The Business of the Supreme Court: A Study in the
Federal Judicial System* (New York: The Macmillan Company, 1928).

This act was the result of protracted debate during the summer of 1789 between Federalists seeking a strong and complete system of federal courts, and anti-Federalists intent on keeping the judicial establishment within the narrowest possible bounds. The Federalists won a limited victory, the statute providing for two judicial levels—district courts in every state and three circuit courts—below the Supreme Court. The circuit courts had no separate judiciary, however. They were to be staffed by the six Supreme Court justices, who would ride circuit between sessions, plus the district judge in whose district the circuit court was sitting.

The act gave to the district and circuit courts jurisdiction in admiralty and in suits between citizens of different states. It conferred little of the potentially broad jurisdiction allowed by the Constitution over cases arising under the Constitution, laws, or treaties, awarding jurisdiction over only a small number of federal crimes, plus penalties and forfeitures made under the laws of the United States. The state courts were allowed to retain jurisdiction concurrent with that of the federal courts in suits between citizens of different states and in numerous types of cases involving the enforcement of federal laws. It was not until 1875 that Congress gave the federal courts the full range of jurisdiction they were capable of exercising under the Constitution.

The act of 1789 also provided for the appointment in each district of a marshal to execute the orders of the court, and of an attorney for the United States to prosecute criminal cases and civil actions in which the United States was a party. Finally, the act set up the office of Attorney General of the United States, whose duty it was "to prosecute and conduct all suits in the Supreme Court in which the United States shall be concerned, and to give his advice and opinion upon questions of law when required by the President of the United States, or when requested by the heads of any of the departments." The Attorney General was not given any supervisory responsibility over the United States attorneys, and the Department of Justice was not created until 1870.

The Judiciary Act of 1789 has been generally hailed as an outstanding piece of legislation, but there were weaknesses in it. The role of the federal court system was limited because the Supreme Court could meet only in the capital, access to which was made difficult by poor transportation; the federal trial courts could meet only at one or at most two places in each state, and had limited jurisdiction. Thus the new system of courts was remote and expensive. From 1789 to 1801 only three cases were appealed from state courts to the Supreme Court. Riding circuit over abominable roads was a judge-killing assignment for the high court's members. Moreover, sitting in circuit courts meant that they reviewed their own decisions when cases were appealed to the Supreme Court.

After their defeat by Jefferson in 1800, the Federalists passed the Judiciary Act of 1801, which terminated circuit riding by the justices. The six-member Court was to be reduced to five when the next vacancy occurred, to avoid tie votes and to give incoming President Jefferson one less vacancy to fill. More district courts were created, and the old circuit court system was abolished in favor of six new courts with increased jurisdiction, manned by resident circuit judges. The fact that all these new judgeships were filled by the outgoing Federalist administration led the Jeffersonians to attack the "midnight judges bill" as judicial jobbery, and it was promptly repealed.

Instead, the Jeffersonians adopted a new act in 1802 providing for six circuits, composed of one Supreme Court justice and one district judge, but allowing the circuit courts to be held by a single judge, a practice that became increasingly common. This act again tied the size of the Supreme Court to the number of circuits, and as the country expanded and more circuits were added, the size of the Supreme Court had to be increased. A seventh member was added in 1807, and in 1837 the size went to nine. A tenth justice was added for a tenth circuit in 1864. President Johnson's difficulties with Congress led it to adopt an act in 1866 reducing the Court to seven, as vacancies occurred, and reorganizing the circuits into nine. Actually, the number of justices did not go below eight. By an act of 1869 the size of the Court was again increased to nine. This statute also drastically curtailed the circuit-riding responsibilities of the justices, but the postwar development of judicial business and the territorial expansion of the country left the pressure on the Court as heavy as ever. By 1890 it had 1,800 cases on its docket.

The problem of the circuit courts also continued unabated. A panel of circuit judges had been provided by the 1869 act, but the number was quite inadequate. By the 1880s, eight-ninths of the litigation in the circuit courts was disposed of by single judges, usually district judges. Cases which came to the circuit courts on appeal from the districts were thus customarily heard by the same judge who had decided the case in the district court.

A remedy was finally found for the Supreme Court's problem in the Circuit Courts of Appeals Act of 1891. A new level of intermediate appellate courts was established, consisting of a court of appeals for each of the nine circuits and the District of Columbia. The old district and circuit courts were retained, but except for certain categories of direct appeal to the Supreme Court, their decisions were routed to the new courts of appeals for final disposition. As a gesture to tradition, the circuit duty of Supreme Court justices was not eliminated, but little was expected of them. The Supreme Court immediately felt the benefits of the act as the flood of litigation it had been receiving was shunted to the circuit courts of appeals. The one obvious error in the 1891 statute was the retention of the circuit courts, which were finally abolished by statute in 1911, through a merger of their jurisdiction with that of the district courts. Thus the present organization of the federal court system was achieved.

Keeping the Supreme Court's business under control required further legislation. Principally the problem was that in a considerable number of situations there was a statutory right of appeal from lower federal courts and from state supreme courts to the Supreme Court. A 1916 act seeking to give the Supreme Court greater discretionary review did not go far enough. With Taft's appointment as Chief Justice in 1921, he took the lead in urging an extension of the discretionary principle, and the Court itself developed a bill which was adopted as the Judiciary Act of 1925.

This act was based on the proposition that the Supreme Court's time had to be conserved for handling issues of national significance. Litigation which did not meet this test was to be left to state courts of last resort and to the circuit courts of appeals. To achieve these purposes, most decisions of the circuit courts of appeals were made reviewable in the Supreme Court only by the writ of certiorari, which the Court granted or denied in its own discretion. Again, cases which previously could be appealed directly from district courts to the Supreme Court were now, with some important exceptions, directed instead to the circuit courts of appeals. Finally, the act confined to two classes the cases which could as a matter of right be taken from the state courts to the Supreme Court: (1) where the validity of a state statute was challenged on federal constitutional grounds and its validity sustained; and (2) where a federal statute or treaty was invoked and its validity denied by a state court.

The size of the Court, which had been stabilized at nine since 1869, again became an issue in 1937 with President Roosevelt's proposal that Congress authorize appointment of one new justice for each sitting justice who remained on the Court after reaching the age of seventy, to a maximum limit of fifteen justices. The plan was generally disliked even by those who disapproved of what the Court had been doing, and it was defeated in Congress.

THE LOWER FEDERAL COURTS

The District Courts

The district courts are the trial courts of the federal system. Cases are heard by a single judge, with participation of a jury when appropriate. There are currently ninety-three district courts, including those located in Puerto Rico, the Canal Zone, Guam, and the Virgin Islands. Each state has at least one federal district court, and some have as many as four. The number of judges per district ranges from one to a high of twenty-seven in the southern district of New York, which covers New York City. In 1975 there were four hundred district judgeships.

About one-third of all the civil suits tried in the district courts involve the government as a party, as either plaintiff or defendant. As for private civil suits, there are three main heads of jurisdiction: (1) federal questions, covering all cases in law and equity arising under the Constitution, laws, and treaties of the United States; (2) diversity of citizenship; and (3) admiralty. In addition, federal courts in the District of Columbia, the Canal Zone, Guam, and the Virgin Islands have general local jurisdiction and law-enforcement responsibilities.

The diversity of citizenship cases constitute one-fourth of all civil cases in the federal courts.[17] The theory of the Constitution in opening the federal courts to suits involving citizens of different states was that the state courts might well be biased against out-of-state litigants, whereas the federal courts would provide a neutral tribunal for all parties. The anti-Federalists opposed giving such jurisdiction to the federal courts, and periodically there have been efforts to abolish it. The present-day objection to diversity jurisdiction is that it congests the federal courts with a tremendous number of cases growing out of essentially local issues which federal

---

[17] In 1974, out of 103,530 civil cases filed in federal district courts, 26,963 were based on diverse citizenship. For a general discussion, see Henry J. Friendly, *Federal Jurisdiction* (New York: Columbia University Press, 1973), Chap. 7.

judges must determine according to state law. While in 1789 there might have been prejudice in state courts against outsiders, it is argued that this possibility is no longer important. These arguments have not prevailed, but in 1958 Congress did limit access to the federal courts in diversity cases by various restrictions.[18]

The federal district courts also deal with a heavy load of criminal prosecutions. Criminal cases begun in 1974 totaled almost 38,000, including prosecutions for violation of the immigration laws, fraud, transportation of stolen automobiles, and violations of the narcotics, liquor, migratory bird, selective service, white slave, and food and drug laws.

A 1968 statute created a system of federal magistrates. Magistrates are attorneys, appointed by district court judges, who serve as officers of the court authorized to issue warrants, fix bail, hold preliminary hearings, conduct trials for petty offenses, and screen petitions which come to the court from prisoners seeking review of their sentences or convictions. There were some 560 magistrates in 1974.[19]

Three-Judge District Courts

There are certain situations where a district court consisting of three district or court of appeals judges must be impaneled. A three-judge trial court was first authorized by Congress in the expediting act of 1903 which empowered the Attorney General, in any proceeding brought by the United States under the Sherman Act or the Interstate Commerce Act which "in his opinion . . . is of general public importance," to file a certificate to that effect with the court where the case was docketed. Thereupon the case was to be given precedence and assigned to a panel of three judges, from whose decision appeal lay directly to the Supreme Court.

A second occasion for use of this device was provided by the Supreme Court's ruling in *Ex parte Young* (1908) that lower federal courts could enjoin state officers from enforcing state statutes on the ground of their unconstitutionality. Congress was alarmed over the prospect of a single federal judge enjoining a state legislative program, and in the Mann-Elkins Act of 1910 and the Judicial Code of 1911, provided that a three-judge court would have to be convened to pass on the constitutionality of state legislation before injunctions could be issued.

The Mann-Elkins Act also created a five-judge Commerce Court which was to hear all appeals of Interstate Commerce Commission cases. In 1913 this court was abolished and injunctions against ICC orders were required to be heard by a three-judge district court. Later statutes set up the same arrangements for certain other federal administrative agencies. In 1937 Congress provided that no interlocutory or permanent injunction against enforcement of an act of Congress on the ground of its alleged unconstitutionality could be issued except by a three-judge court.

Because appeal from decisions of a three-judge district court is directly to the

---

[18] The amount involved in a diversity suit must be at least $10,000, and removal to federal courts from state courts of cases arising under state workmen's compensation laws is forbidden. In 1968 the American Law Institute proposed substantial modifications in diversity jurisdiction. See *Study of the Division of Jurisdiction between State and Federal Courts* (Philadelphia: American Law Institute, 1969).

[19] See "Masters and Magistrates in the Federal Courts," 88 HARVARD LAW REVIEW 779 (1975). *Mathews* v. *Weber* (1976) permitted federal district judges to refer some Social Security and Medicare cases to magistrates for initial review.

Supreme Court and is a matter of right, the Court has tended to interpret strictly the various statutes providing for three-judge courts.[20] In 1950 Congress abolished the three-judge provision for all federal agencies except the ICC. On the other hand, the civil rights era brought many challenges to the constitutionality of state action which had to be tried before three-judge courts.[21] Chief Justice Burger has advocated the abolition of all three-judge courts because of their "waste" of judicial manpower and their erosion of the Supreme Court's discretionary control over its docket. In 1974 the Senate passed a bill (S. 271, 93d Cong.) eliminating the requirement that three-judge courts be convened when a suit was brought attacking the constitutionality of a state or federal law and also abolishing the right of direct appeal to the Supreme Court from these courts, but the bill died in the House.

The Federal Courts of Appeals

The courts of appeals, created by Congress in 1891, and known until 1948 as circuit courts of appeals, constitute the second level of the federal judiciary. Their purpose is primarily to relieve the Supreme Court by hearing appeals from decisions of the district courts, and in practice they are the courts of last resort for the great majority of all federal cases. For judicial purposes the country is divided into ten numbered circuits; an eleventh court of appeals sits in the District of Columbia. Members of the Supreme Court are assigned as supervising justices for each of the circuits. There are from three to fifteen circuit judges in each circuit, and a total of ninety-seven (in 1975) for the eleven courts. A panel of three normally sits on a case.

All final decisions and some intermediate orders of the district courts are subject to review by the courts of appeals. In 1974, 16,400 appeals were taken to the circuit courts, and 13,800 of these were from the district courts. The balance were appeals from federal administrative boards and commissions, such as the Tax Court, the National Labor Relations Board, the Federal Communications Commission, and so on. Trials in the courts of appeals are conducted on the basis of the record made in the original proceeding before the district court or administrative agency. New evidence may not be presented.

THE SUPREME COURT

The Supreme Court is composed of the Chief Justice of the United States and eight associate justices. The Court meets annually in October for its regular term and remains in session, though with periodic recesses, until the following June. The Chief Justice may call the Court into session for special terms during the summer, as was done in 1958 to dispose of the Little Rock segregation controversy and in 1942 to review the death sentences imposed on eight Germans who had come to the

---

[20] *Phillips* v. *United States* (1941); *Swift & Co.* v. *Wickham* (1965); *Gonzalez* v. *Automatic Employees Credit Union* (1974); *MTM, Inc.* v. *Baxley* (1975). See David P. Currie, "The Three-Judge District Court in Constitutional Litigation," 32 UNIVERSITY OF CHICAGO LAW REVIEW 1 (1964); also "The Three-Judge District Court," 77 HARVARD LAW REVIEW 299 (1963).

[21] In 1974 three-judge courts numbered 249 (compared with 320 in 1973), of which 171 dealt with civil rights suits, 51 with review of ICC orders, and 8 with reapportionment issues (down from 32 in 1972).

United States by submarine on a sabotage mission.[22] The Court formerly sat in the old Senate chamber in the basement of the Capitol, but it now occupies a palace of dazzling white marble so elegant that, when it was completed in 1935, one justice suggested that the members of the Court should ride in on elephants.

The Court's Operation

The Court sits for four hours daily, Monday through Wednesday, in an impressive high-ceilinged courtroom, with enormous pillars and red velvet hangings. The justices meet in the robing room behind the drapes shortly before ten o'clock. By tradition, each justice shakes hands with every one of his colleagues. Promptly at ten the court crier smashes his gavel, spectators rise, the velvet curtains part, and the justices come through to take their places behind the long bench.[23]

During its public sessions the Court hears oral arguments in scheduled cases and announces its decisions. For every case on the docket, the record of the proceedings in the lower courts and briefs stating the arguments for each side are filed with the Court. The justices study these materials before the case comes up for hearing. The time for oral argument is strictly limited; except in the most important cases, counsel for each side will have one hour or less to address the Court. When the time is up, a red light goes on at the lectern where the counsel stands facing the court, and he must stop immediately. Legend has it that Chief Justice Hughes once called time on a lawyer in the middle of the word "if."

Counsel seldom have an opportunity to make their arguments without interruption. The justices frequently break in with questions, comments, or requests for clarification. From the questions asked, it is often possible to predict how the individual justices are likely to vote in deciding the case. Probably their minds are not often changed by the oral argument, but it does give counsel a chance to emphasize what they feel are the main points for their side.

On Friday of each week when the Court has been sitting, the justices meet in conference to decide the cases heard that week. These proceedings are absolutely secret. No one other than the justices is present. The Chief Justice presents each case which is ready for decision, making such comments and offering such views as he chooses. Discussion then goes down the table, each associate justice speaking in order of seniority. When all have given their views on the case, voting begins. Now the order is reversed, the most junior justice voting first and the Chief Justice last. This procedure maximizes the role of the Chief Justice, since he has a chance to formulate the issues initially and to break the tie if his colleagues are evenly divided.

Following the vote, the Chief Justice assigns the writing of the "opinion of the Court" to himself or one of the associate justices. However, if there is a divided vote and the Chief Justice is in the minority, then the senior associate justice who voted

---

[22] *Cooper* v. *Aaron* (1958); *Ex parte Quirin* (1942). In 1974 the term was extended to permit hearing the Watergate tapes case, *United States* v. *Nixon*.

[23] For a general discussion of the Supreme Court's operation, see Henry J. Abraham, *The Judicial Process* (New York: Oxford University Press, 1975), Chap. 6. For a personal view of the Court from the inside, see J. Harvey Wilkinson, *Serving Justice: A Supreme Court Clerk's View* (New York: Charterhouse, 1974).

in the majority controls the assigning of the opinion of the Court. Drafts of opinions are circulated among the justices, and the author may revise the final draft on the basis of comments by his colleagues.

In the early years of the Court, it was customary for all justices to give their opinions seriatim in a case, and there was no single opinion of the Court. However, when Marshall became Chief Justice, he saw that the Court would be more influential if it spoke with a single voice, and so he himself wrote the opinion of the Court in almost all important cases.

Justices were still free to write concurring or dissenting opinions, but there was a tendency for them to go along with the opinion of the Court unless their disagreement was sharp. The fame of Justices Holmes and Brandeis as dissenters was based on the quality rather than the quantity of their dissents. However, the Supreme Court's struggle with the New Deal caused dissents to become more frequent, and since the 1943 term nonunanimous opinions have outnumbered the unanimous opinions. Concurring opinions are written by justices who agree with the result reached by the Court but not entirely with the reasons given in the opinion of the Court. The number of concurring opinions written by Supreme Court justices has also increased markedly in the past three decades.

The Court's decisions, formerly announced only on Mondays, since 1965 may be given at the beginning of any session. The author of the opinion of the Court summarizes the main points of his ruling in a few minutes. Dissenters may also outline their disagreement if they wish. No advance notice is ever given as to when a decision in a particular case will be ready, and the opinions are distributed to newsmen only after the decision has been announced from the bench. In the printing operation, each opinion is divided among several printers so they will not know what case they are working on.

The role of the Chief Justice is extremely important, for he can develop a substantial position of leadership on the Court. His formal authority stems primarily from his role as presiding officer at Court sessions and in the conference, and from his power to assign the writing of opinions. But he is also the symbolic head of the Court and the highest officer of the government after the President and Vice President, and if he has the necessary skill, he can use his position to guide the decision-making process toward consensus and keep discussion from bogging down in quibbling and personalities.

Original Jurisdiction

The Supreme Court is primarily an appellate court, but the Constitution does define two categories of cases which can be heard in the Court's original jurisdiction, i.e., without prior consideration by any other court. These are cases in which a state is a party, and those affecting ambassadors, public ministers, and consuls. This grant of original jurisdiction is self-executing and requires no legislation to make it effective. Since it flows directly from the Constitution, Congress can neither restrict it nor enlarge it. This latter point was decided in the case of *Marbury* v. *Madison* (1803), where the Court held a provision of the Judiciary Act of 1789 unconstitutional on the ground that it sought to add to the Supreme Court's original jurisdiction the power of issuing writs of mandamus.

Congress can, however, adopt legislation implementing the constitutional language on original jurisdiction. Thus Congress has provided that the Supreme Court shall have "original and exclusive" jurisdiction of all controversies between two or more states, whereas other cases in which a state is a party can be heard either by the Supreme Court or lower federal courts. Because of such arrangements for concurrent jurisdiction, the Supreme Court generally does not need to accept a suit invoking its original jurisdiction unless it feels there is a good reason why it should. As the Court stated in an 1895 case, its original jurisdiction "is limited and manifestly to be sparingly exercised, and should not be expanded by construction."[24]

Appellate Jurisdiction

All the remaining business of the Supreme Court comes to it in its appellate jurisdiction, which it exercises, as the Constitution says, "with such exceptions, and under such regulations as the Congress shall make." It might have been argued that the Court's appellate jurisdiction, like its original jurisdiction, flowed directly from the Constitution, and did not require legislative authorization. However, the fact is that the Judiciary Act of 1789 did legislate on the subject of appellate jurisdiction, and in 1796 the Court agreed that without a statute prescribing a rule for appellate proceedings, the Court could not assume jurisdiction.[25] In 1810 Marshall held that an affirmative statutory bestowal of appellate jurisdiction implied a denial of jurisdiction not granted.[26]

The consequences of this judicial surrender of control over appellate jurisdiction to Congress were dramatically demonstrated in the post-Civil War case of *Ex parte McCardle* (1869). Stringent Reconstruction measures establishing military rule over the South were enacted by Congress. A Mississippi editor, McCardle, held for trial before a military commission authorized by these acts, petitioned for a writ of habeas corpus under a statute passed in 1867 which gave federal judges power to grant habeas corpus to any person restrained in violation of the federal Constitution or laws, and provided for appeal to the Supreme Court in such cases. McCardle was denied the writ and appealed to the Supreme Court.

That Court had just declared Lincoln's wartime use of military commissions unconstitutional in *Ex parte Milligan* (1866), and Congress feared that it would use the *McCardle* appeal to invalidate the Reconstruction legislation. Consequently in March, 1868, the Radical Republicans rushed through Congress, and repassed over the President's veto, a statute repealing the act of 1867 so far as it granted appeals to the Supreme Court, and withdrawing "any such jurisdiction by said Supreme Court, on appeals which have been, or may hereafter be taken." The Court, which had already heard argument on the *McCardle* case when this act was passed, felt constrained to rule that its authority to render a decision had been abrogated. Congress had withdrawn the Court's jurisdiction in the clearest possible fashion. "Without jurisdiction the court cannot proceed at all in any cause. Jurisdiction is

---

[24] *California* v. *Southern Pacific Co.* (1895).
[25] *Wiscart* v. *Dauchy* (1796).
[26] *Durousseau* v. *United States* (1810).

power to declare the law, and when it ceases to exist, the only function remaining to the court is that of announcing the fact and dismissing the cause."

Under the *McCardle* principle, then, it would be constitutionally possible for Congress to abolish the appellate jurisdiction entirely and leave the Supreme Court with only the handful of cases that can be brought in its original jurisdiction. It is highly unlikely that anything approaching this will ever happen, but in 1957 Senator Jenner sought reprisal against the Court's decisions in certain national security cases by introducing legislation withdrawing the Court's appellate jurisdiction in five specific areas, including cases involving the investigatory power of Congress. This proposal, as modified by Senator Butler, was defeated by the Senate in 1958.[27]

It seems clear that, in the pressure of the times, *McCardle* was wrongly decided. In *Glidden* v. *Zdanok* (1962), Justice Douglas said, "There is a serious question whether the McCardle case could command a majority today." Interpretation of the "exceptions" clause must be consistent with the exercise of the Supreme Court's essential functions under the Constitution.[28]

Methods of Review

Except for the Court's original jurisdiction and in the limited classes of cases where there is an appeal to the Supreme Court as of right, review is sought by filing with the Court a petition for writ of certiorari to a state supreme court or federal court of appeals.[29] This writ, if granted, directs the lower court to send up the record in the case for review. During the 1974 term, there were 4,668 cases on the Supreme Court's docket, including 997 held over from prior terms. They included 12 original jurisdiction cases, 2,308 "paid cases" (i.e., with prepayment of costs), and 1,976 *in forma pauperis* cases (i.e., without prepayment of costs). The latter cases mostly originated with convicts in state or federal prisons. The Court granted full review of 155 of the paid cases and summarily decided 138, for a total of 293 paid cases acted upon. By contrast, the Court granted review of only 19 *in forma pauperis* cases and summarily decided an additional 34, for a total of 53. The great majority of the *in forma pauperis* petitions present no substantial grounds for review.

Certiorari petitions, including pertinent portions of the record, petitioner's brief, and opposing responses, are circulated among all members of the Court, who make substantial use of their law clerks in reviewing the petitions. There can be oral argument on granting petitions, but normally this does not happen. Petitions are granted on the affirmative vote of four justices. The rule of four was adopted when

[27] See C. Herman Pritchett, *Congress versus the Supreme Court: 1957–1960* (Minneapolis: The University of Minnesota Press, 1961), chap. 3; Walter F. Murphy, *Congress and the Court* (Chicago: The University of Chicago Press, 1962).

[28] See Raoul Berger, *Congress v. The Supreme Court* (Cambridge, Mass.: Harvard University Press, 1969), Chap. 9; Leonard G. Ratner, "Congressional Power over the Appellate Jurisdiction of the Supreme Court," 109 UNIVERSITY OF PENNSYLVANIA LAW REVIEW 157 (1960).

[29] Certiorari may be sought to review a federal district court decision while the case is still pending in the court of appeals, but the Supreme Court will grant the writ in these circumstances only if the case is of such "imperative public importance" as to require immediate settlement. See *Aaron* v. *Cooper* (1958) and *Youngstown Sheet & Tube Co.* v. *Sawyer* (1952). In 1974 the Supreme Court took the case of *United States* v. *Nixon* for review directly from the district court, as provided for by Rule 20, *Revised Rules, Supreme Court of the United States* (1967).

the Judiciary Act of 1925 was passed, to reassure Congress that access to the Court by the discretionary writ of certiorari would not be refused too easily.

Review of the flood of certiorari petitions imposes a heavy burden on the justices. The Court's Rule 19 states that review on certiorari "will be granted only where there are special and important reasons therefor." Among the circumstances cited in the rule as justifying the grant of certiorari are the following: where two courts of appeals have rendered conflicting decisions; where a state court or a federal court of appeals has decided an important question of federal law on which the Supreme Court has never passed, or in such a way as to conflict with applicable decisions of the Court; or where a federal court has so far departed from the accepted canons of judicial proceedings as to call for exercise of the Supreme Court's power of supervision.

Usually the Court announces no reason for denial of certiorari. Many petitions, particuarly those *in forma pauperis,* are wholly without merit and ought never to have been filed. When the Court does state a reason, often it is a technical one—for example, that the federal question is not properly presented, or was not passed on below. But some denials are clearly for policy reasons. As Justice Frankfurter said in *Maryland* v. *Baltimore Radio Show* (1950):

> A decision may satisfy all . . . technical requirements and yet may commend itself for review to fewer than four members of the Court. Pertinent considerations of judicial policy here come into play. A case may raise an important question but the record may be cloudy. It may be desirable to have different aspects of an issue further illumined by the lower courts. Wise adjudication has its own time for ripening.

The denial of a writ leaves the decision of the lower court in effect, but it has no other legal significance. It does not mean necessarily that the Supreme Court approves of the decision below, and is in no sense an affirmance of the decree. However, this is a point which is difficult to get across to the public. Denials of certiorari are often cited as precedents, and it must be admitted that in practice they may have such effect, particularly since decisions are reversed in a very high proportion of the cases in which certiorari is granted.

The constantly rising workload of the Supreme Court—4,371 cases were docketed in 1972 as compared with 2,400 ten years earlier—has created concern and stimulated suggestions for reform. In 1972 a report on the Supreme Court's caseload, by a study group appointed by Chief Justice Burger and headed by Paul Freund, concluded that review of the flood of certiorari petitions was draining the energy of the justices and preventing them from giving adequate consideration to the cases they selected to decide.[30] The study group proposed creation of a new

[30] *Report of the Study Group on the Caseload of the Supreme Court* (Washington: Federal Judicial Center, 1972). Comments on the plan include Charles L. Black, Jr., "The National Court of Appeals: An Unwise Proposal," 83 YALE LAW JOURNAL 883 (1974); "The National Court of Appeals: A Constitutional 'Inferior Court'?" 72 MICHIGAN LAW REVIEW 290 (1973); Alexander M. Bickel, "The Overworked Court," 168 THE NEW REPUBLIC 17 (February 17, 1973); Arthur J. Goldberg, "One Supreme Court," 168 THE NEW REPUBLIC 14 (February 10, 1973); Nathan Lewin, "Helping the Supreme Court with Its Work," 168 THE NEW REPUBLIC 15 (March 3, 1973); S. Sidney Ulmer, "Revising the Jurisdiction of the Supreme Court," 58 MINNESOTA LAW REVIEW 121 (1973).

National Court of Appeals immediately below the Supreme Court. Staffed by senior circuit judges on a rotating basis, this court would resolve conflicting rulings among the circuits and screen appeals, passing on perhaps four hundred of the most important cases to the Supreme Court. The plan was not favorably received. Critics, including former Chief Justice Warren, argued that deciding which cases to decide is an essential function of the Supreme Court, and that cutting off access to the Court and denying justices control over their docket would seriously damage the power and prestige of the high court.

SPECIALIZED AND LEGISLATIVE COURTS

In addition to the regular federal courts, Congress has from time to time set up courts for the performance of specialized functions. The oldest of the specialized courts is the Court of Claims, created in 1855, whose function is to try claims against the government. Other specialized courts are the Customs Court, which sits in New York, and the Court of Customs and Patent Appeals. A Commerce Court to review decisions of the ICC was created in 1910, but had an unhappy history and was abolished in 1913. The Emergency Court of Appeals was set up during World War II to try certain suits under the price control statutes. It was staffed by judges from the regular federal courts and was authorized to sit anywhere in the United States.[31] The so-called Tax Court, which reviews tax decisions by the Bureau of Internal Revenue, is legally not a court at all, but a part of the executive branch. The Court of Military Appeals was created by the Uniform Code of Military Justice in 1950 to hear appeals from courts martial on matters of law.

Decisions of the Customs Court are appealed to the Court of Customs and Patent Appeals. Cases from all the other specialized courts go to the Supreme Court on writ of certiorari or certification of questions.

The reason for these specialized courts is primarily to permit certain difficult classes of litigation to be handled by judges who have particular competence in the field. In the case of the Emergency Court of Appeals, it was feared that the wartime program of price control would break down if every federal and state judge in the country could issue injunctions against price control orders, so this power was centralized in a single specialized court.

Congress provides a system of courts for the District of Columbia and for other territories under United States control. For this purpose Congress does not have to rely upon Article III. It is given complete authority to legislate for the District of Columbia by Article I, section 8, and has power to "make all needful rules and regulations" respecting territories of the United States under Article IV, section 3.

As an alternative to the Freund plan, a federal commission headed by Senator Roman L. Hruska proposed in 1975 a seven-member national court to take significant cases on assignment from the Supreme Court or the various circuit courts of appeals. Commission on Revision of the Federal Court Appellate System, *Structure and Internal Procedures: Recommendations for Change* (Washington, D.C., 1975).

[31] A Temporary Emergency Court of Appeals was created by the Economic Stabilization Act of 1970 to hear suits under that statute. See *Fry* v. *United States* (1975).

Courts created by Congress under its authority to legislate for the District or the territories have consequently been called "legislative" courts, in contrast with the "constitutional" courts authorized by Article III.

The practical significance of this distinction is that Congress need not observe the provisions of Article III so far as appointments to and jurisdiction of the legislative courts are concerned. This point has been clear since *American Insurance Co.* v. *Canter* (1828). Congress had created an admiralty court for the territory of Florida, the judges of which were limited to four-year terms of office. This court could have been held unconstitutional because the judges did not enjoy tenure for good behavior. Instead Marshall ruled that the provisions of Article III did not apply to this court, since it was created under congressional power to legislate for the territories. It followed that the judges of a legislative court could not only be given term appointments, but could also be removed by the President, their salaries could be reduced while they were in office, and they could be given jurisdiction other than that specified in Article III.

The test of a legislative court laid down in the *Canter* case was clear enough; it was a geographical test, location in a territory. The same test made the courts of the District of Columbia legislative courts, and the Supreme Court in *Ex parte Bakelite Corp.* (1929) and *Williams* v. *United States* (1933) held that the Court of Customs and Patent Appeals and the Court of Claims were neither confined in jurisdiction nor protected in independence by Article III, but that both had been created by virtue of substantive powers possessed by Congress under Article I. Consequently Congress could give the District of Columbia courts nonjudicial functions such as revisionary powers over grants of patents and rates fixed by the local public utility commission. There was a conceptual hitch, however. Legislative courts had been regarded as exercising no part of the "judicial power of the United States," since they were not created under Article III, whereas the Supreme Court could exercise nothing but "judicial power." How was it possible, then, for the Supreme Court to hear appeals from legislative courts?

When this point was first raised, the Supreme Court concluded that it was not possible. In *Gordon* v. *United States* (1864), Chief Justice Taney ruled that Court of Claims decisions, which were in effect only advisory to the Secretary of the Treasury, could not be reviewed by the Supreme Court. Congress then amended the law to give finality to judgments of the Court of Claims, and on that basis the Court accepted appeals from it.[32] The same thing happened with the revisory power of courts of the District of Columbia over the Federal Radio Commission.[33] Thus the Court developed the rule that in proceedings before a legislative court which are judicial in nature and admit of a final judgment, the Supreme Court will accept appellate jurisdiction—an arrangement which Corwin calls a "workable anomaly."

It was made somewhat less anomalous but somewhat more confusing in 1933 when the Court suddenly decided that the courts of the District of Columbia were *both* legislative and constitutional courts.[34] As regards their organization and the

[32] *DeGroot* v. *United States* (1867).
[33] *Federal Radio Commission* v. *General Electric Co.* (1930).
[34] *O'Donoghue* v. *United States* (1933).

tenure and compensation of their judges, they were constitutional courts controlled by Article III, but as regards their jurisdiction and powers they were both legislative and constitutional courts, and so could be vested with nonjudicial powers while sharing the judicial power of the United States.

The difficulties of this dual status were only partially resolved by the decision in *Glidden Co.* v. *Zdanok* (1962). Congress had sought to clear up the status of the Court of Claims in 1953 by legislation flatly declaring it to have been established under Article III,[35] and it did the same thing for the Court of Customs and Patent Appeals in 1958.[36] The validity of this legislation came into question when judges of these two courts were assigned temporarily by the Chief Justice to sit in regular federal courts which were short of judges because of disability or disqualification. The contention in *Glidden* was that they were not Article III judges, and so could not sit in Article III courts.

By a five to two vote the Supreme Court upheld the Article III status of these judges, but the majority was split as to the reasons. Three justices held that the two courts were now Article III courts because Congress had said so, and they overruled *Bakelite* and *Williams,* which had said they were not. The other two justices in the majority said the two courts had become Article III courts because Congress had withdrawn questionable jurisdiction from those courts since the *Bakelite* and *Williams* decisions, which they would not overrule. The two dissenters, Douglas and Black, thought that these two specialized courts were still performing legislative and executive functions, that *Bakelite* and *Williams* were still the law, and that it was as improper for their judges to be assigned to sit in a regular federal court as it would be for a member of the Interstate Commerce Commission to sit there.

There appears to be something about the legislative court concept which breeds confusion. It might be better if Marshall had never invented it.

STAFFING THE FEDERAL JUDICIARY

The appointment of federal judges is frankly and entirely a political process.[37] During the present century over 90 percent of all judicial appointments have gone to members of the President's party. For example, of the 176 judges named to the federal bench in the first Nixon term, 165 were Republicans. Appointees have typically been active in state or national party affairs, perhaps unsuccessful candidates for office. The posts are also prestigious rewards for administration officials or members of Congress.[38]

---

[35] 67 Stat. 226 (1953).

[36] 72 Stat. 848 (1958).

[37] See Harold W. Chase, *Federal Judges: The Appointing Process* (Minneapolis: The University of Minnesota Press, 1972); Henry J. Abraham, *Justices and Presidents: A Political History of Appointments to the Supreme Court* (New York: Oxford University Press, 1974); John R. Schmidhauser, *The Supreme Court: Its Politics, Personalities, and Procedures* (New York: Holt, Rinehart and Winston, 1960), part I; Robert Scigliano, *The Supreme Court and the Presidency* (New York: The Free Press, 1971), chaps. 4–5.

[38] The political connection of most federal judges became clear during the grand jury investigation of Vice President Agnew in 1973. Every one of the federal district judges in his home state of Maryland disqualified himself from the case because of his ties with Agnew.

In the nomination of judges for the lower federal courts, senators of the President's party play an important role, although not always a dominant one. The Department of Justice, acting through the Deputy Attorney General, also conducts an active search for promising talent. If there is a conflict of views between the senator and the Justice Department, the senator can threaten to block a nomination to which he or she is opposed at the confirmation stage, and so a compromise is usually arranged. Since the courts of appeals cover more than one state, vacancies must be allocated to the various states on some basis satisfactory to the party organizations. When the list of candidates has been narrowed, the FBI runs a full loyalty-security check, and the Justice Department seeks the approval of the American Bar Association Committee on the Federal Judiciary. This committee then conducts its own inquiry, securing the views of the legal profession.[39]

Vacancies on the Supreme Court present major policy problems for the President. He receives suggestions from many sources and particularly from his Attorney General, but he makes his own decisions, and often he has his own ideas on the subject, either as to specific candidates or as to the qualifications he wants. Presidents are usually interested in the political viewpoint of a possible nominee and the line he is likely to take in deciding cases. Of course, predicting the future decisions of a man to be placed in a lifetime position on the bench is risky business. Theodore Roosevelt was unusually careful in picking men who could be expected to vote right on the big issues, and he was very angry when Justice Oliver Wendell Holmes, soon after his appointment to the Court, disappointed his expectations in an important antitrust case. President Taft felt that the most significant thing he had done during his administration was to appoint six justices who shared his conservative views. "And I have said to them," Taft chuckled to newspapermen when his term was expiring, "Damn you, if any of you die, I'll disown you."[40] President Nixon announced on taking office that he would appoint only "strict constructionists" to the Court.

The Senate must confirm all judicial appointees and can thus impose effective restraints on executive choice. Washington saw one of his Supreme Court nominees rejected by the Senate, and in the nineteenth century over 25 percent of the nominations failed to negotiate the Senate hurdle. By contrast, during the first two-thirds of the twentieth century, only one nominee was rejected by the Senate: John J. Parker was defeated in 1930, partly because of the opposition of labor and black organizations. There had been strong conservative opposition to Louis D. Brandeis in 1916, while liberals sought to defeat Charles Evans Hughes in 1931; but both were confirmed by substantial majorities. It was therefore a stunning reversal of precedent when within the space of two years, 1968 to 1970, both President Johnson and President Nixon saw two of their nominees fail to secure confirmation.

Johnson's trouble arose out of his effort to elevate his longtime friend and legal adviser Associate Justice Abe Fortas to the post of Chief Justice. In June, 1968, Earl

[39] See Joel B. Grossman, *Lawyers and Judges: The ABA and the Politics of Judicial Selection* (New York: John Wiley & Sons, Inc., 1965).

[40] Henry F. Pringle, *The Life and Times of William Howard Taft* (New York: Holt, Rinehart and Winston, Inc., 1939), p. 854.

Warren notified Johnson of his desire to retire, effective upon confirmation of his successor. Johnson transmitted Fortas's name to the Senate, at the same time nominating another old friend, Court of Appeals Judge Homer Thornberry of Texas, to the post to be vacated by Fortas. Opposition to Fortas quickly developed for a variety of reasons: partisan politics, objections to the liberal decisions in which he had participated, revelation of Fortas's continuation as presidential adviser while on the bench, and the argument that there was no vacancy since Warren had not actually retired. When a filibuster prevented the Senate from voting on the nomination, Fortas asked the President to withdraw his name, and he remained as Associate Justice.[41] Thus the vacancy for which Thornberry had been nominated was rendered nonexistent, and Warren continued as Chief Justice for one more term and into the Nixon administration.

President Nixon selected Warren Burger as successor to Warren as Chief Justice, and Burger was confirmed almost without opposition. He had been a conservative member of the Court of Appeals for the District of Columbia. The next vacancy was a different matter. It was created by the resignation of Justice Fortas, who was revealed in 1969 to have committed an indiscretion by agreeing to accept an annual fee for advisory services to a private foundation, funded by a man who was under federal investigation at the time and who was subsequently convicted for violations of the Securities and Exchange Act.

President Nixon nominated Appeals Court Judge Clement Haynsworth for the Fortas vacancy. But the Senate had been so alerted to the issues of judicial ethics by the Fortas affair, and the Democrats in the Senate so embarrassed by it, that Haynsworth's record was subjected to intense scrutiny. Certain indications of ethical insensitivity related to stock holdings in companies involved in cases in which he participated, as well as opposition to his conservative political views, led to his rejection by the Senate after a classic battle by a vote of fifty-five to forty-five.

Nixon's next "strict constructionist," G. Harrold Carswell, another appeals court judge, was also rejected by the Senate, fifty-one to forty-five, because of his lack of intellectual qualifications and past opposition to civil rights.[42] Not since 1894 had two successive Supreme Court appointments been defeated in the Senate.

When Justices Black and Harlan retired in the summer of 1971, Attorney General Mitchell submitted to the ABA committee six names of possible nominees, all of whom were unknown nationally or obviously lacking in qualifications for the high court. The committee's response was to rate as unqualified the two candidates listed as Nixon's preferences, ratings which immediately became known to the public. Nixon then dropped these candidates and, without notifying the committee, named two much abler conservatives, Lewis Powell and William Rehnquist.[43]

It is sometimes argued that only persons with previous judicial experience should be given federal judicial appointments. In fact, this frequently happens.

[41] See Robert Shogan, *A Question of Judgment: The Fortas Case and the Struggle for the Supreme Court* (Indianapolis: The Bobbs-Merrill Company, 1972).

[42] See Richard Harris, *Decision* (New York: E. P. Dutton & Co., Inc., 1971).

[43] See James F. Simon, *In His Own Image: The Supreme Court in Richard Nixon's America* (New York: David McKay Company, Inc., 1973).

One-third of the district judges named between 1953 and 1971 had had prior judicial service, while 59 percent of the appointees to the courts of appeals during this period were former judges.[44]

It would be unfortunate, however, if presidential freedom of selection were limited by a judicial experience requirement, particularly at the Supreme Court level. The major questions with which the Supreme Court deals require political judgment more than technical proficiency in private law. If judicial experience had been a prerequisite in the past, many of the greatest Supreme Court justices would have been ineligible for appointment, including Marshall, Story, Taney, Miller, Bradley, Hughes (at his first appointment), Brandeis, Stone, Black, Frankfurter, and Warren.[45] In spite of all criticisms, it should be recognized that the present system of selecting judges has resulted in a federal bench of high prestige, a very satisfactory level of ability, and unquestioned honesty.

JUDICIAL TENURE AND COMPENSATION

Appointment of federal judges for "good behavior" is one of the great pillars of judicial independence. A federal judge can be removed from office only by conviction on impeachment. Only one Supreme Court justice has ever been subjected to impeachment proceedings, Samuel Chase, whose judicial conduct was marked by gross and violent Federalist partisanship. In 1804 the triumphant Jeffersonians sought his removal by impeachment, but failed to secure a conviction. They were successful, however, in impeaching and convicting a district judge, John Pickering, who was a Federalist but also apparently insane. Only seven other federal judges have been impeached, three successfully, and in no case were any partisan political motives involved. But in 1970 Gerald Ford, then House minority leader, sought to initiate impeachment proceedings against Justice William O. Douglas in a transparently partisan effort to remove the Court's most liberal member and clear the way for another Nixon appointment. A House Judiciary subcommittee found no grounds for impeachment.

Federal judges can be indicted for criminal behavior while on the bench, and conviction would of course require resignation. Four judges have been indicted and two convicted.[46]

Whether Congress can effect the removal of a judge from office by abolishing his position is a disputed question. As already noted, the Jeffersonians in 1802

[44] Sheldon Goldman, "Judicial Appointments to the United States Courts of Appeals," 1967 WISCONSIN LAW REVIEW 186, and "Johnson and Nixon Appointees to the Lower Federal Courts," 34 JOURNAL OF POLITICS 936 (1972).

[45] Justice Frankfurter himself, after a detailed study of this problem in 1957, concluded: "One is entitled to say without qualification that the correlation between prior judicial experience and fitness for the functions of the Supreme Court is zero." "The Supreme Court in the Mirror of Justices," 105 UNIVERSITY OF PENNSYLVANIA LAW REVIEW 781 (1957).

[46] Judge Otto Kerner, appealing his conviction for criminal conspiracy in 1974, argued that he could not be tried until after he had been removed by impeachment, but the Supreme Court refused to hear his case, thereby confirming his conviction. *Kerner* v. *United States* (1974). He then resigned.

repealed the statute of 1801 which created sixteen new circuit judgeships for the Federalists to fill. The intent of the 1802 act was to oust the judges who had been appointed to these posts, and the Jeffersonian theory was that they had ceased to be judges when their offices were abolished. Congress took steps to prevent any of the ousted judges from bringing suit by passing a second statute limiting the Supreme Court to one term annually and postponing the next term for fourteen months. By that time the controversy had died down, and the Court was able to avoid a decision on the question.[47] On two subsequent occasions when Congress has abolished federal courts, it has provided for the transfer of their judges to other courts, and this seems to be the more correct constitutional practice.

Congress on occasion creates "temporary" district judgeships, but appointees to these positions have full lifetime tenure. The purpose of a temporary judgeship is temporarily to increase the manpower in a district without increasing the number of authorized judgeships. The next vacancy that occurs after a temporary judgeship has been provided for cannot be filled, thus reducing the judges in the district to the authorized number.

Congress is of course free to encourage the resignation of federal judges by attractive retirement arrangements. The absence or inadequacy of retirement allowances has in the past been responsible for some judges retaining their posts long after they were physically or mentally incapacitated for the work. When Justice Grier had become senile in 1870, a committee of his colleagues, headed by Justice Field, finally waited on him and suggested that he retire. Twenty-six years later Field himself became mentally incompetent. His worried colleagues deputed Justice Harlan to approach Field and ask him if he could recall the course of action he had suggested to Grier. Field finally got the point and, momentarily recovering his acuteness, burst out: "Yes! And a dirtier day's work I never did in my life!" His colleagues then abandoned their efforts, but within a few months Field submitted his resignation.[48]

The age of Supreme Court justices was one of the key issues in President Roosevelt's 1937 "Court-packing" plan. As an aftermath of this controversy, Congress passed a liberalized retirement act which permits federal justices to retire after seventy on full pay without resigning, remaining thereafter subject to recall for further judicial duty in the lower courts.

The provision that a judge's compensation may not be reduced while he is in office is a subsidiary support for judicial independence.[49] In 1920 the Supreme Court in *Evans* v. *Gore* ruled that a federal judge could not be assessed income tax

---

[47] *Stuart* v. *Laird* (1803).

[48] Carl B. Swisher, *Stephen J. Field* (Washington, D.C.: The Brookings Institution, 1930), p. 444. Justice William O. Douglas remained on the Court for eleven months after suffering a stroke, but physical incapacity forced him to retire in November, 1975. He had served for 36½ years on the Supreme Court, the longest period of service in the Court's history.

[49] Judicial salaries as set in 1969 were as follows: Chief Justice, $62,000; Associate Justices, $60,000; Appeals Court judges, $42,500; and District Court judges, $40,000. These salary levels, which were handicapping recruitment of able lawyers to the lower courts, were raised by 5 percent in 1975. In 1976, forty-four federal judges filed suit in the Court of Claims asserting that failure to raise judicial salaries to keep pace with inflation amounted to an unconstitutional reduction of their compensation.

because it would amount to an unconstitutional reduction of his salary. Justices Holmes and Brandeis dissented, Holmes saying that judges were not "a privileged class, free from bearing their share of the cost of the institutions upon which their well-being if not their life depends."

The Court persisted, and in 1925 compounded its error when in *Miles* v. *Graham* it ruled that a judge appointed after the effective date of the tax was also entitled to the immunity. Congress overrode this decision by express legislation, and in 1939 a more sensible Court reopened the matter and overruled *Evans* v. *Gore,* Justice Frankfurter saying in *O'Malley* v. *Woodrough:* "To suggest that [the tax] makes inroads upon the independence of judges . . . is to trivialize the great historic experience on which the framers based the safeguards of Article III."

The immunity of judges from liability for damages for acts committed within their judicial jurisdiction was firmly established at common law, and the Supreme Court recognized this doctrine in *Bradley* v. *Fisher* (1871). This immunity applies even when the judge is accused of acting maliciously or corruptly. The doctrine is not "for the protection of a malicious or corrupt judge, but for the benefit of the public, whose interest it is that the judges should be at liberty to exercise their functions with independence, and without fear of consequences."[50]

---

[50] See also *Pierson* v. *Ray* (1967). For a critical account of the behavior of some federal judges, see Joseph C. Goulden, *The Benchwarmers: The Private World of the Powerful Federal Judges* (New York: Weybright and Talley, 1974). *Imbler* v. *Pachtman* (1976) held that prosecutors are also immune from civil damage suits, even if they deliberately violate the civil rights of defendants.

Chapter 7

Jurisdiction of the Federal Courts

Article III, section 1, provides that the "judicial power of the United States shall be vested in one Supreme Court, and in such inferior courts as the Congress may from time to time ordain and establish." As we know, the Constitution thus left undecided the basic question as to whether there would be a system of lower federal courts, but the First Congress proceeded to create a complete hierarchy of courts.[1]

The "judicial power" is defined in Article III, section 2, which set out the various classes of cases and controversies over which the federal courts can be given jurisdiction. "Jurisdiction" in the judicial sense means the power of a court to hear (or try) a case. A court may exercise judicial power only within its authorized jurisdiction. The terms "judicial power" and "jurisdiction" are often used synonymously. However, so far as the federal courts are concerned, it is necessary to distinguish between "the judicial power of the United States" and "the jurisdiction of the federal courts," because, in spite of the word "shall," the judicial power of the United States is not automatically vested in the lower federal courts by Article III.

These courts are creatures of Congress. It could have failed to establish them in the first place, and presumably it could abolish them if it chose to do so. Consequently Congress has assumed from the beginning that it can control the jurisdiction of the lower federal courts, and the Supreme Court has acquiesced in this

---

[1] See generally Paul M. Bator et al., *Hart and Wechsler's The Federal Courts and the Federal System* (Mineola, N.Y.: The Foundation Press, Inc., 1973); David P. Currie, *Federal Courts* (St. Paul, Minn.: West Publishing Company, 1968); Charles Alan Wright, *Handbook of the Law of Federal Courts* (St. Paul, Minn.: West Publishing Company, 1970).

position in a long series of decisions.[2] The Judiciary Act of 1789 conferred jurisdiction on the lower federal courts, but not all the jurisdiction they were capable of receiving under the federal judicial power.

The situation, then, is that for the lower federal courts to have jurisdiction of a case or controversy, (1) it must be one which the Constitution has defined as within the judicial power of the United States, and (2) an act of Congress must have conferred jurisdiction over such cases on the courts. For example, the Constitution extends federal judicial power to controversies between citizens of different states, but Congress has given the federal courts jurisdiction of such cases only if the amount in controversy exceeds $10,000. The jurisdiction of the Supreme Court is a special problem which was discussed in Chapter 6.

FEDERAL JUDICIAL POWER: SUBJECT MATTER

The judicial power of the United States is defined by Article III on two different bases—subject matter and nature of the parties involved. The subject-matter classifications are (1) all cases in law and equity arising under the Constitution; (2) all cases in law and equity arising under "the laws of the United States"; (3) all cases in law and equity arising under treaties made under the authority of the United States; and (4) all cases of admiralty and maritime jurisdiction. The federal judicial power extends to any case falling in these four fields, regardless of who the parties to the controversy may be.

The Constitution as a Source of Judicial Power

Cases "arising under this Constitution" are those in which an interpretation or application of the Constitution is necessary in order to arrive at a decision. They usually arise when an individual challenges the enforcement against himself of federal or state legislation or executive action, which he asserts to be in violation of federal constitutional provisions. Suits raising a constitutional issue may be filed in the federal courts, or if filed in state courts are subject to review by the Supreme Court after they have progressed through the highest state court to which appeal is possible.[3] The most striking aspect of the American judicial system is the power of courts, both federal and state, to invalidate legislation, both federal and state, on the ground of its conflict with the Constitution. This power of judicial review is so significant that it is reserved for treatment in the following chapter.

Laws and Treaties as Sources of Judicial Power

The "laws of the United States" referred to in Article III are statutes passed by Congress. At first there was some contention that the phrase also covered federal common law. It was asserted that a new political system must carry over and enforce, until revised or repealed, the customary law previously prevailing, which in this case was the English common law. The Supreme Court, however, took the

---

[2] *Turner* v. *Bank of North America* (1799); *United States* v. *Hudson and Goodwin* (1812); *Cary* v. *Curtis* (1845); *Shelden* v. *Sill* (1850).

[3] The case of *Thompson* v. *City of Louisville* (1960) went directly from the Louisville police court to the Supreme Court; it involved two fines of $10 each, and police-court fines of less than $20 on a single charge were not appealable to any other Kentucky court.

general position that "courts which are created by written law, and whose jurisdiction is defined by written law, cannot transcend that jurisdiction"[4] In 1812 it specifically ruled that there was no common law of crimes enforceable by the federal courts.[5]

Under Article VI, "all treaties made, or which shall be made, under the authority of the United States" share with the Constitution and the laws of the United States the status of the "supreme law of the land." A treaty which is self-executing—i.e., which operates of itself, without the aid of any legislative enforcement—thus has the status of municipal law and is directly enforceable by the courts. This distinctive feature of the American Constitution resulted from experience under the Articles, when the fulfillment of treaties entered into by Congress was dependent on the action of state legislatures. Laws and treaties are of course subordinate to the Constitution, but as to each other are on the same level of authority. Thus in the case of a conflict between a law and a treaty, the later one in point of time will be enforced by the courts.[6]

Issues arising under the Constitution, laws, or treaties of the United States are referred to generally as "federal questions." A plaintiff seeking to bring a case in the federal courts on one of these grounds must set forth on the face of his complaint a substantial claim as to the federal question involved. The mere allegation that such a question is present will not suffice; its presence must be clearly shown. The right or immunity created by the Constitution, laws, or treaties must be such that it will be supported if they are given one construction or defeated if given another. The question alleged to exist must not be insubstantial, or have been so conclusively settled as to foreclose the issue entirely. The Supreme Court often declines to review cases because they do not raise a "substantial federal question."

Admiralty and Maritime Jurisdiction

Under the Articles, decisions of state admiralty courts could be taken to an admiralty court of appeals set up by the Congress. The Constitution, in pursuance of its goal of promoting uniform regulation of commerce, provided for admiralty and maritime jurisdiction in the federal courts. The Judiciary Act of 1789 vested this jurisdiction exclusively in the federal district courts,[7] although parties were enabled to avail themselves of common-law remedies in the state courts.

In England admiralty jurisdiction, which dealt with local shipping, harbor, and fishing regulations, extended inland only as far as the ebb and flow of the tide. In a small country like England where practically all navigable streams are tidal, this was an adequate definition, but it did not prove so in the United States. It was gradually expanded until a congressional act of 1845 extended admiralty jurisdiction to all the navigable waters of the country. The Supreme Court upheld this law in the case of *The Genesee Chief* (1852).

[4] *Ex parte Bollman* (1807).
[5] *United States* v. *Hudson and Goodwin* (1812).
[6] *Head Money Cases* (1884).
[7] The general principle of exclusiveness of federal admiralty jurisdiction does not prevent the states from retaining their general or political powers of law enforcement on navigable waters, as was established when the Supreme Court invalidated a federal court conviction for a murder committed in Boston Harbor. *United States* v. *Bevans* (1818).

Admiralty and maritime jurisdiction covers two general classes of cases. The first relates to acts committed on the high seas or other navigable waters, and includes prize and forfeiture cases as well as torts, injuries, and crimes. Locality is the determining circumstance in this class of jurisdiction. The second category relates to contracts and transactions connected with shipping, including seamen's suits for wages, litigation over marine insurance policies, and the like.

FEDERAL JUDICIAL POWER: PARTIES

Apart from the four subject-matter classifications, federal judicial power is defined in terms of parties. Article III extends federal power to controversies (1) to which the United States is a party; (2) between two or more states;[8] (3) between a state and citizens of another state; (4) between citizens of different states; (5) between citizens of the same state claiming lands under grants of different states (a category which quickly became obsolete); (6) between a state, or the citizens thereof, and foreign states, citizens, or subjects; and (7) to all cases affecting ambassadors, other public ministers, and consuls. Matters involving these classes of parties can be brought in the federal courts, no matter what the subject matter.

Suits to Which the United States is a Party

Obviously no constitutional provision would have been necessary to give the United States authority to bring suit as party plaintiff in its own courts. Nor is congressional authorization necessary to enable the United States to sue.[9] Like other parties, however, the United States must have an interest in the subject matter and a legal right to the remedy sought. Thus in 1935 the Supreme Court refused to take jurisdiction of a suit by the United States against West Virginia to determine the navigability of certain rivers in that state on the ground that there were no legal issues, merely differences of opinion between the two governments.[10]

The principal problems arise, not where the United States is a plaintiff, but where it is a defendant. The principle of sovereign immunity establishes that the government cannot be sued without its consent. Where such consent is given by Congress, the United States can be sued only in accordance with the conditions stated. The government has been suable on contracts in the Court of Claims since 1855, but could not be sued in torts until the passage of the Federal Tort Claims Act in 1946. Even under that statute, there are considerable limits on the government's liability for torts of its employees.

Government corporations are in a special category so far as liability to suit is concerned. They have generally been created in order to operate business enterprises for the government with something like the freedom of private corporations, and this includes freedom to sue and be sued. Congress can of course relieve government corporations from liability to suit, but where it makes no provision one way or the

---

[8] The problem of suits between states has already been discussed in Chap. 5.
[9] *Dugan* v. *United States* (1818).
[10] *United States* v. *West Virginia* (1935).

other, the Supreme Court has held the practice of corporate liability to be so well established as to render the corporation subject to suit.[11]

When no consent to sue the government has been given, it may be possible to sue officials acting for the government. In practice it is often very difficult for courts to decide whether a suit which is nominally against a government official is actually a suit against the government. For example, a suit against the Secretary of the Treasury to review a decision about the rate of duty on sugar was held to be suit against the United States because of its effect on the revenue system of the government.[12] One general rule which courts have tended to apply is that a suit in which the judgment would affect the United States or its property is a suit against the United States.[13] On the other hand, cases in which action adverse to the interests of a plaintiff is taken by a government official who is alleged to be acting beyond his statutory authority or under an unconstitutional statute are generally held not to be suits against the government.

The leading case on establishing official liability to suit is *United States* v. *Lee* (1882), which involved the claim of the government to possession of the Robert E. Lee mansion in Arlington, Virginia, through a tax sale. Lee's heirs brought suit for ejectment against the federal officials in charge, and by a five to four vote the Supreme Court held this was not a suit against the United States until it had been determined whether the officers were acting within the scope of their lawful authority. Here the Court found that government possession was based on an unlawful order of the President, and concluded: "No man in this country is so high that he is above the law. No officer of the law may set that law at defiance with impunity."

Controversies between a State and Citizens of Another State

This provision of the Constitution was generally assumed to extend federal jurisdiction only to suits by a state as plaintiff against citizens of another state as defendants. However, in *Chisholm* v. *Georgia* (1793), the Supreme Court imprudently interpreted it as permitting a state to be made a defendant in a suit brought by citizens of another state. Georgia then refused to permit the decree to be enforced, and widespread protests against the Court's action resulted in its prompt reversal by adoption of the Eleventh Amendment. Later the Court itself admitted that the *Chisholm* decision had been erroneous.[14]

Since states cannot be sued by citizens of other states in the federal courts, or in their own courts without their consent, no judicial means may be available to compel a state to honor debts owed to private citizens. As already noted, an effort by citizens of New Hampshire to use their state government as a collection agency to recover on defaulted Louisiana bonds failed.[15] When similar bonds were donated outright to South Dakota, however, that state was successful in collecting from

---

[11] *Keifer & Keifer* v. *Reconstruction Finance Corporation* (1939).
[12] *Louisiana* v. *McAdoo* (1914). See Louis L. Jaffe, "Suits against Governments and Officers: Sovereign Immunity," 77 HARVARD LAW REVIEW 1 (1963); Edgar S. Cahn and Jean C. Cahn, "The New Sovereign Immunity," 81 HARVARD LAW REVIEW 929 (1968).
[13] See *Larson* v. *Domestic & Foreign Commerce Corp.* (1949).
[14] *Hans* v. *Louisiana* (1890).
[15] *New Hampshire* v. *Louisiana* (1883).

North Carolina on them, though four justices thought that even this was a violation of the Eleventh Amendment.[16]

In general, the question as to when a suit is one against a state, and so forbidden by the Eleventh Amendment, is determined on much the same rules as govern federal immunity to suit.[17] Thus, suits against state officers involving state property or suits asking for relief which call for the exercise of official authority are considered suits against the state and so prohibited. But suits against state officials alleged to be acting in excess of their statutory authority or under an unconstitutional statute are maintainable.[18]

Federal legislation can create rights enforceable against states or state officials in spite of the Eleventh Amendment. *Scheuer* v. *Rhodes* (1974) held that parents of students killed by the Ohio National Guard on the Kent State campus in 1970 could bring suit for damages under the Civil Rights Act of 1871 against the Governor of Ohio and other officials for depriving their children of a federal right under color of state law. The immunity of state executive officials is not absolute, the Court said, but depends upon the scope of their discretion and responsibilities and the circumstances existing at the time. *Parden* v. *Terminal Railway* (1964) held that employees of a railroad owned by the state of Alabama could sue the state for injuries under the Federal Employers' Liability Act.[19]

As a plaintiff, suing citizens of another state, a state may act to protect its own legal rights, or as *parens patriae* to protect the health and welfare of its citizens. The *parens patriae* concept will justify suits brought to protect the welfare of the people as a whole, but not to protect the private interests of individual citizens, though this distinction is often difficult to make. In 1945 the Court permitted Georgia as *parens patriae* to sue twenty railroads in its original jurisdiction for alleged rate-fixing conspiracy. "If the allegations of the bill are taken as true," the Court said, "the economy of Georgia and the welfare of her citizens have seriously suffered as the result of this alleged conspiracy."[20]

Under this clause states are limited to civil proceedings. They cannot seek to enforce their penal laws against citizens of other states in the federal courts.[21] Moreover, states may not seek judicial redress which would be inconsistent with the distribution of powers under the federal Constitution.[22]

Controversies between Citizens of Different States

Interesting jurisdictional questions are created by the "diversity of citizenship" clause. For natural persons the tests of state citizenship are domicile in a state, which may be established by residence there, acquisition of property, payment of taxes, or acquisition of the suffrage. If there are multiple parties in a diversity suit,

[16] *South Dakota* v. *North Carolina* (1904).
[17] See *Governor of Georgia* v. *Madrazo* (1828); *Kennecott Copper Co.* v. *State Tax Commission* (1946); Clyde E. Jacobs, *The Eleventh Amendment and Sovereign Immunity* (Westport, Conn.: Greenwood Press, 1972).
[18] See *Osborn* v. *Bank of the United States* (1824).
[19] But the Fair Labor Standards Act did not authorize employees of state nonprofit institutions to sue the state. *Employees of Department of Public Health and Welfare* v. *Missouri* (1973).
[20] *Georgia* v. *Pennsylvania R. Co.* (1945). But in *Ohio* v. *Wyandotte Chemicals Corp.* (1971), the Court declined to permit Ohio to sue companies polluting Lake Erie in its original jurisdiction.
[21] *Wisconsin* v. *Pelican Insurance Co.* (1888).
[22] *Massachusetts* v. *Mellon* (1923).

all the persons on one side of the case must be citizens of different states from all persons on the other side. In the case of corporations the Court has adopted the fiction that all the stockholders of a corporation are citizens of the state of incorporation.[23]

The ease of access to the federal courts thus provided for corporations led to substantial abuses. The classic example was the *Kentucky Taxicab Case* (1928). Here a taxicab company, incorporated in Kentucky and doing business in a Kentucky city, wanted to enter into an exclusive contract to provide taxicab service at a railroad station. Knowing that Kentucky courts would invalidate such a contract as contrary to state law, the corporation dissolved itself and reincorporated the identical business in Tennessee. In its new guise it entered into the contract, and then brought suit in federal court to prevent a competing company from interfering with the carrying out of the contract. Since the federal court was not bound by the Kentucky law, this stratagem succeeded.[24]

The *Kentucky Taxicab Case* would be decided differently today, because in 1938 an extremely important reversal of doctrine occurred on the Supreme Court with respect to the law to be applied in diversity cases. This is an interesting story, which goes back to the original Judiciary Act of 1789. Section 34 of that act provided that in diversity cases at common law the laws of the several states should be the rules of decision of the federal courts. In *Swift* v. *Tyson*, (1842) Justice Story for the Supreme Court decided that "the laws of the several states" referred only to state statutes, and did not cover the unwritten or common law of the states.[25] Thus in the absence of state statutes controlling a case, federal courts were free to adopt and apply such general principles of law as they thought fitting and applicable.

The principle of the *Tyson* case was subsequently extended from negotiable instruments to other matters, such as wills, torts, real estate titles, and contracts, until by 1888 there were twenty-eight kinds of cases in which federal courts were free to apply different rules of law in diversity cases than those of the state courts. Thus in every state the federal and state courts had their own version of commercial common law, with all the attendant confusion that was bound to result, and plaintiffs were free to shop around for the court in which their case would have the best chance of success.

Profound discontent developed with the *Tyson* rule, which was attacked as a wasteful and confused way to handle a delicate problem of federal-state relations. Justice Holmes, who became the spearhead in the fight on *Swift* v. *Tyson*—Miller and Field had preceded him—was motivated not only by respect for state courts, but also by his pragmatic view of law. Law, he said, "does not exist without some definite authority behind it." He had no patience with the notion of a "transcendental body" of law hanging in the air waiting to be divined by the independent judgment of federal courts. An impressive literature of protest against *Swift* v. *Tyson* appeared in the law reviews. Charles Warren in 1923 published an article with newly discovered evidence which seemed to show that Story's interpretation of section 34 was incorrect. Liberals in Congress proposed legislation to terminate the *Tyson* rule.

---

[23] *Strawbridge* v. *Curtiss* (1806); *Muller* v. *Dows* (1877).
[24] *Black & White Taxicab Co.* v. *Brown & Yellow Taxicab Co.* (1928).
[25] See "*Swift* v. *Tyson* Exhumed," 79 YALE LAW JOURNAL 284 (1969).

All this had an effect. In 1934 the Court decided that in a case "balanced with doubt," the federal court's independent judgment should be subordinated to the state decisions.[26] This was the only warning given before the roof fell in. *Erie Railroad* v. *Tompkins* was decided in 1938. Counsel in the case had not questioned the *Tyson* precedent. The interpretation of section 34 was not before the Court. Yet Justice Brandeis not only overruled *Swift* v. *Tyson,* he also held that by its previous interpretation of section 34 the Court had committed an unconstitutional action. This is the first and only time in its history that the Supreme Court has accused itself of having made an unconstitutional decision. What it was saying, in effect, was that if Congress should wish to reinstate the *Tyson* rule, it could not do so without amending the Constitution.

The facts of the *Erie* case may help to show the policy considerations which went into this decision. Tompkins, a citizen of Pennsylvania, was seriously injured by a freight train while he was walking along the railroad right of way. He was a trespasser, and by the common law of Pennsylvania railroads were not liable to trespassers except for wanton or willful negligence. So his attorneys filed suit, not in the state courts of Pennsylvania, but in the federal court in New York, the state in which the railroad was incorporated. The lower federal courts awarded Tompkins a judgment of $30,000, holding that it was unnecessary to consider what Pennsylvania law provided, for the question was one of general law to be decided by the federal courts in the exercise of their independent judgment. To this situation Justice Brandeis reacted by stating this new rule of decision:

> Except in matters governed by the Federal Constitution or by Acts of Congress, the law to be applied in any case is the law of the State. And whether the law of the State shall be declared by its Legislature in a statute or by its highest court in a decision is not a matter of federal concern. There is no federal general common law.

The essential intent of the ruling, Justice Frankfurter said in 1945, was to ensure that, in all diversity cases, "the outcome of the litigation in the federal court should be substantially the same, so far as legal rules determine the outcome of a litigation, as it would be if tried in a State court."[27] At first the Supreme Court's tendency was to push its mandate rather far. For example, the Court held that the *Erie* rule required the enforcement of state procedural as well as substantive law.[28] Again, in situations where the highest state court had not passed on a matter of state law, the Supreme Court held that the federal district court must descend the state judicial hierarchy until it did find a court which had ruled on the matter, and then be guided by that ruling.[29]

However, increasing experience with the *Erie* rule led the Supreme Court to recognize "countervailing factors" which reflect a federal interest in diversity litigation, and where these are deemed to be of overriding importance, to apply federal

---

[26] *Mutual Life Insurance Co.* v. *Johnson* (1934).
[27] *Guaranty Trust Co.* v. *York* (1945).
[28] *Ibid.*
[29] *West* v. *American Telephone & Telegraph Co.* (1940); *Fidelity Union Trust Co.* v. *Field* (1940); but see *King* v. *Order of United Commercial Travelers* (1948).

policy rather than state law.[30] In 1965 Justice Harlan confessed that "up to now Erie and the cases following it have not succeeded in articulating a workable doctrine governing choice of law in diversity actions." His approach toward determining whether to apply a state or federal rule was to inquire whether "the choice of rule would substantially affect those primary decisions respecting human conduct which our constitutional system leaves to state regulation. If so, Erie and the Constitution require that the state rule prevail."[31]

Cases Involving Foreign States and Citizens

The language giving federal jurisdiction over controversies "between a state, or the citizens thereof, and foreign states, citizens or subjects" is not quite as broad as it sounds. Under principles of international law foreign states cannot be sued in American courts without their consent,[32] not even by American states, and conversely foreign powers cannot sue American states in the federal courts.[33] But an American state can sue foreign citizens, foreign states can sue American citizens, American citizens can sue foreigners, and vice versa.

Giving foreign states access to American courts is in accord with the general principle of comity in international law. To be able to sue in American courts, a foreign government must be recognized by the United States, and of course it must submit to the procedures and rules of decisions of American courts.

Cases Affecting Ambassadors, Ministers, and Consuls

When Article III gives the federal courts jurisdiction over cases affecting ambassadors, other public ministers, and consuls, naturally it is referring to diplomatic personnel accredited by foreign states to the United States, not to American ambassadors to other countries.[34] Since ambassadors and ministers representing foreign governments in the United States are exempt from jurisdiction of American courts under international law, the effect of this provision is principally to permit foreign diplomats to bring suit in American federal courts against private individuals.

Consuls are not entitled to the same immunity, and federal courts can take jurisdiction of cases concerning them. They may also be dealt with in state courts where appropriate.[35]

FEDERAL-STATE COURT RELATIONS: CONCURRENCY OF JURISDICTION

Though the Judiciary Act of 1789 provided for a complete system of lower federal courts, the statute, as already noted, withheld from the federal courts much of the jurisdiction they were capable of exercising. In fact, from 1789 to the Civil War the lower federal courts were in effect subsidiary courts, principally designed as protec-

---

[30] See *Textile Workers Union* v. *Lincoln Mills* (1957); Alexander M. Bickel and Harry H. Wellington, "Legislative Purpose and the Judicial Process: The Lincoln Mills Case," 71 HARVARD LAW REVIEW 1 (1957); *Prima Paint Corp.* v. *Flood & Conklin Mfg. Co.* (1967).

[31] *Hanna* v. *Plumer* (1965). See John Hart Ely, "The Irrepressible Myth of Erie," 87 HARVARD LAW REVIEW 693 (1974).

[32] *The Exchange* v. *McFaddon* (1812).

[33] *Monaco* v. *Mississippi* (1934).

[34] *Ex parte Gruber* (1925).

[35] *Popovici* v. *Agler* (1930).

tion to citizens litigating outside their own states. But after the Civil War the new feelings of nationalism motivated Congress to invest the federal judiciary with enormously increased powers. The Removal Act of March 3, 1875, provided that any suit involving a right given by the Constitution, laws, and treaties of the United States could be begun in the federal courts, or if begun in state courts could be removed to the federal courts for disposition.

Jurisdiction over cases within the judicial power of the United States may thus be exercised by either federal or state courts, except in certain areas where Congress has entrusted jurisdiction *exclusively* to the federal courts. Important areas now exclusively within federal jurisdiction include crimes defined by the United States, federal seizures on land or water, admiralty and maritime jurisdiction, bankruptcy proceedings, actions arising under patent and copyright laws, suits for penalties and forfeitures incurred under the laws of the United States, and most of the remedies against the United States or federal agencies that have been specially defined by statute.

States have occasionally sought to place restrictions on the right of removal of civil suits from state courts, particularly in dealing with foreign (i.e., out-of-state) corporations. These efforts have usually been held unconstitutional. *Terral* v. *Burke Construction Co.* (1922) concerned a state law providing that when a foreign corporation removed a suit into federal court, its license to do business within the state would be revoked. The Supreme Court held this was an attempt to curtail the free exercise of a constitutional right, and consequently invalid.

When state courts exercise jurisdiction over cases falling within the judicial power of the United States, they operate under the control of the "supremacy clause" of the Constitution. Article VI, after making the Constitution, laws, and treaties of the United States "the supreme law of the land," continues: "And the judges in every state shall be bound thereby, any thing in the Constitution or laws of any state to the contrary notwithstanding."

Enforcement of this obligation through Supreme Court review of state court decisions, as established in the cases of *Martin* v. *Hunter's Lessee* (1816) and *Cohens* v. *Virginia* (1821), has been discussed in Chapter 4. All things considered, the Supreme Court, like Congress, has been extremely considerate of the position of state courts. This deference is exemplified in its practice of not reviewing a decision of a state court if that decision rests on a nonfederal ground adequate to support it. Section 25 of the Judiciary Act of 1789 limits the Supreme Court to reviewing "final" judgments of the highest state court in which a decision could be had. This ensures that state systems of justice will have full opportunity to settle their own questions before the Supreme Court intervenes.

An interesting aspect of concurrency is the positive obligation which the federal government has sometimes imposed on state courts to enforce federal laws. During the early decades, before the federal courts were so well established, this practice was fairly common. The Fugitive Slave Act of 1793, the Naturalization Act of 1795, and the Alien Enemies Act of 1798, all imposed positive duties on state courts to enforce federal law. In 1799 Congress authorized state trial of criminal offenses under the Post Office Act. Great reliance was placed on state courts for the enforcement of Jefferson's Embargo Acts.

This early effort to relieve the federal courts came to grief. The New England courts were hostile to the Embargo Acts, and the Northern courts generally resisted enforcement of the Fugitive Slave Law. The argument was widely heard that one sovereign cannot enforce the penal laws of another, and the Supreme Court for a time endorsed this position by its holding in *Prigg* v. *Pennsylvania* (1842).

More recently, the Federal Employers' Liability Act of 1908, covering injuries to railroad employees, not only gave concurrent jurisdiction in suits arising under the act to state courts, but even prohibited removal of cases begun in state courts to the federal courts. The purpose was to prevent railroads from fleeing to the federal courts if the injured workman felt he would be better off in the state court. Under this statute a state court can be compelled to enforce federal remedies which are contrary to state policy, the Supreme Court ruled in *Second Employers' Liability Cases* (1912).

The basic constitutional issue was reconsidered in *Testa* v. *Katt* (1947). The Emergency Price Control Act of 1942 provided that persons who had been over-charged in violation of the act could sue for treble damages in any court of competent jurisdiction. When such a suit was brought in Rhode Island, the state supreme court held this to be "a penal statute in the international sense," which state courts could not be required to enforce. The Supreme Court unanimously reversed this ruling, Justice Black reminding Rhode Island that "state courts do not bear the same relation to the United States that they do to foreign countries." Although Congress could not require Rhode Island to provide courts for the enforcement of these suits, since the state does have courts which enforce similar claims, it may require the state to apply the federal law.

A suitor who seeks to defend rights under the federal Constitution, laws, or treaties by filing his suit in federal court cannot be denied his choice of a federal forum merely because state courts are also available to hear such claims. But in *Railroad Commission of Texas* v. *Pullman Co.* (1941), the Court announced a judge-made rule of "equitable abstention," namely, that when an injunction was sought in federal court against a state statute on grounds of its unconstitutionality, the federal courts might suspend action to allow state courts an opportunity to adopt an interpretation of the challenged law that would avoid the constitutional problem. Abstention is not a consistent practice; rather, it is an instrument of judicial diplomacy which the Court uses as a matter of grace and prudence. Abstention cannot be ordered simply to give the state courts the first opportunity to vindicate the federal claim. In *Zwickler* v. *Koota* (1967) the Supreme Court held that abstention should not have been applied in a case where a state statute was attacked as repugnant to the First Amendment on its face.[36]

FEDERAL-STATE COURT RELATIONS: CONFLICTS OF JURISDICTION

A dual system of courts faces, in addition to the confusions of concurrency, the frictions of jurisdictional conflicts. Coercive writs may be sought in one jurisdiction

---

[36] See also *Wisconsin* v. *Constantineau* (1971); *Harris County Commissioners Court* v. *Moore* (1975); *Thermtron Products, Inc.* v. *Hermansdorfer* (1976); "Federal Question Abstention," 80 HARVARD LAW REVIEW 604 (1967).

against the operation of the other. States may try to impose barriers to removal of cases to federal courts. States may attempt to punish in state courts federal officials who commit some transgressions in the execution of their official duties within the state. State courts have on occasion even refused to comply with Supreme Court orders.

Such frictions may require adoption of appropriate federal legislation, but to a considerable extent the two systems of courts handle their own problems by application of principles of comity. Comity, says Corwin, is "a self-imposed rule of judicial morality whereby independent tribunals of concurrent or coordinate jurisdiction exercise a mutual restraint in order to prevent interference with each other and to avoid collisions of authority."[37] Exercise of the principles of comity is most often required where writs of injunction or habeas corpus are used by one system of courts against the other level of government.

Judicial Conflict through Injunctions

In general, neither state nor federal courts may enjoin each other's proceedings or judgments. State courts have been forbidden to take such action by Supreme Court decisions.[38] The reason given has been not the paramount jurisdiction of the federal courts, but rather the complete independence of the two judicial systems in their respective spheres of action.

Federal courts were forbidden to enjoin proceedings in state courts by act of Congress in 1793. But this bar is not applicable where Congress has expressly authorized a stay of proceedings in state courts, or where an injunction is necessary to protect the lawfully acquired jurisdiction of a federal court or to prevent the relitigation of issues previously adjudicated and finally settled by federal court decree.[39]

Congress has also limited the power of federal courts to issue injunctions affecting the states by other statutes. The tax injunction act of 1937 forbids federal district courts to enjoin the collection of state and local taxes where an adequate remedy exists in state courts. Again, the Johnson Act of 1934 forbids the federal courts to enjoin or suspend the operation of public utility rates which have been fixed by state order after reasonable notice and hearing, if there is an adequate remedy in state courts.

Federal courts do, however, exercise the extremely important power of restraining state officials from enforcing unconstitutional state statutes. This power to enjoin state officials from bringing criminal or civil proceedings to enforce an invalid statute was first asserted by the Supreme Court in *Osborn* v. *Bank of the United States* (1824), but the rule then was that an injunction could issue only after a finding of unconstitutionality had been made in a lawsuit. In 1908 this requirement was abandoned in *Ex parte Young,* which held that the attorney general of a state could be enjoined from proceeding to enforce a state statute in the state courts *pending* a determination of its constitutionality.

The *Young* decision was sharply criticized in Congress, which in 1910 passed a

---

[37] *Op. cit.,* p. 626.
[38] *McKim* v. *Voorhies* (1812); *United States ex rel. Riggs* v. *Johnson County* (1868).
[39] "The Federal Anti-Injunction Statute and Declaratory Judgments in Constitutional Litigation," 83 Harvard Law Review 1870 (1970).

law prohibiting the issuance of injunctions by a single federal judge to restrain the enforcement of state laws; a three-judge court was required to sit in all cases seeking "to interpose the Constitution against enforcement of a state policy." The Supreme Court has also since about 1940 tended to exercise a moderating influence on such invalidation of state legislation through injunctions against state officials.[40]

The civil rights problems of the 1960s imposed new strains on relations between federal and state courts, which may be illustrated by the case of *Dombrowski* v. *Pfister* (1965). Officers of a civil rights organization active in Louisiana filed suit in a federal district court requesting an injunction against imminent prosecutions under two state anti-Communist laws. The complaint alleged that the statutes were unconstitutional and that the defendants, who were various state officials, had threatened prosecution solely for the purpose of discouraging the organization's civil rights activities. The Supreme Court held that the provisions of these statutes were so vague and so susceptible of unconstitutional application that their very existence tended to have a "chilling effect upon the exercise of First Amendment rights." Therefore, an injunction should issue immediately, restraining state officials from enforcing or threatening to enforce the statutes until they received an adequate "narrowing construction" in a state declaratory judgment proceeding.

The *Dombrowski* precedent was substantially limited by *Younger* v. *Harris* (1971), involving a California socialist who was charged with violation of the state Criminal Syndicalism Act. This statute had been upheld by the Supreme Court in *Whitney* v. *California* (1927), but *Whitney* had been overruled in 1969 by *Brandenburg* v. *Ohio.* Harris alleged that the very existence of the statute inhibited him in the exercise of his rights of free speech, and on this claim he secured a federal court injunction against prosecution under the statute. However, the Supreme Court reversed, Justice Black arguing that "a federal lawsuit to stop a prosecution in a state court is a serious matter," conflicting with the principles of what he called "Our Federalism"[41]

Huffman v. *Pursue, Ltd.* (1975) held that the *Younger* ban on federal injunctions extended to state civil proceedings as well as criminal prosecutions unless the federal court found that the state proceedings were conducted in bad faith or that the state statute involved was flagrantly and patently unconstitutional. But *Steffel* v. *Thompson* (1974) held that a federal court could issue a declaratory judgment that a state statute was unconstitutional where prosecution under the statute had been threatened but not begun.[42]

In *Hicks* v. *Miranda* (1975), a theater owner brought action in federal court to have the California obscenity law declared unconstitutional and to enjoin officials from seizing certain films. After the federal complaint was filed but before any proceedings of substance had occurred, state criminal proceedings were begun

---

[40] See *Railroad Commission* v. *Rowan & Nichols Oil Co.* (1940, 1941); *Burford* v. *Sun Oil Co.* (1943); *American Federation of Labor* v. *Watson* (1946).

[41] The *Younger* principle was followed in *Samuels* v. *Mackell* (1971) and *Doran* v. *Salem Inn, Inc.* (1975). See "Federal Declaratory Relief from Unconstitutional State Statutes," 9 HARVARD CIVIL RIGHTS–CIVIL LIBERTIES LAW REVIEW 520 (1974).

[42] *Kugler* v. *Helfant* (1975) denied a federal court injunction sought by an indicted New Jersey municipal judge who contended he could not get a fair trial in the New Jersey courts. *Ellis* v. *Dyson* (1975) held that before a federal court could issue a declaratory judgment holding a city loitering ordi-

against the federal plaintiff. This obvious tactic to frustrate the federal case succeeded, as the Supreme Court voted five to four that the *Younger* rule applied. Stewart,
dissenting, thought that this distorted the principle of "Our Federalism" beyond
recognition. If federal courts should not interfere with the legitimate functioning of
state courts, neither should state courts interfere with federal courts.

Judicial Conflict through Habeas Corpus

The first important controversies in this area arose during the Civil War period from
the attempted use of habeas corpus by state courts to release prisoners in federal
custody. The most famous case was *Ableman* v. *Booth* (1859) in which the Supreme
Court took a strong and correct line on national supremacy in dealing with the
action of a Wisconsin judge who had released a prisoner held by a federal officer on
charges of violating the Fugitive Slave Law. As late as 1872, in *Tarble's Case*, Wisconsin again asserted power to release persons in federal custody, and again the
Supreme Court denied this power, saying that neither government "can intrude with
its judicial process into the domain of the other, except so far as such intrusion may
be necessary on the part of the National government to preserve its rightful supremacy in cases of conflict of authority."

The use of habeas corpus by the federal courts to test the constitutionality of
state court convictions for violations of state criminal laws is based on a statute of
1867 extending the remedy of the writ to any person in custody "in violation of the
Constitution, or of any treaty or law of the United States."[43] This measure was
adopted by the Radical Republican Congress in anticipation of Southern resistance
to the new constitutional guarantees. As Justice Brennan has commented: "A remedy almost in the nature of removal from the state to the federal courts of state
prisoners' constitutional contentions seems to have been envisaged."[44]

The result of the 1867 statute has been to create "an utterly unique relationship
between the state and federal sovereigns," under which the "state and federal courts
jointly and severally administer federal law relevant to state criminal proceedings."[45]
The major accommodation between the two systems has been the Supreme Court's
requirement that the defendant exhaust his state remedies, before seeking review on
habeas corpus in a federal district court.[46] However, where a state prisoner fails to
comply with a state procedural requirement and consequently loses the opportunity
to present in the state court federal questions relevant to the power of the state to
hold him in custody, the Supreme Court ruled in *Fay* v. *Noia* (1963) that he is not

---

nance unconstitutional, the plaintiff must demonstrate a genuine, credible threat that he might be arrested under the statute.

  [43] See the comprehensive discussion in "Developments in the Law—Federal Habeas Corpus," 83
HARVARD LAW REVIEW 1038–1280 (1970); also David L. Shapiro, "Federal Habeas Corpus: A Study in
Massachusetts," 87 HARVARD LAW REVIEW 321 (1973). Justice Holmes established habeas corpus as a
postconviction remedy by his eloquent opinion in *Moore* v. *Dempsey* (1923), after he had failed in *Frank*
v. *Mangum* (1915).

  [44] *Fay* v. *Noia* (1963).

  [45] Curtis R. Reitz, "Federal Habeas Corpus: Impact of an Abortive State Proceeding," 74 HAR-
VARD LAW REVIEW 1315, 1324 (1961).

  [46] *Ex parte Hawk* (1944); *Darr* v. *Burford* (1950); *Brown* v. *Allen* (1953); *Pitchess* v. *Davis* (1975).

barred thereby from subsequent resort to the federal courts for relief through habeas corpus.[47]

Applications by convicted state prisoners for habeas corpus from federal courts have increased rapidly—from 127 in 1941 to 7,626 in 1974. In 1953 Justice Jackson made reference in *Brown* v. *Allen* to this multiplicity of petitions, "so frivolous, so meaningless, and often so unintelligible that this worthlessness of the class discredits each individual application." In *Schneckloth* v. *Bustamonte* (1973) Justice Powell, with the support of the other three Nixon justices, attacked "the escalating use, over the past two decades, of federal habeas corpus to reopen and readjudicate state criminal judgment." He contended that the Court had extended habeas corpus "far beyond its historic bounds and in disregard of the writ's central purpose," resulting in unwise use of limited judicial resources, repetitive criminal litigation, and friction between federal and state systems of justice.

Powell was victorious in 1976. In its most significant reversal of Warren Court criminal rulings, the Burger Court in *Stone* v. *Powell* and *Wolff* v. *Rice* held six to three that collateral attacks on state convictions through federal habeas corpus would no longer be permitted where the only challenge to the convictions was the contention that evidence had been secured in violation of the Fourth Amendment, provided the defendant had been given a "full and fair" opportunity to make the Fourth Amendment claim in state court. Powell's opinion stressed that state judges were still obligated by the Supreme Court's holding in *Mapp* v. *Ohio* (1961) to exclude illegally seized evidence, and he was confident that state courts could be relied on to enforce federal constitutional rights. Burger would have gone further; he proposed to wipe out the *Mapp* exclusionary rule, or at least limit it to instances of "egregious, bad faith" conduct by the police. The dissenters were Brennan, Marshall, and White.[48]

The complication of a dual system of courts is one which other leading federal governments, such as Australia, Canada, and India, have avoided. In those countries there is only one federal court, superimposed on a complete system of state courts. By contrast, the American system, as Justice Douglas has noted, may seem to be in many respects "cumbersome, expensive, and productive of delays in the administration of justice. . . . It has required judicial statesmanship of a high order to prevent unseemly conflicts between the two judicial systems." But, he concludes, "the days of crisis have passed; regimes and attitudes of harmony and cooperation have developed; and the tradition of deference of one court system to the other has brought dignity and a sense of responsibility to each."[49]

---

[47] See also *Irvin* v. *Dowd* (1959). *Fay* v. *Noia* overruled the *Darr* v. *Burford* requirement that exhaustion of remedies must include application for review of the state court decision on certiorari to the United States Supreme Court.

[48] In *Francis* v. *Henderson* (1976) the Court held that a defendant in state court who failed to challenge the constitutionality of the grand jury that indicted him had waived his right to raise that issue on federal habeas corpus. See also *Estelle* v. *Williams* (1976).

[49] William O. Douglas, *We the Judges* (Garden City, N.Y.: Doubleday & Company, Inc., 1956), p. 135. Another potential source of conflict between state and federal courts, the authorization given by an 1866 statute to apply for removal of certain civil rights cases from state to federal courts, will be discussed in Chap. 27.

Chapter 8

Judicial Review

The phrase "judicial review" may be applied to several types of processes. It may describe the control which courts exercise over subordinate corporations or units of government, such as municipalities, or over public officials exercising delegated legislative and administrative powers. Courts will customarily review the actions of such officers or units of government to determine whether they are acting within their powers, and will punish or grant redress for acts found to be *ultra vires* (i.e., outside lawful authority). This is the commonest type of judicial review.

Second, federal systems of government have a characteristic form of judicial review, whereby courts are made responsible for enforcing the agreed-on division of functions between the central government and the component state or provincial governments. Such a division of functions is a necessary feature in any federal system, and by the process of judicial review the courts are made responsible for umpiring and enforcing the rules of the federal system. This power necessarily includes authority to declare invalid any state legislation or other state action which infringes on the constitutional authority of the central government or the other states in the federation. It would be extremely difficult to operate a federal system without such an umpire. As already noted, section 25 of the Judiciary Act of 1789 explicitly provided for Supreme Court review of cases decided in state courts where the constitutionality of state statutes was at issue. Justice Holmes once said:

> I do not think the United States would come to an end if we lost our power to declare an act of Congress void. I do think the Union would be imperilled if we could not make that declaration as to the laws of the several states. For one in my place sees how often a local policy prevails with those who are not trained to national views.[1]

The third type of judicial review is the power of the Supreme Court to declare acts of Congress unconstitutional. In more general terms, this is the review by courts over the acts of the legislative and executive departments of the same government. There is no superior-subordinate relationship as there is in the first two types of review. Here the courts, through coordinate parts of the government, nevertheless have the authority to declare actions of the other two branches invalid as contrary to the basic law. That explains why this system is often referred to as one of "judicial supremacy." It is judicial review in this third form which Americans customarily think of when the phrase is employed, for such power is enjoyed by American courts at both the federal and state levels.

It used to be customary to attribute the unique status of the Supreme Court, in comparison with the world's other high tribunals, to the Court's power of invalidating acts of Congress. To a certain extent this was true. No such authority resided in the highest courts of Britain or France. Switzerland, a federation which borrowed somewhat from American experience, deliberately rejected in 1848 the American pattern of judicial review and made the legislature the final interpreter of its constitution. The Canadian and Australian federations did give to their high courts authority to pass on the constitutionality of legislation, but their constitutions, lacking such broad protective standards as due process of law or equal protection of the laws, did not provide as much opportunity for judicial assertion of authority over constitutional interpretation as in the United States.

Within the present century, however, and particularly since World War II, a number of countries—including Argentina, Austria, India, Ireland, Italy, Japan, Norway, the Philippines, West Germany, and Yugoslavia—have established judicial tribunals with power to declare unconstitutional acts of coordinate legislative or executive branches. While the primary model for these developments was been the United States Supreme Court, the systems and the motivation for their adoption vary from country to country. The Japanese court was included in the postwar constitution drafted under General MacArthur. The Italians and Germans were influenced in part by the American example and in part by their experience with dictators. In Ireland and India judicial review was seen as a method of protecting ethnic minorities against majority rule.[2]

---

[1] "Law and the Court," *Speeches* (Boston: Little, Brown and Company, 1934), p. 102.
[2] For a comparative view of the work of constitutional courts in six countries, see Walter Murphy and Joseph Tanenhaus, *Comparative Constitutional Cases* (New York: St. Martin's Press, Inc., 1976); also

THE PREHISTORY OF JUDICIAL REVIEW

The theory on which the American practice of judicial review is based may be summarized as follows: that the written Constitution is a fundamental law, subject to change only by an extraordinary legislative process, and as such superior to common and statutory law; that the powers of the various departments of government are limited by the terms of the Constitution; and that judges are expected to enforce the provisions of the Constitution as the superior law and to refuse to enforce any legislative act or executive order in conflict therewith. What are the foundations of this theory in American thought and experience?

Foundations of Judicial Review

First there is the obvious influence of natural law, the belief that human conduct is guided by fundamental and immutable laws which have natural or divine origin and sanction. In English experience natural law was invoked first as a limitation on the king, and by Coke in the famous *Dr. Bonham's Case* (1610) against Parliament. "When an act of parliament is against common right or reason," said Coke, "the common law will control it and adjudge such act to be void." This view failed to establish itself in England, but in the American Colonies conditions were more propitious. With few lawbooks, and with an increasing disrespect for English legal precedents, the colonists tended to fall back on the Bible or popular notions of natural law as their guides. Locke supplied the systematic statement of this position, concluding: "the fundamental law of Nature being the preservation of mankind, no human sanction can be good or valid against it."

Another factor was the confirmed practice in American experience of reducing the basic laws to writing. The Mayflower Compact of 1620, the Fundamental Orders of Connecticut in 1639, the charters granted to the colonies from 1620 to 1700—always the colonists sought to legitimize and to limit collective action by fundamental written instruments. But the provision of machinery for enforcing these fundamental laws was not given much attention. During the Colonial period there was review machinery of a sort in the powers of disallowance exercised by the Privy Council in England over the acts of colonial legislatures. When the English yoke was thrown off, the initial Revolutionary enthusiasm saw the free popular legislatures as a self-sufficient guarantee against oppression of liberties. But it took only a little experience with all-powerful legislatures to demonstrate the abuses of unchecked authority, and at least three states experimented with special institutional arrangements to protect the fundamental law from encroachment.

Judicial Review in the Convention

It is a never-ending puzzle why judicial review, which has become one of the outstanding features of the operation of the American Constitution, was not even mentioned in that document. What actually happened was that a group in the Conven-

---

Glendon Schubert and David J. Danelski (eds.), *Comparative Judicial Behavior* (New York: Oxford University Press, 1969), and Edward McWhinney, *Judicial Review* (Toronto: University of Toronto Press, 4th ed., 1969).

tion, led by Wilson and Madison, wanted to establish a council composed of the executive and a "convenient number" of the national judiciary, with a veto power over congressional legislation. This plan was defeated three times in the Convention. Several members objected that under this plan judges who would later have to decide on the validity of the law in a case would have prejudged the matter and that the separation of powers would be thus violated. But Madison on June 6 strongly defended the plan. The executive would need both control and support. Associating judges with him in his revisionary capacity would perform both functions and would also enable the judicial department "the better to defend itself against Legislative encroachments," Madison thought.

In the debate on the veto power, then, judicial review in this rather peculiar form was considered and rejected in favor of a purely executive veto. When the original plan failed, its sponsors proposed that the Supreme Court as a whole exercise revisionary powers over legislation. All bills would go both to the President and the Supreme Court, and either could object, whereupon the bill would need to be repassed by a two-thirds vote if either the President or a majority of the Court had objected, and by three-fourths if both had objected. This novel idea was defeated on August 15, three states to eight.

No further effort was made in the Convention to give the Supreme Court explicit revisionary powers over congressional legislation. This does not prove, of course, that the framers were opposed to judicial review as such. But the absence of explicit language did leave room for doubt, and controversy still persists as to their intentions. Charles A. Beard thought that his book, *The Supreme Court and the Constitution,* published in 1912, had settled what Felix Frankfurter in 1924 regarded as an "empty controversy."[3] Beard presented evidence that seventeen of the twenty-five men most influential in the Convention "declared, directly or indirectly, for judicial control." But in 1953 William W. Crosskey concluded after a review of the same evidence that the Constitution had not intended to authorize general judicial review of acts of Congress,[4] and in 1958 Learned Hand took the equivocal position that judicial review was "not a logical deduction from the structure of the Constitution but only a practical condition upon its successful operation."[5]

The debates at the state ratifying conventions have been searched for statements favoring judicial review, particularly by members of the Convention, and some can be found—Marshall in Virginia, Wilson in Pennsylvania, Ellsworth in Connecticut. More attention has been given to Hamilton's clear presentation, in No. 78 of *The Federalist,* of the doctrine of a written constitution as a superior enactment, the preservation of which rests particularly with judges. A "limited constitution," he contended, "can be preserved in practice no other way than through the medium of courts of justice, whose duty it must be to declare all acts contrary to the manifest tenor of the Constitution void." Such authority does not "by any means

---

[3] Charles A. Beard, *The Supreme Court and the Constitution,* with an introduction by Alan F. Westin (Englewood Cliffs, N.J.: Prentice-Hall, Inc., 1962), pp. 1, 35.

[4] *Politics and the Constitution in the History of the United States* (Chicago: The University of Chicago Press, 1953), chap. 28.

[5] *The Bill of Rights* (Cambridge, Mass.: Harvard University Press, 1958), p. 15.

suppose a superiority of the judicial to the legislative power," Hamilton concluded. "It only supposes that the power of the people is superior to both."

THE ESTABLISHMENT OF JUDICIAL REVIEW

With the passage of the Judiciary Act and the inauguration of the federal court system, the fate of judicial review was in the hands of the Supreme Court itself. As we have seen, its initial history did not suggest that it would be able to win a position of respect and power. When John Marshall was named Chief Justice of a Federalist Court in 1801, there were few cases awaiting adjudication, the Jeffersonians were about to assume control of the other two branches of government, and prospects for the Court were dim.

Yet within two years that Court, dominated by Marshall, had successfully asserted its authority to invalidate acts of Congress in one of the cleverest coups of American history. One week before he was to leave office, President Adams appointed forty-two new justices of the peace for the District of Columbia. The formal commissions of appointment had not been made out and delivered by Secretary of State John Marshall, who was holding the two positions simultaneously, when Jefferson became President on March 4, 1801, and he ordered his Secretary of State, James Madison, not to deliver them.

Four of the frustrated appointees, headed by William Marbury, petitioned the Supreme Court for a writ of mandamus to compel Madison to deliver the commissions. Madison ignored a preliminary order issued by Marshall, and then Congress shut the Court down for a year by changing the dates of its sessions, to keep it from passing on the validity of the repeal of the Federalist Judiciary Act of 1801. Consequently Marbury's petition could not be acted on until 1803.

Marshall had a difficult problem to solve. He seemed to face two alternatives. He could order Madison to deliver the commissions, but it was certain Jefferson would countermand the order, and the Court would be exposed as powerless to enforce its order. Or he could avoid a test of strength with the executive by refusing to issue the writ, with the same result of advertising the Court's powerlessness. It is a measure of Marshall's genius that he escaped from this apparent dead end by manufacturing a third alternative, which enabled him to claim for the Court an infinitely greater power than Marbury had asked it to exercise, yet in a fashion which Jefferson could not possibly thwart.

This is how it was done. Marbury had applied for mandamus under section 13 of the Judiciary Act of 1789, which provided that "The Supreme Court . . . shall have power to issue . . . writs of mandamus, in cases warranted by the principles and usages of law, to any courts appointed, or persons holding office, under the authority of the United States." Marbury did not go first to a lower court. Under this statute he filed his petition directly with the Supreme Court. But Article III of the Constitution provides that the Supreme Court shall have original jurisdiction only in cases affecting ambassadors, ministers, and consuls and in cases where a state is a party. Marshall professed to believe that the statutory provision conflicted with the constitutional provision, and that Congress had attempted, contrary to the Constitution, to expand the original jurisdiction of the Supreme Court.

Of course, this was preposterous. Section 13 had been drawn by Oliver Ells-worth, later the third Chief Justice of the United States; it had been passed by the First Congress, which contained many ex-members of the Convention; and it had been actually enforced in 1794 by a Court which contained three ex-members of the Convention. The provision could be, and had been, interpreted in such a way as to raise no questions about adding to the Court's original jurisdiction. It could be taken to mean that the Court had power to issue the writ of mandamus whenever that remedy was appropriate in the disposition of cases properly brought in the Supreme Court, either on appeal or under its original jurisdiction. Thus in a case brought in the Court's original jurisdiction by a state, mandamus would be one of the available remedies. But such an interpretation would not have suited Marshall's purposes.

The proof of Marshall's intent is only too apparent in his opinion. If this was intended as a bona fide holding that the Court lacked jurisdiction to hear the case, he should have made that ruling and then stopped. Jurisdiction is the first thing a court must establish, and if it is found lacking, then the court can do nothing but dismiss the case. Marshall, however, wanted to read Jefferson a lecture. Conse-quently the first question asked in his decision was whether Marbury had a right to the commission. He concluded that he did, and that Madison had wrongfully with-held it. Then he asked a second question—whether the laws of the country afforded Marbury a remedy for the right that Madison had violated. He said that they did. Only after this detour through some interesting political questions did Marshall come to the jurisdictional question as to whether Marbury was entitled to the reme-dy for which he had applied. And only then did Marshall announce his newly discovered conflict between section 13 and Article III.

Admiration for Marshall's skill is of course irrelevant to the basic question. Likewise we may pass over the ethical question presented by Marshall's deciding a case which arose out of his own negligence as Secretary of State. The important matter is the logic of Marshall's demonstration that the Court must have the power to invalidate acts of Congress which it holds to be contrary to the Constitution. The case he makes is a strong one, admittedly profiting from Hamilton's argument in No. 78 of *The Federalist.* Marshall started from the proposition that the government of the United States as created by the Constitution is a limited government, and that "a legislative act, contrary to the constitution, is not law." Then what is the obliga-tion of a court when it is asked to enforce such a statute? For Marshall the answer was obvious.

> If a law be in opposition to the constitution; if both the law and the constitution apply to a particular case, so that the court must either decide that case conformable to the law, disregarding the constitution, or conformable to the constitution, disregarding the law; the court must determine which of these conflicting rules governs the case: this is of the very essence of judicial duty.

After all, Marshall continued, the judicial power extends to cases arising "un-der the constitution." Is the Court to be forbidden to look into the Constitution when a case arises under it? Must it look only at the statute? Further, he noted that the judges take an oath to support the Constitution. It would be nothing less than immoral to compel them to participate as knowing instruments in the violation of the document they have sworn to support.

This argument has been ratified by time and by practice, and there is little point in quibbling with it. Of course the President also takes an oath to support the Constitution. Does not Marshall's argument then give him the right to refuse to enforce an act of Congress which he regards as unconstitutional? Equally questionable was the bland assumption by both Hamilton and Marshall that a judicial finding of repugnance between a statute and the Constitution was "equivalent to an objective contradiction in the order of nature and not a mere difference of opinion between two different guessers."[6] As Thomas Reed Powell says, "they both covered up this possibly question-begging difficulty by saying in somewhat different form that judges are expert specialists in knowing or finding the law." But we now know that constitutional interpretation is a matter of opinion, and that judicial expertise is no guarantee of correctness or wisdom.

Few now find such arguments against judicial review convincing. Yet there is a basic uneasiness which will not die, and which occasionally boils up into bitter conflict, about the supremacy the Supreme Court has assumed in constitutional interpretation. There was, in fact, a less extreme position which the Court could have claimed for itself, which would nonetheless have enabled it to come up with the same disposition of the *Marbury* case. It could have claimed supremacy, not for its interpretations of the Constitution as a whole, but only over those portions of the Constitution pertaining to judicial organization and jurisdiction. Marbury's problem, of course, fell in this area. It could have been argued that the separation of powers principle required each branch to be the interpreter of its own constitutional authority. The judiciary would mark out its own area of constitutional power, but would intervene in the constitutional problems of the other two branches only when disputes arose between them. In *Marbury* v. *Madison*, however, "coequality" was rejected in favor of a policy of judicial supremacy.

This is not the place for a detailed history of the Supreme Court's subsequent use of its power to declare acts of Congress unconstitutional. After *Marbury*, no act of Congress was invalidated until the Missouri Compromise (already repealed) was voided by the disastrous *Dred Scott* decision in 1857. By contrast, from 1865 to 1970, eighty-four acts of Congress were held unconstitutional in whole or in part by the Supreme Court.[7] The climax came in 1935 and 1936 when a Court dominated by four reactionary justices handed down twelve decisions holding acts of Congress unconstitutional.

The "Court-packing" plan which President Roosevelt proposed in 1937 to smash this judicial blockade was by no means the first effort to limit the Supreme Court's powers over congressional legislation. One recurring proposal has been to

---

[6] Thomas Reed Powell, *Vagaries and Varieties in Constitutional Interpretation* (New York: Columbia University Press, 1956), p. 14.

[7] *The Constitution of the United States of America,* Sen. Doc. no. 39, 88th Cong., 1st sess. (Washington: Government Printing Office, 1964), pp. 1387–1401 plus additions by the author. The same source lists 656 state constitutional or statutory provisions and 84 municipal ordinances held unconstitutional by the Supreme Court from 1789 to 1963; pp. 1403–1537.

require an extraordinary majority of the Court to invalidate legislation. In 1868, a bill passed the House which would have required a two-thirds vote of the Court for this purpose. In 1921 a constitutional amendment was proposed in Congress that would have required all but two justices to concur in a declaration of unconstitutionality. Such proposals were motivated by the five to four votes which had been the margin of decision in many important instances.

During the Progessive era in the early part of the twentieth century, the recall of judges was widely advocated and was actually provided for in some states. In 1912 the Progressive party platform advocated, not the recall of judges, but the recall of judicial decisions. LaFollette, in his bid for the Presidency in 1924, proposed an amendment authorizing Congress to reenact a law declared unconstitutional by the Supreme Court, thereby nullifying the decision. After the child labor law was held unconstitutional in 1918, Senator Owen presented a bill to reenact the law with a clause prohibiting the Supreme Court from invalidating it. No action was ever taken along any of these lines.

After his tremendous victory in the 1936 election, President Roosevelt felt strong enough to challenge the Court. As already noted, he chose the device of increasing the size of the Court, which had been juggled several times previously in American history for political purposes, but he presented his plan in a maladroit fashion. He made no reference to the constitutional crisis which had arisen out of the Supreme Court's dogged refusal to keep abreast of the times. Instead he painted a dubious picture of delay in federal court litigation, of the Supreme Court's heavy burden, and of the need for a "constant infusion of new blood." After one of the bitterest political battles in American history, the original plan was defeated in Congress.[8] Instead, a liberalized retirement bill was passed. Moreover, even before the final defeat of the Court-packing plan, the Supreme Court made a historic change of direction (often referred to as "the switch in time that saved nine"), which was confirmed by President Roosevelt's subsequent appointments to the Court.

The *Brown* decision in 1954 ushered in a period during which the Supreme Court was almost constantly in difficulties with some members of Congress and some sections of the populace, but again the institution of judicial review emerged unscathed. It should be obvious that the exercise of such power by the judiciary would not have been tolerated in a democratic government unless it had been wielded with a reasonable measure of judicial restraint and with some attention, as Mr. Dooley said, to the election returns. It therefore becomes appropriate to examine such systematic doctrines or practices as the Court has developed to limit its powers of judicial review.

JUDICIAL SELF-RESTRAINT: JUSTICIABLE QUESTIONS

There are always procedural techniques available to the Court by which it can avoid having to express an opinion on embarrassing or difficult issues. As already noted, the Court has almost complete control over its business through grant or refusal of

---

[8] See Leonard Baker, *Back to Back: The Duel Between FDR and the Supreme Court* (New York: The Macmillan Company, 1967); Robert H. Jackson, *The Struggle for Judicial Supremacy* (New York: Alfred A. Knopf, Inc., 1941).

writs of certiorari. Certiorari, moreover, is granted on the Court's own terms. In the famous 1951 Smith Act case involving prosecution of the leaders of the American Communist Party, *Dennis* v. *United States,* the Court accepted the evidential findings of the court of appeals as final and limited its review to two relatively narrow constitutional issues. When the Court finally granted a full review of Smith Act convictions in a 1957 case, *Yates* v. *United States,* it came to much different conclusions from those it had reached in the *Dennis* case.

The all-too-familiar technique of the law's delay may also be utilized to rescue the Court from difficult situations, by postponing decisions until the heat has gone out of an issue. The Court's castigation of Lincoln's trials of civilians before military tribunals during the Civil War was delivered from the safe vantage point of 1866, and martial law in Hawaii during World War II was voided in 1946. But these methods of judicial self-restraint have not been dignified by the kind or caliber of rationalizations to which we now turn.

Advisory Opinions

The Supreme Court is a court of law, and it has followed a fairly consistent policy of refusing to deal with issues unless they are presented as cases or controversies in the framework of a bona fide lawsuit. In application, this means that the federal courts will not issue advisory opinions indicating what the law would be on a hypothetical state of facts. President Washington in 1793, through his Secretary of State, requested an advisory opinion from the Supreme Court regarding a proposed treaty, but the Court refused the opinion as beyond its competence to give.

If the Supreme Court did give advisory opinions, as supreme courts in several states are obligated to do on request of the governor or legislature, the Court would presumably not have the advantage of arguments by opposing counsel, nor would the opinions be binding should a genuine case or controversy subsequently come along raising the same issue. The granting of advisory opinions would almost certainly result in constant political embroilment and a substantial dissipation of the Court's influence and prestige.

The ban on advisory opinions is not a barrier to declaratory judgment actions, which are sometimes mistakenly confused with advisory opinions. In 1934 Congress passed the Federal Declaratory Judgment Act authorizing the federal courts to declare rights and other legal relations in cases of "actual controversy," and providing that "such declaration shall have the force and effect of a final judgment or decree and be reviewable as such."[9]

The declaratory judgment is a statutory, nontechnical method of securing a judicial ruling in cases of actual controversy, but without requiring the parties to put themselves in jeopardy by taking action based on their conflicting legal interpretations. No coercive order is normally issued in a declaratory judgment proceeding, for the assumption is that once the law has been declared the parties will act according to it. However, the judgment may be made the basis of further relief, if neces-

---

[9] The act was upheld in *Aetna Life Ins. Co.* v. *Haworth* (1937). For an interesting case in which the Court regarded the declaratory judgment as inappropriate, see *Public Affairs Associates* v. *Rickover* (1962). The "case or controversy" requirement was considered in *Ellis* v. *Dyson* (1975).

sary, or quite commonly a petition for writ of injunction is joined with a declaratory judgment action.

"Friendly" Suits

From the principle that a lawsuit must pit against each other parties with adverse legal interests grows the practice in the federal courts of refusing to accept so-called "friendly suits." Obviously, if the interests of the opposing parties are actually not adverse, then motivation for bringing out all the relevant facts will be lacking, and the trial court will have no assurance that justice is being done. Particularly is this important when the constitutionality of a federal statute is being attacked, because both parties might actually be antagonistic to the statute.

Such a situation may be closely approached where a stockholder seeks to enjoin the corporation in which he owns stock from complying with an allegedly unconstitutional statute. Several significant pieces of constitutional litigation have occurred under these circumstances. For example, the federal income tax was declared unconstitutional in a suit brought by a common stockholder to enjoin the corporation's breach of trust by paying voluntarily a tax which was claimed to be illegal.[10]

When a stockholder of the Alabama Power Company sued to enjoin that company from carrying out its contract to sell a portion of its properties to the TVA, Justice Brandeis, speaking for four members of the Court, declared that the Court should decline to permit constitutional issues to be raised by the device of stockholders' suits.[11] That the government's case will at least be adequately presented in such controversies is now guaranteed by the provisions of the act of 1937 requiring that the United States be made a party in any case where the constitutionality of an act of Congress is questioned.

Test Cases

Many suits are carefully planned and brought up to the Supreme Court as "test cases" to secure rulings on disputed constitutional issues. Organizations such as the American Civil Liberties Union and the National Association for the Advancement of Colored People devote much effort to finding good test cases involving constitutional principles on which they hope to draw a favorable ruling from the Supreme Court.

When a new and controversial federal statute is enacted and suits are begun challenging its constitutionality, the Department of Justice customarily selects the case in which it feels the government has the strongest position to carry to the Supreme Court. Sometimes, of course, there is no choice. The case in which the Supreme Court declared the National Industrial Recovery Act unconstitutional, *Schechter Poultry Corp.* v. *United States* (1935), was, as Attorney General Jackson said, "far from ideal as a test case," but circumstances compelled the government to use it.[12]

---

[10] *Pollock* v. *Farmers' Loan & Trust Co.* (1895). See also *Smith* v. *Kansas City Title & Trust Co.* (1921); *Carter* v. *Carter Coal Co.* (1936).

[11] *Ashwander* v. *Tennessee Valley Authority* (1936).

[12] Robert H. Jackson, *The Struggle for Judicial Supremacy* (New York: Alfred A. Knopf, Inc., 1941), p. 113.

Test cases must meet all the requirements of a valid case or controversy. If a case is too obviously "staged" simply for the purpose of drawing a court opinion, the Supreme Court may decline to accept it, as is demonstrated by the famous case of *Muskrat* v. *United States* (1911). In 1906 Congress authorized certain named Indians who had been given allotments of land to sue the United States in the Court of Claims in order to determine the validity of acts of Congress restricting alienation of Indian land and increasing the number of persons entitled to share in it. The Attorney General was designated by the act to defend the case. The Supreme Court dismissed the suits when they were brought, on the ground that the United States had "no interest adverse to the claimants." The United States and the Indians were not in dispute as to their respective property rights. Instead, this was a "made-up" case, the object and purpose of which were "wholly comprised in the determination of the constitutional validity of certain acts of Congress." Thus Congress cannot through legislation create a case or controversy merely by stating an issue and by designating parties to present each side.

Standing to Sue

Not every person with the money to bring a lawsuit is entitled to litigate the legality or constitutionality of government action in the federal courts. In order to have standing to maintain such a suit, the individual must establish the sufficiency of his interest in the controversy, and this involves satisfying the courts on two main points: (1) that his interest is one that is peculiarly personal to him, and not one which he shares with all other citizens generally; and (2) that the interest he is defending is a legally protected interest, or right, which is immediately threatened by government action. In both these respects, however, the Supreme Court in recent years has tended to be less demanding.

The law of standing is generally thought to begin with *Frothingham* v. *Mellon* in 1923. Actually, some sixty years earlier the Court had stated that a plaintiff would not be heard "unless he shows that he has sustained, and is still sustaining, individual damage."[13] But the *Frothingham* case, though the word "standing" is nowhere mentioned, does mark the beginning of the Court's attention to the nature of the plaintiff's interest. Suit had been brought by a Mrs. Frothingham to enjoin the operation of a congressional statute providing grants to the states for programs to reduce maternal and infant mortality. She sought to sustain her standing in court by alleging that she was a taxpayer of the United States and that the effect of the appropriations authorized by this act would be to increase the burden of future taxation and thereby take her property without due process of law.

The Supreme Court unanimously denied her standing to bring the suit. Although taxpayers' suits are rather common in local and state courts, Justice Sutherland pointed out:

> . . . the relation of a taxpayer of the United States to the Federal Government is very different. His interest in the moneys of the Treasury—partly realized from taxation and

---

[13] *Mississippi & Missouri Railroad Co.* v. *Ward* (1863).

partly from other sources—is shared with millions of others; is comparatively minute and indeterminable; and the effect upon future taxation, of any payment out of the funds, so remote, fluctuating and uncertain, that no basis is afforded for an appeal to the preventive powers of a court of equity.

The party who attacks the constitutionality of a federal statute, Sutherland continued, "must be able to show not only that the statute is invalid but that he has sustained . . . some direct injury as the result of its enforcement, and not merely that he suffers in some indefinite way in common with people generally."

Two years later, *Pierce* v. *Society of Sisters* (1925) met the "direct injury" test. Oregon adopted a constitutional amendment in 1922 requiring parents or guardians of children between the ages of eight and sixteen years to send them to a public school, and the failure to do so was a misdemeanor. A religious order which maintained a school got a court order restraining enforcement of the provision, though the direct effect of the act was on parents, not on schools. The Supreme Court affirmed, not only on the ground that the law would cause irreparable injury to the business and property of the religious group, but more importantly because the law "unreasonably interferes with the liberty of parents and guardians to direct the upbringing and education of children under their control." Thus the religious order was permitted to plead the rights of parents to strengthen its own somewhat less direct interest in the situation.[14]

Coleman v. *Miller* (1939) concerned a dispute as to whether the Kansas senate had legally ratified the child labor amendment and was filed by twenty members of the senate who challenged the right of the Lieutenant Governor to cast the tie-breaking vote, by virtue of which the amendment had been adopted. The Court held that these senators "have a plain, direct and adequate interest in maintaining the effectiveness of their votes."

Where a legal right or statutory authorization to sue cannot be demonstrated, judicial review is unavailable, no matter how real or obvious the damage done by government action. The Latin phrase is *damnum absque injuria,* that is, damage not recognized as a basis for judicial relief. *Alabama Power Co.* v. *Ickes* (1938) involved an attempt by a power company to enjoin the New Deal Public Works Administration from making grants to Alabama cities which would permit them to build municipal power systems competing with the established private company. The Supreme Court held that the company lacked standing to challenge the government's action, since it had no monopoly rights in the cities it served. "If its business be curtailed or destroyed by the operations of the municipalities, it will be by lawful competition from which no legal wrong results."

Judicial review over entire areas of governmental action may be limited or entirely foreclosed by inability to establish that rights are involved. Government

---

[14] See also *Barrows* v. *Jackson* (1953), where a California property owner who had breached the obligations of a racial restrictive covenant forbidding sale of property to any but Caucasians was permitted to defend her action by invoking the constitutional rights of non-Caucasians, even though such persons were unidentified and not before the court or directly involved in the case in any way. In *Peters* v. *Kiff* (1972) the Court recognized the standing of a white man to challenge the exclusion of blacks from the grand jury that indicted him and the trial jury that convicted him.

pensions and grants are normally on a privilege basis which does not subject them to judicial review. There is normally no protected interest in contracting with the government.[15] The original concept was that access to the mails was a privilege, but more recently certain rights to postal service have been recognized as justifying judicial review.[16]

In general, the trend has been in favor of increasing opportunities for judicial review and against technical concern about standing. Experience with arbitrary or unreviewable actions of federal administrative agencies led Congress to provide in the Administrative Procedure Act of 1946 that a person "suffering legal wrong because of agency action, or adversely affected or aggrieved within the meaning of a relevant statute, is entitled to judicial review thereof."[17]

The *Frothingham* decision, however, seemed to block the path toward judicial review of any congressional spending legislation. This barrier became of particular concern when Congress in 1965 was considering financial aid to elementary and secondary schools, including religious schools. Both advocates and opponents of aid to parochial schools desired a Supreme Court ruling on its constitutionality but feared that the 1923 decision would tie the Court's hands. However, after passage of the act, the Court found in *Flast* v. *Cohen* (1968) that a taxpayer's suit could be brought to test the grants to religious schools, the reason being that here, unlike in *Frothingham,* the taxpayer was alleging violation of "specific constitutional limitations," namely, the First Amendment religion clauses.

In the *Flast* decision, Justice Harlan distinguished between the traditional "Hohfeldian" plaintiff, who sued to protect or assert his own personal rights, and the ideological or "non-Hohfeldian" plaintiff, who seeks to act "as surrogate for the population at large," and to vindicate "public rights." Clearly the old direct or special interest test had to be modified if non-Hohfeldian plaintiffs were to be granted standing.[18]

This issue was particularly pressing for the conservationists and ecologists of the 1960s and 1970s, who were protesting environmental damage over wide areas affecting great numbers of people. Organizations such as the Sierra Club were generally accorded standing in court, but in one important case, *Sierra Club* v. *Morton* (1972), the Supreme Court ruled that the Club had failed to allege that its members would be affected by a proposed ski resort in a national forest and consequently that the club lacked standing to protest the development under the Administrative Procedure Act.

[15] *Perkins* v. *Lukens Steel Co.* (1940).

[16] *Hannegan* v. *Esquire* (1946); *Lamont* v. *Postmaster General* (1965).

[17] For subsequent review of administrative agency decisions, see *Hardin* v. *Kentucky Utilities Co.* (1968) and *Association of Data Processing Service Organizations* v. *Camp* (1970); also "Judicial Review of Agency Action: The Unsettled Law of Standing," 69 MICHIGAN LAW REVIEW 540 (1971); Kenneth C. Davis, "The Liberalized Law of Standing," 37 UNIVERSITY OF CHICAGO LAW REVIEW 450 (1970).

[18] The phrase "Hohfeldian plaintiff" is that of Louis L. Jaffe and is derived from the work of the American legal scholar Wesley Newcomb Hohfeld, *Fundamental Legal Conceptions as Applied in Judicial Reasoning* (New Haven, Conn.: Yale University Press, 1946). See Louis L. Jaffe, "The Citizen as Litigant in Public Actions: The Non-Hohfeldian or Ideological Plaintiff," 116 UNIVERSITY OF PENNSYLVANIA LAW REVIEW 1033 (1968); Kenneth E. Scott, "Standing in the Supreme Court," 86 HARVARD LAW REVIEW 645 (1973).

This ruling was largely neutralized, however, by *United States* v. *SCRAP* (1973) where the Court granted standing to a volunteer group challenging an Interstate Commerce Commission policy that handicapped recycling operations. Standing, the Court said, "is not confined to those who show economic harm," adding, "aesthetic and environmental well-being, like economic well-being, are important ingredients of the quality of life in our society, and the fact that particular environmental interests are shared by the many rather than the few does not make them less deserving of legal protection through the judicial process." Justice Douglas went further. In the *Sierra Club* case he proposed that a river should be recognized as a plaintiff to speak for "the ecological unit of life that is part of it."[19]

While the Court's standing requirements have been somewhat relaxed, non-Hohfeldian plaintiffs may still encounter difficulties in gaining access to courts. *Laird* v. *Tatum* (1972) rejected, by a vote of five to four, an effort to enjoin the Army from carrying on a program of surveillance of civilian political activities. The majority found that the plaintiffs had not sustained any direct injury and denied that the mere existence of the Army's data-gathering system produced an unconstitutional "chilling effect" on the exercise of First Amendment rights.

A similar decision was *Schlesinger* v. *Reservists Committee to Stop the War* (1974), where a citizen group sought a judicial declaration that it was unconstitutional for members of Congress to hold commissions in the Armed Forces Reserves, the Court holding that the plaintiffs had suffered no concrete injury. Again, a taxpayer's suit, *United States* v. *Richardson* (1974), seeking to compel the Secretary of the Treasury to publish the budget of the Central Intelligence Agency, which is known only to a few key members of Congress, was rejected for lack of standing. In *California Bankers Association* v. *Shultz* (1974), the Court expressed doubt that the association had standing to object to the federal statute requiring banks to keep extensive records of the transactions of their clients.[20]

Class Actions

A class action is a suit brought by one or more persons for themselves and on behalf "of all others similarly situated." The Federal Rules of Civil Procedure authorize class actions where a number of persons have a common legal right and the group is "so numerous as to make it impractical to bring them all before the court." Before a class action can be prosecuted, the judge must determine that such a class exists and that the plaintiffs are members of the class.

The purpose of the class action is to enable claims to be asserted by a large number of persons without formally bringing each person into court. The class action achieves economies of time, effort, and expense by the elimination of repetitious litigation and minimizes the possibility of inconsistent rulings involving common questions or related events.

---

[19] See Christopher D. Stone, "Should Trees Have Standing?" 45 SOUTHERN CALIFORNIA LAW REVIEW 450 (1972).

[20] *Warth* v. *Seldin* (1975) held that organizations and individuals who sought to have the zoning ordinance of a Rochester suburb declared invalid because it excluded persons of low and moderate income from living in the town lacked standing to maintain the suit.

The class suit has been widely employed by civil liberties, consumer, and environmental groups, and retaliatory legislation has been proposed in Congress to limit such suits. For example, President Nixon proposed in 1971 that consumer suits be allowed only after the Justice Department had successfully prosecuted merchants for deceptive practices. The Supreme Court has also taken some steps toward limiting class suits. *Zahn* v. *International Paper Co.* (1973) ruled that for a diversity suit to be maintained, every member of the class must have sustained $10,000 in damages. In *Eisen* v. *Carlisle & Jacquelin* (1974), brought on behalf of all odd-lot purchasers of stock on the New York Exchange over a four-year period, the Court held that the parties initiating a federal class action suit must notify, at their own expense, all other persons in the class.

These decisions may reduce the number of class action suits brought in federal courts and the very large consumer-type suits, but they should have little impact on the smaller class actions which make up the majority of such suits.[21] Likewise, the *Eisen* decision does not necessarily apply in states which permit class actions, of which California is the leader. In 1974 the Los Angeles Superior Court had up to four hundred class actions pending.

JUDICIAL SELF-RESTRAINT: SEPARATION OF POWERS

The Supreme Court operates constantly under the pressures imposed by the necessity of coexistence with its governmental colleagues in a separation of powers system. As a matter of prestige, it cannot allow itself to be put in a position of subservience to the President or Congress, or to be made to look ridiculous by handing down decrees which will not be enforced. But, by the same token, it seeks to reduce to a minimum the situations in which it seems to assert its superiority over Congress and the President. Because the judicial assumption of power to declare acts of Congress unconstitutional is its most striking claim of judicial superiority, the Supreme Court has sought in numerous ways to restrict its performance in this role.

In 1936, Justice Brandeis, concurring in *Ashwander* v. *Tennessee Valley Authority,* undertook to review the standards the Court had developed to avoid passing on constitutional questions. Among them were the following: (1) The Court will not anticipate a question of constitutional law in advance of the necessity of deciding it, nor is it the habit of the Court to decide questions of a constitutional nature unless absolutely necessary to a decision of the case. (2) The Court will not formulate a rule of constitutional law broader than is required by the precise facts to which it is to be applied. (3) The Court will not pass upon a constitutional question, although properly presented by the record, if there is also present some other ground upon which the case may be disposed of. Thus, if a case can be decided on either of two grounds, one involving a constitutional question, the other a question of statutory construction or general law, the Court will decide only the latter. (4) When the validity of an act of the Congress is drawn in question, and even if a serious doubt

---

[21] See Mark L. Rosenberg, "Class Actions for Consumer Protection," 7 HARVARD CIVIL RIGHTS–CIVIL LIBERTIES LAW REVIEW 601 (1972).

of constitutionality is raised, it is a cardinal principle that the Court will first ascertain whether a construction of the statute is fairly possible by which the question may be avoided. Illustrations of the application of these rules by the Court will be found in later chapters.

Turning to judicial-executive relations, respect for the President and a desire to avoid embarrassing clashes with executive authority have clearly been strong motivating factors in the Court's behavior. As Corwin says: "While the Court has sometimes rebuffed presidential pretensions, it has more often labored to rationalize them; but most of all it has sought on one pretext or other to keep its sickle out of this 'dread field.'" He goes on to point out that the tactical situation is such as to make successful challenge of the President somewhat more difficult than that of Congress, for "the Court can usually assert itself successfully against Congress by merely 'disallowing' its acts, [whereas] presidential exercises of power will generally have produced some change in the external world beyond ordinary judicial competence to efface."[22]

Marshall had been one of the first to recognize the judicial untouchability of the President operating in the executive field. So far as the President's "important political powers" were concerned, he said, the principle is that "in their exercise he is to use his own discretion, and is accountable only to his country in his political character, and to his own conscience." In two important post-Civil War cases the Court ratified this doctrine and extended it to include even the President's duty to enforce the law. *Mississippi* v. *Johnson* (1867) was an action by Mississippi seeking to restrain President Johnson from enforcing certain Reconstruction acts on the ground of their alleged unconstitutionality. The state sought to minimize the seriousness of its request to the Court by contending that President Johnson in enforcing these laws was performing a "mere ministerial duty" requiring no exercise of discretion. The Court rejoined that the President's duty to see that the laws were faithfully executed was "purely executive and political," and went on:

> An attempt on the part of the judicial department of the government to enforce the performance of such duties by the President might be justly characterized, in the language of Chief Justice Marshall, as "an absurd and excessive extravagance." It is true that in the instance before us the interposition of the court is not sought to enforce action by the Executive under constitutional legislation, but to restrain such action under legislation alleged to be unconstitutional. But we are unable to perceive that this circumstance takes the case out of the general principles which forbid judicial interference with the exercise of Executive discretion.

A similar effort by Georgia to enjoin the Secretary of War and the generals commanding the Georgia military district from enforcing the Reconstruction acts was likewise frustrated by the Court on the ground that they represented the executive authority of the government.[23] Judicial interposition in the President's conduct of

---

[22] Edward S. Corwin (ed.), *The President: Office and Powers* (New York: New York University Press, 4th rev. ed., 1957), pp. 16, 25.

[23] *Georgia* v. *Stanton* (1868).

foreign affairs is also generally forbidden to the Court by its own self-denying ordinances.[24]

Two major exceptions to the Supreme Court's policy of avoiding adjudication of presidential actions will be examined in Chapter 15. One is the famous *Steel Seizure* case in 1952, where the Court found President Truman's seizure of the steel mills to prevent a strike that would interfere with the flow of munitions to American troops in Korea to be unauthorized by statute and unjustified by inherent presidential powers. The second was *United States* v. *Nixon* (1974), involving the demand of the Watergate special prosecutor for the notorious White House tapes, where the Court gave priority to the obligation to provide a fair trial for the Watergate defendants over Nixon's claim of executive privilege.

The "Political Question" Doctrine

In a substantial number of instances, the Supreme Court has announced its refusal to decide a controversy because it involved a "political question." When this has occurred, considerations of potential conflict with the political branches of the government, such as have just been discussed, have usually been supplemented by professions of doubt as to judicial competence to handle the issues involved or particularly difficult enforcement problems. Significant statements of the political question doctrine as a limitation on judicial action have already been noted in *Luther* v. *Borden* (1849) and *Coleman* v. *Miller* (1939). Chief Justice Hughes said in the latter case that he would not attempt a definition of "the class of questions deemed to be political and not justiciable," but he did indicate that the two dominant considerations were "the appropriateness under our system of government of attributing finality to the action of the political departments, and also the lack of satisfactory criteria for a judicial determination."

As already noted, the political question doctrine was relied on by Justice Frankfurter in *Colegrove* v. *Green* (1946) as a rationalization for judicial refusal to correct population inequalitites in congressional election districts. But Justice Brennan's opinion for the Court majority in *Baker* v. *Carr* (1962) limited the application of the doctrine to separation of powers situations. At present, then, the doctrine amounts to nothing more than a general self-imposed obligation on the Court to show appropriate deference to the President and Congress.

John P. Roche has attacked the political question doctrine as illogical and based on circular reasoning: "Political questions are matters not soluble by the judicial process; matters not soluble by the judicial process are political questions. As an early dictionary explained, violins are small cellos, and cellos are large violins."[25] It is Philippa Strum's opinion that while the political question doctrine is an "anachronism" on an activist Court, nevertheless it is likely to be "dusted off whenever the Court finds it necessary."[26]

[24] See the discussion in Chap. 16; also *Chicago & Southern Air Lines* v. *Waterman S. S. Corp.* (1948).

[25] "Judicial Self-Restraint," 49 AMERICAN POLITICAL SCIENCE REVIEW 762–772 (1955).

[26] *The Supreme Court and "Political Questions": A Study in Judicial Evasion* (University, Alabama: University of Alabama Press, 1974), p. 145. See also Fritz W. Scharpf, "Judicial Review and the Political Question: A Functional Analysis," 75 YALE LAW JOURNAL 517 (1966).

It is now generally assumed that the Supreme Court must be available to answer any constitutional question. Self-restraint counsels the Court to reach constitutional issues reluctantly and to be chary of disagreeing with legislatures or executives, whether national or state. But self-restraint is not the ultimate in judicial wisdom. The Court's primary obligation is not to avoid controversy. Its primary obligation is to bring all the judgment its members possess and the best wisdom that the times afford, to the interpretation of the basic rules propounded by the Constitution for the direction of a free society. The Supreme Court has a duty of self-restraint, but not to the point of denying to the nation the guidance on basic democratic problems which its unique situation equips it to provide.[27]

---

[27] The Burger Court was expected to be more restrained than the Warren Court, but in fact it was also not reluctant to question legislative action. A prime example is *Buckley* v. *Valeo* (1976) in which the Court declared unconstitutional important provisions of the Federal Election Campaign Act of 1974, adopted by Congress to prevent a repetition of the financial scandals of the 1972 presidential campaign. Actually, judicial review was invited by the statute, which authorized "any individual eligible to vote in any election for the office of President" to bring a federal court proceeding "to construe the constitutionality of any provision of this Act." The trial judge was not to make a decision but merely to formulate "questions of constitutionality" to be certified to the court of appeals for the circuit involved, sitting en banc, which was obliged to expedite its decision "to the greatest possible extent," and appeal to the Supreme Court had to be taken within twenty days. The result in *Buckley* v. *Valeo* was that the Supreme Court had to act in advance of any substantial experience with the campaign reforms and handed down what was almost an advisory opinion on hypothetical grounds.

Chapter 9

Membership of Congress

The institutions and powers of the American Congress are provided for in the first article of the Constitution, which comprises in bulk somewhat over half the original document. The major considerations involved in the creation of a bicameral legislature have already been reviewed, as well as the principles which were to control the composition of the two houses. Our more detailed inquiry into the constitutional experience of Congress may begin with an examination of the provisions and practices relating to membership in the House of Representatives and Senate.

THE SENATE

The membership of the Senate, though not its size, is fixed by Article I, section 3, which provides for two senators from each state. Thus the size of the Senate is related directly to the number of states, and with the admission of new states it has grown from an original membership of 26 to its present 100. Article V guarantees that "no State, without its consent, shall be deprived of its equal suffrage in the Senate."

The Constitution originally provided that senators would be chosen from each state by its legislature. This arrangement gave effect to the idea that the Senate represented state governments rather than the people of the states. At first the legislatures were left entirely free to decide how they would select senators. In 1866, however, Congress did intervene to the extent of providing that if the two houses of a state legislature voting separately were unable to agree on a senator, they should meet in joint session and decide the matter by majority vote.

The movement for direct election of senators was motivated partly by the scandals and deadlocks which characterized legislative elections, and partly by the development of a more progressive tone in the country. Some states succeeded in taking the matter largely out of the hands of their legislatures by introducing a form of senatorial primary. Eventually the Seventeenth Amendment was adopted, becoming effective in 1913, and providing for the election of senators by direct popular vote.

APPORTIONMENT OF REPRESENTATIVES

Representation in the House is based on population. For this purpose Article I provided for an "enumeration," or census, to be made within three years after the first meeting of the Congress and to be repeated every ten years thereafter. In determining the basis for representation, all "free persons" and indentured servants were to be counted, plus "three-fifths of all other persons." This latter provision was a delicate method of referring to Negro slaves, whom the slaveholding states wished to include in the electoral base, whereas the other states wanted them excluded, along with "Indians not taxed" (i.e., living in their tribal relationship). Until the first census was taken, Article I, section 2, alloted sixty-five seats to the respective states on the basis of a rough estimate of their populations. The number of representatives was not to exceed 1 for every 30,000 in the electoral base, but each state was to have at least one representative.

The only subsequent constitutional provision affecting representation in the House was made by the Fourteenth Amendment. The abolition of slavery by the Thirteenth Amendment knocked out the three-fifths compromise provision and automatically gave all Negroes full weight for representation purposes. The Fourteenth Amendment recognized this change by language in section 2 apportioning representatives "among the several states according to their respective numbers, counting the whole number of persons in each State, excluding Indians not taxed."

Foreseeing the probable refusal to permit voting by Negroes in the South, the Northern-dominated Congress provided in the same section for reduction in the representation of any state which denied to any of its adult male citizens the right to vote, except for participation in rebellion or other crime. In spite of long-continued and widespread denial of voting rights to Negroes in Southern states, enforcement of this provision was never attempted, and it was regarded as a dead letter in the Constitution.

The actual working out of the apportionment process depends not only upon the decennial census, but also upon subsequent adoption of a new apportionment plan which will give effect to the changes in the state population pattern. The Constitution provides no machinery for this purpose, but it is a task which obviously belongs to Congress. The general procedure was originally that Congress, within a year or two after the census results were available, would pass a reapportionment statute giving effect to the new population figures. Since no state ever liked to have its representation reduced, the total number of seats in the House was increased in every apportionment except one (1842), until it finally reached the figure of 435 under the 1911 statute.

Following the census of 1920 Congress for the first time found itself unable to agree on an apportionment plan, since the alternatives were either to reduce the representation of eleven states or again to increase the size of the House. This experience made it clear that there was no means of compelling Congress to perform its constitutional duty on apportionment. Finally in 1929 a permanent reapportionment statute was adopted for the 1930 census and all subsequent ones. This law freezes the size of the House at 435. After each census the Census Bureau prepares for the President a table showing the number of inhabitants of each state and the number of representatives to which each state would be entitled under two alternative methods of handling the population fractions left over after the state populations have been divided by the country-wide ratio. The President then transmits the information to Congress at the beginning of its next regular session. A reapportionment according to the method of computation employed in the previous apportionment then goes into effect unless within sixty days Congress itself enacts a different one.

DISTRICTING FOR THE HOUSE

Fixing the number of representatives from each state is only the first part of the election process. It is still necessary to divide the states into election districts, unless the representatives are to be elected from the state at large, which was initially a fairly common practice. The districting responsibility is in general left to the states, under the provision of Article I, section 4, that "the times, places and manner of holding elections for Senators and Representatives, shall be prescribed in each state by the legislature thereof."

However, the section goes on to provide that "the Congress may at any time by law make or alter such regulations." Under this authority Congress by the apportionment act of 1842 required every state entitled to more than one representative to be divided by its legislature into districts "composed of contiguous territory," each returning one member. The acts of 1901 and 1911 added a "compact" qualification for districts in an effort to limit the practice of gerrymandering.[1] But the 1929 act omitted any requirement for contiguous, compact, or even equal districts. In *Wood* v. *Broom* (1932) the Supreme Court held that this omission was intentional and had repealed the requirements of the previous laws. Consequently the Court could take no action to correct state redistricting acts setting up gerrymandered districts.

---

[1] Gerrymandering is the practice whereby the majority party in the state legislature draws district lines which will concentrate the strength of the opposition party into as few districts as possible and spread the strength of its own party over as many districts as possible. The usual result of gerrymandering is a number of odd-shaped districts.

The Court initially held itself powerless also to remedy a state's failure to redistrict at all. The case of *Colegrove* v. *Green* (1946) presented the situation of Illinois, where the rural-dominated Legislature refused after 1901 to revise the state's congressional districts because it would have been compelled to increase the proportion of seats going to Chicago. The Supreme Court refused to intervene on the ground that this was a matter for the "exclusive authority" of Congress. If the Supreme Court got involved it would, according to Justice Frankfurter, be entering a "political thicket." Moreover, the Court feared that any relief it could give would be negative; it could declare the existing system invalid, but could not draw new district lines, with the result that Illinois might be thrown into the forthcoming congressional elections, then only a few months away, with the necessity of electing all its House members at large.

This was a four to three decision, and the fourth vote for the majority was cast by Justice Rutledge, who did not agree with Frankfurter's general view that the courts had no responsibility over House districts, but who did favor judicial abstention in this case because he thought intervention just preceding the election would do more harm than good. The three dissenters—Justices Black, Douglas, and Murphy—contended that the failure to redistrict was "willful legislative discrimination" amounting to a denial of equal protection of the laws. Though judicial power to handle legislative districting issues was thus denied by only three members of the Court, the *Colegrove* decision was generally understood as establishing the principle of judicial nonintervention in legislative apportionments or electoral systems, and was cited as a precedent by the Court in refusing to review several subsequent state election cases.[2] But in 1960 the *Colegrove* rule came up for a new examination in *Gomillion* v. *Lightfoot,* an electoral-district controversy in which the Supreme Court did find that it could act. An Alabama state law had redefined the city boundaries of Tuskegee so as to place all but four or five of the city's black voters outside the city limits, without removing a single white voter or resident. The statute was unanimously declared unconstitutional by the Supreme Court.

While the *Gomillion* decision involved racial discrimination in violation of the Fifteenth Amendment, it helped to prepare the way for the more general attack on legislative malapportionment in *Baker* v. *Carr* (1962), already discussed in Chapter 4. In *Wesberry* v. *Sanders* (1964), Justice Black derived the principle of equal congressional districts from certain of Madison's statements at the Constitutional Convention and in *The Federalist,* and more specifically from the language in Article I about the choosing of representatives "by the people of the several States." It was the clear intention of the Convention, he asserted, to make "population . . . the basis of the House of Representatives." He summed up his postion in this concluding paragraph:

> While it may not be possible to draw congressional districts with mathematical precision, that is no excuse for ignoring our Constitution's plain objective of making equal representation for equal numbers of people the fundamental goal for the House of

[2] *South* v. *Peters* (1950); *MacDougall* v. *Green* (1948).

Representatives. That is the high standard of justice and common sense which the Founders set for us.

Following *Wesberry,* the process of congressional redistricting went forward with remarkable speed. The principal problem has been gerrymandering with which, as already noted, the Court has seemed unable to deal.

TERMS

The two-year term for members of the House now seems fairly short, but it must be remembered that it was adopted at a time when democratic theory stressed the need for annual elections. In the Convention, Madison argued that a one-year term would be "almost consumed in preparing for and traveling to and from the seat of national business," and he favored a three-year term.

Proposals for extending the term to four years have often been made, most notably by President Johnson in 1966. Pointing to the accelerating volume of legislation, the increasingly complex problems, the longer sessions of Congress, and the increasing costs of campaigning, he urged a four-year term to attract better men to the House, give them more time to develop an understanding of national problems, and free them from the pressures and costs of biennial campaigns.

President Johnson's proposal called for representatives to be elected at the same time as the President, thus eliminating the midterm elections to the House which now provide some opportunity for public reaction to the administration in power. This feature was widely condemned even by those who favored the four-year term, and no action was taken.

The six-year term for senators is one of the major factors in the peculiar role which the Senate fills in the American system. Legally, the fact that only one-third of the seats fall vacant every two years gives the Senate the status of a "continuing body," compared with the House, which must reconstitute itself every two years.

QUALIFICATIONS

Article I lays down certain qualifications for senators and representatives as to age, citizenship, and residence. A senator must be thirty years of age, nine years a citizen of the United States, and an inhabitant of the state from which he is elected. A representative need be only twenty-five years old and a citizen for seven years, but the residence requirement is the same. By custom a representative must reside not only in the state but in the district from which he is elected.

Members of Congress are disqualified for appointment to executive office by Article I, section 6, which provides: "No person holding any office under the United States, shall be a member of either house during his continuance in office." Thus to accept an executive appointment, a member of Congress must resign his seat, and a federal official who is elected to Congress must resign his post before he takes his seat. Members of Congress, however, have been appointed on many occasions to represent the United States on international commissions and at diplomatic conferences. Such diplomatic assignments are not considered "offices" in the constitutional sense, being for specific, temporary purposes and carrying with them no extra compensation.[3]

A second disqualification affecting congressmen is also stated in Article I, section 6: "No Senator or Representative shall, during the time for which he was elected, be appointed to any civil office under the authority of the United States, which shall have been created, or the emoluments whereof shall have been increased during such time." The purpose of this restriction seems to have been to prevent Congress from feathering the nests of its members by creating jobs to which they could be appointed, but it is a rather inept provision which has achieved no useful purpose on the few occasions it has been invoked.[4]

Each house is authorized by Article I, section 5, to "be the judge of the elections, returns and qualifications of its own members."[5] The "qualifications," it has been established by *Powell* v. *McCormack* (1969), are those stated in the Constitution. In the Convention, Madison opposed a suggestion that Congress itself should have the power to set qualifications for its members, fearing it might be used by a stronger legislative faction to keep out "partizans of a weaker faction." In *The Federalist,* No. 60, Hamilton wrote that the qualifications of legislators were fixed by the Constitution "and are unalterable by the legislature."

However, on several occasions both houses have in effect enforced additional qualifications by refusing to seat duly elected members who met the constitutional qualifications. The Test Oath Act of 1862 imposed as a qualification on all members of Congress (as well as other federal officials) the taking of an oath that they had not participated in rebellion against the United States.

Individual congressmen have been disqualified on several grounds. The House refused to seat a Utah polygamist in 1900. Victor L. Berger of Wisconsin, a Socialist, was refused his seat by the House in 1919 because of his conviction under the Espionage Act for opposing the war. His constituents reelected him, and he was again denied his seat. Before his election for a third time, his conviction was reversed by the Supreme Court, and the House then seated him. In the late 1920s the Senate refused to seat Frank L. Smith of Illinois and William S. Vare of Pennsylvania because of scandals in connection with their campaign funds.

In 1967 Adam Clayton Powell, black Congressman from New York and then the most influential member of his race in a public position, was denied his seat in Congress. There was a judgment of criminal contempt outstanding against him, and his conduct as chairman of the House Education and Labor Committee had been

---

[3] Many members of Congress hold commissions in the Armed Forces Reserves, and it has been objected that this biases them in passing on appropriations and other legislation for the military. In *Schlesinger* v. *Reservists Committee to Stop the War* (1974), a suit to have such membership ruled contrary to the incompatibility clause failed when the Supreme Court held that the plaintiffs lacked standing to raise the issue.

[4] See *Ex parte Levitt* (1937).

[5] In *Roudebush* v. *Hartke* (1972), the Supreme Court held that this provision did not prohibit Indiana from conducting a recount of the 1970 election ballots for U.S. senator. After seven months of failure to decide which candidate had been elected to the Senate from New Hampshire in 1974, the Senate finally gave up the effort and declared the seat vacant, to be filled by a special election. See "The Power of a House of Congress to Judge the Qualifications of Its Members," 81 HARVARD LAW REVIEW 673 (1968).

bizarre and irregular. He then ran in a special election to fill the vacancy and was reelected with 86 percent of the vote. He also filed suit for an injunction ordering the House to seat him. Though he lost in the two lower courts, the Supreme Court in *Powell* v. *McCormack* (1969) ruled that the House had no power to deny a seat to a duly elected member who met the constitutional qualifications for the office. Previous instances of exclusion were held to have been unconstitutional. Congressional interest in preserving its integrity, the Court said, could be safeguarded by censure or expulsion.[6]

EXPULSION AND CENSURE

Congressmen are not subject to impeachment, not being regarded as "civil officers" of the United States. The Constitution does provide, however, that each house may expel its members by a two-thirds vote, or punish them for "disorderly behavior." Congress is the sole judge of the reasons for expulsion. The offense need not be indictable. In 1797 the Senate expelled William Blount for conduct which was not performed in his official capacity nor during a session of the Senate nor at the seat of government. The Supreme Court has recorded in a dictum its understanding that the expulsion power "extends to all cases where the offence is such as in the judgment of the Senate is inconsistent with the trust and duty of a member."[7]

When the Southern states seceded in 1861, their senators were not expelled. The Senate simply noted that the seats had "become vacant." However, two Missouri senators were subsequently expelled for acts against the Union. Formal censure proceedings have been brought against only four of its members in Senate history. Senator Joseph McCarthy was censured in 1954 for conduct "contrary to Senatorial traditions." In 1967 Senator Thomas J. Dodd was censured for conduct tending "to bring the Senate into dishonor and disrepute." Specifically he was charged with using for his personal benefit funds obtained from the public through political testimonial dinners intended to finance his election campaigns.

THE FILLING OF VACANCIES

Vacancies may occur in either house of Congress by death, resignation, expulsion, or the acceptance of a disqualifying office. So far as the House is concerned, Article I, section 2, makes the following provision for special elections: "When vacancies happen in the representation from any state, the executive authority thereof shall issue writs of election to fill such vacancies." For senators, who were originally chosen by state legislatures, section 3 of Article I authorized temporary state executive appointments to fill vacancies occurring during recesses of the legislature. The Seventeenth Amendment superseded this provision with a general authorization to state governors to call a special election, but the amendment also provided "that the

---

[6] In *Bond* v. *Floyd* (1966), the Supreme Court ruled that the Georgia legislature had violated the First Amendment rights of Julian Bond by twice denying him the seat to which he had been elected because he had made public statements opposing the war in Vietnam and the draft.

[7] *In re Chapman* (1897).

legislature of any state may empower the executive thereof to make temporary appointments until the people fill the vacancies by election as the legislature may direct."

In practice almost all states have authorized their governors to proceed on this basis. The result is that Senate vacancies are usually filled immediately by an appointee who serves until the next general election in his state, at which time a senator is elected for the remainder of the original term. On the other hand, the states often leave House vacancies unfilled rather than incur the expense of a special election, particularly if there are only a few months remaining of the term.

PRIVILEGES AND IMMUNITIES OF MEMBERS

Article I, section 6, provides in part: "The Senators and Representatives . . . shall in all cases, except treason, felony and breach of the peace, be privileged from arrest during their attendance at the session of their respective houses, and in going to and returning from the same; and for any speech or debate in either house, they shall not be questioned in any other place." Immunity from arrest during sessions of the legislature was one of the protections asserted by the English Parliament in its struggle with the Crown, and embodied in the English Bill of Rights. It is of comparatively minor significance in the American Constitution. The phrase, "treason, felony or breach of the peace" has been interpreted by the Court as withdrawing all criminal offenses from the scope of the privilege.[8] Thus the only area left for its operation is arrests in civil suits, which were common when the Constitution was adopted, but are now seldom made. The immunity does not apply to service of process in either civil or criminal cases.

Much more important is the freedom of speech guaranteed to congressmen by the provision that they should not be questioned "in any other place" for any speech or debate.[9] The purpose of such legislative immunity is to prevent intimidation of legislators by the executive or holding them accountable before a possibly hostile judiciary. While legislators may abuse their freedom, the constitutional theory is that the public interest will be best served if they are free to criticize, investigate, or take unpopular positions. As Justice Frankfurter said in *Tenney* v. *Brandhove* (1951): "Legislators are immune from deterrents to the uninhibited discharge of their legislative duty, not for their private indulgence but for the public good. One must not expect uncommon courage even in legislators."

The "speech or debate" clause means that congressmen cannot be sued for libel or slander or in any other way held legally accountable for statements made in their official capacity except by the House or Senate. Not only words spoken on the floor of Congress but written reports, resolutions offered, the act of voting, and all things "generally done in a session of the House by one of its members in relation to the business before it" are covered. This was the ruling in *Kilbourn* v. *Thompson* (1881), where the Court held that members of the House were not liable to suit for false

---

[8] *Williamson* v. *United States* (1908).
[9] Legislative immunity was extended to members of state legislatures in *Tenney* v. *Brandhove* (1951).

imprisonment because they had instituted legislative proceedings as a result of which the plaintiff was arrested.

Gravel v. *United States* (1972) interpreted legislative "business" rather strictly, however. In an effort to give wider circulation to the classified Pentagon papers released by Daniel Ellsberg in 1971, Senator Gravel read portions of the papers into the record at a committee session and then arranged with a private firm for their publication. A federal grand jury sought to determine whether any violation of federal law had occurred and demanded Gravel's testimony as to how he secured the papers, which the Senator resisted as an infringement of his legislative immunity. He lost in the Supreme Court, the majority holding that private publication of the papers "was in no way essential to the deliberations of the House" and that Gravel's arrangements with the press "were not part and parcel of the legislative process." The dissenters thought this was "a far too narrow view of the legislative function" and that it was part of a legislator's duty "to inform the public about matters affecting the administration of government."

Legislative immunity may or may not extend to legislative aides or others who carry out legislative purposes. In *Gravel,* the Court held that for the purpose of construing the privilege, the Senator and his aide were to be "treated as one." But in *Dombrowski* v. *Eastland* (1967), the Court ruled that counsel for a Senate committee could be sued for conspiring to violate the civil rights of a group of activists, even though the senator who headed the committee could not be sued. The Court said that the immunity doctrine "is less absolute, although applicable, when applied to officers or employees of a legislative body, rather than to legislators themselves." To the same effect was *Doe* v. *McMillan* (1973), which held that no action could be taken against members of a congressional committee and its staff who prepared and issued a report containing libelous statements about named District of Columbia schoolchildren; but the Court warned that the Government Printing Office or legislative personnel "who participate in distributions of actionable material beyond the reasonable bounds of the legislative task, enjoy no Speech or Debate Clause immunity." Likewise the theory of the *Powell* decision was that while members of the House could not be sued, action could be brought against employees of the House.

In two recent cases the Supreme Court has considered the relationship of the speech or debate clause to criminal prosecutions of congressmen. In *United States* v. *Johnson* (1966), a congressman had made a speech on the floor of the House in return for payment by private interests, and was convicted of conspiring with these interests to defraud the United States. The government contended that the "speech or debate" clause forbade only prosecutions based on the content of a speech, such as libel actions, but not those founded on the antecedent unlawful conduct of accepting a bribe. However, the Supreme Court held unanimously that the purpose of the clause, growing as it did out of the long struggle of Parliament for independence from the king and his courts, was to protect legislators from "intimidation by the executive and accountability before a possibly hostile judiciary," and that consequently any judicial inquiry into the motivation of a congressman's speech was in violation of the Constitution.

But in *United States* v. *Brewster* (1972) the Court interpreted the *Johnson* ruling narrowly to cover only "legislative acts or the motivation for legislative acts." Brewster was charged with accepting a bribe to influence his vote on postal rate legislation. The Court majority concluded that taking a bribe "is not a legislative act," and the ruling was supported by broad policy statements about not immunizing members of Congress from criminal prosecution. The minority contended that immunity not only extends to a congressman's vote but "precludes all extra-congressional scrutiny as to how and why he cast . . . his vote in a certain way." The constitutional intention, said Justice Brennan, was that congressmen would be accountable "solely to a member's own House and never to the executive or judiciary." Considered together, the *Powell, Gravel, Doe,* and *Brewster* decisions reveal an increasing judicial tendency toward supervising and defining the "proper" scope of legislative activity.[10]

---

[10] However, in *Eastland* v. *U.S. Servicemen's Fund* (1975), the Court did give a broad interpretation to the speech and debate clause, holding that it forbade judicial interference with congressional subpoenas that were "within the sphere of legitimate legislative activity."

Chapter 10

Legislative Powers
and Procedure

The first words in the Constitution, following the Preamble, are: "All legislative powers herein granted shall be vested in a Congress of the United States." These grants cover a remarkable variety of powers. The strictly legislative or "lawmaking" role of Congress is exercised by the passing of statutes, which are of four general types: (1) public laws which formulate authoritative rules of conduct, substantive or procedural, applicable generally to all classes of persons or events specified in the statute; (2) private acts which apply to named individuals, usually for the purpose of adjusting claims against the government; (3) revenue acts which provide the government's funds; and (4) appropriation acts which make revenues available for expenditure for specified purposes.

In addition to its lawmaking role, Congress has a number of other functions. Its role in proposing amendments to the Constitution—what may be called its *constituent* power— has already been examined. The *electoral* functions which fall to the House and Senate if no candidate for the Presidency or Vice-Presidency secures a majority in the electoral college, and their joint role in canvassing the electoral vote, will be treated in connection with the discussion of the President, as will also the *executive* authority of the Senate in consenting to the ratification of treaties and giving advice and consent to appointments.

This chapter will discuss the general constitutional principles that have been developed and applied in determining the existence and extent of legislative power as well as the congressional impeachment power, the contempt power, the power to investigate, and the power of administrative supervision, concluding with a brief account of constitutional provisions as to legislative procedure.

PRINCIPLES OF LEGISLATIVE POWER

As the legislative organ of a government of delegated powers, Congress must be able to support any exercise of legislative authority as both authorized and not forbidden by the Constitution. There are two types of authorizations in Article I, section 8. The first seventeen clauses specifically enumerate a series of powers ranging all the way from punishment of counterfeiting to the declaration of war. Then clause 18 is a general authorization "to make all laws which shall be necessary and proper for carrying into execution the foregoing powers, and all other powers vested by this Constitution in the government of the United States, or in any department or officer thereof."

The relationship of this last clause, referred to in the ratification debates as "the sweeping clause," to the enumerated powers preceding it quickly became the subject of controversy between Federalists and Jeffersonians, between broad and strict constructionists. The issue was joined over Hamilton's plan for a national bank, as presented to the First Congress. There was no authorization in the Constitution for Congress to create a bank; in fact, the Convention had specifically refused to grant to Congress even a restricted power to create corporations. On President Washington's invitation, Hamilton and Jefferson submitted their respective views on whether he should sign the bill; they are classical expositions of divergent theories of constitutional interpretation.

Jefferson emphasized the "necessary" in the necessary and proper clause. Since all the enumerated powers could be carried out without a bank, it was not necessary and consequently not authorized. Hamilton, on the other hand, argued that the powers granted to Congress included the right to employ "all the *means* requisite and fairly applicable to the attainment of the *ends* of such power," unless they were specifically forbidden or immoral or contrary to the "essential ends of political society."

The Hamiltonian theory of a broad and liberal interpretation of congressional powers was successful in persuading Washington to sign the bank bill, and it has generally predominated in subsequent constitutional development. In 1819 Marshall gave the definitive statement of this view in the great case of *McCulloch* v. *Maryland.* Congressional authority to create a bank (the second Bank of the United States, incorporated by statute in 1816) was again the issue. Marshall found implied congressional power to establish a bank in its expressly granted powers to collect taxes, to borrow money, to regulate commerce, to declare and conduct a war; for "it may with great reason be contended, that a government, entrusted with such ample powers, on the due execution of which the happiness and prosperity of the nation so vitally depends, must also be entrusted with ample means for their execution." A corporation was such a means. "It is never the end for which other powers are exercised."

Marshall analyzed the necessary and proper clause at length. He rejected the strict Jeffersonian interpretation, which "would abridge, and almost annihilate this useful and necessary right of the legislature to select the means." His final, and famous, conclusion was:

> Let the end be legitimate, let it be within the scope of the constitution, and all means which are appropriate, which are plainly adapted to that end, which are not prohibited, but consistent with the letter and spirit of the constitution, are constitutional.

Perhaps the principal doctrinal challenge of a general character which federal legislative power has had to meet since *McCulloch* v. *Maryland* is "dual federalism," already discussed in Chap. 4. Decisively rejected in *Darby Lumber,* dual federalism experienced a surprising but probably limited revival in *National League of Cities* v. *Usery* (1976), which held that state sovereignty forbids congressional regulation of wages and hours of state and municipal employees.

Notice should also be taken of a view which is at the opposite extreme from dual federalism. This is the theory put forward by James Wilson of Pennsylvania during the Convention period that "whenever an object occurs, to the direction of which no particular state is competent, the management of it must, of necessity, belong to the United States in Congress assembled."[1] This contention of sovereign and inherent power in Congress was repeated by counsel in the case of *Kansas* v. *Colorado* (1907). The steps in the argument were that complete legislative power must be vested either in the state or national governments; that the states are limited to internal affairs; and that "consequently all powers which are national in their scope must be found vested in Congress." The Court rejected this position as in violation of the Tenth Amendment, and held that powers of a national character not delegated to Congress were "reserved to the people of the United States."

In constitutional theory, then, Congress does not derive its authority from any doctrine of sovereign and inherent power. Delegation by the Constitution is the source of federal legislative authority. However, as the subsequent discussion of the commerce power particularly will indicate, Wilson's assertion that Congress must have the power required to deal with national problems has gradually been accepted, and a broad doctrine of implied power, based on the necessary and proper clause, has been a supplemental source of great significance in equipping Congress with authority commensurate with its responsibilities.

DELEGATION OF LEGISLATIVE POWER

There is a Latin saw, *delegata potestas non potest delegari,* which may be translated as meaning that delegated power cannot be redelegated. The Supreme Court accepts this prohibition as applied to Congress. And yet delegation of legislative power is an

---

[1] James De Witt Andrews, *Works of James Wilson* (Chicago: Callaghan and Company, 1896), vol. 1, p. 558.

absolute necessity of practical government and has been practiced from almost the beginning of the Republic. The Supreme Court has recognized this need. Chief Justice Taft once said that the extent and character of permissible delegation "must be fixed according to common sense and the inherent necessities of the governmental co-ordination."[2] The Court has thus been placed in a dilemma, which it has been able to resolve only by tortuous explanations and legal fictions that what is delegation in fact is not delegation in law.

The reasons why Congress must indulge in extensive delegation of legislative power are well known. The legislative machinery is ponderous. Congressmen may succeed well enough in the task of formulating general policies, but lack the time and expert information needed to prescribe the specific methods for carrying out those policies. Moreover, a piece of legislation once enacted is extremely hard to amend, whereas the problems with which the legislation aims to deal may be constantly changing. These legislative limitations have become increasingly obvious with the expansion of governmental intervention into the management of the economy, and in emergency or wartime periods the pressure on Congress to authorize broad delegations of its powers to the executive is especially great. Finally, Congress sometimes uses the delegation technique when it realizes that a problem exists, but is uncertain how to handle it. By delegation the "hot potato" can be passed on to other hands.

Marshall was the first to rationalize a legislative delegation. In *Wayman* v. *Southard* (1825) he distinguished "important subjects, which must be entirely regulated by the legislature itself, from those of less interest, in which a general provision may be made, and power given to those who are to act under such general provisions to fill up the details." This suggestion that delegation may be employed only in dealing with less important subjects has proved completely untenable. On the other hand, the legal fiction that delegation is merely a "filling up the details" of a statute has been a perennially useful one. In *United States* v. *Grimaud* (1911) the Court was confronted with a statute authorizing the Secretary of Agriculture to make rules and regulations with respect to grazing on national forest reservations, which it upheld on the ground that it was "impracticable" for Congress itself to adopt such regulations, covering as they did "local conditions."

Marshall's conception of "filling up the details" of course demands that there be an announced general legislative plan into which the details fit. Consequently the Court has consistently demanded that Congress supply standards to guide and control the acts of delegatees. But the Court has normally been willing to accept rather broad and general standards as meeting constitutional requirements—such as the standard that the Interstate Commerce Commission shall fix rates that are "just and reasonable"[3] or the standard that the Federal Communications Commission shall grant licenses to radio stations when it is in the "public convenience, interest or necessity" to do so.[4]

---

[2] *J. W. Hampton, Jr., & Co.* v. *United States* (1928). For a general discussion see Sotirios A. Barber, *The Constitution and the Delegation of Congressional Power* (Chicago: University of Chicago Press, 1975).

[3] Upheld in *Interstate Commerce Commission* v. *Illinois Central R.R. Co.* (1910).

[4] Upheld in *Federal Radio Commission* v. *Nelson Brothers* (1933).

A special type of delegation is that made in so-called "contingent legislation." Here the delegation is not of power to make rules or fill in details; it is delegation of authority to determine facts or make predictions which are to have the effect of suspending legislation or, alternatively, of bringing it into effect. For example, the McKinley tariff of 1890 authorized the admission of certain articles free of duty but added that if a foreign country producing any of these commodities should impose upon American products duties found by the President to be "reciprocally unequal and unreasonable," then the President would have power to suspend the duty-free status of the foreign commodities, and duties set out in the act would become payable. The Supreme Court upheld this delegation in *Field* v. *Clark* (1892), declaring that the President's role was not that of a legislator but "mere agent of the lawmaking department to ascertain and declare the event upon which its expressed will was to take effect."[5]

Judicial acceptance of delegation was suspended for a brief period during the New Deal. In *Panama Refining Company* v. *Ryan* (1935), the Court invalidated a statute giving the President authority to exclude from interstate commerce oil produced in excess of state regulations. *Schechter Corp.* v. *United States* (1935) held that the National Industrial Recovery Act had gone too far in giving the President authority to promulgate codes of fair competition. One year later, in *Carter* v. *Carter Coal Co.* (1936), the Guffey Coal Act was invalidated, partly because it was held to delegate legislative power to set up a code of mandatory regulations for the coal industry. This time the delegation was doubly condemned since it was not even to government officials but to representatives of the coal industry.

No subsequent statutes have been invalidated on delegation grounds, though there have been numerous opportunities to do so.[6] The broad delegations of the Economic Stabilization Act of 1970, described by Arthur S. Miller as an "economic Gulf of Tonkin resolution" and under which Nixon ordered the wage-price freeze in 1971, never got to the Supreme Court.[7] The Bank Secrecy Act of 1970 requiring banks to maintain whatever reports and records the Secretary of the Treasury believed to be possessed of a "high degree of usefulness" in furthering criminal, tax, or regulatory investigations was upheld by the Court in *California Bankers Association* v. *Shultz* (1974).[8]

[5] See also *J. W. Hampton, Jr. & Co.* v. *United States* (1928).

[6] Agricultural regulatory statutes were upheld in *Currin* v. *Wallace* (1939), *United States* v. *Rock Royal Co-op* (1939), and *Hood & Sons* v. *United States* (1939). The Fair Labor Standards Act was cleared in *Opp Cotton Mills* v. *Administrator of Wage and Hour Division* (1941). Wartime price and rent controls were upheld in *Yakus* v. *United States* (1944) and *Bowles* v. *Willingham* (1944). The Renegotiation Act of 1942 authorizing Department of Defense officials to renegotiate war contracts to avoid excessive profits was approved in *Lichter* v. *United States* (1948). A 1948 statute making not only present but also future state laws applicable to federal enclaves within states was accepted in *United States* v. *Sharpnack* (1958) over the protests of Black and Douglas.

[7] In *Federal Energy Administration* v. *Algonquin SNG, Inc.* (1976), the Supreme Court held that the Trade Expansion Act of 1962, on the authority of which Presidents Nixon and Ford imposed license fees on imported oil for national security reasons, justified their actions and did not unconstitutionally delegate legislative power. In *National Cable Television Assn.* v. *United States* (1974) the Supreme Court, applying the principles of the *Schechter* and *Hampton* cases, construed narrowly a statutory grant of power to the FCC to impose fees for its services in order to avoid a delegation issue.

[8] For a principled attack on delegation by Congress, see Theodore J. Lowi, *The End of Liberalism* (New York: W. W. Norton & Company, Inc., 1969), chap. 5.

THE IMPEACHMENT POWER

Congress functions in a quasi-judicial capacity in the process of impeachment, which is governed by Article II, section 4, providing a means of removing from office "the President, Vice President and all civil officers of the Unites States" on conviction of "treason, bribery, or other high crimes and misdemeanors." Under Article I, the House of Representatives has "the sole power of impeachment." It exercises this power by passing, by majority vote, "articles of impeachment" which perform the function of an indictment.

The Senate is given "the sole power to try all impeachments." At the trial the House acts as the prosecutor through an appointed committee of managers, and the Senate sits as a court. Its presiding officer is the Vice President, unless the impeachment proceedings involve the President, in which case the Chief Justice of the United States presides. This arrangement is specified by the Constitution in order to remove the Vice President from a situation where his own interests would be so directly involved. Though the Senate is under no obligation to follow all the technical rules of judicial procedure, it accords to the accused the principal rights he would have in a law court, including benefit of counsel and compulsory process for obtaining witnesses. The Constitution requires a two-thirds vote of the senators present for conviction.

Impeachment is not applicable to military and naval officers, who are not "civil officers." Members of Congress likewise may not be subjected to impeachment. Though "civil," they are not "officers," for Article I, section 6, provides that "no person holding any office under the United States, shall be a member of either house during his continuance in office."

Impeachment actions have been brought against ten federal judges, four of whom were convicted, and two members of the executive branch, President Andrew Johnson in 1868 and Secretary of War Belknap in 1876. Neither was convicted. Belknap sought to evade trial by resigning his office, but the Senate heard the case anyway, thus establishing the proposition that a civil officer can be impeached after he has left office. In such a case the penalty of "removal from office" which the Constitution specifies as a possible judgment would be impossible, but the other stated penalty of "disqualification to hold and enjoy any office of honor, trust or profit under the United States" could of course still be applied. The Constitution forbids any punishment other than these two for an officer convicted on impeachment, but such a conviction is no bar to subsequent prosecution in the regular courts for any wrongful acts. Prosecution under these conditions would not constitute double jeopardy.

The failure of the Senate, by one vote, to convict Andrew Johnson, and the vindictive partisanship responsible for his impeachment, were generally thought to have so discredited the impeachment device as to preclude its future use against a President. Consequently, as the possible implication of Richard Nixon in the Watergate scandals began to emerge in early 1973, initial suggestions of impeachment were not taken seriously. But the sensational televised hearings conducted by the Senate Select Committee on Watergate, chaired by Senator Sam Ervin; the revelation that White House conversations had been taped; the firing by the President of

Special Prosecutor Archibald Cox; and all the other shattering events of that period resulted in the undertaking of an impeachment inquiry by the House Judiciary Committee, culminating in public hearings in July, 1974.

Two major constitutional issues were raised by these proceedings. First was the meaning of "high crimes and misdemeanors." The phrase, which originated in English parliamentary impeachment practice, is subject to three possible interpretations. One is that offered by Gerald Ford when he was urging the impeachment of Justice Douglas in 1970:

> . . . an impeachable offense is whatever a majority of the House of Representatives considers it to be at a given moment in history; conviction results from whatever offense or offenses two-thirds of the other body considers to be sufficiently serious to require removal of the accused from office.[9]

The second position goes to the other extreme. It asserts that impeachment is limited to serious, indictable crimes. As President Nixon's attorneys argued in their presentation to the House Judiciary Committee: "Not only do the words inherently require a criminal offense, but one of a very serious nature, committed in one's governmental capacity."

The third position, which falls between the other two, is that violation of a criminal statute is not a prerequisite for impeachment so long as the offense is a serious one. The staff lawyers for the Judiciary Committee concluded:

> To confine impeachable conduct to indictable offenses may well be to set a standard so restrictive as not to reach conduct that might adversely affect the system of government. Some of the most grievous offenses against our constitutional form of government may not entail violations of the criminal law.

These issues were debated at length during the Nixon impeachment proceedings. The phrase "high crimes and misdemeanors" was shown clearly to have covered more than indictable offenses in English parliamentary practice. But the President's counsel contended that the broader English practice was a "seventeenth century aberration . . . used as a weapon by Parliament to gain absolute political supremacy at the expense of the rule of law," an aberration that the framers had rejected.

The debates on impeachment at the Constitutional Convention and in the state ratifying conventions were minutely examined. It was noted that when "maladministration" was suggested as a ground for impeachment, Madison rejected it, saying that "so vague a term will be equivalent to a tenure during the pleasure of the Senate." On the other hand, Madison said that the President must be removable for "negligence or perfidy." Edward Rutledge regarded "abuse of trust" as impeachable. Prior American experience with impeachment was also examined. Judge Halsted L. Ritter had been convicted for bringing "his court into scandal and disrepute," hardly indictable offenses.

[9] Irving Brant, *Impeachment: Trials and Errors* (New York: Alfred A. Knopf, Inc., 1972), pp. 5–6.

The majority of the House Judiciary Committee adopted the middle position, which was also clearly the view of the majority of the scholarly community.[10] A minority on the Judiciary Committee, however, insisted that an indictable criminal offense must be proved; as the saying went, they insisted on finding a "smoking gun" at the scene of the crime.

With this division on the committee, it voted three articles of impeachment. The first, charging obstruction of justice by the President in the Watergate coverup, was adopted by a vote of twenty-seven to eleven, with six Republicans joining the twenty-one Democrats. The second alleged abuse of presidential power by misuse of the FBI, CIA, and other government agencies; it was adopted by a vote to twenty-eight to ten. The third, charging Nixon with contempt of Congress by refusing to obey the committee's subpoenas, was more narrowly passed by twenty-one to seventeen. The committee refused to approve two additional articles dealing with Nixon's taxes and the secret bombing of Cambodia.

Eventually the "smoking gun" was supplied by Nixon himself when on August 5, 1974, under pressure of the Supreme Court's unanimous opinion in *United States* v. *Nixon,* he released transcripts of tapes revealing that he had taken command of the coverup only six days after the Watergate break-in, and that he had kept this information from his staff and his counsel. With this damning evidence, the ten Republicans who had supported the President in the votes on all three articles came over to accept the obstruction of justice charge.

A second constitutional issue involved in the Nixon impeachment was whether there was any limit on the investigative powers of the House Judiciary Committee when conducting an impeachment inquiry. The argument for the committee was that the impeachment power of Congress is an intentional breach in the separation of powers principle, and that consequently Congress is the sole judge of what evidence is relevant and can compel its production by the executive. The President's position was that preservation of the integrity of the presidency required that he decide what evidence was relevant to the investigation, and in fact he refused to obey subpoenas for tapes demanded by the committee. However, the committee was able to secure some tapes that had been submitted to Judge Sirica, and on April 30, 1974, Nixon released to the public edited versions of a number of tapes.

The committee chose not to go to court in an attempt to secure additional tapes nor to seek to hold the President in contempt for his refusal. Instead, as just noted, the refusal to honor the committee's subpoenas was made the basis for the third article of impeachment.

Finally, notice should be taken of Raoul Berger's contention that conviction by the Senate on impeachment would be subject to review by the Supreme Court.[11] The

---

[10] See Raoul Berger, *Impeachment: The Constitutional Problems* (Cambridge, Mass.: Harvard University Press, 1973); Charles L. Black, Jr., *Impeachment: A Handbook* (New Haven: Yale University Press, 1974); House Committee on the Judiciary, 93d Cong., 1st sess., *Impeachment: Selected Materials* (Washington: Government Printing Office, 1973); "The Scope of the Power to Impeach," 84 YALE LAW JOURNAL 1316 (1975); E. B. Firmage and R. C. Mangrum, "Removal of the President: Resignation and the Procedural Law of Impeachment," 1974 DUKE LAW JOURNAL 1023.

[11] *Op. cit.,* chap. 3.

constitutional and practical objections to such review are so obvious as to make the proposition, as Charles L. Black said, an "absurdity."[12]

THE LEGISLATIVE CONTEMPT POWER

The power of the English Parliament to punish for contempt of its authority, developed in the centuries of struggle with the Crown, was so firmly established as an inherent legislative power that the framers thought it unnecessary to write it into the Constitution. Contempt proceedings may be brought for such offenses as disturbances in the legislative chamber, for bribing members of Congress, or—most often—for refusing to testify before committees of Congress under subpoena.

Either house can issue its own process, enforceable by its sergeant-at-arms, to cause the arrest and imprisonment of any person found to be in contempt of its authority. There need be no participation by the courts in this procedure. However, legislative imprisonment according to *Anderson* v. *Dunn* (1821), may not be extended beyond the session of the body in which the contempt occurred. Experience with legislative judgments of contempt showed that these proceedings tended to be lengthy and irregular, and the absence of the procedural protections of the law courts was generally disapproved.

Consequently Congress passed an act in 1857 providing that any person refusing to appear before a committee or to answer questions pertinent to an inquiry should, in addition to existing pains and penalties, be deemed guilty of a misdemeanor and be subject to indictment and punishment. In operation this statute requires the following steps. First, the committee before which the alleged contempt occurred must recommend a contempt citation to the parent body, which must vote the citation. The congressional action is then transmitted to the United States attorney, who presents the matter to a federal grand jury. If an indictment is voted, the case is then tried in a federal district court, with appeal to the court of appeals and, if certiorari is granted, to the Supreme Court.

The 1857 act did not preclude the House or Senate from continuing to punish contempts directly, and in fact summary proceedings were common through the nineteenth century. As late as 1934 the Senate convicted a witness of contempt and sentenced him to ten days in jail.[13] Such convictions could be reviewed on habeas corpus, but obviously judicial proceedings under the 1857 act provide much more satisfactory judicial protection of the rights of witnesses. Congress has now completely abandoned any use of its summary procedures.

THE INVESTIGATORY POWER

One of the most significant legislative powers is not even mentioned in the Constitution. The power to investigate is an implied power, supplementary to the power to legislate, to appropriate, to pass on the elections and returns of members, and so on.

---

[12] *Op. cit.,* p. 54.
[13] Carl Beck, *Contempt of Congress* (New Orleans, La.: The Hauser Press, 1959), p. 213.

It is an extremely broad power because the need of Congress for information is broad, but at the same time it is not free from constitutional limitations.

The Supreme Court was initially inclined to construe the investigatory power rather narrowly. In *Kilbourn* v. *Thompson* (1881), three limiting principles were laid down: inquiries could not invade areas constitutionally reserved to the courts or the executive; they must deal with subjects on which Congress could validly legislate; and the resolutions setting up the investigations must suggest a congressional interest in legislating on that subject.

By 1927, however, the Court's attitude was much different. *McGrain* v. *Daugherty* arose out of a Senate inquiry into the connection of the Department of Justice with the Teapot Dome scandal. The brother of the Attorney General sought to avoid testifying on the ground that the Senate was exceeding its proper legislative powers, but the Court disagreed. Granting that Congress had no "general power to inquire into private affairs," here the Senate was looking into the administration of the Department of Justice. Clearly this was a subject on which Congress could legislate and on which information would be useful.

Under this broad "proper legislative purpose" test, what constitutional limits remain on the power of legislative investigation? First, a witness is protected by the ban on self-incrimination in the Fifth Amendment. If he or she "takes the Fifth," claiming that the evidence being requested would tend to be incriminating, the witness can safely decline to answer further questions and is protected from possible prosecution for contempt. While a witness is not admitted to have conclusive power to decide that the answer to a question will tend to be incriminating, on the other hand the witness cannot be forced to reveal the reason for keeping silent, for if it were truly incriminating, then the constitutional protection would have been breached. Consequently a committee chairman must necessarily allow great latitude in permitting the witness to judge the consequences of answering a question.

The principal problem with a Fifth Amendment claim, of course, is that it almost invariably does great damage to the reputation of the claimant and may also be the basis for punitive actions of various kinds. Persons in both public and private employment have lost their jobs as a result of refusing to testify before congressional committees, and Senator Joseph McCarthy pilloried those appearing before his committee as "Fifth Amendment Communists."[14]

Two other defenses were recognized in *McGrain* v. *Daugherty*—a witness may refuse to answer when the committee is exceeding the bounds of its authorization[15] and when the questions are too vague or not pertinent to the matter under inquiry. A witness who refuses to answer on these grounds runs a considerable risk of being successfully prosecuted for contempt.

The First Amendment was offered as a defense for the first time by witnesses appearing before the House Committee on Un-American Activities in the 1940s. They contended that the committee was attempting by forced exposure of their views and activities to abridge their freedom of speech and association and to pun-

---

[14] See *Slochower* v. *Board of Education* (1956), *Lerner* v. *Casey* (1958), *Beilan* v. *Board of Education* (1958), and *Nelson* v. *County of Los Angeles* (1960).

[15] See *United States* v. *Rumely* (1953), and *Deutch* v. *United States* (1961).

ish them for their opinions. This claim met with no success in the courts until 1957 when, in *Watkins* v. *United States,* Chief Justice Warren did recognize the relevancy of the First Amendment, saying, "Abuses of the investigative process may imperceptibly lead to abridgement of protected freedoms." He warned that "there is no congressional power to expose for the sake of exposure." However, he drew back from actually attributing such motives to committee members, and the Court's ruling did not rest on First Amendment grounds. It simply held that the authorization given to the Un-American Activities Committee by the House was unconstitutionally broad.[16]

The *Watkins* decision brought the Court under severe criticism, and various retaliatory measures were proposed in Congress.[17] Two years later the Court retreated from that ruling. *Barenblatt* v. *United States* (1959) involved a college professor who refused to answer questions by the Un-American Activities Committee about his alleged membership in the Communist Party. In a five to four decision, Justice Harlan now ruled that the committee's mandate was not too vague. The "persuasive gloss of legislative history" showed that the House meant the committee to have "pervasive authority to investigate Communist activities." As for the First Amendment, Harlan agreed that "in a different context" the committee's tactics would raise constitutional issues "of the gravest character." But the Communist Party was not "an ordinary political party." Congress had found its goal to be overthrow of the government by force and violence. Since self-preservation is "the ultimate value of any society," the balance between the competing private and public issues at stake had to be struck in favor of public needs.

Justice Black wrote the principal dissent in *Barenblatt.* He attacked Harlan's "balancing" principle, saying it simply gave Congress and the Court the right to ignore the First Amendment. Even if balancing was a proper method of determining the meaning of the First Amendment, Black thought it had been done badly here. Harlan had balanced the right of the government to preserve itself against Barenblatt's right not to talk. What should have been thrown into the scale was the interest of society, of the people as a whole "in being able to join organizations, advocate causes and make political 'mistakes' without later being subjected to governmental penalties for having dared to think for themselves." On the other side of the scale, the congressional interest was vastly overstated as "self-preservation," with no mention that the legislative power to make laws affecting speech and association is limited.

Black also denied that the committee had a "proper legislative purpose." The history of the committee had demonstrated that its "chief aim, purpose and practice" was the illegal one of trying witnesses and punishing them "by humiliation and public shame." He added: "The Court today fails to see what is here for all to see—that exposure and punishment is the aim of this Committee and the reason for its existence."[18]

---

[16] Similarly, in *Sweezy* v. *New Hampshire* (1957), the Court ruled that a state investigation directed to find "subversive persons" was invalid because of absence of legislative control over the investigation.

[17] See C. Herman Pritchett, *Congress Versus the Supreme Court: 1957–1960* (Minneapolis: The University of Minnesota Press, 1961), pp. 45–48.

[18] On the same day as *Barenblatt,* the Court ruled in *Uphaus* v. *Wyman* (1959) that the director of

The Supreme Court went even beyond *Barenblatt* in two 1961 decisions, *Wilkinson* v. *United States* and *Braden* v. *United States.* Wilkinson had gone to Atlanta to organize opposition sentiment against the Un-American Activities Committee which was holding hearings there, and was subpoenaed to appear before the committee within one hour after he arrived in the city. Braden had circulated a petition asking the House not to permit the committee to conduct hearings in the South. He was required to go from Rhode Island to Atlanta for questioning about the petition. A five-judge majority supported the inquiry in both cases, Justice Stewart holding that *Barenblatt* had settled the major issues of congressional authorization and First Amendment relevance.

It thus appeared that the Court had recognized a practically unlimited power of congressional inquiry, but in fact, due partly to changes in the Court's membership, *Braden* and *Wilkinson* marked the end of an era. The Court now began to reverse almost every contempt conviction that came before it. These reversals were accomplished for the most part without challenging the scope of investigatory power or querying the motives of the investigators. They were achieved primarily by strict judicial enforcement of the rules on pertinency, authorization, and procedure plus strict observance of the constitutional standards governing criminal prosecutions.[19]

The Court did invoke the First Amendment in *Gibson* v. *Florida Legislative Investigation Committee* (1963), involving a state rather than a congressional committee. An officer of the NAACP had been ordered to appear before a legislative committee which wanted to find out whether any members of the Association were Communists. Gibson's refusal to bring membership records with him to the hearing was upheld by the Court, on the ground that the state had failed to demonstrate the existence of any substantial relationship between the NAACP and subversive activities which would justify an invasion of its rights to privacy of association.[20]

The tangled case of *Stamler* v. *Willis* (1966, 1969) raised the interesting possibility that a congressional committee could be enjoined from conducting an investigation. In one of its typical proceedings, the Un-American Activities Committee subpoenaed Dr. Jeremiah Stamler for a hearing in Chicago. He declined to answer questions and filed suit to enjoin the hearing on a variety of constitutional grounds, which the court of appeals decided were substantial enough to require trial. In retaliation, the committee started contempt proceedings against Stamler. These two cases, inextricably bound together, moved up and down in the courts until 1973, when the government agreed to drop the contempt proceeding if Stamler would drop his civil suit. This left unreversed the court of appeals holding that a witness called before a congressional committee could counterattack and bring suit ques-

---

a summer camp could be forced to supply the names of all guests at the camp over a two-year period to the New Hampshire attorney general who had been authorized by the state legislature to find out whether there were any "subversive persons" in the state.

[19] Examples are *Deutch* v. *United States* (1961), *Yellin* v. *United States* (1963), *Russell* v. *United States* (1962), *Slagle* v. *Ohio* (1961), and *Gojack* v. *United States* (1966). An exception was *Hutcheson* v. *United States* (1962), where the Court upheld the contempt conviction of a labor union official.

[20] In *DeGregory* v. *Attorney General of New Hampshire* (1966), an inquiry of the same type as those involved in *Sweezy* and *Uphaus* was, like *Gibson,* held to have been justified by no "compelling state interest." The record was found to be "devoid of any evidence that there is any Communist movement in New Hampshire."

tioning the legality of a committee operating in areas affecting First Amendment rights.[21]

Two years later, however, the Supreme Court acted to counter this tactic. The Senate Judiciary Subcommittee on Internal Security, contending that an organization which operated coffeehouses near military bases and helped finance underground newspapers was a subversive threat to the morale of the Armed Forces, subpoenaed its bank records. Since the subpoena was served on the bank, the organization could not contest its validity by defying it and so sought an injunction against the subcommittee, alleging that exposure of the identity of its contributors would dry up donations and violate the organizations's First Amendment rights. The Court in *Eastland* v. *U.S. Servicemen's Fund* (1975), with only Douglas dissenting, ruled that the speech and debate clause forbade judicial interference with congressional subpoenas that were within the sphere of legitimate legislative activity.[22]

By turning contempt-of-Congress prosecutions over to the federal courts, Congress has conceded that judges are to fix the constitutional limits of the investigatory power. Federal judges may naturally feel under some pressure, in handling such cases, to construe the investigatory power rather broadly and to defer to the congressional judgment as to what information is needed for the proper performance of legislative tasks. But the two houses of Congress, precisely because they have turned responsibility for contempt judgments over to the courts, tend to take less responsibility for supervising the work of their committees. When Congress itself tried contempts, the tendency was to consider the circumstances of committee action rather carefully, and often the parent body refused to support a committee contention that a contempt charge was warranted. But now that the courts make the final decision, committee requests for a contempt citation tend to be approved automatically.[23]

The congressional investigatory power has sometimes been shamefully abused, as by the House Committee on Un-American Activities[24] and Senator Joseph McCarthy. But, responsibly used, the power to investigate is a vital safeguard against both governmental and private wrongdoing, as was so forcefully demonstrated by

---

[21] In 1970 a federal judge in the District of Columbia enjoined public distribution of an HISC report on fifty-seven alleged "radical orators" who had spoken on university campuses. The House then ordered a revised report printed and forbade the courts or anyone else from obstructing its distribution. *The New York Times,* December 15, 1970.

[22] On congressional investigations, see M. Nelson McGeary, *The Developments of Congressional Investigative Power* (New York: Columbia University Press, 1940); "Congressional Investigations: A Symposium," 18 UNIVERSITY OF CHICAGO LAW REVIEW 421 (1951); William F. Buckley (ed.), *The Committee and Its Critics* (Chicago: Henry Regnery Company, 1962); Walter Goodman, *The Committee: The Extraordinary Career of the House Committee on Un-American Activities* (New York: Farrar, Straus & Giroux, 1968).

[23] From 1950 to 1965 the House approved every one of the 129 contempt citations requested by the Un-American Activities Committee. Only nine of these citations resulted in final conviction. *The New York Times,* February 8, 1966. One of the rare instances when the House rejected a committee's contempt recommendation occurred in 1971, when the House Commerce Committee sought to hold the Columbia Broadcasting System in contempt for refusing to cooperate in its investigation of the CBS documentary *The Selling of the Pentagon.* The House voted down the citation by a vote of 226 to 181.

[24] The House Committee on Un-American Activities was abolished in 1974 and its duties and staff transferred to the House Judiciary Committee. In 1969 its name had been changed to the House Committee on Internal Security.

the Senate Select Committee on Watergate in 1973 and the House Judiciary Committee impeachment investigation in 1974.[25]

THE POWER OF ADMINISTRATIVE SUPERVISION

The Constitution is not as clear as it might be in allocating responsibility for direction and control of the federal administrative establishment. To be sure, the President has the power to require the opinion in writing of the heads of departments on any subject relating to the duties of their offices, and he has the tremendous leverage which comes with the power to appoint. However, Congress also has a powerful constitutional basis from which to assert supervisory authority. The Senate's advice and consent must be secured for all important appointments. By its legislative authority, Congress can set up, abolish, or modify agencies, offices, and activities. Through its power to appropriate, it controls the nature and extent of administrative programs. Through the power to investigate, it can expose and embarrass officials or operations which are legislatively disapproved.

With these potentialities, it is not surprising that Congress and the President have often been in conflict as to their respective powers of supervision over the federal establishment. But the single-headed Presidency is in an incomparably better position to direct, supervise, and control the administrative branch than is the multitudinous Congress. Experience has been so clear on this point as to convince even Congress, which has gone far toward yielding to the executive two important functions which definitely belong to the legislature—control of finances and departmental organization.

The Budget and Accounting Act of 1921 established the principle and practice of the executive budget, under which the President is responsible for formulating and presenting to Congress a complete and detailed expenditure plan for the following fiscal year. Congress retains authority, in adopting the annual appropriations acts, to modify the executive budget in any way it sees fit. But as a practical matter, the congressional appropriations committees can give only a limited review to expenditure proposals totaling around 400 billion dollars annually.

A congressional appropriation has generally been regarded by the executive as merely an authorization to spend. Consequently Presidents have on numerous occasions, when Congress had appropriated funds for purposes or in amounts which they did not approve, placed part of the appropriation in "reserves" or "impounded" some or all of the funds. Minor controversies between the two branches resulted, but it was not until President Nixon undertook to impound appropriated funds on a massive scale that the issue reached constitutional proportions. He not only made deep cuts in many domestic programs but even terminated congressionally

[25] In November, 1975, the House Intelligence Committee recommended that Secretary of State Kissinger be held in contempt for failure to produce subpoenaed documents pertaining to American foreign relations. At the same time a House subcommittee threatened contempt action against the Secretary of Commerce and the Secretary of Health, Education and Welfare for similar withholding of information. Both controversies were compromised and the contempt actions were dropped. *The New York Times,* December 11, 1975.

approved operations by a total impoundment of their appropriations. The usual targets were appropriations for highway construction, housing, control of water pollution, and other environmental programs, and the usual justification was the need to hold down expenditures to control inflation. Intended recipients of these grants quickly took the administration to court and were generally successful in the lower courts.[26] Likewise, the first case to get to the Supreme Court, *Train* v. *City of New York* (1975) held that an appropriation act which specified that certain sums "shall be allotted" did not permit the administration to withhold any of these funds, even though elsewhere in the act the authorization was for sums "not to exceed" the specified amounts.

Congress, seeing in presidential impoundment a denial of its power to spend, make laws, and override vetoes, undertook to develop legislation that would drastically reduce the opportunity for presidential intervention. At the same time Congress recognized that its own slipshod fiscal practices, which never required appropriations to be considered in relation to anticipated revenues, had furnished the President with justification for his actions. Consequently a serious effort was made to reform congressional budget procedures, which resulted in the Congressional Budget and Impoundment Control Act of 1974. Briefly, the act creates budget committees in each house to oversee expenditures and revenues and establishes a congressional budget office to give Congress the type of expertise now available to the President through his Office of Management and Budget. The act also provides procedures by which Congress can force the President to spend funds he has impounded.[27]

As for organization of the federal establishment, Congress has by a series of reorganization acts authorized the President to prepare reorganization plans for submission to Congress. These plans go into effect automatically unless vetoed by one or both houses of Congress within a specified time period, the provisions for veto varying somewhat in the different statutes.[28] Numerous reorganization plans have been put into effect in this fashion, perhaps the most important being those establishing the Executive Office of the President in 1939; the Department of Health, Education, and Welfare in 1953; and the Office of Management and Budget in 1970.

Although Congress has thus recognized the superior resources of the executive in arriving at budgeting and organizational decisions of a broad legislative character, it has conversely asserted on occasion powers of control over decisions which

---

[26] See "Impoundment of Funds," 86 HARVARD LAW REVIEW 1505 (1973); "Protecting the Fisc: Executive Impoundment and Congressional Power," 82 YALE LAW JOURNAL 1636 (1973); Louis Fisher, *Presidential Spending Power* (Princeton, N.J.: Princeton University Press, 1975), chaps. 7–8.

[27] The President may propose to defer spending to a later time, and such action stands unless overturned by a resolution in either house of Congress. But if the President proposes to rescind the funds entirely, both the House and Senate must approve the action within forty-five days. If either chamber fails to approve, the President must release the funds at the end of the forty-five days.

[28] On the general subject of the "legislative veto," see Joseph P. Harris, *Congressional Control of Administration* (Washington, D.C.: The Brookings Institution, 1964), Chap. 8; Joseph Cooper and Ann Cooper, "The Legislative Veto and the Constitution," 30 GEORGE WASHINGTON LAW REVIEW 467 (1962).

seem clearly administrative in character. Particularly significant have been statutes requiring the approval of congressional committees for specific administrative actions. Attorneys General since at least the time of President Wilson have advised the executive that such legislation is unconstitutional.

LEGISLATIVE PROCEDURE

The constitutional provisions governing legislative procedure require little explication. Article I, section 4, provides that "the Congress shall assemble at least once in every year, and such meeting shall be on the first Monday in December, unless they shall by law appoint a different day." Since by law each Congress terminated on March 4 of the odd years, the "lame duck" session beginning in December of the even years was automatically limited to about three months. This circumstance encouraged legislative filibustering, that is, the deliberate consumption of time in debate in order to prevent the adoption of legislation. Another objection to this time schedule was that congressmen elected in November of the even years did not normally begin service until the next December, thirteen months later. In the meantime, congressmen who had been defeated in November returned to Washington in December and sat in Congress until March 4. The term "lame duck" was applied to these congressmen who, repudiated at the polls, continued to represent their constituents through an entire congressional session. Lame duck Congresses were finally terminated when the Twentieth Amendment, sponsored by Senator Norris, was adopted in 1933. Under its provisions the terms of senators and representatives end at noon on January 3, and the two regular sessions of each Congress begin on that date.

The President is authorized by Article II, section 3, to call "both houses or either of them," into special session. He may indicate in his call the reasons for bringing them into special session, but Congress is in no way limited thereby as to the subjects it can take up.

The presiding officer of the House is its Speaker. The majority party selects its candidate in caucus, and then supports him unanimously when the vote is taken. Unlike the Speaker in the English House of Commons, who must preserve strict impartiality, the American Speaker continues to be a partisan and is in fact the most powerful member of his party in the House. He has a vote and may on rare occasions take the floor to participate in debate.

The Senate has for its presiding officer the Vice President. When serving in this capacity his title is President of the Senate. He has no vote except in case of a tie (Art. I, sec. 3). Giving the Vice President this function in the Senate is a clear defiance of the principle of separation of powers, but the framers apparently concluded that this was the only way to give the Vice President a useful occupation. The Constitution authorizes the Senate to choose a President pro tempore, to preside in the absence of the Vice President, "or when he shall exercise the office of President of the United States." As in the House, the majority party caucuses to agree on the President pro tempore, who is typically chosen on grounds of seniority.

The rules of the Senate guarantee unlimited debate, but in 1917 a rule was adopted permitting cloture to be imposed by a two-thirds vote of senators present and voting (67 if all senators were present). On that basis, cloture was imposed only seventeen times between 1917 and 1975. Repeated efforts of liberals to modify the cloture rule finally achieved a qualified success in 1975, by modification of the rule to require only sixty votes to limit debate. When cloture is voted, thereafter debate is limited to one hour for each senator.

Chapter 11

Taxation and Fiscal Powers

The broadest constitutional grant of fiscal authority to Congress is that in Article I, section 8, clause 1: "The Congress shall have power to lay and collect taxes, duties, imposts and excises, to pay the debts and provide for the common defence and general welfare of the United States."[1] The possession of adequate sources of revenue and broad authority to use public funds for public purposes are essential conditions for carrying on an effective government. Consequently the first rule for judicial review of tax statutes is that a heavy burden of proof lies on anyone who would challenge any congressional exercise of fiscal power. In almost every decision touching the constitutionality of federal taxation, the Supreme Court has stressed the breadth of congressional power and the limits of its own reviewing powers. "The power to tax involves the power to destroy," said Marshall in *McCulloch* v. *Maryland* (1819). The authorization of the Constitution "reaches every subject,"[2] it embraces "every conceivable power of taxation."[3] If the authority to tax is exercised

---

[1] The four terms used to describe governmental levies are broad enough to cover any known form of taxation. "Duties" and "imposts" are interchangeable terms describing customs dues levied on goods imported from foreign countries; "excises" refer to internal revenue taxes on the manufacture, sale, use, or transfer of property within the United States.

[2] *License Tax Cases* (1867).

[3] *Brushaber* v. *Union Pacific R.R.* (1916).

oppressively, "the responsibility of the legislature is not to the courts, but to the people by whom its members are elected."[4] Yet in spite of such statements, the fiscal powers of Congress are not unlimited, and judicial review has a role to play here as elsewhere. The Constitution includes certain specific limitations on the taxing power, and to the interpretations of these restraints we turn first.

SPECIFIC LIMITATIONS ON THE TAXING POWER

Direct Taxation

Article I, section 9, states the following prohibition: "No capitation, or other direct, tax shall be laid, unless in proportion to the census or enumeration herein before directed to be taken." But what is a "direct" tax? When this provision was under discussion in the Constitutional Convention, King asked precisely this question, and according to Madison's notes, "No one answered." The Supreme Court was first called on to give an answer in *Hylton* v. *United States* (1796), when a tax on carriages was attacked as a direct tax, and consequently as one that had to be apportioned among the states on the basis of population. The Court unanimously upheld the tax to be indirect and thus constitutional. The only taxes which the judges thought must clearly be regarded as direct were capitation and land taxes.

During the Civil War, Congress for the first time resorted to income taxation as a source of federal revenue, with no provision for apportionment. The Supreme Court upheld the law in *Springer* v. *United States* (1881) on the ground that an income tax was not a direct tax. Congress thus had every reason to be confident of its authority when in 1894 it levied a tax of 2 percent on incomes in excess of $4,000. This statute was a great victory for the progressive forces of the country, and a sectional triumph for the South and West over the industrial Northeast, where persons with such incomes were mostly located. Before the Supreme Court the tax was depicted as a "Communist march" against the rights of property, and the Court was told that it had never heard nor would ever hear a case more important than this.

The Court handed down two decisions in *Pollock* v. *Farmers' Loan & Trust Co.* (1895). In the first it ruled that, since taxes on real estate are direct taxes, taxes on the income or rents from real estate must similarly be considered direct. The decision also invalidated taxation of income from municipal bonds. However, the Court had been evenly divided, with one member absent because of illness, on the main issue as to whether taxes on the income from stocks and bonds were also to be regarded as direct. In the second decision the Court, by a vote of five to four, ruled that such taxation was direct, and went on to hold the entire tax invalid, thus reversing the law of the preceding hundred years. This surrender of the Court to entrenched wealth, in the same year that it refused to apply the Sherman Act against the sugar trust[5] and upheld the conviction of Eugene V. Debs for violating an

---

[4] *Veazie Bank* v. *Fenno* (1869).
[5] *United States* v. *E. C. Knight Co.* (1895).

injunction during the Pullman strike,[6] earned the Court a popular reputation as a tool of special privilege which was not dispelled for forty years.[7]

A campaign to "repeal" the Court's decision by adoption of a constitutional amendment got under way immediately, and was finally successful in 1913. The Sixteenth Amendment provides: "The Congress shall have power to lay and collect taxes on incomes, from whatever source derived, without apportionment among the several States, and without regard to any census or enumeration." Congress quickly took advantage of the amendment to pass an income tax law, which now provides the principal revenue source for the federal government.

The authorization to tax incomes "from whatever source derived" has been interpreted, in spite of its breadth, as subject to certain limitations.

The Court in *Eisner* v. *Macomber* (1920) held that stock dividends could not be treated as taxable income. Stock dividends were not "income" but capital, and consequently still fell under the apportionment rule. In spite of vigorous subsequent attacks on *Eisner* v. *Macomber*, the principle of the decision has been maintained, though sometimes narrowed in application.

The Uniformity Requirement

After the affirmative grant of power in the first part of Article I, section 8, clause 1, the clause concludes with this proviso: "But all duties, imposts and excises shall be uniform throughout the United States." Since all direct taxes must be apportioned among the states on the basis of population, it follows that only indirect taxes can be subject to the rule of uniformity. This requirement simply means that the thing or activity taxed must be taxed at the same rate throughout the United States. It is "geographical" uniformity that is demanded, the Court ruled in upholding the inheritance tax in *Knowlton* v. *Moore* (1900).[8]

Taxes on Exports

Article I, section 9, clause 5, provides: "No tax or duty shall be laid on articles exported from any state." This provision was demanded by the agrarian states to ensure that the national government could not interfere with export of their surplus agricultural products.[9]

Not every tax bearing on exports is forbidden by this clause. A tax levied directly on the articles exported or on the right to export them is, of course, covered. So are stamp taxes on foreign bills of lading which evidence the exports, and stamp

---

[6] *In re Debs* (1895).

[7] Perhaps not unaffected by the storm it had aroused, the Court refused to use the *Pollock* precedent to invalidate other questioned taxes. An inheritance tax was upheld as an excise in *Knowlton* v. *Moore* (1900); and in *Flint* v. *Stone Tracy Co.* (1911), the Court approved a 1909 statute levying a 1 percent tax on the net income of corporations.

[8] A 1926 amendment to the inheritance tax law permitting a deduction from the federal tax for like taxes paid to a state was held in *Florida* v. *Mellon* (1927) not to be unconstitutional on geographic uniformity grounds because Florida levied no such tax.

[9] Conversely, the states, by Art. I, sec. 10, clause 2, are forbidden, without the consent of Congress, to lay imposts or duties on imports or exports, except what may be absolutely necessary to enforce their inspection laws.

taxes on marine insurance policies covering the exports. But a tax on the income of a domestic corporation engaged in the export business is not an export tax. Nor is a general tax laid on all property equally, including goods intended for export, unconstitutional if it is not levied on goods in the actual course of exportation or because of their intended exportation.

TAXATION FOR NONREVENUE PURPOSES

In addition to these specifically stated limits on the federal taxing power, the Supreme Court has found certain implied restrictions which derive from the inherent nature of the federal system. One major constitutional issue has grown out of congressional efforts to use the taxing power for purposes which are primarily regulatory, and which result in the raising of comparatively little revenue, or sometimes none at all. Does this mixture of motives invalidate a tax statute? Must the taxing power be limited to revenue purposes only? The Supreme Court has not thought so, except in a very few instances and under quite unusual circumstances.

The protective tariff is a clear case of using taxation for goals other than the raising of revenue. The first tariff law was passed in 1789, but the Supreme Court had no occasion to pass on the constitutionality of this form of taxation until 1928. Then, in *J. W. Hampton, Jr., & Co.* v. *United States*, the Court was able to cite in its support some 140 years of practice and the fact that it does bring in revenue. "So long as the motive of Congress and the effect of its legislative action are to secure revenue for the benefit of the general government, the existence of other motives in the selection of the subjects of taxes can not invalidate Congressional action," wrote Chief Justice Taft.

Other regulatory or prohibitory taxes have come before the Court with less impressive genealogy but have been no less firmly upheld. Two types of rationalization can be distinguished in the Court's approach to these problems. The first sustains the questioned tax on the ground that the taxing power is being employed to help enforce another of the federal government's specifically granted powers. In this posture the constitutional case for the tax is strengthened by its auxiliary relationship to an admittedly valid federal purpose. Thus in *Veazie Bank* v. *Fenno* (1869), the Court upheld a 10 percent tax on state bank notes, the admitted purpose of which was to drive them out of existence and leave the field to the notes of the newly authorized national banks. The Court regarded this tax as justified by congressional interest in a sound and uniform currency.[10]

Regulatory or prohibitory taxes have also been upheld, however, even when there was no relationship to other powers of Congress, and where they had to stand or fall on their own merits. In this situation the Supreme Court's reasoning has typically stressed the impropriety of any judicial questioning of the motives of Congress. The classic case is *McCray* v. *United States* (1904), which involved an act of Congress levying a tax of 10 cents per pound on oleomargarine artificially colored

---

[10] Other decisions made on similar reasoning were the *Head Money Cases* (1884) and *Sunshine Anthracite Coal Co.* v. *Adkins* (1940).

yellow to look like butter, and only ¼ cent per pound on uncolored margarine. There could be no doubt that the statute was adopted at the behest of the dairy industry to handicap the sale of a competitive product. But the Court denied that "the motives or purposes of Congress are open to judicial inquiry in considering the power of that body" to enact legislation. The statute was on its face an excise tax, and so it followed that it was within the power of Congress.

The principle of the *McCray* case was again endorsed in *United States* v. *Doremus* (1919), where Congress used a small tax requirement to compel the registration of persons engaged in the narcotics trade, but four justices dissented on the ground that the statute was a bold attempt to exercise police power reserved to the states.

The *Doremus* minority position won control of the Court three years later in *Bailey* v. *Drexel Furniture Co.* (1922), also known as the *Child Labor Tax Case*. This decision invalidated the Federal Child Labor Tax Act, passed in 1919 to replace the 1916 Child Labor Act based on the commerce clause, which the Supreme Court had held unconstitutional in *Hammer* v. *Dagenhart* (1918). The clumsily drafted 1919 law levied a tax of 10 percent on the annual net profits of businesses which at any time during the year employed children in violation of the standards prescribed in the act. The Court, while denying that it had any right or desire to inquire into congressional motives, concluded that this "so-called tax" revealed on its face that it was not a revenue measure, but rather a penalty to regulate child labor. Similarly in *United States* v. *Constantine* (1935), a grossly disproportional federal excise tax, amounting to $1,000, imposed only on retail liquor dealers carrying on business in violation of local law, was declared unconstitutional.

It is not easy for the Court to arrive at such conclusions, for they necessarily involve a finding that Congress has been guilty of improper motives and has used a constitutional subterfuge to accomplish ends which the Constitution forbids. Moreover, the contention that the taxing power of Congress is limited by the regulatory powers reserved to the states by the Tenth Amendment derives from the same dual federalism reasoning embodied in the discredited case of *Hammer* v. *Dagenhart* (1918). Although the Court abandoned dual federalism in interpreting the federal commerce power and specifically overruled *Hammer* v. *Dagenhart* in *United States* v. *Darby Lumber Co.* (1941), some members of the Court illogically continued to apply the doctrine against the federal taxing power.

The principal case is *United States* v. *Kahriger* (1953), where the Court upheld the challenged tax but both majority and minority used dual federalism reasoning. Following the Kefauver nationwide investigation into gambling and racketeering in 1950, Congress levied a tax on persons engaged in the business of accepting wagers and required that they register with the Collector of Internal Revenue. One of the charges against the tax was that it infringed on the police powers of the states. Justice Reed for the majority thought this was a relevant issue and noted that the legislative history indicated a congressional motive to suppress gambling, but finally upheld the statute on the ground that the Court could intervene only if there were provisions in the act "extraneous to any tax need." Justice Frankfurter's dissent, condemning the tax by rationale straight out of *Hammer* v. *Dagenhart*, argued that "when oblique use is made of the taxing power as to matters which substantively are not within the powers delegated to Congress, the Court cannot shut its eyes to what is obviously, because designedly, an attempt to control conduct which the Constitution left to the responsibility of the States, merely because Congress wrapped the legislation in the verbal cellophane of a revenue measure."[11]

Justices Black and Douglas dissented in *Kahriger* on the ground that requiring a person to register and confess that he was engaged in the illegal business of gambling amounted to self-incrimination contrary to the Fifth Amendment. Justice Reed sought to counter the rather obvious logic of this position by contending that the privilege against self-incrimination "has relation only to past acts," whereas the wagering tax was assessed on "the business of wagering in the future." Fifteen years later, in *Marchetti* v. *United States* (1968) and *Grosso* v. *United States* (1968), the Court with only one dissent overruled *Kahriger* and voided the tax on self-incrimination grounds.[12]

INTERGOVERNMENTAL TAX IMMUNITY

A second major implied limitation on congressional power to tax is the immunity to federal taxation of state governments, their property, and activities. This immunity rule rests on no specific language of the Constitution. Rather it is a judicially constructed doctrine, based on certain assumptions by the Supreme Court about the conditions for successful operation of a federal system.

The immunity doctrine was first developed by the Supreme Court, in the famous case of *McCulloch* v. *Maryland* (1819), to protect *federal* activities from *state* taxation. The Bank of the United States, incorporated by Congress in 1816, had a branch in Maryland. The bank was politically unpopular, and in 1818 the state legislature imposed a tax on all banks in the state not chartered by the state legislature, which McCulloch, cashier of the branch bank, refused to pay. Marshall upheld the bank's position. After a notable argument demonstrating the power of Congress to incorporate the bank, which is discussed in Chapter 10, he went on to consider the state's claim to taxing power. The ruling principle, he began, is "that the constitution and the laws made in pursuance thereof are supreme; that they control the constitution and laws of the respective States, and cannot be controlled by them." From this axiom Marshall deduced three corollaries: "1. That a power to create implies a power to preserve. 2. That a power to destroy, if wielded by a different hand, is hostile to, and incompatible with, these powers to create and to preserve. 3. That where this repugnancy exists, that authority which is supreme must control, not yield, to that over which it is supreme." Since the power to tax is, in Marshall's words, "the power to destroy," it followed that the Maryland tax was unconstitutional.[13]

---

[11] See also *Sonzinsky* v. *United States* (1937), where the Court upheld a license tax on manufacturers of, or dealers in, firearms likely to be used in criminal activities, such as sawed-off shotguns and machine guns, but only because the tax was not attended by any "offensive regulation."

[12] Similarly, taxes on unregistered firearms and a marijuana transfer tax were held to violate the Fifth Amendment in *Haynes* v. *United States* (1968) and *Leary* v. *United States* (1969).

[13] The *McCulloch* principle was followed in *Osborn* v. *Bank of the United States* (1824), *Weston* v. *Charleston* (1829), and *Dobbins* v. *Erie County* (1842), the latter case holding that a state had no power to tax the office, or the emoluments of the office, of a federal officer.

State immunity from federal taxation was first asserted by the Court in *Collector* v. *Day* (1871), where the salary of a Massachusetts judge was declared to be immune from the Civil War federal income tax. Justice Nelson grounded the Court's holding directly on the *McCulloch* and *Dobbins* precedents, saying: "If the means and instrumentalities employed by [the federal] government to carry into operation the powers granted to it are, necessarily, and, for the sake of self-preservation, exempt from taxation by the States, why are not those of the States depending upon their reserved powers, for like reasons, equally exempt from Federal taxation?"

Only Justice Bradley pointed to the obvious flaw in this reasoning. State taxation of the instruments of the federal government is a very different thing from federal taxation of the instruments of a state government. State taxation "involves an interference with the powers of a government in which other States and their citizens are equally interested with the State which imposes the taxation." But when Congress levies a tax affecting the states, every state has a voice in the decision through its representatives, and so the states are actually consenting to their own taxation. There is thus a political check on possible abuse of the federal taxing power against the states, whereas a state legislature is subject to no such sense of restraint in levying a tax whose incidence is nationwide.

The doctrine of *Collector* v. *Day* was continued and enlarged in *Pollock* v. *Farmers' Loan & Trust Co.* (1895), which exempted from federal taxation state and local bonds and the interest therefrom. Then, in the 1920s, a conservative Court carried the immunity doctrine to ridiculous extremes. In *Gillespie* v. *Oklahoma* (1922) a state tax applied to income accruing to the lessee of some Indian oil lands was held invalid by a five to four vote, the majority reasoning that the lessee was an instrumentality of the United States used by the government "in carrying out duties to the Indians." Another five to four decision in *Panhandle Oil Co.* v. *Mississippi* (1928) invalidated a state gasoline tax collected on gasoline sold to the federal government. Still another five to four decision, *Long* v. *Rockwood* (1928), held it unconstitutional for a state to tax royalties received from a patent granted by the United States, on the theory that taxing royalties from federal patents would interfere with federal efforts to promote science and invention.

The Court returned to more sober views in the 1930s. The extensions of the immunity principle had rested on the thinnest kind of a Court majority, and represented an extreme view of what constituted a "burden" on government operations. The basis for reversing these decisions had been laid by the dissenting opinions which Justice Holmes and Brandeis, later joined by Stone, had written. It was Holmes who effectively disposed of Marshall's dictum when he rejoined in his *Panhandle* dissent: "The power to tax is not the power to destroy while this Court sits." Holmes left the Court in 1932, and Brandeis early in 1939, so that the major task of translating the minority view of the preceding decade into the majority position of the Roosevelt Court fell to Stone. He had consistently argued that immunity from intergovernmental taxation was not to be supported by merely theoretical conceptions of interference with the functions of government. He demanded that any burdens alleged to result be proved by economic data.

Fox Film Corporation v. *Doyal* (1932) overruled *Long* v. *Rockwood*, decided only four years earlier. *Helvering* v. *Mountain Producers Corporation* (1938) overruled *Gillespie* v. *Oklahoma*, restoring the right to tax oil company income from leased school lands. Next, the long-standing reciprocal exemption of state and federal employees from taxation on their income fell. *Helvering* v. *Gerhardt* (1938) ruled that immunity from federal taxation should not be allowed beyond that vitally necessary for the continued existence of the states. A nondiscriminatory tax on the net income of state employees, concluded Justice Stone for the Court, could not possibly obstruct the performance of state functions.[14]

State activities not considered essential to the preservation of state government had never enjoyed tax immunity. The Court had first ruled to this effect in *South Carolina* v. *United States* (1905), where a state-owned liquor monopoly had been held subject to federal internal revenue taxes. This position was restated in *New York* v. *United States* (1946), upholding federal taxation on the sale of mineral water bottled by the state of New York at Saratoga Springs.

The immunity doctrine is thus no longer a substantial limitation on the congressional taxing power. Of course Congress cannot levy a property tax on a state capitol building, or a stamp tax on writs served by state courts, or any other tax which falls directly on an essential state activity. But of the taxes thus prohibited, the only one of practical importance is the tax on income from state and municipal bonds.[15] Even here, it seems not unlikely that the Court would support Congress if it ever took the initiative in subjecting income from these bonds to the federal income tax.

The same principles now confine federal exemption from state taxation to the "possessions, institutions, and activities of the Federal Government itself."[16] When a state tax falls on a party who is in contractual relationship with the government, the tax is valid, even if it is clear that the tax will be passed on to the government or proportionately increase its costs.[17]

More difficult problems arise when a private party is utilizing government property in manufacture of materials for the government, as often happens on defense contracts. The general distinction here is that the state may not levy a *property* tax on such property, even though it is in private hands and the tax is to be collected from the private taxpayer,[18] but that it may levy a *privilege* tax on the activities of such persons, even though these activities involve the use of government property, and the value or amount of such property is the partial or exclusive basis for measurement of the tax.[19]

[14] Immunity of federal employees from state taxation was denied in *Graves* v. *O'Keefe* (1939). The decision specifically overruled *Collector* v. *Day*.

[15] See *Commissioner of Internal Revenue* v. *Shamberg's Estate* (1945).

[16] *United States* v. *Allegheny County* (1944). In *Department of Employment* v. *United States* (1966) the Court held that the American Red Cross is an instrumentality of the United States, for purposes of immunity from state taxation, and that Congress had not waived that immunity. In *United States* v. *Tax Commission of Mississippi* (1975), the Court held unconstitutional a tax regulation which operated by means of a suppliers' markup to require military installations in Mississippi to pay the equivalent of a state sales tax on liquor sold by the installation.

[17] See *Alabama* v. *King & Boozer* (1941) and *James* v. *Dravo Contracting Co.* (1937).

[18] *United States* v. *Allegheny County* (1944).

[19] *United States and Borg-Warner Corp.* v. *City of Detroit* (1958); *United States* v. *Township of Muskegon* (1958); *City of Detroit* v. *Murray Corporation* (1958).

THE POWER TO SPEND

Revenues are raised by taxation in order to be spent for public purposes. What are the constitutional limitations on the spending power? The basic principle of legislative control over the purse, established by the British Parliament after a long struggle with the Crown, is safeguarded by the provision in Article I, section 9, that "No money shall be drawn from the Treasury, but in consequence of appropriations made by law."[20] But are there any constitutional limits upon the purposes for which Congress may appropriate federal funds? Clearly Congress can spend money to achieve any of the purposes delegated to it by the Constitution, such as regulating commerce among the states or taking the census. But can reliance also be placed upon the rather enigmatic language of the taxing clause which speaks of paying the debts and providing for "the common defence and general welfare"?

Spending and the General Welfare

On occasions it has been urged that the general welfare clause is an independent grant of legislative power to the federal government, quite unrelated to the preceding clause of the same sentence which deals with taxation. In other words, this argument treats the comma after "excises" as though it were a semicolon (as in fact it was up until practically the end of the Constitutional Convention). This position has never been authoritatively accepted. Story contended in his *Commentaries* that adoption of this view would have the tremendous result of transforming the federal government from one of delegated powers into one "of general and unlimited powers."

Rejection of this independent status for the general welfare clause leaves it with what can be called a "purposive" function. However, two purposive theories have been put forward, identified with Madison and Hamilton. Madison asserted that the phrase, "common defence and general welfare," was nothing more than a summary of all the specifically enumerated powers in the subsequent clauses of Article I, section 8. In No. 41 of *The Federalist* he wrote: "Nothing is more natural nor common, than first to use a general phrase, and then to explain and qualify it by a recital of particulars." So Congress could spend only for the express functions stated elsewhere in the Constitution. Hamilton, on the other hand, contended that the general welfare clause conferred a power separate and distinct from the enumerated powers, and that Congress consequently had a substantive power to tax and to appropriate, limited only by the requirement of furthering the general welfare of the United States.

The case of *United States* v. *Butler* (1936) gave the Court an opportunity to settle the argument that Madison and Hamilton had begun. The Agricultural Adjustment Act of 1933 provided for federal payments to farmers who would cooperate in the government's program of price stabilization through production control.

---

[20] See "The CIA's Secret Funding and the Constitution," 84 YALE LAW JOURNAL 608 (1975).

The money paid the farmers was to come from processing taxes on agricultural commodities which were authorized by the same statute. Butler challenged the tax, not as a tax (for it was clearly legal) but as a means of providing money for a program of agricultural production control which he alleged to be an unconstitutional invasion of the powers of the states—in short, "as a step in an unauthorized plan." The Court ratified this stratagem by ruling that the tax and the spending were in fact "parts of a single scheme."

In *Butler* the Court decided that Hamilton was right; the general welfare clause meant that congressional power to spend was "not limited by the direct grants of legislative power found in the Constitution." The only limitation was that taxing and spending, in order to meet the general welfare standard, would have to be on "matters of national, as distinguished from local, welfare."

This was an important victory for the spending power, but the Court immediately proceeded to make it a hollow one by transferring the argument to an entirely new issue. Whether the spending was for national rather than local welfare was of no importance, Justice Roberts concluded for the *Butler* majority, since, as a statutory plan to regulate and control agricultural production, the act invaded the reserved rights of the states and was consequently invalid under the Tenth Amendment. Congress could not "under the pretext of the exertion of powers which are granted" seek to accomplish "a prohibited end."

The *Butler* decision was little more than a nine-day wonder. As a barrier to federal agricultural regulation it was soon bypassed as the type of program it condemned was reenacted by Congress under the commerce power and upheld by a more cooperative Court in *Mulford* v. *Smith* (1939) and *Wickard* v. *Filburn* (1942). As a general threat to the spending power, it was dispelled in 1937 when the Court upheld the tax provisions of the Social Security Act. *Steward Machine Co.* v. *Davis* involved the unemployment compensation section of the act, which provided for a federal payroll tax on employers of a certain percentage of the wages they paid to employees. The proceeds of the tax went into the general federal treasury. If employers paid state taxes into an unemployment fund set up under a satisfactory state law, they could credit such payments against the federal tax up to 90 percent.

The Court denied by a five to four vote that these tax provisions were an attempt to coerce the states or to invade their reserved powers. The states were given, true enough, a compelling inducement to provide unemployment compensation, but the Court viewed this not as coercion but as freedom to adopt such social legislation without putting the employers of some states at a disadvantage compared with employers in other states without unemployment compensation.

A second decision on the same day, *Helvering* v. *Davis*, sustained the Social Security Act system of old-age benefits. The argument on this head had been that the taxing power was being used to benefit a particular class of persons, but the Court believed Congress might reasonably conclude that provision for old-age security would promote the general welfare. The discretion to make such decisions "belongs to Congress, unless the choice is clearly wrong, a display of arbitrary power, not an exercise of judgment."

BORROWING AND MONETARY POWERS

Clauses 2 and 5 of Article I, section 8, give Congress power "to borrow money on the credit of the United States" and "to coin money, regulate the value thereof, and of foreign coin." These authorizations have figured incidentally in several constitutional episodes already discussed. Thus, the holding in *McCulloch* v. *Maryland* (1819) that Congress had the implied power to establish a national bank drew authority in part from clause 5, as did *Veazie Bank* v. *Fenno* (1869) in upholding federal power to tax state bank notes out of existence. However, there are two major crises in American history in which the interpretation of these powers was directly and importantly at issue. The first led up to and was resolved by the *Legal Tender Cases* (1871), the second by the *Gold Clause Cases* (1935).

In Chapter 1 it was pointed out how important the currency problem was in the minds of the members of the Constitutional Convention. Their dislike for "cheap money" led them to prohibit states from coining money, emitting bills of credit, or making anything but gold and silver coin legal tender in payment of debts. Their distrust of paper money even led them to strike out an authorization to Congress to "emit bills of credit" which was included in the original draft of the borrowing clause. However, they did not go so far as to forbid the federal government to issue paper money, and in fact the existence of this power was assumed to be included within the borrowing power as soon as the government began operations.

In connection with the financing of the Civil War, Congress went further and made "greenbacks" (i.e., bills of credit) legal tender at face value in the payment of debts between private individuals. In *Hepburn* v. *Griswold* (1870) the Court by a vote of four to three held the legal tender acts unconstitutional in so far as they required the acceptance of greenbacks in fulfillment of contracts made before the acts were passed, and ruled that creditors would be deprived of due process if compelled to accept depreciated paper money in payment of such debts.

The *Hepburn* holding, if maintained, would have had a tremendous impact, for the nation's economy had adjusted to the use of greenbacks, and many debtors would have been ruined if required to repay their borrowings in hard money. So the popular pressure for reconsideration was very great. On the day the decision was announced, President Grant sent the nominations of two new justices to the Senate. With their votes, the *Hepburn* decision was overruled five to four in the *Legal Tender Cases* (1871).[21]

The new majority held that a congressional power could be implied from a group of expressly granted powers, and by lumping together the war power, borrowing power, and power to coin money, the Court found adequate support for the legal tender provision. As for taking of property without due process, the revised view was that a loss due to the legal tender provision was no more a legal deprivation of property than a loss due to changes in the purchasing power of money. In spite of this emphasis on the war power, *Juilliard* v. *Greenman* (1884) upheld legal tender

---

[21] *Knox* v. *Lee* and *Parker* v. *Davis*.

notes in peacetime. The new amalgam of powers which it cited in support included those to lay taxes, pay debts, borrow money, coin money, and regulate the value of money.

Though the Supreme Court in the *Legal Tender Cases* held that creditors who had merely specified for payment in "lawful money" had to accept legal tender at face value, in *Trebilcock* v. *Wilson* (1872) it added that Congress had not intended to, and possibly could not constitutionally, require creditors who had specified for payment in gold dollars to accept greenbacks at face value. After this decision many creditors insisted on "gold clauses" (i.e., language requiring payment in gold dollars) in bonds, and by 1933 almost all public and private bonds contained such clauses.

The *Gold Clause Cases* (1935) grew out of legislative and executive action in 1933 reducing the gold content of the dollar, with the intention of cheapening money, raising prices, and rescuing agriculture and industry from depression. As elements in the devaluation program, gold payments by the Treasury were suspended, and persons owning gold or gold certificates were required to turn them in to the Treasury in exchange for other currency. Provisions in both private contracts and government bonds for payment in gold were abrogated.

This program of course led to a flurry of litigation. The leading decision came in *Norman* v. *Baltimore & Ohio Railroad Co.* (1935). The holder of a railroad bond promising payment of interest in gold coin of the United States demanded his interest in gold or in an increased number of devalued dollars equal in gold content to the dollars promised before devaluation. By a five to four vote the Court denied this claim. The contract was interpreted as requiring the payment of money, not the delivery of gold bullion. Congress has broad powers of control over the monetary system, and these powers cannot be frustrated by contracts between private parties creating vested rights outside the scope of congressional control. Finally, the Court thought Congress might reasonably conclude that abrogation of the gold clauses in private contracts was an appropriate means of carrying out this revised monetary policy. Justice McReynolds, expressing his dissent, blurted out to the packed courtroom: "As for the Constitution, it does not seem too much to say that it is gone."[22]

Whether Congress could abrogate the gold clause in the government's own contracts was another matter. *Perry* v. *United States* (1935) concerned a government bond issued in 1918 which promised that the principal and interest would be paid in United States gold coin "of the present standard of value." By a vote of eight to one the Court held that the obligation incurred in exercise of the power to borrow money must be given preference over the government's power to regulate the value of money, and consequently that the promise to pay in gold coin could not be abrogated. However, five justices ruled that the person bringing the suit could recover only for actual losses as a result of the government's action, and since there had been none in this case, he was not entitled to sue. Justice Stone in a separate opinion pointed to the Court's dilemma in undertaking to suggest that

---

[22] For an account of the extraordinary measures which President Roosevelt was prepared to take in case the Court had not upheld the government in the *Gold Clause Cases,* see William E. Leuchtenberg, "The Origins of Franklin D. Roosevelt's 'Court-Packing' Plan," in Philip B. Kurland (ed.), *The Supreme Court Review: 1966* (Chicago: The University of Chicago Press, 1966), pp. 352–354.

. . . the exercise of the sovereign power to borrow money on credit . . . may nevertheless preclude or impede the exercise of another sovereign power, to regulate the value of
money; or to suggest that although there is and can be no present cause of action upon
the repudiated gold clause, its obligation is nevertheless, in some manner and to some
extent, not stated, superior to the power to regulate the currency which we now hold to
be superior to the obligation of the bonds.

Congress proceeded to ensure that these dilemmas would cause the Court no further
trouble by passing a statute denying consent to sue the government on these
grounds.

The Commerce Power

The commerce clause has a classic, but deceptive, simplicity. "The Congress shall have power," says Article I, section 8, clause 3, "to regulate commerce with foreign nations, and among the several states, and with the Indian tribes." With this sparse formula the drafters of the Constitution placed in the hands of the federal government a power, the absence of which in the central government under the Articles of Confederation had been largely responsible for the decision to frame a new Constitution.

The language, be it noted, is in terms of a positive grant of power to Congress. The commerce clause does not say what power to "regulate commerce," if any, is left to the states. Nor is any definition attempted of the key words in the clause. As much as any part of the Constitution, this clause has derived its meaning from experience.

Congress undertook the regulation of foreign commerce immediately, but it was quite slow in testing the extent of its constitutional power over commerce among the states. It was not until the adoption of the Interstate Commerce Act in 1887 that the federal government really entered the domestic regulatory field. Consequently, during the first century of the nation's history the commerce clause problems which the Supreme Court was asked to decide grew for the most part out of *state* regulation challenged as infringing the constitutionally protected but largely unexercised power of Congress to regulate commerce among the states.

GIBBONS v. OGDEN

The first case in which the commerce clause figured before the Supreme Court was *Gibbons* v. *Ogden* (1824), one of the landmarks in American constitutional law. It has been customary to credit Marshall with deciding this case in accordance with his own strongly nationalistic views. Actually, his assertion of federal power was less broad and forthright than it might have been. Marshall could write clearly enough when he wanted to, but as Frankfurter says, this opinion "was either unconsciously or calculatedly confused."[1]

Robert Fulton, the inventor, and Robert R. Livingston had been granted an exclusive right by the State of New York to navigate its waters by steamboat. Ogden had a license from them to engage in navigation. Gibbons, on the other hand, was seeking to operate steamboats between New York and New Jersey under a license granted to him by the federal government. Ogden sought to enjoin Gibbons from using vessels within New York waters, to which Gibbons responded that his boats, being licensed under an act of Congress, could not be excluded by any state law. For our present purposes the important part of the Supreme Court's ruling is Marshall's discussion of the character and extent of the congressional power to regulate commerce.

Daniel Webster, appearing before the Supreme Court as counsel for Gibbons, argued for the broadest possible scope of federal power. The authority of Congress to regulate commerce, he contended, "was complete and entire." It went as far as the concept of commerce went, and "in such an age as this, no words embraced a wider field than commercial regulation. Almost all the business and intercourse of life may be connected, incidentally more or less, with commercial regulations." Naturally, in Webster's view, commerce included navigation. Opposing counsel, on the other hand, would limit commerce "to traffic, to buying and selling, or the interchange of commodities," and would exclude navigation from its scope.

Marshall agreed with Webster about navigation being necessarily a part of commerce:

> Commerce, undoubtedly, is traffic, but it is something more: it is intercourse. It describes the commercial intercourse between nations, and parts of nations, in all its branches. . . . The power over commerce, including navigation, was one of the primary objects for which the people of America adopted their government.

But Marshall failed to claim for Congress the "complete and entire" power over commerce for which Webster had contended. He did seem to start out in that direction. Congressional power over commerce with foreign nations, he said, was admittedly complete. It comprehended "every species of commercial intercourse

---

[1] Felix Frankfurter, *The Commerce Clause under Marshall, Taney and Waite* (Chapel Hill, N.C.: The University of North Carolina Press, 1937), p. 17.

between the United States and foreign nations." Moreover, "commerce, as the word is used in the constitution, is a unit, every part of which is indicated by the term."

Now, since commerce is a unit, and since as applied to foreign nations it covers all commercial intercourse, does it not carry the same meaning when applied to commerce "among the several states"? The word "among," continued Marshall, "means intermingled with. A thing which is among others, is intermingled with them. Commerce among the States, cannot stop at the external boundary line of each State, but may be introduced into the interior." Then, having laid the basis for claiming complete federal power to regulate commerce, Marshall drew back.

> It is not intended to say that these words comprehend that commerce which is completely internal, which is carried on between man and man in a State, or between different parts of the same State, and which does not extend to or affect other States. Such a power would be inconvenient, and is certainly unnecessary.

Note that Marshall does not say that such a power was not intended or made possible by the Constitution. He says only that it would be "inconvenient" and "unnecessary" for Congress to exercise such power. Then he adds, in what is the most significant single sentence of the decision: "Comprehensive as the word 'among' is, it may very properly be restricted to that commerce which concerns more States than one." He gives several reasons for this limitation, but the most important is this:

> The genius and character of the whole government seem to be, that its action is to be applied to all the external concerns of the nation, and to those internal concerns which affect the States generally; but not to those which are completely within a particular State, which do not affect other States, and with which it is not necessary to interfere, for the purpose of executing some of the general powers of the government.

Consequently, "the completely internal commerce of a State . . . may be considered as reserved for the State itself."

This whole discussion was largely unnecessary to the actual decision in *Gibbons* v. *Ogden*, which turned on the Court's finding of a conflict between the state and federal statutes. In these circumstances, "the acts of New York must yield to the law of congress," Marshall said. Breaking up the steamboat monopoly was a popular action, but the long-range constitutional importance of the ruling lay in Marshall's rejection of Webster's case for a complete federal power to regulate commerce, and his establishment of a divided authority over commerce, which has been the source of some of the most perplexing problems in American constitutional law.

Subsequently this distinction came to be referred to as that between "interstate" and "intrastate" commerce, and the test for distinguishing between the two categories was whether commerce crossed a state line or not. Marshall, however, did not use these two labels, and his conception of commerce "which concerns more States than one" was considerably more sophisticated. He felt compelled to concede that the "completely internal commerce of a State" was not within federal power, yet he defined such commerce as that which did not "extend to or affect other

States"—certainly not the same thing as saying it is commerce which does not cross a state line.

Marshall's subtle distinctions, however, were soon lost in hard and fast dichotomies. Justice McLean, who thought he was expounding Marshall's views, said in *The Passenger Cases* (1849): "All commercial action within the limits of a State, and which does not extend to any other State or foreign country, is exclusively under state regulation." Chief Justice Taney, whose goals were definitely not those of Marshall, claimed to be stating Marshall doctrine in *The License Cases* (1847) when he spoke of "internal or domestic commerce, which belongs to the States, and over which congress can exercise no control."

INTERSTATE AND INTRASTATE COMMERCE

So it came about that Marshall, who had a unitary conception of commerce, by his decision in *Gibbons* v. *Ogden* laid the basis for splitting commerce among the states into two parts, designated by two terms which he never used. The power of Congress to regulate commerce among the states was assumed to be correctly stated as the power to regulate *interstate* commerce.

Interstate Commerce

Under this approach, the crossing of a state line is the basic justification for federal regulatory authority. Whatever moves across state lines—goods, commodities, persons, intelligence, or whatever—comes within the ambit of congressional power. The breadth of definition which Marshall claimed for "commerce" has been maintained and even expanded. For he qualified "intercourse" by the preceding word "commercial," whereas subsequent decisions of the Supreme Court have made it clear that there need be no actual commercial character to an interstate movement to bring it under the commerce power. The people who cross an interstate bridge "may be as truly said to be engaged in commerce as if they were shipping cargoes of merchandise from New York to Liverpool."[2] In *Caminetti* v. *United States* (1917), the Mann Act, which is based on the commerce power, was held to apply to the transportation of a woman across state lines for immoral purposes, even though no commercial motive was present.

Of course, the major transportation industries offer the classic type of interstate commerce. Congressional power over navigation was settled by the *Gibbons* case, and there was no constitutional doubt as to the power of Congress to pass the Interstate Commerce Act for the regulation of the railroads in 1887. In the *Pipe Line Cases* (1914), the Court upheld federal authority to regulate the transportation of oil and gas in pipelines from state to state, even though the pipelines were not common carriers and transported only the oil and gas of their owners. Regulation of the trucking industry was asserted by the Motor Carrier Act of 1935. Interstate movement of electric power came under federal control in the Federal Power Act of 1935, and the Natural Gas Act of 1938 provided for much the same powers in that field.

[2] *Covington Bridge Co.* v. *Kentucky* (1894).

What is sent across state lines need not be tangible. Federal control over the interstate transmission of intelligence by telegraph was asserted by the Court in 1878, when it said that the powers of the commerce clause "are not confined to the instrumentalities of commerce, or the postal service known or in use when the Constitution was adopted, but they keep pace with the progress of the country, and adapt themselves to the new developments of time and circumstances."[3] Federal control over radio transmission, provided for in 1927 by the Federal Radio Act, was upheld in 1933, Chief Justice Hughes saying: "No state lines divide the radio waves, and national regulation is not only appropriate but essential to the efficient use of radio facilities."[4]

An activity which does not itself involve movement across state lines may be regarded as interstate commerce because of the use of the instrumentalities of such commerce. The classic case is that of the correspondence schools which are interstate commerce because of their necessitous reliance on the United States mails.[5] Regulation of public utility holding companies under the federal act of 1935 was upheld on the ground that their subsidiaries usually operate on an interstate basis, and that the services which the holding company performs for its subsidiaries involve continuous and extensive use of the mails and other facilities of interstate commerce.[6]

In all these decisions the Court has emphasized the unity of interstate transportation. An interstate journey cannot be broken up into the component parts which occur within each state. As Marshall said, "Commerce among the States cannot stop at the external boundary line of each State." In *Wabash Railway Co.* v. *Illinois* (1886) the Court struck down a state claim to regulate the charges for that portion of an interstate journey which took place within the state. "Whatever may be the instrumentalities by which this transportation [from New York to Illinois] is effected, it is but one voyage."

Intrastate Commerce

All this emphasis upon the crossing of a state line as the basic test for commerce logically led to the conclusion that what did not cross a state line was not interstate commerce. Marshall himself appeared to lay the foundation for this position by one of the many dicta propounded in *Gibbons* v. *Ogden*. Speaking of the right of states to enforce inspection laws for the purpose of improving "the quality of articles produced by the labor of a country," he said that these laws "act upon the subject before it becomes an article . . . of commerce among the States." Thus he appeared to divide into two separate, self-contained processes the production of articles and their transportation in commerce. This artificial distinction, which seems inconsistent with his basic conception of the unity of commerce, was developed by later justices into a limitation of tremendous importance on the completeness of the federal commerce power. In application it worked two ways. First, it helped to *uphold state* regulation or taxation as applied to commercial interests which were

---

[3] *Pensacola Telegraph Co.* v. *Western Union Telegraph Co.* (1878).
[4] *Federal Radio Commission* v. *Nelson Bros.* (1933).
[5] *International Text Book Co.* v. *Pigg* (1910).
[6] *Electric Bond & Share Co.* v. *S.E.C.* (1938).

claiming immunity from state control on the ground that interstate commerce was involved. Second, it helped to *defeat federal* regulation by limiting congressional power; and this second effect became more significant after 1890 as Congress began to use its regulatory powers for the first time in a significant fashion.

An illustration of the first category is supplied by *Kidd* v. *Pearson* (1888), involving a state prohibition law which forbade the manufacture of alcohol for sale outside the state. This law was upheld on the ground of the clear distinction between manufacturing and commerce. Manufacture is the fashioning of raw materials into a changed form for use. Commerce is buying and selling and the transportation incidental thereto. If the regulation of commerce included regulation of all manufactures that were intended to be the subject of commercial transactions, the Court said, then "Congress would be invested, to the exclusion of the States, with the power to regulate . . . every branch of human industry."

As an example of the second category, consider what the production-distribution distinction did to the enforcement of the Sherman Act. In *United States* v. *E. C. Knight Co.* (1895) this statute was held inapplicable to a sugar monopoly which had acquired nearly complete control of the manufacture of refined sugar within the United States. The reason was simple. "Commerce succeeds to manufacture, and is not a part of it." Commerce among the states does not begin until goods "commence their final movement from the State of their origin to that of their destination." The monopolistic acts here charged "related exclusively to the acquisition of the Philadelphia refineries and the business of sugar refining in Pennyslvania, and bore no direct relation to commerce between the States." In other decisions the Court applied the same principle to mining,[7] lumbering,[8] fishing, farming, oil production,[9] and generation of hydroelectric power.[10]

The Beginning of Interstate Commerce

This separation between production and distribution has enormous practical consequences. If the Congress cannot regulate production, and the states cannot burden interstate distribution, it becomes vital to determine just where one process stops and the other begins. In general, the rule is that interstate commerce begins when goods are delivered to a common carrier for transit outside the state, or when they actually start a continuous journey between two states. The local movement of goods preparatory to their delivery to a common carrier is not part of the interstate journey. After the continuous interstate journey has begun, temporary interruptions in the course of transportation do not legally break the continuity of the journey.[11]

The Ending of Interstate Commerce

Determination of the point at which an interstate journey ends and state authority resumes is an equally important problem. Marshall dealt with such an issue in the second commerce case which his Court decided, *Brown* v. *Maryland* (1827). In this case the goods involved were imports from abroad into Maryland, and that state

[7] *United Mine Workers* v. *Coronado Coal Co.* (1922); *Oliver Iron Mining Co.* v. *Lord* (1923).
[8] *Coe* v. *Errol* (1886).
[9] *Champlin Refining Co.* v. *Corporation Commission* (1932).
[10] *Utah Power and Light* v. *Pfost* (1932).
[11] *Coe* v. *Errol* (1886).

sought to levy a license tax on the importer. Article I, section 10, forbids the states to lay duties on imports, and Marshall, searching for a practical rule on the subject, held that imported goods retained their character as imports as long as they remained unsold in the original package. The "original package" doctrine has continued to be used as a judicial rule of thumb. So far as interstate (as opposed to foreign) commerce is concerned, its effect is to forbid states to exert their police power on goods shipped in from other states while remaining in the original packages, unsold, unbroken, and unused. Stated positively, this doctrine protects the first sale of goods within the state while in the original package. Since the original package has this important protective character, it is not surprising that numerous controversies have arisen as to just what the original package is in different circumstances.[12]

THE POWER TO "REGULATE"

Although the federal power to regulate commerce is thus not a "complete" power, wherever the power does exist it is "plenary." Consequently the breadth of regulatory power which Congress may exercise within its recognized scope of authority has seldom been successfully questioned. Efforts to read restrictive interpretations into the word "regulate" have almost uniformly failed. Regulation, the Court has said, means not only protection and promotion, but also restriction and even prohibition.

The railroad field was the first in which Congress really tested the extent of its regulatory authority. The Interstate Commerce Act of 1887, setting up a regulatory commission with rather limited powers, was upheld by the Court in *Interstate Commerce Commission* v. *Brimson* (1894) as a necessary and proper means of enforcing congressional authority. In 1916 Congress took what then seemed the rather extreme step of providing in the Adamson Act for the eight-hour day and specifying wage and overtime rates on the railroads. The Court by a bare five to four margin approved the statute in *Wilson* v. *New* (1917) as necessary to prevent the interruption of commerce by a nationwide strike. The even more drastic plan for recapture of excess rail earnings in the Transportation Act of 1920 was upheld by the Court in 1924.[13]

The Commerce Power as a National Police Power

A severe test of congressional power over commerce was presented when Congress began, around the turn of the century, to explore the possibilities of using the commerce clause as a kind of national police power. An act of 1895 made it unlawful to transport lottery tickets into a state from another state or a foreign country. By a five to four vote the law was upheld in *Champion* v. *Ames* (1903). Harlan's opinion overruled the objection that regulation did not extend to complete prohibition and accepted the prevention of harm to the public morals as an appropriate goal of the commerce power, without any showing of effect on the safety or efficiency of commerce. The states were free to take action against intrastate traffic in

---

[12] *Austin* v. *Tennessee* (1900); *Cook* v. *Marshall County* (1905).
[13] *Dayton–Goose Creek R. Co.* v. *United States* (1924).

lottery tickets. Why then could not Congress provide that "commerce shall not be polluted by the carrying of lottery tickets from one State to another"? The Court was clearly aware that if Congress could not prohibit the interstate traffic in lottery tickets, a no-man's-land would be created where neither federal nor state regulation could enter.

On the authority of *The Lottery Case,* the Supreme Court upheld the Food and Drug Act of 1906, which prohibited the introduction of impure foods and drugs into the states by means of interstate commerce.[14] The Mann Act (1910), forbidding the transportation of women in interstate commerce for the purpose of prostitution and debauchery, was upheld in 1913 on the basis of these precedents.[15] "Of course it will be said that women are not articles of merchandise," the Court wrote, "but this does not affect the analogy of the cases." The applicable principle was the simple one "that Congress has power over transportation 'among the several States'; that the power is complete in itself; and that Congress, as an incident to it, may adopt not only means necessary but convenient to its exercise, and the means may have the quality of police regulations."

The Child Labor Decision

This technique of closing the channels of interstate commerce, which had been uniformly successful in meeting constitutional tests, was then applied by Congress in the Federal Child Labor Act of 1916. This statute prohibited transportation in interstate commerce of the products of factories, mines, or quarries where children under the age of fourteen had been permitted to work more than eight hours a day or six days a week or at nights. In the historic case of *Hammer* v. *Dagenhart* (1918) the statute was declared unconstitutional by a five to four vote.[16]

The power to regulate commerce, said Justice Day for the majority, is the power "to control the means by which commerce is carried on," not the right "to forbid commerce from moving." To establish the correctness of this view the Court, of course, had somehow to deal with the contrary precedents just reviewed. Instead of overruling them, Day labored to explain that lottery tickets, impure food, and prostitutes are harmful in and of themselves, whereas goods produced by child labor "are of themselves harmless." In the case of the harmful categories, their regulation in interstate commerce could only be satisfactorily achieved by banning their movement altogether. But with harmless commodities, prohibition of their interstate movement by Congress was unconstitutional. This astounding argument was fittingly answered by Justice Holmes in his dissent.

> The notion that prohibition is any less prohibition when applied to things now thought evil I do not understand. But if there is any matter upon which civilized countries have agreed . . . it is the evil of premature and excessive child labor. I should have thought that if we were to introduce our own moral conceptions where in my opinion they do

---

[14] *Hipolite Egg Co.* v. *United States* (1911).

[15] *Hoke* v. *United States* (1913).

[16] For an interesting account of the development of this case, see Stephen B. Wood, *Constitutional Politics in the Progressive Era: Child Labor and the Law* (Chicago: University of Chicago Press, 1968).

not belong, this was preëminently a case for upholding the exercise of all its powers by the United States.

The more reputable part of Day's argument rested on the well-established doctrine that manufacturing, mining, and the like are intrastate commerce, subject to local regulation. In this statute Congress professed to observe the distinction between production and distribution and in form regulated only the latter. But in fact, Day said, the aim was "to standardize the ages at which children may be employed in mining and manufacturing within the States." Congress cannot use *its* admitted powers to oust the states from the exercise of *their* admitted powers. "The grant of authority over a purely federal matter was not intended to destroy the local power always existing and carefully reserved to the States in the Tenth Admendment to the Constitution."

This is a classic statement of the doctrine of dual federalism—that the powers delegated to the national government are nevertheless limited by the reserved powers of the states. When this view had been pressed upon the Court in *The Lottery Case*, Harlan had rejected it in positive fashion: "If it be said that the act of 1895 is inconsistent with the Tenth Amendment, reserving to the States respectively or to the people the powers not delegated to the United States, the answer is that the power to regulate commerce among the States has been expressly delegated to Congress."

Holmes subjected Day's logic to more extensive analysis in his *Hammer* dissent. Certainly what Congress had done—forbidding the transportation of goods in interstate commerce—was within the power expressly given to Congress by the commerce clause, if considered only as to its immediate effects. If it was to be declared unconstitutional, it would have to be because of its possible reaction upon the conduct of the states—in this case, because of its effect upon their freedom to permit child labor. "But if an act is within the powers specifically conferred upon Congress, it seems to me that it is not made any less constitutional because of the indirect effects that it may have, however obvious it may be that it will have those effects, and that we are not at liberty upon such grounds to hold it void."

Holmes went on to point out how often the exercise of a federal power limited state freedom. For example, federal taxation of state bank notes had driven them out of circulation. But his main emphasis was upon the admitted right of Congress to regulate interstate commerce. When states seek to send their products across a state line, "they are no longer within their rights. If there were no Constitution and no Congress their power to cross the line would depend upon their neighbors. Under the Constitution such commerce belongs not to the States but to Congress to regulate."

Obviously Holmes was right, but the majority view in *Hammer* v. *Dagenhart* remained at least in theory the official interpretation until the decision was overruled in 1941. Influential as it may have been, it was never anything but an exception to the general rule, which as stated by Harlan in *The Lottery Case* is that the power to regulate commerce "is plenary, is complete in itself, and is subject to no limitations except such as may be found in the Constitution." It was the general rule, not the exception, which the Court followed in upholding the power of Congress over interstate commerce in stolen motor vehicles in 1925[17] and kidnapped persons in 1936.[18]

THE CONCEPT OF "EFFECT UPON COMMERCE"

In spite of this emphasis on transportation across state lines as the basis for congressional power over commerce, there were other doctrinal developments on the Supreme Court which laid the basis for the twentieth-century growth of the commerce power. This expansion came about primarily by application of the concept of "effect upon commerce." Under this doctrine, Congress could regulate not only commercial activities where state lines were crossed, but also activities which *affected* interstate commerce.

As all else in this field, the effect doctrine traces back to Marshall's opinion in the *Gibbons* case. There he said, in spelling out the area of commercial regulation remaining in the hands of the states under the commerce clause, that "it is not intended to say that these words comprehend that commerce . . . which does not extend to or affect other States." When the double negative is eliminated, this is an affirmation that Congress *can* regulate commerce within a state which affects other states.

By 1900 it was clear that congressional power over commerce would have to be freed from its exclusively "interstate" connotations if substantial expansion of congressional power over the industrial and commercial life of the country was to occur. Marshall's effect doctrine was available for this purpose. Of course, "effect" is a vague word; it may be useful if we endeavor to classify various types of situations where activities of a geographically intrastate character have such obvious impact on commerce among the states as to make application of the effect doctrine reasonable.

Effect Through Intermingling

First we may note that it is possible for intrastate commerce to be physically so intermingled or intertwined with interstate commerce that the two cannot practically be divided for regulatory purposes; under these circumstances interstate commerce can simply not be regulated without also regulating intrastate commerce. A good example of this situation is supplied by *Southern Railway Co.* v. *United States* (1911). The case arose when the company hauled on its interstate railroad in *intrastate* traffic three cars not equipped with safety couplers as required by the federal Safety Appliance Act. The statute specifically applied, not only to equipment used in interstate commerce, but also to cars "used in connection therewith." The Court approved this assertion of federal control over railroad cars which did not them-

---

[17] *Brooks* v. *United States* (1925).

[18] *Gooch* v. *United States* (1936). The federal Travel Act of 1970, which makes criminal the use of facilities of interstate commerce for carrying on illegal activities such as gambling, was upheld in *Erlenbaugh* v. *United States* (1972) as applied against persons who shipped racing "scratch sheets" from Chicago into Indiana by train. But see *Rewis* v. *United States* (1971).

selves cross state lines, saying: "This is so, not because Congress possesses any power to regulate intrastate commerce as such, but because its power to regulate interstate commerce is plenary and consequently may be exerted to secure the safety of the persons and property transported therein and of those who are employed in such transportation, no matter what may be the source of the dangers which threaten it."

"Stream of Commerce"

A second situation is the so-called "stream of commerce." The case commonly regarded as the fount of this notion was *Swift & Co.* v. *United States* (1905). Chicago stockyards firms had been charged with conspiracy in restraint of trade, and they objected that the purchase and sale of cattle in Chicago was not commerce among the states. Justice Holmes replied for the Court:

> Commerce among the States is not a technical legal conception, but a practical one, drawn from the course of business. When cattle are sent for sale from a place in one State, with the expectation that they will end their transit, after purchase, in another, and when in effect they do so, with only the interruption necessary to find a purchaser at the stock yards, and when this is a typical, constantly recurring course, the current thus existing is a current of commerce among the States, and the purchase of the cattle is a part and incident of such commerce.

By similar reasoning, Chief Justice Taft upheld federal regulation of stockyards in *Stafford* v. *Wallace* (1922) and grain exchanges in *Chicago Board of Trade* v. *Olsen* (1923).[19]

The Shreveport Doctrine

Still a third type of situation in which the effect of local commerce on interstate commerce has achieved constitutional significance is illustrated by the famous *Shreveport Rate Case* (1914). The situation was that Shreveport, Louisiana, competed with Houston and Dallas, Texas, for the trade of the intervening Texas territory. Interstate rates from Shreveport to Texas cities, regulated by the ICC, were higher than the intrastate rates fixed by the Texas Railroad Commission from Dallas and Houston to the same cities for comparable distances. Thus Shreveport was placed at a competitive disadvantage because of the interstate character of its commerce into Texas. The ICC agreed that it could not permit interstate traffic to be thus burdened, and issued an order requiring Texas *intrastate* rates from Dallas and Houston to be equalized with the interstate rates from Shreveport into Texas.

Justice Hughes wrote a strong opinion for the Court upholding federal power to exercise such control over intrastate commerce. The commerce power of Congress is "complete and paramount. . . . It is of the essence of this power that, where it exists, it dominates. Interstate trade was not left to be destroyed or impeded by the rivalries of local governments." Congress was given power by the commerce clause

[19] For a recent illustration of "stream of commerce" reasoning, see *Allenberg Cotton Company, Inc.* v. *Pittman* (1974).

to see "that the agencies of interstate commerce shall not be used in such manner as to cripple, retard or destroy it." Consequently,

> Wherever the interstate and intrastate transactions of carriers are so related that the government of the one involves the control of the other, it is Congress, and not the State, that is entitled to prescribe the final and dominant rule, for otherwise Congress would be denied the exercise of its constitutional authority and the State, and not the Nation, would be supreme within the national field.

Direct versus Indirect Effect

These various rationalizations of federal control might appear to open the way for complete exclusion of state regulation, and an achievement of that completeness of the federal commerce power for which Webster had argued in the *Gibbons* case. The Supreme Court, however, did not mean to go so far as that, and consequently there runs through all these cases an insistence by the Court that it is holding back something from the completeness of federal power. It is not *any* effect on commerce, however minimal, which justifies congressional control over intrastate activities. The Court tried a variety of semantic devices in the 1920s and 1930s in an attempt to indicate what kinds of effects justify federal control and what do not—the relation must be "close," the effect must be "substantial"—but the test most often suggested as a standard for judicial review of congressional action was "directness" as opposed to "indirectness" of effect.

The Court first began to talk in terms of direct and indirect effects in the early antitrust cases. Thus in the *Sugar Trust Case* (1895) the Court held that the chance "trade or commerce might be indirectly affected" by a sugar company merger was not enough to entitle the government to a Sherman Act decree. At this point the Court's dogma was that sale of a product was incidental to its production, and could never affect commerce other than incidentally or indirectly. But as time went on the Court became less sure on this point. In Holmes's opinion in the *Swift* case, sales became an element in an interstate stream, an integral part of an entire interstate movement. Chief Justice Taft in the *Chicago Board of Trade* case went even further in defining the kind of effect which justified federal control as "whatever amounts to more or less constant practice, and threatens to obstruct or unduly to burden the freedom of interstate commerce."

Clearly the direct-indirect test was a slippery one, with which different courts could get different results. Where Congress or its agent, the ICC, had definitely claimed an area of intrastate commerce under the effect doctrine, the Court tended to acquiesce. As Taft said in the *Chicago Board of Trade* case, "It is primarily for Congress to consider and decide the fact of the danger [to commerce] and meet it. This court will certainly not substitute its judgment for that of Congress in such a matter unless the relation of the subject to interstate commerce and its effect upon it are clearly non-existent."

But where the statute was a general one, like the Sherman Act, then the Court had to satisfy itself, as an original proposition, that the facts of the particular case demonstrated not merely the *existence*, but the *directness* of the effects upon commerce. In the three decades following the *Swift* decision in 1905, a predominantly conservative Court did find such directness in most of the important controversies, thus expanding the federal commerce power. The result of this expansion was not only to justify federal regulation of business, but also to permit the Court to strike at labor unions and their practices under federal law.

Early applications of the Sherman Act against labor organizations, as in the *Danbury Hatters Case*,[20] led Congress to attempt to exempt labor unions from its scope by section 6 of the Clayton Act (1914). However, the Court substantially interpreted this provision out of existence, and found directness of effect on commerce in such intrastate labor actions as a violent strike by the United Mine Workers against a coal company [21] and a secondary boycott by the stonecutters' union in the *Bedford Cut Stone* case of 1927.[22]

This was the status of the law and the Court's holdings when the National Recovery Administration legislation came up for judicial review in the famous case of *Schechter Poultry Corp.* v. *United States* (1935). The NRA was a major reliance of the New Deal in its attack on the Depression. Under the statute, codes of fair practice had been adopted for most of the industries of the country, large and small, fixing minimum wages and maximum hours, and regulating unfair or destructive competitive practices. President Roosevelt's high hopes for the NRA as a kind of partnership between capital and labor had not been fulfilled, and it was near collapse by the time the Supreme Court mercifully administered the *coup de grâce* in 1935. Our concern, however, is with the constitutional theory of the decision.

The statute's assertion of federal control was over transactions "in or affecting interstate or foreign commerce." The Schechter Corporation was a Brooklyn slaughterhouse operator which purchased live poultry in New York or Philadelphia, trucked it to the Brooklyn plant, slaughtered it, and then sold it to local retail dealers in Brooklyn. The live poultry code did not concern transportation or the practices of commission men. It dealt with hours and wages in the slaughterhouse and the company's local selling practices. Chief Justice Hughes for a unanimous Court held that these activities of the Schechter Corporation were not "transactions in interstate commerce."

Consequently the Schechter Corporation could be brought under the NRA only by one of the several "effect" notions. Would the "stream of commerce" doctrine apply? The Court said no. "So far as the poultry here in question is concerned, the flow in interstate commerce had ceased." Was there a direct effect upon interstate commerce which would justify the regulation? Again the answer was negative. Any effects present were indirect. The distinction between direct and indirect effects, Hughes said, "is clear in principle," but he impliedly admitted that he could not state it by falling back on illustration from individual cases the Court had decided in the past. What he was clear about, however, was that "the distinction between direct and indirect effects of intrastate transactions upon interstate commerce must be recognized as a fundamental one, essential to the maintenance of our

[20] *Loewe* v. *Lawlor* (1908).

[21] *Coronado Coal Co.* v. *United Mine Workers* (1925).

[22] *Bedford Cut Stone Co.* v. *Journeymen Stone Cutters' Assn.* (1927). See also *Local 167 I.B.T.* v. *United States* (1934).

constitutional system. Otherwise . . . there would be virtually no limit to the federal power and for all practical purposes we should have a completely centralized government." And he added, after mentioning the government's contention that such centralized powers were necessary to meet the economic emergency in the country: "It is not the province of the Court to consider the economic advantages or disadvantages of such a centralized system. It is sufficient to say that the Federal Constitution does not provide for it."

One year later a sharply divided Court did a reprise on this theme in *Carter* v. *Carter Coal Co.* (1936), which invalidated the coal industry codes set up under the Bituminous Coal Conservation Act of 1935. This time it fell to Justice Sutherland to write the opinion, and he dared to do what Hughes had been unwilling to attempt in the *Schechter* case, namely, to define the difference between a direct and an indirect effect on commerce.

> The word "direct" implies that the activity or condition invoked or blamed shall operate proximately—not mediately, remotely, or collaterally—to produce the effect. It connotes the absence of an efficient intervening agency or condition. And the extent of the effect bears no logical relation to its character. The distinction between a direct and an indirect effect turns, not upon the magnitude of either the cause or the effect, but entirely upon the manner in which the effect has been brought about. If the production by one man of a single ton of coal intended for interstate sale and shipment . . . affects interstate commerce indirectly, the effect does not become direct by multiplying the tonnage, or increasing the number of men employed, or adding to the expense or complexities of the business, or by all combined.

Sutherland then went on to underline the application of these principles to the current problem:

> Much stress is put upon the evils which come from the struggle between employers and employees over the matter of wages, working conditions, the right of collective bargaining, etc., and the resulting strikes, curtailment and irregularity of production and effect on prices; and it is insisted that interstate commerce is *greatly* affected thereby. But . . . the conclusive answer is that the evils are all local evils over which the federal government has no legislative control. The relation of employer and employee is a local relation. . . . And the controversies and evils, which it is the object of the act to regulate and minimize, are local controversies and evils affecting local work undertaken to accomplish that local result. Such effect as they may have upon commerce, however extensive it may be, is secondary and indirect. An increase in the greatness of the effect adds to its importance. It does not alter its character.

This opinion was the dead end of the directness-indirectness dogma. It illuminated as by a flash of lightening a judicial dream world of logical abstractions, where there was no difference between one ton of coal and a million tons of coal, where considerations of degree were not cognizable by the law. Production was local. A production crisis in every part of the country simultaneously could never add up to a national problem with which Congress could deal; it could never have anything other than an indirect effect on commerce.

Sutherland sought to demonstrate that this fantastic result was required by the precedents. But the effect doctrine had been proved to be flexible enough to accommodate earlier legislative efforts to deal with intrastate commercial activities. "A survey of the cases," said Cardozo, dissenting along with Brandeis and Stone, "shows that the words [direct and indirect] have been interpreted with suppleness of adaption and flexibility of meaning." He was thinking of Holmes in the *Swift* case, Hughes in the *Shreveport* holding, Taft in *Chicago Board of Trade* v. *Olsen*. These were pragmatic and realistic appraisals of the federal commerce power which expose Sutherland's elaborate conceptualism in the *Carter* case as absurdly irrelevant to the issues before the country. The commerce power, Cardozo summed up, should be "as broad as the need that evokes it."[23]

THE COMMERCE POWER AFTER 1937

Neither the Court nor the country could live with the doctrine of *Carter* v. *Carter Coal Co.* Within a year the standard stated by Justice Cardozo in dissent there became the majority view of the Court. The vehicle for this return to reality was *National Labor Relations Board* v. *Jones & Laughlin Corp.* (1937), involving the constitutionality of the National Labor Relations Act. This case was decided some two months after President Roosevelt had sent his Court-packing plan to Congress, while the Court was still the center of violent political controversy. The decision, which saw Chief Justice Hughes and Justice Roberts joining the liberal trio of Brandeis, Cardozo, and Stone in upholding the statute, was widely regarded as the Court's contribution toward restoration of peaceful relations by acceptance of the New Deal.

The Wagner Act

The National Labor Relations Act, popularly known as the Wagner Act, aimed to protect the right of employees to organize into labor unions and to bargain collectively with their employers. The statute defined certain types of interference with these rights as unfair labor practices and set up the NLRB with authority to compel employers to cease and desist from such practices. There was widespread employer resistance to the statute, and obviously it could not be applied to production industries if the *Schechter* and *Carter* view of the commerce clause was correct.

   The key jurisdictional provision in the Wagner Act was that empowering the NLRB to forbid any person from engaging in any unfair labor practice "affecting commerce." The Jones & Laughlin Company was one of the nation's major steel producers, with integrated operations in several states. The particular unfair labor acts charged in this case took place in one of the company's Pennsylvania plants, and the constitutional question was whether these practices had a sufficient effect upon commerce to justify congressional control. Chief Justice Hughes said:

[23] A more recent example of the effect doctrine is found in *Perez* v. *United States* (1971), involving the Consumer Credit Protection Act of 1968, in which Congress struck at "loan sharking," i.e., the use by organized crime of extortionate means to collect payments on loans. Justice Stewart, dissenting, thought that loan sharking was a "wholly local activity," but the Court majority ruled that "extortionate credit transactions, though purely intrastate, may in the judgment of Congress affect interstate commerce."

In view of respondent's far-flung activities, it is idle to say that the effect would be indirect or remote. It is obvious that it would be immediate and might be catastrophic. We are asked to shut our eyes to the plainest facts of our national life and to deal with the question of direct and indirect effects in an intellectual vacuum.

This, of course, was precisely what Sutherland had done in the *Carter* opinion. Hughes continued:

When industries organize themselves on a national scale, making their relation to interstate commerce the dominant factor in their activities, how can it be maintained that their industrial labor relations constitute a forbidden field into which Congress may not enter when it is necessary to protect interstate commerce from the paralyzing consequences of industrial war?

The stress which the Hughes opinion placed on the importance and nationally integrated character of the steel industry certainly suggested that these factors were important in justifying the Court's decision. But on the same day the Court also upheld the application of the Wagner Act to a trailer manufacturer [24] and to a small manufacturer of men's clothing [25] on the authority of the *Jones & Laughlin* decision. Apparently a business did not after all need to be one whose interruption by strike would be "catastrophic" in order to justify coverage by the statute.

For a couple of years after the *Jones & Laughlin* decision, there was a flurry of cases searching for loopholes in its doctrine, but none was found.[26] After 1939 cases testing the constitutional coverage of the NLRB virtually disappeared from the Supreme Court's docket. The Board did continue to run into an occasional unfavorable decision in the federal courts of appeals, but it appeared to be almost literally true that in no labor relations case over which the NLRB was willing to claim jurisdiction as affecting commerce would the Supreme Court deny the validity of the claim. Indeed, the NLRB eventually undertook voluntarily to limit its own jurisdiction, setting up categories of cases which it could have legitmately handled but which it announced it would not accept.

The Fair Labor Standards Act

As the Wagner Act furnished the occasion for bringing down the *Schechter* and *Carter* decisions, it fell to another labor statute, the Fair Labor Standards Act, to demolish *Hammer* v. *Dagenhart*. This 1938 statute, also called the Wages and Hours Act, was the last major piece of New Deal legislation adopted. The formula it employed was similar to that of the 1916 federal child labor law, Congress making it unlawful to ship in interstate commerce goods produced in violation of the wage and hour standards set by the act. The coverage of the act was not as broad as that of the Wagner Act. Where that statute had applied to unfair labor practices "affect-

---

[24] *NLRB* v. *Fruehauf Trailer Co.* (1937).
[25] *NLRB* v. *Friedman–Harry Marks Clothing Co.* (1937).
[26] *See Consolidated Edison Co.* v. *NLRB* (1938); *Santa Cruz Fruit Packing Co.* v. *NLRB* (1938); *NLRB* v. *Fainblatt* (1939). Later cases upholding a broad interpretation of NLRB authority are *Polish Alliance* v. *Labor Board* (1944), *Guss* v. *Utah Labor Board* (1957), and *NLRB* v. *Reliance Fuel Oil Corp.* (1963).

ing commerce," the Fair Labor Standards Act was made applicable to employees "engaged in commerce or in the production of goods for commerce."

The basic decision upholding the constitutionality of this act was *United States v. Darby Lumber Co.*, announced unanimously by the Court in 1941. As Justice Stone said, there would have been little need for any extended discussion of the constitutional issue, since Congress was asserting its clear power over the movement of goods across state lines, if it had not been for *Hammer* v. *Dagenhart*. Stone's attention was consequently devoted primarily to disposing of that derelict on the stream of the law.

> In that case it was held by a bare majority of the Court over the powerful and now classic dissent of Mr. Justice Holmes . . . that Congress was without power to exclude the products of child labor from interstate commerce. The reasoning and conclusion of the Court's opinion there cannot be reconciled with the conclusion which we have reached, that the power of Congress under the Commerce Clause is plenary to exclude any article from interstate commerce subject only to the specific prohibitions of the Constitution.
>
> *Hammer* v. *Dagenhart* has not been followed. The distinction on which the decision was rested that Congressional power to prohibit interstate commerce is limited to articles which in themselves have some harmful or deleterious property— a distinction which was novel when made and unsupported by any provision of the Constitution— has long since been abandoned. . . .
>
> The conclusion is inescapable that *Hammer* v. *Dagenhart* was a departure from the principles which have prevailed in the interpretation of the Commerce Clause both before and since the decision and that such vitality, as a precedent, as it then had has long since been exhausted. It should be and now is overruled.

The *Darby* decision, clear-cut as it was, did not suffice to settle the jurisdictional questions under the Fair Labor Standards Act in the definitive fashion that the *Jones & Laughlin* decision had achieved for the Wagner Act. Two reasons account for the continuing stream of wage and hour cases after 1941. First, the absence of any administrative tribunal like the ICC or the NLRB to perform enforcement functions under the act withheld from the courts, in Frankfurter's words, "the benefit of a prior judgment, on vexing and ambiguous facts, by an expert administrative agency."[27]

Second is the fact that Congress in enacting the statute did not see fit to exhaust its constitutional power over commerce. By failing to make the Wages and Hours Act applicable to all employment "affecting commerce," Congress prevented the Court from using the Wagner or Sherman Act precedents. In FLSA cases it had to be established to the satisfaction of the courts in each instance that the employees involved were engaged "in commerce" or "in the production of goods for commerce."

Application of these statutory standards required the drawing of some rather fine lines. Since type of work done by the employee, and not the nature of the

[27] *10 East 40th Street* v. *Callus* (1945).

employer's business, determines coverage, it was possible for an employer to have some workers who were covered and others who were not. Thus an examination of the nature of the duties of individual employees and their relation to interstate commerce or the production of goods for commerce was usually required to settle a disputed case. The original act specified that "an employee shall be deemed to have been engaged in the production of goods if such an employee was engaged . . . in any process or occupation necessary to the production thereof, in any State." Because the Court tended to interpret this language as authorizing a fairly broad coverage of fringe workers,[28] Congress in 1949 amended the statute to apply only to workers "directly essential" to production. In 1961 another amendment expanded the act's coverage to every employee "in an enterprise engaged in commerce or in the production of goods for commerce," thus liquidating the necessity to distinguish among employees in the same enterprise.[29] The amendment included as "enterprises" hospitals and schools, whether public or private, a provision upheld in *Maryland v. Wirtz* (1968) against charges that such use of the commerce clause violated state sovereignty.[30]

Agricultural Regulation

The initial New Deal effort to handle the farm problem by invoking the federal taxing power was defeated by the Court in the *Butler* decision. Congress soon found a stopgap after *Butler* in soil conservation, for which farm payments similar to those of the unconstitutional production control program were available. As a more permanent approach, Congress turned to marketing controls. The Agricultural Marketing Act of 1937, under which milk marketing agreements were set up to control prices in the major milksheds of the country, was held constitutional by the Court in two 1939 decisions involving the New York and Boston areas. The Court said that since most of the milk under agreements moved in interstate commerce and the intrastate milk was inextricably mixed with interstate milk, the regulation of prices of all milk in these markets was a valid exercise of the commerce power.[31]

The Agricultural Adjustment Act of 1938 utilized a new control device, marketing quotas. In 1939 such quotas on tobacco marketing were upheld by the Court in *Mulford* v. *Smith*. The Court emphasized that the statute did not purport to limit production but merely to control the sales of tobacco in interstate commerce so as to prevent the flow of commerce from causing harm. But how tenuous a relationship to interstate commerce the Court was willing to accept was dramatically demonstrated in *Wickard* v. *Filburn* (1942). Here a farmer raising 23 acres of wheat, none of it intended for interstate commerce since all was to be consumed on the farm or

---

[28] See *Kirschbaum* v. *Walling* (1942); *Borden Co.* v. *Borella* (1945); *Martino* v. *Michigan Window Cleaning Co.* (1946).

[29] The amendment also provided that any company doing an annual business in excess of 1 million dollars was engaged in interstate commerce for purposes of the act.

[30] But in an unexpected five to four decision, *National League of Cities* v. *Usery* (1976) overruled *Wirtz* and held federal wage and hour requirements for state and municipal employees unconstitutional on the *Hammer* v. *Dagenhart* theory that the commerce power is limited by state "sovereignty."

[31] *United States* v. *Rock Royal Cooperative* (1939); *Hood & Sons* v. *United States* (1939). See also *United States* v. *Wrightwood Dairy Co.* (1942).

fed to stock, was held to have such an effect on interstate commerce as to be liable to the marketing penalties imposed by the act of 1938.

As Justice Jackson recognized, the Court, in spite of the "great latitude" permitted to the commerce power in its post-1937 decisions, had not yet held that production might be regulated "where no part of the product is intended for interstate commerce or intermingled with the subjects thereof." Now in *Wickard* v. *Filburn* it was prepared to do so, and Jackson's justification of this result is the high-water mark of commerce clause expansionism. The guiding principle is that, "even if appellee's activity be local and though it may not be regarded as commerce, it may still, whatever its nature, be reached by Congress if it exerts a substantial economic effect on interstate commerce, and this irrespective of whether such effect is what might at some earlier time have been defined as 'direct' or 'indirect.' "[32]

Navigable Streams and Federal Power Projects

Another important area of congressional interest concerns navigable waters and the hydroelectric power derived from them. Here the basic decision is *United States* v. *Appalachian Electric Power Co.* (1940). The Federal Water Power Act of 1920 made it unlawful to construct a dam for water power development in a navigable water of the United States without first securing a license from the Federal Power Commission. This license controls service, rates, and profits of the licensee, and provides for recapture of the project by the government after fifty years on payment of the net investment therein.

In the *Appalachian* case the contention was that the New River in West Virginia was not navigable, and that even it it were, the government had no right to impose the conditions set forth in the license, since most of them had nothing to do with navigation or its protection. The Court held that the New River was navigable and announced a revised test of navigability which greatly increased federal authority. The Court also held that the government's power over navigable waters was not restricted to control relating to navigation. The power being exercised was the commerce power, of which navigation is only a part. "Flood protection, watershed development, recovery of the cost of improvements through utilization of power are likewise parts of commerce control. . . . Navigable waters are subject to national planning and control in the broad regulation of commerce granted the Federal Government."

Of course the federal government may itself build dams in navigable streams under its commerce power. Attempts to question the legitimacy of and the motives behind the construction of federal multiple-purpose dams where power generation was an important factor have uniformly failed. The Boulder Canyon Project Act of 1928 was upheld in *Arizona* v. *California* (1931). The constitutionality of the TVA power-development program was supported by a federal trial court in 1938 against an attack by eighteen private power companies, but the Supreme Court found it unnecessary to pass on the constitutional issue, holding that the utilities had suf-

---

[32] The constitutionality of the Wholesome Meat Act of 1967, providing for federal regulation of meat plants selling intrastate, was never questioned.

fered no legal injury from TVA activities and consequently had no ground for bringing the suit.[33]

The Sherman Act

The breadth of the commerce clause has also been demonstrated in Sherman Act prosecutions. In 1942 the Department of Justice secured indictments against an underwriters' association which represented a membership of nearly two hundred fire insurance companies, charging conspiracy to fix rates and monopolize trade and commerce. This prosecution challenged a famous Supreme Court decision dating back to 1869, *Paul* v. *Virginia*, which had held that the writing of insurance was a local activity, not interstate commerce. "These contracts are not articles of commerce in any proper meaning of the word." the Court said. The effect of the decision was to uphold a state law requiring insurance companies not incorporated in the state to secure a license and deposit bonds with the state treasurer before doing business in the state.

On the basis of this decision, the insurance business developed into one of gigantic proportions in the nation while retaining constitutionally its local status. But in *United States* v. *South-Eastern Underwriters Assn.* (1944), the Supreme Court terminated this anomalous situation. Justice Black, speaking for a four-judge majority, started by noting that *Paul* v. *Virginia* and all the other precedents holding insurance business not to be commerce were cases where the validity of state statutes had been at issue, and the question had been the extent to which the commerce clause might automatically deprive states of the power to regulate insurance. It was in these circumstances that the Court had consistently upheld state regulatory authority. The *South-Eastern* case was the first in which the Court had been asked to pass on the applicability of a federal statute to companies doing an interstate insurance business.

Coming at the problem from this angle, an entirely different line of precedents became applicable. All the cases in which the transportation or movement across state lines of lottery tickets, stolen automobiles, kidnapped persons, and the like, had been held to be interstate commerce and subject to federal regulation were the controlling authorities. If activities of these variegated sorts were interstate commerce, then Black felt that "it would indeed be difficult now to hold that no activities of any insurance company can ever constitute interstate commerce." Although a contract of insurance might not in itself be interstate commerce, the entire transaction of which it is a part is a chain of events crossing state boundaries. "No commercial enterprise of any kind which conducts its activities across state lines has been held to be wholly beyond the regulatory power of Congress under the Commerce Clause. We cannot make an exception of the business of insurance."[34]

---

[33] *Tennessee Electric Power Co.* v. *T.V.A.* (1939). See also *Oklahoma ex rel. Phillips* v. *Guy Atkinson Co.* (1941).

[34] After this decision Congress passed a statute permitting the states to continue to regulate and tax the insurance business, and exempted it from any federal statutes, with the exception of the Sherman Act and three others. The Supreme Court upheld this statute in *Prudential Insurance Co.* v. *Benjamin* (1946) and *Robertson* v. *California* (1946).

In *Goldfarb* v. *Virginia State Bar* (1975), the Court held that minimum fee schedules for legal

The Court did, however, make a wholly illogical exception for organized baseball. In *Flood* v. *Kuhn* (1972), baseball's reserve clause, under which the club first signing a player has continuing and exclusive right to his services, was upheld. Baseball had been given exemption from the antitrust laws in two earlier decisions.[35] *Flood* conceded that baseball was obviously interstate commerce but ruled that the long-standing exemption it had enjoyed from the Sherman Act was an "established aberration" in which Congress had acquiesced and which Congress, not the Court, would have to correct.[36]

It should be noted that the language of the Sherman Act, which forbids all conduct "in restraint of trade or commerce among the several states," is broader than that in other trade regulation statutes such as the Clayton and Robinson-Patman Acts, which make illegal certain price discriminatory and anticompetitive practices "in commerce." The Burger Court in its 1974 term relied on this statutory difference to hold that one of the largest suppliers of janitorial services in the country and a provider of paving materials for interstate highways were not "in commerce" and so were not covered by these two statutes.[37]

The Commerce Clause and Civil Rights

In a 1946 decision sustaining the "death sentence" provision of the Public Utility Holding Company Act, the Supreme Court said: "The federal commerce power is as broad as the economic needs of the nation."[38] Recent experience has shown that it is also as broad as the social needs. In the Civil Rights Act of 1964 Congress undertook to ban racial discrimination in public accommodations throughout the country. The constitutional foundations for the statute were the commerce clause and the equal protection clause. However, in *Heart of Atlanta Motel, Inc.* v. *United States* (1964) and *Katzenbach* v. *McClung* (1964), the Supreme Court found the commerce clause alone fully adequate to support the statute.

The act applied to three classes of business establishments—inns, hotels, and motels; restaurants and cafeterias; and theaters and motion picture houses—if their operations "affect commerce." The act defined what it meant by affecting commerce. Any inn, motel, or other establishment which provides lodging to transient guests affects commerce per se. Restaurants and cafeterias affect commerce if they serve interstate travelers or if a substantial portion of the food they serve or products they sell have "moved in commerce." Motion picture houses and theaters affect commerce if they customarily present films or performances which "move in commerce."

---

services relating to residential real estate transactions, published and enforced by the organized bar, constituted price fixing in violation of the Sherman Act. Interstate commerce was sufficiently affected for Sherman Act purposes in that significant amounts of funds furnished for financing purchase of homes came from outside the state. See also *Hospital Bldg. Co.* v. *Trustees of Rex Hospital* (1976).

[35] *Federal Baseball Club* v. *National League* (1922); *Toolson* v. *New York Yankees* (1953).

[36] Other sports do not enjoy this exemption. See *United States* v. *International Boxing Club* (1955); *Radovich* v. *National Football League* (1957).

[37] *United States* v. *American Building Maintenance Industries* (1975) and *Gulf Oil Corp.* v. *Copp Paving Company* (1974).

[38] *American Power & Light Co.* v. *SEC* (1946). The "death sentence" was a statutory requirement that holding companies be simplified and reorganized, and their operations limited to those of an integrated public utility system.

The two 1964 test cases were brought by an Atlanta motel and a Birmingham restaurant. The Court, noting that it was applying principles "first formulated by Chief Justice Marshall in *Gibbons* v. *Ogden*," unanimously upheld the act as applied to both. Only two questions need be asked, said Justice Clark for the Court: did Congress have a rational basis for finding that racial discrimination by places of public accommodation affected commerce; and were the means it selected to eliminate that evil reasonable and appropriate? The answer to both was in the affirmative. The fact that Congress was using the commerce power to legislate against "moral wrongs" was irrelevant so far as the constitutional foundation for the enactment was concerned.[39]

The commerce-based Civil Rights Act of 1964 also provided in Title VII against discrimination in employment and created the Equal Employment Opportunity Commission. The Equal Pay Act of 1963 forbade discrimination in compensation on the basis of sex. The Civil Rights Act of 1968 in Title VIII prohibited discrimination on the basis of race, color, religion, or national origin in the sale or rental of housing.

In the 1968 Civil Rights Act Congress demonstrated that the commerce power could be employed to restrain as well as to protect civil rights. Reacting to the 1967 riots in the cities and the apparent connection with the disturbances of traveling radicals and "black power" agitators, Congress attached a rider to the 1968 statute making it a federal crime to use the facilities of interstate commerce or to cross state lines for the purpose of inciting a riot or violence.[40]

*   *   *

In 1976 the only cloud on the federal commerce power was that cast by the Burger Court's ruling in *National League of Cities* v. *Usery*. Here Rehnquist sought to revive the long discredited notion that the commerce power is limited by the reserved powers of the states under the Tenth Amendment, writing: "There are attributes of sovereignty attaching to every state government which may not be impaired by Congress, not because Congress may lack an affirmative grant of legislative authority to reach the matter but because the Constitution prohibits it from exercising the authority in that manner." He thought that if Congress could determine wage and hour standards for state employees, "there would be little left of the state's separate and independent existence." This ruling, which Brennan called "mischievous," marked the first time the Court had struck down major congressional economic legislation since the judicial attack on the New Deal in the 1930s, and it seemed likely, if it survived, to have only limited applicability.

---

[39] The statute was successfully invoked in *Daniel* v. *Paul* (1969) against a segregated amusement park in Arkansas which claimed to be a private club but sold "memberships" for 25 cents. The Court held that the act applied because the "club" advertised for patronage from an audience which the management knew included interstate travelers and because the food served moved in interstate commerce. See generally Paul R. Benson, Jr., *The Supreme Court and the Commerce Clause, 1937–1970* (New York: Dunnellen, 1971).

[40] Violation of this statute was charged in the 1969 prosecution of the Chicago Seven for disturbances at the 1968 Chicago Democratic convention. See discussion in Chap. 20.

Chapter 13

The Commerce Power
and the States

In the Republic's early years, Congress, which admittedly possessed regulatory power over commerce among the states, generally failed to exercise it or used it very incompletely. The states, on the other hand, were continually adopting legislation which, intentionally or not, touched interstate commerce. It then became the duty of the Supreme Court to decide whether the Constitution left room for the states to exercise those controls, or whether regulatory power belonged exclusively to Congress. The Court is now in the second century of its wrestling with these issues, and no end is in sight.

THE EXCLUSIVENESS ISSUE

Whether and to what extent the commerce power is an exclusive power of Congress was a major focus of Marshall's three discussions concerning the commerce clause. In *Gibbons* v. *Ogden* (1824) New York State had clearly undertaken to assert authority over interstate navigation using New York waters. In *Brown* v. *Maryland* (1827) the state had levied a rather heavy license tax on importers of foreign articles and had forbidden them to sell the goods they imported until they paid the tax. In *Willson* v. *Black-Bird Creek Marsh Co.* (1829) a dam built across a navigable creek under authority of a Delaware law had been broken by a vessel. When the owners of the dam brought an action of trespass against the owner of the vessel, he defended on the ground that the creek was a navigable highway which had been unlawfully obstructed by the dam.

After Marshall, problems of similar character came before the Taney Court. In *The License Cases* (1847) liquor purchased in one state was sold in another state without the vendor's obtaining the license required by law in the state of sale. *The Passenger Cases* (1849) arose when New York and Massachusetts imposed on masters of ships coming into the state from foreign ports a tax for each passenger aboard, the proceeds of which were used to defray the costs of examining passengers for contagious diseases and to maintain a hospital for those found to be diseased.

The Concurrent Power Theory

Judicial discussion in this series of cases developed several theories of exclusiveness in federal-state relations under the commerce clause. The first may be called the theory of "concurrent power." According to this view no field of regulation was exclusively reserved to Congress by the commerce clause. Both Congress and the states had authority to range over the entire field of commerce. The only limitation on state power to regulate commerce was the supremacy clause of Article VI; that is, a federal statute would definitely displace any conflicting state statute. In the absence of such conflicting legislation, the states would be free to go as far as they liked.

This argument was made on behalf of the state in *Gibbons* v. *Ogden.* It was contended that the state had the regulatory power prior to the adoption of the Constitution, and that it was retained by the Tenth Amendment. The affirmative grant of regulatory power to Congress did not oust the states, "unless in its own nature . . . the continued exercise of it by the former possessor is inconsistent with the grant," which was alleged not to be the case here. To support the concurrent theory, the analogy of the taxing power was used. The Constitution gives Congress power to lay and collect taxes, but this grant clearly does not interfere with the exercise of the same power by the states. Why does not the same situation prevail with respect to the commerce power?

Marshall met this argument head on and refuted it. The commerce and taxing powers are similar neither in their terms nor their nature.

> The power of taxation . . . is a power which, in its own nature, is capable of residing in, and being exercised by, different authorities at the same time. . . . When, then, each government exercises the power of taxation, neither is exercising the power of the other. But, when a State proceeds to regulate commerce with foreign nations, or among the several States, it is exercising the very power that is granted to Congress, and is doing the very thing which Congress is authorized to do.

The Dormant Power Theory

At the opposite pole from the concurrent power doctrine was the so-called "dormant power" theory. Where the former gave maximum range to state authority, the latter reduced state power to a minimum. Stated succinctly, the dormant view was that the grant of commerce power to Congress, even though unexercised by Congress, necessarily prevented the states from regulating commerce and invalidated any regulations which impinged on commerce.

Justice Johnson's concurring opinion in *Gibbons* v. *Ogden* forthrightly adopted this view; New York's action in granting a monopoly affecting interstate commerce was invalid whether or not there was conflicting legislation by Congress, he contended. But Marshall avoided taking a position on the issue. In discussing state power, he said, "we may dismiss . . . the inquiry, whether it is surrendered by the mere grant to congress, or is retained until congress shall exercise the power. We may dismiss that inquiry because it has been exercised, and the regulations which congress deemed it proper to make, are now in full operation." In the *Black-Bird* case there was, in Marshall's view, no conflicting federal act (though actually Willson's vessel was licensed under the same federal statute as Gibbons's boat had been), but again Marshall avoided deciding that the state act authorizing damming of a navigable creek was "repugnant to the power to regulate commerce in its dormant state" by holding that the state power being used was the police power rather than the commerce power.

Thus the dormant power theory won no explicit official endorsement from the Court, but at the same time it was not definitively rejected, as the concurrent notion had been. So it continued to figure in Supreme Court discussions. It was avowed by part of the Court in *The License Cases* (1847), where the justices were so badly split that no opinion for the Court was possible. Two years later in *The Passenger Cases* (1849), the dormant power theory finally achieved a victory as the Court held state taxing power to have been abridged "by mere affirmative grants of power to the general government." This was Taney's characterization of the opinion, and naturally he protested it, saying: "I cannot foresee to what it may lead." Actually it led nowhere, for in another three years the dormant doctrine was abandoned by every member of the Court except one in the great case of *Cooley* v. *Port Wardens of Philadelphia* (1852). Before we get to that point, however, we must trace the fortunes of still another unsuccessful doctrine of the period.

The Mutual Exclusiveness Theory

This third theory is that of "mutual exclusiveness." The defeat of the concurrent doctrine in the *Gibbons* case had established that there must be some degree of exclusiveness in the congressional commerce power, some areas of regulation from which the states were excluded. The question was, how much exclusiveness, and how was it to be determined? One possible answer was that the field of commercial regulation was divided into two parts by a definite line. On one side of the line the federal government could regulate; the other side belonged to the states; each had to keep out of the other's territory. Their powers, in short, were mutually exclusive.

Marshall seemed in the *Gibbons* case to mark off a sphere of regulation belonging exclusively to the states. He referred there to "that immense mass of legislation, which embraces everything within the territory of a State, not surrendered to a general government." Becoming more specific, he alleged that "inspection laws, quarantine laws, health laws of every description, as well as laws for regulating the internal commerce of a state, and those which respect turnpike roads, ferries, etc., are component parts of this mass. No direct general power over these objects is granted to congress; and, consequently, they remain subject to state legislation."

Similarly, though he did not state it so clearly, Marshall appeared to argue that Congress had exclusive jurisdiction over its sphere, and thus neither the state nor the nation could exercise the powers of the other. But then he very cleverly recaptured for the federal government much of the authority which he had appeared to give away to the states. "It is obvious," he says, "that the government of the Union, in the exercise of its express powers . . . may use means that may also be employed by a State, in the exercise of its acknowledged powers." In other words, to regulate commerce among the states it may be necessary to regulate commerce within a state. Thus he grafted onto his talk about mutually exclusive state and national powers what Crosskey calls the "doctrine of inevitable concurrency as to the means of their execution."[1] But of course this confusion made no difference, because Marshall decided the case on the quite different ground of collision between a state and a federal act.

This strange performance may make some sense if we note that mutual exclusiveness was Jeffersonian doctrine, put forward to protect state claims in opposition to federal power. Marshall may have felt that he could best restrain this view by appearing to accept it while at the same time smothering its impact in a welter of words. In the *Black-Bird* case he continued his apparent tactics of mollification of states' rights sentiment without yielding up the substance of federal power. State authorization of the dams was justified, Marshall said, by "the circumstances of the case." The legislative aims were the draining of swamps, with consequent improvement of health and enhancement of property values. Thus it was action taken under the state's police power, not a regulation of commerce, that was involved, and there was no need to avow or disavow mutual exclusiveness. It was not until the *Cooley* discussion in 1852 that the Court definitely rejected mutual exclusiveness, its suport by that time having dwindled, as in the case of the dormant power theory, to one member of the Court.

The Selective Exclusiveness Theory

The winner in this doctrinal conflict was the theory of "selective exclusiveness." Interestingly enough, this was precisely the view Webster had urged on the Court in his original *Gibbons* argument. His contention there was "that the power of Congress to regulate commerce was complete and entire, and, to a certain extent, necessarily exclusive." By this he meant that some, but not all, areas of commercial regulation were absolutely foreclosed to the states by the constitutional grant of power to Congress. Who would decide in which areas Congress had exclusive power? Presumably that would fall to the Supreme Court. Marshall knew that if he agreed with Webster, he would have to claim for the Court a breadth of discretion-

[1] W. W. Crosskey, *Politics and the Constitution in the History of the United States* (Chicago: The University of Chicago Press, 1953), p. 695.

ary power which was bound to be unpopular with the Jeffersonians. It was perhaps for this reason that he failed to adopt straight-forwardly Webster's doctrine of selective exclusiveness, but sought to achieve much the same result by the devious route of mutual exclusiveness plus inevitable concurrency in means of execution.

In any case, Webster was finally vindicated by *Cooley* v. *Port Wardens of Philadelphia* (1852). A state act of 1803 provided that ships in the port of Philadelphia arriving from or bound to any foreign port must engage a local pilot. Failure to do so would result in a fine equal to half the cost of pilotage, payable to the board of wardens of the port to the use of a fund for superannuated pilots and their dependents. By an act of 1789 Congress had in effect adopted all then-existing state harbor regulations and provided that pilots should continue to be regulated in conformity "with such laws as the States may respectively hereafter enact for the purpose, until further legislative provision shall be made by Congress."

Justice Curtis, writing the Court's opinion, was confronted first of all with the necessity of finally deciding one way or the other on the dormant power theory. For if the mere grant of the commercial power to Congress *ipso facto* deprived the states of all power to regulate pilots, then Congress could not confer on the states the power thus to legislate, and the act of 1789 would be void. So the Court had to start from first principles.

> The grant of commercial power to congress does not contain any terms which expressly exclude the States from exercising an authority over its subject-matter. If they are excluded, it must be because the nature of the power, thus granted to congress, requires that a similar authority should not exist in the States. . . . But when the nature of a power like this is spoken of . . . it must be intended to refer to the subjects of that power, and to say they are of such a nature as to require exclusive legislation by congress.

Thus Curtis shifted gears from the theoretical problem of the "nature" of the commerce power to the pragmatic examination of the "subjects" of that power. In this real world Curtis's first observation was that the subjects of regulation are "exceedingly various" and "quite unlike in their nature." Such heterogeneity of subjects quickly led Curtis to conclude that the rules by which they were regulated must be similarly adaptable. Whereas "some imperatively demand . . . a single uniform rule, operating equally on the commerce of the United States in every port," others "as imperatively demand . . . that diversity, which alone can meet the local necessities."

This analysis clearly doomed the dormant power theory, and Curtis wrote its epitaph in these words: "It is the opinion of a majority of the court that the mere grant to congress of the power to regulate commerce, did not deprive the States of power to regulate pilots." Instead, Curtis accepted the principle of selective exclusiveness as the Court's rule for the future, in these two pregnant sentences:

> Either absolutely to affirm, or deny that the nature of this power requires exclusive legislation by congress, is to lose sight of the nature of the subjects of this power, and to assert concerning all of them, what is really applicable but to a part. Whatever subjects

of this power are in their nature national, or admit only of one uniform system, or plan of regulation, may justly be said to be of such a nature as to require exclusive legislation by congress.

Subjects lacking in these characteristics, by the same token, were not within the exclusive power of Congress. Pilotage laws, Curtis concluded, were in this latter category.

The Act of 1789 contains a clear and authoritative declaration by the first congress, that the nature of this subject is such, that until congress should find it necessary to exert its power, it should be left to the legislation of the States; that it is local and not national; that it is likely to be best provided for, not by one system, or plan of regulation, but by as many as the legislative discretion of the several States should deem applicable to the local peculiarities of the ports within their limits.

The *Cooley* decision marks the end of the formative period for constitutional theory on federal-state relations under the commerce clause. From this period certain basic principles emerged. First, the commerce clause, by its own force and effect, gave Congress exclusive power to regulate certain kinds of commerce and voided any state infringement on those areas.

Second, the rule developed by the Court conceded that there were areas where commerce among the states or with foreign nations might constitutionally be regulated by the states. Marshall had sought to leave room for such state action by giving it another name—regulation of a "police" character. This was sheer quibbling, which Taney properly exposed in *The License Cases*.

Third, in the determination of this question of constitutional power, the Supreme Court was to be an active participant. True, the grant of regulatory power is to Congress. But Congress gives its attention to commerce only sporadically, whereas the Court is continuously on tap. For well over a century since *Cooley* it has consistently performed the role of umpire, enforcing the laws of Congress against conflicting state laws, invalidating state statutes discriminating against commerce, and determining whether the states are entering fields belonging to the national government under the Constitution.

STATE REGULATION AND COMMERCE

Thomas Reed Powell used to say that he could easily state the principles of the commerce clause in three sentences: "Congress may regulate interstate commerce. The states may also regulate interstate commerce, but not too much. How much is too much is beyond the scope of this statement."[2] The Supreme Court cannot evade the question of "how much is too much" that easily. In fact, this is precisely the issue it has faced in literally hundreds of cases since *Cooley* was decided.

In these federal-state commercial controversies, the decisions are complicated and often seem contradictory. It is hard to derive understandable principles out of

[2] Thomas Reed Powell, *Vagaries and Varieties in Constitutional Interpretation* (New York: Columbia University Press, 1956), p. ix.

the welter of factual situations with which the Court has dealt. Admittedly the issues are complex, but it must be frankly recognized that part of the confusion results from the fact that the judicial decisions have reflected, in Justice Rutledge's words, "not logic alone, but large choices of policy, affected . . . by evolving experience of federalism."[3]

It is easy to say that the conflict has been between a nationalism as represented by Marshall and the states' rights interests which Taney symbolized. But these are labels which do little toward promoting an understanding of judicial motivation over the years. Nearly all the members of the Court have been nationalists in the sense that they knew the economic history of the Confederation and were resolved to prevent fractionalization of American commerce or the setting up of trade barriers around each state.

But a nationalist view on the question of state regulation of commerce may be motivated, not by concern for an unobstructed national market, but by a laissez-faire hostility toward business regulation or taxation in general. If these motives are involved, then there may be a liberal-conservative tinge to the decisions, and the judicial lineups may seem somewhat confused. In the preceding chapter, the liberal position was that of justifying a broad extend of federal power under the commerce clause, as against conservative restrictions on federal regulatory authority. But in these federal-state conflicts, the liberal doctrine has called for limiting the inhibitions which the federal commerce clause imposes on the states, while the conservative has emphasized federal power as a limitation on state regulation or taxation.

Take the case of *Di Santo* v. *Pennsylvania* (1927). Pennsylvania required that persons selling steamship tickets to or from foreign countries had to be licensed. Filing of a bond was involved, and a showing that the person was actually an agent for steamship companies. The law was plainly designed to prevent fraud on the public, but the Court majority struck it down as a regulation of foreign commerce, over the dissent of Holmes, Brandeis, and Stone. It is fairly clear that the decision did not register an intent to protect commerce, but simply distaste for all business regulation. In *California* v. *Thompson* (1941) a liberalized Court overruled the *Di Santo* decision, and in numerous other cases made it evident that its dominant motive was to clear the channels for a reasonable amount of state regulation or revenue.

State Regulation in the Absence of Federal Legislation

Turning to the cases, it is helpful to divide them into two categories. First we may consider those in which state legislation impinging on commerce among the states is challenged and there is no conflicting federal legislation. Here the alleged conflict is directly with the commerce clause, and the Court must decide whether state regulation is consistent with the area of free trade carved out by the Constitution itself.

In such situations the Court may conclude that the state regulation is either valid or invalid. A holding of validity will be basically on the grounds developed by Curtis in the *Cooley* decision, namely, that the problem is essentially a local one in

---

[3] *Prudential Insurance Co.* v. *Benjamin* (1946).

which there is no necessity for a uniform national rule. The case of *Bob-Lo Excursion Co.* v. *Michigan* (1948) well illustrates this situation. The Michigan civil rights act had been invoked against a Detroit amusement park company which operated an excursion steamer to an island on the Canadian side of the Detroit River. The company had refused to transport a black girl to the island, and in court the defense was that the state law could have no applicability to foreign commerce. The Supreme Court majority, however, held that this commerce was only technically foreign, and was in fact "highly local," the island being "economically and socially, though not politically, an amusement adjunct of the city of Detroit." Moreover, there was nothing in the Michigan law "out of harmony, much less inconsistent, with our federal policy in the regulation of commerce between the two countries." The Court concluded: "It is difficult to imagine what national interest or policy, whether of securing uniformity in regulating commerce, affecting relations with foreign nations or otherwise, could reasonably be found to be adversely affected by applying Michigan's statute to these facts or to outweigh her interest in doing so."

Commonly associated with the assertion that the situation is essentially local is the supporting rationalization that the state law constitutes no burden on commerce. Even where a law does have some clearly burdening effects, it may still be rescued by showing that the burden falls uniformly on the commerce affected without discrimination in favor of any group or locality. An interesting example of this position is found in *South Carolina Highway Department* v. *Barnwell Brothers* (1938).

South Carolina law prohibited on the highways of that state motor trucks and trailers wider than 90 inches and heavier than 20,000 pounds. These limits were substantially stricter than those in adjacent states, so that trucks meeting legal requirements elsewhere might not be able to operate in South Carolina. A general federal statute regulated interstate trucks, but it did not cover size and weight. In these circumstances the Court permitted the state law to stand. The "essentially local" requirement of the *Cooley* case was met. "Few subjects of state regulation," said Justice Stone, "are so peculiarly of local concern as is the use of state highways." Certainly the statute imposed a burden on commerce, but it fell on all truckers equally. If there had been any evidence that the state was seeking to favor its own citizens, the result would probably have been different.[4]

When the Court majority tips the scale in the other direction, and state legislation is invalidated, the discussion usually still follows the line of the *Cooley* case, but the answers are different. The Court finds that in the particular situation, unless a national, uniform rule is enforced, the burden on commerce will be too serious to be borne. Again, the best way of getting a sense of the argument is to give examples.

In *Southern Pacific Co.* v. *Arizona* (1945), Arizona had passed a train-length law prohibiting operation within the state of trains more than fourteen passenger cars or seventy freight cars in length. The statute was justified as a safety measure, the hazards to trainmen from "slack action" being allegedly greater on longer trains.

---

[4] A New Mexico newspaper and radio station were enjoined from accepting or publishing within the state a Texas optometrist's advertising, under a state law forbidding price advertising on eyeglasses. The Court in *Head* v. *New Mexico Board of Examiners* (1963) upheld the statute as a valid exercise of the police power and not discriminatory against interstate commerce or operating to disrupt its uniformity.

The railroad brotherhoods who sponsored the legislation were also perhaps not unmindful of the fact that it would create more jobs. The Court majority concluded that the claims for increased safety were slight and dubious, and were outweighed by the "national interest in keeping interstate commerce free from interferences which seriously impede it and subject it to local regulation which does not have a uniform effect on the interstate train journey which it interrupts." If there was to be regulation of train lengths, the Court indicated that it would have to come from Congress, since national uniformity was "practically indispensable to the operation of an efficient and economical national railway system." There might seem to be some conflict between this decision and *Barnwell Brothers*, but the Court explained that states have a much more extensive control over their highways than over interstate railroads.

In *Morgan* v. *Virginia* (1946) the Virginia law requiring the separation of white and colored passengers on all motor carriers within the state was invalidated so far as it affected buses in interstate travel. Having just asserted in the *Southern Pacific* case that states had unusual powers of control over motor vehicle traffic, the Court now had to make clear that this point had no particular relevance to the present case. The important thing was whether an undue burden would result from permitting local rules to govern seating in interstate buses. The Court held that there would be real disturbances to the comfort of passengers and their freedom of choice in selecting accommodations. "It seems clear to us that seating arrangements for the different races in interstate motor travel require a single, uniform rule to promote and protect national travel."[5]

Bibb v. *Navajo Freight Lines* (1959) saw the Court strike down an Illinois statute requiring plastic contour rear-fender mudguards on trucks operating in the state, and making the conventional mudflap, which is legal in forty-five states, illegal in Illinois. The Court regarded this as a nondiscriminatory but nevertheless unconstitutionally severe burden on commerce.[6]

Where the burden takes the form of a complete obstruction to commerce, then the case against the state regulation involved is very strong indeed. In *Edwards* v. *California* (1941) the Court held unconstitutional a California statute making it a misdemeanor for anyone knowingly to bring or assist in bringing into the state a nonresident "indigent" person.

State Power Where Federal Legislation Exists

Now we turn to situations where Congress has adopted legislation regulating interstate commerce, with which state action is alleged to conflict. The Court's problem in these cases is simpler—to decide whether Congress has completely occupied the field, or whether it has left some room for nonconflicting state legislation. There is

---

[5] In *Colorado Anti-Discrimination Commission* v. *Continental Air Lines* (1963) an airline was charged with violation of the state antidiscrimination act because of refusal to hire a black pilot. The airline contended that the *Morgan* case required interstate carriers to be free from diverse state regulations in the field of racial discrimination. But the Supreme Court held that there was no such need for uniform regulation in this situation, and that the act imposed no undue burden on the airline.

[6] *Great Atlantic & Pacific Tea Co.* v. *Cottrell* (1976) held that Mississippi could not bar Louisiana milk satisfying Mississippi health standards simply because Louisiana had not signed a reciprocity agreement with Mississippi. See also *Dean Milk Co.* v. *City of Madison* (1951).

likely, nevertheless, to be opportunity for considerable difference of opinion even here, since legislative intent is often difficult to appraise.

Perhaps the most interesting group of recent cases concerns those in which state labor laws have been attacked as in conflict with the national labor relations acts.

Most of the cases have gone against the states, on the ground that Congress had preempted the field by its regulatory legislation. An important decision was *Hill* v. *Florida* (1945), where a state statute providing for compulsory licensing of labor union business agents was held to conflict with the purposes of the Wagner Act. State laws interfering with the right to strike, in public utilities as well as in private businesses, have been invalidated.[7]

Similarly, states have been forbidden to enjoin peaceful picketing[8] or to award damages therefor.[9] Relief, by damages or otherwise, has been denied for unfair labor practices.[10] State antitrust laws cannot be used to prevent the effectuation of collective bargaining agreements[11] or to enjoin a strike as a restraint of trade.[12] Since the Railway Labor Act expressly sanctions union shop agreements, a state right-to-work law cannot be invoked to abrogate such agreements.[13] In general, states have not been permitted to duplicate remedies provided by federal legislation.[14]

Perhaps the most important decision upholding state power against federal preemption claims in the labor field was *Allen-Bradley Local* v. *Wisconsin Employment Relations Board* (1942), in which the Court held that federal legislation was not intended to impair a state's powers to punish or in some instances to prevent offensive conduct relating to "such traditionally local matters as public safety and order and the use of streets and highways." In this case state action was approved against mass picketing, threats of physical violence against workers, and obstruction of access to a plant by strikers.[15]

Another significant decision favorable to the states was *DeVeau* v. *Braisted* (1960). The New York–New Jersey waterfront compact, dealing with labor racketeering in New York Harbor, and state legislation implementing it, disqualified felons from holding office in waterfront labor organizations. The Supreme Court held that congressional consent to the compact eliminated any ground for the contention that such regulations conflicted with federal labor legislation, though a minority believed the situation to be indistinguishable from *Hill* v. *Florida*.

This issue of federal preemption and federal-state statutory conflict has been

---

[7] *International Union* v. *O'Brien* (1950); *Amalgamated Association* v. *Wisconsin Employment Relations Board* (1951); *Motor Coach Employees* v. *Missouri* (1963).

[8] *Garner* v. *Teamsters Union* (1953). For a more general treatment of the picketing problem, see Chap. 20.

[9] *San Diego Unions* v. *Garmon* (1957, 1959).

[10] *Guss* v. *Utah Labor Board* (1957).

[11] *Teamsters Union* v. *Oliver* (1959).

[12] *Weber* v. *Anheuser-Busch, Inc.* (1955).

[13] *Railway Employees Department* v. *Hanson* (1956).

[14] *Garner* v. *Teamsters Union* (1953).

[15] See also *United Automobile Workers* v. *Wisconsin Employment Relations Board* (1956). In *Brotherhood of Locomotive Engineers* v. *Chicago R.I & P.R. Co.* (1966) an Arkansas "full-crew" law was upheld against the charge that a 1963 act of Congress had preempted the field.

faced in many fields other than labor relations.[16] An interesting case from another area is *Huron Portland Cement Co.* v. *Detroit* (1960), where the Court upheld a conviction for violation of Detroit's smoke-abatement ordinance by a vessel in the Detroit harbor, even though the ship was operating in interstate commerce and its boiler met the standards of federal legislation.

Congressional Legitimization of State Regulations

There has been a notable line of cases upholding the right of Congress to legitimize state trade barriers where the motivation had general public approval. This technique was first employed to assist states which wished to prohibit the sale of intoxicating liquor. In 1890 the Court ruled in *Leisy* v. *Hardin* that Iowa could not, "in the absence of congressional permission to do so," prevent the first sale in the original package of liquor brought into the state. Within a few months Congress reacted to this decision by passing the Wilson Act rendering intoxicating liquor upon arrival in a state or territory "subject to the operation and effect of the laws of such state or territory enacted in the exercise of its police powers, to the same extent as though such . . . liquors had been produced in such state or territory, and . . . not . . . exempt therefrom by reason of being introduced therein in original packages or otherwise." The Court promptly sustained the validity of this legislation in *In re Rahrer* (1891), saying: "No reason is perceived why, if Congress chooses to provide that certain designated subjects of interstate commerce shall be governed by a rule which divests them of that character at an earlier period of time than would otherwise be the case, it is not within its competency to do so."

Congress then went further, and passed the Webb-Kenyon Act of 1913 over the veto of President Taft, whose Attorney General told him it was unconstitutional. This statute prohibited the shipment of liquor into any state where it was intended to be used in violation of state law. Thus it had the effect of divesting liquor of the protection of its interstate character even before it had begun to move in commerce and before it had come into the state where its illegal use was intended. The Supreme Court upheld the law, saying it was but an extension of the principle of the Wilson Act, for the purpose of "making it impossible for one State to violate the prohibitions of the laws of another through the channels of interstate commerce."[17] The substance and much of the exact language of the Webb-Kenyon Act were subsequently written into the Twenty-first Amendment. "Since that amendment," said Justice Brandeis in 1939, "the right of a State to prohibit or regulate the importation of intoxicating liquor is not limited by the commerce clause."[18]

---

[16] See the discussion of *Pennsylvania* v. *Nelson* (1956), and the preemption controversy to which it gave rise in Congress, in Chap. 4. In *Railroad Transfer Service* v. *Chicago* (1967), involving a transfer service for passengers and baggage between Chicago railroad stations, the Court held that the Interstate Commerce Act had preempted the field and invalidated attempts by the city to require the service to secure a license which gave the city a veto power over its operations.

[17] *Clark Distilling Co.* v. *Western Maryland R. Co.* (1917).

[18] *Finch Co.* v. *McKittrick* (1939). These legislative techniques for divesting liquor of its character as interstate commerce were almost exactly repeated in dealing with the products of convict labor. See *Whitfield* v. *Ohio* (1936) and *Kentucky Whip & Collar Co.* v. *Illinois Central R. R. Co.* (1937).

STATE TAXATION AND THE IMPORTS-EXPORTS CLAUSE

State taxation of commerce presents special problems not met in the preceding discussion of state regulation. For one thing, another provision of the Constitution is here called into play as a supplement to the commerce clause, the imports-exports clause of Article I, section 10. This clause reads, in part: "No state shall, without the consent of Congress, lay any imposts or duties on imports or exports, except what may be absolutely necessary for executing its inspection laws." Another differentiating factor is that, as we saw earlier in this chapter, the taxing power is admittedly a concurrent power, whereas the commerce power is not.

Both the imports-exports clause and the commerce clause were first applied to a state effort to tax foreign commerce in the famous case of *Brown* v. *Maryland* (1827). Here a state act required importers of foreign articles to have a license in order to be able to sell these goods. The state contended that this was an occupational tax, not a tax on imports, but Marshall pierced through this verbiage. "No goods would be imported if none could be sold." However, he recognized that freedom of imports from taxation could not be a perpetual immunity. At some point imports must become assimilated with the general mass of property in a state and subject to state taxation. Marshall suggested the "original package" doctrine for determining when this point was reached:

> It is sufficient for the present to say, generally, that when the importer has so acted upon the thing imported, that it has become incorporated and mixed up with the mass of property in the country, it has, perhaps, lost its distinctive character as an import, and has become subject to the taxing power of the State; but while remaining the property of the importer, in his warehouse, in the original form or package in which it was imported, a tax upon it is too plainly a duty on imports to escape the prohibition in the constitution.

Although Marshall was rather tentative in putting forth the original package doctrine, it proved to have great survival value. For 132 years, as Justice Frankfurter said in 1959, the Court followed the doctrine "without a single deviation." Indeed, in *Hooven & Allison Co.* v. *Evatt* (1945) the Court apparently extended its principle to apply not only to imports for sale, but also to imports for the importer's own use or consumption.

There never was any logical reason, however, to grant imports original package protection from non-discriminatory state taxes. The original purpose of the imports clause was to prevent discrimination against foreign goods, and to bar taxes that would benefit states through which imports first passed at the expense of interior states of final destination and use. In *Michelin Tire Co.* v. *Wages* (1976) the Court finally saw this point and upheld state taxation on all imports, provided such taxes were imposed equally on all goods, foreign and domestic, and were not levied on goods still in transit. Decisions to the contrary, going back to *Low* v. *Austin* (1872), were overruled.

The Twenty-first Amendment, which leaves the states completely unconfined by traditional commerce clause limitations when they restrict the importation of intoxicating liquors for distribution or consumption within their borders, does not repeal the imports-exports clause. Consequently the states are still forbidden to tax liquor imports while in the original package.[19] Similarly, states may not prohibit the sale of untaxed liquor to airline passengers leaving on overseas flights, for delivery to them on arrival at their foreign destination.[20]

STATE TAXATION AND COMMERCE

The Supreme Court has examined the impact of state taxes on interstate commerce in a staggering number of cases, but from the decisions two general principles emerge more or less clearly. First, the Court has generally been resolved that state tax power shall not be used to discriminate against interstate commerce. Second, it has been equally certain that the status of interstate commerce should not be used to permit business operations to escape paying a fair share of local tax burdens. Application of these conflicting principles has been most difficult, partly because of the impossibility of being certain about the final incidence of the disputed taxes.

Implementing the first principle is the rule that property cannot be taxed while it is actually in interstate transit.[21] When interstate transit has terminated, the goods become immediately taxable and the original package gives no protection.[22] However, a tax which falls with intentional discriminatory incidence on goods originating outside the state is unconstitutional.[23]

Robbins v. *Shelby County Taxing District* (1887) ruled that, when delivery of goods was made from outside the state in consequence of a contract of sale entered into within the state, state taxes could not constitutionally be levied.[24] But states have largely plugged this tax loophole by "use" taxes, levied at the same rate as state sales taxes, imposed on the use of goods purchased outside the state.[25]

A state has no power to refuse or tax the privilege of doing an interstate business.[26] But where a corporation is doing both an intrastate and interstate business, the state can levy a privilege tax on the doing of the intrastate business.[27] States may, of course, attempt to do by indirection what they cannot do directly, and they will fail if the Court finds that the company's interstate business is being burdened,[28] but a "franchise" tax has been upheld if it is merely a "just equivalent" of other taxes.[29]

---

[19] *Department of Revenue* v. *James B. Beam Distilling Co.* (1964).

[20] *Hostetter* v. *Idlewild Bon Voyage Liquor Corp.* (1964).

[21] *State Freight Tax Case* (1873). But it may be difficult to determine when interstate transit actually begins: *Coe* v. *Errol* (1886).

[22] *Woodruff* v. *Parham* (1869); *Sonnenborn Bros.* v. *Cureton* (1923).

[23] *Welton* v. *Missouri* (1876).

[24] This rule was followed in *McLeod* v. *Dilworth* (1944), *Freeman* v. *Hewit* (1946), and *Nippert* v. *City of Richmond* (1946).

[25] Upheld in *Henneford* v. *Silas Mason Co.* (1937). For problems in the collection of use taxes, see *Nelson* v. *Sears, Roebuck & Co.* (1941), *General Trading Co.* v. *State Tax Cmsn.* (1944), *Miller Bros.* v. *Maryland* (1954), and *National Bellas Hess, Inc.* v. *Illinois* (1967).

[26] *Crutcher* v. *Kentucky* (1891).

[27] *Pacific Telephone & Telegraph Co.* v. *Tax Cmsn.* (1936).

[28] *Western Union Tel. Co.* v. *Kansas ex rel. Coleman* (1910).

[29] *Railway Express Agency* v. *Virginia* (1959); *Colonial Pipeline Co.* v. *Traigle* (1975).

Where concerns do both local and interstate business, with their property being employed in both types of commerce, various apportionment formulas have been used, which the Supreme Court has approved provided the result was a fair measure for the protection provided by the state.[30] Apportioned taxes based on corporate net income have generally been regarded as not a burden on interstate commerce,[31] but state taxes on corporate gross receipts are more questionable, making possible burdensome "multiple taxation" by all the states in which the corporation did business.[32] However, in *General Motors Corp.* v. *Washington* (1964), a tax measured by gross wholesale sales of motor vehicles and parts in the state, even though unapportioned, was upheld on the ground that taxable local business was so mingled with interstate business that the state was justified in attributing all sales in Washington to its local activity.

The apportionment principle, originating largely in connection with railroad transportation, has not been so directly applicable to navigation and air transport. For vessels the general rule is that they are taxable only at their home port, unless they have acquired actual situs in another state by continuous employment there, and this rule prevents multiple taxation.[33] However, in 1949 the apportionment principle was successfully applied by Louisiana to a barge line operating on the Mississippi.[34] Minnesota was able to utilize a version of the home port theory in winning the Court's approval for a personal property tax on the entire air fleet of Northwest Airlines, a Minnesota corporation, even though only a fraction of the fleet was in the state on tax day.[35]

Taxation of motor vehicles has largely avoided apportionment problems. Every truck entering a state can be charged a toll for its use of state highways, and the only question is whether the tax is within reasonable bounds. Since the basic decision in *Hendrick* v. *Maryland* (1915) comparatively few taxes on motor vehicles have been declared invalid on commerce grounds.[36] A "use and service charge" of $1 for all passengers enplaning at the Evansville, Indiana, airport was upheld by the Court in 1972 as a reasonable charge to help defray the costs of airport construction and maintenance and so not a burden on commerce "in the constitutional sense."[37]

Since the 1930s the Supreme Court has manifested an increased unwillingness to strike down state tax measures on constitutional grounds. Perhaps the initial cause was the desperate financial situation of the states during the Depression, when the Court clearly felt under some compulsion to approve the new taxes developed to save the states from bankruptcy. Another factor was the uncertainty of some justices as to the validity of their credentials as tax umpires. Around 1940 Justices

---

[30] *Western Union Tel. Co.* v. *Massachusetts* (1888); *Pullman's Palace Car Co.* v. *Pennsylvania* (1891).
[31] *Northwestern States Portland Cement Co.* v. *Minnesota* (1959).
[32] *Joseph* v. *Carter & Weekes Stevedoring Co.* (1947).
[33] *Gloucester Ferry Co.* v. *Pennsylvania* (1885); *Old Dominion S.S. Co.* v. *Virginia* (1905).
[34] *Ott* v. *Mississippi Barge Line Co.* (1949).
[35] *Northwest Airlines* v. *Minnesota* (1944).
[36] Examples of taxes upheld are *Aero Mayflower Transit Co.* v. *Georgia Public Service Cmsn.* (1935), *Dixie Ohio Express* v. *State Revenue Cmsn.* (1939), and *Capitol Greyhound Lines* v. *Brice* (1950). Taxes were held unacceptable in *Interstate Transit* v. *Lindsey* (1931) and *Ingels* v. *Morf* (1937).
[37] *Evansville-Vanderburgh Airport Authority District* v. *Delta Airlines* (1972).

Black and Douglas, joined for a time by Frankfurter, revived the Taney doctrine that the responsibility of enforcing the commerce clause involves so much discretion that it belongs more appropriately to Congress.[38] Although this "leave-it-to-Congress" attitude enjoyed some minor successes, the Court soon returned to its role as umpire of the federal system. As Frankfurter said in *Freeman* v. *Hewit* (1946), "The Commerce Clause was not merely an authorization to Congress to enact laws for the protection and encouragement of commerce among the States, but by its own force created an area of trade free from interference by the States."[39]

[38] See Taney's dissent in *Pennsylvania* v. *Wheeling Bridge Co.* (1852); the dissent of Black, Douglas, and Frankfurter in *McCarroll* v. *Dixie Greyhound Lines* (1940); and Black's concurring opinion in *Northwest Airlines* v. *Minnesota* (1944).

[39] See generally Laurence H. Tribe, "Intergovernmental Immunities in Litigation, Taxation, and Regulation: Separation of Powers Issues in Controversies About Federalism," 89 *Harvard Law Review* 682 (1976).

Chapter 14

Qualifications and Election of the President

The creation of the Presidency of the United States by the Constitutional Convention was political invention of a very high order. While there can have been in 1787 no conception of the powerful and multifaceted office which history and practice were to make of the Presidency, the basis was laid for this development by the bold decisions of the Founders.

Their duality of views on the presidential office has already been noted. On one side was the preference for an executive which would be nothing more than an institution for carrying the will of the legislature into effect, with an incumbent appointed by and accountable to the legislature. On the other side was the strong-executive faction, which wanted a single-headed office independent of the legislature. As the Convention deliberated, the key decisions increasingly favored the latter view.

In the controversy over ratification of the Constitution, fear of these strong executive powers was one of the motives most widely exploited by opponents of the new charter. Hamilton in No. 67 of *The Federalist* ridiculed the efforts that had been made to present the office as possessed of practically royal prerogatives. As for the unity of the executive, he contended that far from being a danger, it made the institution more susceptible of popular surveillance and control, while at the same time guaranteeing energy in the office, "a leading character in the definition of good government."

What the "energy" of George Washington and his successors has made of the office cannot be recounted here. Our concern is the much narrower one of examining the basis which the specific provisions of Article II, as judicially interpreted, have provided for the presidential office, and the authority which these provisions have conferred, or the limits they have imposed, upon presidential power. Thus confined, much of the flesh and blood of the Presidency is outside the scope of our consideration. For the Supreme Court has only infrequently been called on to resolve the constitutional issues of the Presidency. Where executive action has impinged on private rights, or occasionally in cases of conflict between the President and Congress, judicial intervention to define the constitutional situation has been successfully invoked. But over the broad political reaches of presidential power the judicial influence has been minor. In the area of the present chapter, which deals with the qualifications and electoral arrangements for the Presidency, judicial interpretation has seldom been important.

QUALIFICATIONS

The Constitution provides that "No person except a natural born citizen, or a citizen of the United States, at the time of the adoption of this Constitution, shall be eligible to the office of President." The clause making eligible persons who were citizens of the United States at the time of the adoption of the Constitution was of only temporary significance, but it was necessary since every adult in the United States in 1787, who had been born in this country, had been born a British subject.

Every person born in the United States and subject to its jurisdiction is a citizen and, of course, a natural-born citizen. Persons born abroad and acquiring citizenship by the process of naturalization are thus excluded from eligibility to the Presidency. But persons born abroad to American citizen parents are considered natural-born American citizens.[1]

The other qualifications of the President as stated in Article II are that he shall have attained the age of thirty-five years, and have been for fourteen years a resident within the United States. Although these are the only constitutional qualifications which must be met for eligibility to the Presidency, in effect Congress has added to them by providing that persons convicted of various federal crimes shall, in addition to other penalties, be incapable of holding office under the United States.

PRESIDENTIAL ELECTION AND THE CONSTITUTION

The Original Plan

The constitutional solution of the problem of presidential selection was to provide that each state should "appoint, in such manner as the legislature thereof may

---

[1] Congress so provided by Act of March 26, 1790, 1 Stat. 415.

direct, a number of electors, equal to the whole number of Senators and Representatives to which the State may be entitled in the Congress." That the electors should not be holders of federal office was guaranteed by the further provision that "no Senator or Representative, or person holding an office of trust or profit under the United States, shall be appointed an elector."

The choosing of the President was thus to be in the hands of a selected group of citizens in each state, equal in number to that state's congressional delegation. But the resemblance to Congress went no further. Instead of assembling in the capital, the electors were to "meet in their respective States, and vote by ballot for two persons, of whom one at least shall not be an inhabitant of the same State with themselves." The results of the vote were to be transmitted to the president of the Senate, who would open the sealed certificates in the presence of both houses, and the votes would then be counted. The person with the greatest number of votes was to be the President, provided he had a majority of the whole number of electors. If two candidates were tied, and both had more than a majority, the House was immediately to choose between them. If no candidate had a majority, then the House would choose from the five highest on the list. In either event the House was to vote by states, "the representation from each State having one vote," with a majority required to elect. After the choice of the President, the person having the next greatest number of votes was to be Vice President, and in the event of a tie, the Senate was to choose between the contenders.

The intention of the framers as to the role of the electors was not entirely clear. Hamilton thought the electors could freely choose candidates for President on the basis of their own judgment and experience, but others have argued that the electoral plan was a step toward, not away from, popular election and that the electors were to be bound by pledges they had given in securing appointment.[2] In any case, the unanimity of agreement on Washington prevented any difficulties arising in the first two elections.

With the development of political parties, the electoral plan was immediately in trouble. The result of the 1796 balloting was to give the Presidency and Vice-Presidency to different parties, with John Adams and Thomas Jefferson ranking first and second in the electoral voting.

This was a minor defect, however, compared with the result in 1800. Jefferson and Aaron Burr, as the Republican candidates for President and Vice President, were both named by each Republican elector, so that a tie resulted. Everyone understood that Jefferson was the Presidential choice, but the tie threw the election into the House, voting by states. It took prolonged balloting before the House finally elected Jefferson in February, 1801.

Problems under the Twelfth Amendment

This experience exposed a constitutional defect so serious that immediate repair was needed. Consequently the Twelfth Amendment was adopted in 1804, and it still

[2] Lucius Wilmerding, Jr., *The Electoral College* (New Brunswick, N.J.: Rutgers University Press, 1958), pp. 19–22.

controls the electoral process. It made the following changes: (1) the electors were to ballot separately for President and Vice President; (2) if no candidate for President received a majority, the House, voting as before by states, was to choose "from the persons having the highest numbers not exceeding three on the list"; (3) the Vice President also had to receive a majority of the electoral votes, and if no one achieved a majority, the Senate was to choose between the two highest candidates; (4) if the choice of President fell to the House, and it had not made a choice by March 4, the Vice President was to act as President; and (5) it was specifically provided that no person constitutionally ineligible to the office of President should be eligible to that of Vice President.

This was an improvement, but the election of 1824 showed how unsatisfactory was the alternative of selection by the House. The breakdown of the congressional caucus in that election caused votes to be cast for a number of candidates, the three highest being Andrew Jackson with ninety-nine, John Quincy Adams, eighty-four, and William H. Crawford, forty-one. Henry Clay, Speaker of the House and one of the defeated candidates, swung the vote to Adams, to the vast outrage of the Jackson forces, who claimed that the House was morally bound to select the candidate with the highest electoral vote. The subsequent development of a mature two-party system kept further electoral difficulties from arising until 1876.

The Hayes-Tilden election controversy was an incredibly tangled affair. The truth seems to be that the Democrats stole the election in the first place, and the Republicans then stole it back. There was no doubt that Tilden, the Democratic candidate, had a popular majority. He was conceded 184 electoral votes, one less than a majority, and Hayes had 165, while 20 were in dispute. Disagreement centered on Louisiana, South Carolina, and Florida, from which rival sets of returns had been sent in amid charges of fraud and violence, and Oregon, where one elector was in dispute. A majority of the Senate was Republican and a majority of the House was Democratic. If the president of the Senate decided which votes to count, Hayes would win, whereas if the election was thrown into the House, Tilden would be elected.

The Twelfth Amendment provides that the president of the Senate should open the certificates, but does not say who should do the counting or decide what votes to count. With the two houses hopelessly deadlocked, a completely extraconstitutional compromise was eventually enacted at the end of January, 1877. A fifteen-man Electoral Commission was created, composed of five members of the House (three Democrats and two Republicans), five Senators (three Republicans and two Democrats), and five members of the Supreme Court. Four of the justices were designated in the act by reference to their judicial circuits, and they were evenly divided as to parties. The fifth justice, chosen by these four, was Joseph P. Bradley of New Jersey, a Republican, whose vote gave the Republicans an eight to seven margin on each of the issues before the Commission, electing Hayes by a vote of 185 to 184.

Thus was the country rescued from the consequences of a faulty electoral system by a device entirely unknown to the Constitution. In 1887 Congress by statute provided that any dispute over appointment of electors was to be conclusively settled by the state itself, provided it did so at least six days before the time for the meeting of the electors. If a state failed to perform this function and its electoral vote remained in dispute, it would not be counted unless both houses of Congress agreed. So the 1876 dilemma need not be reenacted, and no subsequent presidential election has posed the threat of comparable breakdown in electoral machinery. But certain basic characteristics of the electoral college system remain as perennial subjects of controversy.

ELECTORAL COLLEGE PROBLEMS

Distortion of the Popular Vote

The first objection to the electoral college system is the disproportion it usually yields between the electoral vote and the popular vote. The electoral college margin of the winning candidate is typically much greater than his majority in the popular vote. This does no real harm, of course, and may even have some psychological value when it results in giving a clear electoral college majority to a candidate who secured only a plurality in the popular vote.[3]

But electoral college distortion can also have the opposite consequence of deflating a popular vote majority or plurality into an electoral vote minority. In three presidential elections—1824, 1876, and 1888—the winning candidate did not lead in the popular vote. However, in two of these three cases, it is hardly fair to blame the electoral system for the perversion of the popular mandate. In 1824 this responsibility rests on the House for failing to select the popular favorite, Jackson, and similarly in 1876 it was the Electoral Commission which made the decisions that kept Tilden out of office. Thus the 1888 experience, when Harrison was elected with 100,000 fewer popular votes than Cleveland, is the only bona fide case of the electoral college yielding a minority President. Nevertheless, it may well be argued that even one case is one too many, and that the mere existence of such a possibility is a grave defect in an electoral system.

The Unit Vote

Actually, the major reason for this potentiality of electoral miscarriage is not a constitutionally required feature of the electoral system. The primary cause of distortion is the practice (which, with minor exceptions, all states have followed for well over a century) of each state casting its electoral votes as a unit for the candidate securing a majority or plurality of the popular votes in that state, rather than using some plan of proportional division of the electors.

The Constitution does not control the manner in which the states shall "appoint" their electors, and a great variety of means have been employed. In the first

---

[3] On electoral college problems and proposals for reform, see Neal Peirce, *The People's President* (New York: Simon and Schuster, 1967); James David Barber (ed.), *Choosing the President* (Englewood Cliffs, N.J.: Prentice-Hall, Inc., 1974); Lawrence D. Longley and Alan G. Braun, *The Politics of Electoral College Reform* (New Haven, Conn.: Yale University Press, 1972); Wallace S. Sayre and Judith H. Parris, *Voting for President* (Washington, D.C.: The Brookings Institution, 1970); Judith Best, *The Case Against Direct Election of the President* (Ithaca, N.Y.: Cornell University Press, 1975); Nelson W. Polsby and Aaron Wildavsky, *Presidential Elections* (New York: Charles Scribner's Sons, 4th ed., 1975).

three presidential elections, choice of electors by the state legislatures was the usual method. Thereafter popular election became the rule, and at first several states used the district plan, which meant that a state's electoral vote could be divided among the candidates. By 1832, however, all states had abandoned the district plan, and it has since been employed only rarely. With the statewide general ticket system of choosing electors, it is virtually impossible for a split result to occur. No state is likely to abandon the present plan on its own initiative, for a proportional division of its vote while other states retained the block principle would minimize its electoral college importance.

The unit-vote system makes each of the big states, where the parties are usually rather evenly balanced, a glittering jackpot. The parties must give major attention to capturing votes in the large states, where the potential payoff is so great, while largely disregarding the smaller states. The candidates are usually selected from the large states, and the parties must direct their appeals to the interests of their urban and industrial residents. Moreover, with the entire electoral vote of each large state subject to determination by the margin of a few thousand votes, bad weather, fraud, appeals to minority groups, and other fortuitous circumstances may determine the choice of President.

Another effect of the unit-vote system is that it prevents voters who supported the losing candidate in each state from having any impact on the electoral result. Though a candidate may secure only 51 percent of the popular votes, he is awarded the entire electoral vote of the state, and those who opposed him are in effect coerced by the system into supporting him. In 1966 the state of Delaware filed an unusual suit with the Supreme Court in its original jurisdiction, contending that the unit-voting system abridged the political rights of individuals by canceling each state's minority votes, gave the large states a favored position, created the possibility of minority Presidents, and in general guaranteed distortion and debasement in the electoral process. The Supreme Court dismissed the suit.[4]

Other Distorting Factors

The unit system of casting electoral votes is not the only cause of the typical lack of correspondence between the electoral and popular results. There is in addition the overweighting of the electoral vote of the less populous states, which results from giving each state, large or small, two electoral votes on the basis of its two Senators.

A further factor in causing skewed electoral results is the varying rate of voter turnout in the states. In the South, where the real contests until recently were decided in the Democratic primaries, the final elections tended to be routine, attracting relatively few voters. The past disfranchisement of Negro voters in the area also contributed to low turnout, so that in general each electoral vote case by a Southern state represented only a fraction of the voters per electoral vote elsewhere.

Finally, shifts in population and varying rates of population growth among the states between census periods cause additional disproportion between popular and electoral votes. In the election of 1960 each state still cast the number of electoral

---

[4] *Delaware v. New York* (1966).

votes it had been awarded under the census of 1950. Thus California had only thirty-two electoral votes in the 1960 election, whereas her population as shown by the 1960 census would have entitled the state to forty votes.[5]

The Status of Electors

A second disturbing feature of the present system is the status of the electors. Successful operation of the electoral college system requires that the electors regard themselves as automatons, whose sole function is to cast an electoral vote for the candidates of their party. General acceptance of the automatic character of the electors' function is reflected in the fact that their names do not even appear on the ballot in almost three-fourths of the states. However, in recent elections there have been organized efforts in certain Southern states to claim for electors the freedom of choice which presumably was theirs in the original constitutional theory. In part this freedom has been asserted by individual electors. But it has also been claimed by state legislatures which have provided for unpledged slates of electors, under no instructions from the electorate and completely free to vote their own choices in the electoral college.

In 1948 a Democratic elector from Tennesee, who was also on the slate of electors for the States' Rights Dixiecrats, cast his electoral vote for Thurmond instead of Truman. In 1956 one of Alabama's Democratic electors refused to support Stevenson and cast his vote for an Alabama circuit judge.

In 1960 several slates of electors unpledged to any candidate were on state ballots. Georgia's twelve Democratic electors were not pledged to support Kennedy, and only five of Alabama's eleven Democratic electors were so pledged. In Mississippi there were two sets of Democratic electors, one unpledged, while in Louisiana the States' Rights party's electors were unpledged. In the actual balloting the six unpledged Alabama electors and all eight Mississippi electors voted for Senator Harry F. Byrd of Virginia. So did one of the Republican electors from Oklahoma, Henry D. Irwin. After Kennedy's narrow victory at the polls, Irwin and an Alabama attorney made contact with all the victorious electors of both parties urging them to withhold their electoral votes or to vote for a third candidate, in the hope that Kennedy would be deprived of his electoral vote majority and the election be thrown into the House. But the plan failed, and no elector except Irwin violated his pledge. In the 1964 electoral vote there were no defections, but there was one in each of the 1968 and 1972 elections.[6]

Election by the House

A third feature of the present system which is almost universally condemned is the choice of a President by the House, voting by states, in the event that no candidate receives a majority of the electoral vote. Since the Twelfth Amendment has been in effect, this has happened only once, in 1824, and it yielded a result in conflict with the voters' choice. Much more serious results are possible if the experience is ever

---

[5] The same ten-year time lag will affect the 1980 election.

[6] An Alabama statute requiring electors to vote for the nominees of their party was upheld by the Supreme Court in *Ray* v. *Blair* (1952).

repeated, as it very nearly was in 1948. Had Truman lost Ohio and California—and his combined majority in these two states was 25,472 out of 6,700,000 votes cast— the election would have been thrown into the House, because of the success of the third-party candidate in four states.

In the House as constituted on January 3, 1949, twenty-one state delegations had a Democratic majority, twenty had a Republican majority, three were evenly divided, and four represented states carried by the States' Rights ticket. It is hard to overestimate the turmoil which would have been involved in getting twenty-five of these delegations to agree on Truman, Dewey, or Thurmond in the short period from January 3 to noon of January 20, the hour when the new President's term was to begin. If no President had been selected by that time, then the Vice President, chosen from between Alben Barkley and Earl Warren by the Senate, which had fifty-four Democrats, would have begun to act as President.

Again, in 1960 a shift of only a few thousand votes in key states carried by Kennedy with narrow margins would have left him, as well as Nixon, without an electoral college majority and enabled the Byrd electors to throw the choice of President into the House. In 1968, for the first time in history, there was a complete slate of electors for three candidates in every state. George Wallace hoped to throw the election into the House, but though he received 9.9 million votes (13.5 percent) and though there was a difference of only 500,000 votes between Nixon and Humphrey, the luck of the electoral college translated Nixon's 43.4 percent of the popular vote into 56 percent (302 votes) of the electoral total.

PROPOSALS FOR ELECTORAL REFORM

Reform of the electoral college system has been perennially discussed, but the difficulty of taking action has always been that there was no consensus on an alternative. A principal reason for this inability to agree on any change in the electoral arrangements is that, in spite of the defects pointed out above, many persons feel, with considerable justification, that the present system has worked reasonably well. It has produced Chief Executives comparable in quality, if not generally superior, to those of other democratic nations. It has met crises successfully. No President has had to be chosen by the House since 1824. No President has been elected with fewer popular votes than his opponent since 1888. The method has been a strong source of support for the two-party system by handicapping the development of third parties. Although twelve men who received less than 50 percent of the popular vote have been elected President,[7] only three were supported by less than 45 percent of the electorate—Lincoln with 39.79 percent in 1860, Wilson with 41.85 percent in 1912, and Nixon with 43.4 percent in 1968.

Defenders of the present system admit, of course, that the casting of electoral votes by state units gives predominant campaign importance to the large states, the large cities, and key minority groups in the large cities. But their response is that it

---

[7] This figure would be increased to fifteen by adding the three Presidents—Adams (1824), Hayes (1876), and Harrison (1888)—who were elected despite the fact that they had fewer popular votes than their opponents.

is appropriate for urban influences to control in electing the President because state legislatures and the U.S. Senate are overweighted in representation of rural areas and the small states. Thus one imbalance tends to correct the other.

The Proportional-Vote Plan

The proportional-vote was originally referred to as the Lodge-Gossett amendment after its two initial sponsors. This plan would give candidates for the Presidency such proportion of the electoral vote in each state as the candidate received of the total vote cast for the Presidency in that state, percentages being figured to three places beyond the decimal point. This plan would make the relation between the electoral and popular vote exactly proportional, but would not correct the distortions arising from the small state advantage in electoral votes, differences in the rate of turnout, or census lag in dividing electoral votes among the states.

Fears have been expressed that the proportional electoral count might encourage the formation of third parties or a whole group of splinter parties. The present block system has been a barrier to the success of third parties, for unless they can get the top vote in one or more states, they get no credit at all for their popular votes in the electoral college. But under a proportional system of recording the vote, all votes cast are given effect and the chances of a party with a mere plurality vote winning the Presidency are increased. For this reason the Lodge-Gossett plan, when before the Senate in 1950, was revised by addition of the Lucas amendment, requiring a 40 percent plurality in the electoral vote to elect a President. If no candidate had such a proportion, the election would be thrown into Congress, the House and Senate, sitting jointly, to elect the President from the top two candidates.

In addition to reflecting more accurately the popular strength of the candidates, the proportional plan would retain the importance of the states in the electoral process, and would encourage turnout and the growth of the second party in previously one-party states, since every vote cast would be given effect in the count. Objections to the plan, in addition to its possible encouragement of splinter parties, are that the large states would lose their present commanding position, while the small states would not give up their advantage of two electoral votes regardless of size, and that it would still be possible for a candidate to be elected President with fewer popular votes than his opponent. Indeed, if the votes in the 1960 election had been counted by the proportional system, Nixon, with 113,000 fewer votes than Kennedy, would have been elected with 266.075 electoral votes to 265.623 for Kennedy.

The District-Vote Plan

The district plan, originally sponsored by Senator Mundt, would require electors to be chosen by districts, using either the existing congressional districts or the same number of districts drawn specifically for presidential elections. The two electoral votes awarded to each state by reason of its Senate seats would of course continue to be subject to statewide election. Unlike the proportional plan, which dispenses with electors, the district plan would retain the position of elector, and the candidate for elector receiving a plurality of the votes in his district would be elected. If no candidate achieved a majority in the electoral vote, the President would be chosen from among the highest three candidates by the senators and representatives sitting jointly and voting as individuals.

The arguments for the district plan are that it would eliminate the electoral distortions and emphasis on the large states that result from the unit-vote plan; that by using congressional districts it would give exactly the same kind of representative quality to the electoral vote as is found in Congress; and that, unlike the proportional plan, it would discourage third parties because they would have to carry individual congressional districts in order to have any electoral impact.

Against the district plan the arguments are that it is preferable to have different bases for the election of President and members of Congress; that the temptation to gerrymander congressional districts would be too great to control, since gerrymandering would now pay off twice, in both congressional and presidential elections; that many states would continue to vote as a unit, since the winning party is often dominant in the entire state; and that rural and one-party states would be advantaged at the expense of urban areas.

Direct Election

The simplest and most direct plan for electing the President would be to abandon the electoral college system entirely, ignore state lines, and throw all the voters of the nation into a single electorate for choice of the President. The case for this method is overwhelming. The votes of all individuals would be equal. Since all votes count in the national total, political activity would be encouraged in all areas, including previously one-party states.

The direct nationwide vote is the most democratic system. The President, as the only elected national official (along with the Vice President), should be chosen by the nation and responsible to it. Only direct election can guarantee that the man elected President will be the one with more popular votes than any other candidate. Under the unit, proportional, or district plan it is possible for a candidate to lose in the popular vote and win in the electoral vote; all three systems are lotteries where the relation between the popular and electoral votes is subject to chance.

Direct election would of course eliminate the electoral vote advantage now enjoyed by the small states, and for this reason it was long assumed that a constitutional amendment abolishing the electoral vote system could never secure ratification by three-fourths of the states. But in fact the small-state advantage has been more than offset by the advantage the unit system gives to the large states. Increasingly it has become evident that the only practicable way to remedy these inequities is to abandon the states as electoral areas.

Direct election would create some problems calling for decision. An absolute majority of the popular votes could hardly be required for election; as already noted, fifteen past Presidents polled less than 50 percent of the vote. On the other hand, if a plurality is sufficient to elect, this might encourage splinter parties to enter candidates and fragment the national vote. A President who took office on the basis of a 30 percent plurality would be in a very weak position to exercise national leadership.

But if 40 percent or some other minimum plurality is adopted, provision must be made for the eventuality that no candidate may achieve that minimum. There are two possibilities. One is a runoff election limited to the top two candidates. The other is election by Congress, with members of both houses sitting jointly and voting as individuals. The first is democratic but expensive and a complete novelty at the national level. The second is less democratic but simpler and sanctioned by past practice.

After Wallace's third-party threat to the electoral system in 1968, interest in the direct election alternative increased sharply. In 1969 a constitutional amendment sponsored by Senator Birch Bayh and supported by President Nixon passed the House by a vote of 339 to 70. However, it failed in the Senate in 1970 when two efforts to stop a filibuster were defeated. Opponents of the direct election plan argue that it would eliminate critical leverage for metropolitan areas underrepresented elsewhere in the political system, that it would undermine the two-party system, and that it would weaken the presidential mandate as splinter party candidates eroded the winner's electoral base.

TERM AND TENURE

The decision of the Convention for a four-year term was based in large part on the delegates' preference for presidential re-eligibility. When Washington declined a third term, he did so for reasons of personal convenience. But when Jefferson announced in 1807 that he would withdraw after two terms, he stressed Washington's example and raised the issue to one of principle, arguing that indefinite re-eligibility would undermine the elective system and turn the Presidency into a life tenure post. The subsequent examples of Madison, Monroe, and Jackson gave the two-term tradition almost unassailable validity.

The first concerted attack on the two-term tradition came in 1876 from a group of Republican politicians who wanted Grant to run for a third term, but the resistance was overwhelming. In 1908 Theodore Roosevelt, having served three and a half years of McKinley's term and one term in his own right, stated that "the wise custom which limits the President to two terms regards the substance and not the form," and stated flatly that "under no circumstances will I be a candidate for or accept another nomination." However, by 1912 he had changed his mind, and unsuccessfully sought a third term. Calvin Coolidge found himself in somewhat the same position in 1928, but he never definitely stated his view on the application of the two-term tradition in his case, merely announcing that he did not "choose to run for President in 1928."

Thus it was left for Franklin Roosevelt definitely to breach the tradition in 1940, when the electorate concluded that maintenance of the two-term limit was less important than retaining his experienced leadership in a world at war. Election for a precedent-shattering fourth term was quickly followed by Roosevelt's death on April 12, 1945.

The tragic denouement of this experiment with unlimited re-eligibility, combined with pent-up Republican frustration over four successive defeats by the same candidate, quickly produced a move for writing the two-term rule into the Constitution. When the Republicans won control of the Eightieth Congress they immediately pushed through such an amendment, which was ratified in 1951. The Twenty-second Amendment provides that no person shall be elected to the office of President more than twice, and that no person who has held the office of President, or acted as President, for more than two years of a term to which some other person was elected President, shall be elected more than once. This provision would have made Theodore Roosevelt ineligible in 1912 and Coolidge in 1928, but not Johnson in 1968.

In support of the two-term limit, it can be argued that the physical toll of eight years in the Presidency under present conditions is all that any man can safely endure and that it is desirable to have an automatic limit on presidential ambitions. On the other hand, this provision forecloses the possibility of retaining an experienced President for a third term in times of emergency, and it may substantially weaken the authority of the President in the closing years of his second term.

SUCCESSION

Apart from the expiration of his term, the President's tenure in office may be terminated by resignation, impeachment, inability to perform his duties, or death. Eight Presidents have died in office, and there have been three instances when substantial doubt existed about the ability of the President to perform his duties. Andrew Johnson was impeached but not convicted, while Richard Nixon averted impeachment and certain conviction by resigning.

The Status of the Vice President

The constitutional provision for these contingencies is found in Article II, section 1, as follows: "In case of the removal of the President from office, or of his death, resignation, or inability to discharge the powers and duties of the said office, the same shall devolve on the Vice President." Another relevant provision is in the Twelfth Amendment, which requires that the Vice President have the same qualifications as the President.

The vagueness of the constitutional language on succession has been the cause of much controversy. What is it that devolves upon the Vice President when the President dies, resigns, or is impeached? Is it the "office" of President, or only the "powers and duties" of the office? Was it intended that the Vice President become President, or that he simply "act" as President until a new President was elected?

An excellent case can be made for the latter alternative, both on the basis of the language of the Constitution and on what is known about the intention of the framers from other evidence. Certainly the drafters intended that only an acting President be installed under the circumstances described in the latter part of the same paragraph, which provides: "And the Congress may by law provide for the case of removal, death, resignation or inability, both of the President and Vice President, declaring what officer shall then act as President." The point is then driven home by the rest of the paragraph: "And such officer shall act accordingly, until the disability be removed, or a President shall be elected." There is also the language of the Twelfth Amendment, which prescribes what shall be done if no candidate secures the requisite majority of votes in the electoral college or the House: "Then the Vice President shall act as President, as in the case of the death or other constitutional disability of the President."

There was no need to construe the constitutional language on succession until 1841, when President Harrison died after only one month in office. It therefore fell to Vice President John Tyler to establish the practice in this all-important respect. Tyler was on his Virginia farm when Harrison died on April 4, and the Cabinet sent him a notice of the fact, addressing him as Vice President. Tyler took the oath prescribed by the Constitution on April 6, but the certificate of the judge who administered the oath noted that Tyler deemed himself "qualified to perform the duties and exercise the powers and offices of President . . . without any other oath" than the one he had taken as Vice President. He nevertheless took the presidential oath, since "doubts may arise, and for greater caution."

This statement of Tyler's would indicate that he initially thought of himself as an acting President, and his Cabinet appears to have taken the same position. However, on April 9 Tyler issued an "inaugural address" in which he spoke of himself as having been called "to the high office of President of this Confederacy." The claim was not accepted without controversy. John Quincy Adams recorded in his diary on April 16 his view that Tyler's position was "in direct violation both of the grammar and context of the Constitution." When Congress met on May 31, the customary resolutions were proposed informing the President that Congress was ready to proceed to business. Amendments were offered in both houses to strike out the word "President" and insert instead "Vice President, now exercising the office of President," but they were defeated. Thus the institution of acting President was strangled at birth.

The Twentieth Amendment terminated any possible doubt on this matter by providing, in section 3: "If, at the time fixed for the beginning of the term of the President, the President elect shall have died, the Vice President elect shall become President." The Twenty-fifth Amendment added: "In case of the removal of the President from office or of his death or resignation, the Vice President shall become President."

Succession beyond the Vice President

The Constitution authorizes Congress to declare what "officer shall . . . act as President" in case neither the President nor Vice President is living or able to serve. Congress acted on this authorization in 1792, by passing a statute which provided for the succession first of the President pro tempore of the Senate and then of the Speaker of the House. It was not contemplated that these officials would have much time in office, however, for the statute required immediate steps to be taken for choosing a successor through the electoral college, who would be elected for a full four-year term. If any President had ever been elected under this statute, the synchronization of presidential elections with congressional would of course have been destroyed. But the act of 1792 never had to be utilized.

In 1886 Congress adopted a different theory of presidential succession, providing that the heads of the seven Cabinet departments then existing, beginning with the Secretary of State, should constitute the line of succession after the Vice President. This act repealed the 1792 provision requiring immediate election of a new President, but it substituted therefor a direction to the acting President to assemble Congress within twenty days if it were not in session, thus apparently intending to give Congress a chance to arrange for election of a President if it should see fit to do so.

Thus the law stood when Harry Truman became President to serve out the last three years and nine months of Franklin Roosevelt's fourth term. Truman was disturbed by the fact that during this long period when there would be no Vice President, succession would go to the man whom he named as Secretary of State. He felt that it was undemocratic for him to be in a position to name his successor, and in a special message to Congress on June 19, 1945, he urged revision of the 1886 law to place the Speaker of the House and the President pro tempore of the Senate ahead of the Cabinet in the line of succession. The Republican Eightieth Congress adopted these proposals in the Presidential Succession Act of 1947.

Under this statute the Speaker of the House, upon resigning as Speaker and as a member of the House, is to act as President when a successor to the Presidency is needed and there is no Vice President. If there is no Speaker, or if he fails to qualify, the President pro tempore of the Senate, upon resigning his post and his Senate seat, is to act as President. In either event the acting President is to serve for the remainder of the current presidential term, unless he is filling in because the President elect or Vice President elect had failed to qualify or the President was temporarily disabled; in such a situation his status would terminate if and when the President did qualify or the disability was removed. Cabinet officers follow in the line of succession according to the seniority of their departments.[8] A Cabinet officer must resign his departmental headship on taking the presidential oath of office, but his occupancy of the office would last only until there was a Speaker or President pro tempore available to succeed him. The statute clearly states that the title of all successors taking presidential office under the act will be "Acting President."

The act of 1947 was a bad piece of legislation.[9] Placing the Speaker and President pro tempore ahead of the Secretary of State and other Cabinet members was ill-advised, considering that Secretaries of State have tended to be men of greater stature, ability, and prominence than the heads of the two houses of Congress. Moreover, having the succession pass to congressional officers opens the way for transfer of party control over the Presidency, if Congress is controlled by the party which lost the last presidential election. Finally, since the Speaker or President pro

---

[8] The order of departments is as follows: State, Treasury, Defense, Attorney General, Post Office, Interior, Agriculture, Commerce, and Labor. The newest Cabinet departments, all created since 1947—Health, Education and Welfare; Housing and Urban Development; and Transportation—are not included in the line of succession

[9] See Joseph E. Kallenbach, "The New Presidential Succession Act," 41 AMERICAN POLITICAL SCIENCE REVIEW 931 (1947).

tempore serves out the remainder of the four-year term after taking office, even though the congressional term to which he was elected may have expired in the meantime, there is the possibility of a new kind of "lame duck" President.

The constitutional flaws in the statute are equally serious, running counter as it does to the theory of separation of powers. The Constitution requires that the person named by Congress as a successor must be an "officer" of the United States. It also declares that no person holding "any office under the United States" is eligible to a seat in Congress. Consequently a member of Congress cannot be an "officer of the United States," and so is ineligible to act as President. The act of 1792 was clearly unconstitutional, because it provided that the acting President was to retain his seat in Congress and his post as President pro tempore or Speaker. The 1947 act chose the other horn of the dilemma, requiring the Speaker or President pro tempore to resign his legislative post and seat *before* becoming Acting President. But it is only as they hold these posts that they are entitled to act as President. Thus the 1947 act seems also to be clearly contrary to the Constitution.

The Twenty-fifth Amendment

In 1965 Congress sought to solve the succession problem by insuring that the Vice-Presidency would never be vacant for long. The Twenty-fifth Amendment, ratified in 1967, provides in section 2 that "whenever there is a vacancy in the office of the Vice President, the President shall nominate a Vice President who shall take office upon confirmation by a majority vote of both houses of Congress."

The Amendment was widely praised, but the first occasion for its use revealed entirely unanticipated difficulties. In 1973 Vice President Spiro Agnew pleaded no contest to charges of income tax evasion and resigned. Nixon then named Gerald Ford, House minority leader, as Vice President; he took office on December 6, 1973, after confirmation by bipartisan votes of 387 to 35 in the House and 92 to 3 in the Senate. Nine months later, Nixon, facing certain impeachment and conviction, also resigned, making Ford President. Ford, in turn, selected Nelson Rockefeller as Vice President, but a long delay in his confirmation left the nation for four months without a Vice President.

Thus the Twenty-fifth Amendment not only failed to prevent a vacancy in the Vice-Presidency but, much more important, produced the astounding result of placing in office both a President and a Vice President neither of whom had been elected to those posts. President Ford, moreover, owed his selection to his discredited predecessor.

This experience led to consideration of alternative methods of filling vice-presidential vacancies, and there were even serious suggestions that the office be abolished.[10] Vice-presidential nominees have usually been hurriedly selected at party conventions for reasons of political balance rather than competence. The office is an awkward one, with no duties except to preside over the Senate unless the President

---

[10] Arthur Schlesinger, Jr., "Is the Vice Presidency Necessary?" 233 THE ATLANTIC 37 (May 1974) and "On the Presidential Succession," 89 POLITICAL SCIENCE QUARTERLY 475 (1974).

wishes to find other work for the Vice President to do. If the office were abolished, a vacancy in the Presidency could be filled temporarily by the Speaker of the House or the Secretary of State as Acting President while a special election was held.

PRESIDENTIAL INABILITY

The Constitution takes account of the President's possible "inability to discharge the powers and duties of the said office," and, as in the case of death or removal, the Vice President is directed to take over. However, unlike death or removal, inability may be only a temporary condition which can pass away and leave the President as fit as ever to continue his duties. If the original constitutional intention that the Vice President would be only an Acting President under all contingencies had come to fruition, there would be little difficulty in the Vice President's filling in temporarily for a disabled President. But the fact that the office of Acting President is unknown to our history in other eventualities has resulted in some doubt as to its applicability in cases of inability.[11]

Three American Presidents have suffered serious disability during their terms of office. President Garfield was shot on July 2, 1881, and lingered on until his death on September 19. During this period he was able to perform only one official act, the signing of an extradition paper. A majority of Garfield's Cabinet believed that any performance of presidential functions by Vice President Arthur would automatically oust Garfield from the Presidency, on the theory that there could not be two Presidents at the same time. Consequently Arthur took no action.

On September 26, 1919, President Wilson suffered a collapse and was disabled for many weeks. For over three months he saw no one except his wife and the doctors. Mrs. Wilson gave him such state papers as she thought he could handle; others were referred by her to Cabinet members. Secretary of State Lansing, at the onset of the President's illness, tried to secure support for having Vice President Marshall take over Wilson's powers and duties, but was unsuccessful. Then Lansing took the initiative in calling several Cabinet meetings. When Wilson heard of this, he regarded it as an assumption of Presidential authority, and requested Lansing's resignation.[12]

President Eisenhower had three serious illnesses in a little over two years. He had organized the Presidency for the first time on the staff principle with which he was familiar from his military experience, with substantial delegations of authority which kept many of the normal concerns of his predecessors from coming to his attention. He had moreover made greater use of his Vice President than had been customary in the past. During Eisenhower's convalescences the role of the Vice President was somewhat expanded, including the chairing of Cabinet meetings and sessions of the National Security Council, but the primary responsibility for keeping

[11] See generally John D. Feerick, *From Failing Hands: The Story of Presidential Succession* (New York: Fordham University Press, 1965).

[12] See Richard Hansen, *The Year We Had No President* (Lincoln, Nebr.: University of Nebraska Press, 1962); Gene Smith, *When the Cheering Stopped* (New York: William Morrow & Company, Inc., 1964).

the wheels turning was assumed by the White House staff, headed by Sherman Adams.

Each of these emergencies created a temporary power vacuum and aroused concern about constitutional unpreparedness for handling situations of such great potential danger. Each emergency could have been eased by having the Vice President become Acting President for a temporary period. This did not occur, a principal reason being uncertainty as to the effect this assumption of responsibility would have on the status of the disabled President.

In the absence of any legislation or constitutional consensus on this problem, President Eisenhower wisely took the initiative and in March, 1958, made public an agreement he had reached with Vice President Nixon concerning a possible future inability. This agreement called for the Vice President to serve as "acting President, exercising the powers and duties of the office until the inability had ended." Then the President "would resume the full exercise of the powers and duties of the office." President Kennedy entered into a similar agreement with Vice President Johnson in 1961, as did President Johnson with Vice President Humphrey in 1965.

Section 3 of the Twenty-fifth Amendment gave constitutional recognition to the Eisenhower-Nixon type of arrangement by providing that the President, if unable to discharge the powers and duties of his office, could transfer them to "the Vice President as Acting President" by filing a written declaration of inability with the President of the Senate and the Speaker of the House. The President could resume his powers and duties by a written declaration to the same two officers.

The most difficult problem that the drafters of the Twenty-fifth Amendment foresaw was the possibility that the President might suffer a mental illness and not recognize his inability.[13] Stripping a President of his office against his will is a grave prospect, yet the need for such action could arise. Section 4 consequently provided a formula which it was hoped would protect all interests in such a crisis. The Vice President and a majority of the Cabinet "or such other body as Congress may by law provide" were authorized to declare the President unable to serve by written notice to the heads of the two houses of Congress, and on the filing of such a declaration the Vice President would become Acting President.

The President could resume his powers by written notice to the two houses that the inability had ceased to exist. However, if the Vice President and a majority of the Cabinet (or other designated body) within four days thereafter notified Congress that in their opinion the President had not recovered from his disability, then Congress would have to decide the issue. It would assemble within forty-eight hours and reach a decision within twenty-one days. If two-thirds of both houses voted that the President was unable to discharge his duties, the Vice President would continue as Acting President. Otherwise the President would resume his office.[14]

---

[13] Questions have been raised concerning the mental stability of President Nixon during the period prior to his resignation. See Theodore H. White, *Breach of Faith: The Fall of Richard Nixon* (New York: Atheneum Publishers, 1975); Bob Woodward and Carl Bernstein, *The Final Days* (New York: Simon and Schuster, Inc., 1976).

[14] During the last weeks of Nixon's presidency, when he faced impeachment and the government seemed to be coming to a standstill, there were some suggestions that he "take the Twenty-fifth" and step aside temporarily, allowing Vice President Ford to serve as Acting President until Nixon's status was

The process of nominating presidential candidates has not been considered in this chapter, since it is not controlled by constitutional provisions. It should be noted, however, that the methods by which the Republican Party raised 60 million dollars for the 1972 campaign, and the corrupting effect of so much money, resulted in adoption by Congress of the 1974 Election Campaign Act and of similar statutes by a number of states.[15] Moreover, discontent with existing nominating procedures was increased by the fiasco of the 1972 Democratic convention, which was selected on strictly representative principles yet nominated an unelectable candidate.

The increasing number of states holding presidential primaries (thirty in 1976) and the resulting physical and financial burdens on candidates have led to proposals for regional primaries or a national presidential primary.[16]

---

determined. Obviously the Twenty-fifth Amendment was not intended for this kind of situation.

[15] The 1974 act took the form of amendments to the Federal Election Campaign Act of 1971. Its principal provisions (1) limited political contributions to candidates for federal elective office by an individual or group to $1,000, or by a political committee to $5,000; (2) limited expenditures by individuals or groups on behalf of a candidate to $1,000, and by a candidate from his personal or family funds to various specified amounts depending on the federal office sought; (3) restricted overall primary and general election expenditures by candidates to various specified amounts; (4) required political committees to keep detailed records of contributions and expenditures and to file quarterly reports; (5) created the Federal Election Commission as the administering agency, consisting of two members appointed by the President pro tempore of the Senate, two by the Speaker of the House, and two by the President (all subject to confirmation by both houses of Congress), plus the Secretary of the Senate and the Clerk of the House as ex officio nonvoting members. Public financing of major party presidential nominating conventions and primary and general election campaigns was provided by amendments to the Internal Revenue Code, the funds to be disbursed by the FEC.

In *Buckley* v. *Valeo* (1976) the Supreme Court upheld the limits on contributions as being appropriate legislative weapons against the reality or appearance of improper influence by large campaign contributors, and likewise ruled that the disclosure and record-keeping requirements were constitutional. Public funding of conventions, primaries, and elections was also upheld as a use of public money to facilitate and enlarge public discussion and participation in the electoral process. However, the limits on election expenditures were held to violate the First Amendment, restricting protected political expression. Also, the composition of the FEC was constitutionally objectionable, in that Congress had usurped the President's appointing power in the case of four of its six members. The Court gave Congress thirty days to reconstitute the Commission.

[16] James W. Davis, *Presidential Primaries: Road to the White House* (New York: Thomas Y. Crowell Company, 1967); Judith H. Parris, *The Convention Problem: Issues in Reform of Presidential Nominating Procedures* (Washington, D.C.: The Brookings Institution, 1972).

Executive Powers in General

In turning to a general discussion of presidential authority, it is particularly important to recall the limitations of this volume. It is not a constitutional history. It is not a compendium of governmental practice under the Constitution. Thus, in discussing the subject of executive powers under the Constitution there can be no thought of undertaking any detailed account, either chronological or analytical, of the development of the theory or practice of executive power. Our concern is the more limited one of focusing attention on the problems of interpretation and controversy to which the constitutional language pertaining to executive power has given rise. For reasons having to do with the separation of powers, already noted, the courts have usually been reluctant to intervene in controversies over executive power. Nevertheless, there have been opportunities for some strikingly important expressions of judicial opinion on these problems.

THE PRESIDENT AND LAWMAKING

We begin with the paradox that some of the President's most important executive powers are legislative. They are legislative in the sense that the Constitution gives him a role to play in relation to Congress as an institution and in relation to its adoption of legislation.

First, the President has certain functions in connection with the convening and adjourning of Congress. The regular annual sessions of Congress are stipulated by the Constitution, but the President is authorized by Article II, section 3, "on extraordinary occasions, [to] convene both houses, or either of them," in special session, a power which has often been exercised. He has the power to adjourn Congress, but only in case the two houses disagree with respect to the time of adjournment, an eventuality which has never occurred.

Again, the President has an important role as the initiator of legislative programs, based on the following language from Article II, section 3: "He shall from time to time give to the Congress information of the state of the Union, and recommend to their consideration such measures as he shall judge necessary and expedient." Accordingly, a "State of the Union" message is submitted to Congress by the President, usually in person. at the beginning of each regular session, followed by the annual budget message plus special messages from time to time. Executive influence on formulation of the legislative program, of course, does not stop here. The policy leadership of the administration is continuously manifested by the preparation of draft bills, testimony before congressional committees by department heads and other officials of the executive branch, and use of the President's vast powers as party leader and manipulator of public opinion.

Approval of Legislation

The role of the President in the final approval of legislation is carefully safeguarded by the Constitution. Under Article I, section 7, "every bill" and "every order, resolution, or vote to which the concurrence of the Senate and House of Representatives may be necessary" must be presented to the President for approval or disapproval. There are only three exceptions to this general rule of presidential participation. First, the requirement is by its terms not applicable to actions affecting only a single house, such as adopting rules of procedure, appointing officers and employees, establishing special committees, or passing resolutions not purporting to have any legislative effect. Second, as already noted in Chapter 2, the President does not participate formally in the process of proposing amendments to the Constitution.

Third, joint actions of the two houses in the form of *concurrent resolutions* are customarily not submitted to the President. Concurrent resolutions are adopted by both houses of Congress, but normally not for strictly lawmaking purposes. They are used, for example, in correcting errors in bills after they have been adopted, setting up joint committees of the two houses, or fixing the time for adjournment. Technically it would seem that the concurrent resolution is an evasion of the constitutional requirements. The evasion, however, is unimportant so long as concurrent resolutions are not used for lawmaking purposes. But there have been instances where this limitation was not observed, and under these conditions the concurrent resolution is a potential threat to the constitutional right of the President to participate in the lawmaking process.[1]

---

[1] For example, the Lend-Lease Act of 1941 delegated certain temporary powers to the President, the expiration date being June 30, 1943. However, the act provided that the powers would lapse earlier if Congress should pass a concurrent resolution declaring that they were "no longer necessary to promote

Executive Veto Power

The President's power to veto legislation is referred to as a "qualified" or "suspensive" veto, since it can be overridden by a two-thirds vote of both houses. Nevertheless, it is scarcely possible to overestimate the contribution which the veto power makes to executive authority. The number of times the President exercises the veto is of course no index to its importance. The mere existence of the power is a constant factor in congressional thinking, and legislative planning is generally circumscribed by realization of the necessity of producing measures which the President will be willing to sign.

Thinking and practice with respect to use of the veto power have varied greatly during our history. The first six Presidents usually vetoed bills only on the ground that they were unconstitutional or technically defective. Jackson was the first President to adopt a policy of vetoing bills simply because he considered them objectionable in aim and content, but even so he vetoed only twelve bills in eight years. Only fifty-one vetoes were recorded up to the Civil War.

Eight Presidents—the most recent being Garfield—never vetoed a single measure. Grover Cleveland and Franklin Roosevelt, on the other hand, used the veto 414 and 631 times respectively. No presidential veto was overridden until Tyler's administration, and it still occurs very infrequently. Even Franklin Roosevelt, who originated more than one-third of all the vetoes in American history up to that time, was reversed only nine times. Eisenhower, with 181 vetoes, was overridden only twice. In his first year, six of Ford's 37 vetoes were overridden.

If the President decides to veto a bill, he returns it unsigned within ten days to the house in which it originated, accompanying it with a statement of his objections. The veto stands unless, with a quorum present, it is overridden by a two-thirds vote in each house. On the question of repassage of the bill, the way each member votes must be recorded, which imparts a greater sense of responsibility to the action.

The President can permit a bill to become law without his signature by failing to return it with his signature within ten days after he has received it. This procedure is used when the President does not approve of a bill, but feels it impossible or impolitic to veto it. However, in these circumstances the bill will become law only if Congress is still in session after the ten days have expired. If Congress adjourns within the ten-day period, the bill does not become law, and is said to have been given a "pocket veto." A pocket veto is an absolute veto, since the adjournment of Congress prevents any attempt at repassage of the bill.[2]

---

the defense of the United States." See a defense of the constitutionality of the provision in Edward S. Corwin, *The President: Office and Powers, 1787–1957* (New York: New York University Press, 4th rev. ed., 1957), pp. 129–130, and President Roosevelt's objection in Robert H. Jackson, "A Presidential Legal Opinion," 66 HARVARD LAW REVIEW 1353 (1953). See also D. W. Buckwalter, "The Congressional Concurrent Resolution: A Search for Foreign Policy Influence," 14 MIDWEST JOURNAL OF POLITICAL SCIENCE 434 (1970).

[2] Adjournment of the first session of a Congress amounts to "adjournment" for purposes of the pocket veto, the Supreme Court held in *The Pocket Veto Case* (1929). But Nixon's effort to use the pocket veto during a five-day Christmas recess in 1970 was invalidated in *Kennedy* v. *Sampson* (1973), and when this decision was upheld by the Court of Appeals for the District of Columbia, the Justice Department decided not to appeal. However, in 1974 President Ford announced that on the advice of the Attorney

The President must by practice accept or reject a bill *in toto;* he has no "item veto." Thus there is a temptation for Congress to attach legislation which the President is known to oppose, as a "rider" to some vitally important bill. Numerous proposals to give the President an item veto, primarily with respect to appropriations measures, have uniformly failed.[3]

THEORIES OF EXECUTIVE POWER

When we turn from the President as participant in lawmaking to the President as operating head of the executive branch, the first relevant constitutional provision is the initial sentence of Article II: "The executive power shall be vested in a President of the United States of America." There has been considerable disagreement as to whether these words comprise a grant of power or are a mere designation of office. If the latter view is taken, then the executive power must be defined by the more or less specific authorizations to the President found elsewhere in Article II, such as the power to grant pardons, to receive ambassadors, to make appointments, or to take care that the laws be faithfully executed.

But is there any reason for concluding that this more restrictive view of executive powers is the correct or preferable one? The main argument against the broader concept is based on a supposed logical difficulty. Why, it is said, should Article II start out with a general grant of executive power and then be followed by more specific grants? Chief Justice Taft sought to dispose of this query by explaining that the specific grants lend emphasis "where emphasis was regarded as appropriate."[4] On the basis of extensive research into eighteenth-century practices and terminology, Crosskey concludes that draftsmanship of that period typically made use of "a general proposition followed by an incomplete enumeration of particulars, or things which, arguably, are particulars, included within the antecedent general expression."[5]

But perhaps the best reason for regarding the initial sentence of Article II as a grant of power is that only by this method is the President equipped with the broad authority which the chief executive of a state must have. The prime characteristic of executive power is that it is "residual." The executive is always in session, always available to fill in gaps and meet emergencies. In contrast, as Locke says, "the law making power is not always in being, and is usually too numerous and so too slow for the dispatch requisite to execution."[6]

If further support is needed for the position that the "executive power" phrase is a broad grant of power, it can be found in an action of the First Congress,

---

General he reserved the right to use the pocket veto during congressional recesses, a position he abandoned in 1976. *Congressional Quarterly Weekly Report,* April 17, 1976, p. 887.

[3] Nixon's effort to achieve the purposes of the item veto by use of the impounding power is discussed in Chap. 10. See also Jong R. Lee, "Presidential Vetoes from Washington to Nixon," 37 JOURNAL OF POLITICS 522 (1975).

[4] *Myers* v. *United States* (1926).

[5] W. W. Crosskey, *Politics and the Constitution in the History of the United States* (Chicago: The University of Chicago Press, 1953), p. 379.

[6] John Locke, *Of Civil Government,* book 2, chap. 14.

commonly referred to as the "decision of 1789." In setting up the new department of foreign affairs, the House fell into a debate as to how the secretary of the department would be removed. Some members thought the Senate's consent would be necessary, just as in appointment, and others said Congress could provide any arrangement for removal it saw fit under the "necessary and proper" clause. The language actually put into the statute, "whenever the said principal officer shall be removed from office by the President," reflected the majority conclusion that the President already had the right of removal on the basis of his "executive power" under the Constitution.

The only other language approaching the executive power provision in breadth of authorization is the sentence in Article II, section 3: "He shall take care that the laws be faithfully executed." Although this is a notably broad grant of power, it also served the limiting function of emphasizing the American notion of the executive as subordinate to the law, in contrast with the wide prerogative powers of the English executive.

For a satisfactory indication of how these two general grants of executive power have been interpreted and what they have meant in practice, nothing less than a history of the Presidency would be adequate. But fortunately for our purposes, an understanding of the two principal contrasting interpretations of executive power can be supplied by two Presidents, Theodore Roosevelt and William H. Taft. Roosevelt wrote his activist personality and expansive attitude into constitutional law with his "stewardship" conception of the presidential office. His theory was

> . . . that the executive power was limited only by specific restrictions and prohibitions appearing in the Constitution or imposed by the Congress under its Constitutional powers. . . . I declined to adopt the view that what was imperatively necessary for the Nation could not be done by the President unless he could find some specific authorization to do it. My belief was that it was not only his right but his duty to do anything that the needs of the Nation demanded unless such action was forbidden by the Constitution or by the laws.[7]

Taft found this position incompatible with his more sedentary view of the Presidency. In lectures which he gave in 1916 after his Presidential term, he said:

> The true view of the Executive functions is, as I conceive it, that the President can exercise no power which cannot be fairly and reasonably traced to some specific grant of power or justly implied and included within such express grant as proper and necessary to its exercise. Such specific grant must be either in the Federal Constitution or in an act of Congress passed in pursuance thereof. There is no undefined residuum of power which he can exercise because it seems to him to be in the public interest.[8]

The issue that emerges here, then, is whether the President must always be able

---

[7] Theodore Roosevelt, *Autobiography* (New York: The Macmillan Company, 1913), pp. 388–389.
[8] William Howard Taft, *Our Chief Magistrate and His Powers* (New York: Columbia University Press, 1916), pp. 139–140.

to cite a law of the United States or a specific constitutional authorization in support of his actions, or whether the broad "executive power" with which he is vested justifies any actions he conceives as being in the public interest, so long as there is no conflict with existing legislation or constitutional provisions. Locke put this issue in its classical form. Pointing to the relative characteristics of executive and legislature already quoted, he concluded that the executive must always be equipped with discretionary and prerogative powers.

> For the legislators not being able to foresee and provide by laws for all that may be useful to the community, the executor of the laws, having the power in his hands, has by the common law of Nature a right to make use of it for the good of the society, in many cases where the municipal law has given no direction, till the legislative can conveniently be assembled to provide for it. Many things there are which the law can by no means provide for, and those must necessarily be left to the discretion of him that has the executive power in his hands, to be ordered by him as the public good and advantage shall require; nay, it is fit that the laws themselves should in some cases give way to the executive power, or rather to this fundamental law of Nature and government—viz., that, as much as may be, all the members of the society are to be preserved.

The Supreme Court found it necessary to take a position on this issue in *In re Neagle* (1890), and it lined up with Locke. The *Neagle* case grew out of a highly bizarre set of facts. Supreme Court Justice Field, whose judicial circuit included California, had had his life threatened by a disappointed litigant named Terry, and the Attorney General assigned a United States marshal to protect Field while riding the circuit in that state. When Terry appeared about to make a physical attack on Field, the marshal, Neagle, killed him. There was some local feeling favorable to Terry, and Neagle was arrested and held by state authorities on a charge of murder. The United States sought Neagle's release on habeas corpus under a provision of the federal statutes making the writ available to one "in custody for an act done or omitted in pursuance of a law of the United States."

The problem was that Congress had enacted no *law* authorizing the President or the Attorney General to assign marshals as bodyguards to federal justices. But the Supreme Court did not propose to interpret "law" so narrowly. "In the view we take of the Constitution . . . any obligation fairly and properly inferrible from that instrument, or any duty of the marshal to be derived from the general scope of his duties under the laws of the United States, is a 'law,' within the meaning of this phrase."

It would be unthinkable, said the Court, which admittedly had a more than academic interest in the matter, for a sovereign government to have "within the domain of its powers no means of protecting . . . judges" in the discharge of their duties. The power must exist somewhere, and the only question is where. The legislature could pass a law, but it had not done so. Then, in language practically paraphrasing Locke, the Court turned to the President, whom it found admirably equipped for performing such a function, through his Cabinet, his appointees, his executive departments, his control over the Armed Forces, through all those who "aid him in the performance of the great duties of his office, and represent him in a thousand acts."

There is "a peace of the United States," the Court went on, and by necessity and design the President is the principal conservator of that peace. The President's duty to see that the laws are faithfully executed is consequently not "limited to the enforcement of acts of Congress . . . according to their *express terms*" but includes also "the rights, duties and obligations growing out of the Constitution itself, our international relations, and all the protection implied by the nature of the government under the Constitution." Thus the duty assigned to the marshal in this affair was properly considered to arise "under the authority of the law of the United States."

This broad interpretation of the laws which the President was obliged faithfully to execute was underlined five years later in the case of *In re Debs*. As already noted, President Cleveland sent troops to Chicago to deal with a railway strike and had his Attorney General secure a federal court injunction against the strikers. There was no explicit statutory basis for the injunction, but the Supreme Court sustained it on the broad ground that: "Every government, entrusted, by the very terms of its being, with powers and duties to be exercised and discharged for the general welfare, has a right to apply to its own courts for any proper assistance in the exercise of the one and the discharge of the other." Here again the theme was that the right of self-preservation must belong to a government, whether claimed by statute or not, and that the executive was constitutionally entitled to act in such cases.

In contrast to these strong supports for the doctrine of inherent or implied presidential powers, stands the 1952 decision in the famous *Steel Seizure Case (Youngstown Sheet and Tube Co.* v. *Sawyer)*. A few hours before a nationwide steel strike was to begin on April 9, 1952, President Truman issued an executive order directing the Secretary of Commerce to take possession of and operate the steel mills of the country. The President based his action on a contention that the work stoppage would jeopardize national defense, particularly in Korea. The next morning he sent a message to Congress reporting his action, and a second message on April 21. The steel companies obeyed the Secretary's orders under protest, and brought suit for injunction against him in the District of Columbia district court. On April 30, Judge Pine granted a preliminary injunction restraining the Secretary from continuing the seizure. The case went to the Supreme Court with almost unprecedented speed, and on June 2, the Court held by a six to three vote that the President had exceeded his constitutional powers.

Chief Justice Vinson's opinion for the three dissenters was in the spirit of the *Neagle* and *Debs* cases. His theory of the President's seizure was that its purpose was "to faithfully execute the laws by acting in an emergency to maintain the status quo, thereby preventing collapse of the legislative programs [military procurement and anti-inflation] until Congress could act." Admittedly there was no statutory authorization for the seizure in the Taft-Hartley Act, which Congress had passed in 1947 to deal with nationwide strikes. But Vinson regarded the constitutional grant of "executive power" to the President, and his constitutional responsibility to execute the laws, as providing inherent power for such presidential action. His reading of the Constitution and his interpretation of the purpose of the Founders was that "the Presidency was deliberately fashioned as an office of power and independence." His illustrations ran all the way from Washington's vigorous suppression of the Whiskey Rebellion, Jefferson's initiative in the Louisiana Purchase, and Lincoln's wholly unauthorized Emanicipation Proclamation, down to President Roosevelt's World War II nonstatutory seizures of aircraft and industrial plants.

Judge Pine's decision in the district court had challenged such an interpretation of executive powers under the Constitution. He denied that the President had any "inherent" powers not traceable to an express grant in the Constitution. As his sole authority for this position, he cited the passage from Taft's book already quoted. Judge Pine dismissed Roosevelt's stewardship theory as one which does not "comport with our recognized theory of government." The numerous instances in American history where Presidents have acted on a theory of inherent powers he dismissed as "repetitive, unchallenged, illegal acts."

Judge Pine's action in enjoining the steel seizure was upheld by the Supreme Court, but his denial of inherent powers to the President was not ratified by the Court. Only Black and Douglas approved the Pine position that the President was limited to expressly granted powers. Like Judge Pine, they took up dogmatic positions based on a hard-and-fast interpretation of the separation of powers. Black disposed of the entire controversy in thirteen paragraphs, and his argument was on such a plane of lofty moral and constitutional generalities that he did not bother to cite a single Supreme Court decision bearing on the substantive issue. But the other majority justices did not accept this separation of powers dogma. Frankfurter specifically attached a paragraph to Black's opinion for the Court in order to warn that "the considerations relevant to the legal enforcement of the principle of separation of powers seem to me more complicated and flexible than may appear from what Mr. Justice Black has written."

Consequently we must turn away from Black and Douglas to the other four majority justices in search for the real doctrine of the steel decision. All four of their opinions recognize that American constitutional law is a pragmatic affair. Jackson, for example, stressed the folly of any rigorous notions about strict separation of the branches of government. Successful operation of our system requires a combination of "separateness" with "interdependence," "autonomy" with "reciprocity." He thought that "presidential powers are not fixed but fluctuate, depending upon their disjunction or conjunction with those of Congress." He believed that when the President "takes measures incompatible with the expressed or implied will of Congress, his power is at its lowest ebb," and because he was convinced that the President had done that here, he found the action unconstitutional.

Frankfurter likewise approached the problem as a matter of balancing the equities in this particular instance between the two democratic branches of the government, to both of which the Supreme Court owed deference. Examination of congressional actions pertaining to use of presidential seizure powers from 1916 to the passage of the Taft-Hartley Act convinced Frankfurter that Congress had "deemed seizure so drastic a power as to require it to be carefully circumscribed whenever the President was vested with this extraordinary authority." When considering the Taft-Hartley bill, Frankfurter went on, Congress gave considered attention to the seizure device and on "a balance of considerations . . . chose not to lodge this power in the President." It is true that Congress did not write into the act a statutory prohibition on presidential seizure, but it "expressed its will to withhold this power from the President as though it had said so in so many words."

In *New York Times Co.* v. *United States* (1971), involving the government's attempt to enjoin the press from publishing the so-called Pentagon Papers,[9] the court likewise rejected, by a vote of six to three, a presidential claim to inherent power to protect national defense secrets that was unsupported by statutory authorization. But two of the majority justices, Stewart and White, were willing to grant the existence of a "sovereign prerogative" power to protect the confidentiality of materials related to the national defense and only voted against the President because they could not say that disclosure of the Pentagon Papers would "surely result in direct, immediate, and irreparable damage to our Nation or its people." Another majority justice, Marshall, stressed that, as in the *Steel Seizure* case, Congress had refused to adopt legislation that would have given the President the power he sought here. Speaking for the three dissenters, Harlan would have granted the President's inherent power to act, subject only to a judicial determination that the issue lay within "the proper compass of the President's foreign relations power" and a determination by the Secretary of State or Secretary of Defense that "disclosure of the subject matter would irreparably impair the national security."[10]

THE POWER OF APPOINTMENT

Basic to executive authority is the President's power to appoint the officials of the administration. Article II, section 2, provides:

> [The President] shall nominate, and by and with the advice and consent of the Senate, shall appoint ambassadors, other public ministers and consuls, judges of the Supreme Court, and all other officers of the United States, whose appointments are not herein otherwise provided for, and which shall be established by law; but the Congress may by law vest the appointment of such inferior officers, as they think proper, in the President alone, in the courts of law, or in the heads of departments.

This language establishes four different methods of appointment—by the President with Senate confirmation, by the President alone, by the courts of law, and by the heads of departments. Congress has no appointment power, except, under Article I, to choose its own officers.[11] Nevertheless, Congress is involved very deeply in the process of appointment, as the following discussion will indicate.

Qualifications and Disqualifications

In creating offices, Congress can specify the qualifications to be possessed by appointees to those offices. Familiar statutory requirements relate to citizenship, resi-

---

[9] A forty-seven-volume classified study made by direction of the Secretary of Defense as to how the United States became involved in the Vietnam war, which was made available to the press by Daniel Ellsberg. See Neil Sheehan et al., *The Pentagon Papers* (New York: Bantam Books, 1971).

[10] See Peter D. Junger, "Down Memory Lane: The Case of the Pentagon Papers," 23 CASE WESTERN RESERVE LAW REVIEW 3 (1971).

[11] In *Buckley* v. *Valeo* (1976) the Court held that the six members of the Federal Election Commission, four of whom were appointed by Congress, were "officers of the United States" and consequently must be appointed by the President.

dence, age, political affiliation, professional attainments, and so on. Congress has even provided on occasion that presidential appointments shall be made from among a small number of persons named by others. Thus an act of 1920 required that the Railroad Labor Board consist of three men to be appointed from six nominees by employees, and three to be chosen from six nominees by carriers. The civil service system is, of course, a general limitation on the executive appointment power.

Senatorial Confirmation

The requirement that appointments by the executive shall be subject to approval by the upper house of the legislature is peculiar to the United States, and to the several countries of Central and South America that have used the American Constitution as a model. The Senate's advice and consent is given by a majority of a quorum. The distinction between "officers" who need Senate confirmation and "inferior officers" who do not is entirely in the discretion of Congress. The Constitution apparently assumes that these two categories will cover the field, but in extraconstitutional practice a third and very numerous category, "employees," is recognized, who may be appointed by officers whose status is lower than that of department head.

When the framers of the Constitution spoke of the Senate's "advice" on nominations, they apparently were thinking of collective advice by the Senate acting as a kind of council for the President. But the Senate has never functioned as such a council, and it is obviously impractical for it to offer advice on appointments in any collective fashion. However, advice is given by individual senators, which is made very effective by the practice of "senatorial courtesy." A nomination to a federal office within a state, on which the senator or senators of that state from the President's party have not been consulted, will almost invariably be refused confirmation if the aggrieved senator chooses to make an appeal to his colleagues. Where the appointment is to an office in Washington, it is normal procedure to consult with the senator of the state from which the appointee comes, but if this is not done the rule of senatorial courtesy is less likely to be applied when confirmation is requested. If the Senate does refuse confirmation for a high-level appointment, it is usually for broad policy reasons, not because the rule of senatorial courtesy has been ignored.

Recess Appointments

Article II, section 2, clause 3, provides: "The President shall have power to fill up all vacancies that may happen during the recess of the Senate, by granting commissions which shall expire at the end of their next session." The word "happen" does not mean that the vacancy must have actually developed while the Senate was in recess. A vacancy occurring during a Senate session, which for any reason remains unfilled by the end of the session, can be filled by a recess appointment. This, plus the fact that a recess appointee can serve throughout the next session of the Senate, opens up the possibility of the President's using recess appointments to keep in office men whom the Senate would refuse to confirm, and this has occasionally happened. In fact, President Jefferson appears to have kept Robert Smith as his Secretary of the

Navy for four years without Senate confirmation by this device. Congress has moved against such practices by legislation providing that if the vacancy exists while the Senate is in session, the recess appointee may receive no salary until he has been confirmed by the Senate.

THE POWER OF REMOVAL

Surprisingly, the Constitution makes no express provision for the removal of federal officials except through the process of impeachment, which is an unwieldy and quite impractical device, useful only on extraordinary occasions. This gap has been filled by executive practice, legislative provisions, and judicial interpretation.

Two principal constitutional issues have arisen in connection with removals. First, is removal solely an executive function, or can the Senate claim a share in removing officials who were appointed subject to Senate confirmation? Hamilton in No. 77 of *The Federalist* expressed the opinion that the consent of the Senate "would be necessary to displace as well as to appoint." But the First Congress, faced with this issue in setting up the Department of State, acted on the theory, as we have already seen, that the President alone possessed the removal power.

In fact Congress tacitly recognized the existence of an unrestrained presidential removal power from 1789 to 1867, and it developed into one of his most effective instruments for control of the executive branch. In 1867, however, Congress passed the Tenure of Office Act, which forbade the removal by the President of department heads without consent of the Senate. President Johnson's attempt to remove his Secretary of War in violation of this act was one of the charges in his impeachment. Following Johnson's term the act was modified, and it was completely repealed in 1887, without ever having been the subject of constitutional test.

Meanwhile, however, Congress had passed in 1876 a law providing that postmasters of the first, second, and third class, appointed for four-year terms, should be subject to removal by the President "by and with the advice and consent of the Senate." The Supreme Court finally had occasion to rule on this law in 1926, in the famous case of *Myers* v. *United States*. President Wilson removed Myers, a first-class postmaster in Portland, Oregon, in 1920 before his four-year term was up, without seeking Senate consent. Myers brought suit in the Court of Claims for his salary for the balance of his four-year term, and the Supreme Court held by a vote of six to three that the law of 1876 was unconstitutional.

Chief Justice Taft's opinion for the Court was one of the longest and most elaborate in its history. First, he relied upon the "decision of 1789," and the subsequent practice of untrammeled removal power. The Tenure of Office Act of 1867 he dismissed as a temporary divergence from legislative policy resulting from partisan controversy. Second, and more importantly, he derived the principle of the removal power directly from the Constitution, specifically from the grant of "executive power" and the "faithful execution of the laws" clause. Obviously, said the Chief Justice, the President "alone and unaided could not execute the laws. He must execute them by the assistance of subordinates." It follows that "in the absence of any express limitation respecting removals, that as his selection of administrative officers is essential to the execution of the laws by him, so must be his power of removing those for whom he cannot continue to be responsible."

Chief Justice Taft went on to develop this argument in language which seemed to be illumined by his own experience in the presidential office. He said:

> When a nomination is made, it may be presumed that the Senate is, or may become, as well advised as to the fitness of the nominee as the President, but in the nature of things the defects in ability or intelligence or loyalty in the administration of the laws of one who has served as an officer under the President, are facts as to which the President, or his trusted subordinates, must be better informed than the Senate, and the power to remove him may, therefore, be regarded as confined, for very sound and practical reasons, to the governmental authority which has administrative control.

Indeed, there is an imperative need for the President to be able to remove his immediate subordinates, to whom the President delegates exercise of his discretion and discharge of his political duties. Since there is nothing in the Constitution that would permit a distinction between these officials and those engaged in more normal duties, Taft concluded that an unrestricted power to remove attaches to all positions filled by the President.

The Taft opinion failed to convince three members of the Court, including Holmes and Brandeis. Holmes thought the arguments based on constitutional grants of executive power were "spider's webs inadequate to control the dominant facts." However, the Taft decision was sound law because it was sound politics and sound administration in equating the powers of the President with his responsibilities. Where the opinion was unsound was in its attempt to decide more than the case called for. Taft veered off from considerations applicable to a postmastership into dicta about executive officials not in a position of direct responsibility to the President, saying:

> There may be duties of a quasi-judicial character imposed on executive officers and members of executive tribunals whose decisions after hearing affect interests of individuals, the discharge of which the President can not in a particular case properly influence or control. But even in such a case he may consider the decision after its rendition as a reason for removing the officer, on the ground that the discretion regularly entrusted to that officer by statute has not been on the whole intelligently or wisely exercised. Otherwise he does not discharge his own constitutional duty of seeing that the laws be faithfully executed.

This dictum challenged the statutory basis on which Congress had established the Interstate Commerce Commission in 1887, the Federal Trade Commission in 1914, and the Federal Tariff Commission in 1916. To be sure, the statutes setting up these agencies did not require Senate concurrence in removals, but the commissioners were in each case made removable by the President "for inefficiency, neglect of duty, or malfeasance in office," and the clear implication of this statutory language was that the President was forbidden to remove on any other ground. A restriction of a different sort was placed in the Budget and Accounting Act of 1921, making the

Comptroller General subject to removal (aside from impeachment) only by joint resolution of Congress and then only after a hearing which established incapacity, inefficiency, neglect of duty or malfeasance, or conduct involving moral turpitude.

Such legislation raised the second major issue concerning the removal power. Granting that removal is solely an executive function, can the exercise of this executive power be regulated by law? The *Myers* decision was correctly interpreted by Congress as challenging the validity of any restrictions on the President's removal power. Consequently as new quasi-judicial commissions or regulatory agencies were set up, no such restrictive language was inserted in their statutes.[12]

A test of Taft's dictum was inevitable, and it took the form of *Humphrey's Executor* v. *United States* (1935). Humphrey, first appointed to the Federal Trade Commission by President Coolidge, was reappointed by President Hoover in 1931 for a seven-year term. His views were not in accord with the philosophy of the New Deal, and President Roosevelt in 1933 requested Humphrey's resignation, saying: "I do not feel that your mind and my mind go along together on either the policies or the administering of the Federal Trade Commission, and, frankly, I think it is best for the people of this country that I should have a full confidence." When the resignation was not forthcoming, the President removed him. Humphrey died shortly afterwards but his executor brought suit in the Court of Claims for his salary from the time of removal until his death.

The Supreme Court ruled unanimously that this action had exceeded the President's authority. In view of the fact that the removal was based squarely on Chief Justice Taft's dictum in the *Myers* case, it was, of course, necessary for Justice Sutherland, who wrote the *Humphrey* decision, to disavow the Taft theory. This he did by pointing out that the officer involved in the *Myers* case, a postmaster, was "restricted to the performance of executive functions," and rather lowly ones at that. In contrast, Humphrey was a member of "an administrative body created by Congress to carry into effect legislative policies embodied in the statute," performing its duties "without executive leave." In fact, Sutherland continued, a Federal Trade Commissioner "occupies no place in the executive department and . . . exercises no part of the executive power vested by the Constitution in the President." The Federal Trade Commission is a "quasi-legislative or quasi-judicial" agency, which Congress intended to discharge its duties "independently of executive control." Forbidding the President to remove its commissioners except for cause is a legitimate way of implementing that policy, "for it is quite evident that one who holds his office only during the pleasure of another, cannot be depended upon to maintain an attitude of independence against the latter's will."

Sutherland challenged not only the dicta of Taft's opinion, but also its basic constitutional theory. He ignored Taft's interpretation of the executive power clause as a grant of authority. He appeared to whittle down presidential power to two categories. First, there were the prerogatives explicitly granted to the President in

---

[12] The statutes setting up the Federal Power Commission, reorganized in 1930, and the Federal Communications Commission and the Securities and Exchange Commission, both created in 1934, lack any limitation on the President's removal power.

the Constitution. The impact of the "decision of 1789," Sutherland said, was limited to this category, since it concerned the Secretary of State, an officer who was "purely executive . . . responsible to the President, and to him alone, in a very definite sense." The second category of presidential responsibility was for those officials who exercised only nondiscretionary or ministerial powers, such as postmasters. Apart from these two classes of officials, it appeared that Congress was free to impose such limitations as it chose upon the removal power. Congress reacted immediately to the *Humphrey* decision by writing into the National Labor Relations Act, then in the process of enactment, the most stringent provision it had yet applied to a regulatory commission: "Any member of the Board may be removed by the President, upon notice and hearing, for neglect of duty or malfeasance in office, but for no other cause."

Arthur E. Morgan attempted unsuccessfully to use the *Humphrey* decision to invalidate his removal as chairman of the TVA by President Roosevelt in 1938.[13] But in 1958 the Court applied and extended the *Humphrey* doctrine in *Wiener* v. *United States.* Wiener was removed from the War Claims Commission by President Eisenhower to make way for a deserving Republican. Though the statute erecting the commission had placed no limitation on the President's right to remove its members, the Court held that from the quasijudicial nature of the agency it could be assumed that "Congress did not wish to have hang over the Commission the Damocles' sword of removal by the President for no reason other than that he preferred to have on that Commission men of his own choosing." Under the *Wiener* decision, then, the President's power of removal, which normally can be exercised at his discretion, may be exercised on quasijudicial agencies only for cause, regardless of whether Congress has so provided.

The legislation establishing the federal civil service system and providing certain protections for the tenure of government employees is, of course, a valid limitation on the executive power of removal. Similarly, a legislative requirement for the removal of civil servants engaging in political activities has twice been held constitutional by the Supreme Court.[14] The removal of federal employees on loyalty-security grounds, carried out after 1947 under executive orders issued by Presidents Truman and Eisenhower, is discussed in Chapter 23.

EXECUTIVE PRIVILEGE

The Presidency of Richard Nixon brought to a head some long-standing concerns about the awesome power of the executive office and the lack of means for enforcing presidential responsibility. Since Franklin Roosevelt, the presidential office had burgeoned at the expense of Congress, and it had become accepted doctrine that a powerful President was required to deal with national problems. But Nixon went

---

[13] *Morgan* v. *TVA* (1941). See C. Herman Pritchett, *The Tennessee Valley Authority: A Study in Public Administration* (Chapel Hill, N.C.: The University of North Carolina Press, 1943), pp. 203–216.

[14] *United Public Workers* v. *Mitchell* (1947); *U.S. Civil Service Commission* v. *National Assn. of Letter Carriers* (1973).

beyond previous Presidents in several important respects, particularly in the degree to which he centralized power in the White House and in his attitude of distrust and near-contempt for Congress.

The Watergate scandals destroyed Nixon's "imperial Presidency" and provoked an unprecedented examination of the constitutional position of the office.[15] Separation of powers problems that previously had been only subjects for speculation by constitutional scholars suddenly erupted in newspaper headlines and TV commentaries. One major issue was the validity of the claim of "executive privilege" which Nixon had earlier put forth to justify refusal to respond to congressional requests for information and which he now raised in denying White House tapes and other records demanded by the congressional investigating committees, the Watergate special prosecutor, and judges in several Watergate cases. His position was that executive privilege had been asserted by all Presidents going back to Washington, that his discussions with members of the White House staff were protected by the necessity of confidentiality, and that the principle of separation of powers guarantees each of the branches of government the right to defend itself against incursions by the other branches.

While it is true that earlier Presidents had on occasion refused to submit information requested by Congress, the instances were considerably fewer than Nixon claimed, while the phrase "executive privilege" and the defense of confidentiality dated back only to the Eisenhower administration.[16] As the Senate Watergate Committee began operations in 1973, Nixon forbade any of his White House aides to testify before it, a position from which he quickly withdrew under pressure, and in fact the Ervin Committee did hear testimony from all relevant White House aides.

Nixon also refused to submit White House tapes subpoenaed by both the Senate Committee and the House Judiciary Committee in its impeachment inquiry. However, the Watergate special prosecutor, Archibald Cox, went to court in his demand that the tapes be made available to the Watergate grand jury and was upheld by Judge John Sirica. Recognizing that there was some need to protect presidential confidentiality, Sirica indicated that he would himself review the subpoenaed materials to screen out any matter where executive privilege was validly invoked, and that he would then pass the rest on to the grand jury. Sirica's ruling was upheld by the Court of Appeals for the District of Columbia in *Nixon* v. *Sirica* (1973), and Nixon then complied without carrying an appeal to the Supreme Court.

The Supreme Court's turn to speak on executive privilege came in 1974. In preparation for the major Watergate coverup trial, special prosecutor Leon Jawor-

---

[15] See Arthur M. Schlesinger, Jr., *The Imperial Presidency* (Boston: Houghton Mifflin Company, 1973); Frederick C. Mosher et al., *Watergate: Implications for Responsible Government* (New York: Basic Books, Inc., 1974); Rexford G. Tugwell and Thomas E. Cronin (eds.), *The Presidency Reappraised* (New York: Praeger Publishers, 1974).

[16] See Raoul Berger, *Executive Privilege: A Constitutional Myth* (Cambridge, Mass.: Harvard University Press, 1974); also "Executive Privilege and Congressional Inquiry," 12 UCLA Law Review 1044, 1364 (1965). For a critique of Berger's rejection of all executive privilege claims, see Ralph K. Winter, Jr., "The Seedlings for the Forest," 83 Yale Law Journal 1730 (1974).

ski[17] subpoenaed some sixty-four tapes. Judge Sirica ordered compliance, and his decision was upheld by the Supreme Court in *United States* v. *Nixon* (1974).[18] The Court unanimously denied the President's right to make a final, unreviewable claim of executive privilege.

> Neither the doctrine of separation of powers, nor the need for confidentiality of high-level communications, without more, can sustain an absolute, unqualified, presidential privilege of immunity from judicial process under all circumstances.

The Court did grant that there was a limited executive privilege with a constitutional base—mentioning particularly the need to protect military, diplomatic, or sensitive national security secrets—and assured that the courts would recognize claims of confidentiality related to the President's ability to discharge his constitutional powers effectively.[19] But no national security claims were involved here. There was only "the generalized assertion of privilege," which "must be considered in light of our historic commitment to the rule of law" and "must yield to the demonstrated specific need for evidence in a pending criminal trial."

PRESIDENTIAL IMMUNITIES

President Nixon's involvement in the Watergate coverup raised other legal issues concerning presidential immunities. As just noted, subpoenas were upheld against Nixon in two cases. There had been some doubt whether the President was subject to subpoena because of the obvious enforcement problem if he chose to resist. The principal precedent was Chief Justice Marshall's subpoena to President Jefferson in the 1807 treason trial of Aaron Burr. While Marshall's opinion clearly rejected the contention that the President was immune from subpoena, the later developments in the case were somewhat confused and the subpoena was not actually enforced.[20]

In *Mississippi* v. *Johnson* (1867), the Supreme Court declined to issue an injunction against the President, pointing out that if he refused obedience, the Court

---

[17] Jaworski had succeeded Archibald Cox after the "Saturday night massacre," when Attorney General Elliott Richardson and Assistant Attorney General William Ruckelshaus resigned rather than carry out Nixon's order to fire Cox, who was then removed by Solicitor General Robert H. Bork as Acting Attorney General. See J. Anthony Lukas, *Nightmare* (New York: The Viking Press, 1976).

[18] For comment on the decision, see Paul A. Freund, "On Presidential Privilege," 88 HARVARD LAW REVIEW 13 (1974). All the documents in the case are collected in Leon Friedman (ed.), *United States* v. *Nixon: The President before the Supreme Court* (New York: Chelsea House Publishers, 1974).

[19] The Court was criticized by some for this admission, since it was the first time the Court had ever explicitly recognized the legitimacy of a claim of executive privilege. In *United States* v. *Reynolds* (1953), a suit under the Tort Claims Act arising from the death of three civilians in a military plane crash, the government contended that executive department heads had power to withhold any documents from judicial view if they deemed it in the public interest to do so. The Court found it unnecessary to accept this position, deciding *Reynolds* on a narrower ground. Philip Kurland criticized executive privilege as "a tool for the preclusion of legislative oversight, which is the only real check on abuse of executive power." To counter the Court's concession in *Nixon,* he argued that Congress should provide a statutory definition of the doctrine and a strict assertion of the conditions under which the privilege could be claimed by Presidents. (*Los Angeles Times,* June 22, 1975.) See also "Symposium: *United States* v. *Nixon,*" 22 *UCLA Law Review* 1–140 (1974).

[20] *United States* v. *Burr* (1807). See Raoul Berger, "The President, Congress, and the Courts—Subpoenaing the President: Jefferson v. Marshall in the Burr Case," 83 YALE LAW JOURNAL 1111 (1974).

would be "without power to enforce its process." When Judge Sirica subpoenaed Nixon's tapes for use of the Watergate grand jury, he considered it immaterial "that the court has not the physical power to enforce its order to the President." He simply relied on "the good faith of the executive branch." In fact, Nixon did yield to both subpoenas, though prior to the Supreme Court's decision in *United States* v. *Nixon* his counsel had refused to give assurance that Nixon would obey a Supreme Court order. It was generally agreed that if such resistance had occurred, it would have been cause for immediate impeachment.

A second issue raised by Watergate was whether a President is subject to criminal indictment while in office. The Watergate grand jury was convinced by the evidence it received that Nixon had participated in the coverup, and it wished to indict him along with the other principals. It was dissuaded, however, by Jaworski, who—taking it upon himself to decide this constitutional question—told the grand jury that the President was constitutionally protected against indictment.[21] Consequently, Nixon was merely named as an "unindicted coconspirator" by the grand jury. In accepting the case of *United States* v. *Nixon,* the Supreme Court agreed to consider whether an incumbent President can be named in this manner; but after consideration, the justices ruled that the issue was irrelevant and so failed to express an opinion on it.

The Constitution makes it clear that after a President leaves office he can be prosecuted for criminal acts performed in office, even if he has already been convicted on impeachment for those acts (Art. I, sec. 3). Nixon faced the prospect of various legal actions following his resignation. A proposal that Congress grant him immunity from criminal prosecution was dropped, and in any event it could have had no binding effect. President Ford's pardon foreclosed any federal criminal prosecutions, but Nixon remained liable to suit in civil cases.

A third issue concerns the ownership of presidential papers and records. Past practice has proceeded on the assumption that Presidents own their papers and take them with them when they leave the White House.[22] However, because of the circumstances under which Nixon left office and the relevance of his tapes and papers to ongoing criminal investigations, Congress passed the Presidential Recordings and Materials Preservation Act of 1974, which required the General Services Administration to issue protective regulations for the Nixon materials. In *Nixon* v. *Administrator of General Services* (1976) a three-judge court in the District of Columbia upheld the statute, concluding that the invasion of privacy was not unreasonable since the act served national interests of overriding importance.

[21] For the opposing view that a President can be prosecuted while in office, see Raoul Berger, "The President, Congress, and the Courts—Must Impeachment Precede Indictment?" 83 YALE LAW JOURNAL 1111, 1123 (1974).

[22] It should be realized that this practice developed when the Presidency was practically a personal office, with only a few assistants and secretaries. Since 1939, when the Executive Office of the President was established, the Presidency has become institutionalized. There were 14 staff agencies in the Nixon White House, 36 special assistants, and 3,400 executive employees in all. The explosion in "presidential" papers is indicated by the following data: Hoover, in one term, accumulated a million pages; Roosevelt, in three terms, 10.5 million pages; Eisenhower, in two terms, 11 million pages; Kennedy, in less than one term, 13 million; Johnson, in one and one-half terms, 17 million; and Nixon, in one and one half terms, 42 million pages. The notion that these papers are the personal property of the President obviously requires rethinking. (*The New York Times,* September 10, 1975.)

THE POWER TO PARDON

Article II, section 2, provides that the President "shall have power to grant reprieves and pardons for offenses against the United States, except in cases of impeachment." A pardon is usually thought of as an act of grace to correct a conviction or sentence which seems mistaken, harsh, or disproportionate to the crime. However, American Presidents have on numerous occasions used the pardoning power to grant amnesty to an entire group.[23] Congress also has the power to grant amnesties; it has done so in remitting penalties incurred under national statutes[24] and by providing immunity from prosecution for persons testifying before courts or congressional investigating committees.[25] However, Congress cannot interfere with the President's right to issue amnesties.[26]

The effect of a pardon is to grant exemption from the punishment the law inflicts for a crime. Since imprisonment and fine are the normal punishments, a pardon frees a convicted criminal from serving any uncompleted term of imprisonment and from paying any unpaid fine. Loss of certain civil and political rights is often an additional penalty for conviction of crime. Since a pardon will restore these rights, one may still be sought on behalf of persons who have completed their sentences and paid their fines.

In *Ex parte Garland* (1867) the Supreme Court ruled that the result of a pardon is to wipe out completely all effects of the conviction for crime, Justice Field stating: "When the pardon is full, it releases the punishment and blots out of existence the guilt, so that in the eye of the law the offender is as innocent as if he had never committed the offence."[27]

Marshall early stated the rule that a pardon must be accepted to be valid,[28] which was followed in *Burdick* v. *United States* (1915). President Wilson had offered a full pardon for all offenses against the United States to one Burdick, whose testimony was wanted by a federal grand jury. Burdick, however, refused to accept the pardon, and the Supreme Court unanimously backed him.[29]

The only directly stated limitation on the President's pardoning power is that it does not apply to cases of impeachment, thus preventing the President from undoing the effect of such legislative punishment. A conviction for criminal contempt of court can be pardoned, but civil contempt actions, whose purpose is to enforce the rights of litigants, cannot be frustrated by a pardon.

The validity of a "conditional" pardon was upheld in *Schick* v. *Reed* (1974).[30] On review of a soldier's murder conviction and death sentence imposed by court-

---

[23] Upheld in *Armstrong* v. *United States* (1872).
[24] *The Laura* (1885).
[25] *Brown* v. *Walker* (1896).
[26] *United States* v. *Klein* (1872).
[27] But see *Carlesi* v. *New York* (1914) for a limitation on this principle.
[28] *United States* v. *Wilson* (1833).
[29] But see *Chapman* v. *Scott* (1925) and *Biddle* v. *Perovich* (1927).
[30] A precedent was *Ex parte Wells* (1855). The *Schick* decision also presumably upheld the commutation granted by President Nixon in 1971 to James Hoffa, former head of the Teamsters Union, with the condition that he was barred from engaging in Teamster activities until 1980.

martial, President Eisenhower had commuted the sentence to life imprisonment, with the condition that the prisoner would never be eligible for parole. Marshall, dissenting, contended that the Court's 1972 ruling in *Furman* v. *Georgia* declaring capital punishment unconstitutional had voided the original sentence, leaving simple life imprisonment with eligibility for parole as the only legal alternative. He also contended that the President could not use his pardoning power to create unauthorized punishments.

President Ford's pardon of Richard Nixon, to whom Ford owed his office, was the most controversial in American history. To avert certain impeachment and conviction, Nixon had resigned effective August 9, 1974. By so doing he retained pension rights and other perquisites extended by law to ex-Presidents, which he would have forfeited had he been convicted on impeachment. The impeachment proceedings were thereby aborted, the Judiciary Committee simply submitting a final report to the House. Actually the impeachment proceedings could have been continued even after the resignation and in spite of the pardon, since the pardoning power does not apply to cases of impeachment.

Ford's pardon of Nixon, which had been negotiated secretly without consultation with any responsible political figures and announced on September 8 with bombshell effects, raised several constitutional questions. First, it was alleged that the pardon violated the spirit of the constitutional ban on pardons in cases of impeachment. More significant was the challenge to the timing and scope of the pardon. Ford granted "a full, free and absolute pardon unto Richard Nixon for all offenses against the United States which he, Richard Nixon, has committed or may have committed or taken part in during the period from January 20, 1969 through August 9, 1974."

On September 8 Nixon had not been impeached by Congress or indicted for any crime, though he had been named as an unindicted coconspirator in the Watergate coverup case. Since Nixon had admitted no criminal acts, it appeared that Ford had made an executive finding of guilt in referring to crimes which Nixon "has committed." Also, the pardon guaranteed Nixon absolute immunity from federal criminal prosecution at a time when possible criminal acts on his part were still actively under investigation.

It is true that at the Constitutional Convention language proposing that pardons could be granted only "after conviction" was rejected on the ground that "pardon before conviction might be necessary in order to obtain the testimony of accomplices." Moreover, in *Ex parte Garland* (1867), a closely divided Court held that the pardoning power "may be exercised at any time after . . . commission [of the offense], either before legal proceedings are taken, or during their pendency, or after conviction and judgment." However, this statement was dictum, and since the Court speaks of "offenses," it can be argued that until there has been a confession or at least an indictment, there is no "offense" and thus no power to pardon.

The public reaction to the Nixon pardon was highly unfavorable and, together with the revelation that Nixon had considered the possibility of pardoning himself and his Watergate associates before resigning, led to proposals for a constitutional amendment which would bar pardons prior to conviction.

Chapter 16

Control of Foreign Relations

The doctrine of "political questions," we noted in Chapter 8, is available for the Supreme Court's use when an issue of private right which it is asked to decide turns on considerations largely outside judicial competence or authority. It is significant that the political questions doctrine has been perhaps most often invoked by the Court to avoid decisions relating to the conduct of American foreign relations. An early instance was *Foster* v. *Neilson* (1829), where the Court refused to rule on the location of the boundary between Spain and the United States in 1804 because this was "more a political than a legal question," and one on which the courts must accept the decisions of the "political departments."

The development of constitutional principles in the foreign relations field is thus more properly traced through the medium of diplomatic history than constitutional law, and the present chapter will be accordingly of limited scope. The Supreme Court has nevertheless on several occasions stated principles of primary importance in the guidance and rationalization of American practice in the field of foreign relations.[1] Of course the federal courts administer general international law

---

[1] A highly useful general work is Louis Henkin, *Foreign Affairs and the Constitution* (Mineola, N.Y.: The Foundation Press, 1972).

in so far as it is applicable in cases coming before them, but that is a different problem and one outside the confines of the present study.

THE NATURE OF FEDERAL POWER

The provisions of the Constitution pertaining to foreign relations all take the form of assignments of particular functions to the various branches of the government. These specifically mentioned powers by no means cover the whole range of foreign affairs, and there is no grant of authority over foreign relations in broad terms comparable, say, with the authorization to regulate commerce among the states. On the other hand there are no provisions expressly denying or limiting the federal government's full authority to conduct external relations as a sovereign nation in a world of sovereign nations.

The framers were in fact well aware that there was no choice in this matter. The central government they were instituting would be fatally disabled if it lacked authority to deal with its peers or to meet the ever-recurring crises arising out of its relations abroad. As Hamilton said in No. 23 of *The Federalist*: "The circumstances that endanger the safety of nations are infinite, and for this reason no constitutional shackles can wisely be imposed on the power to which the care of it is committed." Thus the first principle in this area is that governmental power over foreign relations is plenary. The manner of its exercise is in certain respects specified by the Constitution, and the location of responsibility is defined. But the federal government's basic authority to conduct foreign relations is constitutionally unlimited.

What is the constitutional source of this authority, which goes far beyond the sum of the particular functions mentioned in the document? The answer is that authority over foreign affairs is an inherent power, which attaches automatically to the federal government as a sovereign entity, and derives from the Constitution only as the Constitution is the creator of that sovereign entity. As Justice Sutherland said in *United States* v. *Curtiss-Wright Export Corporation* (1936): "The investment of the federal government with the powers of external sovereignty did not depend upon the affirmative grants of the Constitution. The powers to declare and wage war, to conclude peace, to make treaties, to maintain diplomatic relations with other sovereignties, if they had never been mentioned in the Constitution, would have vested in the federal government as necessary concomitants of nationality."

For this reason, Sutherland continued, the source of foreign relations authority contrasted sharply with federal power over internal affairs. "In that field, the primary purpose of the Constitution was to carve from the general mass of legislative powers *then possessed by the states* such portions as it was thought desirable to vest in the federal government, leaving those not included in the enumeration still in the states." But the Constitution could not transfer power over external affairs in this way from the states to the nation because "the states severally never possessed international powers." Rather, on the separation of the colonies "acting as a unit" from Great Britain, "the powers of external sovereignty passed from the Crown not to the colonies severally, but to the colonies in their collective and corporate capacity as the United States of America." Even before the Declaration of Independence, the Colonies were acting through a common agency, the Continental Congress, and when "the external sovereignty of Great Britain in respect of the colonies ceased, it immediately passed to the Union." Thus the Union, existing before the Constitution, "was the sole possessor of external sovereignty and in the Union it remained without change save in so far as the Constitution in express terms qualified its exercise."

Presumably the purpose of Sutherland's conceptualistic analysis, which seems strikingly at variance with the actual historical facts of the Revolutionary period,[2] was to establish that the federal government's power over foreign affairs was inherent, plenary, and exclusive, but it seems an unnecessarily involved way of achieving those ends. Surely the inherent nature of the power to conduct foreign affairs can be deduced from the right of a nation to self-preservation in a world of nations, without elaborate hypotheses about the location and transfer of sovereignty in a revolutionary period. That the power is plenary is established by the absence of any expressed constitutional limitations on its exercise. That the power is exclusive as against the states is sufficiently established by Article I, section 10, which flatly forbids states to enter into "any treaty, alliance, or confederation," or to grant "letters of marque and reprisal." The third clause of section 10 carries further prohibitions, though these may be waived with the consent of Congress. The clause reads:

> No state shall, without the consent of Congress, . . . keep troops, or ships of war in time of peace, enter into any agreement or compact . . . with a foreign power, or engage in war, unless actually invaded, or in such imminent danger as will not admit of delay.

In fact, the consent of Congress has never been asked for any of these purposes, and the clause must now be read as an unqualified bar to the acts specified. Thus the complete incapacity of the states for foreign relationships is fully established by the letter of the Constitution and by practice.

Neither is Sutherland's theory necessary to prevent any possible encroachment on federal authority by the states through their "reserved powers" under the Tenth Amendment. In discussing the commerce clause, we saw how the doctrine of dual federalism for a time made reserved state powers an instrument for denying full exercise by the federal government of its directly granted powers to regulate commerce among the states. But dual federalism never got a foothold in the field of foreign relations, as *Ware* v. *Hylton* (1796) demonstrates. During the Revolutionary War Virginia passed a law sequestering British property and providing that debts owed by citizens of the state to British subjects could be discharged by payment to a designated state officer. This statute was clearly a valid exercise of state powers under international law. However, the treaty of peace between the United States and Great Britain controverted this arrangement and preserved the right of British creditors to collect such debts. The Supreme Court held that this exercise by the United States of its treaty power had the effect of nullifying the conflicting Virginia law.

---

[2] See the excellent article by Charles A. Lofgren, "*United States* v. *Curtiss-Wright Export Corporation*: An Historical Reassessment," 83 YALE LAW JOURNAL 1 (1973), in which he concludes that Justice Sutherland's history was "shockingly inaccurate."

THE ROLE OF THE PRESIDENT

The principal theoretical writers on government whose works were known and read by the framers—Blackstone, Locke, Montesquieu—were unanimous in contending that the power to conduct foreign relations must rest with the executive. In spite of this fact, the Constitution allocated the power to declare war to Congress, where the authority had vested under the Articles of Confederation. It made the Senate's consent necessary to the ratification of treaties, and by a two-thirds vote. It made the Senate's advice and consent a condition to the appointment of ambassadors. When account is taken of the general lawmaking and appropriating powers of Congress, the exercise of which may be essential to the formulation and execution of foreign policy decisions, it is clear that, as Corwin says, "The Constitution, considered only for its affirmative grants of powers capable of affecting the issue, is an invitation to struggle for the privilege of directing American foreign policy."[3]

For this struggle the President is powerfully equipped by the general characteristics of executive power already noted, by his constitutional authority as Commander in Chief, and by his recognized position as "the Nation's organ for foreign affairs."[4] The Supreme Court has repeatedly recognized the President's primacy and special position in this area, as a further look at the *Curtiss-Wright* decision will demonstrate. The controversy in that case involved a joint resolution adopted by Congress in 1934 authorizing the President by proclamation to prohibit the sale within the United States of arms to certain South American belligerent states. The President promptly issued such a declaration. A conviction for violation of the proclamation and joint resolution was attacked on the ground that the statute constituted an unlawful delegation of legislative power to the President, because action was left to the "unfettered discretion" of the executive with no statutory standards to guide his decision.

As noted in Chapter 10, the Court had just used such grounds to invalidate federal statutes in the *Panama Refining, Schechter,* and *Carter Coal Co.* cases. But in *Curtiss-Wright* Justice Sutherland pointed out that the delegations in those three cases had "related solely to internal affairs," whereas the "whole aim" of the resolution challenged here was "to affect a situation entirely external to the United States." In this latter area the President possessed not only the powers given him by statute, but also "the very delicate, plenary and exclusive power of the President as the sole organ of the federal government in the field of international relations." Sutherland went on:

> It is quite apparent that if, in the maintenance of our international relations, embarrassment . . . is to be avoided and success for our aims achieved, congressional legislation which is to be made effective through negotiation and inquiry within the international field must often accord to the President a degree of discretion and freedom from statutory restriction which would not be admissible were domestic affairs alone involved.

[3] Edward S. Corwin (ed.), *The President: Office and Powers,* 1787–1957 (New York: New York University Press, 4th rev. ed., 1957), p. 171.

[4] This phrase goes back to a statement made by John Marshall in the House of Representatives in 1799. See *ibid.,* pp. 177–178. See Raoul Berger, "The Presidential Monopoly of Foreign Relations," 71 MICHIGAN LAW REVIEW 1 (1972).

Moreover, he, not Congress, has the better opportunity of knowing the conditions which prevail in foreign countries. . . . He has his confidential sources of information. He has his agents in the form of diplomatic, consular and other officials.

In the light of these circumstances, the Court concluded that delegations of legislative power to the President in matters involving foreign relations could not be judged by the same standards that would be applied in internal affairs.

More specifically, what powers does the President exercise in his role as "sole organ" of foreign relations for the nation? First of all, he is the channel for communications to and from other nations. He appoints the members of the diplomatic corps through whom official contacts are maintained abroad and receives their reports through the Department of State. Negotiations with foreign countries are conducted under his direction. In collaboration with the Secretary of State he determines the policies to be followed in dealing with foreign nations. [5]

Second, the power of recognizing foreign governments follows from the presidential role in sending and receiving diplomatic representatives. President Washington established the controlling precedent in this area when he received Citizen Genêt and then some months later demanded his recall by France, without consulting Congress on either occasion. Constitutional authority for decisions on the establishment of diplomatic relations—as in the recognition of Russia in 1933, or the Nixon-Kissinger visit to Communist China in 1972, or the break with Castro's Cuba—rest on the President alone, as the Supreme Court recognized in *United States* v. *Belmont* (1937).

Third, the President can use his control of the Armed Forces to implement his foreign policy and to enforce American rights or interests abroad. In 1844 Tyler disposed the naval and military forces so as to protect Texas against Mexican reprisals because of the pending treaty for annexation of Texas to the United States. Theodore Roosevelt in 1903 "took Panama," as he put it, and later sent the fleet around the world to demonstrate American power and interest in world affairs. President Wilson ordered the arming of American merchant vessels as a countermove to German unrestricted submarine warfare in March, 1917. Three Presidents sent troops into the Vietnam quagmire. Ford used air and naval forces in 1975 against Cambodia to rescue the American vessel *Mayaguez*. Troops have been repeatedly employed to protect American lives and property in foreign countries.

These are powers of tremendous impact—so great, in fact, that they largely cancel out the most important grant of external authority to Congress, the power to declare war.

Treaties

On the other hand, the necessity of securing Senate consent by a two-thirds vote for the ratification of treaties has proved in practice to be a real limitation on executive policy making. The framers thought of the Senate as a kind of council with which

---

[5] During the Nixon administration, Secretary of State William P. Rogers was largely eclipsed by Henry Kissinger, presidential assistant for national security. Kissinger became Secretary of State in 1973 but also retained his White House national security post until 1975.

the President would sit while treaties were under negotiation and from which he would get advice. In fact President Washington tried to use the Senate in this way in August, 1789, going to the Senate chamber in person and presenting seven issues pertaining to a proposed treaty with the Southern Indians on which he wished "advice and consent." The senators preferred not to discuss the matter in the presence of the President, and voted to refer it to a committee of five. Washington, quite indignant, exclaimed: "This defeats every purpose of my coming here," and subsequently withdrew with what William Maclay called "a discontented air." Washington did go back two days later for the Senate's answers to his questions, but the whole experience was so unfortunate that the effort has never been repeated.

Treaties are consequently negotiated by the executive, though congressional leaders are normally appointed to the American delegation to important international conferences as well as to the United Nations. When treaties are sent to the Senate in completed form, their fate is unpredictable. John Hay once wrote: "A treaty entering the Senate is like a bull going into the arena; no one can say just how or when the final blow will fall—but one thing is certain, it will never leave the arena alive."[6] This is highly exaggerated, but the shambles which Senate intervention has sometimes made of United States foreign policy has led many students to conclude that consent to treaty ratification by a majority vote of the two houses of Congress would be preferable to the present arrangement.

The Senate can defeat a treaty entirely or consent to ratification with amendments. This latter action requires the President, if he still favors the treaty, to secure the acceptance of these amendments by the foreign power involved before the treaty can be ratified. The Senate may also attach reservations, which do not alter the content of the treaty itself but do qualify the obligations assumed under the treaty by the United States.

Executive Agreements

Partly because of the hazards of Senate treaty approval, the President has made extensive use of "executive agreements" with foreign countries.[7] Since these agreements are not treaties in name, they are not subject to the constitutional requirement of Senate consent. They may be employed for minor matters which it would be inappropriate to embody in a treaty, but in the twentieth century many executive agreements have dealt with matters of major importance. Thus Japanese immigration into the United States was governed for seventeen years by the "Gentlemen's Agreement" of 1907, and the controversial Potsdam and Yalta Pacts were executive agreements.

[6] William R. Thayer, *The Life and Letters of John Hay* (Boston: Houghton Mifflin Company, 1915), vol. 2, p. 393. In 1974 the Senate Foreign Relations Committee voted out the Geneva protocol on chemical warfare which had been submitted for ratification in 1926.

[7] Congress has periodically but unsuccessfully sought to restrict the use of executive agreements as a means of avoiding submission of treaties to the Senate. The famous Bricker Amendment of the 1950s had this as one of its purposes. In 1972 discovery by the Senate of a number of secret foreign commitments, particularly an agreement permitting use of Spanish bases in return for American grants, led Congress to adopt the so-called Case Amendment, which requires the Secretary of State to submit to Congress within sixty days the text of any international agreement made by the executive branch. In 1975 some members of Congress were urging a congressional procedure, similar to that proposed in the Bricker Amendment, for disapproving executive agreements.

Executive agreements are often based on acts of Congress authorizing them. If not, they are usually said to find their constitutional authority in the President's power as Commander in Chief or in his position as the sole organ of international relations. Efforts to distinguish the legal effects of executive agreements from treaties have generally been unsuccessful. One contention has been that the force of an executive agreement terminates with the end of the administration which entered into it, but this is not true. For example, the 1940 destroyer deal with Britain provided for United States leases extending ninety-nine years on the British bases involved.

A further contention is that agreements, unlike treaties, are not "law of the land" unless authorized or approved by Congress, and so not noticeable by the courts. But in *United States* v. *Belmont* (1937) the Supreme Court specifically denied this view, holding that the recognition of Soviet Russia in 1933 and the accompanying executive agreements constituted an international compact which the President was authorized to enter into without consulting the Senate. Moreover, such agreements had the same effect as treaties in superseding conflicting state laws. To similar effect was the decision in *United States* v. *Pink* (1942).[8]

CONGRESS AND FOREIGN RELATIONS

In addition to the power of Congress to declare war and the special role of the Senate in ratifying treaties and confirming ambassadorial appointments, Congress can exercise great influence over foreign policy through its general powers of legislation, appropriation, and investigation.[9] Congress early seized power from the President on the matter of neutrality. In 1793 President Washington, on the outbreak of war between Britain and France, issued a proclamation asserting the intention of the United States to be "friendly and impartial" toward both belligerents. Hamilton wrote a defense of the constitutional right of the President to issue such a proclamation, but the action was offensive to Jeffersonian views of executive power. In 1794 Congress superseded the executive proclamation by passing the first neutrality act, and this precedent has been subsequently accepted as establishing legislative authority over the neutrality issue.

Congress possesses specific constitutional authority to define and punish offenses against the law of nations as well as to regulate foreign commerce. Congress may use its general lawmaking power to frustrate or limit executive foreign policy. In 1924 Congress adopted the Japanese Exclusion Act over the protests of President Coolidge and Secretary of State Hughes, with damaging effects on American foreign relations. The authority to negotiate reciprocal trade agreements, a basic instrument of foreign policy after 1934, had to be won anew from Congress every two or three years. More recently a favorite legislative device has been to impose statutory bans on trade with, or aid to, countries in congressional disfavor.

---

[8] The Supreme Court has not determined whether an executive agreement will supersede an earlier act of Congress with which it is in disagreement. See *United States* v. *Guy W. Capps, Inc.* (1955).

[9] See Arthur Schlesinger, Jr., "Congress and the Making of American Foreign Policy," 51 FOREIGN AFFAIRS 78 (1972).

Congressional legislative power may also step into the breach caused by failure of the treaty process to function successfully. After the defeat of the Treaty of Versailles, it was a joint resolution of Congress which finally brought American participation in the war against the Central Powers to a legal conclusion in 1921. Moreover, it should be noted that American adherence to the United Nations was accomplished by congressional statute, the United Nations Participation Act of 1945.

The appropriations power gives legislative control over any executive policy which requires funds for its implementation, and the fact that appropriations measures must originate with the House serves somewhat to balance the Senate's special role in the foreign relations field. Since the inauguration of the Marshall Plan in 1947, the appropriation for foreign aid has annually precipitated lengthy and often acrimonious debates over foreign policy, and the executive recommendations are almost invariably substantially reduced.

The House and Senate can also use their general investigatory powers to influence foreign policy. During the 1930s Senator Nye's investigations of the armaments industry did much to encourage an isolationist attitude toward foreign involvements. Senator Fulbright, who was at odds with President Johnson on Vietnam, used his powerful position as chairman of the Senate Foreign Relations Committee to conduct "educational" hearings on China policy and the North Atlantic Treaty Organization as well as Vietnam.

Conscious of the desirability of congressional support for the use of troops outside the country, President Eisenhower in 1955 requested Congress to adopt a joint resolution authorizing his employment of the armed forces to protect Formosa from Chinese attack. Again in 1957 Congress voted support for the President if he should determine there was necessity for use of force against Communist aggression in the Middle East.

These precedents were utilized by President Johnson in 1964. At a time when there were only 20,000 American troops in Vietnam, and after alleged North Vietnamese torpedo boat attacks on two United States destroyers in the Gulf of Tonkin, the President asked Congress for a joint resolution of support to strengthen his hand in dealing with the Vietnam situation. Almost unanimously Congress adopted the so-called Tonkin Gulf Resolution approving and supporting "the determination of the President, as Commander in Chief, to take all necessary measures to repel any armed attack against the forces of the United States and to prevent further aggression."

In the aftermath of the Vietnam debacle, Congress undertook to play a more active role in foreign relations, highlighted by an arms embargo against Turkey in 1974 following the Turkish invasion of Cyprus, and a ban on funds and military aid to factions in the Angola civil war in 1975. Both actions were strongly condemned by the executive as congressional meddling in foreign affairs. Disclosure of CIA covert activities and assassination plots abroad led both the House and Senate to create special intelligence committees in 1975 to investigate these reports, and to consider how Congress might begin to exercise some oversight and control over the activities of this agency.

CONSTITUTIONAL ASPECTS OF THE TREATY POWER

Article VI provides: "This Constitution, and the laws ·of the United States which shall be made in pursuance thereof; and all treaties made, or which shall be made, under the authority of the United States, shall be the supreme law of the land." Two problems growing out of this language need consideration here: first, the relationship between treaties and acts of Congress; and second, the relationship of treaties and the treaty-making power to the Constitution itself.

Treaties and Acts of Congress

Article VI sets treaties and acts of Congress on a par—both are "the supreme law of the land." How then are conflicts between treaties and statutes adjusted? First it is necessary to distinguish between "self-executing" and "non-self-executing" treaties. A treaty is self-executing when it requires no congressional legislation to put it into effect. Thus the provisions of a treaty defining the rights of aliens in the United States would automatically become the "supreme law of the land," and the courts would be obliged to enforce them. A non-self-executing treaty is one in which obligations of future action are undertaken by the political departments of the government. A treaty of alliance with a foreign power, or a treaty which required the appropriation of money by Congress would be illustrations. The courts have no power to enforce such treaties should the government fail to honor the obligation it has undertaken.

In general, where a treaty and a statute conflict, the later in point of time supersedes the earlier. There are exceptions, however. All acts of Congress prevail over earlier conflicting treaties, but a non-self-executing treaty does not supersede an earlier conflicting act of Congress.[10]

Constitutional Scope of Treaties

According to Article VI, laws must be made "in pursuance" of the Constitution in order to have status as supreme law of the land, but treaties need be made only "under the authority of the United States." Considerable effort has been made to conjure up from this difference in wording the bogey of a treaty power which is unlimited by the Constitution. Some substance seems to be given to these fears by the fact that the Supreme Court has never held a treaty unconstitutional. But such fears, to the extent that they were genuine, were completely unfounded.

First, the provision that treaties need be made only "under the authority of the United States" was required to validate treaties made *before* the Constitution was adopted, particularly the important peace treaties which concluded the Revolutionary War. Second, the Court has on several occasions clearly announced that the treaty power is subject to the Constitution. Perhaps the most explicit earlier holding to this effect came in *Geofroy* v. *Riggs* (1890). Justice Field there began by admitting that "the treaty power, as expressed in the Constitution, is in terms unlimited," but he went on to note that it was subject to those implied "restraints which are found

---

[10] See *Head Money Cases* (1884).

in that instrument against the action of the government or of its departments, and those arising from the nature of the government itself and of that of the States." Since this language was a little vague, Field added: "It would not be contended that [the treaty power] extends so far as to authorize what the Constitution forbids, or a change in the character of the government or in that of one of the States, or a cession of any portion of the territory of the latter, without its consent."

Any doubt which could have remained on the subjection of the treaty power to the Constitution after this decision was completely extinguished by *Reid* v. *Covert* (1957). Justice Black, after quoting Article VI, said:

> There is nothing in this language which intimates that treaties and laws enacted pursuant to them do not have to comply with the provisions of the Constitution. . . . It would be manifestly contrary to the objectives of those who created the Constitution, as well as those who were responsible for the Bill of Rights—let alone alien to our entire constitutional history and tradition—to construe Article VI as permitting the United States to exercise power under an international agreement without observing constitutional prohibitions. In effect, such construction would permit amendment of that document in a manner not sanctioned by Article V.

The Supreme Court's decision in *Missouri* v. *Holland* (1920) dealt with another important aspect of the treaty power. This case arose out of the efforts of the United States to impose limits on the shooting of migratory birds. The first congressional statute passed for this purpose was declared an unconstitutional exercise of federal commerce power in two federal district court decisions, on the ground that the birds were owned by the states in their sovereign capacity for the benefit of their people. The United States then entered into a treaty with Great Britain, reciting the dangers of extermination of birds in their annual migrations between the United States and Canada, providing for closed seasons and other forms of protection, and agreeing that the two powers would take or propose to their legislatures necessary measures for making the treaty provisions effective. In pursuance of this treaty, Congress passed a statute in 1918 prohibiting the killing of migratory birds except in accordance with federal regulations.

The Supreme Court, through Justice Holmes, upheld enforcement of this statute against the charge that the treaty and legislation were an unconstitutional interference with the rights of the states. In part his conclusion rested upon the evanescent nature of the state claim to ownership of the birds. "The whole foundation of the State's rights is the presence within their jurisdiction of birds that yesterday had not arrived, tomorrow may be in another State and in a week a thousand miles away." But more positively his case was based on recognition of the fact that here was "a national interest of very nearly the first magnitude" which could be protected "only by national action in concert with that of another power. . . . But for the treaty and the statute there soon might be no birds for any powers to deal with."

Holmes did not intend to see the only effective means of protecting this national interest frustrated by "some invisible radiation from the general terms of the Tenth Amendment." For "it is not lightly to be assumed that, in matters requiring national action, 'a power which must belong to and somewhere reside in every civilized government' is not to be found." In this instance the authority was to be found in the treaty power. Holmes hastened to add that he did not "mean to imply that there are no qualifications to the treaty-making power"; one such limitation, he suggested, would be any explicit "prohibitory words . . . found in the Constitution." But there were none applicable to this situation. The general deduction which he drew was that "there may be matters of the sharpest exigency for the national well being that an act of Congress could not deal with but that a treaty followed by such an act could."

There is at first glance something startling about a situation whereby ratification of a treaty gives Congress constitutional powers it did not possess in the absence of the treaty. But this result is an inevitable consequence of the plenary nature of federal power over foreign affairs. The division of functions between federal and state governments made by the Constitution relates only to internal affairs. The complete incapacity of the states for foreign relationships requires that the federal government have authority to deal with all matters which are of legitimate concern to American foreign relations.

CONTROL OVER PASSPORTS

The Passport Act of 1856, codified and reenacted in 1926, provides that "The Secretary of State shall be authorized to grant and issue passports . . . under such rules as the President shall designate and prescribe. . . ." Subsequent legislation authorized the Secretary of State, as incident to the issuance of passports, to control travel by American citizens abroad. Motivated by the cold war after World War II, the State Department in 1947 adopted a policy of refusing passports to Communists or persons whose travel would "prejudice the orderly conduct of foreign relations" or "otherwise be prejudicial to the interests of the United States." During the following decade, a substantial number of persons, most of whom denied being Communists, were refused passports. In the Internal Security Act of 1950, Congress added statutory support to this policy by forbidding passports to members of Communist organizations ordered to register with the Attorney General.

The first test of these restrictions to reach the Supreme Court was *Kent* v. *Dulles* (1958), in which Justice Douglas held:

> The right to travel is part of the "liberty" of which the citizen cannot be deprived without the due process of law of the Fifth Amendment. . . . Freedom of movement across frontiers in either direction . . . was a part of our heritage. Travel abroad . . . may be necessary for a livelihood. It may be as close to the heart of the individual as the choice of what he eats, or wears, or reads.

Having decided this much, the Supreme Court found it unnecessary to take up the more difficult question of how far this liberty might be curtailed without infringing on due process, because five justices concluded that Congress had not authorized the kinds of curtailment which the State Department had been practicing.

The State Department, while announcing that passport applicants would no longer be required to answer questions about Communist Party membership, immediately appealed to Congress to adopt legislation confirming the powers it had been exercising. Surprisingly, Congress failed to act. This left, as the only expressly applicable statute, the Internal Security Act, the registration provisions of which the Court held constitutional in 1961.[11] This brought the passport provisions of the act into effect, and the State Department promptly used them to deny passports to two leading American Communists. The Supreme Court held the legislation unconstitutional in *Aptheker* v. *Secretary of State* (1964).

Justice Goldberg ruled for the Court that the language was unconstitutional on its face because it prohibited the granting of passports to any member of a registered Communist organization, regardless of whether his membership was knowing or unknowing, regardless of his degree of activity in the organization and his commitment to its purpose, or regardless of the purposes for which he wished to travel. After all, he might simply want "to visit a relative in Ireland, or . . . read rare manuscripts in the Bodleian Library of Oxford University." Justice Clark for a three-judge minority thought these were "irrational imaginings" and argued that, at least as applied to admitted Communist leaders, the statute should be upheld.

The Court did not say in *Aptheker* that the right to travel was absolute. It merely held that this particular limitation was too broad and indiscriminate in its scope. In *Zemel* v. *Rusk* (1965), the Court upheld the State Department's refusal to validate passports for travel to Communist Cuba. The broad language of the Passport Act of 1926, which the Court had held in the *Kent* case did not authorize State Department denial of passports to Communists, was here thought to justify the practice of geographical area limitations on travel. The Court majority found that there had been a frequent practice of area restrictions on passports in the decade prior to 1926; thus it could be inferred that Congress intended by the broad language of the act to maintain such authority in the executive—authority that could be supported by "the weightiest considerations of national security."

Another, and more persuasive, difference from the *Kent* situation was that there the action was taken against an individual because of his views or affiliations, whereas area limitations are imposed "because of foreign policy considerations affecting all citizens." Thus the Court felt there was no possible First Amendment claim that the individual was being restrained from travel because of his views.

Enforcement of these area restrictions proved quite frustrating for the State Department. A newspaperman who went to Cuba without a passport was indicted on his return under the Immigration and Nationality Act of 1952, which forbids reentry of an American citizen into the United States without a valid passport. The Court of Appeals for the Fifth Circuit held this provision unconstitutional as a denial of the fundamental right of free ingress.[12] Preferring not to take this case to the Supreme Court, the Department of Justice chose to rely instead on a statute forbidding citizens to depart from the country without a valid passport. But there was no specific language in the statute punishing violation of State Department area restrictions, and the Court in *United States* v. *Laub* (1967) and *Travis* v. *United*

---

[11] *Communist Party* v. *Subversive Activities Control Board* (1961).
[12] *Worthy* v. *United States* (1964).

States (1967) held that the criminal indictments must be dismissed. "Crimes are not to be created by inference," said Justice Fortas.

This ruling left open to the State Department the sanction of canceling the passports of persons who visited off-limits countries. But after another Court reversal on this issue,[13] the State Department in 1968, while continuing to declare certain countries off limits to American travelers, abandoned its efforts to deny passports to persons wishing to visit those countries or to revoke passports of those who traveled to restricted countries.

[13] *Lynd* v. *Rusk* (1967).

Chapter 17

The President
as Commander in Chief

In No. 74 of *The Federalist* Alexander Hamilton wrote: "Of all the cares or concerns of government, the direction of war most peculiarly demands those qualities which distinguish the exercise of power by a single hand." He was defending the "propriety" of the Commander in Chief clause (Art. II, sec. 2) which reads: "The President shall be Commander in Chief of the army and navy of the United States, and of the militia of the several states, when called into the actual service of the United States." This provision, he added, was "so consonant to the precedents of the State constitutions in general, that little need be said to explain or enforce it." It would amount, he said in No. 69, "to nothing more than the supreme command and direction of the military and naval forces, as first general and admiral of the Confederacy," while the more significant powers of declaring war and of raising and regulating fleets and armies were exercised by Congress.

LINCOLN AND THE WAR POWER

Hamilton did not foresee the tremendous reservoir of power that this constitutional language was to provide for the President. It was President Lincoln who, in his resolve to maintain the Union, linked together the Presidential power to take care that the laws be faithfully executed with that of Commander in Chief to yield a result approaching constitutional dictatorship.

For ten weeks after the fall of Fort Sumter until he called Congress into special session, Lincoln met the emergency by a series of actions which were for the most part completely without statutory authorization, though they were subsequently ratified by Congress. He added 40,000 men to the Army and Navy, closed the Post Office to "treasonable correspondence," paid out 2 million dollars from unappropriated funds in the Treasury, proclaimed a blockade of Southern ports, suspended the writ of habeas corpus in several areas, and caused the arrest and military detention of persons suspected of treasonable practices.

Lincoln's inauguration of military operations without authorization by Congress was upheld by the Supreme Court in the *Prize Cases* (1863). The President had declared a blockade of Confederate ports in April, 1861, and this case concerned four vessels which had been captured and taken as prizes by Union naval vessels. To decide this issue of private rights, the Court had to consider questions of the highest political significance. If it held that the conflict was not a war because it had not been declared so by Congress, then the laws of war would not apply and the prizes would have been illegally taken. If it held that the blockade was legal, but in the process recognized the Confederacy as an independent sovereign, recognition of the Confederate States by foreign governments would be encouraged, with vastly damaging effects for the Union cause.

By a narrow margin the Court avoided both of these positions. Five justices held that the insurrection was a state of war under domestic and international law, so that the President's blockade and the capture of prizes was legitimate. This "greatest of civil wars," Justice Grier said, "sprung forth suddenly from the parent brain, a Minerva in the full panoply of *war*. The President was bound to meet it in the shape it presented itself, without waiting for Congress to baptize it with a name; and no name given to it by him or them could change the fact." Moreover, it was the President who had to determine "what degree of force the crisis demands." The President's blockade proclamation was conclusive evidence for the Court that a state of war existed which demanded recourse to such a measure. At the same time the Court majority accorded no rights of sovereignty to the South.

The Court thus took the view urged by Richard Henry Dana, one of the counsel in the case, that "War is *a state of things,* and not an act of legislative will." In contrast, the minority contended that the conflict was a "personal war" of the President "until Congress assembled and acted upon this state of things."

THE POWER TO DECLARE WAR

The members of the Constitutional Convention had considered the allocation of the war-making power only very briefly. The original draft from the Committee on Detail gave Congress the power "to make war." After a brief debate, the word "make" was changed to "declare," perhaps to assure the President the power to repel attacks or perhaps to make clear that the President, not Congress, would *conduct* the war. As early as 1793 Hamilton and Madison were disagreeing over the intention of the Convention. Hamilton argued that since war making was by nature an executive function, Congress could exercise only those aspects which the Constitution specifically granted to the legislature. Madison, on the other hand, asserted that war making was a legislative function and that any exceptions in favor of the executive must be strictly interpreted.

This debate has continued over almost two centuries and can never be settled. But Charles Lofgren's careful reexamination of the original understanding convinces him that the intention was to give Congress the power to "commence" war, whether declared or not.[1]

In practice, of course, the President's control over the armed forces and responsibility for the conduct of foreign relations has made Congress a distinctly secondary participant in decisions on inauguration of military action. The only wars that Congress declared and which it had a significant role in instigating were the War of 1812 and the Spanish-American War of 1898. In the Mexican War of 1846 and in World Wars I and II Congress simply recognized the existence of a state of war by its declaration.

In the present century, both Roosevelts, Wilson, Truman, Eisenhower, Kennedy, Johnson, Nixon, and Ford have all moved American troops into action or across national frontiers with little or no effort to secure advance congressional assent. Since 1950, there have been presidential moves into Korea, Lebanon, Cuba, the Dominican Republic, Vietnam, Laos, and Cambodia—as well as distant naval operations, undercover plots, military advisory programs, and aerial overflights of foreign countries that risked conflict—with no opportunity for congressional review.

The War in Vietnam

The disastrous American involvement in Indochina was accomplished by the use of Commander-in-Chief powers by four different Presidents. After the initial commitment of American advisers and a small number of troops in Vietnam by Presidents Eisenhower and Kennedy, President Johnson used the occasion of an alleged, and almost certainly nonexistent, North Vietnamese torpedo-boat attack on two United States destroyers in the Gulf of Tonkin to ask Congress for a joint resolution of support to strengthen his hand. Almost unanimously, Congress adopted the Gulf of Tonkin Resolution approving and supporting "the determination of the President, as Commander in Chief, to take all necessary measures to repel any armed attack against the forces of the United States and to prevent further aggression."

President Johnson subsequently relied on this resolution as authorizing and justifying the tremendous escalation of military operations in Vietnam and the bombing of North Vietnam, whereas many congressmen came to feel that there had been no such intention and that they had been manipulated into a position where they had to approve the resolution or give an impression of national disunity. Assistant Secretary of State Katzenbach, testifying before the Foreign Relations Committee of the Senate on August 17, 1967, argued that the Gulf of Tonkin Resolution

---

[1] Charles A. Lofgren, "War-Making Under the Constitution: The Original Understanding," 81 YALE LAW JOURNAL 672 (1972). See also Francis D. Wormuth, "The Nixon Theory of the War Power: A Critique," 60 CALIFORNIA LAW REVIEW 623 (1972).

gave the President as much authority as a declaration of war would have. In fact, he alarmed the senators by referring to declarations of war as "outmoded" and contended that a declaration of war would not "correctly reflect the very limited objectives of the United States with respect to Vietnam."

Efforts by members and committees of Congress to recapture some control of the war-making power were tremendously accelerated in 1970 by President Nixon's precipitate expansion of military activities into Cambodia without any prior consultation with Congress, but they had only limited success. The Cooper-Church Amendment of 1970 banned the use of funds for American ground combat forces in Laos, Thailand, and Cambodia. Later that year Congress repealed the Gulf of Tonkin Resolution, but this had no effect, since by then the official justification for continued military operations was the necessity to protect American troops until they could be withdrawn from Vietnam. Various "end the war" and withdrawal resolutions failed, but Congress did eventually order the bombing of Cambodia stopped by August 15, 1973.

The War Powers Act

Ultimately, congressional frustration over its own impotence produced an important new statute, the War Powers Act, passed in 1973 over President Nixon's veto. The law sets a sixty-day limit on any presidential commitment of United States troops abroad without specific congressional authorization. The commitment can be extended for another thirty days if necessary for the safe withdrawal of troops. Unauthorized commitments can be terminated prior to the sixty-day deadline through congressional adoption of a concurrent resolution, a measure that does not require presidential signature. Moreover, the act requires the President to consult with Congress in every possible instance before introducing United States Armed Forces into hostilities or into situations where imminent involvement in hostilities is clearly indicated. While President Nixon condemned the statute as an unconstitutional and dangerous restriction on the power of the Commander in Chief to meet emergencies, some members of Congress voted against it on the opposite ground that the statute in fact recognized the President's right to start a war.

As the South Vietnamese regime was collapsing in April, 1975, President Ford felt obliged, because of the limitations imposed by the War Powers Act, to ask Congress for authorization to use United States troops if necessary to evacuate American citizens and their dependents from Saigon. A Vietnam aid bill containing such authority was approved by a conference committee on April 25, but before the House could act on the report, American troops had carried out the evacuation on April 28 and 29. The bill was then defeated on May 1, on the ground that conditions had made it moot.

Within two weeks another situation occurred calling for application of the War Powers Act—the seizure of the American merchant vessel *Mayaguez* by Cambodian naval forces on May 12, 1975. Not until the sea and air rescue operation ordered by President Ford, including bombing of the Cambodian mainland, was under way on May 14 did he call congressional leaders to the White House to "advise" them of the military moves. The President contended that his action as Commander in Chief was consistent with the War Powers Act, and though a few congressional leaders disagreed, there was widespread support, both in Congress and in the country, for Ford's prompt and decisive action. The *Mayaguez* incident suggested that the War Powers Act was unlikely to prove a very effective limitation on presidential military initiatives.

The Vietnam War in the Courts

The judiciary has never played an extensive role in determining the constitutional limits of the presidential war power. Summing up his study of the Commander in Chief, Clinton Rossiter concluded that the Supreme Court has been asked to examine only "a tiny fraction of [the President's] significant deeds and decisions as commander in chief, for most of these were by nature challengeable in no court but that of impeachment—which was entirely as it should have been. The contours of the presidential war powers have therefore been presidentially, not judicially, shaped: their exercise is for Congress and the people, not the Court, to oversee."[2]

Efforts to secure judicial review of the constitutionality of the congressionally undeclared war in Indochina were almost uniformly unsuccessful. A variety of tactics were employed to develop litigable cases which the courts might agree to hear. In *Katz* v. *Tyler* (1967), a draft objector claimed that the American operation in Vietnam was a war of aggression outlawed by the 1945 Treaty of London.[3] The trial judge dismissed the suit for lack of standing, and the Supreme Court refused to grant certiorari.

In *Mitchell* v. *United States* (1967) the Court likewise denied certiorari in another case based on the Treaty of London, where the trial judge had barred from evidence any testimony as to the legality of the war or about alleged atrocities by American forces in Vietnam as not germane to the charge of failing to report for induction. Justice Douglas dissented, on the ground that these claims presented "sensitive and delicate questions" which should be answered, adding that there is "a considerable body of opinion that our actions in Vietnam constitute the waging of an aggressive 'war.' "

The Court also denied certiorari in *Mora* v. *McNamara* (1967), where three soldiers had refused to go to Vietnam on the ground that it was an illegal war, but this time Justice Stewart joined Douglas in thinking the case should be heard. The appeal, he said, raised questions of great magnitude as to whether the Vietnam action was war in the constitutional sense, and if so, whether the President could send men to fight there when no war had been declared by Congress.

In an effort to force the Supreme Court to confront the Vietnam issue, the Massachusetts legislature in 1970 passed a law providing that Massachusetts ser-

---

[2] Clinton Rossiter, *The Supreme Court and the Commander in Chief* (Ithaca, N.Y.: Cornell University Press, 1951), p. 126.

[3] The Treaty of London, often called the Nuremberg Charter, was signed by United States representatives but not submitted to the Senate for ratification. It makes soldiers in an aggressive war individually responsible as war criminals, even if they acted under orders.

vicemen could refuse to take part in armed hostilities in the absence of a declaration of war by Congress. The state attorney general was authorized to bring an action in the name of the state in the original jurisdiction of the Supreme Court, seeking a declaration that the military action in Vietnam was unconstitutional and an injunction forbidding the Secretary of Defense to send any citizen of Massachusetts to Vietnam until Congress had declared war. The Supreme Court in *Massachusetts* v. *Laird* (1970) denied the state's motion to file the suit, though Douglas, Harlan, and Stewart dissented.

The case was then filed in federal district court in Boston, but Judge Wyzanski held that the Supreme Court's action meant that Massachusetts lacked standing and that the controversy lacked justiciability. This decision was affirmed by the Court of Appeals for the First Circuit, that body relying principally on the fact that the Vietnam war was "a product of the jointly supportive actions of the two branches to whom the congeries of the war powers have been committed." Only if one of the two branches should be opposed to the continuance of hostilities would the court take a different view of its responsibility. The "steady Congressional support" for the war which the appeals court cited was of course the Gulf of Tonkin Resolution and the appropriations which Congress had consistently voted to finance the war.

Sarnoff v. *Shultz* (1972) was a suit brought against the Secretary of the Treasury to enjoin disbursements under the Foreign Assistance Act of 1961 in aid of American military operations in Vietnam. The suit was dismissed on the ground that it presented a "political question" beyond judicial cognizance. The Supreme Court denied certiorari over the dissent of Douglas and Brennan, who thought it presented a spending issue that might be litigable under the doctrine of *Flast* v. *Cohen* (1968).[4]

In *Holtzman* v. *Schlesinger* (1973), a federal district judge enjoined the Secretary of Defense from continuing military action in Cambodia as being unauthorized by Congress. The injunction was promptly stayed by the Court of Appeals for the Second Circuit. Holtzman, a Congresswoman from New York, then appealed on August 1 to Justice Marshall, as Circuit Justice, to vacate the stay. While granting that the Cambodian war might ultimately be adjudged to have been unlawful, Marshall concluded that granting the application would exceed his legal authority. Holtzman then applied to Justice Douglas who, while recognizing that he owed great deference to Marshall's ruling, nevertheless vacated the stay on August 4, because he regarded this as a capital case in which "someone is about to die" in Cambodia. Later that day Marshall, having communicated with the other members of the Court by phone, reversed Douglas's action and reentered the stay. Douglas dissented, charging that "telephone disposition of this grave and constitutional issue is not permissible." On August 6, when the bomb load of an American B-52 fell short and struck the Cambodian town of Neak Luong, 137 people were killed.

---

[4] Two additional cases that the Supreme Court declined to review, *Berk* v. *Laird* (1971) and *Orlando* v. *Laird* (1971), are discussed in Leon Friedman and Burt Neuborne, *Unquestioning Obedience to the President: The ACLU Case against the Legality of the War in Vietnam* (New York: W. W. Norton & Company, Inc., 1972). See also Michael Tigar, "Judicial Power, the 'Political Question' Doctrine, and Foreign Relations," 17 UCLA LAW REVIEW 1135 (1970).

THE STATE OF WAR

The War Power of Congress

There have been several alternative theories about the source of the war power of Congress. In No. 23 of *The Federalist* Hamilton seemed to assume that the war power derived from the specific provisions of Article I, section 8, which in clauses 11 to 14 authorizes Congress:

> To declare war, grant letters of marque and reprisal, and make rules concerning captures on land and water;
> To raise and support armies, but no appropriation of money to that use shall be for a longer term than two years;
> To provide and maintain a navy;
> To make rules for the government and regulation of the land and naval forces.

But in *Penhallow* v. *Doane* (1795), the Supreme Court suggested that the war power was an attribute of sovereignty and so not dependent upon these specific grants. Marshall in *McCulloch* v. *Maryland* (1819) derived the power to "conduct" a war from the authorization to "declare it."

No matter what the constitutional theory, the judicial result has almost invariably been to support a war power coextensive with war's "felt necessities." Conscription was attacked in the *Selective Draft Law Cases* (1918) on the grounds that the Constitution gave Congress no such power, that conscription amounted to involuntary servitude, and that it encroached on the constitutional power of the states over the militia, but the Court rejected all these contentions.

The war power of course does not require the existence of a state of war for its exercise. Even in the more sheltered times of the nineteenth century, it was necessary to prepare for war in time of peace. The Supreme Court found occasion to defend this obvious principle in *Ashwander* v. *Tennessee Valley Authority* (1936), where it supported the peacetime maintenance and operation of the Wilson Dam nitrate and power plants, built under the National Defense Act of 1916, on the ground that they were "national defense assets."

After hostilities end, there is necessarily a period before the state of war is legally terminated and the country readjusts to a peacetime economy. Congressional reliance on its war powers to deal with the problems of the postwar period has seldom been questioned. During World War I the so-called Wartime Prohibition Act was passed on November 22, 1918, eleven days after the armistice. In *Hamilton* v. *Kentucky Distilleries* (1919), the Court unanimously refused to "enquire into the motives of Congress," but noted in support of the legislation "that the treaty of peace has not yet been concluded, that the railways are still under national control by virtue of the war powers, that other war activities have not been brought to a close, and that it cannot even be said that the man power of the nation has been restored to a peace footing." The Court upheld postwar rent control for the District of Columbia in 1921 in *Block* v. *Hirsh*, though by 1924 it did conclude that the emergency had come to an end, and with it the case for rent control.[5]

[5] *Chastleton Corp.* v. *Sinclair* (1924).

Similar questions were raised at the close of World War II. The rent control statute passed in 1947 was upheld in *Woods* v. *Miller Co.* (1948). Justice Douglas warned, however, that the Court did not intend to permit the war power to "be used in days of peace to treat all the wounds which war inflicts on our society," to the point where it would "swallow up all other powers of Congress" and the Ninth and Tenth Amendments as well.

Another important ruling in this period was *Ludecke* v. *Watkins* (1948), involving deportation of a German national in 1946 under the Alien Enemy Act of 1798, which was operative only during periods of a "declared war." Five justices held that the Court could not question the President's power to take such action, but Justice Black thought "the idea that we are still at war with Germany in the sense contemplated by the statute . . . is a pure fiction."

The Ending of War

In the absence of any constitutional language indicating how wars are to be ended, judicial responsibility has again been to recognize the political decisions. As for the actual cessation of hostilities by armistice or otherwise, that is, of course, a decision for the President to make. Termination of the legal state of war is effected normally by negotiation of a treaty, but there is American experience with other methods. The Civil War was ended by presidential proclamation, World War I by joint resolution of Congress. "Whatever the mode," said the Supreme Court in *Ludecke* v. *Watkins* (1948), termination of a state of war "is a political act."

Occupation of Territory

Territory conquered by the United States comes under the control of the President. In a whole series of controversies arising out of incidents following the Mexican War, the Civil War, and the Spanish-American War, the Supreme Court repeatedly denied any right to review presidential actions in these circumstances. The President's authority to establish a government for conquered territory comes neither from the Constitution nor the laws of the United States, but only from the law of war.

Following a period of military occupation, the President has full authority to establish a system of civil government for conquered territory, which may, however, be superseded by congressional legislation. If the territory is to be retained permanently by the United States, Congress must adopt legislation creating a civil government. But until this is done, the President is the sole source of governmental authority in the area.[6]

THE PRESIDENT AND THE ARMED FORCES

As Commander in Chief the President is the ceremonial, legal, and administrative head of the Armed Forces.[7] He appoints the officers of the services, though Con-

---

[6] The sole exception was the case of *Jecker* v. *Montgomery* (1851). See *Santiago* v. *Nogueras* (1909).

[7] The President's position as Commander in Chief gives him the status of a member of the Armed Forces. President Lincoln's assassination was treated as a military crime for this reason—the killing of

gress determines the grades to which appointments may be made and may specify the qualifications of the appointees, who must also be confirmed by the Senate. The President has an unlimited power to dismiss officers from the service in time of war, but in time of peace Congress has provided that dismissal shall be only in pursuance of the sentence of a general court-martial. He may adopt rules and regulations for the government, safety, and welfare of the Armed Forces, in subordination to Congress's constitutional power "to make rules for the government and regulation of the land and naval forces."

The President may involve himself in such direction of military movements and strategy and the actual conduct of military operations as he sees fit. President Washington accompanied his troops into the field at the time of the Whiskey Rebellion in 1792. One need think only of President Lincoln's telegraphic orders and personal visits to his generals in the field, or President Roosevelt in the chart room of the White House mapping the grand strategy of World War II, or President Johnson personally approving the targets to be bombed in North Vietnam, to appreciate the tremendous potential of the President's role.

As commander of the Armed Forces the President is in control of the most incomparably powerful machinery of coercion in the country. He may use this power to enforce national laws and treaties within the United States, and he is the agent for enforcing the guarantee which Article IV, section 4, gives to the states against invasion and domestic violence.[8]

THE PRESIDENT AND MARTIAL LAW

Suspension of the Writ of Habeas Corpus

"Martial law" is a general term covering military rule in domestic areas. In varying degrees it involves military assumption of normal civil lawmaking and enforcement functions. A necessary instrument of a system of martial law is suspension of the writ of habeas corpus, which permits civil or military authorities to hold persons in jail indefinitely without placing charges against them or bringing them to trial.

The Constitution provides in Article I, section 9: "The privilege of the writ of habeas corpus shall not be suspended, unless when in cases of rebellion or invasion the public safety may require it." Suspension of the "privilege" of the writ means that, though courts may continue to issue the writ, the jailer to whom the writ is directed is relieved of the responsibility of obeying the order to produce the prisoner in court. The Constitution undoubtedly contemplated that Congress should have power to suspend the writ when required by public safety, since the clause is located in the legislative article of the Constitution. However, President Lincoln, acting on his own authority, suspended it several times during the Civil War. In the Habeas

---

the Commander in Chief while he was actually in command of the national forces in his headquarters city. A military tribunal of nine officers tried the assassins, and no civil court ever looked into the commission's jurisdiction or proceedings.

[8] Two early Supreme Court decisions, *Martin* v. *Mott* (1827) and *Luther* v. *Borden* (1849), dealing with presidential action in calling out the militia, emphasize that the President is not judicially accountable for his emergency use of the Armed Forces.

Corpus Act of March 3, 1863, Congress, in carefully chosen language, said that the President was authorized to suspend the writ "during the present rebellion," but without indicating where the authorization came from. Before this act was passed, however, there had been a notable clash between Lincoln and Chief Justice Taney over the issue.

In May, 1861, Taney, sitting in the circuit court in Baltimore, under statutory authority from the Judiciary Act of 1789 granted the writ requested by John Merryman, who had been arrested and confined in Fort McHenry because of his secessionist activities. The military authorities refused to honor the writ, and Taney's effort to arrest the commanding general for contempt was likewise frustrated. Taney wrote an opinion holding unconstitutional Lincoln's suspension of the privilege, and directed the clerk of the court to send a copy to the President. "It will then," he added, "remain for that high officer, in fulfillment of his constitutional obligation to take care that the laws be faithfully executed, to determine what measures he will take to cause the civil processes of the United States to be respected and enforced." Lincoln continued to exercise the power which Taney had held unconstitutional, though Merryman was shortly turned over to civil authorities and indicted for treason.

Military Trials of Civilians

In a proclamation of September 24, 1862, President Lincoln coupled suspension of habeas corpus with an order that all persons "guilty of any disloyal practice affording aid and comfort to rebels" should be liable to trial and punishment by "courts-martial or military commissions." This order was effective throughout the United States and was a direct challenge to the authority of the regular civil courts. Although Congress subsequently ratified the habeas corpus suspension by its act of 1863, it never gave statutory support to trial of civilians by military commissions, which had to rest solely on the President's power as Commander in Chief.

The Court eventually ruled trial by military commissions unconstitutional, but not until the Civil War had been over for a year, in the case of *Ex parte Milligan* (1866). Milligan was arrested at his home in Indiana late in 1864, tried by a military commission, and sentenced to be hanged. In May, 1865, Milligan got a writ of habeas corpus from the federal court in Indianapolis, and the Supreme Court unanimously ruled that the President had no power to order trial of civilians by military courts in areas where the regular courts were open and operating.

There was a considerable similarity between Lincoln's military commissions and the situation that prevailed in Hawaii during the greater part of World War II. Under authority of the Hawaii Organic Act, the Governor of Hawaii declared martial law immediately after the Japanese attack on December 7, 1941; the President approved his action two days later. Civil and criminal courts were forbidden to try cases, military tribunals being set up to replace them. Some criminal cases were still being tried by military courts as late as 1944. In *Duncan* v. *Kahanamoku* (1946), the Supreme Court held that when Congress had granted the Governor of Hawaii the power to declare martial law, it had not meant to supersede constitutional guarantees of a fair trial which apply elsewhere in the United States or to "authorize the supplanting of courts by military tribunals."

THE PRESIDENT AND MILITARY JUSTICE

Military Trials for Military Personnel

The Armed Forces maintain a system of courts-martial for punishment of offenses by their members, under regulations prescribed by Congress. Articles of War were adopted for the Army by Congress in 1789, and for the Navy in 1800. The procedures embodied in the Articles were those of the Revolutionary War, aimed at enforcing discipline rather than administering justice, and they became increasingly unacceptable to the citizen soldiers of World Wars I and II. These protests were recognized by the adoption in 1950 of the Uniform Code of Military Justice, a sweeping overhaul of military law which gave a man in uniform more procedural rights than he would have had as a suspect in civilian courts at that time. In fact, the Code anticipated the major Supreme Court decisions of the next decade by providing free legal counsel in general courts-martial, requiring warning of rights before a suspect could be questioned, and providing free transcripts and counsel for appeals.[9]

In general, courts-martial are totally distinct from the civilian courts, constituting completely separate systems of justice. Courts-martial exercise no part of the judicial power of the United States. The decision of a court-martial must be affirmed by the appropriate command officers and in certain cases by a board of review appointed by a judge advocate general, and a final appeal may be taken on matters of law to the Court of Military Appeals. This is a bench of three civilian judges set up by the Uniform Code of Military Justice, appointed for fifteen-year terms by the President with the advice and consent of the Senate.

Article 76 of the Code makes the findings and sentences of courts-martial "final and conclusive" and "binding upon all . . . courts . . . of the United States." However, the writ of habeas corpus furnishes a method whereby detention as a result of a court-martial decision can be reviewed by the civil courts. Such review is strictly limited to the issue of jurisdiction of the court-martial, which may be challenged on the ground that the offense charged was not within its cognizance, that the court was not constituted according to law, or that the punishment exceeded the limits imposed by the Code. Conformity of court-martial procedures to applicable constitutional standards may also be examined.

The relationship of the guarantees of the Bill of Rights to military trials is somewhat complex. The right to indictment by grand jury is specifically made inapplicable to "cases arising in the land and naval forces," and there is of course no right to trial by jury. Initially it was assumed that only those constitutional rights specifically authorized by Congress applied in courts-martial, and in fact legislation did guarantee the privilege against self-incrimination and the rights to confrontation, counsel, and compulsory process. But in *Wade* v. *Hunter* (1949) the Supreme Court held that the Fifth Amendment's ban on double jeopardy also applied to courts-martial, and in *United States* v. *Tempia* (1967) the Court of Military Appeals applied all the standards of the Supreme Court's decision in *Miranda* v. *Arizona*

---

[9] *Middendorf* v. *Henry* (1976) ruled that counsel need not be furnished to servicemen accused of minor offenses at summary courts-martial. By contrast, *Argersinger* v. *Hamlin* (1972) held that in the regular courts no person could be imprisoned even for a petty offense unless there had been representation by counsel.

(1966) for the regular courts to the military legal system. The theory of the *Tempia* decision is that the entire framework of constitutional rights applies in the armed services "except insofar as they are made inapplicable either expressly or by necessary implication."

In addition to absence of grand jury indictment and trial by jury, the principal objection to court-martial procedure has been "command influence." The commanding officer appoints the pretrial investigating officers, authorizes searches and arrests, convenes the court-martial, decides whether the accused shall remain in pretrial confinement, selects the prosecutor and often the defense counsel, chooses the members of the court (the equivalent of jurors), decides whether a sentence to confinement will be deferred pending appeal, and makes the initial review of the case. Proposals have been made in Congress to eliminate command influence by establishing in the Armed Forces a separate and independent court-martial command, modeled after the civilian courts.[10]

On occasions the Supreme Court has been critical of the court-martial system, comparing it unfavorably with the civil courts. In *United States ex rel. Toth* v. *Quarles* (1955), Justice Black said that "from the very nature of things, courts have more independence in passing on the life and liberty of people than do military tribunals." This attitude motivated the Court in *Toth* to deny the right of the Air Force to subject a civilian ex-serviceman to court-martial for a crime allegedly committed during his period of military service.

The same inclination to limit the jurisdiction of courts-martial was even more evident in *O'Callahan* v. *Parker* (1969), where the Court reviewed the conviction of a soldier who, while on an evening pass, had broken into a Honolulu hotel room and assaulted a girl. This time it was Justice Douglas who stressed that courts-martial are not "an independent instrument of justice" but rather a "specialized part of the overall mechanism by which military discipline is preserved." By a vote of six to three, the Court held that where a member of the Armed Forces was charged with the commission of a crime cognizable in a civilian court, alleged to have been committed off post and while on leave, there was no justification for a court-martial that would deprive the serviceman of his constitutional rights to indictment by grand jury and trial by jury.[11]

The "service-connected" issue was raised again in *Schlesinger* v. *Councilman*

---

[10] Criticism of military justice was heightened by the record in the My Lai atrocity cases. Out of a total of twenty-five enlisted men and officers charged in connection with the 1968 mass murders in Vietnam, only six were brought to trial and only one—Lt. William Calley—was convicted. When widespread public sympathy was manifested for Calley—arising partly from the feeling that he had been made a scapegoat for the misdeeds of his superiors—President Nixon issued a public statement pointing out that as Commander in Chief he would ultimately review the conviction. This was an extraordinary illustration of "command influence," which the Army captain who had prosecuted the Calley case publicly condemned as subjecting military justice to "political influence." Calley's conviction was set aside in 1974 by a federal judge on the ground that massive publicity about his case had denied him a fair trial, but this ruling was reversed and the conviction reinstated by the Court of Appeals for the Fifth Circuit in 1975. The Supreme Court refused review; *Calley* v. *Hoffman* (1976). See generally Joseph W. Bishop, Jr., *Justice under Fire: A Study of Military Law* (New York: Charterhouse, 1974).

[11] In *Relford* v. *Commandant* (1971), the Court itemized twelve tests to aid in determining whether an offense was "service-connected."

(1975) by a soldier brought before a general court-martial on a marijuana charge, but he also challenged the entire legitimacy of the military justice system as denying due process of law. The Court rejected this charge, saying that "implicit in the congressional scheme embodied in the Code is the view that the military court system generally is adequate to and responsibly will perform its assigned task. We think this congressional judgment must be respected and that it must be assumed that the military court system will vindicate servicemen's constitutional rights."

For the three dissenters, Brennan denied that this was a service-connected offense. Rather, it was a "common everyday type of drug offense that federal courts encounter all over the country every day." It does not become a service-connected crime "merely because the participants are servicemen." This decision, Brennan held, violated the "basic constitutional tenet that subordinates the military to civil authority—restrict[ing] military cognizance of offenses to the narrowest jurisdiction deemed absolutely necessary, and preclud[ing] expansion of military jurisdiction at the expense of the constitutionally preferred civil jurisdiction."

The unpopular Vietnam war, fought with a largely conscript army, created strains within the Armed Forces, resistance to military discipline, and new claims for First Amendment rights of criticism and free discussion. The best-known case was that of Captain Howard Levy, who talked against the war and refused to teach his medical skills to the Green Berets, an elite combat force, on the ground that they were guilty of calculated atrocities in Vietnam. At his court-martial, Levy's defense charged that two articles of the Uniform Code were unconstitutional as infringing on rights of free speech and also vague and unduly broad in violation of the Fifth Amendment. Article 133, dating back to the Revolutionary War, proscribes "conduct unbecoming an officer and a gentleman," and Article 134 forbids "all disorders and neglects to the prejudice of good order and discipline."

The Supreme Court denied certiorari to review the court-martial verdict of guilt in *Levy* v. *Corcoran* (1967). Review was then sought by the habeas corpus route, but eventually the Supreme Court ruled against Levy's claims by a vote of five to three in *Parker* v. *Levy* (1974). For the majority, Justice Rehnquist held that the two questioned articles were neither unduly vague nor overbroad and that Levy's conduct in publicly urging enlisted personnel to refuse to obey orders that might send them into combat was unprotected under the most expansive notions of the First Amendment. Because of the factors differentiating military from civilian society, Congress was permitted to legislate with greater breadth and flexibility, and the standards for judicial review should be those applicable to economic affairs, not First Amendment rights. Justice Stewart, dissenting, said he found it "hard to imagine criminal statutes more patently unconstitutional than these vague and uncertain General Articles. . . ."[12]

Military Trials for Military Dependents

Whether military courts may assert jurisdiction over dependents accompanying American servicemen stationed abroad in occupied territory or at American mili-

---

[12]See also *Secretary of the Navy* v. *Avrech* (1974); *Greer* v. *Spock* (1976).

tary bases has given the Supreme Court some trouble. The Uniform Code of Military Justice makes subject to its provisions "all persons serving with, employed by, or accompanying the armed forces without the continental limits of the United States." In *Reid* v. *Covert* (1957) and *Kinsella* v. *Krueger* (1957), cases in which wives of military personnel living on American bases in England and Japan had killed their husbands, the Court held that subjecting civilians "accompanying" the Armed Forces to courts-martial was unconstitutional.

There was some disagreement on the Court as to whether this reasoning was applicable only when capital crimes were involved. However, in *Kinsella* v. *United States ex rel. Singleton* (1960), the Court majority ruled that military trial of service dependents for noncapital offenses was also unconstitutional. Moreover, American civilian employees of the Armed Forces abroad cannot be tried by military courts for either capital or non-capital offenses, according to *McElroy* v. *United States ex rel. Guagliardo* (1960) and *Grisham* v. *Hagan* (1960).

Military Trials of Enemies

Courts-martial or military commissions have occasionally been set up by the President, under statutory authorization or his inherent powers as Commander in Chief, to deal with military crimes committed by others than the Armed Forces of the United States. As already noted, a military commission was created to try the assassins of President Lincoln. In 1942 President Roosevelt established a military commission to try eight German saboteurs who had been landed in this country by submarine with the assignment of blowing up factories and bridges. When the case before the tribunal was nearly completed, counsel for the saboteurs, despite an executive order denying them all access to civil courts, got a writ of habeas corpus contending for their right to trial in a civil court.

The Supreme Court unanimously upheld the military trial in *Ex parte Quirin* (1942). It was unnecessary to determine the extent of presidential authority as Commander in Chief, since Congress had provided for the trial of offenses against the law of war by such commissions, and the acts charged against the saboteurs were offenses against the law of war. The constitutional requirements of grand jury indictment and jury trial were held inapplicable to the trial of such offenses by military commissions. As for the *Milligan* decision, which was particularly relied on by counsel for the saboteurs, the Court pointed to the obvious factual differences in that case and held it inapplicable. The significance of the *Quirin* decision is its firm establishment of the authority of the civil courts to examine the jurisdiction of presidentially appointed military commissions.

Following World War II certain Japanese generals who had commanded troops in the Pacific theater were placed on trial before an American military commission in the Philippines. The Supreme Court in *In re Yamashita* (1946) again took jurisdiction, and again upheld the authority of the commission. Its procedures had been particularly under attack, for under the regulations prescribed by General MacArthur the commission had admitted hearsay and opinion evidence, and had allowed defense counsel inadequate time to prepare their defense. But the Court majority held that the commission's procedures and its rulings on evidence were reviewable only by the superior military authorities, not by the courts. Justices Murphy and Rutledge, however, filed eloquent dissents objecting to "departures from constitutional norms inherent in the idea of a fair trial."

Hirota v. *MacArthur* (1948) differed from the *Yamashita* case in that the Japanese defendants involved had been tried for war crimes before a military tribunal set up by General MacArthur as the agent for the Allied Powers which had defeated Japan. The defendants sought to file habeas corpus petitions directly with the Supreme Court, but their motions were denied on the grounds that courts of the United States could have no jurisdiction over this tribunal because of its international character. It was not "a tribunal of the United States."[13]

THE PRESIDENT AND THE HOME FRONT

Control of the Economy

Insofar as the economic controls increasingly demanded by twentieth-century warfare have been based on congressional enactments, their general judicial ratification has already been noted. There have been some instances, however, where a President has acted without specific statutory support under his general powers as Commander in Chief.

In both World War I and II presidential action was taken to seize industrial plants, an interference with the use of private property which admittedly could be justified only on grounds of wartime necessity. President Wilson's seizures were based on statutory authorization, but from 1941 to 1943 President Roosevelt made numerous seizures without any supporting legislation, simply referring to his general authority as President and Commander in Chief. The plants seized were ones important to war production in which labor-management disagreements were threatening, or had already resulted in, stoppage of production. Ultimately Congress authorized presidential seizures of manufacturing and production facilities by the Smith-Connally Act of 1943.

Only one court test of these wartime seizures eventuated, and it led to no definitive ruling by the Supreme Court. After a three-year struggle between Montgomery Ward and the War Labor Board, the President in 1944 ordered the Secretary of War to take possession of the company's properties. The government itself then went to court, seeking an injunction forbidding the company officers from interfering with the seizure. A federal district judge held that Montgomery Ward was engaged in "distribution," not "production," and consequently the statute did not authorize seizure of its facilities, nor did he think the President could take such action under his general war powers. The court of appeals, however, interpreted production more broadly and thereby found statutory support for the seizure. The

---

[13] See Richard H. Minear, *Victors' Justice: The Tokyo War Crimes Trial* (Princeton, N.J.: Princeton University Press, 1971).

Supreme Court accepted the case, but then dismissed it as moot because the Army had turned the properties back to the company.[14]

President Truman's seizure of the nation's steel mills in 1952 did not come in a period of declared war, and Justice Black's opinion for the Court in *Youngstown Sheet & Tube Co.* v. *Sawyer* refused to give any consideration to claims that the action could be justified by his status as Commander in Chief. Justice Jackson undertook a more thoughtful statement of reasons for this holding.

> We should not use this occasion to circumscribe, much less to contract, the lawful role of the President as Commander-in-Chief. I should indulge the widest latitude of interpretation to sustain his exclusive function to command the instruments of national force, at least when turned against the outside world for the security of our society. But, when it is turned inward, not because of rebellion but because of a lawful economic struggle between industry and labor, it should have no such indulgence. . . . The purpose of lodging dual titles in one man was to insure that the civilian would control the military, not to enable the military to subordinate the presidential office. No penance would ever expiate the sin against free government of holding that a President can escape control of executive powers by law through assuming his military role.

The Japanese Evacuation

The enforced evacuation of Japanese and Japanese-Americans from the West Coast early in World War II by combined executive-legislative action must be regarded, in spite of its subsequent ratification by the Supreme Court, as one of the most unfortunate episodes in the long history of the war power under the Constitution. The deeply rooted opposition to Orientals on the West Coast, combined with the hysteria of the early war period, built up a tremendous pressure to take action against the over 100,000 persons of Japanese ancestry in the area. On February 19, 1942, President Roosevelt issued an executive order empowering the Secretary of War to designate military areas from which any or all persons might be excluded in order to prevent espionage and sabotage. Under this authorization the three West Coast states and part of Arizona were proclaimed military areas and all persons of Japanese ancestry, 70,000 of whom were American citizens, were cleared from these areas. Congress on March 21, 1942, passed a law ratifying and confirming the executive order.[15]

The inevitable constitutional tests of this harsh and unprecedented treatment of American citizens and aliens lawfully resident in the United States, with its untold suffering and loss of property, presented the Supreme Court with a difficult problem. Was it to hold these procedures contrary to due process, or to justify them on the ground that the responsible civil and military leaders claimed they were a military necessity? As usual, the law's delays gave the Court a period of grace before it had to answer. The decision in *Hirabayashi* v. *United States* did not come until June,

[14] *Montgomery Ward and Co.* v. *United States* (1945).

[15] See Jacobus TenBroek, Edward N. Barnhart, and Floyd W. Matson, *Prejudice, War and the Constitution* (Berkeley: University of California Press, 1954); Morton Grodzins, *Americans Betrayed: Politics and the Japanese Evacuation* (Chicago: University of Chicago Press, 1949).

1943. Moreover, the circumstances of the case provided an opportunity for the Court to avoid the more difficult constitutional questions. Shortly before the evacuation program had been undertaken, the Army had adopted a curfew regulation requiring all aliens and persons of Japanese ancestry to be in their residences between 8 P.M. and 6 A.M. Hirabayashi, an American-born citizen of alien Japanese parents, was convicted of failure both to obey the curfew and to report for registration for evacuation. Sentence for the two offenses was made to run concurrently.

The Supreme Court took advantage of this fact to limit its review to the curfew, clearly a less drastic interference with liberty than the enforced evacuation, and unanimously upheld it as a temporary emergency war measure. Under the circumstances that existed at the time, the Court concluded that it was not unreasonable for those charged with the national defense to feel that the Japanese constituted a peculiar danger to national security. Racial discriminations are odious and usually unconstitutional, because justified by no proper legislative purpose. But "in time of war residents having ethnic affiliations with an invading enemy may be a greater source of danger than those of a different ancestry."

In *Korematsu* v. *United States,* decided in December, 1944, the constitutionality of the evacuation program, then in effect for over two and a half years, could no longer be avoided, and the Court upheld it by a divided vote. The majority opinion followed the lines of the earlier decision, holding that the military authorities were not unjustified in concluding that the Japanese residents of the Coast area constituted a potentially grave danger to the public safety, a danger so great and pressing that there was no time to set up procedures for determining the loyalty or disloyalty of individual Japanese. Actually the Court made no effort to use that valuable prerogative of judicial review, the "wisdom of hindsight," to challenge the military conclusions, though it certainly was apparent by the end of 1944 that the fears of sabotage and treachery by West Coast residents of Japanese descent were entirely groundless. Only Justice Murphy charged that the case made by the military had not been based on any demonstrated public necessity, but upon "an accumulation of much of the misinformation, half-truths and insinuations that for years have been directed against Japanese Americans by people with racial and economic prejudices." Justices Roberts and Jackson also dissented, the latter suggesting that even if the military decision was justified, the Court should refuse to enforce it, because Court approval would give constitutional sanction to "a military expedient that has no place in law under the Constitution."

The Court partially recouped its reputation as the defender of individual liberties by *Ex parte Endo* (1944), decided the same day as *Korematsu.* Here the Court upheld the right of a Japanese-American girl, whose loyalty to the United States had been established, to a writ of habeas corpus freeing her from a relocation camp. Justice Douglas's opinion avoided any ruling on the constitutionality of the detention program as a whole by pointing out that neither statute nor executive order anywhere specifically authorized detention. Justice Roberts, concurring in the result, thought the Court had ignored its responsibility to meet squarely the constitutional issue created by the government's action in depriving an admittedly loyal citizen of her liberty for a period of years. The weekend before the *Endo* ruling, and apparently in anticipation of it, the Army ordered the release of all loyal Japanese-Americans from the relocation camps.

In 1947 President Truman's Commission on Civil Rights described the evacuation as "the most striking mass interference since slavery with the right to physical freedom," and recommended that the evacuees be at least partly compensated for their property losses. Congress responded by passing the Evacuation Claims Act of 1948, under which some thirty-seven million dollars was paid to 26,500 claimants.[16]

---

[16] See also *Honda* v. *Clark* (1967).

Chapter 18

Constitutional Basis for Protection of Individual Rights

The one essential quality of constitutionalism, says McIlwain, is as a legal limitation on government. Tom Paine wrote that a constitution is "to liberty, what a grammar is to language." Of course, a written constitution is not necessary to the protection of civil liberties, as English experience so well demonstrates. And the most elaborate safeguards in a written constitution will be meaningless unless the country to which they apply has a tradition which makes freedom a value of the highest order, and unless there are the resources, the opportunities, and the will to protect the principles of an open society from attack or frustration.

The American tradition of civil liberty is composed of many strands. Basic is the Christian-Hebraic belief in the worth of the individual, and acceptance of a moral obligation to shape the institutions of society so that they will promote the unfolding and the enrichment of human character. Centuries of struggle in England to achieve political institutions which would aim toward equality before the law and equalization of political power, resulting in such documents as Magna Carta (1215), the Petition of Right (1628), and the Bill of Rights (1689), were a living part of the early American tradition. The writings of the seventeenth- and eighteenth-century political philosophers, particularly Locke, with their notions about natural law and the origins of government in a compact freely entered into by its citizens, were an essential element in American Revolutionary thought. The Declaration of Independence put these ideas about liberty and equality into classic phraseology.

All this was the heritage of the new nation, the "common law" of American liberties. If it had never been spelled out in a written constitution, it would nonetheless have continued to be effective in guiding the political decisions of the developing commonwealth.

THE BILL OF RIGHTS

As a matter of fact, the theory of the Constitutional Convention was that the traditional liberties did not need much in the way of specific constitutional protection. The basic concept of limited national government was to be achieved by division of functions, separation of powers, checks and balances, calculated to frustrate any drive toward dictatorial power. The drafters of the Constitution relied on the open spaces of the American continent to guarantee escape from confining situations. They saw the boundless resources of the country as insurance of economic opportunity. They conceived that the broad expanse of the Republic would encompass such a variety of interests as to make combination into a domineering majority difficult. Said Madison in No. 10 of *The Federalist:*

> The smaller the society, the fewer probably will be the distinct parties and interests composing it . . . and . . . the more easily will they concert and execute their plans of oppression. Extend the sphere, and you take in a greater variety of parties and interests; you make it less probable that a majority of the whole will have a common motive to invade the rights of other citizens.

Thus individual liberty did not need to be planned for. It would come automatically as the by-product of a system of economic opportunity, social mobility, and political responsibility.

Although this seems to have been the dominant theory of the Convention, it was departed from in a few instances. There are in fact several provisions which bear more or less closely on issues of civil liberty: protection against suspension of the writ of habeas corpus; prohibition of the passage of bills of attainder or ex post facto laws by either Congress or the state legislatures; the ban on religious tests as a qualification for public office; the requirement of trial by jury; the restrictions on conviction for treason; and the guarantee to citizens of each state of all privileges and immunities of citizens in the several states.

When the proposed Constitution went to the states for ratification, it quickly became apparent that the framers' view of civil liberties as needing no special protection in the new charter was not widely shared. In several of the important states ratification was secured only on the understanding that amendments protecting individual rights would be immediately added to the Constitution. In his first inaugural address, Washington urged Congress to give careful attention to the demand for these amendments.

Madison took the lead in bringing together the various suggestions for amendments, which he presented to the House on June 8, 1789. His original idea was that they should be incorporated into the body of the Constitution at the places where they would appropriately belong. Most of the proposals had to do with limiting the power of Congress over citizens, and these were to follow the clause in Article I, section 9, prohibiting congressional adoption of bills of attainder and ex post facto laws. The new language to be inserted at this point would have prohibited Congress from abridging the freedom of religion, of speech, press, or assembly, and of bearing arms. There were also restrictions on quartering troops, prosecuting citizens for crime, and inflicting punishment. Changes aiming at a fuller guarantee to the citizen of a fair trial by a jury in his own district and the benefits of the common law were to be worked into the jury trial provision of Article III.

When the House took up consideration of the amendments, Roger Sherman of Connecticut objected to the insertion of new material into, and the deletion of superseded material from, the original Constitution, and he was eventually able to convince the House that the amendments should be appended to the Constitution, each complete, independent, and understandable in itself. The House proposals went to the Senate on August 24. Twelve amendments were approved by the Senate, and after concurrence by the House, they were sent to the states on September 25, 1789.

Two of these proposed amendments ultimately failed of ratification. The first had to do with the ratio between population and the number of representatives in the House, and the second would have postponed the effect of any alteration in the compensation of congressmen until an election had intervened. The remaining ten amendments were ratified by the necessary eleven states (there being fourteen states in the Union by that time) on December 15, 1791.

The ten amendments can be thought of as falling into four categories. The First, and justly the most famous of the amendments, covers freedom of speech, press, assembly, and religion. The Second and Third, which are of little contemporary significance, deal with the right of the people to keep and bear arms,[1] and the quartering of soldiers in private homes. The Fourth through the Eighth are concerned primarily with procedural protections in criminal trials, but other matters are also covered, such as the prohibition on taking of private property for public use without just compensation. Finally, the Ninth and Tenth Amendments are simply declaratory of the existing constitutional situation. The Ninth Amendment provides that the enumeration of certain rights in the Constitution shall not be construed to deny or disparage others retained by the people. The Tenth concerns primarily state powers rather than individual rights, and thus has little bearing on the discussion of the present section of this volume.

Only gradually did the conception grow that these ten amendments constituted

---

[1] The Second Amendment ties "the right of the people to keep and bear arms" to the need to maintain a "well regulated militia." Consequently, the Supreme Court in *United States* v. *Cruikshank* (1875) held that the amendment protected only the right of the states to maintain and equip a militia and did not guarantee to individuals the right to bear arms. In *United States* v. *Miller* (1939), the Court ruled that unless a defendant could show that his possession of a firearm in violation of federal statutes had "some reasonable relationship to the preservation or efficiency of a well regulated militia," he could not challenge a gun control statute on Second Amendment grounds. See "Firearms: Problems of Control," 80 HARVARD LAW REVIEW 1328 (1967).

a great Bill of Rights.[2] About half the state constitutions at the time did not include a bill of rights in their provisions, and it could be argued that these ten amendments accomplished no substantial changes in the constitutional pattern. They took away from Congress few powers which it could reasonably have been thought to have had before the amendments were ratified, and the procedural limitations on criminal trials would no doubt have been carried over from the common law in any event. Unquestionably, however, these provisions have had a tremendous value in the development of American constitutional thinking and practice.

CIVIL RIGHTS PROBLEMS TO THE CIVIL WAR

Three-quarters of a century elapsed after the Bill of Rights was added to the Constitution before any more amendments dealing with civil liberties were adopted. No detailed account of the application of constitutional guarantees during that period can or need be attempted. The ex post facto clause was early given a definitive and restricted interpretation in *Calder* v. *Bull* (1798). The Alien and Sedition Acts of 1798 raised some constitutional questions, but they never got to the Supreme Court. As the nineteenth century wore on, all other issues paled into obscurity in the fierce light of the slavery controversy, until that issue was excised by the brutal surgery of the Civil War. The Court's involvement in civil liberties issues during the first half of the nineteenth century was infrequent, but the little that did happen was inextricably involved in subsequent constitutional thought, and it is impossible to understand the post-Civil War amendments without some grasp of the Court's prior actions in four major respects.

The Bill of Rights and the States

First we may look at the differences of opinion which arose as to whether the provisions of the Bill of Rights, and more particularly the first eight amendments, were applicable to the federal government alone, or whether they also affected the states. It may seem surprising that doubt on such a fundamental point could have been left in the drafting of the amendments, but the fact is that only two of the amendments are specifically stated as restraints upon the United States. They are the First Amendment, which is by its terms made applicable only to Congress, and one clause of the Seventh which provides that "no fact tried by jury, shall be otherwise reexamined in any court of the United States, than according to the rules of the common law." All the other amendments, from the Second through the Eighth, state general libertarian principles, with no indication that their protective effect is only against federal action.

Nevertheless, the Supreme Court as early as 1833, in a unanimous opinion written by Chief Justice Marshall, ruled that these amendments were inapplicable to the states. This was the famous case of *Barron* v. *Baltimore,* and the specific issue was whether the city of Baltimore, by street grading which had diverted streams

---

[2] See Zechariah Chafee, Jr., *How Human Rights Got into the Constitution* (Boston: Boston University Press, 1952); Irving Brant, *The Bill of Rights: Its Origin and Meaning* (Indianapolis: The Bobbs-Merrill Company, Inc., 1965).

from their natural courses and rendered Barron's wharf unusuable, had deprived him of property without due process of law, contrary to the Fifth Amendment. Obviously his claim could not stand unless the Fifth Amendment applied to state and local governments.

The issue, said Marshall, was of great importance but not of much difficulty.

> The constitution was ordained and established by the people of the United States for themselves, for their own government, and not for the government of the individual states. . . . The powers they conferred on this government were to be exercised by itself; and the limitations on power, if expressed in general terms, are naturally, and, we think, necessarily applicable to the government created by the instrument.

Following this appeal to logic, Marshall turned to history. It was well known that the ratification of the Constitution was not secured without immense opposition. "In almost every convention by which the constitution was adopted, amendments to guard against the abuse of power were recommended. These amendments demanded security against the apprehended encroachments of the general government—not against those of the local governments."

Finally, Marshall's appeal was to the textual provisions of the original Constitution. He called attention to sections 9 and 10 of Article I, both containing a series of prohibitions on legislative action. But in section 9 the language is general, whereas in section 10 all the prohibitions are imposed specifically on the states. Thus section 9 forbids ex post facto laws and bills of attainder generally, while in section 10 the ban is repeated for the states. Whenever a constitutional provision was meant to affect the states, Marshall concluded, "words are employed which directly express that intent. . . . These amendments contain no expression indicating an intention to apply them to the state governments. This court cannot so apply them."

These are powerful arguments, and they have been fully incorporated into American constitutional development. Nevertheless, *Barron* v. *Baltimore* did not represent a universally accepted view.[3] When it came time to draft the post-Civil War amendments, one of the leading motives of some members of Congress was precisely to liquidate the effects of this decision.

The Meaning of Privileges and Immunities

The second dilemma of the pre-Civil War period concerned the meaning of Article IV, section 2—the privileges and immunities clause. The provision that "the citizens of each state shall be entitled to all privileges and immunities of citizens in the several states" was perhaps the vaguest of all the civil rights language in either the original Constitution or the amendments, and a difficult problem was thereby created for reviewing courts. By all odds the best known of the early judicial efforts along this line was that of Justice Bushrod Washington, sitting in federal circuit court in *Corfield* v. *Coryell* (1825). This case, already noted in Chapter 4, involved a New Jersey statute which prohibited any person not a resident of New Jersey from gath-

---

[3] See William W. Crosskey, *Politics and the Constitution in the History of the United States* (Chicago: The University of Chicago Press, 1953), pp. 1056–1082.

ering oysters in the state. Washington held that this act was not a violation of Article IV, section 2, because the privileges and immunities which the Constitution protects are those "which are, in their nature, fundamental; which belong, of right, to the citizens of all free governments." He went on to suggest quite a list of rights which met this test: protection by the government; enjoyment of life and liberty; the right to acquire and possess property; the right of a citizen of one state to pass through, or reside in, other states for purposes of trade or profession; protection by the writ of habeas corpus; the right to institute and maintain court actions; exemption from higher taxes than are paid by other citizens of the state; and the elective franchise, as regulated by the laws of the particular state in which it is exercised. "These, and many others which might be mentioned, are, strictly speaking, privileges and immunities."

This language of Washington's, which was well known and widely quoted, sounds, as Fairman says, like "pure natural law." It does not seek to discover the nature of these privileges and immunities by reference to the Bill of Rights or any other part of the Constitution. Rather Washington speaks simply of "fundamental" rights, belonging to "the citizens of all free governments," and then throws in a hodgepodge of activities, some of which, such as the practice of a profession or exercise of the elective franchise, obviously are subject to a wide variety of state regulations. According to Washington, the provision established a uniform, nationwide set of standards, applicable to all states. In effect he revised the sentence to read: "The citizens of each state shall be entitled to all privileges and immunities of citizens of the United States in the several states." This position, as developed and applied into the Civil War period and beyond, Crosskey calls the "old Republican view" of the privileges and immunities clause, a part of the "common faith" of that party. As such it had a great importance in the drafting and adoption of the Fourteenth Amendment.

Opposed to the "Washington–old Republican" interpretation of the privileges and immunities clause was another, which was in fact probably the one intended by the framers. The language can be read as meaning simply that a citizen of one state going into another state is not to be discriminated against because of his out-of-state origin. As a matter of fact, Washington's opinion in *Corfield* v. *Coryell* was so broad that it may seem to support this interpretation also. On this basis there is no need to search for any natural law or fundamental standards; the privileges and immunities to which an individual is entitled are those which are standard in that state, applied without discrimination. Under this view the clause is read as though it said: "The citizens of each state shall be entitled in each of the other states to all privileges and immunities of the citizens of the state in which they shall happen to be."

Under this second interpretation the clause does not bulk so large in its import for civil liberties. It is more of an instrument for interstate adjustment and comity. As the preamble of the corresponding provision in the Articles of Confederation put it, the intent was "the better to secure and perpetuate mutual friendship and intercourse among the people of the different states in this Union." But it seems clear that Representative Bingham, the "old Republican" who subsequently carried the privileges and immunities clause over from Article IV into the Fourteenth Amendment, saw in it a much more potent instrument, a guarantee of certain basic rights, variously defined as those specified elsewhere in the Constitution or, more broadly, as those belonging of right to the citizens of all free governments.

Constitutional Issues of Slavery

The most important and notorious of the Supreme Court's decisions on the slavery issue, the case of *Dred Scott* v. *Sandford* (1857), has a bearing on the matter just dealt with, and on the drafting of the Fourteenth Amendment.[4] A Negro named Dred Scott, a slave in Missouri, had been taken by his owner into the state of Illinois, where slavery had been forbidden by the Northwest Ordinance of 1787, and also into the territory of Upper Louisiana (Minnesota), where slavery was forbidden by the Missouri Compromise. Having then been returned to Missouri, Scott brought suit for his freedom in a Missouri court, on the ground of his periods of residence in free territory. His claim was denied by the state supreme court, which held that Scott's legal status was determined by the law of the state in which he resided.

Taking advantage of the fact that a citizen of New York had become Scott's owner, Scott's friends then brought a similar suit in the federal courts based on diversity of citizenship. The issue of Scott's citizenship, which could have been crucial to the case, was minimized by the judge. He held that citizenship, for purposes of federal court jurisdiction, meant only residence and the power to own property. Consequently he permitted the case to be tried, and ruled against Scott on the merits of his claim to freedom.

The Supreme Court's decision was delayed until just after Buchanan's inauguration in 1857. Ignoring the complex whirl of events in which the case had its setting, we need note only two of the Court's main holdings, as announced by Chief Justice Taney. First, no Negro slave could be a citizen with power to sue in the federal courts. Scott had not become a free man by reason of the Missouri Compromise, because it was unconstitutional. Unless he had some other claim to freed status, he was still a slave and so without right to bring suit in the federal courts.

Second, and more fundamental, Taney contended that Negroes had been regarded as persons of an inferior order when the Constitution was adopted, and that it had not considered them as "citizens." Consequently, all persons of African descent, whether slaves or not, were barred from access to the federal courts under the diversity of citizenship clause and indeed, from the enjoyment of any rights or protections under the Constitution. Specifically, Taney wrote that "persons" of Dred Scott's "class" were not "a portion of this people" or "constituent members of this sovereignty." They were "not included, and were not intended to be included, under the word 'citizens' in the Constitution, and can therefore claim none of the rights and privileges which that instrument provides for and secures to citizens of the United States."

What were the rights and privileges of citizens of the United States which Taney thus foreclosed to all persons of African descent? In addition to the right to

---

[4] See Carl B. Swisher, *History of the Supreme Court of the United States: The Taney Period, 1836–1864* (New York: Macmillan Publishing Company, 1974), vol. 5, chap. 24.

sue in the federal courts, there was eligibility to the Congress or the Presidency, which is limited to citizens of the United States. But what about rights guaranteed by the Constitution to "the people" or to "persons" generally? Taney's use throughout his opinion of "the people" of the American Union as synonymous with "citizens of the United States" certainly suggests that these broader guarantees were no more effective than the narrower ones.

But what about Article IV, section 2? If a state gives its free Negro residents the status of state citizens, would they not be able to claim protection in other states for the privileges and immunities of state citizenship? Taney said no. In his view Article IV, section 2, protected only the rights of citizens of the United States. Each state, he said, might confer "the character of citizen" upon anyone it thought proper, but such a citizen would not be entitled to "the privileges and immunities of a citizen in the other states." To put a "citizen" of any given state on a plane of "perfect equality" with the citizens of every other state as to rights of person and property would be, in effect, to make him a citizen of the United States. And since the Court had started out by saying that persons of Dred Scott's class could not be citizens of the United States, obviously the privileges and immunities clause had to be interpreted so as not to open a loophole in that doctrine.

So the privileges and immunities clause, under the pressure of the slavery issue, was given a very restricted interpretation indeed. Its protections were available only to those citizens of the states who were also citizens of the United States. This prevented the clause from protecting Negroes. But Taney then went on to remove its protection further by holding that it covered only citizens of the United States who were temporarily in other states. There they were entitled to the minimum privileges and immunities generally prevailing in that state. But a state was left perfectly free to create inequalities in rights among its *own* citizens.

The Meaning of Due Process

The due process clause of the Fifth Amendment closely approaches the privileges and immunities clause in vagueness. The Supreme Court has confessed that "few phrases of the law are so elusive of exact apprehension as this."[5] But "due process" did have something in the way of an ascertainable history. It was generally thought to be descended from the Latin phrase "per legem terrae" in the Magna Carta of 1215. In chapter 39 of that document the King promised: "No freeman shall be arrested, or imprisoned, or disseized, or outlawed, or exiled, or in any way molested; nor will we proceed against him, unless by the lawful judgment of his peers or by the law of the land."

The Petition of Right of 1628 prayed that "freemen be imprisoned or detained only by the law of the land, or by due process of law, and not by the King's special command without any charge." In 1819 Daniel Webster tried his hand at defining due process in his argument in the *Dartmouth College* case, describing it as "the general law; a law, which hears before it condemns, which proceeds upon inquiry, and renders judgment only after trial," so that "every citizen shall hold his life,

---

[5] *Twining* v. *New Jersey* (1908).

liberty, property, and immunities, under the protection of the general rules which govern society."

The *Dartmouth College* decision did not turn on the due process clause, however, and actually it was not until 1856 that the Supreme Court first interpreted it, in the case of *Murray's Lessee* v. *Hoboken Land & Improvement Company*. An act of Congress had authorized the Treasury Department, without recourse to judicial process, to issue warrants against and make a levy on the property of federal revenue collectors found to be indebted to the United States. The complaint was made that this was a taking of property without due process of law. The Supreme Court upheld the statute, on the ground that the procedure prescribed was not in conflict with any specific provisions of the Constitution, nor with the settled usages under English common and statute law which had been carried over into the practice of this country.

These, then, are the most important pre–Civil War contributions (both positive and negative) made by the Supreme Court to the understanding of civil liberties under the Constitution. The lines of judicial interpretation thus opened up were of great significance when Congress undertook those postwar modifications in the Constitution which John Frank has referred to as constituting "the second American Revolution."

DRAFTING OF THE FOURTEENTH AMENDMENT

Of the three post–Civil War amendments, only the Fourteenth need concern us here. The Thirteenth Amendment, abolishing slavery and involuntary servitude, became effective in December, 1865. While achieving its immediate purpose, it was quickly seen to be inadequate to the task of making the freedmen into free people. The principal application of the Thirteenth Amendment has been to invalidate state "peonage" legislation,[6] but in *Jones* v. *Alfred H. Meyer Co.* (1968), the Supreme Court adopted an interpretation of the amendment under which it applies to all racial discrimination stemming from former slave status.[7] The Fifteenth Amendment, forbidding abridgement of the right to vote because of race, color, or previous condition of servitude, took effect in March, 1870, and will be discussed in Chapter 30.

The formative period of the Fourteenth Amendment was between January 12,

---

[6] Peonage usually involves an employer giving an employee an advance of wages and then compelling the worker to stay on the job until the debt is worked off. A number of state statutes have allowed or fostered such a system of indentured labor. See *Bailey* v. *Alabama* (1911) and *Pollock* v. *Williams* (1944).

There are exceptional circumstances in which compulsory labor is permissible. A state may require able-bodied persons to devote a reasonable amount of their time to such public duties as jury service or repair of the roads [*Butler* v. *Perry* (1916)]. Forced service for military purposes is not interpreted as involuntary servitude [*Selective Draft Law Cases* (1918)]. Nor does the Thirteenth Amendment cover special professions which operate under conditions requiring continued service for a specified time, such as seamanship [*Robertson* v. *Baldwin* (1897)]. In *Heart of Atlanta Motel* v. *United States* (1964) the Court found "no merit" in the contention that, by requiring appellant to rent rooms to blacks against its will, Congress was subjecting the motel to involuntary servitude.

[7] See discussion in Chap. 28.

1866, when the first drafts were considered by the Joint Committee on Reconstruction, and June 13 of the same year, when the House concurred in the Senate version. What was it that the Congress, under control of Republican Reconstructionists, was trying to do? Its basic motivation was undoubtedly to protect the rights of the newly freed Negroes, to establish constitutional guarantees which would be effective when, as ultimately would happen, military control was withdrawn from the Southern states. The "Black Codes" of those states had been grossly discriminatory, forbidding Negroes to own property, to have access to the courts, and so on. Since *Barron* v. *Baltimore* had limited the effect of the Bill of Rights to the federal government, the only provision in the Constitution as it then existed which might cover the Negro was the privileges and immunities clause. However, the *Dred Scott* decision, as just noted, eliminated this possibility. Thus new guarantees were needed.

The first move of the Thirty-ninth Congress was toward statutory protection. A civil rights bill was introduced by Senator Trumbull of Illinois on January 5, 1866, and became law on April 9 by passage over President Johnson's veto, two months before the Fourteenth Amendment was adopted by Congress. The Civil Rights Act provided that persons born in the United States were citizens of the United States, and that such citizens, without regard to color, were entitled in every state and territory to the same rights to contract, sue, give evidence, and hold property as were enjoyed by white citizens, and to the equal benefit of all laws for the security of person and property. Any person who under color of law caused any such civil right to be denied would be guilty of a federal offense.

By the Civil Rights Act the federal government asserted its power to control civil rights *within* the several states for the purpose of preventing discrimination against the newly freed Negroes. Where did it get this power? Senator Trumbull cited three sources—the Thirteenth Amendment, the privileges and immunities clause, and the Declaration of Independence. "Liberty and slavery," he said, "are opposite terms." Consequently an unjust encroachment upon liberty was "a badge of servitude which, by the Constitution, is prohibited." As for privileges and immunities, he was relying upon the *Corfield* v. *Coryell* interpretation which saw them as "such fundamental rights as belong to every free person . . . the great fundamental rights of life, liberty, and the pursuit of happiness, and the right to travel, to go where he pleases. This is the right which belongs to the citizen of each State." The Declaration of Independence he threw in for good measure.

However, Trumbull's arguments failed to convince some in Congress who were wholly in favor of the bill. Particularly, Representative John A. Bingham of Ohio, an important member of the Joint Committee on Reconstruction, challenged reliance on the privileges and immunities clause because it gave no enforcement authority to Congress. The Thirteenth Amendment argument was not accepted. Consequently there was a strong feeling among the Republican Reconstructionists that the civil rights of the freedmen must be put on a firmer constitutional footing, and one that would not be subject to repeal by a later Congress. Thus discussion of the Fourteenth Amendment proceeded concurrently with the action on the Civil Rights Act.

It is not possible to examine in detail the evolution of the amendment from the first drafts submitted in the Joint Committee on January 12 to its final passage.[8] But we can get a sense of the developmental process by noting the successive versions of the first section proposed by Bingham, whose role entitled him to rate as "father" of the amendment. His first draft said simply: "The Congress shall have power to make all laws necessary and proper to secure to all persons in every State within this Union equal protection in their rights of life, liberty and property."

We note two things about this language. First, it would supply the constitutional authority for legislation which Bingham felt to be lacking for the Civil Rights Act. Second, it was concerned with giving Congress power to protect civil rights, rather than with stating standards of protection which would be enforceable directly by the courts. This latter point deserves underlining, for it is essential to understanding the spirit of the times. The Presidency under Johnson was in eclipse. The Supreme Court, in the aftermath of the *Dred Scott* decision, was at very nearly the lowest point in its history. Congress was in the saddle, and the first thing that occurred to its members was that Congress should undertake the protection of civil liberties by legislation and by securing whatever authority was necessary for such legislation.

On January 27 a revised Bingham draft proposed to give Congress legislative power "to secure all persons in every State full protection in the enjoyment of life, liberty and property; and to all citizens of the United States in every State the same immunities and equal political rights and privileges." This was poor drafting. How much protection is "full" protection? Did the "same immunities" mean the same throughout the nation, or merely the same for white and Negro in each state? Bringing "political" rights into the amendment added a whole new field of concern.

The Joint Committee rejected this draft by a tie vote, so Bingham tried again. This time his proposal ran: "Congress shall have power to make all laws which shall be necessary and proper to secure to citizens of each State all privileges and immunities of citizens in the several States; and to all persons in the several States equal protection in the rights of life, liberty and property."

The text was reported to the two houses on Feberuary 13. In the House Bingham explained that both parts of his proposal were already in the Constitution and binding on the states, and that he was merely adding the power of Congress to enforce them. Since this contention is in flat contradiction to the holdings of *Barron* and *Dred Scott,* it must be assumed that Bingham was intending to repeal those decisions.

If this was Bingham's view and purpose, then one essential element was missing from his formulation. He had failed to do anything about repealing another of the doctrines of the *Dred Scott* case, namely, that persons of African descent, whether slaves or not, could not be citizens of the United States under the Constitution. The

[8] See Horace E. Flack, *The Adoption of the Fourteenth Amendment* (Baltimore: The Johns Hopkins Press, 1908); Joseph B. James, *The Framing of the Fourteenth Amendment* (Urbana, Ill.: The University of Illinois Press, 1956); Charles Fairman, "Does the Fourteenth Amendment Incorporate the Bill of Rights? The Original Understanding," 2 STANFORD LAW REVIEW 5–139 (1949) and "The Supreme Court and the Constitutional Limitations on State Governmental Authority," 21 UNIVERSITY OF CHICAGO LAW REVIEW 40–78 (1953); William W. Crosskey, "Charles Fairman, 'Legislative History,' and the Constitutional Limitations on State Authority," 22 UNIVERSITY OF CHICAGO LAW REVIEW 1–143 (1954).

Civil Rights Act did have a provision guaranteeing the status of Negroes as citizens of the United States, but the draft of the Fourteenth Amendment did not, and during the House discussion no one suggested that it was needed.

After a three-day House debate at the end of February, further consideration of Bingham's draft was postponed. In April the Joint Committee undertook further revisions, and on April 28 the first section of the Fourteenth Amendment, in what was to be its final form save only for the first sentence defining citizenship, was adopted. It was again the work of Bingham. In contrast to the draft which the House had debated, this version was not merely a grant of power to Congress. It was a direct obligation on the states. Moreover, the long debate as to whether the amendment should leave the states free to set their own standards on civil rights and merely seek to prevent unequal application of those standards, or whether it should set up general standards of treatment to which the practices in each state must conform, was finally settled. It would do both. So there was an equal protection clause which guaranteed no discrimination, though without the "life, liberty and property" language of the earlier draft. But there was also the privileges and immunities clause carried over from Article IV, section 2, and made applicable to "citizens of the United States." And to this was now added the due process clause from the Fifth Amendment.

The House passed this version on May 10. The Senate took it up on May 23, and there it was handléd by Jacob M. Howard of Michigan. It was in fact Howard who, seeing the need for a definition of citizenship, subsequently added the first sentence of the present amendment to fill that gap. Howard devoted more attention to explaining the privileges and immunities clause to the Senate than to the other parts of the first section. He agreed that the privileges and immunities guaranteed by Article IV were somewhat vague, and thought it would be "a somewhat barren discussion" to determine what they were. "But it is certain," he added, "the clause was inserted in the Constitution for some good purpose."

Whatever these privileges and immunities were—and Howard quoted from Justice Washington in *Corfield* v. *Coryell*—they "are secured to the citizen solely as a citizen of the United States and as a party in their courts. They do not operate in the slightest degree as a restraint or prohibition upon State legislation." The Supreme Court, as we have just seen, had ruled to this effect in the *Dred Scott* case. Moreover, the first eight amendments were in the same situation, because of *Barron* v. *Baltimore*. Howard specifically recited the provisions of these amendments and said that the privileges and immunities clause of the Fourteenth Amendment would make this "mass of privileges, immunities, and rights, some of them secured by the second section of the fourth article . . . some by the first eight amendments of the Constitution," effective on the states. "The great object of the first section of this amendment is . . . to restrain the power of the States and compel them at all times to respect these great fundamental guarantees."

With regard to the equal protection and due process clauses, he pointed out that they would "disable a State from depriving not merely a citizen of the United States, but any person, whoever he may be, of life, liberty, or property without due process of law, or from denying to him the equal protection of the laws of the State."

Similarly in the House Bingham had stressed the difference between the protection of "citizens" in the first clause and "persons" in the second and third clauses, and had said that the amendment would protect the "inborn rights of every person," both "citizen and stranger."

It is not feasible to report the additional debate in detail. The Senate approved the resolution, as amended, on June 8, and the House accepted the revised version on June 13. Thus, with the concurrence of the necessary states, were added to the Constitution three important new standards for the protection of civil liberties against state action. Equal protection, a general guarantee against discrimination, was the most specific of the new provisions. The other two—due process, and privileges and immunities—were concepts without precise contours which would have such meaning as they might be given by Congress and, more importantly, by the Supreme Court.[9] To this process of spelling out the implications for individual liberties of the Bill of Rights and the Fourteenth Amendment, we now turn, giving attention first to freedom of speech and press.

[9] A very useful source on the legislative history of the Thirteenth, Fourteenth, and Fifteenth Amendments is Alfred Avins (ed.), *The Reconstruction Amendments' Debates* (Richmond, Va.: Virginia Commission on Constitutional Government, 1967).

Chapter 19

The Judicial Approach
to the First Amendment

"Congress shall make no law . . . abridging the freedom of speech, or of the press."
This great principle of an open society was incorporated into the Constitution when
the First Amendment was ratified on December 15, 1791. No one who has even the
faintest understanding of how democratic self-government functions can harbor any
doubt as to the fundamental importance of freedom of ideas. The case against
suppression of opinion was put in perhaps its most perfect literary form for modern
times by Justice Holmes's dissent in the case of *Abrams* v. *United States* (1919):

> Persecution for the expression of opinions seems to me perfectly logical. If you have no
> doubt of your premises or your power and want a certain result with all your heart you
> naturally express your wishes in law and sweep away all opposition. To allow opposition
> by speech seems to indicate that you think the speech impotent, as when a man says that
> he has squared the circle, or that you do not care whole-heartedly for the result, or that
> you doubt either your power or your premises. But when men have realized that time
> has upset many fighting faiths, they may come to believe even more than they believe
> the very foundations of their own conduct that the ultimate good desired is better
> reached by free trade in ideas—that the best test of truth is the power of the thought to
> get itself accepted in the competition of the market, and that truth is the only ground

upon which their wishes safely can be carried out. That at any rate is the theory of our Constitution.

Holmes is here making a "utilitarian" defense of free speech, basing its justification on its value to society. But freedom to speak may also be defended as a natural right which individuals must enjoy if they are to achieve the full potentialities of their intellectual and moral endowments. Interference with such rights would on this basis be objectionable, not because society was deprived of truths it might otherwise have discovered, but because individuals were thwarted in the development and expression of their rational faculties.

Our task, however, is not to discuss generally the philosophical or moral or social case for freedom of expression but rather to examine more specifically the meaning and effect which the libertarian principles of the First Amendment have achieved in American experience through judicial interpretation and enforcement.[1]

THE ENGLISH HERITAGE AND THE INTENTION OF THE FRAMERS

In *Robertson* v. *Baldwin* (1897) the Supreme Court said: "The law is perfectly well settled that the first ten amendments to the Constitution, commonly known as the Bill of Rights, were not intended to lay down any novel principles of government, but simply to embody certain guaranties and immunities which we had inherited from our English ancestors."

If the First Amendment was in fact intended to be limited to principles inherited from our English ancestors, then Blackstone's famous definition of the liberty of the press would be a principal guide to its meaning:

> The liberty of the press is indeed essential to the nature of a free state; but this consists in laying no previous restraints upon publications, and not in freedom from censure for criminal matter when published. Every freeman has an undoubted right to lay what sentiments he pleases before the public; to forbid this, is to destroy the freedom of the press; but if he publishes what is improper, mischievous or illegal, he must take the consequence of his own temerity.[2]

If the First Amendment ratifies Blackstone's understanding of freedom of the press and of speech, then it is a protection only against previous restraint, or censorship. This is of course an important guarantee and one which has been fully incorporated into American reasoning. Banning of books, preventing newspapers from being published, forbidding or breaking up peaceful assemblies—such actions are associated with dictatorships; they are not permissible under the First Amendment.

But Blackstone offered no principle which would protect speakers or publishers from punishment for what they had said or written. He would permit punishment, not only for speech or publication which is illegal or criminal, but also for matter

---

[1] For a broad consideration of the libertarian philosophy, see Thomas I. Emerson, *The System of Freedom of Expression* (New York: Random House, Inc., 1970).

[2] Blackstone, *Commentaries,* IV, 151, 152.

which is "improper" or "mischievous." His rules would allow broad scope for governmental prosecutions against those who had exercised the right of free speech or free press. English practice, in fact, permitted wide latitude for severe action against the crime of "seditious libel"—that is, defaming or criticizing the government or its officers. If the First Amendment carried over the English law of seditious libel, then freedom of speech and press in America were subject to serious limits.

That this English legacy had in fact persisted was evident when Congress adopted the Sedition Act of 1798. This statute provided punishment for making false, scandalous, and malicious statements against the government of the United States, either house of Congress, or the President, with intent to defame them or bring them into contempt or disrepute, or to stir up the hatred of the people against them, or bring about sedition in any of its various forms. The act was broad enough to make criminal virtually any criticism of the government.

The Federalist members of Congress who passed this legislation as a device for punishing their Jeffersonian critics obviously did not regard it as barred by the First Amendment. However, the violent public reaction against the numerous prosecutions instituted under the act indicated that the Federalists were in error. The act expired by its own terms in 1801 without ever reaching the Supreme Court for a constitutional test. Many convictions were secured under it, but the fines levied were subsequently repaid by act of Congress, and President Jefferson pardoned all those who had been found guilty under the act. Eventually the Sedition Act was formally declared to have been unconstitutional by the Supreme Court in *New York Times* v. *Sullivan* (1964).[3]

RELATION OF THE FIRST AMENDMENT TO THE STATES

As we saw in Chapter 18, the provisions of the Bill of Rights were declared in *Barron* v. *Baltimore* (1833) to be limitations only on Congress, and of course the First Amendment is specific in its reference to Congress. Consequently at the state level, where infringements on speech or press freedom were most likely to occur, such violations would not give rise to federal questions or be subject to Supreme Court adjudication. This point was made clear in a 1922 case, *Prudential Insurance Co.* v. *Cheek,* where the Court said that "the Constitution of the United States imposes upon the States no obligation to confer upon those within their jurisdiction . . . the right of free speech."

However, since the 1870s the Court had been interpreting the due process clause of the Fourteenth Amendment to protect economic freedoms and property rights against state action, and it had shown no hesitation to strike down state legislation on what came to be known as "substantive due process" grounds. In the 1923 case of *Meyer* v. *Nebraska,* the Court was confronted with a situation where a property right and a censorship issue were closely allied. Wartime hysteria had

---

[3] For historical analyses see Walter Berns, "Freedom of the Press and the Alien and Sedition Laws: A Reappraisal," in Philip B. Kurland (ed.), *The Supreme Court Review: 1970* (Chicago: University of Chicago Press, 1970), pp. 109–160; Leonard W. Levy, *Legacy of Suppression: Freedom of Speech and Press in Early American History* (Cambridge, Mass.: The Belknap Press, Harvard University Press, 1960).

caused the Nebraska legislature to forbid the teaching of German even in private schools, but the Supreme Court saw this as an attack on the livelihood of German language teachers and ruled that the "liberty" to teach a foreign language was protected by the Fourteenth Amendment due process clause. Then in 1925 the Court, in *Pierce* v. *Society of Sisters,* invalidated a Ku Klux Klan–backed Oregon constitutional amendment, aimed at parochial schools, which denied parents the "liberty" of sending their children to private schools. Again the Court pointed out that this law would destroy the property rights of religious schools.

It was by this property-oriented, substantive due process route that the Supreme Court came to its precedent-shattering decision in *Gitlow* v. *New York* (1925), only one week after the *Pierce* decision. In the course of upholding the conviction of a prominent Communist under the New York criminal anarchy statute, Justice Sanford for the conservative Court made this astounding concession: "We may and do assume that freedom of speech and of the press . . . are among the fundamental rights and 'liberties' protected . . . from impairment by the States." This issue had not been argued before the Court, and the holding was unnecessary to the decision of the *Gitlow* case. It was in this offhand manner that the historic decison was made enormously enlarging the coverage of the First Amendment and the jurisdiction of the Supreme Court to guarantee the freedom of speech and press against state or local action as well as against Congress.

THE CLEAR AND PRESENT DANGER TEST

The usual reason for seeking to control or punish speech is that the speech threatens to result in dangerous or illegal acts. Ideas do have consequences. "Words," as Judge Learned Hand said in the *Masses* case, "are not only the keys of persuasion, but the triggers of action."[4] The shout of "Fire" in a crowded theater can directly cause the most deadly panic. A person may be persuaded by speech or writing to commit murder. Words may lead to the development of a plan for overthrowing the government.

It is clear that words which directly incite to illegal acts are themselves tainted with illegality. The common law recognized the crime of incitement to violence, and the First Amendment has never been understood as extending its sanctuary to speech criminal in purpose and intent. But it immediately becomes apparent there are questions of degree involved here. How closely related must the speech be to the crime in order to taint the speech with illegality? How clear must the purpose be to incite to crime? What degree of immediacy must there be in the situation? And, since these questions are going to be determined in legal prosecutions, who will be responsible for doing so—the trial judge, or the jurors?

At one extreme, the theory can be adopted that words do not become criminal until they have a tendency to produce immediate breach of the peace. But if this is the rule to be applied, then no new legislation or judicial standards are needed, for the common-law rules on criminal solicitation or incitement cover the case.

[4] *Masses Publishing Co.* v. *Patten* (1917).

But the lawmakers and the public are often unwilling to confine restrictive powers over speech within such narrow limits, particularly in crisis situations. They may begin to move against speech merely because it is unpopular. They may say, as Justice Sanford did in *Gitlow* v. *New York* (1925): "The State cannot reasonably be required to measure the danger from every . . . utterance in the nice balance of a jeweler's scale. A single revolutionary spark *may* kindle a fire that, smouldering for a time, *may* burst into a sweeping and destructive conflagration."

This "remote and indirect tendency" test was in fact operative prior to the adoption of the First Amendment. The English common law of sedition made words criminal if they cast blame on the government or its officials, on the ground that bringing them into disrepute would *tend* to overthrow the state. The American Sedition Act of 1798 adopted this same standard, but in other respects the act was an advance on the common law of criminal sedition in that it entrusted criminality to the jury rather than the judge, and admitted truth as a defense. This act was rejected by the political process, and the authority of the "remote and indirect tendency" test which it embodied was at least somewhat impaired. But no other standard was stated, nor was there judicial need for one in the federal courts until World War I when enforcement of the Espionage Act of 1917 and the Sedition Act of 1918 forced the issue onto the Supreme Court's calendar.

Justice Holmes was the Court's spokesman in its initial encounters with the free speech problem. The Espionage Act, which prohibited the making of false statements intended to interfere with the successful prosecution of the war, as well as acts obstructing recruiting or causing insubordination in the Armed Forces, was at issue in *Schenck* v. *United States* (1919). The defendants had mailed circulars to men eligible for the draft, declaring conscription to be unconstitutional despotism and urging them to assert their rights. Holmes spoke for a unanimous Court in finding that such speech was not protected by the First Amendment because of the "clear and present danger" that it would result in illegal action:

> The character of every act depends upon the circumstances in which it is done. . . . The most stringent protection of free speech would not protect a man in falsely shouting fire in a theatre and causing a panic. . . . The question in every case is whether the words used are used in circumstances and are of such a nature as to create a clear and present danger that they will bring about the substantive evils that Congress has a right to prevent. It is a question of proximity and degree.

Then he added, with particular reference to the problems of the *Schenck* case: "When a nation is at war many things that might be said in time of peace are such a hindrance to its effort that their utterance will not be endured so long as men fight and that no Court could regard them as protected by any constitutional right."[5]

Thus the clear and present danger test proved a rather illusory protection to freedom of speech in wartime. It was, in effect, a rationalization for sending men to

---

[5] In the same month, March, 1919, Holmes wrote two more unanimous opinions for the Court upholding convictions in Espionage Act cases—*Frohwerk* v. *United States* (1919) and *Debs* v. *United States* (1919).

jail because of their speech, though it did insist that the relationship between speech and illegal acts must be proximate, not remote and indirect. Professor Zechariah Chafee, Jr., praised the *Schenck* ruling as supplying "for the first time an authoritative judicial interpretation in accord with the purpose of the framers of the Constitution."[6]

In the fall of 1919 Holmes, along with his colleague, Louis D. Brandeis, sought to show that the test did have protective value, but the two justices were unable to carry the Court majority with them. The crime in *Abrams* v. *United States* was printing and circulating pamphlets attacking the government's action in sending American troops to Vladivostok and Murmansk in the summer of 1918 and calling for a general strike of munitions workers. Holmes's dissent is probably his most famous piece of rhetoric; but here we need note only the effort he made to sharpen up and strengthen the clear and present danger test by these words:

> We should be eternally vigilant against attempts to check the expression of opinions that we loathe and believe to be fraught with death, unless they so imminently threaten immediate interference with the lawful and pressing purposes of the law that an immediate check is required to save the country. . . . Only the emergency that makes it immediately dangerous to leave the correction of evil counsels to time warrants making any exception to the sweeping command, "Congress shall make no law . . . abridging the freedom of speech."

Holmes was again unsuccessful in *Gitlow* v. *New York* (1925). Justice Sanford for the majority denied that the clear and present danger test was even applicable as a test of the New York criminal anarchy act. Brandeis made a final effort to restate the test in *Whitney* v. *California* (1927), involving conviction of a Communist under the California syndicalism act. A legislative declaration that a danger exists which justifies restrictions on speech and assembly creates, he said, merely a "rebuttable presumption." If the conditions alleged by the legislature do not, in fact, exist, then the courts, guided by the clear and present danger test, must refuse to enforce the statute. Brandeis admitted that the standards for the test had not yet been clearly fixed, and he undertook once more the task of formulation:

> To courageous, self-reliant men, with confidence in the power of free and fearless reasoning applied through the processes of popular government, no danger flowing from speech can be deemed clear and present, unless the incidence of the evil apprehended is so imminent that it may befall before there is opportunity for full discussion. If there be time to expose through discussion the falsehood and fallacies, to avert the evil by the processes of education, the remedy to be applied is more speech, not enforced silence. Only an emergency can justify repression. . . . Moreover, even imminent danger cannot justify resort to prohibition of these functions essential to effective democracy, unless the evil apprehended is relatively serious. Prohibition of free speech and assembly is a measure so stringent that it would be inappropriate as the means for averting a relatively trivial harm to society. . . . The fact that speech is likely

---

[6] Zechariah Chafee, Jr., *Free Speech in the United States* (Cambridge, Mass.: Harvard University Press, 1941), p. 82.

to result in some violence or in destruction of property is not enough to justify its suppression. . . . Among free men, the deterrents ordinarily to be applied to prevent crime are education and punishment for violations of the law, not abridgment of the rights of free speech and assembly.

The subsequent history of the clear and present danger test—its development in the 1930s and 1940s and its decline in the 1950s and 1960s—will be found in later chapters. But at this point it may be noted that from 1919 to 1927 its successive statements were eloquent but it kept no one out of jail.

LEGISLATIVE REASONABLENESS

Looking back, we see that the clear and present danger test was, at first, not a test for the validity of legislation—the Espionage Act was admittedly constitutional— but only a test for determining how closely words had to be related to illegal acts in order to be infected with their illegality. Even in *Gitlow,* Holmes did not appear to challenge the New York statute. He merely doubted whether Gitlow's "redundant discourse" was included in the statutory prohibition. It was not until *Whitney* that clear and present danger was definitely set forth as a basis on which courts, and indeed, all Americans, could "challenge a law abridging free speech and assembly by showing that there was no emergency justifying it."

This development brought the clear and present danger test into direct conflict with an earlier standard of judicial review; namely, that legislative conclusions embodied in statutes must be upheld by courts if there is any basis on which a "reasonable man" could have reached the same conclusion as the legislature. The reasonable man theory was embraced by the majority in *Gitlow* and *Whitney.* Those decisions held that the function of the Court, when confronted with a statute alleged to infringe basic civil liberties, was limited to judging whether a reasonable man could have reached the legislature's conclusion as to the existence of a danger demanding that protective action be taken. As Sanford said in *Gitlow*: "Every presumption is to be indulged in favor of the validity of the statute." Legislatures should be rebuked only if they act "arbitrarily or unreasonably."

Now there is sound authority for the reasonable man theory of judicial review. Holmes himself was ordinarily one of the most ardent exponents of this test. As he said in his famous dissent to *Lochner* v. *New York* (1905), he would not invalidate any statute "unless it can be said that a rational and fair man necessarily would admit that the statute proposed would infringe fundamental principles as they have been understood by the traditions of our people and our law." Of course, *Lochner* was not a civil liberties case; the issue was whether New York could limit the hours of employment in bakeries. But in 1923 Holmes did apply the reasonable man test in what came very close to being a civil liberty case, *Meyer* v. *Nebraska.* The Court majority here, as previously noted, held invalid a state law which was aimed to prevent the teaching of the German language in the primary schools. Holmes refused to go along with this judgment, because he believed that whether children in their early years should hear and speak only English at school was "a question upon which men reasonably might differ and therefore I am unable to say that the Constitution of the United States prevents the experiment being tried."

This quotation epitomizes the doctrine upon which Holmes's reputation for liberalism was based. The reasonable man theory was a method of letting the legislatures have their own way. A conservative Supreme Court, from 1880 on, had insisted on the right to substitute its judgment for that of Congress or the state legislatures as to the constitutionality of laws which changed the rules respecting rights and uses of property. Holmes thought that the Court had no such license from the Constitution to override the views of popularly elected legislatures, except to veto statutes for which no case could possibly be made that would satisfy a reasonable man. This was the core of his liberalism.

Why, then, did Holmes appear to abandon the reasonable man test in the civil liberties field? And could it be liberalism to advocate a doctrine of narrow judicial review in dealing with economic regulation and broad judicial review over regulations limiting freedom of speech and press? This apparent paradox was explained in two different ways on the Roosevelt Court, and the divergence was the basis for some of its classic arguments.

PREFERRED POSITION

One explanation, adopted on numerous occasions and associated with the judicial quartet of Black, Douglas, Murphy, and Rutledge, was that the reasonable man test, although appropriate in all other fields, did not apply where the basic freedoms of the First Amendment were at issue. There, it was contended, the judiciary had to hold itself and legislatures to higher standards because of the "preferred position" which the Constitution gives to First Amendment freedoms. Stated in an extreme form, the argument is that any law touching communication is infected with presumptive invalidity. A more moderate statement is that, because First Amendment values are so essential to a free society, legislative action infringing those values must be shown to be not only "reasonably" adapted to the attaining of valid social goals but justified by overwhelmingly conclusive considerations.

The development of the preferred position view must be indicated rather summarily. Holmes himself never made this argument. Its origin might be found in Justice Cardozo's statement in a 1937 decision that First Amendment liberties were on "a different plane of social and moral values." Freedom of thought and speech, he said, is "the matrix, the indispensable condition, of nearly every other form of freedom. . . . Neither liberty nor justice would exist if they were sacrificed."[7] A somewhat similar position was taken a little earlier in the same year, in the case of *Herndon* v. *Lowry*. But the credit for the invention is usually given to Justice Stone, in a footnote which he appended to a 1938 decision.[8]

The case in question concerned application of a congressional act prohibiting transportation of certain types of compounded milk products in interstate commerce, and Stone was rehearsing the familiar arguments for the reasonable man theory of judicial review:

[7] *Palko* v. *Connecticut* (1937).
[8] *United States* v. *Carolene Products Co.* (1938). For the interesting history of this footnote, see Alpheus T. Mason, *Harlan Fiske Stone: Pillar of the Law* (New York: The Viking Press, Inc., 1956), pp. 512–516.

The existence of facts supporting the legislative judgment is to be presumed, for regulatory legislation affecting ordinary commercial transactions is not to be pronounced unconstitutional unless in the light of the facts made known or generally assumed it is of such a character as to preclude the assumption that it rests upon some rational basis within the knowledge and experience of the legislators.

At this point occurred the footnote:

There may be narrower scope for operation of the presumption of constitutionality when legislation appears on its face to be within a specific prohibiton of the Constitution, such as those of the first ten amendments, which are deemed equally specific when held to be embraced within the Fourteenth. . . . It is unnecessary to consider now whether legislation which restricts those political processes which can ordinarily be expected to bring about repeal of undesirable legislation, is to be subjected to more exacting judicial scrutiny under the general prohibitions of the Fourteenth Amendment than are most other types of legislation. . . . Nor need we enquire . . . whether prejudice against discrete and insular minorities may be a special condition, which tends seriously to curtail the operation of those political processes ordinarily to be relied upon to protect minorities, and which may call for a correspondingly more searching judicial inquiry.

This is admittedly a tentative and qualified pronouncement; Frankfurter, who vigorously challenged the whole preferred position argument as "mischievous," was justified in concluding that it "did not purport to announce any new doctrine" and that, if it had, a footnote would hardly have been an "appropriate way" of doing so.[9] But within a year and a half the idea which Stone had at least suggested leaped from the footnotes to become the doctrine of an almost unanimous Court, Justice Frankfurter included, in the 1939 handbill cases.[10] Speaking through none other than Justice Roberts, the Court said:

In every case, therefore, where legislative abridgement of the rights [to freedom of speech and press] is asserted, the courts should be astute to examine the effect of the challenged legislation. Mere legislative preferences or beliefs respecting matters of public convenience may well support regulation directed at other personal activities, but be insufficient to justify such as diminishes the exercise of rights so vital to the maintenance of democratic institutions. And so, as cases arise, the delicate and difficult task falls upon the courts to weigh the circumstances and to appraise the substantiality of the reasons advanced in support of the regulation of the free enjoyment of the rights.

McReynolds was the only dissenter.

The "preferred position" phrase was apparently not actually employed until Stone, by then Chief Justice, used it in 1942 in his dissent from *Jones* v. *Opelika*, where the Court majority upheld municipal license taxes on booksellers as applied to Jehovah's Witnesses and cited the fact that these were general tax ordinances, not levies aimed at this particular group. In reply Stone observed:

[9] *Kovacs* v. *Cooper* (1949).
[10] *Schneider* v. *Irvington* (1939).

The First Amendment is not confined to safeguarding freedom of speech and freedom of religion against discriminatory attempts to wipe them out. On the contrary, the Constitution, by virtue of the First and Fourteenth Amendments, has put those freedoms in a preferred position. Their commands are not restricted to cases where the protected privilege is sought out for attack. They extend at least to every form of taxation which, because it is a condition of the exercise of the privilege, is capable of being used to control or suppress it.

One year later Justice Douglas restated this thought, but now for the Court majority, in *Murdock* v. *Pennsylvania* (1943), which overruled *Jones* v. *Opelika*: "Freedom of press, freedom of speech, freedom of religion are in a preferred position." The phrase reappeared in several subsequent decisions. Even Justice Jackson, whose subsequent thoughts were most antagonistic to the preferred position argument, lent it support in his 1943 holding in the second flag-salute case.[11] Perhaps the strongest of all the statements along this line was that by Justice Rutledge in *Thomas* v. *Collins* (1945):

> Any attempt to restrict those liberties must be justified by clear public interest, threatened not doubtfully or remotely, but by clear and present danger. The rational connection between the remedy provided and the evil to be curbed, which in other contexts might support legislation against attack on due process grounds, will not suffice. These rights rest on firmer foundation. Accordingly, whatever occasion would restrain orderly discussion and persuasion, at appropriate time and place, must have clear support in public danger, actual or impending. Only the gravest abuses, endangering paramount interests, give occasion for permissible limitation.

The task of rebutting the preferred position doctrine was principally assumed by Justice Frankfurter. It was his contention that Holmes by the clear and present danger test had not really challenged the reasonable man theory or intended to develop an alternative to it as a test for the validity of legislation. He was dismayed by the uses to which the Roosevelt Court began to put the clear and present danger test. He contended that it was being used for a purpose other than Holmes had intended—namely, to determine the constitutionality of legislation; that it was being applied in much different areas than Holmes had contemplated, including contempt of court proceedings and violation of petty police regulations; and that the spirit of its use was much different than Holmes would have approved. In dissenting from the Court's decision in *Bridges* v. *California* (1941), he charged that Justice Black's employment of the clear and present danger test with preferred position embellishment was an unthinking "recitation of phrases that are the shorthand of a complicated historic process." In *Pennekamp* v. *Florida* (1946) he came close to denying any meaning at all to the doctrine, saying: " 'Clear and present danger' was never used by Mr. Justice Holmes to express a technical legal doctrine or to convey a formula for adjudicating cases. It was a literary phrase not to be distorted by being taken from its context."

In *Kovacs* v. *Cooper* (1949) Justice Frankfurter, reacting against Justice Reed's

---

[11] *West Virginia State Board of Education* v. *Barnette* (1943).

acceptance of the "preferred position" phrase in the Court's opinion, made the clearly mistaken claim that this doctrine had "never commended itself to a majority of this Court." But in the same opinion he gave evidence of the persuasiveness of the preferred position idea when he agreed that "those liberties of the individual which history has attested as the indispensable conditions of an open as against a closed society come to this Court with a momentum of respect lacking when appeal is made to liberties which derive from shifting economic arrangements."

THE ABSOLUTIST–LITERALIST POSITION

Beyond the preferred position argument stands the contention that the First Amendment gives *absolute* protection to the freedoms it names. This approach asserts that the First Amendment means literally what it says—that Congress shall *make no law* which has the effect of limiting, or reducing in compass, freedom of speech and press. On this reasoning any law passed by Congress which abridges the freedom of speech or press is unconstitutional on its face, and the circumstances alleged to justify it need not even be considered.

The principal proponent of the absolutist position on the Supreme Court was Justice Black, who summarized his argument in *Smith* v. *California* (1959) as follows:

> I read "no law abridging" to mean *no law abridging.* The First Amendment, which is the supreme law of the land, has thus fixed its own value on freedom of speech and press by putting these freedoms wholly "beyond the reach" of *federal* power to abridge. No other provision of the Constitution purports to dilute the scope of these unequivocal commands of the First Amendment. Consequently, I do not believe that any federal agencies, including Congress and this Court, have power or authority to subordinate speech and press to what they think are "more important interests."

The tenets of the absolutist doctrine, however, were developed most completely by Alexander Meiklejohn. He writes:

> No one who reads with care the text of the First Amendment can fail to be startled by its absoluteness. The phrase, "Congress shall make no law . . . abridging the freedom of speech," is unqualified. It admits of no exceptions. To say that no laws of a given type shall be made means that no laws of that type shall, under any circumstances, be made. That prohibition holds good in war as in peace, in danger as in security.[12]

Meiklejohn distinguished between public and private speech. It is public speech, concerned with public issues, for which absolute protection is essential, because in a self-governing system the citizens are the rulers and must be free to examine and discuss all ideas relating to the public issues they must decide:

---

[12] Alexander Meiklejohn, *Free Speech and Its Relation to Self-government* (New York: Harper & Row, Publishers, Incorporated, 1948), pp. 17, 26–27. An expanded version of his views is contained in *Political Freedom: The Constitutional Powers of the People* (New York: Harper & Row, Publishers, Incorporated, 1960). See also his "The First Amendment is an Absolute," in Philip B. Kurland (ed.), *The Supreme Court Review, 1961* (Chicago: University of Chicago Press, 1961), pp. 245–266.

Just so far as, at any point, the citizens who are to decide an issue are denied acquaintance with information or opinion or doubt or disbelief or criticism which is relevant to that issue, just so far the result must be ill-considered, ill-balanced planning for the general good. . . .When a question of policy is "before the house," free men choose to meet it not with their eyes shut, but with their eyes open. To be afraid of ideas, any idea, is to be unfit for self-government. Any such suppression of ideas about the common good, the First Amendment condemns with its absolute disapproval. The freedom of ideas shall not be abridged.

Meiklejohn sought support for his view from another protection of speech found in the Constitution which has unquestioningly been treated as an absolute right. That is the provision in Article I, section 6, to the effect that members of Congress "shall not be questioned in any other place" for "any speech or debate in either house."

The parallel is an interesting one: Congress "shall make no law," and congressmen "shall not be questioned." We have already seen in Chapter 9 that the congressional right of free speech is taken at its face value. Congressmen are absolutely protected from prosecution because of what they have said in Congress or its committees or its official publications. The Constitution makes a similar judgment, say the absolutists, concerning freedom of speech, because of the importance of freedom of discussion to democratic self-government. The Constitution knows how to grant qualified rights, if that is its purpose and intent. Take the due process clause of the Fifth Amendment. It does not state an absolute prohibition. It does not say that persons shall not be deprived of life, liberty, or property. It says that persons *may* be so deprived, provided due process of law is followed. Life, liberty, and property are qualified rights under the Fifth Amendment. But freedom of speech under the First Amendment is limited by no such qualifications.

Literalism-absolutism does create some problems for its advocates. A purely literal reading of the First Amendment, which applies by its terms only to Congress, would have prevented the Court from extending the amendment's coverage to the states as was done in the *Gitlow* case. Chafee denies that Meiklejohn's supposed boundary between public and private speech actually exists: "There are public aspects to practically every subject."[13] To Meiklejohn's charge that Holmes subverted the First Amendment by permitting it to be breached whenever there was a clear and present danger, Chafee responds that the only practicable alternative to Holmes's limited immunity for speech was not absolute immunity but no immunity at all. Black's absolutism led him into a quixotic attack on the validity of the entire law of libel.[14] It is significant that Justice Murphy, as devoted a civil libertarian as ever sat on the Court, admitted in *Chaplinsky* v. *New Hampshire* (1942): "It is well understood that the right of free speech is not absolute at all times and under all circumstances."

[13] Book review, 62 *Harvard Law Review* 891 (1949).

[14] See Chap. 22; also Edmond Cahn, "Mr. Justice Black and First Amendment 'Absolutes': A Public Interview," 37 NEW YORK UNIVERSITY LAW REVIEW 37 (1962).

BALANCING

The converse of the absolutist position that the government has *no* power to limit expression in constitutionally protected areas is that the government has *some* power to limit expression in all areas. The extent of this power must be determined in every case by balancing the case for freedom against the case for order or security.

The clear and present danger test was, of course, a form of balancing, but the scales were definitely tipped in favor of freedom; as Justice Brandeis said, the apprehended evil must be not only clear and present but also "relatively serious" and so "imminent" that it could not be averted by the processes of education. Advocates of the preferred position for civil liberties also allowed for balancing, but freedom's thumb on the scales was even heavier here.

The more recent proponents of balancing on the Supreme Court, principally Justice Harlan, have weighed freedom against order with no preferences. The basic notion of the balancers, as Emerson has expressed it, is "that the court must, in each case, balance the individual and social interest in freedom of expression against the social interest sought by the regulation which restricts expression."[15]

The balancing formula was applied in the 1950s in cases where the Court was passing on the validity of congressional action against Communists. Initially utilized by Chief Justice Vinson in *American Communications Association* v. *Douds* (1950), it was perhaps most clearly stated by Justice Harlan in *Barenblatt* v. *United States* (1959) for the Court majority in upholding the power of congressional investigation. In some circumstances, Harlan said, the First Amendment would protect an individual from disclosing his associational relationships to a congressional committee. But a witness does not have the right to resist inquiry in all circumstances. Consequently there must be "a balancing by the courts of the competing private and public interests at stake in the particular circumstances shown." Harlan then proceeded to review the individual and the governmental interests at stake, and concluded that "the balance . . . must be struck in favor of the latter."

Justice Black, dissenting in *Barenblatt,* argeed that balancing might be employed by courts to test the validity of a law which "primarily regulates conduct" but which has a minor effect on speech or "indirectly" affects ideas. But he vigorously denied that laws directly abridging First Amendment freedoms could be justified by a balancing process. Such action was a direct challenge to his absolutist interpretation of First Amendment protections. He also protested that Harlan had misused the balancing test because he had balanced "the right of the Government to preserve itself, against Barenblatt's right to refrain from revealing Communist affiliations." The real interest in Barenblatt's silence, Black felt, was not a mere personal one. It was "the interest of the people as a whole in being able to join organizations, advocate causes and make political 'mistakes' without later being subjected to governmental penalties for having dared to think for themselves. . . . It is these inter-

---

[15] Thomas I. Emerson, "Toward a General Theory of the First Amendment," 72 YALE LAW JOURNAL 877 (1963); *Toward a General Theory of the First Amendment* (New York: Random House, Inc., 1966), pp. 53–54.

ests of society, rather than Barenblatt's own right to silence, which I think the Court should put on the balance against the demands of the Government, if any balancing process is to be tolerated."

Emerson criticizes balancing because it "frames the issues in such a broad and undefined way, is in effect so unstructured, that it can hardly be described as a rule of law at all." It provides "no hard core of doctrine to guide a court," but rather casts it loose "in a vast space . . . to strike a general balance in the light of its own best judgment. . . . If a court takes the test seriously, the factual determinations involved are enormously difficult and time-consuming, and quite unsuitable for the judicial process." But in fact the test does not allow courts to exercise any real degree of independent judgment, because it gives "almost conclusive weight to the legislative judgment."[16]

On the other hand, Dean Alfange, Jr., feels that the balancing doctrine has been unfairly abused by liberals because it has been unfairly used by its proponents. He defends balancing of interests as a central feature of sociological jurisprudence; it is an activist technique, well adapted to the settlement of First Amendment cases; it is essential to "an accurate appraisal of reality." He concludes: "The alternative to balancing is to prepackage decisions by setting up objective standards in advance, which, because of their unavoidable abstractness, cannot be made adequate to deal with the constantly varying factual situations which each case presents."[17]

THE TWO-LEVEL THEORY

Finally, the Supreme Court has on occasion sought to solve some of its First Amendment problems by dividing expression into two levels—one level to which the First Amendment applies and a second level of expression which does not deserve constitutional protection. The Court first spelled out this theory in the case of *Chaplinsky* v. *New Hampshire* (1942). Chaplinsky, threatened with arrest after creating a public disturbance by his open denunciations of all religion as a "racket," had told a city marshal of Rochester, New Hampshire, that "you are a God damned racketeer" and "a damned Fascist and the whole government of Rochester are Fascists or agents of Fascists." The Court upheld Chaplinsky's conviction for violating a state statute against calling anyone "offensive or derisive" names in public. Justice Murphy, writing for a unanimous Court, said:

> There are certain well-defined and narrowly limited classes of speech, the prevention and punishment of which has never been thought to raise any Constitutional problem. These include the lewd and the obscene, the profane, the libelous, and the insulting or 'fighting' words—those which by their very utterance inflict injury or tend to incite an immediate breach of the peace. It has been well observed that such utterances are no

---

[16] See also criticisms of balancing in Laurent B. Frantz, "The First Amendment in the Balance," 71 YALE LAW JOURNAL 1424–1450 (1962); Martin Shapiro, *Freedom of Speech: The Supreme Court and Judicial Review* (Englewood Cliffs, N.J.: Prentice-Hall, Inc., 1966), chap. 3.

[17] "The Balancing of Interests in Free Speech Cases: In Defense of an Abused Doctrine," 2 LAW IN TRANSITION QUARTERLY 1, 22 (1965).

essential part of any exposition of ideas, and are of such slight social value as a step to truth that any benefit that may be derived from them is clearly outweighed by the social interest in order and morality.

This conception that only speech which has "social value" is protected by the First Amendment solved the Court's immediate problem in the *Chaplinsky* case, but it has difficult and serious implications which have made the two-level theory of dubious value.

APPRAISAL

The various doctrines just reviewed are obviously related to the results which their judicial practitioners wished to achieve and the conceptions they had of their judicial responsibilities. In fact, Martin Shapiro, referring to the "polemical origins" of these doctrines, goes so far as to say that it is a "grave error to take them seriously instead of viewing them in their true light as the superficial ploys of the deeper struggle between activist and modest [self-restraint] tendencies on the Court."[18] Without going this far, one can point up the relations between these doctrines and their consequences for judicial review.

The absolutist position involves a maximum of judicial challenge to legislatures with a minimum exercise of judicial judgment, because the absolutist automatically strikes down any legislation which abridges protected liberties. The two-level theory is another manifestation of absolutism, but at the other end of the scale; expressions on the lower level are absolutely unprotected, so the judge need neither challenge legislative infringements on expression at that level nor exercise judicial judgment.

The reasonable man test and the balancing technique as employed on the Court may be paired. Both are doctrines of judicial self-restraint and rationalizations for letting legislatures have their own way. The test of reasonableness, as Felix S. Cohen wrote, "makes of our courts lunacy commissions sitting in judgment upon the mental capacity of legislators."[19] Since legislators are seldom lunatics, their actions are seldom without some justification in reason.

The clear and present danger test and the preferred position doctrine are also closely related. Both require judges to take at least a moderately activist stance and to exercise responsible judgment in determining whether the First Amendment has been breached. These tests do not give the automatic answers of the absolutists, but, in contrast to the pseudo-standards of the reasonableness and balancing doctrines, they do supply positive and workable standards to guide judicial judgment.[20]

With this introduction to the principal standards developed by or available to the Supreme Court for interpreting First Amendment freedoms, we now turn to an examination of their application in specific fields of protected expression.

[18] *Op. cit.,* p. 87.

[19] L. K. Cohen (ed.), *The Legal Conscience: Selected Papers of Felix S. Cohen* (New Haven: Yale University Press, 1960), p. 44.

[20] See Shapiro, *op. cit.,* Chap. 4, for a strong defense of the clear and present danger and preferred position tests.

Chapter 20

Freedom of Speech

The First Amendment provides that "the freedom of speech" shall not be abridged by law. Communication by speech is by definition a social experience, which must involve the interaction of at least two persons. Here is the beginning of a community interest in the speech process. Suppose two persons are discussing politics in a private home. Certainly there is no case for governmental restraint here. But wait! What if the discussion becomes an argument and voices are raised, to the annoyance of neighbors? Or suppose one of the discussants applies offensive language to the other, who resents it and starts a brawl? Suppose a weapon is drawn? At some point along the way a speech situation in which the government could have no interest has turned into a matter justifying public intervention, and all this with only two participants.

As we increase the number of discussants and move them from a private to a public location, the opportunities for public intervention are multiplied. Suppose an unpopular group wants to meet in a public school auditorium. Suppose demonstrators convene in a public park or parade on a public street, thereby creating traffic problems and making it likely that persons unsympathetic to the demonstrators will happen by and be tempted to display their opposition. Suppose that loudspeakers being used at an outdoor meeting annoy by their noise, regardless of the words used, other members of the public rightfully in the area.

Obviously there is no end to the complications that can arise in a speech situation as we move out from a constitutionally protected core into areas where preservation of speech rights must compete with other allowable public interests. Because, as Justice Jackson said in *Kunz* v. *New York* (1951), "the vulnerability of various forms of communication to community control must be proportioned to their impact upon other community interests," it will be helpful to distinguish three different communication situations—pure speech (speech without conduct), speech plus conduct, and symbolic speech (conduct without speech).

PURE SPEECH

"Pure speech" is a concept created by the Supreme Court. It was first developed in the Court's labor picketing decisions, to take account of the fact that picketing is more than speech. In the 1940 case of *Thornhill* v. *Alabama* the Court broadly assimilated peaceful picketing to freedom of speech, and so protected it by the First Amendment against abridgement. But very soon the Court concluded that this was a partially incorrect conception of picketing, and began to qualify this position. As Justice Douglas said in a 1942 decision: "Picketing by an organized group is more than free speech, since it involves patrol of a particular locality and since the very presence of a picket line may induce action of one kind or another, quite irrespective of the nature of the ideas which are being disseminated."[1] In *Cox* v. *Louisiana* (1965) Justice Goldberg speaks of those "who communicate ideas by pure speech," as contrasted with those "who would communicate ideas by conduct such as patrolling, marching, and picketing on streets and highways." Again in the same opinion he refers to "speech in its pristine form." Pure speech would include, we can assume, communication taking place by the spoken word in face-to-face contacts, addresses or remarks at meetings, speech amplified by mechanical means or on the channels of the various communications media. Pure speech can range from dull expositions to the most emotional harangues. The distinctive qualities of pure speech are that it relies for its effect only on the power of the ideas or emotions that are communicated by speech and that usually the audience is a voluntary one which chooses to listen to the speaker's message.

Because pure speech situations generally cause no interference with or inconvenience to those not involved in the communication process, justification for community control is at an absolute minimum. In fact, legislation permitting the restriction or punishment of pure speech is generally regarded as invalid on its face. For example, in *Street* v. *New York* (1969), the Court dealt with a New York statute making it a misdemeanor to mutilate or cast contempt on the American flag "by words or act," and it held that punishment "merely for speaking defiant or contemptuous words" was unconstitutional.

There are, however, many borderline situations where exception may be taken to the general rule. In Chapter 19 we noted that *Chaplinsky* v. *New Hampshire* (1942) held "fighting words" to be unprotected by the First Amendment, since they were

[1] *Bakery and Pastry Drivers Local* v. *Wohl* (1942).

so likely to cause a breach of the peace. The "fighting words" holding, though never overruled, has been narrowly interpreted.[2] In *Gooding* v. *Wilson* (1972) a Georgia statute punishing "opprobrious words or abusive language, tending to cause a breach of the peace," was invoked to convict a black man who had called a white police officer a "son of a bitch" and had threatened to kill him, choke him, or cut him to pieces. The Supreme Court reversed the conviction because the Georgia courts had not narrowed this statutory language to apply only to "fighting words."

The federal statute punishing threats to kill the President was involved in the case of *Watts* v. *United States* (1969). A speaker at a public rally on the Washington Monument grounds said that if he was drafted for the Vietnam War and given a rifle, "the first man I want to get in my sights is L. B. J." The Supreme Court reversed his conviction on the ground that any statute making criminal "a form of pure speech" must be strictly interpreted, and this "political hyperbole" was not regarded as a true threat but only as "a very crude offensive method of stating a political opposition to the President."

Statutes punishing public use of "offensive" language or public swearing have likewise been held to strict standards.[3] *Cohen* v. *California* (1971) concerned a young man who had expressed his opinion of the Vietnam war by wearing in public a jacket bearing the words "Fuck the Draft." He was convicted of disturbing the peace by "offensive conduct." Justice Harlan for the Court held that he had engaged in pure speech, not conduct, and reversed on the ground that use of this four-letter word was unlikely to cause "violent reaction" and that the state lacked authority as a guardian of public morality to try to remove the word from the public vocabulary. In this latter connection Harlan took issue with Murphy's assumption in the *Chaplinsky* case that only speech which is an essential part of an "exposition of ideas" and of "social value as a step to truth" is entitled to constitutional protection. In a very perceptive passage Harlan wrote:

> . . . much linguistic expression serves a dual communicative function: it conveys not only ideas capable of relatively precise, detached explication, but otherwise inexpressible emotions as well. In fact, words are often chosen as much for their emotive as their cognitive force. We cannot sanction the view that the Court, while solicitous of the cognitive intent of individual speech, has little or no regard for that emotive function which practically speaking, may often be the more important element of the overall message sought to be communicated.

Of course, "shouting fire in a theater" has been regarded as a classic type of punishable speech ever since Justice Holmes used this example in *Schenck* v. *United*

---

[2] As John Hart Ely says, the category of "fighting words" is "no longer to be understood as a euphemism for either controversial or dirty talk but requires instead an unambiguous invitation to a brawl." See "Flag Desecration," 88 Harvard Law Review 1482, 1493 (1975).

[3] In *Eaton* v. *City of Tulsa* (1974), a witness in court referred to an alleged assailant as "chicken shit." His conviction for contempt of court was reversed by the Supreme Court, which held that this "single isolated use of street vernacular, not directed at the judge or any officer of the court," did not constitute contempt. See also *In re Little* (1972), *Papish* v. *University of Missouri* (1973), and *Lewis* v. *New Orleans* (1974).

States (1919). A more up-to-date version of this offense would be saying that there is a bomb on a plane. *Kovacs* v. *Cooper* (1949) ruled that limits can be set for sound amplification of speech in public places.[4]

Serious limitations on the political speech of government employees were imposed by the Hatch Act, which forbade civil servants to take an active part in political management or campaigns. The Supreme Court upheld the law by a four to three vote in *United Public Workers* v. *Mitchell* (1947). Citing long-standing concern with the spoils system, Justice Reed said: "To declare that the present supposed evils of political activity are beyond the power of Congress to redress would leave the nation impotent to deal with what many sincere men believe is a material threat to the democratic system." In a later test case, *U.S. Civil Service Commission* v. *National Association of Letter Carriers* (1973), the Supreme Court by a six to three margin reiterated its support for the statute.[5] A bill repealing many of the Hatch Act restrictions was vetoed by President Ford in 1976.

In a surprising 1976 decision, *Elrod* v. *Burns,* the Court went further and by a five to three vote declared the spoils system unconstitutional. Firing public employees because they belong to the wrong party, said Brennan, penalizes political beliefs and "clearly infringes First Amendment interests." An exception was made for those in policy-making or confidential positions. The ruling seemed to offer wide vistas for lawsuits by discharged public employees.

Following the scandalous use of funds in the 1972 Nixon campaign, Congress adopted a new campaign finance law in 1974 which limited both contributions and expenditures, required disclosure of campaign contributions, and provided for public financing of presidential elections.[6] The statute was attacked in *Buckley* v. *Valeo* (1976) on the ground that limitations on contributions and expenditures curbed the First Amendment freedom of contributors and candidates to express themselves in the political marketplace. The Court upheld the limitations on direct contributions to political candidates as representing "only a marginal restriction upon the contributor's ability to engage in free communication." However, the Court did conclude that expenditure limitations would seriously limit access to the expensive mass media which are "indispensable instruments of effective political speech," and so were unconstitutional. The statute also violated the First Amendment by forbidding individuals or groups to make expenditures "relative to particular candidates," such as buying newspaper or television advertising, so long as such expenditures were made independently of the candidate or his agents.

SPEECH PLUS CONDUCT

"Speech plus," as the Court sometimes refers to speech plus conduct, involves the communication of ideas by patrolling, marching, and picketing on sidewalks, streets, or other public areas. "Speech plus" is a constitutional hybrid. Insofar as it

---

[4] Compare *Saia* v. *New York* (1948).

[5] In *Broadrick* v. *Oklahoma* (1973) the Court likewise upheld a state statute similar to the Hatch Act. A federal employee who was fired after criticizing his supervisor was held not to have been denied freedom of speech in *Arnett* v. *Kennedy* (1974).

[6] *Schwartz* v. *Vanasco* (1976) invalidated a New York "fair campaign" law designed to curb smear tactics, on the ground that it was so broad it could "chill" legitimate political speech.

is speech, it is protected. Insofar as it is conduct, it is subject to regulation where good cause is shown. Picketing and demonstrating involve physical movement of the participants, who rely less upon the persuasive influence of speech to achieve their purposes and more upon the public impact of assembling, marching, and patrolling. Their purpose is to bring a point of view—by signs, slogans, singing, or their mere presence—to the attention of the widest possible public, including those uninterested or even hostile. Demonstrators are likely to seek maximum exposure by going where they will be seen and heard by the most people, which increases the possibility of traffic problems, inconvenience to the public, and breach of the peace.

Communication by use of the streets or other public areas is guaranteed by the concept of the "public forum."[7] It is interesting to note that Holmes, while a member of the Massachusetts supreme court, upheld a Boston ordinance which required a permit from the mayor for persons to "make any public address" on Boston Common. A legislature, he said,

> as representative of the public . . . may and does exercise control over the use the public may make of such places. . . . For the Legislature absolutely or conditionally to forbid public speaking in a highway or public park is no more an infringement of the rights of a member of the public than for the owner of a private house to forbid it in his house.[8]

This early Holmes ruling had to be distinguished or disregarded as dictum when the Supreme Court in the 1930s and 1940s began seriously to consider the constitutional status of meetings in public places. *Hague* v. *C.I.O.* (1939), the first such encounter, grew out of a Jersey City ordinance which prohibited assemblies "in or upon the public streets, highways, public parks or public buildings" without a permit from the director of public safety. Under Mayor Hague, who became famous for his boast, "I am the law," the CIO was denied use of public halls in Jersey City on the ground that it was a Communist organization. Members of the CIO were searched when coming into the city, were threatened with arrest if they discussed the Wagner Act, were arrested for distributing printed matter, and were forcibly ejected from the city and put on the boat for New York.

The Supreme Court by a five to two vote held that these invasions of liberty could not be defended as valid police regulations. "Wherever the title of street and parks may rest," wrote Justice Roberts, "they have immemorially been held in trust for the use of the public and time out of mind have been used for the purpose of assembly, communicating thoughts between citizens and discussing public questions." Their use for communication of views on national questions may be regulated in the interests of all, but may not in the guise of regulations, be abridged or denied.

So it was established that individuals and groups have a right of access to the public forum for discussion of public issues. This means that speakers can mount soapboxes on street corners, or address groups in public parks. But it does not

---

[7] See Harry Kalven, Jr., "The Concept of the Public Forum," in Philip B. Kurland (ed.), *The Supreme Court Review: 1965* (Chicago: The University of Chicago Press, 1965), p. 23; Geoffrey R. Stone, "Fora Americana: Speech in Public Places," in Philip B. Kurland, (ed.), *The Supreme Court Review: 1974* (Chicago: University of Chicago Press, 1974), p. 233.

[8] *Commonwealth* v. *Davis* (1895); upheld by the U.S. Supreme Court, *Davis* v. *Massachusetts* (1897).

follow that their access to the public forum is an absolute right beyond restraint or regulation in the public interest.[9] After all, sidewalks, streets, and parks serve other purposes in addition to communication. In an effort to accommodate and reconcile these conflicting interests, legislatures and city councils have rather generally provided for some form of restraint on access to the public forum, thereby creating potential First Amendment problems.

Permit Systems

The duty and responsibility of governmental authorities to keep the streets open obviously justifies them in requiring that persons desiring to parade on the streets secure permits. The Court so held in *Cox* v. *New Hampshire* (1941), where it unanimously approved the conviction of a group of Jehovah's Witnesses who had marched single file along a downtown city street, carrying placards to advertise a meeting, without securing the special license required by state statute for "parades or processions" on a public street. The statute was held to be a reasonable police regulation, administered under proper safeguards. The Court made clear that it was treating the license requirement as merely a traffic regulation and that the conviction was not for conveying information or holding a meeting. As Justice Reed said in a later case, *Poulos* v. *New Hampshire* (1953), involving the same statute: "Regulation and suppression are not the same, and courts of justice can tell the difference."

The constitutionality of a permit system can be challenged in two ways. First, the ordinance or statute may be so restrictive, or give such discretionary power to public officials to deny permits, as to be unconstitutional on its face. For example, a city ordinance of Birmingham, Alabama, authorized a city commission to refuse a parade permit if "in its judgment the public welfare, peace, safety, health, decency, good order, morals or convenience require that it be refused." In *Walker* v. *Birmingham* (1967) the Supreme Court intimated that this ordinance was unconstitutional on its face, and it specifically so held in *Shuttlesworth* v. *Birmingham* (1969).

Kunz v. *New York* (1951) invalidated a New York City ordinance which made it unlawful to hold public worship meetings on the street without first obtaining a permit from the police commissioner. The Court majority regarded the ordinance as giving to "an administrative official discretionary power to control in advance the right of citizens to speak on religious matters on the streets of New York . . . with no appropriate standards to guide his action."

Second, the permit regulations, though phrased with due regard for constitutional requirements, may be administered in a discriminatory or repressive fashion. The authorities may deny permits to some groups, or seek to confine parades to remote areas of the city, or find that demonstrations are never compatible with traffic requirements. In *Niemotko* v. *Maryland* (1951) a group of Jehovah's Witnesses requesting use of a city park for religious services was denied a permit by the city council, after a hearing where the Witnesses were queried about their alleged refusal to salute the flag and their interpretation of the Bible. The Supreme Court conclud-

---

[9] In *Lehman* v. *City of Shaker Heights* (1974), the Supreme Court held that buses on a municipally owned transit system were not a "public forum" and that a candidate for political office could be refused advertising space on the buses without violating his free speech rights.

ed that the permit was denied because of dislike for the group's views and unanimously held such action not only an infringement on freedom of speech but also a denial of equal protection of the law.

Injunctions

In addition, or as an alternative, to control by permits, demonstrations may be limited by court injunctions, which can be fashioned by the judge to specify the form and area of demonstration and even the number of participants. Injunctions may also protect the right to demonstrate. The famous Selma march led by Martin Luther King, Jr., in 1965 took place under the protection of an injunction forbidding interference by Governor George Wallace. Judge Frank Johnson, in issuing the injunction, said: "[The] extent of the right to assemble, demonstrate and march peaceably along the highways and streets in an orderly manner should be commensurate with the enormity of the wrongs that are being protested and petitioned against." Judge Johnson regarded the wrongs here as "enormous."[10]

When a permit for a demonstration has been refused or an injunction has been issued against it, the demonstrators have two choices. They can go ahead with their demonstration and risk arrest, or they can bring court action to secure review of the ban. Martin Luther King, Jr., took the first course in 1963 when he and some of his followers, having been denied a Birmingham parade permit, defied a state court injunction against racial demonstrations while tensions were high. He contended that the injunction denied his constitutional rights, and he feared that his protest movement would lose its momentum if he paused to litigate the injunction. For the majority Justice Stewart admitted that the injunction raised substantial constitutional issues, but held that it should have been challenged in court, not disobeyed. He sympathized with the "impatient commitment" of the civil rights leaders to their cause, but said, "Respect for judicial process is a small price to pay for the civilizing hand of law, which alone can give abiding meaning to constitutional freedom."[11] Justice Brennan for the minority charged that the Court was ignoring the doctrine of constitutional supremacy and raising Alabama's judicial ruling "above the right of free expression guaranteed by the Federal Constitution."[12]

Restricted Areas

There are certain types of public areas or buildings where the right to demonstrate may be forbidden because of serious conflict with other public interests. Traffic considerations may foreclose demonstrations in highly congested areas. Thus Justice Goldberg said in *Cox* v. *Louisiana* (1965) that no one could "insist upon a street meeting in the middle of Times Square at the rush hour as a form of freedom of speech or assembly." Justice Black would have gone further. In the same case he denied that "speech plus" is speech at all, and would have given the state "general

---

[10] *Williams* v. *Wallace* (1965).

[11] *Walker* v. *Birmingham* (1967). But see the holding in *Carroll* v. *President and Commissioners of Princess Anne* (1968) that an ex parte injunction was incompatible with the First Amendment.

[12] See Norman G. Rudman and Richard C. Solomon, "Who Loves a Parade? *Walker* v. *City of Birmingham*," 4 LAW IN TRANSITION QUARTERLY 185 (1967).

power . . . to bar all picketing on its streets and highways." But this was a minority view, directly in conflict with the *Hague* principle that the use of streets and public places "for purposes of assembly, communicating thoughts between citizens, and discussing public questions [is] a part of the privileges, rights, and liberties of citizens."

Statutes prohibiting the obstruction of "public passages" (i.e., streets and sidewalks) are clearly constitutional if applied in a nondiscriminatory fashion.[13] However, such a statute was invalidated in the *Cox* case because it made a specific exemption for labor picketing.[14]

A civil rights demonstration on the grounds of the South Carolina state capitol by some two hundred black students was upheld by the Court in *Edwards* v. *South Carolina* (1963) as the exercise of "basic constitutional rights in their most pristine and classic form." Meetings and demonstrations on the grounds of the United States Capitol have been forbidden since 1882, but this ban was declared unconstitutional by the court of appeals for the District of Columbia in a judgment upheld by the Supreme Court in 1972.[15]

Demonstrations in the vicinity of the White House were governed until 1967 by an informal agreement that the District of Columbia police would be given prior notice. But a gathering of 30,000 pro-Israeli demonstrators in Lafayette Park across from the White House in June, 1967, led the National Park Service to issue regulations requiring permits for demonstrations and limiting the number of demonstrators to one hundred on the White House sidewalk and five hundred in Lafayette Park. These regulations were invalidated by the Court of Appeals for the District of Columbia in 1969, but the court did hold that there should be a notification of intent to assemble fifteen days prior to a demonstration.[16]

In 1949 Congress passed a statute making it illegal to picket or parade in or near a building housing a federal court, with the intention of interfering with the administration of justice or influencing judges or jurors in the discharge of their duties. This statute resulted from the picketing of federal courthouses by partisans of the defendants during trials involving leaders of the Communist Party, and was adopted by Congress at the urging of the organized bar and the federal judiciary. Several states, including Louisiana, enacted statutes on the same model. In the case of *Cox* v. *Louisiana,* this statute was invoked against Cox, whose demonstrators had taken up positions 125 feet from the courthouse.

Justice Goldberg for the Court found this law to be "a statute narrowly drawn to punish specific conduct that infringes a substantial state interest in protecting the judicial process." It was "on its face a valid law dealing with conduct subject to

[13] See *Cameron* v. *Johnson* (1968).
[14] *Grayned* v. *Rockford* (1972) upheld an ordinance forbidding noisy and disruptive picketing outside public schools, but *Police Department of Chicago* v. *Mosley* (1972) declared a school antipicketing ordinance unconstitutional because it made an exception permitting labor picketing.
[15] *Chief of the Capitol Police* v. *Jeanette Rankin Brigade* (1972).
[16] *A Quaker Action Group* v. *Hickel* (1970). See "Regulation of White House Demonstrations," 119 UNIVERSITY OF PENNSYLVANIA LAW REVIEW 668 (1971). In *Greer* v. *Spock* (1976) the Court upheld the authority of the armed services to ban political candidates and demonstrators from military bases, saying that the business of a military installation is "to train soldiers, not to provide a public forum."

regulation so as to vindicate important interests of society . . . the fact that free speech is intermingled with such conduct does not bring with it constitutional protection." Justice Black was even stronger in his support for the statute, saying: "The streets are not now and never have been the proper place to administer justice."

A public library was the scene of a peaceful sit-in by five blacks protesting its racially discriminatory policies in *Brown* v. *Louisiana* (1966). In spite of Justice Black's argument that "order and tranquility" are essential to the operation of libraries and that they are not permissible places for demonstrations, Justice Fortas for the five-judge majority held that by their "silent and reproachful presence" where they had a right to be, the protesters were exercising their constitutional right to petition the government for the redress of grievances. But later that year, in *Adderly* v. *Florida* (1966), the Court took a different view of a demonstration on the grounds of a county jail, protesting segregation in the jail. Now speaking for the majority, Black held that jail grounds, where security is essential, are not open to the public and cannot be the site of demonstrations.

Whether demonstrators have a right of access to the grounds of shopping centers, which are technically private property, has been troublesome. In *Amalgamated Food Employees Union* v. *Logan Valley Plaza* (1968) the Court upheld the right of a labor union to picket a store in a shopping center where there was no other feasible way to convey the facts of a labor dispute to the public. The Court relied on *Marsh* v. *Alabama* (1946), which had approved the right to distribute religious literature in the business district of a company-owned town. But in *Lloyd Corp.* v. *Tanner* (1972) it was distribution of handbills that was involved, which the Court refused to protect because there were "adequate alternative avenues of communication" that would not infringe on private property rights. *Hudgens* v. *NLRB* (1976) was another labor picketing situation, but the Court now not only declined to follow *Logan Valley;* Stewart's opinion contended that the guarantee of free expression was completely inapplicable to shopping centers, and that *Lloyd* had overruled *Logan Valley.* However, three of the six-judge majority denied that *Logan Valley* had been overruled.

Privacy Problems

Picketing or demonstrating in residential areas raises privacy issues but was upheld by dictum in *Gregory* v. *Chicago* (1969). There, some one hundred predominantly black activists had marched on the sidewalks around the home of Mayor Daley to protest policies of the Chicago superintendent of schools. Residents of the wholly white area, resenting the intrusion, threatened the marchers with violence; the police, fearing a riot, arrested some of the demonstrators, five of whom were found guilty of disorderly conduct. The Supreme Court reversed the convictions as unsupported by evidence and also expressed the opinion that such a march, "if peaceful and orderly, falls well within the sphere of conduct protected by the First Amendment."[17]

May the state protect individuals in their homes from unwanted communica-

---

[17] See "Picketers at the Doorstep," 9 HARVARD CIVIL RIGHTS–CIVIL LIBERTIES LAW REVIEW 95 (1974).

tions? *Martin* v. *City of Struthers* (1943) tested an ordinance which made it unlawful for a person distributing "handbills, circulars or other advertisements" to ring the doorbell or otherwise summon the occupant of a residence to the door for the purpose of receiving such material. The ordinance was applied against a member of Jehovah's Witnesses who was distributing a dodger announcing a meeting and lecture. The motivation for the ordinance was to protect the daytime sleep of residents of this industrial town, since many of them were employed on night shifts in factories.

By a six to three vote, the Supreme Court invalidated the ordinance. Justice Black noted that "for centuries it has been a common practice in this and other countries for persons not specifically invited to go from home to home and knock on doors or ring doorbells to communicate ideas to the occupants or to invite them to political, religious, or other kinds of public meetings." To be sure, door-to-door visitation might be a nuisance or a blind for criminal activities. But it was also a customary part of the techniques of many political, religious, and labor groups, and "is essential to the poorly financed causes of little people."

Breard v. *Alexandria* (1951) upheld an ordinance against house-to-house canvassing applied against salesmen of magazine subscriptions. But *Hynes* v. *Borough of Oradell* (1976) held unconstitutionally vague an ordinance requiring persons canvassing house to house in political campaigns to give advance written notice to the police department.

Picketing in Labor Disputes

Picketing in labor disputes has a long history and presents special problems. Initially all labor picketing was regarded by the courts as tortious conduct and illegal. Gradually the view developed that peaceful picketing by strikers who had a direct economic interest to serve might be permitted by the state, but "stranger picketing" remained outside the law. In 1921 the Supreme Court cautiously admitted that "strikers and their sympathizers" might maintain one picket "for each point of ingress and egress" at a plant or place of business. Unless severely limited in this way, the Court concluded, picketing "indicated a militant purpose, inconsistent with peaceable persuasion."[18]

It is a long jump from 1921 to 1940, when in the case of *Thornhill* v. *Alabama* Justice Murphy put peaceful picketing of all kinds under the protection of the free speech clause, saying: "in the circumstances of our times the dissemination of information concerning the facts of a labor dispute must be regarded as within that area of free discussion that is guaranteed by the Constitution."[19]

But picketing is more than a form of communication. It is likely that many people respect picket lines simply to avoid trouble or charges of being antiunion rather than because they are intellectually persuaded by the signs pickets carry. On many picket lines the purpose is not so much publicity as it is economic coercion.

---

[18] *American Steel Foundries* v. *Tri-City Central Trades Council* (1921).
[19] The way had been prepared for *Thornhill* by Justice Brandeis's holding in *Senn* v. *Tile Layers' Protective Union* (1937).

Moreover, picketing in labor disputes often results in violence. Almost immediately after *Thornhill* the Court had to begin qualifying the right to picket. In *Milk Wagon Drivers Union* v. *Meadowmoor Dairies* (1941), the Court held that the Illinois courts were justified in enjoining all picketing in a labor dispute which had been so marred by past violence that it was believed impossible for future picketing to be maintained on a peaceful basis. But the likelihood of violence was not the only ground on which the Court proved willing to support restrictions on picketing. In *Carpenters and Joiners Union* v. *Ritter's Cafe* (1942), Ritter was having a residence built by nonunion labor, but the pickets were operating around his cafe, a mile away, where the pressure would hurt him more. By a five to four vote the Court ruled that Texas had the right to restrict picketing to the area within which a labor dispute arises.

More important as illustrating the conflict between rights of communication and other lawful social interests was a series of cases beginning in 1949. *Giboney* v. *Empire Storage & Ice Co.* (1949) upheld an injunction against a union that was picketing to force an employer to agree to a restraint of trade that was illegal under state law. *Hughes* v. *Superior Court of California* (1950) approved an injunction against a citizen group that was demanding that a store's employees be in proportion to the racial origin of its customers. In *International Brotherhood of Teamsters* v. *Hanke* (1950), the injunction, which the Court approved, had been issued simply to prevent a union from dictating business policy to self-employed used-car dealers. An effort by pickets to force an employer to coerce his employees into joining the union was successfully enjoined in *International Brotherhood of Teamsters, Local 695* v. *Vogt* (1957). Thus it appears that legislatures and judges are largely free to define public purposes and protect public interests which may override picketing rights. As Justice Frankfurter said in the *Hughes* case: "Picketing, not being the equivalent of speech as a matter of fact, is not its inevitable legal equivalent. Picketing is not beyond the control of a State if the manner in which picketing is conducted or the purpose which it seeks to effectuate gives ground for its disallowance."

SYMBOLIC SPEECH AND EXPRESSION

Symbolic speech involves the communicating of ideas or protests by conduct, such as burning a draft card or pouring blood over draft files to express opposition to the Vietnam war. Such action serves as a surrogate for speech and conveys an ideational message perhaps more effectively than speech would do. But is symbolic speech for that reason entitled to the full constitutional protection of normal speech?

The Supreme Court had an early encounter with this question in *Stromberg* v. *California* (1931), involving a state law which made it a felony to display a red flag as an "emblem of opposition to organized government." Conviction of the director of a children's summer camp for raising a red flag every morning was reversed by the Supreme Court on the ground that the statutory language was so loose as to threaten free political discussion.

A much more significant form of symbolic speech was the sit-in movement, which developed in the early 1960s to protest racial discrimination primarily in

Southern eating places. As a protest, blacks would take seats at lunch counters and, if refused service, continue to sit there until arrested or ousted by force. They were customarily charged either with breach of the peace resulting from trespass, or criminal trespass (that is, remaining on private property after being requested to leave).

Ordinarily, trespass on private property is clearly illegal and subject to punishment. Does it gain a protected status when it is employed as a form of expression, as a social protest? A sit-in, Justice Harlan readily conceded in *Garner* v. *Louisiana* (1961), "was a form of expression within the range of protections afforded by the Fourteenth Amendment." It was

> . . . as much a part of the "free trade in ideas" . . . as is verbal expression, more commonly thought of as "speech." It, like speech, appeals to good sense and to "the power of reason as applied through public discussion" . . . just as much as, if not more than, a public oration delivered from a soapbox at a street corner. This Court has never limited the right to speak, a protected "liberty" under the Fourteenth Amendment . . . to mere verbal expression.

However, Harlan went on to deny that the Fourteenth Amendment would protect "demonstrations conducted on private property over the objection of the owner," which of course was the issue in the sit-in cases. Black put the same view even more forcibly in *Bell* v. *Maryland* (1964): "Unquestionably petitioners had a constitutional right to express these views [against refusal of service] wherever they had an unquestioned legal right to be." But they had no legal right to be on the premises of the restaurant against the owner's will. "The right to freedom of expression is a right to express views—not a right to force other people to supply a platform or a pulpit."

The Court as a whole, however, never endorsed the view that sit-ins involving trespass were illegal. Though it decided a dozen sit-in cases between 1960 and 1964, it never found one that would require it to pass squarely on the constitutional situation of sit-in trespassers.[20] Eventually the federal Civil Rights Act of 1964, plus similar state statutes, terminated the constitutional issue by making racial discrimination in public accommodations unlawful.[21]

The clearest instance of Court approval for symbolic speech came in *Tinker* v. *Des Moines School District* (1969). School officials had forbidden pupils to wear black armbands as a protest against Vietnam on the ground that this gesture might cause controversy in the school. The Court, however, upheld the students, saying that "apprehension of disturbance is not enough to overcome the right to freedom of expression." By contrast, the Court refused in *United States* v. *O'Brien* (1968) to grant the legitimacy of symbolic draft card burning. Chief Justice Warren wrote: "We cannot accept the view that an apparently limitless variety of conduct can be

---

[20] See *Boynton* v. *Virginia* (1960), *Peterson* v. *Greenville* (1963), and *Lombard* v. *Louisiana* (1963).
[21] See *Bell* v. *Maryland* (1964) and *Hamm* v. *City of Rock Hill* (1964).

labeled 'speech' whenever the person engaging in the conduct intends thereby to express an idea."[22]

Another, and rather common, form of protest against the Vietnam war involved mutilation or unconventional treatment of the American flag. Various federal and state statutes make such conduct punishable. The Supreme Court has appeared to assume that abuse of the flag can be made illegal, but it has nevertheless usually found grounds for reversing convictions by strict interpretation of the statutes involved.[23] *Street* v. *New York* (1968) has already been noted. In *Smith* v. *Goguen* (1974), where a youth had worn a small flag on the seat of his pants, the statute punishing "contemptuous" treatment of the flag was held unconstitutionally vague and overbroad. At the time of the Cambodian invasion, a college student hung a flag upside down with a peace symbol attached outside his window. The Court in *Spence* v. *Washington* (1974) reversed his conviction for improper use of the flag, holding that he was engaged in a form of communication, but *Sutherland* v. *Illinois* (1976) declined a review of convictions for flag burning to protest Vietnam.

While public nudity has in some instances been regarded as a form of expression entitled to constitutional protection, in *California* v. *LaRue* (1972) regulations of the state Alcoholic Beverage Control Department forbidding nude entertainment in bars and other licensed establishments were upheld, Justice Rehnquist concluding that the activity in question partook "more of gross sexuality than of communication."

SPEECH AND BREACH OF THE PEACE

In all states there are statutes defining and punishing such misdemeanors and crimes as breach of the peace, disorderly conduct, inciting to riot, and the like. Speech can be, and often is, the direct cause of incitement to breach of the peace. A group assembled to hear speakers or to communicate ideas by demonstrating or picketing can easily develop into a disturbance of the public tranquillity. Law-enforcement officers and courts are continually required to balance the claims of free speech against the claims of law and order.

Reviewing the Supreme Court's experience with these difficult problems, we find that three stages in the judicial analysis can be distinguished. First, the Court must determine whether the speech involved in the prosecution for breach of the peace is of a type which enjoys constitutional protection. Normally there is no difficulty in deciding this issue favorably. The assertion in *Chaplinsky* v. *New Hampshire* (1942) that certain types of speech—"the lewd and obscene, the profane, the libelous, and the insulting or 'fighting' words"—are so lacking in social utility as to forfeit any claim to First Amendment protection has been largely reconsidered by the Court. In the overwhelming majority of speech prosecutions, there can be no doubt that the First Amendment is applicable. The principal problem, as we have seen, comes in connection with symbolic speech.

[22] See a critique of this decision by Dean Alfange, Jr., "Free Speech and Symbolic Conduct: The Draft-Card Burning Case," in Philip B. Kurland (ed.), *The Supreme Court Review, 1968* (Chicago: University of Chicago Press, 1968), pp. 1–52.

[23] See John Hart Ely, "Flag Desecration," 88 HARVARD LAW REVIEW 1482 (1975).

The second question to be asked is whether the ordinance or statute under which the speaker is being prosecuted, both on its face and as judicially applied in the instant case, validly states or recognizes the constitutional status which protected speech enjoys under the First Amendment. The best case to illustrate this requirement is *Terminiello* v. *Chicago* (1949). The controversy there arose out of a speech on the fascist model made under riotous conditions in a Chicago auditorium in 1946. Following the affair Terminiello was found guilty of disorderly conduct under an ordinance covering "all persons who shall make, aid, countenance, or assist in making any improper noise, riot, disturbance, breach of the peace, or diversion tending to a breach of the peace."

This case seemed to offer the Supreme Court an opportunity and an obligation to consider the facts of this disturbance against a background of free speech theory which would give due weight to the right of a speaker to address willing listeners in a private hall, and the nature of the community's obligation to defend that right against violent interruptions from outsiders. But a five-judge majority, speaking through Justice Douglas, never reached this issue. It appeared from an examination of the record that the trial judge had charged the jury that "breach of the peace" consists of any "misbehavior which violates the public peace and decorum" and that the "misbehavior may constitute a breach of the peace if it stirs the public to anger, invites dispute, brings about a condition of unrest, or creates a disturbance, or if it molests the inhabitants in the enjoyment of peace and quiet by arousing alarm."

The Court majority held that this construction of the ordinance was as relevant and as binding as though the "precise words had been written into the ordinance." Consequently, the issue was whether an ordinance which penalized speech that might "invite dispute" or "bring about a condition of unrest" was constitutional. Justice Douglas's brief opinion, almost without argument and completely without reference to the facts of the riotous meeting, concluded that speech could not be censored or punished on such grounds but only where it was shown likely "to produce a clear and present danger of a serious substantive evil that rises far above public inconvenience, annoyance, or unrest." Consequently, the conviction was reversed.

If the Court had not invalidated the ordinance by this construction, it would have had to proceed to the third stage of the analysis and determine whether the danger of breach of the peace resulting from the speech was so real that it overrode the claims of constitutional protection. This is precisely what the dissenters in *Terminiello*, who found no fault with the ordinance, did. Justice Jackson supplied a detailed summary of the factual situation on which the prosecution was based and which was in the trial judge's mind as he charged the jury. He conveyed some sense of the inflammatory situation at the meeting by quoting at length from the stenographic record of Terminiello's speech and his testimony at the trial. For Jackson, who had been Allied prosecutor in the Nazi war crimes trials at Nuremberg, this exhibition of political, racial, and ideological conflict was not an isolated or unintended collision of forces. "It was a local manifestation of a worldwide and standing conflict between two groups of revolutionary fanatics, each of which had imported to this country the strong-arm technique developed in the struggle by which their kind has devastated Europe." American cities have to cope with this problem. They should not be paralyzed by sweeping decisions which would encourage hostile ideological forces to use city streets as battlegrounds, with resulting destruction of public order.

Another case which illustrates the full three-stage analysis, in which the Court was unanimous, is *Cantwell* v. *Connecticut* (1940). Here a member of Jehovah's Witnesses was on a public street seeking converts. In accordance with the practice of his sect, he carried a phonograph and records, which he sought to play for anyone who would listen. He stopped two pedestrians and requested that they listen to a record. They agreed. The record was a violent attack on all organized religious systems and particularly the Catholic Church, which was characterized in offensive terms. The listeners, both Catholics, were angered. They felt like hitting him, but when they made known their displeasure, Cantwell packed up his phonograph and left. The incident did not draw a crowd or impede traffic, and no blows were struck. Nevertheless, Cantwell was charged with the common-law offense of inciting a breach of the peace, and convicted.

The Supreme Court reversed the conviction. First, the speech was protected; it was "an effort to persuade a willing listener to buy a book or to contribute money in the interest of what Cantwell, however misguided others may think him, conceived to be true religion." Second, the law was valid. Third, there had been no danger of breach of the peace. There had been "no assault or threatening of bodily harm, no truculent bearing, no intentional discourtesy, no personal abuse." Justice Roberts summed up the constitutional principles that should govern such a case:

> In the realm of religious faith, and in that of political belief, sharp differences arise. In both fields the tenets of one man may seem the rankest error to his neighbor. To persuade others to his own point of view, the pleader, as we know, at times, resorts to exaggeration, to vilification of men who have been, or are, prominent in church or state, and even to false statement. But the people of this nation have ordained in the light of history, that, in spite of the probability of excesses and abuses, these liberties are, in the long view, essential to enlightened opinion and right conduct on the part of the citizens of a democracy.

A federal breach of the peace statute which presents serious questions of constitutionality is the Anti-Riot Act of 1968. Reacting to the violent demonstrations of that period and believing that they were caused by certain activists moving through the country, Congress attached a rider to the 1968 Civil Rights Act making it a crime to travel in interstate commerce for the purpose of inciting riots. Violation of the statute was charged against the Chicago Seven in connection with the violence at the 1968 Democratic convention. Five of the defendants were convicted, but the court of appeals reversed for errors in the trial.[24] However, by a vote of two to one,

---

[24] *United States* v. *Dellinger* (1972). See discussion of the case in "Invoking Summary Criminal Contempt Procedures," 69 MICHIGAN LAW REVIEW 1549 (1971). During the Indian occupation of Wounded Knee, South Dakota, in 1973, at least fifty persons were arrested in various states under the Anti-Riot Act when they crossed state lines in autos with food and clothing for the "rioters" at Wounded Knee.

the appeals court upheld the constitutionality of the act. It had not by 1976 been passed on by the Supreme Court.[25]

THE EXPECTATION OF VIOLENCE

To secure a conviction for breach of the peace involving speech, we have seen that the peace need not be actually broken. It may be enough that the speech tended with sufficient directness toward a breach of the peace. But who is to make this determination, and on what grounds?

Initially, of course, the chances of violence must be appraised by the police or other law-enforcement officers present at the scene of the potential disturbance, in deciding whether to arrest the speaker. Then the prosecuting attorney must prove to a trial judge and jury, using primarily evidence supplied by the police, that a breach of the peace had been committed or incited. Finally, the record of the trial-court proceedings will be reviewed by one or more appellate courts to determine whether the conviction can be supported on the facts and the law. Each stage of judicial review moves further away from the immediacy of the events, and relies more and more on a cold written record. On what basis can judges thus remote from the controversy challenge the judgment of the police who were on the scene?

A policeman's lot in a trouble spot is not a happy one. He must appraise the chances of violence, and determine how long he can let the speech or demonstration go on without interfering, in the hope that violence will not actually break out. If he determines that he must intervene, he must decide which of the participating parties offers the greater threat to the peace. Should he arrest the speaker or those who are threatening the speaker? And how will he later prove in court that his judgment was the one called for by his obligation to preserve the peace?

Only a comparatively few Supreme Court decisions speak to these issues. *Feiner v. New York* (1951) involved a university student who made a rather inflammatory speech on a Syracuse streetcorner to some seventy-five listeners. Two policemen, aware of a certain "restlessness" in the crowd, demanded that Feiner stop and, when he refused, arrested him. Feiner's conviction for disorderly conduct was upheld by the Supreme Court. The evidence as to whether "a clear danger of disorder" threatened as a result of the speech, Chief Justice Vinson said, had been weighed by the trial court, and the conclusion had been affirmed by two higher state courts. Feiner had a right to speak, but he did not have a right to "incite to riot." But Justice Douglas, dissenting, thought that the record indicated no likelihood of riot. "It shows an unsympathetic audience and the threat of one man to haul the speaker from the stage. It is against that kind of threat that speakers need police protection. If they do not receive it and instead the police throw their weight on the side of those who would break up the meetings, the police become the new censors of speech."

The *Feiner* case did, indeed, approve a formula which could make police suppression of speech quite simple. Any group which wished to silence a speaker could

[25] See the excellent discussion and materials on this issue in Lionel H. Frankel, *Law, Power, and Personal Freedom* (St. Paul, Minn.: West Publishing Company, 1975), pp. 695–728.

create a disturbance in the audience, and that would justify police in requesting the speaker to stop. If the speaker refused, he would be guilty of disorderly conduct.

By 1963, when *Edwards* v. *South Carolina* was decided, the civil rights revolution was in full swing and the Court had had more time to think about police obligations in handling speakers and demonstrators. In the *Edwards* situation a peaceful demonstration on the South Carolina state capitol grounds was ordered to disperse, and when the demonstrators refused, they were arrested and subsequently convicted of the common-law crime of breach of the peace.

With only one dissent, the Supreme Court reversed the conviction. The reasoning followed the three stages already described. First, the students were exercising "basic constitutional rights in their most pristine and classic form." Second, the offense had not been defined in "a precise and narrowly drawn regulatory statute" aimed at "certain specific conduct." Rather, they were convicted of an offense "so generalized" that it was admittedly "not susceptible of exact definition." As in the *Terminiello* case, South Carolina law as interpreted and applied here had sought "to make criminal the peaceful expression of unpopular views," which the Fourteenth Amendment does not permit.

Although this holding would have been sufficient to decide the case, the Court, perhaps mindful of the criticism it had received in *Terminiello* for ignoring the factual situation, went on to the third stage. On the basis of its own "independent examination of the whole record," the Court denied that there had been sufficient danger of breach of the peace to justify the police demand to disperse. The students had "peaceably assembled" and "peaceably expressed their grievances." Not until they were warned to "disperse on pain of arrest did they do more." Even then, there was only a "religious harangue" and the singing of songs. "There was no violence or threat of violence on their part, or on the part of any member of the crowd watching them. Police protection was 'ample.' "

In *Cox* v. *Louisiana* (1965) there was, in addition to the charges noted earlier, also a breach of the peace conviction. The Court found *Cox* strikingly similar to *Edwards* and reversed the conviction, Goldberg holding the speech and assembly involved here constitutionally protected and the law applied "unconstitutionally broad." The Court's independent examination of the record, supported by a television news film of the events which the Court viewed, indicated that the meeting was "orderly and not riotous." The fear of violence was based on the presence of a group of 100 to 300 tense and agitated white citizens who were looking on from across the street. But they were separated from the students by seventy-five armed policemen, a fire truck, and the fire department, and the evidence indicated that they could have handled the crowd. Only after this finding of an absence of danger did Justice Goldberg note, as an additional reason for reversing the conviction, that the breach of the peace statute involved here was "unconstitutionally vague in its overly broad scope."

REDRESS FOR VIOLATION OF SPEECH RIGHTS

Protection of free speech rights has been almost entirely in the hands of courts as they develop and apply constitutional standards in trying prosecutions for alleged speech offenses of the type discussed in this chapter. There has been no recent congressional legislation to protect speech rights; the civil rights acts of 1957, 1960, 1964, 1965, and 1968 dealt primarily with public accommodations, racial segregation, voting, and housing. In fact, Congress was more likely to limit speech rights, as by the Anti-Riot Act of 1968 and the investigations conducted by Senator Joseph McCarthy and the House Committee on Un-American Activities. The principal administrative agencies in the civil rights field are the Commission on Civil Rights, created by the 1957 act, and the Civil Rights Division in the Department of Justice, but neither has been much concerned with speech rights.

This means that positive action to enforce speech rights and to secure redress for abuse of those rights must depend primarily on the initiative of individuals or civil rights groups. Their recourse to the courts may be to seek injunctive protection, as we have seen. Also, redress in the form of money damages may be sought under the Civil Rights Act of 1871, which provides that:

> Every person who, under color of any statute, ordinance, regulation, custom, or usage, of any State or Territory, subjects, or causes to be subjected, any citizen of the United States or other person within the jurisdiction thereof to the deprivation of any rights, privileges, or immunities secured by the Constitution and laws, shall be liable to the party injured in an action at law, suit in equity, or other proper proceeding for redress. [42 U.S.C., sec. 1983]

Only recently have suits under section 1983 been successful, whether for deprivation of speech or any other civil rights. In *Tenney* v. *Brandhove* (1951), damages were sought against a California legislative investigating committee by a man who contended that a hearing had been held to intimidate him and prevent him from exercising his free speech rights. The Supreme Court ruled that the committee members had legislative immunity from suit. *Pierson* v. *Ray* (1967) arose out of a demonstration by a group of white and black clergymen against segregated interstate bus terminal facilities. Convictions in police court of breach of the peace were subsequently reversed on appeal, and the clergymen then sued the police judge under section 1983. But the Supreme Court ruled that the statute had not abolished the traditional immunity of judges for acts within their judicial role.

State executive officers, however, do not share legislative or judicial immunity. In *Scheuer* v. *Rhodes* (1974), a suit brought by parents of students killed at Kent State University in 1970, the Supreme Court held that the Governor of Ohio and officials of the National Guard had no absolute immunity to suit. However, in the resulting civil suit the jury exonerated all the defendants.[26]

The first substantial awards for violations of rights of speech and assembly came in 1975, when a Washington, D.C., jury in a class action suit brought by the American Civil Liberties Union awarded some 12 million dollars in varying amounts to 1,200 persons who were arrested during the 1971 Mayday antiwar demonstrations as they listened to speeches on the steps of the United States Capitol.[27]

[26] *The New York Times*, August 28, 1975.
[27] *The New York Times*, January 17, 1975.

Interestingly enough, this suit did not rely on section 1983 but charged direct violation of the First and Eighth Amendments.

ACADEMIC FREEDOM

Involvement of the courts in constitutional claims of academic freedom sharply increased during the troubled times on American campuses in the late 1960s and 1970s. So far as students are concerned, the issues were generally free speech claims for student newspapers and campus assemblies and due process in disciplinary actions taken by authorities against students. On the free expression issue, the principal Supreme Court decisions have been *West Virginia State Board of Education* v. *Barnette* (1943), holding that students cannot be required to salute the flag as a part of school exercises, and *Tinker* v. *Des Moines School District* (1969), where Fortas, upholding the right of students to wear black armbands in protest against the Vietnam war, said: "In our system, state-operated schools may not be enclaves of totalitarianism."

The principal due process ruling was *Goss* v. *Lopez* (1975), which held that before students could be suspended from public schools, they must be given notice of charges and an opportunity to defend themselves. *Wood* v. *Strickland* (1975) added that in a student suit against school officials for violation of civil rights, the officials were not entitled to good faith immunity if they reasonably should have known that their acts violated the students' constitutional rights.[28]

So far as teachers are concerned, academic freedom issues usually arise out of dismissal or discipline because of views or associations. The association problem will be discussed in Chapter 23. In one of those cases, *Keyishian* v. *Board of Regents* (1967), Brennan said:

> Our Nation is deeply committed to safeguarding academic freedom, which is of transcendent value to all of us and not merely to the teachers concerned. That freedom is therefore a special concern of the First Amendment, which does not tolerate laws that cast a pall of orthodoxy over the classroom.

Teacher tenure has been rather effectively protected by the American Association of University Professors. The Supreme Court's entry into the field came in *Pickering* v. *Board of Education* (1968), where it ruled that a high school teacher could not be dismissed because he had written a letter to the local newspaper critical of the handling of funds by the school board.[29] In *Perry* v. *Sinderman* (1972), a

---

[28] The Supreme Court has rejected the review of many cases raising student academic freedom issues. In 1974 the Court granted review of a case involving censorship of a high school paper (*Indianapolis School Commissioners* v. *Jacobs*) but then reversed its action. The Court declined to rule on a case of school discipline for long hair in *Olff* v. *East Side Union High School* (1972). On the long hair issue, see 84 HARVARD LAW REVIEW 1702 (1971). *Baker* v. *Owen* (1975) upheld corporal punishment.

[29] However, the Court has refused to review several more recent cases of teacher firing. See *Meinhold* v. *Taylor* (1973) and *Hetrick* v. *Martin* (1973). But in *Hortonville Joint School District* v. *Hortonville Education Assn.* (1976) the Court ruled that a school board empowered by state law to hire and fire teachers did not violate the teachers' constitutional rights to due process by firing those engaged in an illegal strike.

junior college professor was discharged after ten years, allegedly because of his public criticism of the college administration. The Court held that he had an "expectancy" of tenure, that he was entitled to a hearing, and that if his removal was because of his views, his free speech rights had been violated. But *Board of Regents v. Roth* (1972) ruled that a professor who was not rehired after one year had no constitutional right to a statement of reasons or a hearing.[30]

---

[30] A few examples of the extensive literature in this field are Charles Alan Wright, "The Constitution on the Campus," 22 VANDERBILT LAW REVIEW 1027 (1969); "Common Law Rights for Private University Students," 84 YALE LAW JOURNAL 120 (1974); Paul D. Carrington, "Civilizing University Discipline," 69 MICHIGAN LAW REVIEW 393 (1971).

Chapter 21

Freedom of the Press

When Blackstone wrote that "the liberty of the press consists in laying no *previous* restraints upon publications," he was stating a principle which had become established in England by 1695 and in the colonies by 1725. The issue had thus been closed for decades by the time the First Amendment was adopted. Whatever other doubts there might have been about its intent, there could be no question that it was meant to restate the ban on previous restraints of the press.

The tradition of press freedom is firmly established in the United States.[1] There has of course been censorship in wartime. In the heat of political controversy, as for example over the abolition of slavery, presses have been destroyed, newspapers have been burned or refused delivery through the mails. Newspapers can be shut down by strikes of their employees. They may fail because of economic pressures, a fate which has left so many American cities as one-newspaper towns. Access to the news can be "managed" by public officials. The Nixon administration carried on an orchestrated attack against the press. The lot of the publisher or distributor of unpopular doctrine can be made difficult in various ways. But the fact remains that *legal* efforts to restrain the freedom of the press have been comparatively few.

[1] But see Leonard W. Levy, *Legacy of Suppression: Freedom of Speech and Press in Early American History* (Cambridge, Mass.: The Belknap Press, Harvard University Press, 1960).

FREEDOM FROM OVERT PRIOR RESTRAINT

The basic right of the publisher is that he shall not be required to have government permission to publish or be subjected to a governmental ban on publication. When Blackstone was defining freedom of the press, licensing of publishers was the typical means of government control, and that is obviously unconstitutional under the First Amendment. But in the Supreme Court's first great anticensorship decision, *Near* v. *Minnesota* (1931), control took the form of a statute providing for the abating, as a public nuisance, of "malicious, scandalous and defamatory" newspapers or periodicals and the enjoining of anyone maintaining such a nuisance. The paper involved was a Minneapolis weekly devoted to attacks on the law enforcement officers of the city, who were charged with permitting "Jewish gangsters" to control illegal operations in the area and with deriving graft from those activities.

The statute as applied against this paper was declared unconstitutional by a five to four vote. The minority of Butler, Van Devanter, McReynolds, and Sutherland defended the statute on the ground that it did not constitute prior restraint as that idea had been historically understood. "It does not authorize administrative control in advance such as was formerly exercised by the licensers and censors but prescribes a remedy to be enforced by a suit in equity." Instead of arbitrary administrative action this statute guaranteed the due process of the law courts. Moreover, since the injunction could be issued only *after* a malicious or defamatory publication had appeared and been adjudged a nuisance, it was not a *previous* restraint but the abating of a nuisance already committed. But Chief Justice Hughes replied for the majority that the object of the statute was not punishment but suppression, and concluded: "This is of the essence of censorship."

The second major point of the dissenters was that the reasonable man rule should be applied here. "The Act was passed in the exertion of the State's power of police, and this court is by well established rule required to assume, until the contrary is clearly made to appear, that there exists in Minnesota a state of affairs that justifies this measure for the preservation of the peace and good order of the State." Butler went on: "It is of the greatest importance that the States shall be untrammeled and free to employ all just and appropriate measures to prevent abuses of the liberty of the press."

Hughes in reply did not assert that the protection against previous restraint was "absolutely unlimited." He did, however, deny that it was normally within the legislative range of choice to pass previous restraint legislation, or that there was any obligation on courts to presume the validity of such legislation. The legitimacy of prior restraints could be recognized only in "exceptional cases." He specified four such exceptional situations. One was where the success of the nation's Armed Forces was at stake in time of war, and here he quoted from Holmes in the *Schenck* case, though he did not directly invoke the clear and present danger test. Another was when the "primary requirements of decency" were enforced against obscene publications. The third arose where the security of community life had to be protected "against incitements to acts of violence and the overthrow by force of orderly government." Fourth, it might be necessary for equity courts "to prevent publications in order to protect private rights." Only the last two could conceivably be relevant in the *Near* case, but Hughes held them inapplicable. The purpose of the statute was not to redress individual or private wrongs. As for the chance that the circulation of scandal might tend to disturb the public peace, "the theory of the constitutional guaranty is that even a more serious public evil would be caused by authority to prevent publication."

Near v. *Minnesota* was followed in 1936 by a decision invalidating an effort to discourage publications by discriminatory taxation, a type of restraint that had been common in English and early American history. In 1934 the Louisiana legislature, under the control of Huey Long, enacted a 2 percent tax on gross receipts from advertising on all firms publishing newspapers or periodicals having a circulation of more than 20,000 copies per week. It was denominated as a license tax on the privilege of engaging in the business of selling advertising but was clearly aimed at city newspapers, which on the whole were opposed to the Long regime, whereas the country press was favorable to Long.

In *Grosjean* v. *American Press Co.* (1936), the Supreme Court unanimously held the tax unconstitutional. Newspapers were of course not immune from any of the ordinary forms of taxation:

> But this is not an ordinary form of tax, but one single in kind, with a long history of hostile misuse against the freedom of the press. . . . The tax here involved is bad not because it takes money from the pockets of the appellees. . . . It is bad because, in the light of its history and of its present setting, it is seen to be a deliberate and calculated device in the guise of a tax to limit the circulation of information to which the public is entitled in virtue of the constitutional guaranties.

The First Amendment does not, however, entitle publishers to any special exemption from governmental regulation of business practices which may be constitutionally applied to businesses generally. The Wagner Act regulating labor relations was held applicable to the press by a five to four vote in *Associated Press* v. *National Labor Relations Board* (1937). Similarly the antitrust provisions of the Sherman Act and the wage and hour requirements of the Fair Labor Standards Act have been held applicable to the publishing industry.[2]

In *Mills* v. *Alabama* (1966) the Supreme Court held unconstitutional, as applied to the editor of a Birmingham newspaper, a state law making it a crime to electioneer or solicit votes on election day in support of, or in opposition to, any proposition being voted on. The editor had published on election day an editorial urging voters to approve a change to the mayor-council form of city government for Birmingham, a change that was generally understood to be aimed at establishing a more moderate racial policy in the city by eliminating its two most prominent segregationist officials. The state supreme court sustained the criminal conviction of the editor, on the ground that the law was a reasonable election regulation and served the salutary purpose of protecting the public from confusing last-minute charges when, because

---

[2] *Associated Press* v. *United States* (1945); *Lorain Journal* v. *United States* (1957); *Citizen Publishing Co.* v. *United States* (1969); *Oklahoma Press Publishing Co.* v. *Walling* (1946).

of lack of time, they could not be answered or their truth determined. Justice Black said it was "difficult to conceive of a more obvious and flagrant abridgement of the constitutionally guaranteed freedom of the press."

Handbills

Anyone with a hand printing press is a publisher for purposes of the First Amendment, with full rights not to be hampered by government restrictions in the publishing and circulation of the printed product. This has been established by a series of Supreme Court decisions on handbills.

The first was *Lovell* v. *Griffin* (1938), in which the Supreme Court unanimously condemned as unconstitutional a municipal ordinance requiring official permission to distribute publications. The ordinance covered distribution "by hand or otherwise" of "literature of any kind," which was made a nuisance unless written permission in advance was obtained from the city manager. Counsel for the city argued that the ordinance was justified because of the "sanitary problem in removing from . . . streets papers, circulars and the other like materials." Moreover, it was contended that the petitioner in this case, who was a member of Jehovah's Witnesses selling their literature from door to door, was not a member of the press, and so not "in the class of persons who are entitled to invoke the constitutional provisions touching the freedom of the press."

The Supreme Court held the ordinance "invalid on its face." It was an absolute prohibition of distribution without permit, "not limited to ways which might be regarded as inconsistent with the maintenance of public order or as involving disorderly conduct, the molestation of the inhabitants, or the misuse or littering of the streets." The First Amendment was appropriately invoked, because liberty of the press necessarily embraced the distribution of pamphlets and leaflets. "These indeed have been historic weapons in the defense of liberty, as the pamphlets of Thomas Paine and others in our own history abundantly attest. The press in its historic connotation comprehends every sort of publication which affords a vehicle of information and opinion."

Subsequent decisions widened the protection afforded distribution of handbills.[3] In *Talley* v. *California* (1960), the Court declared unconstitutional a state law which required all handbills to have printed on them the names and addresses of the persons who prepared, distributed, or sponsored them. The purpose was to provide a method of identifying those who might be responsible for fraud, false advertising, or libel, but the Court majority thought the identification requirement would tend to restrict freedom of expression. Three dissenting justices were not convinced that the

---

[3] See *Schneider* v. *Irvington* (1939) and *Jamison* v. *Texas* (1943). *Organization for a Better Austin* v. *Keefe* (1971) upheld the action of a racially integrated citizen organization in distributing leaflets critical of a real estate broker's alleged "blockbusting" and "panic peddling" activities in a Chicago area. The Court ruled that any invasion of the broker's right to privacy by distribution of these leaflets in the suburb where the broker resided was not sufficient to support an injunction against peaceful distribution of informational literature, and a claim that the literature was intended to exercise a coercive impact on the broker did not remove the literature from the reach of the First Amendment.

Constitution protects the "freedom of anonymous speech." It should be noted that First Amendment protection does not extend to commercial handbills.[4]

The Pentagon Papers Case

The most significant challenge to press freedom in American history occurred in 1971 when the Nixon administration secured injunctions against *The New York Times* and the *Washington Post* to prevent them from continuing their publication of the so-called Pentagon papers. These papers came from a many-volumed study, made at the direction of the Defense Department, of the circumstances leading to United States involvement in the Vietnam war. The study was classified as secret, but Daniel Ellsberg, who had access to the volumes through his employment by a private research agency, violated government security rules and furnished copies to the press. After considering the matter for several months, *The New York Times* began publication of the papers on June 13, 1971, and several other newspapers followed shortly thereafter.[5]

Judicial action proceeded with incredible speed. The government went into court in New York on June 15, asking for an injunction against further publication, and in Washington against the *Washington Post* on June 18. The Courts of Appeals for the Second Circuit and for the District of Columbia acted on June 19. The Supreme Court agreed to accept the cases on June 25, heard argument on June 26, and handed down a six to three decision quashing the injunctions on June 30.

The Supreme Court, badly divided, gave its ruling in *New York Times* v. *United States* in a three-paragraph per curiam opinion, simply holding that the government had not met the "heavy burden" of justifying any system of prior restraint. All nine justices then proceeded to state their own views. For Black and Douglas, the issue was clear and plain: "every moment's continuance of the injunctions against these newspapers amounts to a flagrant, indefensible, and continuing violation of the First Amendment." Brennan's position differed only in that he seemed to accept the possibility that in extreme cases the government might present proof of great danger to national interests justifying an injunction, which it had not done here. Marshall, drawing on the holding in the *Steel Seizure Case,* particularly stressed the fact that Congress had on two occasions declined to pass legislation that would have given the President the power he was now seeking to have the courts exercise. "When Congress specifically declines to make conduct unlawful it is not for this Court to redecide those issues—to overrule Congress," he concluded.

Stewart and White completed the six-judge majority. White, like Marshall, stressed the absence of any congressional authorization for prior restraints in such circumstances and could find no inherent power in the executive or the courts "to authorize remedies having such sweeping potential for inhibiting publications by the press." Stewart thought that the Constitution had made the President responsible for protecting the confidentiality necessary to carry out responsibilities in the fields

---

[4] *Valentine* v. *Chrestensen* (1942).

[5] See Martin Shapiro, *The Pentagon Papers and the Courts* (San Francisco: Chandler Publishing Company, 1972); Sanford J. Ungar, *The Papers and the Papers* (New York: E. P. Dutton & Co., Inc., 1972); *The Pentagon Papers* (New York: Bantam Books, 1971).

of international relations and national defense and that the courts could not be asked, in the absence of specific laws or regulations, to take over this function. Both Stewart and White, however, expressed concern that the national interest had been damaged by the publications and inferred that they believed criminal proceedings could be brought against the publishers.

The dissenters were Chief Justice Burger and Justices Harlan and Blackmun. All protested the speed with which the cases had been heard. Burger heatedly castigated the newspapers for accepting "stolen property." Blackmun warned that if publication of the papers prolonged the war or further delayed the freeing of United States prisoners, "then the Nation's people will know where the responsibility for these sad consequences rests."

While the result in *New York Times* was clear enough, the Court's opinions do not add up to a sound defense of freedom of the press. It would appear that at least four members of the Court, and possibly five, believed that the newspapers could be criminally punished for their action. This view was particularly spelled out by White, who said that "failure by the Government to justify prior restraints does not measure its constitutional entitlement to a conviction for criminal publication." He cited various provisions of the criminal code as possibly relevant and added: "I would have no difficulty in sustaining convictions under these sections . . . "

The Department of Justice appeared to be less certain than White that statutorily defined crimes had been committed in the Pentagon Papers case. The indictments secured against Daniel Ellsberg had to fall back on generalized charges of espionage, theft, and conspiracy. The case was a weak one. The "theft" was of information, not of documents. The documents were copied by Ellsberg and returned. Can "information" be stolen? Was the espionage law violated when the information "stolen" was not given to a foreign power? Moreover, there is no law, only executive orders, setting up the classification system and pertaining to the disclosure of classified information. The collapse of the Ellsberg prosecution due to illegal action by the government prevented any definitive answer to these questions.

But the experience did call attention to the absence of any Official Secrets Act in the United States. A massive revision of the federal criminal code presented to Congress in 1975 would have filled this gap by making it a crime to pass national defense information or any classified information to unauthorized persons. [6] Adoption of such a threatening new instrument of government secrecy appeared unlikely.[7]

---

[6] The [proposed] Criminal Justice Reform Act, S. 1, 94th Congress.

[7] Congress took an important action to limit government secrecy when it passed the Freedom of Information Act in 1966, which was intended to increase popular control of government and to encourage agency responsibliity. The act requires that identifiable agency records be disclosed to any person who requests them and provides a judicial remedy for improper withholding of information by an agency. The act was strengthened by amendments in 1974, over President Ford's veto. The act has been very extensively used to pry materials out of the files of the FBI and other agencies. However, there are exemptions in the act, covering the production of certain kinds of records, which have been interpreted by the Supreme Court to prevent disclosure in such cases as *Environmental Protection Agency* v. *Mink* (1973) and *Administrator, Federal Aviation Administration* v. *Robertson* (1975). See "The Freedom of Information Act and the Exemption for Intra-Agency Memoranda," 86 HARVARD LAW REVIEW 1047 (1973); Norman Dorsen and Stephen Gillers, *None of Your Business: Secrecy in America* (New York: The Viking Press, Inc., 1974); "The Freedom of Information Act: A Seven Year Assessment," 74 *Columbia Law Review* 896 (1974).

INDIRECT PRIOR RESTRAINT

The Post Office

In *Ex parte Jackson* (1878), Justice Field observed: "Liberty of circulating is as essential to that freedom [of the press] as liberty of publishing; indeed, without the circulation, the publication would be of little value." By this test access to the Post Office should be a constitutional right, but this has not been the case. Exclusion of lottery tickets from the mails was upheld in *Jackson* and also in *In re Rapier* (1892). Field reconciled his approval of this ban with his views on freedom of circulation by saying, "In excluding various articles from the mail, the object of Congress has not been to interfere with the freedom of the press . . . but to refuse its facilities for the distribution of matter deemed injurious to the public morals." The same rationale was used to justify exclusion of obscene matter from the mails, which will be discussed in Chapter 22.

About 1940 the Post Office, without any statutory authority and with the cooperation of the Bureau of Customs, progressed from obscenity to "foreign political propaganda," confiscating periodicals and books regarded as politically questionable which were mailed to residents of the United States. The Russian newspapers *Pravda* and *Izvestia* were typical of the materials intercepted. This practice was stopped by President Kennedy's Executive Order in 1961. The next year Congress retaliated by passing a statute specifically authorizing the Postmaster General to detain "communist political propaganda" and to deliver it only upon the addressee's request. In *Lamont* v. *Postmaster General* (1965) the Supreme Court unanimously declared this statute unconstitutional, holding that to force an addressee to request in writing that his mail be delivered was an abridgement of First Amendment rights.

Another type of Post Office prior restraint relates to the granting of second-class mailing privileges. The circulation of publications carried at second-class rates is in effect subsidized by the government, for the rates are much less than the third-class rates which would otherwise have to be paid. Thus second-class mailing privileges are absolutely essential if a periodical publication is to compete successfully in its field.

During the First World War the power over second-class privileges was one of two weapons used to effect, with Supreme Court approval, a blatant censorship of the press. The second weapon was the Espionage Act of 1917, one entire title of which was devoted to use of the mails. It provided that any newspaper published in violation of any of the provisions of the act would be nonmailable. The law was promptly applied to *The Masses,* a revolutionary antiwar monthly journal, its August, 1917, issue being excluded from the mails.[8] Postmaster General Burleson then refused to grant the September or any future issues second-class privileges, on the ground that since the magazine had skipped the August number, it was no longer a periodical, since it was not regularly issued!

This same one-two punch, as administered to a socialist paper published by Victor Berger, the *Milwaukee Leader,* was upheld by the Supreme Court in *Milwaukee Publishing Co.* v. *Burleson* (1921). Justice Clarke for the majority took the position that second-class rates were a privilege withdrawable by the Postmaster Gener-

---

[8] *Masses Publishing Co. v. Patten* (1917).

al when a publication failed to conform to the law. Justice Brandeis thought this power would make the Postmaster General "the universal censor of publications," and Justice Holmes added: "The United States may give up the Post Office when it sees fit, but while it carries it on the use of the mails is almost as much a part of free speech as the right to use our tongues, and it would take very strong language to convince me that Congress ever intended to give such a practically despotic power to any one man."

These protests proved ineffective, and again in World War II precisely the same technique was employed. In fields unrelated to national security, however, some support for the Holmes-Brandeis position on the powers of the Postmaster General with respect to second-class mail was given by the Supreme Court's 1946 decision in *Hannegan* v. *Esquire.* Postmaster General Walker sought to withdraw second-class privileges from *Esquire,* on the ground that the magazine did not meet the statutory test of being "published for the dissemination of information of a public character, or devoted to literature, the sciences, arts, or some special industry." He argued that the material in *Esquire,* although not obscene in a technical sense, was so close to it that it was "morally improper and not for the public welfare and the public good."

A unanimous Supreme Court held that Congress had not meant to grant the Postmaster General rights of censorship when it attached these conditions to the second-class privilege. Under the statute he was limited to determining whether a publication "contains information of a public character, literature or art"; he was not granted "the further power to determine whether the contents meet some standard of the public good or welfare." The Holmes-Brandeis dissent in *Milwaukee Publishing Co.* was noted, with the comment: "Grave constitutional questions are immediately raised once it is said that the use of the mails is a privilege which may be extended or withheld on any grounds whatsoever."

Newsmen's Privilege

By common law or statute, certain relationships such as lawyer-client, priest-penitent, doctor-patient, and husband-wife are privileged—that is, those involved cannot be forced in court proceedings to reveal what passed between them. Newsmen argue that they should have a similar privilege with respect to their confidential informants, on the ground that often information will be given to them only if they can promise not to reveal their sources.[9] Accepting this premise, many states have adopted "shield laws" which do guarantee the confidentiality of reporters' news sources.

The Supreme Court, however, rejected the claim of confidentiality by a vote of five to four in *Branzburg* v. *Hayes* (1972). A reporter who had developed contacts in the Black Panther organization in San Francisco, and another who had published stories about drug activities in Kentucky, were subpoenaed to appear before grand juries to be questioned about their knowledge of illegal activities. Both refused, claiming that requiring them to give testimony to a grand jury would deny press

[9] See "Reporters and Their Sources: The Constitutional Right to a Confidential Relationship," 80 YALE LAW JOURNAL 317 (1970); Vince Blasi, "The Newsman's Privilege: An Empirical Study," 70 MICHIGAN LAW REVIEW 229 (1971).

freedom by making them in effect government agents, destroying their credibility as newsmen, and drying up their news sources.

Justice White for the Court dismissed these claims rather brusquely. His main theme, repeated time and again in the opinion, was that newsmen have the same obligation "as other citizens . . . to answer questions relevant to an investigation into the commission of crime." He was uncertain how much burden would be imposed on news gathering by refusing to grant newsmen's privilege, but in any event the public interest in pursuing and prosecuting crimes must take precedence. None of the traditional types of infringement on press freedom was involved here, White noted—no prior restraint, no command to publish, no tax, no penalty for publishing, no denial of access to confidential sources. If grand juries should abuse their powers (as some clearly had[10]), White promised that the courts would intervene. His final "pragmatic" point, that the press was powerful and "far from helpless to protect itself from harassment or substantial harm," rather overlooked the fact that it is not "the press" but individual newsmen who must weigh the prospect of going to jail for defying a grand jury subpoena, as a considerable number have done.

Justice Stewart, dissenting in *Branzburg,* attacked White's "simplistic and stultifying absolutism" which was insensitive to "the critical role of an independent press" and willing to approve annexing "the journalistic profession as an investigative arm of the government." As Stewart saw it, "a corollary of the right to publish must be the right to gather news," and "the right to gather news implies, in turn, a right to a confidential relationship between a reporter and his source." He was convinced that the absence of this right would "either deter sources from divulging information or deter reporters from gathering and publishing information."

The *Branzburg* decision led Senator Sam Ervin to make a gallant but unsuccessful effort to draft a federal shield law. Actually there was considerable disagreement within the publishing fraternity as to whether a shield law was desirable. Some feared that any law on this subject would seem to grant the legitimacy of statutory regulation of the press, and they would prefer to rely simply on the First Amendment, which they contend the Court wrongly interpreted in *Branzburg.*[11]

Another defeat for newsmen's claims came in *Saxbe* v. *Washington Post* (1974), where the Court upheld, five to four, a federal prison regulation under which media representatives, while given general permission to interview inmates, were forbidden to request interviews with particular prisoners. Similar California prison regulations were upheld in *Pell* v. *Procunier* (1974).

---

[10] See David J. Fine, "Federal Grand Jury Investigation of Political Dissidents," 7 HARVARD CIVIL RIGHTS–CIVIL LIBERTIES LAW REVIEW 432 (1972).

[11] Robert G. Dixon, "The Constitution Is Shield Enough for Newsmen," 60 AMERICAN BAR ASSOCIATION JOURNAL 707 (1974). The Department of Justice has been aware of possible abuses of grand jury power and issued in 1970 *Guidelines for Subpoenas to the News Media,* which required the Attorney General's personal approval of subpoenas issued to news media representatives. The regulations stated that the Department did not consider the press as "an investigative arm of the government" and warned that in every case where a subpoena was considered, its limiting effect on the exercise of First Amendment rights "should be carefully weighed against the public interest in the fair administration of justice." In 1975 Attorney General Edward H. Levi extended these regulations to cover the subpoenaing of confidential material from authors, documentary film producers, or anyone else "engaged in reporting on public affairs." *The New York Times,* November 20, 1975.

FREE PRESS AND FAIR TRIAL

A free press problem of increasing importance and difficulty relates to the right of newspapers to publish information and comment about current criminal proceedings. The right to a fair trial, as will be discussed in more detail in Chapter 26, includes among other features the right to trial by an unbiased jury. A fair trial requires that the judge and jury make their judgments solely on the basis of the evidence introduced in the courtroom, and of course they must be subjected to no outside pressures in reaching their decisions.

The American tradition of press freedom has given newspapers complete freedom to report the facts of criminal investigations and prosecutions. From the time a crime is committed, newspapers undertake to publish every bit of information they can secure concerning the crime and the criminal, usually with the cooperation of the police and prosecutors. They recount the evidence and the previous criminal record, if any, of the suspect. In particularly gruesome crimes, the press may whip up feeling against the person charged. "Trial by newspaper" may be so complete and effective that the task of securing a jury which has not prejudged the case becomes very difficult. Occasionally a newspaper will go so far as to attempt to exert editorial presure on the judge or jury while the case is still being tried.

In such a situation there is a fundamental conflict between two constitutional rights—a fair trial and a free press. The basic justification for freedom of the press is that untrammeled public discussion and expression of all conceivable views offers the best chance of achieving truth and wisdom. Public policy making must be subjected to the influence of popular pressures. But in a trial at law the purpose is to safeguard the proceedings as fully as possible *from* popular pressures. The whole judicial apparatus is aimed at limiting a jury or judge to consideration of relevant and probative facts bearing on the controversy. Admittedly there is and must be popular interest in and discussion of the way the judicial function is performed. But while a case is pending in court the public interest in the evenhanded administration of justice requires that the judge and jury be subject to no dictates or pressures but those of their own judgment and consciences.

The Contempt Power

The power of judges to punish for contempt, which was examined in Chapter 6, is the principal instrument by which a judge can protect proceedings in his court from newspaper pressure. However, American judges are seriously limited in their use of the contempt power to restrain out-of-court comments about current court proceedings. The English practice is much more restrictive in this connection than the American. Only the barest facts may be published in England concerning a pending prosecution, and anything remotely smacking of comment on the case would lay the offender open to contempt charges. The American tradition, with its great reliance upon elected judges at the state and local level, its rough-and-ready standards of justice on the frontier, and its general hostility toward restraints, has been much less willing to concede the immunity of judicial proceedings from outside comment. In addition, summary punishment procedures tend to arouse greater resentment when applied to contempts occurring out of court than when committed in the presence of the court.[12]

These attitudes were reflected in a federal statute adopted in 1831 which forbade summary punishments except in the case of misbehavior in the presence of the court, "or so near thereto as to obstruct the administration of justice." This act effected a substantial limitation on the contempt power, but near the turn of the century some federal district courts again undertook summary punishment for publications. The Supreme Court gave approval to this trend in *Toledo Newspaper Co.* v. *United States* (1918), holding that a newspaper publishing objectionable comments about a judge and his conduct of pending litigation was "so near thereto" as to justify summary punishment. Justice Holmes, dissenting with Brandeis, denied that there had been any obstruction of justice, saying: "I think that 'so near as to obstruct' means so near as actually to obstruct—and not merely near enough to threaten a possible obstruction." He added that "a judge of the United States is expected to be a man of ordinary firmness of character."

The *Toledo* decision was overruled in 1941 by *Nye* v. *United States* as the Court adopted the Holmes position that "so near thereto" means physical proximity. Consequently newspapers are protected by statute from summary punishment for comments on federal judicial decisions.

So far as state courts are concerned, the freedom of newspapers from contempt prosecutions derives from the Fourteenth Amendment and the Supreme Court's decision in *Bridges* v. *California* (1941). A radical labor leader, Harry Bridges, and a conservative, labor-baiting newspaper, the *Los Angeles Times,* had with unique impartiality been brought to book for contempt. The newspaper was cited by a California judge who was trying a case involving assault by labor union members on nonunion truck drivers. At a time when the defendants had been found guilty, but not yet sentenced, the *Times* said editorially: "Judge A. A. Scott will make a serious mistake if he grants probation to Matthew Shannon and Kennan Holmes. This community needs the example of their assignment to the jute-mill." As for Harry Bridges, while a motion for a new trial was pending in a case involving a dispute between an AFL and a CIO union, he sent a telegram to the United States Secretary of Labor calling the judge's decision "outrageous," threatened that an attempt to enforce it would tie up the entire Pacific Coast, and warned that his union did "not intend to allow state courts to override the majority vote" in NLRB elections.

The Supreme Court reversed both contempt citations by a narrow five to four margin. Justice Black for the majority held there would have to be "a clear and present danger" that such comments would obstruct justice in order for the contempt citations to be justified, and he saw no such threat. To accept the possibility that such publications would in themselves have a "substantial influence upon the course of justice would be to impute to judges a lack of firmness, wisdom, or honor,—which we cannot accept as a major premise."

Justice Frankfurter made a strong attack on the application of the clear and present danger test in these circumstances. Holmes had no thought of using it for such a purpose, he contended.

[12] See Ronald L. Goldfarb, *The Contempt Power* (New York: Columbia University Press, 1963).

A trial is not a "free trade in ideas," nor is the best test of truth in a courtroom "the power of the thought to get itself accepted in the competition of the market." A court is a forum with strictly defined limits for discussion. . . . We cannot read into the Fourteenth Amendment the freedom of speech and of the press protected by the First Amendment and at the same time read out age-old means employed by states for securing the calm course of justice. . . . To assure the impartial accomplishment of justice is not an abridgement of freedom of speech or freedom of the press. . . . In fact, these liberties themselves depend upon an untrammeled judiciary whose passions are not even unconsciously aroused and whose minds are not distorted by extrajudical considerations.

This argument was continued in two subsequent cases, *Pennekamp* v. *Florida* (1946) and *Craig* v. *Harney* (1947), both of which freed newspapers from contempt charges. By this line of decisions, Justices Jackson and Frankfurter charged in *Shepherd* v. *Florida* (1951), the Supreme Court had "gone a long way to disable a trial judge from dealing with press interference with the trial process."

Pretrial Publicity

The Court was also reluctant to attempt control of pretrial publicity.[13] Not until 1961, in *Irvin* v. *Dowd*, did the Court reverse a state conviction because of pretrial publicity. Here the defendant was a man accused of six murders, whose confession had been issued by the police in press releases which were intensively publicized. Because of the popular indignation generated by the publicity, one change of venue to an adjoining county was granted, but feeling was high there also, and a second change was refused. Convincing evidence of prejudice against the defendant was demonstrated when it took four weeks to select the jury from a panel of 430, of whom 268 had to be excused because of fixed opinions of guilt. Eight of the twelve jurors selected, though claiming not to have fixed opinions, thought the defendant was guilty. The Supreme Court unanimously concluded: "With his life at stake, it is not requiring too much that petitioner be tried in an atmosphere undisturbed by so huge a wave of public passion and by a jury other than one in which two thirds of the members admit, before hearing any testimony, to possessing a belief in his guilt."

In *Rideau* v. *Louisiana* (1963) the pretrial publicity was compounded by television. A man accused of murder made a confession, which he subsequently repeated in a filmed television "interview" with the sheriff. The film was shown three times on the local television station; three of the members of the jury which tried him two months later had seen the film. The Supreme Court reversed the conviction on the ground that a change of venue should have been granted so that the jury could have been drawn "from a community of people who had not seen and heard Rideau's televised 'interview.' "

Problems in Conduct of the Trial

The televising of a trial was held in *Estes* v. *Texas* (1965) to be inherently prejudicial to a fair trial. But the case which focused national attention on the fair trial problem was the scandalous press involvement in the nationally famous trial of Dr. Sam

---

[13] See *Maryland* v. *Baltimore Radio Show* (1950) and *Stroble* v. *California* (1952).

Sheppard for the murder of his wife in 1954. One Cleveland newspaper in particular conducted a campaign to cast suspicion on Sheppard, to get him indicted, and to convict him in the eyes of the public. Every action in the case took place in a carnival of publicity. The coroner's inquest was held in a school gymnasium with live broadcasting. When Sheppard was brought in to the city hall under arrest, scores of newscasters, photographers, and reporters were awaiting his arrival. In the courtroom three of the four rows of benches were assigned to the communications media, and a press table was even erected inside the bar of the court, so close to Sheppard that he could not consult with his lawyers without being overheard. The jurors were subjected to constant publicity; their pictures appeared in Cleveland newspapers more than forty times.

The Supreme Court, appalled by this travesty of justice, reversed the conviction in *Sheppard* v. *Maxwell* (1966); in the course of the opinion, Justice Clark suggested what the judge should have done to control the trial. First, he should have adopted stricter rules governing the use of the courtroom by newsmen. Their number should have been limited, and their conduct more closely regulated. (They even handled exhibits lying on the counsel table during recesses.) Second, the judge should have "insulated" the witnesses; instead they were interviewed at will by newsmen. Third, "the court should have made some effort to control the release of leads, information and gossip to the press by police officers, witnesses, and the counsel for both sides." The prosecution repeatedly made alleged "evidence" available to the news media which was never offered in the trial. As for the highly distorted reports of the trial in the papers, Clark thought the judge "should have at least warned the newspapers to check the accuracy of their accounts."

The American Bar Association responded to this challenge with the Reardon report proposing rules which would limit statements for dissemination to the public on pending criminal cases by lawyers, court attachés, and law-enforcement officers. From the time of arrest or filing of a charge until the end of the trial, information could not be released outside of court on such matters as prior criminal record, existence or contents of any confession, performance of examinations, identity of prospective witnesses, or possible guilt or innocence. These rules would be made effective as to lawyers through the ABA Canons of Professional Ethics, enforceable by disciplinary proceedings, and as to law-enforcement agencies by internal regulations. On the touchy question of enforcement against the press, the ABA committee recommended use of the contempt power in limited instances while cases were actually on trial.

The American Newspaper Publishers Association sharply attacked these proposals. They contended that any interference with news sources concerning criminal investigations and prosecutions would be censorship and that a free press requires not only freedom to print without prior restraint but also free and uninhibited access to information. They denied that pretrial and intrial reporting had any real bearing on the outcome of criminal cases, and contended that the press was actually a positive influence in assuring a fair trial.[14]

[14] See Alfred Friendly and Ronald L. Goldfarb, *Crime and Publicity: The Impact of News on the Administration of Justice* (New York: The Twentieth Century Fund, 1967).

The net result of this heightened concern about prejudicial publicity was to encourage judges all over the country to issue "gag orders" when dealing with sensational prosecutions.[15] In *Nebraska Press Assn.* v. *Stuart* (1976) the press was barred for eleven weeks from reporting the fact of a confession in a gruesome murder case even though it was testified to in a preliminary court hearing open to the public. The Supreme Court unanimously struck down this order as unconstitutional prior restraint. Burger's opinion did not absolutely forbid all gag orders, and he seemed to leave open the possibility that judges might achieve the same purposes by closed court hearings, but they would have to bear a "heavy burden of demonstrating, in advance of trial, that without prior restraint a fair trial will be denied."[16]

It is a good thing that police and prosecutors have been warned to avoid prejudicial publicity, and the press could well practice some self-limitation. But there are other protections for the integrity of the criminal trial process than gag orders. The voir dire examination of potential jurors, and the availability of challenges of jurors, offer substantial guarantees against prejudice. Change of venue must be granted on a showing of local feeling against the defendant.[17] The jury can be protected from publicity during the trial by sequestration. Motions for mistrial can be granted, and convictions can be voided on appeal.[18] These alternatives offer substantial protection against trials unfair because of prejudicial publicity and are preferable to judicial control by prior restraints on the news media.

ACCESS TO THE PRESS

The basic concept of press freedom has been that of John Stuart Mill and Oliver Wendell Holmes—a marketplace of ideas in which free competition will result in the

---

[15] Andrew M. Schatz, "Gagging the Press in Criminal Trials," 10 HARVARD CIVIL RIGHTS–CIVIL LIBERTIES LAW REVIEW 608 (1975).

[16] While the Court was unanimous in *Nebraska Press,* Burger's disinclination to hold gag orders unconstitutional under all conditions was supported only by White, Blackmun, Powell, and Rehnquist, and even White confessed "grave doubts" that gag orders ever would be justifiable. Brennan, speaking for Stewart and Marshall as well, held all gag orders "constitutionally impermissible," and Stevens indicated he might well agree with Brennan "if ever required to face the issue squarely."

On the same day that *Nebraska Press* was decided, the Court refused to review the contempt conviction of William Farr, a Los Angeles newsman, for refusing to reveal the name of an attorney who had given Farr information concerning the Manson murder case in violation of the judge's gag order (*Farr* v. *Pitchess* [1976]). The Court also declined to review the case of four Fresno newsmen held in contempt for a story involving grand jury proceedings where a gag order had been imposed *(Rosato* v. *Superior Court* [1976]).

In *Evans* v. *Fromme* (1976) the judge in the trial of Lynette Fromme for the attempted assassination of President Ford had enjoined the showing of a documentary film, in which Miss Fromme was portrayed as a member of the Manson family, in 26 counties until a jury has been selected and sequestered. The Supreme Court denied review.

[17] *Groppi* v. *Wisconsin* (1971); *Murphy* v. *Florida* (1975).

[18] The conviction of Lt. William Calley for the My Lai murders by court-martial was voided in 1974 by a federal district judge primarily on the ground of prejudicial pretrial publicity, but his ruling was reversed by the Court of Appeals for the Fifth District, which held that any harm to the accused had been remedied by scrupulous care in choosing the jury and by other safeguards. *The New York Times,* September 11, 1975.

But two months later the same court voided the conviction of the kidnapper of an Atlanta newspaper editor on the ground of prejudicial publicity. Following his release and before the trial, Reg Murphy, the editor, had published a long narrative account of the kidnapping, and other extensive media coverage was also regarded by the Court of Appeals as prejudicial. *The New York Times,* November 29, 1975.

truth winning out. Insofar as American newspapers are concerned, the situation is quite different. Economic realities have killed hundreds of newspapers, and the one-newspaper town has now become the norm. Earlier efforts by the government to enforce competition between newspapers by bringing Sherman Act prosecutions have now been succeeded by legislation seeking to save failing newspapers by authorizing competitors to pool operations and facilities.[19]

Popular access to the "free marketplace of ideas" is of course subject to the decisions of the editors and publishers. While all papers welcome letters and news items, decisions on what to publish are controlled by available space and editorial policy. A newspaper is not a public utility. It is the essence of First Amendment rights that a paper's contents or policies in selecting news may not be dictated by government. The press cannot be forced to be "fair," at least in its news or editorial columns.

This issue was clarified by the Supreme Court's decision in *Miami Herald Publishing Co.* v. *Tornillo* (1974). A Florida "right to reply" law provided that if a newspaper attacked the personal character or official record of any political candidate, the paper was obligated to print, without charge, any reply the candidate might make to the attack. While the case for compulsory access to news columns had been ably argued by Jerome A. Barron in a widely noted article,[20] the Court unanimously viewed the statute as a clear attempt at government control over the exercise of editorial judgment. Even Justice White, who had not been too friendly to the press in the *Branzburg* case, here said, "this law runs afoul of the elementary First Amendment proposition that government may not force a newspaper to print copy which, in its journalistic discretion, it chooses to leave on the newsroom floor."

COMMERCIAL SPEECH

In *Valentine* v. *Chrestensen* (1942), a clever attempt by the exhibitor of a submarine to bring a commercial handbill under the protection of the *Lovell* and *Schneider* decisions failed.[21] The *Chrestensen* decision gave rise to the concept that the First Amendment did not apply to "commercial speech," which was furthered by the Court's decision in *Pittsburgh Press Co.* v. *Pittsburgh Commission on Human Relations* (1973). A "human relations" ordinance was construed in this case to forbid local newspapers from carrying help-wanted advertisements in sex-designated columns. Such advertisements, the Court said, are "classic examples of commercial speech." But Stewart, one of four dissenters, was alarmed; he thought that if "a government agency can force a newspaper publisher to print his classified advertising pages in a certain way in order to carry out governmental policy . . . I see no reason why Government cannot force a newspaper publisher to conform in the same way in order to achieve other goals thought socially desirable."

It appears, however, that the Supreme Court intended to define "commercial

---

[19] See Keith Roberts, "Antitrust Problems in the Newspaper Industry," 82 HARVARD LAW REVIEW 319 (1968).

[20] "Access to the Press—A New First Amendment Right," 80 HARVARD LAW REVIEW 1641 (1967).

[21] See "Freedom of Expression in a Commercial Context," 78 HARVARD LAW REVIEW 1191 (1965).

speech" very narrowly. In *New York Times* v. *Sullivan* (1964)), a major decision to be discussed more fully in Chapter 22, a Birmingham police commissioner who sued the newspaper for libel contended that the allegedly libelous statements were not protected by the First Amendment because they appeared in a paid advertisement. The Court's reply was that this "was not a 'commercial' advertisement in the sense in which the word was used in *Chrestensen*." This ad, which had been submitted by persons active in the civil rights movement, "communicated information, expressed opinion, recited grievances, protested claimed abuses, and sought financial support on behalf of a movement whose existence and objectives are matters of the highest public interest and concern."

The *New York Times* precedent was followed in *Bigelow* v. *Virginia* (1975), where a newspaper had published, contrary to Virginia law, an advertisement for a legal abortion service in New York. Justice Blackmun, upholding the paper, distinguished the *Pittsburgh* case. Here the ad "conveyed information of potential interest and value to a diverse audience—not only to readers possibly in need of the services offered, but also to those with a general curiosity about, or genuine interest in, the subject matter or the law of another State . . . and to readers seeking reform in Virginia." Going even further, *Virginia Pharmacy Board* v. *Virginia Consumer Council* (1976) ruled that states could not forbid pharmacists to advertise the prices of prescription drugs, for even "purely commercial" advertising was entitled to some First Amendment protection in a "free enterprise economy."

SPECIAL PROBLEMS OF RADIO AND TELEVISION

In spite of the importance of the electronic media as channels of news and discussion, they have been fatally handicapped in their claims for full First Amendment protection by the fact that their existence depends upon government licenses. Licenses are granted by the Federal Communications Commission in its discretion on a showing of "public interest, convenience and necessity," and are subject to renewal every five years. They can be revoked or suspended for violation of statutory standards or FCC rules. While these sanctions are rarely used, FCC control, guidance, or criticism is expressed in many other ways.[22]

The FCC is forbidden by its statute to exercise powers of censorship over the media, yet broadcast programming is one of the factors likely to be taken into account in deciding whether the "public interest" is being served by a station. Section 315(a) of the Federal Communications Act, the "equal time" provision, requires that if one political candidate receives time on the air, his opponents must be granted equal amounts of broadcast time. The broadcasting of obscene or profane language is forbidden by statute, and the industry is subject to the antitrust laws.

But it is an FCC policy, the "fairness doctrine," which in application has pro-

[22] To give only one example, an FCC policy statement which appeared to prohibit stations from playing "drug related" songs on the air was upheld in *Yale Broadcasting Co.* v. *FCC* (1973). See "Morality and the Broadcast Media: A Constitutional Analysis of FCC Regulatory Standards," 84 HARVARD LAW REVIEW 664 (1971). In 1976 the television media brought suit charging that the FCC had violated their First Amendment rights by coercing the networks into accepting the "family hour" concept, an early evening period during which the level of sex and violence would be reduced.

vided the clearest insight into the constitutional status of broadcasters. From the beginning the FCC stressed the obligation of licensees to devote a reasonable amount of time to coverage of public issues and to provide an opportunity for presentation of contrasting points of view. In 1967 the FCC issued rules making more specific its requirement that when personal attacks or political editorials were broadcast, the station must notify the persons involved and give them a reasonable opportunity to respond over the station's facilities.

In *Red Lion Broadcasting Co.* v. *Federal Communications Commission* (1969), the Supreme Court upheld the fairness regulations by a three-step reasoning process. First, because the limited number of broadcast channels requires government allocation and licensing, a First Amendment right in this field "comparable to the right of every individual to speak, write, or publish," is simply impossible. Second, since licensees must be selected and given monopoly rights, they must be subject to further regulation to prevent the abuses of private censorship. But, third, the government's power does have constitutional limits, and Congress intended the regulatory schemes to give broadcasting "the widest journalistic freedom consistent with its public obligations." Only the minimal regulation necessary to ensure the individual's right to receive information and society's need for an informed electorate is permitted.

Applying these principles, Justice White in *Red Lion* held for the Court that the FCC fairness doctrine had struck a fair balance. The FCC had not refused to permit a station to express its own views; it had not censored a program. All it had done was to say that, once a station's facilities were used for a personal attack on an individual, he or she must be permitted to reply. The contrast with the *Tornillo* decision, striking down a right-to-reply law affecting newspapers, is obvious.[23]

While the result achieved by the fairness doctrine in *Red Lion* seems proper, its extension would have serious potentialities. For example, in 1972 NBC broadcast a documentary stressing abuses in the nation's private pension systems. After a complaint of biased presentation had been filed, the FCC ruled that the program had in fact been unfair and ordered NBC to balance the broadcast by another program. NBC refused and appealed to the Court of Appeals for the District of Columbia, which in *Accuracy in Media* v. *NBC* (1974) reversed the FCC and cautioned the agency "not to intervene or burden or second-guess the journalist" except in the clearest cases of abuse by broadcasters.[24]

CBS has had a policy of refusing to accept paid editorial advertisements. The case of *CBS* v. *Democratic National Committee* (1973) involved refusal to sell time to a group which wished to express its views on the Vietnam war. The Supreme Court ruled that Congress had intended "private broadcasting to develop with the widest journalistic freedom consistent with its public obligations," and did not require the FCC "to mandate a private right of access to the broadcast media."

---

[23] See Louis L. Jaffe, "The Editorial Responsibility of the Broadcaster: Reflections on Fairness and Access," 85 HARVARD LAW REVIEW 768 (1972); Richard A. Kurnit, "Enforcing the Obligation to Present Controversial Issues: The Forgotten Half of the Fairness Doctrine," 10 HARVARD CIVIL RIGHTS–CIVIL LIBERTIES LAW REVIEW 137 (1975).

[24] The Supreme Court declined review in 1976. The Court also let stand an appeals court ruling that

The First Amendment was successfully invoked by a television station in *Cox Broadcasting Corp.* v. *Cohn* (1975), where a station which identified a deceased rape victim during trial of the alleged rapists was sued by the father of the victim for invasion of his right of privacy. The Court held that the First Amendment forbade imposing sanctions for an accurate publication obtained from official court documents open to public inspection.[25]

the FCC has no authority to require the Corporation for Public Broadcasting to provide "objectivity and balance" in the programs it funds and supplies to noncommercial broadcasting stations (*Accuracy in Media, Inc.* v. *FCC* [1976]). Under the fairness doctrine the Polish-American Congress requested television time to rebut some "Polish jokes" on the Dick Cavett show, but the FCC and lower court refusal to intervene was upheld by the Supreme Court in *Polish-American Congress* v. *FCC* (1976).

[25] For a further discussion of the invasion of privacy by publication, see Chapter 22.

Obscenity and Libel

Historically two types of expression have been denied the protection of the First Amendment—the obscene and the libelous. Punishment for such publications was long thought to require no constitutional justification. In *Near* v. *Minnesota* (1931), Chief Justice Hughes simply assumed that one of the exceptions to the rule of no prior restraint was enforcement of "the primary requirements of decency . . . against obscene publications," and he likewise took it for granted that the law of criminal libel rested upon a "secure foundation." The same view was reflected in Justice Murphy's acceptance in *Chaplinsky* v. *New Hampshire* (1942) of "the lewd and obscene" and "the libelous" as classes of speech "the prevention and punishment of which has never been thought to raise any Constitutional problem." In both fields the Supreme Court has more recently found it necessary to reconsider these earlier views.[1]

[1] Among the many serious discussions of obscenity, see Harry M. Clor, *Obscenity and Public Morality* (Chicago: University of Chicago Press, 1969); Charles Rembar, *The End of Obscenity* (New York: Random House, Inc., 1968); Richard H. Kuh, *Foolish Figleaves? Pornography in—and out of—Court* (New York: The Macmillan Company, 1967); Harry Kalven, Jr., "The Metaphysics of the Law of Obscenity," in Philip B. Kurland (ed.), *The Supreme Court Review, 1960* (Chicago: University of Chicago Press, 1960), pp. 1–45; Louis Henkin, "Morals and the Constitution: The Sin of Obscenity," 63 COLUMBIA LAW REVIEW 391 (1963); Harry M. Clor (ed.), *Censorship and Freedom of Expression* (Chicago: Rand

OBSCENITY

Legal restraints on obscenity and legal standards governing the degree of frankness in discussion of sexual matters date in England from the passage of Lord Campbell's Act in 1857. A few years later, in the United States, the crusading zeal of Anthony Comstock led to the passage of regulatory legislation in many states. Congress enacted a statute in 1872 making unmailable obscene or indecent publications or devices.

Why did legislatures act against obscenity, and why did American judges for so long assume the constitutionality of such legislation? In general, there seem to have been two kinds of concerns. First, obscenity has been regarded as bad in and of itself. It is indecent. It is a violation of good moral standards. It appeals to "prurient interest" and "stimulates impure sexual thoughts." It arouses feelings of disgust and revulsion or, alternatively, it induces unhealthy psychological excitement. In the words of the federal postal law, the obscene is the "lewd," the "lascivious," the "filthy."

Second, obscenity may be regarded as criminally punishable because of its evil effects on individuals and society. Obscene material, it is alleged, will have a tendency to deprave the minds or characters of persons exposed to it. It will corrupt the public morals. It will lead to immoral or antisocial sexual conduct. It will result in the advocacy of improper sexual values.

It was this second approach which was embodied in the first widely accepted legal definition of obscenity, that framed in 1868 by Justice Cockburn in the English case of *Queen* v. *Hicklin*. He said: "I think the test of obscenity is this, whether the tendency of the matter charged as obscenity is to deprave and corrupt those whose minds are open to such immoral influences, and into whose hands a publication of this sort may fall."

Under the pressure of this "effects" test, Justice Cockburn had to specify *who* was being depraved and corrupted, and his answer was, "those whose minds are open to such immoral influences." It was this feature of the *Hicklin* test which rendered it ultimately unacceptable, for, as Judge Learned Hand said in *United States* v. *Kennerly* (1913), it "would forbid all which might corrupt the most corruptible." Hand did not think that "society is prepared to accept for its own limitations those which may perhaps be necessary to the weakest of its members. . . . To put thought in leash to the average conscience of the time is perhaps tolerable, but to filter it by the necessities of the lowest and least capable seems a fatal policy."

The *Hicklin* test ignored literary and other social values, judged a whole book by passages taken out of context, and tested for obscenity by the tendency of the passages alone to deprave the minds of those open to such influence and into whose hands the book might come. Nevertheless, this test became so thoroughly established in the United States that in 1913 Judge Learned Hand felt compelled to give it effect in the *Kennerly* decision, even though he personally rejected it in the following memorable language:

McNally & Company, 1971); *The Report of the Commission on Obscenity and Pornography* (New York: Random House, Inc., 1970).

I hope it is not improper for me to say that the rule as laid down, however consonant it may be with mid-Victorian morals, does not seem to me to answer to the understanding and morality of the present time. . . . I question whether in the end men will regard that as obscene which is honestly relevant to the adequate expression of innocent ideas, and whether they will not believe that truth and beauty are too precious to society at large to be mutilated in the interests of those most likely to pervert them to base uses.

It was not until the 1930s that this remarkably sage counsel began to be effective in judicial decisions.[2] In the celebrated *Ulysses* case of 1934, Judge Augustus N. Hand in the court of appeals explicitly repudiated the *Hicklin* rule and replaced it with this new standard:

While any construction of the statute that will fit all cases is difficult, we believe that the proper test of whether a given book is obscene is its dominant effect. In applying this test, relevancy of the objectionable parts to the theme, the established reputation of the work in the estimation of approved critics, if the book is modern, and the verdict of the past, if it is ancient, are persuasive pieces of evidence; for works of art are not likely to sustain a high position with no better warrant for their existence than their obscene content.[3]

The abandonment of the *Hicklin* test permitted more civilized judgments on literary works, but it left the legal tests for obscenity vague, and it did nothing toward reconciling obscenity prosecutions with free speech theory. It was this task which the Supreme Court finally undertook in the *Roth* case.

The Two-Level Theory

Roth v. *United States* (1957) and its companion case, *Alberts* v. *California*, required the Court to rule on the constitutionality of both federal and state obscenity laws. The task, so long avoided, turned out to be surprisingly easy. Justice Brennan, writing for the majority, held there was no First Amendment problem because obscenity was "not within the area of constitutionally protected speech." The First Amendment extends to "all ideas having even the slightest redeeming social importance—unorthodox ideas, controversial ideas, even ideas hateful to the prevailing climate of opinion. . . . But implicit in the history of the First Amendment is the rejection of obscenity as utterly without redeeming social importance." Since obscenity is not "protected speech," there is no necessity to show any connection with unlawful action in order to justify criminal punishment. Rather, "convictions may be had without proof either that obscene material will perceptibly create a clear present danger of antisocial conduct, or will probably induce its recipients to such conduct." It is sufficient to allege, as had been done in these cases, that the materials circulated had incited "impure sexual thoughts."

So the obscene is not constitutionally protected. But what is obscene? That was the question which the Court now had to answer, and it was not so easy. Brennan made clear that he did not mean to say all discussions of sex were obscene; indeed,

[2] See *United States* v. *Dennett* (1930); *United States* v. *One Obscene Book Entitled "Married Love"* (1931); *United States* v. *One Book Entitled "Contraception"* (1931).
[3] *United States* v. *One Book Entitled "Ulysses"* (1934).

sex is "a great and mysterious motive force in human life . . . one of the vital problems of human interest and public concern." Consequently it was necessary to find a legal test for obscenity to supplant the *Hicklin* test which would fully protect the right to deal with sexual subjects. This is the test he proposed: "whether to the average person, applying contemporary community standards, the dominant theme of the material taken as a whole appeals to prurient interest."

The improvements in this standard over *Hicklin* are obvious. It is the average person, not the most susceptible person, whose morals are to be protected. The dominant theme of the material taken as a whole is the basis for judgment, not isolated passages from a book. Applying contemporary community standards recognizes that obscenity is a relative concept. Since the trial courts in both *Roth* and *Alberts* had defined obscenity consistently with this standard, Justice Brennan concluded that the convictions should be upheld.

Justices Douglas and Black, dissenting, denied Brennan's basic constitutional premise that obscenity can be punished because of the thoughts it provokes, with no proof that it has incited overt acts or antisocial conduct. "The test of obscenity the Court endorses today gives the censor free range over a vast domain. To allow the State to step in and punish mere speech or publication that the judge or the jury thinks has an *undesirable* impact on thoughts but that is not shown to be a part of unlawful action is drastically to curtail the First Amendment."

Justice Harlan also dissented so far as enforcing the federal statute was concerned. The charge against Roth was selling a book which tended to "stir sexual impulses and lead to sexually impure thoughts." He suggested that much of the great literature of the world could be stigmatized under such a view of the statute, and he believed that the federal government had no power "to bar the sale of books because they might lead to any kind of 'thoughts.' " But so far as the constitutionality of the state law was concerned, he felt obliged to accept as not irrational the legislature's conclusion that distribution of certain types of literature might induce criminal or immoral sexual conduct. He approved application of the state law in the *Alberts* case because his own "independent perusal" of the material convinced him that its suppression would not unconstitutionally "interfere with the communication of 'ideas' in any proper sense of that term."

Because the *Roth* decision upheld the constitutionality of obscenity laws, and because it flatly denied that obscenity was entitled to any constitutional protection under the First Amendment, the opinion when it was first handed down was widely considered to be a forecast of strong judicial support for further obscenity prosecutions. Certainly the four dissenters regarded the *Roth* reasoning as dangerously broad. Harlan, for example, found "lurking beneath its disarming generalizations" a number of problems which left him with "serious misgivings" as to the future effect of the decision.

Limiting the Obscenity Concept

However, it soon appeared that the Court recognized the dangers of the two-level theory and intended to define the concept of obscenity very strictly. In *Kingsley International Pictures Corp.* v. *Regents* (1959), a film version of *Lady Chatterly's*

Lover had been banned because it portrayed approvingly an adulterous relationship. Justice Stewart for a unanimous Court reversed this action. What New York had done was to censor a motion picture "because that picture advocates an idea"—the idea "that adultery under certain circumstances may be proper behavior." This idea might well be contrary to moral standards, religious precepts, and legal codes. But, said Stewart, the Constitution does not protect only those ideas "that are conventional or shared by a majority. It protects advocacy of the opinion that adultery may sometimes be proper, no less than advocacy of socialism or the single tax." There can be no prosecution, then, for "thematic obscenity." Ideas cannot be obscene.

The next important step in limiting the obscenity concept was taken in *Manual Enterprises, Inc.* v. *Day* (1962), where Justice Harlan wrote the opinion. As already noted, he had been concerned over the breadth of the "prurient interest" test announced in *Roth*, and in *Manual* he was able to narrow it by adding a second test. In his view, "prurient interest" was only another way of stating the *Hicklin* "effect" test of depraving and corrupting. He believed that conviction for obscenity should require proof of *both* the elements analyzed earlier in this chapter; there must be prurient interest effect *and* "patent offensiveness." He pointed out that some acknowledged masterpieces of art or literature might have a dominant theme appealing to prurient interest, and he would rank such works as obscene only if their "indecency" was self-demonstrating. On the basis of the patent offensiveness test, Harlan absolved of obscenity the material involved in *Manual*—magazines with photographs intended to appeal to male homosexuals. He found the magazines to be "dismally unpleasant, uncouth, and tawdry," but not "beyond the pale of contemporary notions of rudimentary decency."

A third test, likewise restrictive of the scope of the obscenity concept, was put forward by Justice Brennan in *Jacobellis* v. *Ohio* (1964). Its foundation was his statement in the *Roth* case that obscenity is "utterly without redeeming social importance." At that time he had simply been defending the two-level theory and justifying the constitutionality of laws against obscenity. But his statement was also relevant as a test *for* obscenity. If it is true that obscenity is "utterly without redeeming social importance," then it must be equally true that anything *with* redeeming social importance cannot be obscene. This was what Brennan spelled out in the *Jacobellis* case, which dealt with censorship of the film "The Lovers." He wrote that

> . . . material dealing with sex in a manner . . . that has literary or scientific or artistic value or any other form of social importance, may not be branded as obscenity and denied the constitutional protection. Nor may the constitutional status of the material be made to turn on a "weighing" of its social importance against its prurient appeal, for a work cannot be proscribed unless it is "utterly" without social importance.

Thus the Court had by 1964 set up three tests for obscenity—prurient interest appeal, patent offensiveness, and utterly without redeeming social value. In the famous *Fanny Hill* case of 1966 (*A Book Named "John Cleland's Memoirs of a Woman of Pleasure" v. Attorney General of Massachusetts*) the Court made it clear that the three tests were separate and that a book had to fail all three before it could be adjudged obscene. The supreme court of Massachusetts had granted that the book might have "some minimal literary value," but did not think that gave it any social importance. Since it appealed to prurient interest and was patently offensive, the state court held it obscene. Justice Brennan for the Supreme Court ruled that this was a misinterpretation of the social value criterion. "Each of the three federal constitutional criteria is to be applied independently; the social value of the book can neither be weighed against nor canceled by its prurient appeal or patent offensiveness." Since the state court admitted the book had a "modicum of social value," that was enough to rescue it from the charge of obscenity.

Though the justices encountered some difficulties in applying these standards, there did emerge a clear majority view that there was a class of materials, called "hard-core pornography," which was not protected by the First Amendment. Some members of the Court believed that nothing else would meet the Court's three tests for obscenity. Justice Harlan said in *Manual Enterprises:* "At least one important state court and some authoritative commentators have considered *Roth* and subsequent cases to indicate that only 'hard-core' pornography can constitutionally be reached under this or similar state obscenity statutes." But, as Chief Justice Warren asked in *Jacobellis:* "Who can define 'hard-core pornography' with any greater clarity than 'obscenity'?" Justice Stewart in the same case confessed: "I shall not attempt . . . to define the kinds of material I understand to be embraced within [hard-core pornography]; and perhaps I could never succeed in intelligibly doing so. But I know it when I see it, and the motion picture involved in this case is not that."

The Pandering Test

The Supreme Court's obscenity decisions undoubtedly contributed toward an increase in the openness with which sexually stimulating materials were published and advertised. When the magazine *Eros*, announced as a quarterly "devoted to the subjects of Love and Sex," was founded in 1962 by Ralph Ginzburg, he said in an advertisement that it was "the result of recent court decisions that have realistically interpreted America's obscenity laws and that have given to this country a new breath of freedom of expression. . . . *Eros* takes full advantage of this new freedom of expression. It is *the* magazine of sexual candor."

Ginzburg had misinterpreted the extent of the new freedom. He was prosecuted and convicted under the federal obscenity statute for the publication of *Eros* and certain other materials and sentenced to five years in prison. The Supreme Court, some members of which had apparently become concerned over the commercial exploitation of sex resulting from its earlier decisions, unexpectedly affirmed the conviction by a vote of five to four in *Ginzburg* v. *United States* (1966).

In justification for this ruling, Justice Brennan for the majority announced a new, fourth test for obscenity—the setting or context in which the publications claimed to be obscene were presented to the public. The Court conceded that Ginzburg's publications "standing alone . . . might not be obscene." But when viewed "against a background of commerical exploitation of erotica solely for the sake of their prurient appeal," a different conclusion was justified.

Each of the accused publications, the Court found, had been "originated or

sold as stock in trade of the sordid business of pandering." The "leer of the sensual-
ist" permeated the advertising. The publisher "deliberately emphasized the sexually
provocative aspects of the work, in order to catch the salaciously disposed." He
engaged in the "exploitation of interests in titillation by pornography." The magazine was even mailed from Middlesex, New Jersey, after arrangements to mail it
from Intercourse, Pennsylvania, had proved unsuccessful.

Justice Brennan did not state the new "context" test very precisely. He simply
affirmed for the Court that "the question of obscenity may include consideration of
the setting in which the publications were presented as an aid to determining the
question of obscenity." He did not discuss the relationship of the context test to the
other three tests, except to say that "in close cases evidence of pandering may be
probative with respect to the nature of the material in question and thus satisfy the
Roth test." But surely the holding is that the setting test can override the other three,
since materials otherwise not clearly obscene can become "illicit merchandise" because of the way in which they are presented.

In *Mishkin* v. *New York* (1966), decided the same day as *Ginzburg,* the Court by
a vote of six to three upheld the criminal conviction of a man who published and
arranged for the writing of books concerned largely with deviant sexual practices.
The New York courts applied hard-core pornography as their obscenity standard,
which of course met the Supreme Court's constitutional requirements. The principal
feature of interest in *Mishkin* was its treatment of the "average person" aspect of the
Roth test. Counsel for Mishkin argued that books emphasizing flagellation, fetish-
ism, lesbianism, and masochism such as were here at issue were so deviant that they
would not appeal to the prurient interest of an "average" person, but instead would
"disgust and sicken" him. Justice Brennan countered this legalism by the following
adjustment of "the prurient-appeal requirement to social realities": "where the material is designed for and primarily disseminated to a clearly defined deviant sexual
group, rather than the public at large, the prurient-appeal requirement of the *Roth*
test is satisfied if the dominant theme of the material taken as a whole appeals to the
prurient interest in sex of the members of that group."

The Warren Court Reconsiders

Appearing to recognize that its confusing obscenity decisions had created what C.
Peter Magrath called a "disaster area," in 1967 the Court took a new tack.[4] A brief
and uncomplicated *per curiam* opinion in *Redrup* v. *New York* recapitulated the
Court's past problems in reaching a consensus and suggested that in the future it
would uphold obscenity convictions only where the statute "reflected a specific and
limited state concern for juveniles," or where "individual privacy" had been assaulted by obscene material "in a manner so obtrusive as to make it impossible for an
unwilling individual to avoid exposure to it," or where there was "pandering" of the
Ginzburg type.

Pursuant to this new and promising line, the Court in *Ginsberg* v. *New York*

---

[4]"The Obscenity Cases: Grapes of Roth," in Philip B. Kurland (ed.), *The Supreme Court Review,
1966* (Chicago: University of Chicago Press, 1966), pp. 7–78.

(1968) upheld a state statute prohibiting the sale of obscene materials to minors under seventeen years of age. Congress picked up the point about imposing obscenity on captive audiences and in 1967 passed a law providing that persons receiving in the mail material that they regarded as obscene could demand the removal of their names from the firm's mailing list, after which a second mailing would be basis for prosecution. This law was upheld in *Rowan* v. *Post Office Department* (1970).

In *Stanley* v. *Georgia* (1969), however, none of the three *Redrup* justifications was present. In fact, this was an egregious case where federal and state agents equipped with a warrant to search a private home for gambling evidence found instead some obscene films which they proceeded to view and then confiscate, charging the resident with possession of obscene matter. Justice Marshall's opinion was a ringing defense of every person's right to "satisfy his intellectual and emotional needs in the privacy of his own home" and a denial of the state's right "to control the moral content of a person's thoughts." The decision was unanimous, but three justices would have preferred to rest the case on a finding of unconstitutional search and seizure.

The Burger Court Takes Over

If, as *Stanley* held, private possession of obscene materials is constitutionally privileged, it might seem to follow that there is a constitutional right to receive such materials through any modes of distribution as long as adequate precautions are taken to prevent their dissemination to unconsenting adults and minors. In *United States* v. *Reidel* (1971), a prosecution for mailing allegedly obscene material, the trial court did in fact hold that "if a person has the right to receive and possess this material, then someone must have the right to deliver it to him." But the Supreme Court declined to accept this logic. *Stanley* did not overrule *Roth*, White held. Obscenity was still unprotected by the First Amendment, and the government could exclude it from the mails.[5] *United States* v. *Thirty-seven Photographs* (1971), decided at the same time, upheld seizure of obscene photographs taken from the luggage of a returning foreign traveler as he went through customs. White's opinion upheld the power of Congress "to exclude noxious articles from commerce," even if the photos were for private use, but two of the six-judge majority concurred only on the understanding that commercial use of the photographs was intended in this case.[6]

Black, Douglas, and Marshall dissented. Black wryly suggested that the right of private possession of obscenity recognized by *Stanley* was now effective "only when a man writes salacious books in his attic, prints them in his basement, and reads them in his living room."

By 1973, with four Nixon appointees, the Court was ready for a new effort to clear up the obscenity mess. In *Miller* v. *California* (1973), Chief Justice Burger set out to "formulate standards more concrete than those in the past." First, he accept-

[5] In *United States* v. *Orito* (1973), the Court upheld the federal law forbidding the knowing transportation of obscene material by common carrier in interstate commerce. See also *Hamling* v. *United States* (1974).

[6] However, in *United States* v. *12 200-Ft. Reels of Super 8 MM. Film* (1973), a later Court held that Congress had the constitutional power to proscribe the importation of obscene matter even though the material was for the importer's private, personal use and possession.

ed the *Roth* "prurient interest" and "contemporary community standards" test. However, he rejected the Warren Court's notion that "community" meant the "national community." It would be an "exercise in futility" to seek such a national consensus, he said; the nation is too big and diverse. "It is neither realistic nor constitutionally sound to read the First Amendment as requiring that the people of Maine or Mississippi accept public depiction of conduct found tolerable in Las Vegas, or New York City." In *Miller* the jury had been instructed to evaluate the materials with reference to contemporary standards in California, and this was held to be constitutionally adequate.

Second, Burger revised the *Manual* "patent offensiveness" test to read, "whether the work depicts or describes, in a patently offensive way, sexual conduct specifically defined by the applicable state law." To aid state legislatures, Burger gave some examples of what he had in mind: "representations or depictions of intimate sexual acts, normal or perverted, actual or simulated." and "representations or depictions of masturbation, excretory functions, and lewd exhibition of the genitals."

Finally, Burger rejected the "utterly without redeeming social value" test which, he said, placed on prosecutors the impossible task of proving a negative. He substituted for it this test: "whether the work, taken as a whole, lacks serious literary, artistic, political, or scientific value."

With these new or revised tests, Burger proudly announced that for the first time since *Roth* a Court majority had agreed on "concrete guidelines to isolate 'hard core' pornography from expression protected by the First Amendment." Abandoning the "casual" standards announced in *Redrup*, he asserted that the Court was now providing "positive guidance to the federal and state courts alike."

Several other obscenity cases were decided the same day. *Paris Adult Theatre I* v. *Slaton* (1973) held that "adult" theaters were not protected by the First Amendment merely because they exhibited for consenting adults only. Specifically rejected was the *Redrup* position that the state's concern was only with protecting children and unconsenting adults. There are, Burger said, "legitimate state interests at stake in stemming the tide of commercialized obscenity . . . in the quality of life and the total community environment . . . [and] the public safety itself." Answering the argument that there is no conclusive proof of a connection between antisocial behavior and obscenity, Burger replied: "From the beginning of civilized societies, legislators and judges have acted on various unprovable assumptions."

Miller and its four companion cases were all decided by a five to four vote, with Stewart joining Douglas, Brennan, and Marshall in dissent. Principal interest attaches to Brennan's agonizing reappraisal of his position. Having been a principal formulator of the Court's obscenity views since *Roth*, he now concluded that all their efforts had failed to "bring stability to this area of the law without jeopardizing fundamental First Amendment values." None of the available formulas had reduced the Court's vagueness to a tolerable level, nor would Burger's new formulations help. Parenthetically, Brennan expressed some distaste at being charged with deciding "whether a description of human genitals is sufficiently 'lewd' to deprive it of constitutional protection." And why should it be thought that the First Amendment protects only expressions of "*serious* literary or political value"?

The only solution, Brennan concluded, was to abandon the idea he himself had authored in *Roth*, namely, "that there exists a definable class of sexually oriented expression that may be totally suppressed." Save only for the juvenile and unconsenting adult exceptions, he would hold that "the First and Fourteenth Amendments prohibit the state and federal governments from attempting wholly to suppress sexually oriented materials on the basis of their allegedly 'obscene' contents."

Rather embarrassingly for Burger's claims that a new day had dawned and that the Court had returned to local communities the right to decide what was obscene, a Georgia jury promptly held *Carnal Knowledge,* a widely acclaimed and nationally distributed film, obscene. The Court in *Jenkins* v. *Georgia* (1974), having viewed the film, felt compelled to reverse the finding. Cautioning that *Miller* did not mean to give local juries unbridled discretion, Justice Rehnquist said that this movie did not depict sexual conduct in a patently offensive way and so could not be held obscene under the *Miller* tests.

There is no reason to agree with Burger that *Miller* has solved the Court's obscenity problems. Rather, the prospect of applying local community standards in this field presents a serious threat to national distribution of books, magazines, and films. In 1976 a crusading United States attorney in Memphis secured a jury conviction of eleven persons variously connected with the film, "Deep Throat," some merely as actors, on a charge of "national conspiracy to transport interstate an obscene motion picture."[7]

The Techniques of Morals Censorship

Legislative limitations on the circulation of allegedly obscene literature usually employ the technique of subsequent punishment. In addition to the normal protection of criminal punishment procedures thus provided, *Smith* v. *California* (1959) held that a bookseller must be proved to be aware of the obscene contents of a book to justify a conviction. If a seller were absolutely liable for having obscene books in his possession, the Court believed that he would tend to restrict the books he sold to those he had personally inspected, which would be a serious bar to the free flow of communications.

Prior restraint cannot be employed against allegedly obscene books because obscene literature does not lose the protection of the First Amendment until its status under *Roth* has been determined in court. In *Bantam Books, Inc.* v. *Sullivan* (1963) a statute creating a public commission which threatened book distributors

---

[7] The Court's recognition of local community standards as decisive in obscenity cases has led to "forum shopping." Since mailing of pornographic material can be proceeded against either in the community where it was mailed or where it was received, prosecutors have a choice of forums. In 1975 postal authorities sent to Los Angeles for advertised "adult material" and had it delivered to a pseudonym in New Hampshire, where they brought prosecution, on the assumption that a New Hampshire jury would be more likely to convict than one in Los Angeles. The federal court in New Hampshire, however, granted a defense motion to transfer the case to Los Angeles. In a similar case transferred from Iowa to Los Angeles, the government contended that Iowa community standards should nevertheless be used. The federal judge in Los Angeles agreed and then dismissed the charges on grounds that a Los Angeles jury could not determine what Iowa standards were. *The New York Times,* July 11, 1975. But in *Novick, Haim and Unique Specialties Inc.* v. *U.S. District Court* (1975), the Supreme Court refused to hear a request from two Los Angeles men, charged with sending obscene materials through the mails, that they be tried in Los Angeles rather than Louisiana. See also *Marks* v. *United States* (1976).

Young v. *American Mini Theatres* (1976) approved the use of zoning ordinances to restrict the proliferation of "adult" movie theaters and bookstores.

with prosecution if they handled objectionable literature was held unconstitutional as prior restraint. But a procedure under which an injunction was secured, followed by prompt trial, after which the offending material could be seized by the sheriff and destroyed, was upheld in *Kingsley Books* v. *Brown* (1957). Chief Justice Warren, dissenting, charged that book seizure "savors too much of book burning," and the Court subsequently struck down search and seizure statutes which provided slightly less procedural protection.[8]

State censorship of motion pictures was approved by the Court in the 1915 case of *Mutual Film Corp.* v. *Industrial Commission of Ohio*. The motion picture of that era was of course only an entertaining novelty rather completely devoid of any ideational content, and it was readily assimilated to burlesque or other theatrical spectacles which were customarily subjected to control on moral grounds. Moreover, the 1915 decision antedated the Court's concern with civil liberties problems.

Over the years both motion pictures and the Court changed. The movies came somewhat closer to being commentaries on the social scene, and in documentary films and newsreels they rivaled the newspapers in reporting current events, yet censorship continued to be practiced. It was not until 1952, in *Burstyn* v. *Wilson,* that the 1915 censorship opinion was finally reversed and motion pictures were recognized as coming at least partly under the protection of the First Amendment.[9] However, *Burstyn* did not ban all prior restraints on motion pictures; it merely held that the charge in this case, which was "sacrilege," was not an acceptable ground. Subsequent rulings took the same line.[10] Consequently, movie censorship is not unconstitutional on its face, as book censorship would be, but the Court imposed such strict procedural limitations on state and local censorship boards in *Freedman* v. *Maryland* (1965) that they have been abandoned or rendered ineffective.[11]

In *Southeastern Promotions, Ltd.* v. *Conrad* (1975), city officials in Chattanooga had refused to rent a city auditorium for performance of the rock musical *Hair* on the ground that it was obscene. The Court reversed, holding that prior restraint of a theatrical production in a public forum, though not necessarily unconstitutional per se, could be imposed only under the procedural safeguards set forth in *Freedman*.

Roaden v. *Kentucky* (1973) held that seizure of a film by a sheriff without a constitutionally sufficient warrant was essentially the same restraint on expression as seizure of all books in a bookstore and was unreasonable prior restraint under the Fourth and Fourteenth Amendments. But *Heller* v. *New York* (1973) upheld a film seizure where the judge issuing the warrant saw the entire film before signing the seizure warrant; an adversary hearing prior to seizure was not required.

---

[8] *Marcus* v. *Search Warrant* (1961), and *A Quantity of Copies of Books* v. *Kansas* (1964). In *Blount* v. *Rizzi* (1971), a statute allowing the Post Office to stop the mail of businesses found in administrative hearings to sell pornographic matter was held unconstitutional because it did not provide sufficient procedural protections.

[9] See Ira H. Carmen, *Movies, Censorship, and the Law* (Ann Arbor, Mich.: University of Michigan Press, 1966).

[10] *Times Film Corp.* v. *Chicago* (1961).

[11] The *Freedman* requirements are as follows: (1) the burden of proving that the film is obscene rests on the censor; (2) the censor must either pass the film within a brief period or go to court to restrain its showing; (3) the procedure must assure a prompt judicial decision.

LIBEL

First some definitions and distinctions are in order. *Libel* is the defamation of character by print or other visual presentation such as television. *Slander* is defamation by oral presentation. Defamation itself needs definition. The Sedition Act of 1798 spelled out the concept as "false, scandalous and malicious writing . . . with the intent . . . to bring into contempt or disrepute; or to excite . . . the hatred of the good people of the United States."

Prosecutions for libel can be *civil* or *criminal*. The theory of a criminal prosecution is that libel is an offense against the peace and good order of the community, likely to incite acts of physical retaliation. In earlier times when there were no laws punishing defamation, dueling developed as a method by which wounded feelings of honor could be avenged. Criminal punishment for libel provides a lawful means of redress and is designed to avert the possibility that libelous utterances will provoke an enraged victim to breach of the peace. Libels of the government or public officials may be made criminally punishable, as by the Sedition Act of 1798. Criminal libel statutes provide for fines and sentences of imprisonment within defined limits. The act of 1798 specified maximum sentences of $5,000 fine and five years in prison.

A civil prosecution for libel is a suit for monetary damages brought by the victim against the publisher of the libel. The civil suit has generally tended to supplant criminal prosecutions for libel in the area of private defamation. As Justice Brennan said in *Garrison* v. *Louisiana* (1964), the civil remedy "enabled the frustrated victim to trade chivalrous satisfaction for damages [and] substantially eroded the breach of the peace justification for criminal libel laws."

Damages in a civil suit may be of two types—*compensatory* and *punitive*. Compensatory damages are intended to reimburse the individual for actual financial loss resulting, for example, from loss of employment or earning power or reputation occasioned by the libel. The amount of such losses can be reasonably well established by evidence. Punitive damages are exemplary in character, intended to compensate the victim for his suffering and to punish the libeler for malicious intent. There is no objective standard for determining the amount of punitive damages, and they have tended to escalate in recent years. When Theodore Roosevelt won a libel suit after he had left the Presidency against a newspaper which had charged he cursed and was intoxicated while campaigning, he was awarded damages of 6 cents. But more recently a college football coach who had been accused in a *Saturday Evening Post* story of giving his team's signals to an opponent was awarded $60,000 in compensatory damages and 3 million dollars in punitive damages, which was cut to $460,000 on appeal. A television actor who lost his job because he was blacklisted by a right-wing organization was awarded damages totaling 2.25 million dollars, which was cut to $550,000 on appeal.

Seditious Libel

Seditious libel is defamation of the government and its officials and is punished criminally. American experience with seditious libel was strongly influenced by English practice. The English law of seditious libel permitted punishment for publications tending to bring into hatred or contempt, or to excite disaffection against, the king, the government, Parliament, or the administration of justice. The English law of libel was initially developed by the Star Chamber, which made no use of a jury. After the Star Chamber was abolished in 1641, the King's Bench was influenced by its tradition and permitted juries only a limited role, such as finding facts as to authorship or publication, reserving for the bench the question of whether these facts constituted a libel. A long line of oppressive libel prosecutions finally led to Fox's Libel Act in 1792, which allowed the jury to find a general verdict in cases of criminal libel. The American Sedition Act of 1798 also entrusted the determination of criminality to the jury, and in addition admitted truth as a defense.

It was the contention of Zechariah Chafee in his influential book, *Free Speech in the United States,* that the First Amendment was intended to abolish the law of seditious libel, a position also accepted by Justice Holmes. This view has been questioned by Leonard Levy, who argues that it was not until after adoption of the act of 1798 that opinion crystallized against seditious libel.[12] He points out that Jefferson, although he attacked the act of 1798 and its use against his partisans, was willing to see his Federalist opponents prosecuted for seditious libel in the states after he became President.

As already noted, the Sedition Act was never passed on by the Supreme Court before it expired in 1801. But in *New York Times Co.* v. *Sullivan* (1964), the Court flatly ruled the act had been inconsistent with the First Amendment "because of the restraint it imposed upon criticism of government and public officials." In fact, Justice Brennan, who wrote the opinion for the Court, suggested that the right to criticize official conduct was "the central meaning of the First Amendment."

So far as prosecutions for libel on government are concerned, then, the Supreme Court has held, as reiterated by Justice Brennan in *Rosenblatt* v. *Baer* (1966), that "the Constitution does not tolerate [them] in any form." There is complete freedom to criticize government and public policies. But the government acts through individual public officials. Does that mean there is also complete freedom to criticize or defame public officials? That is a different problem, to which we now turn.

Libel of Public Officials

Prosecutions for alleged libel of public officials may be either civil or criminal. The case of *New York Times Co.* v. *Sullivan* (1964) was a civil suit. *The New York Times* had printed as a paid advertisement a criticism of the treatment of Negroes in Montgomery, Alabama. The ad was submitted by reputable persons, but it was later discovered that it contained some factual errors. The police commissioner of Montgomery, though not mentioned in the ad either by name or specific reference to his office, contended that criticism of the Montgomery "police" constituted a libel of him. The case was tried in Alabama.

The trial judge ruled that the statements in the ad were "libelous per se." He instructed the jury that legal injury was implied from the bare fact of publication, that compensatory (or general) damages did not need to be alleged or proved but

---

[12] Leonard W. Levy. *Legacy of Suppression* (Cambridge, Mass.: The Belknap Press, Harvard University Press, 1960), and *Jefferson and Civil Liberties: The Darker Side* (Cambridge, Mass.: The Belknap Press, Harvard University Press, 1963).

were presumed, and also that "falsity and malice" were presumed, thus justifying punitive damages as well. The judge refused to require that the verdict differentiate between compensatory and punitive damages.

The Alabama jury awarded damages of $500,000, an amount one thousand times greater than the maximum fine provided by the Alabama criminal defamation statute. Another commissioner who sued on the basis of the same ad also got a $500,000 judgment, eleven additional libel suits were filed against *The Times* seeking a total of 5.6 million dollars, while five suits asking 1.7 million dollars were brought at the same time against the Columbia Broadcasting System based on its coverage of Alabama civil rights controversies. This indicates the magnitude of the threat to the solvency of major communications media which these libel proceedings had raised.

The Supreme Court unanimously reversed the *Sullivan* libel judgment on the ground that the Alabama libel law, as applied against *The New York Times*, failed to provide safeguards for freedom of speech and press required by the Constitution. The earlier statements in such cases as *Near* and *Chaplinsky* that the Constitution does not protect libelous publications were now qualified. A libel law, like any other, must meet constitutional standards; "libel can claim no talismanic immunity from constitutional limitations."

The *New York Times* case, Justice Brennan said for the Court, had to be considered "against the background of a profound national commitment to the principle that debate on public issues should be uninhibited, robust, and wide-open, and that it may well include vehement, caustic, and sometimes unpleasantly sharp attacks on government and public officials." This advertisement, as an expression of grievance and protest on a major public issue, clearly qualified for constitutional protection.

Had it forfeited that standing by the falsity of some of the statements and the alleged defamation of the police commissioner? The Court did not think so. Erroneous statement is inevitable in free debate. "A rule compelling the critic of official conduct to guarantee the truth of all his factual assertions—and to do so on pain of libel judgments virtually unlimited in amount" would be fatal to robust debate on public issues. It would impose a "pall of fear and timidity . . . upon those who would give voice to public criticism." A defense for "erroneous statements honestly made" is essential to the survival of First Amendment freedoms.

The Court did, however, attach one important reservation to this broad constitutional protection for freedom of comment. Defamatory falsehood relating to official conduct would be actionable if made with "actual malice," that is, "with knowledge that it was false or with reckless disregard of whether it was false or not." But actual malice would have to be proved. Recognizing that this particular case might be tried again, the Court thought it wise to warn that the facts presented in the Alabama trial would not sustain a finding of actual malice on the part of *The New York Times*. Nor did the Court find any sufficient evidence in the record to transmute the general, "impersonal" criticisms of Alabama government into personal criticism, and hence potential libel, of the officials of that government.[13]

Justices Black, Douglas, and Goldberg would have gone further than the Court.

[13] The Court applied the principles of the *New York Times* civil suit to a prosecution for criminal

They argued for "absolute, unconditional" freedom of publications from libel suits. Black contended that the press must have "an absolute immunity for criticism of the way public officials do their public duty." He charged that "state libel laws threaten the very existence of an American press virile enough to publish unpopular views on public affairs and bold enough to criticize the conduct of public officials." The "actual malice" test, he thought, was "an elusive, abstract concept, hard to prove and hard to disprove." It would be an uncertain, "evanescent protection for the right critically to discuss public officers."

Though the Court did not give criticism of public officials the complete protection for which Black argued, *New York Times* did leave public officials very largely defenseless against any except the most vicious attacks, thus adopting the Harry Truman maxim that "If you can't stand the heat, stay out of the kitchen." Some members of the Court were disturbed by this prospect. In *Rosenblatt* v. *Baer* (1966), Stewart expressed fear that the Court, in protecting the right of free discussion under the First Amendment, was neglecting "the right of a man to the protection of his own reputation from unjustified invasion and wrongful hurt. . . . The protection of private personality . . . is left primarily to the individual States under the Ninth and Tenth Amendments." He would not permit the First Amendment to undermine the right of the states to safeguard the "rights and value of private personality [which] far transcend mere personal interests. Surely if the 1950s taught us anything, they taught us that the poisonous atmosphere of the easy lie can infect and degrade a whole society." He would prevent a state from converting its law of defamation into a law of seditious libel, but that was as far as he would go. The same concern was evinced by Fortas in *St. Amant* v. *Thompson* (1968) in these words: "The First Amendment does not require that we license shotgun attacks on public officials in virtually unlimited open-season. The occupation of public officeholder does not forfeit one's membership in the human race."[14]

A word should be said about libelous utterances *by* public officials. As we have already seen, members of Congress enjoy an absolute immunity from legal liability for any statements they may make in their official capacity. The Supreme Court's decision in *Barr* v. *Matteo* (1959) extended immunity from libel prosecution to all federal administrative officials for statements made within the "outer perimeter" of their official duty. Thus government officials have absolute protection against prosecution for libel, whereas persons who allegedly libel government officials have the qualified protection provided by the actual malice rule.

Libel of "Public Figures"

Following the *New York Times* decision, the Supreme Court was not long in extending constitutional safeguards against libel suits beyond public officials to "public figures," that is, private citizens who had thrust themselves into public controversies

---

defamation in *Garrison* v. *Louisiana* (1964). The "actual malice" rule was interpreted in *Time Inc.* v. *Pape* (1971).

[14] In a message to Congress on campaign reform, on March 8, 1974, President Nixon proposed that a federal libel law be considered to give political candidates and public officials greater protection from attacks in the press and by opponents. He wanted to encourage "good and decent people" to run for office without "fear of slanderous attacks."

or who had a status in life that commanded wide interest and legitimate public attention.

Associated Press v. *Walker* (1967) concerned a well-known right-winger, General Edwin A. Walker, who filed suits totaling more than 20 million dollars against the Associated Press and television companies because of statements they made about his activities on the University of Mississippi campus during the rioting in 1962. He was reported as having "assumed command of the crowd" and having "led a charge of students against federal marshals." He won one jury award of 3 million dollars, reduced by the judge to 2.25 million dollars, and another of $800,000, reduced by the judge to $500,000.

This latter award was unanimously set aside by the Supreme Court in *Associated Press* v. *Walker* (1967), though there was disagreement on the reasoning. Five justices thought the *New York Times* rule limiting libel to "malicious falsehoods" should apply equally to public officials and "public figures," whereas the other four justices, led by Harlan, would allow damages to "public figures" on a showing of "highly unreasonable conduct constituting an extreme departure from the standards of investigation and reporting ordinarily adhered to by responsible publishers." On neither standard was Walker held entitled to damages. Harlan noted that Walker's appearance on the campus during the rioting was "hot news" which had to be written quickly and, though there might have been errors in the dispatch, there was not "the slightest hint of a severe departure from accepted publishing standards."

In a second case, *Curtis Publishing Co.* v. *Butts* (1967), these two different standards resulted in a split on the Court. A five-judge majority upheld the libel judgment of $460,000 won by the former athletic director of the University of Georgia against *The Saturday Evening Post* for an article charging him with giving his team's plays to an opponent. Writing for the majority, Harlan pointed out that, unlike the *Walker* case, the *Saturday Evening Post* story was not "hot news," and charged that the magazine had ignored "elementary precautions" and conducted an inadequate investigation in preparing the article. Chief Justice Warren joined the Harlan group of four from the *Walker* case to provide the fifth vote for this position.

The "public figure" rule has been applied in several subsequent cases. In *Greenbelt Cooperative Publishing Assn.* v. *Bresler* (1970), the "public figure" was a real estate developer who had applied for zoning variances. In *Monitor Patriot Co.* v. *Roy* (1971), a newspaper article had characterized a candidate for the state legislature as a "former small-time bootlegger." The Court held that candidates for public office must be treated the same as public officials and that a publication charging criminal conduct, no matter how remote in time or place, against a candidate would have the full protection of the *New York Times* rule.

During Barry Goldwater's candidacy for President in 1964, Ralph Ginzburg's magazine *Fact* pictured him as mentally unstable on the basis of opinions solicited from a large number of psychiatrists. A jury found a "reckless disregard of truth" in the preparation of the article and awarded Goldwater a judgment of $75,000. The Supreme Court declined review in *Ginzburg* v. *Goldwater* (1970), over the protest of Black and Douglas.

Defamation of Private Individuals

In *Gertz* v. *Robert Welch, Inc.* (1974), Justice Powell recapitulated the case for applying the *New York Times* rule to public officials and public figures, thereby making it harder for them to secure redress for the harm inflicted on them by defamatory falsehoods:

> The first remedy of any victim of defamation is self-help. . . . Public officials and public figures usually enjoy significantly greater access to the channels of effective communication and hence have a more realistic opportunity to counteract false statements than private individuals normally enjoy. Private individuals are therefore more vulnerable to injury, and the state interest in protecting them is correspondingly greater.

But this rationale did not appear to have been persuasive to the Court three years earlier, when *Rosenbloom* v. *Metromedia* (1971) was decided. There the Court came close to abandoning the "private individual" distinction as a guide to decision in libel cases. A news distributor had been arrested and charged with distribution of obscene magazines. A radio newscast repeated the charge and used the term "smut distributors." Subsequently a jury acquitted Rosenbloom on instructions of the judge that the nudist magazines were not obscene. Rosenbloom then sued the station for defamation and got a substantial award, which was reversed on appeal.

The Court's opinion was a confusing one, with eight justices announcing their views in five separate opinions, none of them commanding more than three votes. Brennan's judgment for the Court held that Rosenbloom's status as a private individual who had not voluntarily chosen to become involved in the public arena was irrelevant. The controlling consideration was that the issue raised by his arrest was "a subject of public or general interest" in which the community had a vital concern, namely, proper enforcement of the criminal laws on obscenity. Brennan consequently would apply the *New York Times* rule "to all discussion and communication involving matters of public or general concern, without regard to whether the persons involved are famous or anonymous."

The Court continued erosion of the private individual distinction in *Old Dominion Branch No. 496* v. *Austin* (1974), where a letter carrier who refused to join the union, and who had been listed as a "scab" in the union publication, lost his $45,000 defamation judgment when the Supreme Court held that the *New York Times* rule covered all participants in labor disputes.[15]

In *Gertz* v. *Robert Welch, Inc.*, however, the Court finally found a bona fide "private individual" who was constitutionally entitled to sue a traducer for defamation, and in the process it overruled *Rosenbloom*. Gertz was a Chicago lawyer who had been retained to sue a policeman by a family whose son the policeman had killed. The John Birch Society magazine published an article saying that the suit was part of a communist campaign against the police, that Gertz was a "Leninist," a "Communist-fronter," and, by implication, that he had an extensive criminal record. Justice Powell's opinion asserted that Gertz was a private individual, no mat-

---

[15] See also *Linn* v. *United Plant Guard Workers* (1966).

ter how much attention he might receive as counsel in a newsworthy lawsuit, and that he was entitled to defend his reputation by a libel suit. However, under the *Gertz* ruling publishers continued to be protected by the negligence rule; private individuals must prove failure of the publisher to exercise normal care.

Time Inc. v. *Firestone* (1976) involved a Florida court decision upholding a jury verdict of $100,000 against *Time* magazine for referring to a divorcee as an "adulteress" when the decree had not specifically found the woman guilty of adultery. Applying the *Gertz* rule, the Court limited "public figures" to those who thrust themselves "into the forefront of particular public controversies in order to influence the resolution of the issues involved." Participants in divorce proceedings, even if sensational, do not meet this test. Though the divorce decree was very loosely drawn and "full of talk about adultery," the Court held that publishers could be held liable for a reporter's negligent misreading of a court decision, even if the news story was "a rational interpretation of an ambiguous document." The case was returned to the Florida courts for a finding on the issue of negligence. [16]

Invasion of Privacy by Publication

In dealing with cases charging invasion of privacy by publication, the Supreme Court has tended to employ the same standards used in its libel decisions.[17] The leading case is *Time Inc.,* v. *Hill* (1967). In 1952 a Pennsylvania family named Hill had been held hostage in their home for nineteen hours by three escaped convicts. A novel portraying a similar incident was published in 1953, and was made into a play which appeared on Broadway in 1955. *Life* magazine made a feature story of the play, which it linked directly to the experience of the Hills, even taking pictures of the actors in the house where the Hills lived when the incident occurred. In fact, both the book and play were highly fictionalized accounts, differing in many respects from the family's experience.

The Hills sued for damages under a state law protecting privacy and were awarded $30,000. The Supreme Court by a vote of five to four set the judgment aside. Justice Brennan stressed that the risk of exposure to publicity is "an essential incident of life in a society which places a primary value on freedom of speech and of press." The press cannot be saddled with "the impossible burden of verifying to a certainty the facts associated in news articles with a person's name, picture or portrait, particularly as related to non-defamatory matter." However, Brennan thought the press could be held to the same standard he had previously developed for libel suits in *New York Times* v. *Sullivan* (1964), namely, that "knowing or reckless falsehood" could not be protected. Since it was not clear that the trial judge had charged the jury in these terms, the Court reversed the judgment, though leaving the way open for a new trial. Justice Fortas regarded the article as a "reckless and irresponsible assault" upon the Hill family, and did not believe that the Court was adequately protecting the constitutional right of privacy.

---

[16] In *Triangle Publications* v. *Montandon* (1975), the Court let stand a $150,000 libel judgment against *TV Guide* for a program listing that implied a television personality was a call girl.

[17] See Donald E. Brown, "The Invasion of Defamation by Privacy," 23 STANFORD LAW REVIEW 547 (1971).

As we have just seen, by 1974 the Court had come closer to sharing Fortas's concern about privacy, and this new attitude found expression in *Cantrell* v. *Forest City Publishing Co.* (1974). The *Cleveland Plain Dealer* published a feature story discussing the impact upon a local family of the father's death in a bridge collapse. The story contained a number of inaccuracies and false statements. In fact, it described and attributed various quotations to the widow, though she was not at home when the reporter made his visit. The Supreme Court upheld an award for invasion of privacy. While there was some confusion as to whether the trial court had applied the common law or the *New York Times* definition of malice, in any event the story contained "knowing falsehoods."[18]

Group Libel

The case of *Beauharnais* v. *Illinois* (1942) raised the interesting question whether groups, as well as individuals, can be libeled. Is it possible, or desirable, to offer legal protection to groups against defamatory statements? There is of course general acceptance of the importance of groups in a democratic society, and it is likewise clear that defamatory statements about a group can have serious adverse effects upon members of that group. Nevertheless, groups are not persons, and they are legitimate subjects of public discussion. Any conception that comments about groups are limited by laws against criminal defamation is bound to impose substantial barriers to uninhibited discussion of public issues.

The problem of group defamation was presented in its most horrifying form by Hitler's success in calculated exploitation of anti-Semitism. This represented a kind of evil which can destroy the fabric of civilized communities, and it is not surprising that, in the United States, efforts to control what the Indiana Legislature called "hate racketeering" were adopted. Actually, the Illinois law involved in *Beauharnais* had been passed in 1917, reflecting the state's reaction to earlier racial problems. The statute made it unlawful to publish or exhibit any writing, picture, drama, or moving picture which portrays "depravity, criminality, unchastity, or lack of virtue of a class of citizens, of any race, color, creed or religion . . . [or] exposes the citizens of any race, color, creed or religion to contempt, derision, or obloquy or which is productive of breach of the peace or riots."

Joseph Beauharnais, head of an organization called the White Circle League, circulated on Chicago street corners anti-Negro leaflets which were in the form of petitions to the mayor and city council. The leaflets made defamatory and derogatory comments about Negroes and asked the use of the police power to protect the white race from their "rapes, robberies, knives, guns and marijuana." The leaflets also appealed for persons to join the White Circle League and asked for financial contributions. Beauharnais was convicted of violating the statute and was fined $200.

---

[18] See also *Cox Broadcasting Corp.* v. *Cohn* (1975). In *Paul* v. *Davis* (1976) the Louisville police had circulated a flyer to local merchants containing the names and photographs of several hundred persons labeled as "active shoplifters." One person included had been arrested on a shoplifting charge eighteen months earlier, but the charge had been dropped before trial. The Court ruled, five to three, that his privacy had not been invaded, and that due process protected only his liberty and property, not his reputation and good name.

The Supreme Court upheld the conviction and statute by a five to four vote, Justice Frankfurter writing the opinion. Every state, he noted, provides for the punishment of libels directed at individuals. Clearly, it is libelous falsely to charge a person "with being a rapist, robber, carrier of knives and guns, and user of marijuana." The question, then, is whether the Fourteenth Amendment prevents states from punishing libels "directed at designated collectivities and flagrantly disseminated." His answer was that the Illinois Legislature might reasonably have decided to seek ways "to curb false or malicious defamation of racial and religious groups, made in public places and by means calculated to have a powerful emotional impact on those to whom it was presented." Where the individual is "inextricably involved" in the group, speech which could be libelous if directed to the individual may also be treated as libelous when directed at the group.

Justices Black, Douglas, Reed, and Jackson dissented, though Jackson's position differed from that of the other three. To Black, this decision manifested the shocking results of the reasonable man test in the civil liberties field. By treating the Illinois statute as a libel law, Frankfurter had taken the case out of the context of all the Court's free speech decisions on "the bland assumption that the First Amendment is wholly irrelevant. It is not even accorded the respect of a passing mention." Such a law, Black was sure, would present "a constant overhanging threat to freedom of speech, press and religion."

Justice Jackson agreed with the majority on the constitutionality of the group libel law, but thought that convictions would have to meet the clear and present danger test by taking into account the "actual or probable consequences" of the libel. In this case there should have been an appraisal of the particular form, time, place, and manner of the communication. Is a leaflet inherently less dangerous than the spoken word, because less "emotionally exciting?" Is the publication "so foul and extreme" as to defeat its own ends? Perhaps its appeal for money, "which has a cooling effect on many persons," would negate its inflammatory tendencies. Perhaps it would impress the passer-by "as the work of an irresponsible who needed mental examination." By failing to insist on such an inquiry into the circumstances, Jackson thought the majority had failed to achieve a constitutional balance between state power and individual rights.

Subsequent developments have demonstrated the error of the *Beauharnais* decision and undermined its authority. It failed to consider the close relationship between group libel and seditious libel.[19] It sought to remove important areas of public discussion from the protection of the First Amendment. It failed to understand, as the Court later put it in the *New York Times* case, the constitutional flaw in a law which "dampens the vigor and limits the variety of public debate." Even hatemongers have rights in a free society.

Group libel laws punish the act of discussion itself.[20] If the debate becomes too vigorous, the breach of the peace laws are available. It is significant that when

[19] Harry Kalven, Jr., *The Negro and the First Amendment* (Chicago: University of Chicago Press, 1965), chap. 1.

[20] But see the very thoughtful and challenging defense of the *Beauharnais* decision by Hadley Arkes, "Civility and the Restriction of Speech: Rediscovering the Defamation of Groups," in Philip B.

Illinois revised its criminal code in 1961, the three criminal libel laws on the books were merged into a single brief statute keyed to breach of the peace. On the other hand, it should be noted that England, faced for the first time with racial problems, has adopted the group libel formula. The Race Relations Act of 1965 makes it unlawful to stir up in a public place "hatred against any section of the public in Great Britain distinguished by color, race or ethnic or national origins."[21]

Kurland (ed.), *The Supreme Court Review, 1974* (Chicago: University of Chicago Press, 1974), pp. 281–336.

[21] See Anthony Lester and Geoffrey Bindman, *Race and Law in Great Britain* (Cambridge, Mass.: Harvard University Press, 1972).

Chapter 23

Freedom of Association

There is no provision in the Constitution specifically protecting freedom of association, yet the right of individuals to organize into groups for political, economic, religious, and social purposes is universally recognized. The constitutional basis for this freedom must be derived from the right of assembly and the freedoms of speech, press, and religion. The Supreme Court has remarked upon "the close nexus between the freedoms of speech and assembly," and noted how "effective advocacy of both public and private points of view, particularly controversial ones, is undeniably enhanced by group association."[1]

Because it is so closely linked with these First Amendment freedoms, discussion of associational freedom in this volume is partly subsumed under other headings—for example, in dealing with political parties, labor unions, and religious groups. In this chapter our concern is primarily with unpopular organizations whose rights of association have been under the most pressure.

Associative freedom, of course, is not absolute for any group, any more than are the freedoms of speech, press, and assembly. The freedom of group life is always subject to some degree of regulation in the public interest. Totalitarians carry this

[1] *National Association for the Advancement of Colored People* v. *Alabama* (1958).

regulation to the point of completely subjecting all groups to the purposes of the state. Anarchists go to the other extreme in proposing that the state abdicate its functions to groups. The liberal state seeks to encourage the maximum of group freedom compatible with general public welfare.[2]

In recent American experience, the organization whose associational rights have been under greatest pressure is the Communist Party. To meet the threat which communism appeared to present to American security after the Russian Revolution established a basis for the Party's world-wide operations, much restrictive and punitive legislation was passed both by Congress and the state legislatures, and reviewing courts have had to struggle with very difficult problems in reconciling traditional and basic associative freedoms with society's right to counter organized efforts conceived to threaten its way of life and undermine national security.

THE COMMUNIST PARTY AND GUILT BY ASSOCIATION

The Supreme Court's introduction to the interpretation of statutory restrictions on radicals came during and immediately after World War I, involving the Espionage Act of 1917 and the Sedition Act of 1918. Both enactments had to be construed in a wartime setting, which hardly encouraged the Court to be venturesome in protecting the speech rights of the assorted Socialists, pacifists, pro-Germans, Communists, and anarchists who were prosecuted under those statutes. The more significant of the decisions—particularly the *Abrams, Schenck*, and *Debs* cases—have already been commented on, and the ineffectiveness of the clear and present danger test, first developed in these cases, has been noted.

The "Red scare" stirred up by the Bolshevik revolution persisted for some time after the war, particularly in the form of the raids conducted by Attorney General A. Mitchell Palmer and his efforts toward the deportation of alien radicals. But the national return to normalcy largely took the federal government out of the anti-Communist field, and the Sedition Act was repealed in 1921. There remained the states, many of which had legislation on the books aimed at radicals of various sorts. Some of these laws had been passed after the assassination of President McKinley in 1901 by an anarchist, and were directed at "criminal anarchy" or "criminal syndicalism." It was a New York statute of this sort which was involved in *Gitlow* v. *New York* (1925).

The Supreme Court's unanticipated concession in the *Gitlow* case—that the First Amendment applied to the states by way of the Fourteenth—opened the way for Supreme Court review of all state laws under which political radicals were convicted; and in *Whitney* v. *California* (1927) the Court appeared to adopt the rule of guilt by association. Miss Whitney's crime, under the California Syndicalism Act, was that she participated, without protest, in the convention which set up the Communist Labor party of California and was elected an alternate member of its state executive committee. She testified that it was not her purpose that this party should

---

[2] See generally "Developments in the Law—Judicial Control of Actions of Private Associations," 76 HARVARD LAW REVIEW 983–1100 (1963); Robert A. Horn, *Groups and the Constitution* (Stanford, Calif.: Stanford University Press, 1956).

be an instrument of terrorism or violence, or violate any law, but the party was found to have been formed to teach criminal syndicalism, and as a member of the party she participated in the crime.

The Supreme Court upheld this conviction on the ground that "united and joint action involves . . . greater danger to the public peace and security than the isolated utterances and acts of individuals," but Justices Brandeis and Holmes did not agree. Brandeis said:

> The felony which the statute created is a crime very unlike the old felony of conspiracy or the old misdemeanor of unlawful assembly. The mere act of assisting in forming a society for teaching syndicalism, of becoming a member of it, or of assembling with others for that purpose is given the dynamic quality of crime. There is guilt although the society may not contemplate immediate promulgation of the doctrine. Thus the accused is to be punished, not for contempt, incitement or conspiracy, but for a step in preparation, which, if it threatens the public order at all, does so only remotely. The novelty in the prohibition introduced is that the statute aims, not at the practice of criminal syndicalism, nor even directly at the preaching of it, but at association with those who propose to preach it.

The Hughes Court of the 1930s, however, refused to accept the *Whitney* rule of guilt by association. In three important decisions—*Stromberg* v. *California* (1931), *DeJonge* v. *Oregon* (1937), and *Herndon* v. *Lowry* (1937)—the convictions of admitted Communists were reversed because they had not personally been guilty of violating any criminal law. For example, DeJonge had addressed a Communist Party meeting, and that party might have illegal objectives. But, said Hughes, "Notwithstanding those objectives, the defendant still enjoyed his personal right of free speech and to take part in a peaceable assembly having a lawful purpose, although called by that Party."

The Smith Act

What was destined to become the most famous of the anti-Communist measures was the Alien Registration Act of 1940, better known as the Smith Act. Actually, alien registration was only one of the five purposes of the act. Its major importance was as a peacetime sedition act, the first federal peacetime restrictions on speaking and writing by American citizens since the ill-fated Sedition Act of 1798. Section 2 of the statute made it unlawful knowingly to advocate or teach the overthrow of any government in the United States by force or violence, to print or distribute written matter so advocating, or organize or knowingly become a member of any group which so advocates. Section 3 made punishable conspiracy to accomplish any of these ends.

The language of the Smith Act was less drastic than the Sedition Act of 1798 in that it forbade only the advocacy of force, and not mere political criticism of government officials. But it was more restrictive in at least one respect. The law made it a crime to belong to an organization that was subsequently found to advocate the overthrow of the government by force, regardless of what the individual said or did. The act did not mention the Communist Party by name, but there can be no doubt that the framers of the statute believed the Party advocated force and violence and intended the act to apply to it and its members.

In 1948 the Truman administration, apparently goaded by the Republican charges of being "soft on communism," began a dramatic prosecution in New York of eleven leaders of the American Communist Party under the Smith Act. The indictment made two charges against them: (1) willfully and knowingly conspiring to organize as the United States Communist Party a society, group, and assembly of persons who teach and advocate the overthrow and destruction of the government of the United States by force and violence, and (2) knowingly and willfully advocating and teaching the duty and necessity of overthrowing and destroying the government by force and violence. No overt revolutionary acts other than teaching, advocating and conspiring were alleged.

The trial before Judge Harold R. Medina was full of sensation and lasted for nine months. The ultimate conviction was upheld by the court of appeals, Chief Judge Learned Hand writing the opinion. The Supreme Court then granted certiorari limited to questions of the constitutionality of the Smith Act, "inherently or as construed and applied in the instant case." By vote of six to two, with Chief Justice Vinson writing the opinion, the Court confirmed the convictions in *Dennis* v. *United States* (1951).

The major issue confronting the Court was how to reconcile with the free speech guarantee of the Constitution convictions which treated speaking and teaching as criminal offenses. For, admittedly, the eleven had taken no action with the immediate intention of initiating a revolution. Vinson sought to validate the statute by construing it as being "directed at advocacy, not discussion." But that did not solve the problem completely. For advocacy has two aspects. It is action against which, when aimed toward unlawful ends, the government had the undoubted power to protect itself. But it also "contains an element of speech," as Vinson agreed; and consequently his opinion for the Court majority had inevitably to return to the clear and present danger test.

Vinson's argument amounted to a substantial reinterpretation of the Holmes-Brandeis doctrine, which he purported to follow. The actual formula he adopted was that used by Learned Hand in the court of appeals: "whether the gravity of the 'evil,' discounted by its improbability, justifies such invasion of free speech as is necessary to avoid the danger." Obviously, said Vinson, the clear and present danger test "cannot mean that before the Government may act, it must wait until the *putsch* is about to be executed, the plans have been laid and the signal is awaited . . . . We must therefore reject the contention that success or probability of success is the criterion."

Jackson and Frankfurter each added their own interpretations of clear and present danger. For Jackson, the problem was easy. Holmes and Brandeis had developed this test in cases which presented only "technical or trivial violations . . . arising before the era of World War II revealed the subtlety and efficacy of modernized revolutionary techniques used by totalitarian parties." Jackson would save the test, "unmodified, for application as a 'rule of reason' in the kind of case for which it was devised," namely, hot-headed speeches on street corners or circulation of a few incendiary pamphlets. But when the issue is the probable success of a world-wide revolutionary conspiracy, it is futile for the courts to attempt prophecy in the guise of a legal decision. "The judicial process simply is not adequate to a trial of such far-flung issues."

Justice Black, dissenting, charged that the Court's decision repudiated "directly or indirectly" the clear and present danger rule: "I cannot agree that the First Amendment permits us to sustain laws suppressing freedom of speech and press on the basis of Congress' or our own notions of mere 'reasonableness.' Such a doctrine waters down the First Amendment so that it amounts to little more than an admonition to Congress." He would hold Section 3 of the Smith Act "a virulent form of prior censorship of speech and press," and "unconstitutional on its face."

Douglas's dissent wanted to know how clear and present danger could have been determined when the record contained no evidence on the "strength and tactical position" of the Communist Party in the United States. In the absence of such evidence, he himself could see no danger from these "miserable merchants of unwanted ideas." "Free speech—the glory of our system of government—should not be sacrificed on anything less than plain and objective proof of danger that the evil advocated is imminent."

The Court, however, had cut itself off from consideration of the evidence relied on to prove the alleged conspiracy by its questionable action in granting certiorari limited only to the constitutionality of the statute. Actually the government's case was a most peculiar one. The evidence presented at the trial was primarily concerned with what was in the basic texts of Marxism-Leninism extending all the way back to 1848, as distributed by the Communist Party and discussed at their meetings. The guilt of the Communist leaders was established by connecting them with the organization of the Party and the teaching of these texts. By allowing the validity of convictions based on such textual analyses to be established by default, the Supreme Court permitted the assumption that it had accepted the principle of guilt by association; illegal conspiracy could be established by demonstrating activities—any kind of activities—in furtherance of the organizational work of the Communist Party.

The *Dennis* decision encouraged the government to bring similar prosecutions, based on similar evidence, against the lesser Party leaders throughout the country. The government was almost uniformly successful in these subsidiary suits, in none of which did the Supreme Court grant certiorari until October, 1955, when it agreed to review the conviction of fourteen California Communists. This time no limitation was imposed on the grant of certiorari, and the result was the shattering decision in *Yates* v. *United States* (1957). By a vote of six to one the Court, while not challenging the constitutionality of the Smith Act as established by the *Dennis* decision, reversed the convictions of five of the fourteen defendants and laid down conditions for Smith Act trials which made it much more difficult to secure any future convictions.

Justice Harlan, writing the majority opinion, completely abandoned the clear and present danger test, contending that *Dennis* had actually been based on the distinction between "advocacy of abstract doctrine," which is protected, and "advocacy directed at promoting unlawful action," which is not protected. He continued:

The essence of the *Dennis* holding was that indoctrination of a group in preparation for future violent action, as well as exhortation to immediate action, by advocacy found to be directed to "action for the accomplishment" of forcible overthrow, to violence "as a rule or principle of action," and employing "language of incitement" . . . is not constitutionally protected when the group is of sufficient size and cohesiveness, is sufficiently oriented towards action, and other circumstances are such as reasonably to justify apprehension that action will occur.

Evidence in the *Yates* record sufficient to support convictions for this second type of advocacy was, Harlan said, "strikingly deficient":

At best this voluminous record shows but a half dozen or so scattered incidents which, even under the loosest standards, could be deemed to show such advocacy. Most of these were not connected with any of the petitioners, or occurred many years before the period covered by the indictment. We are unable to regard this sporadic showing as sufficient to justify viewing the Communist Party as the nexus between these petitioners and the conspiracy charged.

What the Court was saying was that evidence of activity in the Communist Party would not meet the requirements in this case. Some of the Party's activities might be wholly lawful. The defendants could be convicted only on the basis of their individual acts other than their mere relations with the Party. On this basis five of the defendants were completely cleared. There was no evidence in the record to connect them with the conspiracy charged except that they had long been members and officers of the Communist Party of California.

As for the other nine defendants, the Court was not prepared to go so far. There was evidence involving them—Party classes, an "underground apparatus," board meetings held in a devious and conspiratorial manner—which might meet the Court's tests. "We are not prepared to say, at this stage of the case, that it would be impossible for a jury, resolving all conflicts in favor of the Government and giving the evidence . . . its utmost sweep, to find that advocacy of action was also engaged in when the group involved was thought particularly trustworthy, dedicated, and suited for violent tasks."

The Black-Douglas dissents in the *Dennis* case were partially vindicated by the *Yates* decision, though again in *Yates* Black and Douglas found themselves in disagreement with the majority opinion. While concurring in the result, they would have held the Smith Act completely unconstitutional and directed the acquittal of all defendants. In fact, this latter result was achieved six months later when the Department of Justice "reluctantly" requested the trial court to dismiss the indictments against the remaining nine defendants on the ground that "the evidentiary requirements laid down by the Supreme Court" could not be satisfied. Also on the basis of the *Yates* ruling, indictments were dismissed against six Communists in Pittsburgh and eleven in Puerto Rico; courts of appeals reversed convictions of seven who had been tried in Hawaii, four in Seattle, five in New Haven, and four in Philadelphia. It appeared that the Smith Act had been rendered virtually useless as an instrument for jailing Communists and that the more than one hundred convictions under the act had been largely illegal.

Thus the Court, which had appeared to accept guilt by association in *Dennis,* in *Yates* moved back toward its traditional insistence on proof of individual wrong-doing. But section 2 of the Smith Act, which makes unlawful mere membership in a group advocating forcible overthrow of the government, remained to be construed by the Court. When it came up for review in the case of *Scales* v. *United States* (1961), the Court was asked to hold it unconstitutional because it imputed guilt on the basis of associations and sympathies rather than because of concrete personal involvement in criminal conduct.

The Court, however, upheld the constitutionality of section 2 by interpreting it as applying only to "knowing," "active," members who had a "specific intent to bring about violent overthrow." Specific intent could be established by evidence showing "the teaching of forceful overthrow, accompanied by a contemporary, though legal, course of conduct clearly undertaken for the specific purpose of rendering effective the later illegal activity which is advocated."

The Court majority found that Scales was linked to illegal advocacy by this kind of evidence. Douglas, dissenting along with Warren, Black, and Brennan, contended that Scales was charged with no unlawful acts and therefore that the Court had legalized guilt by association. The majority sought to refute this charge by reversing another section 2 conviction on the same day in *Noto* v. *United States* (1961). In Noto's trial, Justice Harlan ruled, the kind of evidence that had convicted Scales was lacking. Justice Black interpreted the *Noto* decision as telling the government that it had not had sufficient up-to-date information on the present policies of the Communist Party, and he added: "I cannot join an opinion which implies that the existence of liberty is dependent upon the efficiency of the Government's informers."

The government's success in the *Scales* case was not followed up, and Smith Act prosecutions were largely abandoned. In *Brandenburg* v. *Ohio* (1969), the Court pronounced an obituary on the entire line of cases criminalizing association, beginning with *Whitney,* which was specifically overruled. Striking down the Ohio criminal syndicalism act in *Brandenburg,* the Court stressed *Yates,* not *Dennis,* and *Noto,* not *Scales.* Black and Douglas used the occasion to read their own personal obsequies over the clear and present danger test, which Douglas said had been distorted beyond recognition in *Dennis* and which in any event was "not reconcilable with the First Amendment."[3]

THE INTERNAL SECURITY ACT OF 1950

The Internal Security Act of 1950, which got its start as the Mundt-Nixon bill in 1948 and was passed over President Truman's veto, sought to cripple the Communist Party by the device of registration. The statute ordered Communist organiza-

---

[3] The defunct Smith Act would be revived by the proposed Criminal Justice Codification Act, S. 1, 94th Congress, which provided for imprisonment for fifteen years and $100,000 fine for membership in an organization advocating the incitement to action which "at some future time would facilitate" the destruction of the government "as speedily as circumstances will permit" and where "intent" for such change can be shown.

tions to register with the Attorney General, and a Subversive Activities Control Board (SACB) was established to determine which organizations shoud be required to register. Upon issuance of such an order by the board, the organization was required to register, disclose names and addresses of its officers, and give an accounting of sources of money and expenditures. Among the sanctions incurred by a registered organization were the following: its mail and radio broadcast had to be identified as Communist propaganda; members could not hold nonelective federal positions; they committed a crime if they applied for or used a United States passport; and their right to work in defense plants was limited.[4]

The SACB was organized in November, 1950. The Attorney General almost immediately filed a petition to compel the Communist Party of the United States to register as a Communist-action organization. After many misadventures, the board finally got a favorable ruling from the Supreme Court eleven years later in *Communist Party* v. *Subversive Activities Control Board* (1961). The Party had contended that the registration provisions were fraudulent and that the real purpose of the statute was to impose impossible requirements in order to lay a foundation for criminal prosecution of the Party and its officers and members—in effect "outlawing" the Party. There is much evidence that this was in fact the intention of Congress, but the Court accepted the statute as a bona fide registration law and upheld it on that basis. The Court majority declined to consider the constitutionality of any of the sanctions which the act applied to registered organizations on the ground that, since the Party had not yet registered, they had not come into effect. Justice Frankfurter wrote:

> Although they become operative as soon as a registration order is made final, their application remains in a very real sense problematical. We cannot now foresee what effect, if any, upon the Party the denial of tax exemption will have. . . . We do not know that, after such an order is in effect, the Party will wish to utilize the mails. . . . It is wholly speculative now to foreshadow whether, or under what conditions, a member of the Party may in the future apply for a passport, or seek government or defense-facility or labor-union employment, or, being an alien, become a party to a naturalization or a denaturalization proceeding. None of these things may happen.

Naturally, these things did happen. The registration order having been upheld by the Supreme Court, prosecutions were brought against two leaders of the Communist Party to revoke their passports. In *Aptheker* v. *Secretary of State* (1964), the Court declared the passport provisions of the 1950 statute unconstitutional because they too broadly and indiscriminately restricted the right to travel.

The government had no more success in compelling enforcement of the registration requirement. The Party's officials refused to register after the 1961 decision

---

[4] Title II of the Internal Security Act, designated the Emergency Detention Act, gave the government power, in the event of war, invasion, or insurrection, to seize and hold persons who could be expected to attempt acts of espionage or sabotage even though they had as yet committed no crime. This authority was repealed in 1971, with a provision prohibiting such detention without specific congressional authorization. See Richard Longaker, "Emergency Detention: The Generation Gap, 1950–1971," 27 WESTERN POLITICAL QUARTERLY 395 (1974).

and were upheld by a federal appeals court, which ruled that no one could be forced by a registration proceeding to declare his association with a party that had been labeled criminal. The Supreme Court denied certiorari.[5] The SACB, persevering, then brought action to require individual party members to register. In *Albertson* v. *SACB* (1965), the Supreme Court unanimously held that this would constitute compulsory self-incrimination.

Following the failure of two more SACB efforts to compel alleged "Communist-front" organizations to register,[6] this record of futility was completed in *United States* v. *Robel* (1967), where the Court declared unconstitutional by a vote of six to two the provision of the McCarran Act making it a crime for any member of a Communist-action organization "to engage in any employment in any defense facility." The Court was not prepared to rescue this provision, as it had done with section 2 of the Smith Act in *Scales* v. *United States* (1961), by interpreting it as applying only to active members with the specific intent to overthrow the government. Rather the precedent applied was *Aptheker*, and the statute was invalid because its language swept "indiscriminately across all types of associations with Communist-action groups, without regard to the quality or degree of membership . . . . The statute quite literally establishes guilt by association alone, without any need to establish that an individual's association poses the threat feared by the Government in proscribing it."

POLITICAL TRIALS AND THE CONSPIRACY CHARGE

The prosecutions of Communist Party members can be regarded as "political trials" in the sense that they were charged with opposition to the established political regime and threatening the safety of the state.[7] In the late 1960s and early 1970s, old-line Communists were largely replaced by opponents of the war in Vietnam, the New Left, "black power" radicals, and various violent underground movements as the principal perceived threat to the political order. The two most significant prosecutions in this period were those of Dr. Benjamin Spock and four others in 1968 for encouraging resistance to the draft and the Chicago Seven in 1970 for violation of the federal Anti-Riot Act at the 1968 Democratic convention.[8]

These two cases highlighted the special constitutional issues in securing a fair "political trial." One is the unusual degree of government discretion in determining whom to prosecute. In the Spock case, the five defendants scarcely knew each other before they were indicted, and they were selected almost at random to stand trial as surrogates for and warning to the entire peace movement. Again, the selection of the

[5] *Communist Party* v. *United States* (1963).

[6] *American Committee for Protection of Foreign Born* v. *SACB* (1965) and *Veterans of the Abraham Lincoln Brigade* v. *SACB* (1965). After a concerted effort by the Nixon administration in 1971 and 1972 to find something for the SACB to do, it was finally allowed to die in 1973 by failure to appropriate funds for it.

[7] See Otto Kirchheimer, *Political Justice: The Use of Legal Procedures for Political Ends* (Princeton, N.J.: Princeton University Press, 1961).

[8] See Jessica Mitford, *The Trial of Dr. Spock* (New York: Alfred A. Knopf, Inc., 1969); Jason Epstein, *The Great Conspiracy Trial* (New York: Random House, Inc., 1970); Jack Nelson and Ronald J. Ostrow, *The FBI and the Berrigans: The Making of a Conspiracy* (New York: Coward, McCann & Geoghegan, 1972).

eight original Chicago defendants from among the thousands who participated in the convention riots was pure prosecutorial discretion. Other characteristics of political trials are related to the public tension and near-hysteria which may be generated by such occasions and the disruptive courtroom behavior which the defendants may engage in to demonstrate their contempt for the regime.

A special constitutional problem in such trials is the common reliance on charges of conspiracy. An indictment for criminal conspiracy offers peculiar advantages for the government because it is easier to prove and more difficult to defend against than other criminal charges. A criminal conspiracy at common law occurs when two or more persons enter into an agreement to commit an unlawful act or to achieve a lawful object by unlawful means. The essence of the offense is making the agreement; under common law nothing more in the way of carrying out the conspiracy is required to justify conviction.[9]

There are other features of the law of conspiracy that make it attractive to prosecutors. Two individuals can be convicted for agreeing to perform an act that, if accomplished by one person, would not even be indictable. Individuals may be charged with conspiracy to commit an illegal act as well as with the illegal act itself,[10] and the statutory penalty for conspiring may be greater than for the substantive crime. Furthermore, because conspiratorial agreements are typically secret and thus difficult to prove, courts relax the normal rules of evidence in conspiracy cases.

Because of these characteristics, Jackson said in *Dennis* v. *United States* that he considered "criminal conspiracy a dragnet device capable of perversion into an instrument of injustice in the hands of a partisan or complacent judiciary." Nevertheless, since the law of conspiracy had "an established place in our system," he saw no reason not to apply it against concerted action claimed to undermine the government. Vinson's opinion for the Court in *Dennis* ignored the conspiracy issue, but Douglas, dissenting, did not. He wrote:

> Never until today has anyone seriously thought that the ancient law of conspiracy could constitutionally be used to turn speech into seditious conduct. . . . To make lawful speech unlawful because two men conceive it is to raise the law of conspiracy to appalling proportions.

The case against criminal charges for crimes of expression was also considered by the Court of Appeals for the First Circuit in reviewing the conviction of Dr. Spock and his codefendants. All three judges were disturbed by the conspiracy convictions and in fact reversed the jury findings of guilt for two of the four appellants. However, only one judge, Frank M. Coffin, rejected the punishment of political speech on the conspiracy theory as a violation of the First Amendment.[11]

[9] See "Conspiracy and the First Amendment," 79 YALE LAW JOURNAL 872 (1970); "Developments in the Law—Criminal Conspiracy," 72 HARVARD LAW REVIEW 920 (1959).

[10] *Iannelli* v. *United States* (1975) held that it is not double jeopardy to be convicted of conspiracy to violate a statute as well as the substantive offense of violating it.

[11] See *United States* v. *Spock* (1969); Thomas Church, Jr., "Conspiracy Doctrine and Speech Offenses: A Reexamination of *Yates* v. *United States* from the Perspective of *United States* v. *Spock*," 60 *Cornell Law Review* 569 (1975).

THE PUBLIC SERVICE AND SUBVERSION

An important motive of legislation or administrative action aimed at the Communist Party has been to keep its members out of public employment or other posts where they would be in a position to undertake subversive activities.

Loyalty Oaths

Both federal and state laws customarily require public employees to take some kind of oath of loyalty to the government. An oath denying membership in the Communist Party was first upheld by the Supreme Court in *Garner* v. *Board of Public Works* (1951), Justice Frankfurter saying: "In the context of our time, such membership is sufficiently relevant to effective and dependable government, and to the confidence of the electorate in its government."

However, the Court quickly imposed some limits on such oaths. In *Wieman* v. *Updegraff* (1952), the Court unanimously insisted that the mere fact of membership was not sufficient grounds for exclusion from the public service; it must be a "knowing" association.

By 1966 a majority of the Court was ready to go further, and *Elfbrandt* v. *Russell* apparently reversed the *Garner* decision, by striking down an Arizona loyalty-oath law which provided punishment for anyone taking the oath who was or later became a knowing member of an organization having for one of its purposes the overthrow of the government. Justice Douglas for a five-judge majority relied on the principle of the *Aptheker* case. To punish mere knowing membership was to adopt the rule of guilt by association; beyond knowing membership there also had to be a "specific intent" to further the illegal aims of the organization before punishment was justified.

Loyalty-oath statutes have also been invalidated on other grounds. In *Cramp* v. *Board of Public Instruction* (1961), a Florida act requiring state employees to swear that they had never lent their "aid, support, advice, counsel, or influence to the Communist Party" was held lacking in "terms susceptible to objective measurement" and so failed to inform what the state commanded or forbade. *Baggett* v. *Bullitt* (1964) involved two Washington provisions which required teachers to swear that they were not "subversive persons" and that they would "by precept and example promote respect for the flag . . . reverence for law and order and undivided allegiance to the government of the United States." The Court held these provisions "invalid on their face because their language is unduly vague, uncertain and broad."

In *Whitehill* v. *Elkins* (1967), the Court declared unconstitutional the Maryland law requiring state employees to swear they were not subversive persons which it earlier upheld per curiam in *Gerende* v. *Board of Supervisors* (1951). The *Gerende* decision was now distinguished on the ground that at that time the attorney general of the state had interpreted the law to apply only to persons attemping to alter the form of government by force or violence.

The net result of these decisions was to limit loyalty oaths to little more than pledges of support for the federal and state constitutions and to deflate the oath fad, which had been carried to ridiculous extremes. For example, a California constitutional provision required all individuals and organizations claiming exemption from state property taxes to file loyalty oaths; the Court voided it in *Speiser* v. *Randall*

(1958).[12] *Cole* v. *Richardson* (1972) did uphold an oath which, in addition to support for the Constitution, required a pledge to "oppose the overthrow of the government . . . by force, violence or by any illegal or unconstitutional method." But Burger's opinion implied that no one took these oaths seriously or literally. They imposed no obligation of "specific, positive action," but merely committed officials "to live by the constitutional processes of our system."

A very famous non-Communist oath, applying not to public officials but to labor union officers, was that required by the Labor Management Relations Act of 1947, better known as the Taft-Hartley Act. Section 9(h) of this act denied the protections and services of the act to any labor organization unless each of its officers filed an affidavit with the National Labor Relations Board "that he is not a member of the Communist Party or affiliated with such party, and that he does not believe in, and is not a member of or support any organization that believes in or teaches, the overthrow of the United States Government by force or by any illegal or unconstitutional methods." Here for the first time in this series of measures the Communist Party was definitely named.

In *American Communications Association* v. *Douds* (1950), the Supreme Court upheld the validity of the oath. The congressional purpose, according to Chief Justice Vinson, was to remove political strikes as an obstruction to interstate commerce. Congress had such power under the commerce clause unless results were achieved which were forbidden by other provisions of the Constitution. He agreed that political freedoms were limited by the statute because its effect was to exert "pressures upon labor unions to deny positions of leadership to certain persons who are identified by particular beliefs and political affiliations." Normally, beliefs and affiliations are "irrelevant to permissible subjects of government action," but that does not mean they are "never relevant." Here the Court conceived that beliefs and affiliations bore a reasonable relation to the apprehended evil. The persons identified by the statute did not cause damage by speech, and it was not their speech that the statute sought to restrain, but rather their use of force through the political strike. "Speech may be fought with speech. . . . But force may and must be met with force."

The Taft-Hartley oath was repealed in 1959. It had proved ineffective, since Communists were willing to take the oath, which meant that the only sanction was a perjury prosecution presenting serious difficulties of proof. Congress substituted a provision making it a crime for a member of the Communist Party to serve as an officer or employee of a labor union (73 Stat. 519, 536). In *United States* v. *Brown* (1965) the Court by a five to four vote held this provision unconstitutional as a bill of attainder.

Removal of Public Employees

The loyalty oath was supplemented in many jurisdictions by statutory programs for the removal of public employees on loyalty grounds. The New York law was upheld by the Court in *Adler* v. *Board of Education* (1952). This law required the Board of Regents to make, after notice and hearing, a listing of organizations which it found

---

[12] *Communist Party of Indiana* v. *Whitcomb* (1974) invalidated a loyalty oath for political parties to get on the ballot.

to advocate, advise, teach, or embrace the doctrine that the government should be overthrown by force or violence or any unlawful means. Membership of a schoolteacher in any such listed organization was "prima facie evidence for disqualification for appointment to or retention in" any school position, but before an individual was severed from or denied employment, there was to be a full hearing and the right of judicial review.

The Court upheld the law by a six to two vote. For the majority, Minton contended that the "guilt by association" point had been disposed of by the *Garner* opinion, and he added:

> We adhere to that case. A teacher works in a sensitive area in a schoolroom. There he shapes the attitude of young minds towards the society in which they live. In this, the state has a vital concern. . . . That the school authorities have the right and the duty to screen the officials, teachers, and employees as to their fitness to maintain the integrity of the schools as a part of ordered society, cannot be doubted. One's associates, past and present, as well as one's conduct, may properly be considered in determining fitness and loyalty. From time immemorial one's reputation has been determined in part by the company he keeps.

The *Adler* decision was eventually overruled by a five to four vote in *Keyishian* v. *Board of Regents* (1967), a case brought by professors in the New York State university system. Brennan for the majority disposed of *Adler* on the ground that the Court there had not considered charges that the statutory standards were too vague and uncertain in their application, and also because of intervening decisions holding that "mere membership" in the Communist Party could not be constitutionally penalized.

Another rather common state action has been the removal of public employees who refuse to give information about alleged subversive connections, whether by taking the Fifth Amendment before a legislative committee or by some other method. In three important cases the Court divided five to four on the constitutional aspects of such action. In the first, *Slochower* v. *Board of Higher Education of New York City* (1956), a Brooklyn College professor had taken the Fifth Amendment before a Senate committee on all questions covering his political associations before 1941. He was discharged under a provision of the New York charter that whenever an employee utilized the privilege against self-incrimination to avoid answering a question relating to his official conduct his employment tenure "shall terminate" and the office "shall be vacant." The Court majority, speaking through Justice Clark, held that the charter provision as interpreted here had converted the employee's claim of privilege "into a conclusive presumption of guilt. Since no inference of guilt was possible from the claim before the federal committee, the discharge falls of its own weight as wholly without support."

Justice Clark went on to express the view that Slochower had no "constitutional right" to his job, and that it would be perfectly proper for "the city authorities themselves to inquire into Slochower's fitness." This was precisely what happened in *Lerner* v. *Casey* (1958) and *Beilan* v. *Board of Public Education, School District of Philadelphia* (1958). Lerner was a New York subway conductor, Beilan a public school teacher. Lerner refused to tell New York City authorities whether he was a member of the Communist Party, and was dismissed as a person of "doubtful trust and reliability" because of his "lack of candor." Beilan refused to tell his superintendent whether he had held a certain position in the Communist Party in 1944, and later took the Fifth Amendemnt before a House committee; he was dismissed for "incompetency." The Court majority upheld the official action in both cases. Again, in *Nelson* v. *County of Los Angeles* (1960), the majority upheld a discharge for insubordination based on refusal to answer questions before the House Un-American Activities Committee, a decision which came very close to overruling *Slochower.*

A different type of removal action was held unconstitutional by the Court in *Shelton* v. *Tucker* (1960). An Arkansas statute required every teacher in the public schools and state colleges, as a condition of employment, to file annually a list of every organization to which he had belonged or contributed in the preceding five years. Justice Stewart for the majority agreed that the state had a right to investigate the competence and fitness of persons hired as teachers, but considered such an "unlimited and indiscriminate" inquiry a threat to associational freedom going "far beyond what might be justified in the exercise of the State's legitimate inquiry into the fitness and competency of its teachers."

The Federal Loyalty-Security Program

President Truman set up a loyalty program for federal employees in 1947, and President Eisenhower continued it in somewhat revised form in 1953. All employees and applicants for employment were required to undergo a loyalty check, in which the FBI assisted in an investigative role. The Department of Justice prepared a list of subversive organizations to help guide the decisions of agency loyalty boards. Hearings were held by these boards when damaging information was received concerning an employee or applicant, but some of the customary protections of the hearing procedure—particularly the right to be informed of the source of the charges and the right to confront the persons making the accusations—were not guaranteed in these proceedings.

The loyalty-security program was widely attacked as denying procedural due process. In *Joint Anti-Fascist Refugee Committee* v. *McGrath* (1951), the Court majority held that the Attorney General had not accorded necessary procedural protections to the organizations he labeled as subversive, the listing being made, as Justice Frankfurter said, "without notice, without disclosure of any reasons justifying it, without opportunity to meet the undisclosed evidence or suspicion on which designation may have been based, and without opportunity to establish affirmatively that the aims and acts of the organization are innocent."

On the more serious question of whether the hearings accorded individual civil servants met due process standards, the Court divided four to four in *Bailey* v. *Richardson* (1951). No one would contend that, in order to discharge a federal employee for inefficiency, his superiors should hold a quasi-judicial hearing and provide for judicial review of the decision. But removals under the loyalty-security program were not ordinary removals. A loyalty charge put an employee on trial not only for his job but for his reputation and his professional standing. Removal on loyalty grounds might make it impossible for him to secure any other employment for which he was fitted. He was condemned as a person unworthy of trust and confidence. These considerations convinced four members of the Court that loyalty hearings must meet full due process standards.

In several subsequent cases the Supreme Court considered aspects of the loyalty-security system, but largely avoided the constitutional issues.[13] However, in *Greene* v. *McElroy* (1959), which dealt with the industrial security program in effect for private plants doing work for the government that involved access to secret information, the Court did object strongly to loyalty hearings which "failed to comport with our traditional ideas of fair procedure."

As a consequence of the *Greene* decision President Eisenhower issued an executive order which significantly enlarged the right of accused security risks in industrial establishments to confront and cross-examine their accusers. Procedural protections in the loyalty hearings of government employees were also generally improved by the agencies involved.[14]

Admission to the Bar

The Supreme Court upheld the Illinois supreme court in denying admission to the bar to a conscientious objector in *In re Summers* (1945), but in *Konigsberg* v. *State Bar of California* (1957) it reversed a denial of admission on character grounds involving alleged connections with the Communist Party.[15] The California bar then gave the applicant another hearing and again refused him admission, this time specifically on the ground that his refusal to answer questions concerning possible Communist Party membership had obstructed a full investigation into his qualifications. The Court upheld this action in 1961 by a five to four vote, concluding that a committee can require a bar applicant "to provide unprivileged answers to questions having a substantial relevance to his qualifications."[16]

The Court again reversed itself by a five to four vote in two 1971 cases, *Baird* v. *State Bar of Arizona* and *In re Stolar*, both involving bar applicants who declined to answer questions concerning their beliefs about government and their possible affiliations with subversive organizations. Referring to such inquiries as "relics" of the McCarthy era, Justice Black held that "views and beliefs are immune from bar association inquisitions." However, in *Law Students Civil Rights Research Council* v. *Wadmond* (1971), the Court rejected by another five to four vote a contention that the "character and general fitness" requirement for admission to the New York bar was unconstitutional.

---

[13] *Peters* v. *Hobby* (1955); *Cole* v. *Young* (1956); *Service* v. *Dulles* (1957); *Taylor* v. *McElroy* (1959); *Vitarelli* v. *Seaton* (1959). See also *Harmon* v. *Brucker* (1958).

[14] But see *Cafeteria & Restaurant Workers Union* v. *McElroy* (1961). A useful general study is Ralph S. Brown, Jr., *Loyalty and Security: Employment Tests in the United States* (New Haven, Conn.: Yale University Press, 1958).

[15] The same position was taken in *Schware* v. *New Mexico Board of Bar Examiners* (1957).

[16] The Court reached the same result in *In re Anastaplo* (1961). For an account of the *Anastaplo* case by the protagonist, see George Anastaplo, *The Constitutionalist: Notes on the First Amendment* (Dallas, Tex.: Southern Methodist University Press, 1971), Appendix F.

THE NAACP AND THE POOR

Aside from the Communist Party, the only organization whose associational rights have been seriously litigated before the Supreme Court is the NAACP. After the *Brown* decision in 1954, the activities of the NAACP in seeking to promote school desegregation aroused great hostility in most of the Southern states. Its members were subjected to economic coercion and often to physical violence. There were also many efforts through legislation and court action to hamper or terminate the work of the organization.

Alabama, like other states, has a statute requiring out-of-state corporations to register and meet certain requirements before doing business in the state. The NAACP, organized under the laws of New York, had a regional office in Alabama, but did not comply with the statute, from which it considered itself exempt. After 1954 the organization was particularly active in the state seeking enforcement of the Supreme Court's ruling against racial segregation in the public schools. In retaliation Alabama officials brought court action in 1956 to enjoin the association from conducting business in the state, in the course of which the organization was ordered to produce its records, including names and addresses of all members in Alabama. The association filed the qualifying forms required by statute and produced all records requested except the membership lists, the disclosure of which it contended the state could not constitutionally compel. For this failure the organization was held in contempt and fined $100,000.

The Supreme Court ruled in *NAACP* v. *Alabama* (1958) that compelled disclosure of the membership lists would abridge the rights of members to engage in lawful association in support of their common beliefs. For the association was able to make

> . . . an uncontroverted showing that on past occasions revelation of the identity of its rank-and-file members has exposed these members to economic reprisal, loss of employment, threat of physical coercion, and other manifestations of public hostility. . . . Under these circumstances, we think it apparent that compelled disclosure of . . . membership is likely to affect adversely the ability of petitioner and its members to pursue their collective effort to foster beliefs which they admittedly have the right to advocate, in that it may induce members to withdraw from the Association and dissuade others from joining it because of fear of exposure of their beliefs shown through their associations and of the consequences of this exposure.

The Court had to deal with an embarrassing precedent, *Bryant* v. *Zimmerman* (1928), which had upheld, as applied to the Ku Klux Klan, a New York law requiring disclosure of membership lists. But the 1928 ruling had stressed the nature of Klan activities, involving unlawful intimidation and violence, which the Court contrasted with the lawful nature of NAACP activities.[17]

The NAACP has concentrated much of its effort on court suits to compel desegregation, and here also it has been subjected to pressure. A Virginia law, typical of those in many other states, forbids the stirring up of litigation or the

[17] For subsequent developments in this case, see *NAACP* v. *Alabama* (1964).

improper solicitation of legal business. This legislation was aimed at "ambulance chasing" and other unethical legal practices, but because the NAACP admittedly seeks out test cases on which it can go to court, it was accused of violating the statute in Virginia.

In *NAACP* v. *Button* (1963) the Supreme Court upheld the association's litigation procedures, and in the decision recognized litigation as "a form of political expression." The Court said that "in the context of NAACP objectives, litigation is not a technique of resolving private differences; it is a means of achieving the lawful objectives of equality of treatment by all government, federal, state, and local, for the members of the Negro community in this country." Indeed, "for such a group, association for litigation may be the most effective form of political association."[18]

Finally, note may be taken of the recognition of associational rights of the poor in *U.S. Department of Agriculture* v. *Moreno* (1973). A 1971 amendment to the Food Stamp Act rendered ineligible any household containing an individual unrelated to any other member of the household. The legislative history of the amendment clearly showed that the intention was to prevent "hippie communes" from securing food stamps. Brennan's opinion for the Court held the amendment unconstitutional, on equal protection grounds, as a classification not rationally related to any legitimate governmental interest. But Douglas, concurring, saw this as an associational issue:

> As the facts of this case show, the poor are congregating in households where they can better meet the adversities of poverty. This banding together is an expression of the right of freedom of association that is very deep in our traditions.

---

[18] In *Brotherhood of Railroad Trainmen* v. *Virginia ex rel. Virginia State Bar* (1964) and *United Mine Workers* v. *Illinois State Bar Assn.* (1967), the Court followed the *Button* case in upholding forms of group legal service to organization members.

Chapter 24

Religious Freedom
and Establishment

Freedom to worship God according to the dictates of individual conscience was one of the dominant motives in the founding of the American Colonies, and it might have been expected that provisions guaranteeing that right would have an important place in the Constitution. In fact, the Founders left the original Constitution almost devoid of language on the relationships of government and religion, thus conforming with their general practice in the civil liberties field. The sole exception was the provision of Article VI that "no religious test shall ever be required as a qualification to any office or public trust under the United States." Even this language was protested by Roger Sherman of Connecticut, who thought prohibition of religious tests for office was unnecessary, "the prevailing liberality being a sufficient security against such tests."

Actually, the "prevailing liberality" had not kept religious tests from being rather common in the Colonies and states. The early constitutions of several states disfranchised or excluded from office Catholics, Jews, and nonbelievers. In Massachusetts and Maryland, the office of governor was closed to all except Christians. In four more states, the governor had to be a Protestant. New York and Virginia were exceptional in taking no account of religious opinion for officeholding.

The adoption of the First Amendment repaired the omissions of the original

Constitution on religious freedom by the addition of the following language: "Congress shall make no law respecting an establishment of religion, or prohibiting the free exercise thereof." The states were thus specifically excluded from the ambit of the First Amendment, though many states had similar provisions in their own constitutions. In 1940, however, the Supreme Court held that the free exercise clause in the First Amendment had been made applicable to the states by the Fourteenth Amendment's guarantee of "liberty." This step was a logical sequence to the Court's ruling in the 1925 *Gitlow* decision applying the free speech and press provisions of the First Amendment to the states. Clearly, freedom to propagate religious convictions is hardly distinguishable from free speech generally, and the Supreme Court so held in *Cantwell* v. *Connecticut*.[1]

It was not until 1947, in *Everson* v. *Board of Education of Ewing Township,* that the Supreme Court had occasion to deal with the state-religion relationships in an establishment context. But when it did so, it assumed without discussion that the establishment provision of the First Amendment was just as binding on the states as the freedom of religion language.

Judicial interpretation of the free exercise and establishment principles has been affected by the differences in their developmental history. The principle of religious freedom or toleration was the older and the more firmly grounded in 1791. The tragic results of religious persecution and discrimination, of punishment for matters of conscience and belief, had long been demonstrated in England and on the continent by the time of the founding of the American nation, and the theoretical and practical case for toleration was well developed in English writing.

The establishment provision, on the other hand, was in flat contradiction to the English practice then current, and some variety of establishment was found in several of the American states at the time the Constitution was adopted. Thus the principle of separation of church and state was an American invention whose application remained to be worked out in practice.[2]

FREE EXERCISE OF RELIGION

The two religion clauses are actually so interrelated that it is difficult to discuss them separately. Free exercise demands that the state avoid coercion with respect to religious beliefs and activities, and there is little overt or intentional state discrimination of this kind at the present time. But many government programs with purely secular purposes, such as compulsory education or public assistance, have coercive features which some religions or religiously motivated individuals may find objectionable. Yet if the state makes exceptions to take account of religious objections, it

[1] Six years earlier, in *Hamilton* v. *Board of Regents* (1934), Justice Cardozo had anticipated this ruling by writing in a concurring opinion: "I assume for present purposes that the religious liberty protected by the First Amendment against invasion by the nation is protected by the Fourteenth Amendment against invasion by the states."
[2] See generally Richard E. Morgan, *The Supreme Court and Religion* (New York: The Free Press, 1972); David Fellman, *Religion in American Public Law* (Boston: Boston University Press, 1965); Philip B. Kurland, *Religion and the Law* (Chicago: Aldine Publishing Co., 1962); Leo Pfeffer, *God, Caesar and the Constitution: The Court as Referee of Church-State Confrontation* (Boston: Beacon Press, 1975).

may then be viewed as giving positive assistance to religion in violation of the establishment clause. The problem is that too much coercion may deny free exercise, while exemption from coercion in response to religious objections may be favoritism amounting to establishment.

Free Exercise and Freedom of Expression

Free exercise of religion is closely related to freedom of expression generally, and it is natural that principles from the broader field can be used, sometimes without further refinement, to dispose of free exercise issues. In fact, one of the most important actions ever taken by the Supreme Court to guarantee free exercise of religion did not even rely on First Amendment principles. This was the case of *Pierce* v. *Society of Sisters* (1925), in which a Catholic religious order sued to test the constitutionality of an Oregon law requiring all children to attend only public schools for the first eight grades. In upholding the constitutional right of children to attend nonpublic schools where religious education could be provided, the Court struck down the law simply as an interference with the "business and property" of private and parochial schools.

It is possible for other constitutional provisions to be invoked to protect free exercise. For example, in *Niemotko* v. *Maryland* (1951) some Jehovah's Witnesses were arrested for making proselyting speeches in a public park without having secured a permit to do so. The Court held that permission had been denied because the city officials disliked the Witnesses and their views, and consequently the convictions violated the equal protection clause. Again, *Lovell* v. *Griffin* (1938) protected the right of Jehovah's Witnesses to sell the sect's literature from door to door without a permit, on free press grounds. *Saia* v. *New York* (1948) upheld the right of a Jehovah's Witnesses preacher to use a sound truck in a public park for his sermons, on free speech reasoning.

Another important principle which carries over from the speech field is the ban on prior restraint. In *Cantwell* v. *Connecticut* (1940), the Court held that a state statute requiring approval of a county official for any person to solicit from house to house for religious or philanthropic causes amounted to "a censorship of religion." *Murdock* v. *Pennsylvania* (1943) ruled that municipal license fees on transient merchants or book agents could not be applied to Jehovah's Witnesses who went from door-to-door offering religious tracts for sale. A New York ordinance requiring a police permit for public worship meetings on city streets was invalidated in *Kunz* v. *New York* (1951).

By reliance on general free expression principles to handle religious freedom claims, the Court has to that extent avoided the necessity of developing any special doctrinal content or tests for enforcement of the free exercise clause. It has assumed that the right to distribute religious pamphlets is no different from the right to distribute pamphlets dealing with other kinds of ideas. It has assumed that religious meetings in public parks deserve the same claim to protection as political rallies.

There are some obvious reasons for equating political and religious freedoms. If religious freedom is not the same as political freedom, then it must enjoy either less or more protection. The first alternative would result in discrimination against religious groups, which is not compatible with the free exercise clause. The second would amount to preference for religious freedom over general speech and press claims, and would raise possible establishment problems. This is the dilemma the Court must face when and if it undertakes to discuss religious freedom as a value separate from the general context of other civil liberties.[3]

The Secular Regulation Rule

The most general principle that has been developed to achieve neutrality of the state with respect to religion is the secular regulation rule. This rule holds that there is no constitutional right to an exemption, on free exercise of religion grounds, from the compulsion of general regulations dealing with nonreligious matters.

The secular regulation rule is based on the distinction between belief and action. Religious beliefs admittedly must have absolute protection, but actions, even though purporting to be taken for religious reasons or as part of religious observances, must conform with the regulations established by the community to protect public order, health, welfare, and morals. This interpretation of the free exercise clause can be traced back to Jefferson who, in a letter to the Danbury Baptists, praised the religion clauses of the First Amendment as permitting "the legislative powers of the government [to] reach actions only, and not opinions. . . ." He saw no interference with natural rights, because the individual "has no natural right in opposition to his social duties."[4]

Jefferson was too optimistic. Experience has shown only too clearly that religious beliefs often require, or are used to justify, unorthodox, bizarre, or even dangerous kinds of practices ranging all the way from polygamy to use of drugs and snake handling. De Tocqueville referred to the large number of "strange sects" in the United States, and observed that "religious insanity is very common."[5]

A regulation which is alleged to impinge on religious belief can be challenged under the secular regulation rule on two grounds: (1) that the regulation is not reasonably related to a valid secular purpose and (2) that there is a religious discrimination on the face of the statute or regulation.

The secular regulation rule was first developed and applied in dealing with the Mormon practice of polygamy. A congressional statute had made polygamy illegal in the territories of the United States, and in *Reynolds* v. *United States* (1878) the Court upheld the constitutionality of the statute against the Mormon contention that polygamy was required by their religion and that consequently punishing polygamy would deny them the free exercise of their religion. The Court thought the situation was exactly the reverse. Since a law against polygamy in the territories was clearly within the constitutional powers of Congress as a general secular regulation, the Mormons were actually asking for favored treatment from the law, namely,

---

[3] See Donald A. Giannella, "Religious Liberty, Nonestablishment, and Doctrinal Development: Part I. The Religious Liberty Guarantee," 80 HARVARD LAW REVIEW 1381 (1967).

[4] Quoted in *Reynolds* v. *United States* (1878).

[5] Alexis de Tocqueville, *Democracy in America* (New York: Alfred A. Knopf, Inc., 1948), vol. 2, p. 134, note 19. In *Pack* v. *Tennessee ex rel. Swann* (1976) snake handling and the drinking of poison in a religious ritual were enjoined as a public nuisance.

exemption from a statute which would be enforced on all others whose religious principles did not include polygamy.

Compulsory vaccination for smallpox was resisted, sometimes on religious grounds, but in *Jacobson* v. *Massachusetts* (1905) the Court upheld the legislation as a secular regulation reasonably in accord "with the common belief and . . . maintained by high medical authority."

The resistance of Jehovah's Witnesses to the compulsory flag salute in the public schools presented the Supreme Court with a particularly perplexing secular regulation issue. The Witnesses instruct their children that saluting the flag constitutes worship of a "graven image," and is contrary to Bible teaching. The conflict in conscience thus set up in schools requiring the salute was brought to the Supreme Court in *Minersville School District* v. *Gobitis* (1940), where the Court decided, with only Justice Stone dissenting, that the compulsory flag salute did not infringe the constitutional rights of the protesting children.

Justice Frankfurter argued that this was "legislation of general scope not directed against doctrinal loyalties of particular sects." The free exercise clause did not, he said, relieve the individual from obedience to a general law not aimed at the promotion or restriction of religious beliefs. The mere possession of religious convictions which contradict the relevant concerns of a political society does not relieve the citizen from the discharge of political responsibilities. The only question was whether a school board was justified in thinking that requiring the flag salute would help to further legitimate educational ends, and Frankfurter did not see how the Supreme Court could deny that the school board might legitimately hold such a view.

Justice Frankfurter's position was thus that the state had a constitutional right to compel all school children to salute the flag. There was no discrimination against those who had religious scruples against this ceremony. In fact, as in the *Reynolds* case, if their religious scruples were regarded as exempting them from the exercise, they would be receiving preference because of their religion over all other students who had no such scruples.

The *Gobitis* decision unleashed a wave of persecution against the Witnesses, and the ruling was rather generally condemned in the press.[6] Justice Stone, the sole dissenter, accepted religious objections as a valid ground for refusing to salute the flag. He thought that, while voluntary expressions of loyalty might promote national unity, compulsory exercises by children in violation of their own and their parents' religious convictions were not so important a method of promoting national unity as to override the constitutional guarantee of free exercise.

Three years later, *West Virginia State Board of Education* v. *Barnette* (1943) accomplished the important result of reversing the *Gobitis* holding while at the same time avoiding Stone's solution of religious preference. Justice Jackson for the new majority stated the issue as whether any child, regardless of religious belief, could be compelled to engage in a compulsory flag-salute exercise. He answered: "We think the action of the local authorities in compelling the flag salute and pledge tran-

---

[6] David R. Manwaring, *Render unto Caesar: The Flag-Salute Controversy* (Chicago: The University of Chicago Press, 1962).

scends constitutional limitations on their power and invades the sphere of intellect and spirit which it is the purpose of the First Amendment . . . to reserve from all official control." Since the state could not compel *any* student to engage in the flag salute, there was no need to develop a justification for giving preferential treatment to particular religious groups.

Prince v. *Massachusetts* (1944) involved a state law forbidding boys under twelve and girls under eighteen from selling newspapers on the street. A nine-year old girl, accompanied by her aunt, who was a Jehovah's Witness, sold literature of the Witnesses on downtown streetcorners at night. The Court, by a vote of five to four, upheld the statute as reasonable and nondiscriminatory. Propagandizing activities on the public streets were thought likely to result in the same kinds of problems "whether in religious, political or other matters," and Massachusetts was justified in concluding that an absolute prohibition of involvement of children was necessary to accomplish the state's purpose.

Justice Murphy, one of the dissenters, did not doubt the right of the state to have general child welfare regulations, but he insisted that when they infringed on a religious exercise, then there had to be a grave, immediate, and substantial danger as justification. He could see no such dangers in this situation. He thought that the evils a legislature might normally envisage with children on the streets would not be present when there was a religious motivation involved.

Various state decisions have upheld laws forbidding commercial fortune-telling when applied to palm reading as a religious practice, or laws prohibiting the handling of snakes in religious services. Faith healers cannot use religious liberty as a defense in prosecutions for the unlicensed practice of medicine. In *United States* v. *Ballard* (1944) the Court held that a cult leader could be prosecuted for mail fraud, provided the jury was not allowed to pass on the truth of the religious claims he made but only his good faith in professing to believe them.

Alternatives to the Neutrality Principle

While the secular regulation rule is appealing in its simplicity and apparent even-handedness, in application it may prove senselessly harsh, failing to take into account the impact of regulations on the religious life of individuals or groups or the relative importance of the public purpose served by the regulation. A significant recognition of the undesirability of such rigidity occurrred in 1961, when the secular regulation rule was applied to uphold Sunday closing laws, but with a qualification which was to result in a substantial modification in the Court's subsequent attitude on free exercise problems. Two of the *Sunday Closing Cases, Gallagher* v. *Crown Kosher Super Market* and *Braunfeld* v. *Brown,* involved challenges to Sunday closing laws in two states by Orthodox Jewish merchants who contended that, since their religion required that they close their shops on Saturday, a Sunday closing law limited them to a five-day work week and was a restraint of the free exercise of their religion.

Two justices agreed with this position. Justice Stewart thought that the state could not constitutionally compel "an Orthodox Jew to choose between his religious faith and his economic survival." Justice Douglas felt that when a state uses its coercive powers "to compel minorities to observe a second Sabbath, not their own," the state was aiding and preferring one religion over another, contrary to the Constitution.

The Court majority, however, speaking through Chief Justice Warren, upheld the Sunday closing laws as secular regulations. While they had admittedly been religious in their origin, the Court regarded them now as purely an effective device for providing a uniform day of rest. Moreover, the laws were secular regulations which did not make any religious activity unlawful, merely more expensive.

However, Warren's opinion made an important addition to the secular regulation rule. This is the key sentence: "If the State regulates conduct by enacting a general law within its power, the purpose and effect of which is to advance the State's secular goals, the statute is valid despite its indirect burden on religious observances *unless the State may accomplish its purpose by means which do not impose such a burden.*" (Italics added.) This is substantially a new test for secular regulations, which now will be upheld against claims of interference with free exercise only if there appear to be no practicable alternative means whereby the legislative purpose can be accomplished. Applying the test in *Braunfeld,* the Chief Justice evaluated the availability of alternative means for achieving the secular goal of a common day of rest, and found none that seemed practicable.

The potentialties of this new test became apparent when in *Sherbert* v. *Verner* (1963) its effect was to invalidate a state law. A Seventh Day Adventist textile worker was discharged for refusal to work on Saturday, and no other work was available in the area for one who would not work on Saturday. She filed a claim for unemployment compensation, which was denied on the ground that her refusal to accept suitable work meant that she was not "available for work" as required by statute.

Justice Brennan for the Court ruled that this denial of benefits was a burden on the free exercise of the woman's religion. Admittedly the law had a valid secular purpose. But the pressure on her to violate her Sabbath was as much an infringement on the free exercise of her religion as a fine imposed for Saturday worship. Sunday observers are protected from having to make such a choice. The opinion does not rely on this claim of discrimination, however. It rests rather on the ground that there is an available alternative here which will preserve the free exercise of religion—namely, to grant exemption from the statute for refusal to work for religious reasons. This requirement that a state must grant preference to religious reasons for refusing to work over nonreligious reasons disturbed Justices Harlan and White, dissenting, who would have applied the traditional secular regulation rule.[7]

The *Sherbert* holding was subsequently applied in state courts to overturn the conviction of Navajo members of the Native American Church for using peyote in their religious ceremonies;[8] to free a woman from a contempt sentence for refusal on religious grounds to serve on a jury;[9] and to hold that children could not be compelled to stand while the national anthem was being played in school.[10]

---

[7] The Saturday employment issue was raised again in *Parker Seal Co.* v. *Cummins* (1976).
[8] *People* v. *Woody* (1964).
[9] *In re Jenison* (1963).
[10] *Sheldon* v. *Fannin* (1963).

In addition to the "less drastic means" test, the secular regulation rule may be ameliorated by judicial balancing of interests. *Wisconsin* v. *Yoder* (1972) presented a classic confrontation between state compulsory education laws and the adamant insistence of the Old Order Amish that their children cease public school attendance after the eighth grade. Further education, they contended, was unnecessary for the simple agricultural life led by the sect and would, in fact, expose the children to secular influences imperilling their religious values. Experience in several states demonstrated that the Amish would not yield on their principles, no matter how much coercion was applied.

The Court concluded, almost unanimously (Douglas was in partial dissent) that enforcement of the law would deny free exercise of the Amish religion and that there was no state interest of sufficient magnitude to override their claims for protection. The Amish beliefs were not matters of personal preference but "of deep religious conviction, shared by an organized group, and intimately related to daily living," pervading and determining "virtually their entire way of life." Secondary schooling, by exposing Amish children to "worldly influences" contrary to their beliefs, would substantially interfere with their religious development and their "integration into the way of life of the Amish faith community at the crucial adolescent state of development."

An earlier instance of judicial recognition of religious claims occurred in *Murdock* v. *Pennsylvania* (1943), where the Court held that Jehovah's Witnesses' practice of their religion by offering their literature for sale from door to door did not subject them to municipal license taxes. "The hand distribution of religious tracts is an age-old form of missionary evangelism," said Justice Douglas, and "selling" the literature to defray expenses did not make it a commercial operation.[11]

Congress as well as the Court has authorized religiously motivated exceptions to secular regulations, most notably in connection with conscientious objection to military service.[12] Every American conscription law has granted exemption from military service to conscientious objectors who met the statutory definition. The Draft Act of 1917 gave exemption to objectors affiliated with a "well-recognized religious sect or organization . . . whose existing creed or principles [forbid] its members to participate in war in any form." This limitation of exemption to members of particular sects seems clearly invalid as a discrimination against other religions, but in fact the Secretary of War ruled that "personal scruples against war" would be considered as constituting conscientious objection.[13]

In adopting the 1940 Selective Training and Service Act Congress made it unnecessary to belong to a pacifist religious sect if the claimant's own opposition to

---

[11] *Murdock* reversed the Court's holding in *Jones* v. *Opelika* (1942), decided only a year earlier.

[12] Decisions denying naturalization to alien conscientious objectors unwilling to swear that they would defend the United States by force of arms—*United States* v. *Schwimmer* (1929), *United States* v. *Macintosh* (1931), *United States* v. *Bland* (1931)—were reversed in *Girouard* v. *United States* (1946).

[13] The general constitutionality of the draft act was upheld in *Arver* v. *United States (Selective Draft Law Cases)* (1918).

war was based on "religious training and belief." This phrase was defined in the 1948 act as follows: ". . . an individual's belief in a relation to a Supreme Being involving duties superior to those arising from any human relation, but [not including] essentially political, sociological, or philosophical views or a merely personal moral code."

The Supreme Court construed this language in *United States* v. *Seeger* (1965). The case involved three young men, none of whom was a member of an orthodox religious group or willing to declare a belief in a Supreme Being. However, none was "an avowedly irreligious person or . . . an atheist." All were found by the Court to have a sincere and meaningful belief which occupied a place in their lives "parallel to that filled by the orthodox belief in God." The Court interpreted the statutory phrase "Supreme Being" as meaning not the orthodox God but a "broader concept of a power or being, or a faith, 'to which all else is subordinate or upon which all else is ultimately dependent.' " The language denying the rights of conscientious objection based upon a "merely personal moral code" meant "a moral code which is not only personal but which is the sole basis for the registrant's belief and is in no way related to a Supreme Being."

Following *Seeger* Congress amended the statute to delete the reference to a "Supreme Being" but continued to provide that "religious training and belief" did not include "essentially political, sociological or philosophical views, or merely personal moral code." In *Welsh* v. *United States* (1970) the registrant was explicit in denying that his views were religiously based. But Justice Black for the Court read Welsh's statement of beliefs against the taking of life as being held "with the strength of more traditional religious convictions" and interpreted the statute as exempting "from military service all those whose consciences, spurred by deeply held moral, ethical, or religious beliefs, would give them no rest or peace if they allowed themselves to become a part of an instrument of war."

While Harlan concurred in the result, he believed that Black had "performed a lobotomy" on the act by reading out of it the theistic religious requirement which Congress had clearly intended as a condition for exemption. However, such a theistic basis of classification seemed to Harlan contrary to the establishment clause, and so, rather confusingly, he concurred in Black's test, "not as a matter of statutory construction, but as a touchstone for salvaging a congressional policy of long standing that would otherwise have to be nullified." White, Burger, and Stewart dissented.[14]

While the Court finessed the religious preference dilemma in *Welsh*, other cases in which exemption from secular rules was granted to religious devotees came perilously close to unconstitutional favoritism to religion. As Justice Frankfurter protested in the Second Flag Salute case: "The validity of secular laws cannot be measured by their conformity to religious doctrines. It is only in a theocratic state that ecclesiastical doctrines measure legal right or wrong."

Moreover, recognition of the right of religious claimants to override secular

---

[14] "The Legal Relationship of Conscience to Religion: Refusals to Bear Arms," 38 UNIVERSITY OF CHICAGO LAW REVIEW 583 (1971).

regulations inescapably involves determining what religion is. To carry out a policy of preference for religious freedom, the Supreme Court must either define religion itself, or allow groups and individuals to make their own definitions of religion.

The Court's initial tendency was to undertake its own definition of religion, as was demonstrated in the Mormon cases. In *Davis* v. *Beason* (1890) the territory of Idaho had made it a prerequisite to exercise of the franchise that the voter take an oath he was not a member of any organization which advised or practiced the "crime of bigamy or polygamy." Davis, a Mormon, was denied the right to vote. Since he was not himself a polygamist, he had lost the franchise because of his belief in polygamy as expressed in his church membership. To uphold the statute the Court had to deny that polygamy could be a religious belief, and to do this it sought to develop an objective test or definition of religion: "The term 'religion' has reference to one's views of his relations to his Creator, and to the obligations they impose of reverence for his being and character, and of obedience to his will." Religious liberty permits each individual "to entertain such notions respecting his relations to his Maker and the duties they impose as may be approved by his judgment and conscience, and to exhibit his sentiments in such form of worship as he may think proper, not injurious to the equal rights of others."

On the basis of this definition, the Court somehow concluded that polygamy could not be "a tenet of religion." Rather it was, by "the general consent of the Christian world in modern times," a crime, and "crime is not the less odious because sanctioned by what any particular sect may designate as religion." Similarly in *Church of Jesus Christ of Latter-day Saints* v. *United States* (1890) the Court found that the Mormon Church could not be considered a religious corporation, because one of its principal tenets, polygamy, was merely supposed or imagined to be religious. As a parallel, the Court pointed to the Thugs of India, who "imagined that their belief in the right of assassination was a religious belief; but their thinking so did not make it so."

More recently, however, the Court has tended to allow groups and individuals to define religion for themselves, and to recognize opinion and action religiously motivated in good faith as constitutionally protected, even though this means accepting views which seem, as Justice Douglas said in the *Ballard* case, "incredible, if not preposterous, to most people." In *Murdock* v. *Pennsylvania,* as we have seen, the Court allowed Jehovah's Witnesses to decide for themselves that selling their literature from door to door was part of their religion. In *Fowler* v. *Rhode Island* (1953) the Court said: "It is no business of courts to say that what is a religious practice or activity for one group is not religion under the protection of the First Amendment."

Black Muslim prison inmates were initially denied the right to practice their religion in prison. The reasons given by prison administrators were that the sect was not a religion but rather a political and racist movement and that their preachings of hatred for white people would be dangerous in prison. But in *Cooper* v. *Pate* (1963), the Supreme Court reversed the refusal of a lower court to hear the complaint of a Black Muslim that he was denied access to religious publications and certain other privileges because of his religious beliefs. Subsequent decisions have established that Muslims must be allowed to have the Koran, to be visited by Islamic ministers, and to hold religious services. Similar rights for Buddhists were recognized in *Cruz* v. *Beto* (1972), and American Indian prisoners belonging to the Native American Church have won the right to wear their hair longer than prison rules normally allow.[15] But the Church of the New Song, founded in 1970 by two inmates of the Atlanta federal prison, whose religious observances required sherry and steak and monthly fruit baskets and movies, was less successful in winning recognition as a religion.

Theism is coming to be regarded as no longer a necessary element in religion. In *Torcaso* v. *Watkins* (1961), a Maryland requirement of a "declaration of belief in the existence of God" as a qualification for public office in the state was declared unconstitutional by a unanimous Court, as an invasion of "freedom of belief and religion." Government may not "aid those religions based on a belief in the existence of God as against those religions founded on different beliefs."

Denial of Religious Claims

In spite of the new permissiveness, the Supreme Court does, of course, reserve the right to disallow claims for religious status. In *Gillette* v. *United States* (1971), the Court declined to stretch the statutory exemption for conscientious objectors to cover draftees who did not object to all wars but only to particular wars (specifically, the war in Vietnam). While the moral case against participation in "unjust wars" has an ancient and honorable lineage in religious thought,[16] the Court could not reconcile it with the express statutory command that exemption be based only on opposition "to participation in war in any form."

Similarly, *Johnson* v. *Robison* (1974) rejected the claim that statutory denial of veterans' educational benefits to conscientious objectors who had performed alternate civilian service violated religious freedom and equal protection. The American Friends Service Committee and two of its employees failed in their effort to secure refund, as a method of bearing witness to their religious opposition to participation in war in any form, of that part of their taxes used for military purposes.[17]

The refusal of Jehovah's Witnesses to permit blood transfusions because of the Biblical injunction against "eating blood" has created tragic dilemmas. There have been many cases where, because the patient or family members refused consent, hospital authorities or doctors have sought court orders authorizing transfusions. If a child is involved (even an unborn child[18]), the courts have invariably ordered the transfusion. With adults, the problem is more difficult, but again most courts have acted on the theory that there is no constitutional right to die and that attempted suicide is a crime. If there are minor children who might become charges of the state in case of the death of a parent, that is a further consideration.

The Supreme Court has regularly denied certiorari in cases raising this issue.[19]

[15] The U.S. Army has recognized the right of members of the Sikh religion to wear turbans and have long hair and beards. *The New York Times,* January 8, 1974.

[16] See John A. Rohr, *Prophets without Honor: Public Policy and the Selective Conscientious Objector* (Nashville, Tenn.: The Abingdon Press, 1971).

[17] *United States* v. *American Friends Service Committee* (1974).

[18] *Raleigh Fitkin–Paul Morgan Memorial Hospital* v. *Anderson* (1964).

[19] For example, *State* v. *Perricone* (1962), *George* v. *United States* (1966).

Only one state supreme court appears to have held that the state should not intervene. *In re Brooks' Estate* (1965) was an Illinois case where an adult woman without minor children was dying and the hospital obtained a court order appointing a conservator who approved the transfusion, but she died in spite of it. The state supreme court, hearing the case after her death, ordered the appointment expunged on the ground that her refusal had created no clear and present danger and that the order had interfered with her basic constitutional rights.

The opposing view, taken by most courts, is exemplified by the New Jersey supreme court in *John F. Kennedy Memorial Hospital* v. *Heston* (1971), involving a twenty-two-year-old unmarried woman. The court upheld the court-ordered transfusion, suggesting that the hospital might have been guilty of malpractice had it failed to use established medical procedures and that it was reasonable to resolve the issue by permitting the hospital and staff "to pursue their functions according to their professional standards."[20]

An emerging issue of the deepest moral and religious significance is whether persons who have suffered irreversible brain damage should be kept alive by massive artificial means. In 1975 a suit filed in the New Jersey courts by the parents of Karen Ann Quinlan, asking that she be permitted to "die with dignity," stimulated national consideration of the right to die. On the one hand, it is argued that a failure to use all available means to preserve life amounts to murder and opens the door to "mercy killings." On the other hand, there is the alarming prospect of hospitals and nursing homes filling up with machine-sustained organisms devoid of all human qualities whose "life" is maintained by a huge commitment of societal resources.

The Liberty of Churches

While courts will become involved in the internal affairs of churches only with the greatest reluctance, there are disputes, particularly those involving property rights, which they cannot avoid. State courts have accepted suits brought by individuals for reinstatement of membership, suits filed for reinstatement of a pastor or to prevent a discharged pastor from conducting services, cases involving the right of a church to buy and sell property, and cases concerning burial rights. In suits between competing factions of a local congregation, the general rule is that the will of the majority prevails, and courts will limit their inquiry to determining which is the majority. But where hierarchical or centrally organized churches are involved, the courts will follow the decision of the proper institutional authority.[21]

ESTABLISHMENT OF RELIGION

There have been two general views as to the intention of the establishment clause. One position holds that it was meant to outlaw only the kind of establishment that existed in Europe in 1791, namely, an official, publicly supported church. This view contends that the evil in establishment is the preferential treatment of one religion

[20] See also *Application of President and Directors of Georgetown College* (1964); John J. Paris, "Compulsory Medical Treatment and Religious Freedom," 10 *University of San Francisco Law Review* 1 (1975).
[21] See *Watson* v. *Jones* (1872), *Kedroff* v. *St. Nicholas Cathedral of Russian Orthodox Church* (1952), and *Kreshik* v. *St. Nicholas Cathedral* (1960); also *Serbian Eastern Orthodox Diocese* v. *Milivojevich* (1976).

over others. It argues that the establishment clause does not forbid state contacts with religion or state support of religious activities so long as all religions are treated equally and no discrimination is involved.

The other view contends that establishment refers to any government support of or connection with religion. This position holds that the no-establishment principle requires the complete separation of church and state, and forbids any public financial support to religious institutions, even if made available on a nonpreferential basis. The Supreme Court has consistently espoused this second position, and the supporting arguments for this interpretation can be summarized briefly.

First there is the evidence supplied by the framing of the First Amendment. Congress considered and rejected language that would clearly have adopted the first position stated above. In the Senate three motions, all aimed directly and narrowly against laws preferring one "sect" or "denomination" over others, were defeated. However, the Senate then adopted another comparatively narrow ban: "Congress shall make no law establishing articles of faith or a mode of worship." The House, which had previously adopted broad prohibitory language against laws "establishing religion," rejected the Senate's version. A conference committee of the two houses, including James Madison as chairman of the House conferees, abandoned the Senate proposal and drafted the present language which forbids "an establishment of religion" rather than merely an established church.

Second, the phrase "establishment of religion" must be given the meaning that it had in the United States in 1791, rather than its European connotation. In America there was no establishment of a single church, as in England. Four states had never adopted any establishment practices. Three had abolished their establishments during the Revolution. The remaining six states—Massachusetts, New Hampshire, Connecticut, Maryland, South Carolina, and Georgia—changed to comprehensive or "multiple" establishments. That is, aid was provided to all churches in each state on a nonpreferential basis, except that the establishment was limited to churches of the Protestant religion in three states and to those of the Christian religion in the other three states. Since there were almost no Catholics in the first group of states, and very few Jews in any state, this meant that the multiple establishment practices included every religious group with enough members to form a church. It was this nonpreferential assistance to organized churches that constituted "establishment of religion" in 1791, and it was this practice that the amendment forbade Congress to adopt.

Third, Jefferson and Madison were the dominant figures in developing the constitutional policy on establishment, and they both espoused strict separation of church and state. A bill providing for tax support of religion had been presented to the Virginia Legislature in 1784. Those who professed no religion were permitted by the bill to direct that their tax be used for general educational purposes. Madison attacked this bill in his famous "Memorial and Remonstrance against Religious Assessments," which was so persuasive that the bill was not even presented in the 1785 session. Instead, Jefferson's Act for Establishing Religious Freedom was passed by the Virginia Legislature.

During their terms as President, moreover, both Jefferson and Madison took very strict positions on establishment. Both believed that presidential proclamations of Thanksgiving Day were contrary to the Constitution. They also regarded as unconstitutional tax exemption for churches, payment from government funds to chaplains in Congress and the armed services, and nonpreferential land grants for the support of churches. It is significant that a 1796 treaty with Tripoli, a Moslem country, negotiated under President Washington and ratified by the Senate, stated that there was no ground for religious differences between the two nations because "the government of the United States of America is not, in any sense, founded on the Christian religion."

Current understanding sees the no-establishment principle as based upon two interrelated values.[22] One is religious voluntarism, a recognition that the growth and advancement of a religious sect must come from the voluntary support of its members. The second is political noninvolvement, the best interests both of the state and the church demanding that the political process be substantially insulated from religious pressures and interfaith dissension. The mixture of religion with politics is an explosive one, an historic evil that the establishment clause recognized and sought to defuse.[23] On the other hand, religion is a vital force in society, and its manifestations cannot be hermetically sealed off from secular life. Consequently, even though the goal of political noninvolvement in religion is generally accepted, there has been a wide variety of views and practices in applying the principle.

Benevolent Neutrality

The Supreme Court's first full discussion of the establishment problem[24] came in the case of *Everson* v. *Board of Education of Ewing Township* (1947), where the five-judge majority embraced what may be called the "benevolent neutrality" theory. A New Jersey statute authorized local boards of education to make rules and contracts for transportation of children to and from schools, whether public or private. Under this statute the Ewing township board arranged to reimburse parents of public and Catholic school pupils for money expended by them for transportation of their children on the regular public transportation system.

A taxpayer brought suit challenging on constitutional grounds the right of the board to reimburse parents of parochial school students, but lost in the Supreme Court by a five to four vote. Justice Black's opinion for the majority (including Douglas, Murphy, Vinson, and Reed) dealt principally with the objection that the statute amounted to an establishment of religion. To assist in applying the establishment clause to the New Jersey bus problem, Black reviewed European and

---

[22] Donald A. Gianella, "Religious Liberty, Nonestablishment, and Doctrinal Development: Part II. The Nonestablishment Principle," 81 HARVARD LAW REVIEW 513 (1968).

[23] Mark DeWolfe Howe, *The Garden and the Wilderness: Religion and Government in American Constitutional History* (Chicago: University of Chicago Press, 1965).

[24] The issue was ignored in a 1930 case, *Cochran* v. *Louisiana State Board of Education,* where it might have been exploited. The state of Louisiana under a free textbook program was supplying books to students in parochial as well as public schools. The constitutional objection raised was that this involved a taking of property for private use contrary to the due process clause. The Court ruled, however, that the appropriation of tax funds was for a public purpose, and thus upheld the program.

American colonial history of government-supported churches, concluding that the First Amendment means at least this much:

> Neither a state nor the Federal Government can set up a church. Neither can pass laws which aid one religion, aid all religions, or prefer one religion over another. Neither can force nor influence a person to go to or to remain away from church against his will or force him to profess a belief or disbelief in any religion. No person can be punished for entertaining or professing religious beliefs or disbeliefs, for church attendance or non-attendance. No tax in any amount, large or small, can be levied to support any religious activities or institutions, whatever they may be called, or whatever form they may adopt to teach or practice religion.

On the basis of these principles Black acknowledged that the New Jersey statute approached the "verge" of constitutional power. Indeed, looking at the establishment of religion clause as forbidding the contribution of "tax-raised funds to the support of an institution which teaches the tenets and faith of any church"—and Black admitted this is what the provision means—it would be hard to support the statute. But he escaped from the necessity of reaching this conclusion by moving over to the free exercise of religion clause, which he interpreted as commanding New Jersey not to "hamper its citizens in the free exercise of their own religion." The state must not exclude any individuals, "because of their faith, or lack of it, from receiving the benefits of public welfare legislation."

Fearful that this argument might prove too much, Black hurried on to say that of course a state could limit its provision of transportation assistance to public school children only. But in fact, he added, the states have generally not taken this line. They already furnish many services to church schools with general approval, such as fire and police protection, sidewalks, and public highways. The First Amendment "requires the state to be a neutral in its relations with groups of religious believers and non-believers; it does not require the state to be their adversary. State power is no more to be used so as to handicap religions than it is to favor them." His argument closed with the contention that this New Jersey action did not constitute "the slightest breach" in the wall between church and state, which "must be kept high and impregnable."

The principle of the *Everson* case, then, is that it does not violate the establishment clause to permit religious institutions to share in social gains from government programs that are religiously neutral. The benefits here went to the children and their parents, not to the religious schools. It was a similar "child benefit" theory that the Court embraced in *Board of Education* v. *Allen* (1968) to uphold a New York statute requiring school districts to purchase and "loan" textbooks to pupils in parochial and private as well as in public schools. Justice White saw this as simply making "available to all children the benefits of a general program to lend school books free of charge."

Justice Black disagreed that the *Everson* principle covered *Allen*. Schoolbooks were different from bus fares. Though required to be secular, the books selected would "inevitably tend to propagate the religious views of the favored sect." He was

also alarmed at the incursion into politics of the "powerful sectarian religious propa-
gandists who have succeeded in securing passage of the present law to help religious
schools carry on their sectarian religious purposes." However, the Court reiterated
its approval of textbook-loan programs in *Meek* v. *Pittinger* (1975).[25]

The pupil benefit theory was the justification for the provisions in the "GI Bill"
passed by Congress in 1944, under which returning veterans could attend denomi-
national schools to which federal payments were made directly. Similarly, all children who attend tax-exempt schools were made eligible for the benefits of the National School Lunch Act. Under various federal statutes, such as the National
Defense Education Act, Congress has provided for loans or grants to colleges and
universities for buildings or educational programs. Religious institutions of higher
learning have generally been eligible for such aid, with the limitation that no funds
can go for buildings used for religious instruction or for chapels or for schools of
divinity or theology.

Prior to 1965, no substantial federal financial aid in the elementary and secondary education field had ever been provided. The principal reason why all the proposals for federal aid to education failed of enactment in Congress was Catholic
refusal to support legislation which did not include aid for religious schools. President Johnson successfully bypassed this barrier and secured passage of the Elementary and Secondary Education Act of 1965 by proposing a variation of the pupil
benefit theory under which funds would go primarily to schools serving children
from low-income families. The act as passed made grants available under various
programs for improving the education of students in both religious and public
schools.

The High Wall—No Aid Theory

The strict, as opposed to the benevolent, view on church-state separation draws its
symbolic support from Jefferson's warning that a "high wall" must be maintained
between the government and religion. It was this wall that Black insisted he was
preserving "high and impregnable" in *Everson,* but the four dissenters there felt that
Black's rhetoric was inconsistent with his conclusion. It reminded Jackson of
Byron's Julia, who, while "whispering 'I will ne'er consent,'—consented." Rutledge's
masterly dissent in *Everson* invoked what he held to be the true teaching of Jefferson
and Madison, whose writings were analyzed at length. As a practical matter Rutledge contended that no line could be drawn between payment of bus fare and
payment for larger, but no more necessary, items in religious education.

One year later, in *McCollum* v. *Board of Education* (1948), all the justices except
Reed agreed that the high wall had been breached. The public schools of Champaign, Illinois, had a "released time" program of religious education under which
public school children, on consent of their parents, attended classes in Protestant,
Catholic, or Jewish religious instruction during school hours and in the school building. The religious teachers were not paid by the schools, but were under the supervi-

---

[25] "Sectarian Books, the Supreme Court, and the Establishment Clause," 79 Yale Law Journal
111 (1969); Paul A. Freund, "Public Aid to Parochial Schools," 82 Harvard Law Review 1680 (1969).

sion of the school superintendents, and attendance was compulsory for participants in the program.

Justice Black, speaking for six justices, held that under this plan tax-supported school buildings were being used in disseminating religious doctrines, and the state's public school machinery was being employed to provide pupils for religious classes—a clear violation of the *Everson* principle. Justice Jackson, concurring, agreed that the Champaign religious classes went beyond permissible limits, but he was worried over the prospect of the Supreme Court's becoming a "super board of education for every school district in the nation." Without a clearer statement of legal principles to provide guidance to both educators and judges than Black's opinion provided, he feared that the wall of separation between church and state was likely to become "as winding as the famous serpentine wall designed by Mr. Jefferson for the University he founded."

The *McCollum* decision created a furore in church circles, for similar released time programs were widely in effect throughout the country. It was against this background that the Court was offered a second opportunity to consider the issue, in ruling on the New York program of released time religious education in *Zorach* v. *Clauson* (1952). The New York plan called for religious instruction outside the schools, thus differing sufficiently from the Champaign arrangement to win the approval of six justices, including three who had voted against the Champaign plan (Douglas, Vinson, and Burton) and two who had not been on the Court at the time of the earlier decision (Clark and Minton).[26]

Under the New York City program, students were released from classes during the school day, on written request of their parents, in order to attend religious exercises or classes in religious centers off the school grounds. Those not released stayed in the school classrooms. The churches made weekly reports to the schools of children who had not reported for religious instruction. Because the program involved "neither religious instruction in public school classrooms nor the expenditure of public funds," Douglas ruled for the majority that the *McCollum* case was not controlling. The situation was merely that of schools closing their doors or suspending their operations "as to those who want to repair to their religious sanctuary for worship or instruction. . . . The public schools do no more than accommodate their schedules to a program of outside religious instruction." But this latter statement cannot possibly be squared with the facts, as the dissenters (Black, Jackson, and Frankfurter) promptly pointed out. The schools do not close their doors or suspend their operations. Students who do not participate in the religious program are compelled to attend other school activities. Thus the state in the New York program was clearly making "religious sects beneficiaries of its power to compel children to attend secular schools." As Jackson put it, the school "serves as a temporary jail for a pupil who will not go to Church."[27]

[26] See "The 'Released Time' Cases Revisited: A Study of Group Decisionmaking by the Supreme Court," 83 YALE LAW JOURNAL 1202 (1974).

[27] See Frank J. Sorauf, "*Zorach* v. *Clauson:* The Impact of a Supreme Court Decision," 53 AMERICAN POLITICAL SCIENCE REVIEW 777 (1959); "The Released Time Case," in C. Herman Pritchett and Alan F. Westin (eds.), *The Third Branch of Government* (New York: Harcourt, Brace & World, Inc., 1963), pp.

Two outstanding "high wall" decisions are *Engel* v. *Vitale* (1962) and *School District of Abington Township* v. *Schempp* (1963). The first arose out of the action of the New York State Board of Regents, which has general supervisory authority over the state public schools, in composing a twenty-two-word prayer so bland that it was thought to be nonsectarian and recommending its daily recital in the public schools as part of a general program of moral and spiritual training. By a vote of six to one (Stewart), the Supreme Court held that a prayer "composed by governmental officials as a part of a governmental program to further religious beliefs" was clearly an establishment of religion.[28]

At issue in the *Schempp* case were the practices in two Pennsylvania and Maryland schools of beginning the day with reading of the Bible or recitation of the Lord's Prayer. The Court held these likewise to be unquestionably religious exercises and so, again with only Stewart dissenting, unconstitutional.

Justice Black's opinion in *Engel* relied largely on the unhappy history of evils resulting from establishment, in both England and the American Colonies. He did not invoke the free exercise clause for two reasons. First, the prayer was considered "denominationally neutral" or nonsectarian. Second, participation in the prayer on the part of pupils was voluntary, which might be regarded as taking care of those who objected to the prayer. Justice Black apparently thought that under these conditions it would be difficult to demonstrate an interference with any pupil's free exercise of religion, although he admitted that "indirect coercive pressure upon religious minorities" could exist under the plan.

The reaction to the *Engel* decision, particularly since it came only three months after the controversial ruling in *Baker* v. *Carr,* was explosive in the extreme. Only a minority of those expressing their opinions—and this minority notably included President Kennedy—appeared to have made an effort to understand the Court's position. For most, their conclusion was simply that the Supreme Court was against prayer. The Court was variously charged with "tampering with America's soul," with having stated its "disbelief in God Almighty." A representative in Congress from Alabama cried out: "They put the Negroes in the schools and now they've driven God out." A number of constitutional amendments were immediately introduced in Congress to authorize prayers in the public schools.

Time was to show that sober second thought would yield more understanding of and support for the Court's position than the initial reactions indicated. The Court itself, unmoved by the outcry against *Engel,* in the next term reiterated its position in the *Schempp* case. From the Court's previous decisions Clark drew this rule: "To withstand the strictures of the Establishment Clause there must be a secular legislative purpose and a primary effect that neither advances nor inhibits religion." The constitutional command is for a "wholesome" neutrality. Such neutrality would not prevent study of the Bible or of religion in public schools "when presented objectively as part of a secular program of education." Nor did "the concept of neutrality, which does not permit a State to require a religious exercise

---

118–148. In *Smith* v. *Smith* (1976) the Court refused to reconsider the *Zorach* decision.

[28] See Louis H. Pollak, "Public Prayers in Public Schools," 77 HARVARD LAW REVIEW 62 (1963).

even with the consent of the majority of those affected, collide with the majority's right to free exercise of religion." The free exercise clause prohibits the use of state action to deny the rights of free exercise to anyone, but "it never meant that a majority could use the machinery of the State to practice its beliefs."

The *Schempp* decision also spelled out why the Court was invoking the establishment rather than the free exercise clause. As Justice Clark said, "It is necessary in a free exercise case for one to show the coercive effect of the enactment as it operates against him in the practice of his religion," whereas no coercion need be shown to support an establishment violation. Consequently it is much easier to satisfy the "standing" requirement in an establishment suit than in a free exercise case. In fact, the issue of standing, which in *Doremus* v. *Board of Education* (1952) the Court used to avoid deciding a Bible-reading case, was practically ignored by the Court in the *Engel* and *Schempp* cases.[29]

The opposition aroused by *Engel* was revived by *Schempp*, though it did not reach the same degree of intensity. Amendments to permit voluntary prayers and Bible reading in the schools have been proposed in every session of Congress. Senator Dirksen's amendment in 1966 came within nine votes of the required two-thirds majority in the Senate. In practice, the evidence is that the rulings are ignored or evaded in many schools.[30]

Compulsory chapel at the nation's military academies, an obvious challenge to the high wall, was declared unconstitutional by the Court of Appeals for the District of Columbia in 1972, and the Supreme Court refused certiorari in *Laird* v. *Anderson* (1972). However, the Court has made clear that it has no intention of opposing all manifestations of religion in public life, such as chaplains in Congress and in the Armed Forces, Thanksgiving Day proclamations, or "In God We Trust" on coins.[31]

Strict Neutrality

A different formula for achieving the strict separation sought by the high wall theory was proposed by Philip B. Kurland in an influential 1961 law review article,[32] a position subsequently adopted by Justice Harlan as a rule for decision. Kurland proposed that "the freedom and separation clauses should be read as a single precept that government cannot utilize religion as a standard for action or inaction because these clauses prohibit classification in terms of religion either to confer a benefit or to impose a burden." In other words, neutrality would be achieved by never mentioning religion in a statute or taking it into account in an administrative decision.

Harlan employed this approach in his *Allen* concurrence, asserting that the New York textbook law did not "employ religion as its standard for action or

[29] See the criticism on this point by Arthur E. Sutherland, Jr., "Establishment According to Engel," 76 HARVARD LAW REVIEW 25 (1962).

[30] See Kenneth M. Dolbeare and Phillip E. Hammond, *The School Prayer Decisions: From Court Policy to Local Practice* (Chicago: University of Chicago Press, 1971); W. K. Muir, Jr., *Prayer in the Public Schools: Law and Attitude Change* (Chicago: University of Chicago Press, 1967).

[31] See Justice Brennan's opinion in the *Schempp* case, and *Aronow* v. *United States* (1970).

[32] "Of Church and State and the Supreme Court," 29 UNIVERSITY OF CHICAGO LAW REVIEW 1–96 (1961).

inaction." He justified tax exemption for churches in *Walz* v. *Tax Commission* (1970) by the same neutrality rationale. The Court, he warned, must be alert to spot "religious gerrymanders, that is, legislation singling out religious institutions for favored treatment." But in *Walz* the exemption included educational and charitable institutions as well as religious, and so he concluded that "the radius of legislation encircles a class so broad that . . . religious institutions could be thought to fall within the natural perimeter."

The decision in *Epperson* v. *Arkansas* (1968) also employed strict neutrality reasoning. In that case a state statute forbidding the teaching of evolution in public schools and publicly supported colleges and universities was held to violate the rule that government "must be neutral in matters of religious theory, doctrine, and practice." The Court said, "the overriding fact is that Arkansas' law selects from the body of knowledge a particular segment which it proscribes for the sole reason that it is deemed to conflict with . . . a particular interpretation of the Book of Genesis by a particular religious group."[33]

It should be understood that the Kurland-Harlan position, while attractive in its simplicity, would prevent any accommodation of religious claims such as the Court approved in releasing the Amish from school attendance laws and would render invalid the exemption granted by Congress in 1965 to the Amish—who believe that any form of insurance shows a lack of faith in God—from the social security system.

Secular Tests

More appealing to most members of the Court than the strict neutrality test has been some formula for distinguishing secular from religious purposes. Justice Clark was the first to propose a simple test for this purpose in his *Schempp* opinion: "To withstand the strictures of the Establishment Clause there must be a secular legislative purpose and a primary effect that neither advances nor inhibits religion." Also in *Schempp,* Brennan tried his hand at a somewhat more complex set of standards; what the establishment clause forbids, he said, are "those involvements of religious with secular institutions which *(a)* serve the essentially religious activities of religious institutions; *(b)* employ the organs of government for essentially religious purposes; or *(c)* use essentially religious means to serve governmental ends, where secular means would suffice." Obviously Bible reading and school prayers were condemned by either the Clark or Brennan formulas.

Brennan repeated his three-part rule in the *Walz* case, where he discovered two basic secular justifications for granting real property tax exemptions to religious organizations. First, along with other private, nonprofit organizations, they "contribute to the well-being of the community in a variety of nonreligious ways, and thereby bear burdens that would otherwise have to be met by general taxation, or be left undone, to the detriment of the community." Second, religious organizations

---

[33] In 1975 both a federal district judge and the Tennessee supreme court ruled unconstitutional a 1973 Tennessee law requiring textbooks to provide equal space to Biblical theories on the creation of the universe. *The New York Times,* August 21, 1975.

"uniquely contribute to the pluralism of American society by their religious activities."

Free Exercise Accommodation

Still another rationale stresses the obligation to avoid governmental action that would interfere with the free exercise of religion. *Sherbert* v. *Verner* held that an infringement of free exercise rights can only be justified by a "compelling state interest"—moreover, a compelling state interest that cannot be satisfactorily achieved by some less drastic means that will avoid the free exercise burden. This would not amount to "establishing" a religion by giving it a preferential position; rather, it would simply recognize "the governmental obligation of neutrality in the face of religious differences." Similarly, in *Wisconsin* v. *Yoder,* the Court found that, "however strong the State's interest in universal compulsory education, it is by no means absolute" and in this situation not of "sufficient magnitude to override the interest claiming protection under the Free Exercise Clause."

Establishment on the Burger Court

The Warren Court had not been too seriously divided in the religion cases. There were votes of five to four in *Everson* and six to three in *Allen* and *Zorach,* but *McCollum, Engel,* and *Schempp* each drew only one dissenting vote. It could have been anticipated that the Burger Court would have more trouble, with harder problems to solve. For one thing, the decision in *Flast* v. *Cohen* (1968) had opened the way for court tests of the constitutionality of the Education Act of 1965, with its aid to parochial schools under a poverty formula. Again, religious schools were having progressively more severe financial trouble, and state legislatures were responding with ingenious formulas for granting them financial aid. In addition, President Nixon was pressing for federal aid to the parochial schools.

As it turned out, while the rhetoric changed somewhat, the Burger Court had not by 1976 substantially modified the constitutional law of establishment. In *Walz* v. *Tax Commission* (1970), the Court could hardly have been expected to challenge the time-honored practice of tax exemption for churches. Only Douglas took the strict view that tax exemption was the equivalent of a direct subsidy to churches. Burger, speaking for the Court, followed the benevolent neutrality line of allowing some "room for play in the joints." His interpretation of the religion clauses was that they were intended "to insure that no religion be sponsored or favored, none commanded, and none inhibited," and his practical guide for testing any state relationship to religion was whether it involved "excessive entanglement."

Excessive entanglement was to become part of the standard rhetoric of the Burger Court. Burger's opinion in *Lemon* v. *Kurtzman* (1971) was based almost entirely on "entanglement" reasoning. This case involved a Rhode Island program of salary supplements paid to teachers of secular subjects in nonpublic schools and a Pennsylvania program of reimbursement to nonpublic schools for teachers' salaries, textbooks, and instructional materials used in the teaching of specific subjects. The programs were invalidated because entanglement would result from the "comprehensive, discriminating, and continuing state surveillance" that would inevitably be required to enforce the secular purpose limitations, as well as from the "divisive political potential" of these programs. "The potential for political divisiveness related to religious belief and practice is aggravated in these two statutory programs by the need for continuing annual appropriations and the likelihood of larger and larger demands as costs and populations grow." Only White dissented.

On the same day that *Lemon* was decided, however, the federal program of construction grants for colleges and universities, which included church-related institutions, passed the entanglement test in *Tilton* v. *Richardson* (1971). Naturally no grants were available for buildings used for worship or sectarian instruction, but it was contended that in a church-related college sectarian influences would permeate the entire institution. Burger's opinion rejected this view. There was a substantial difference in this regard between institutions of higher education and parochial elementary and secondary schools. Religious indoctrination is not a substantial purpose of the church-related colleges, and in any event "college students are less impressionable and less susceptible to religious indoctrination." Also, many church-related institutions have a "high degree of academic freedom." Douglas, Black, and Marshall, dissenting, were not convinced. Government surveillance would have to continue, Douglas asserted, as long as the buildings lasted.

These issues returned to the Court in 1973 and were decided in almost identical fashion. *Committee for Public Education and Religious Liberty* v. *Nyquist* involved three financial aid plans for New York nonpublic schools—money grants for maintenance and repair of buildings, tuition reimbursement for parents of pupils in nonpublic schools, and tax relief to parents failing to qualify for tuition reimbursement. Powell, commenting on "the ingenious plans for channeling state aid to sectarian schools that periodically reach this Court," held that the New York aid plans so clearly had the "impermissible effect of advancing religion, it is not necessary to consider whether such aid would yield an entanglement with religion."

Sloan v. *Lemon* (1973) brought up to the Court a Pennsylvania parent reimbursement plan to replace the teacher salary plan invalidated by *Lemon* v. *Kurtzman*. As in *Nyquist,* this program was declared unconstitutional as advancing religion. The third case, *Levitt* v. *Committee for Public Education and Religious Liberty* (1973), struck down a New York program to reimburse nonpublic schools for costs incurred in connection with examinations and maintenance of student records. Burger held that such services, "some secular and some potentially religious," were constitutionally different from bus rides or state-loaned textbooks. But there was a fourth case—*Hunt* v. *McNair* (1973), involving a college building construction program from South Carolina—which included church-related institutions; it was approved on the precedent of *Tilton* v. *Richardson.*

Pennsylvania, undaunted, came back to the Court with still another program in *Meek* v. *Pittinger* (1975). This time the state proposed to finance for nonpublic schools auxiliary services such as counseling, testing, speech and hearing therapy, and "other secular, neutral, nonideological services," to lend instructional materials and equipment, and to lend textbooks acceptable for use in public schools. The Supreme Court upheld the textbook loan but declared the other parts of the program unconstitutional. Stewart took the occasion to provide still another "convenient, accurate distillation" of the Court's rules on establishment, which came down to three tests: the statute must have a secular legislative purpose, it must have a primary effect that neither advances nor inhibits religion, and the statute and its administration must avoid excessive government entanglement with religion.

In *Roemer* v. *Board of Public Works of Maryland* (1976) the Burger Court modified somewhat its position on entanglement. Maryland had a program of annual financial state grants to colleges in the state, including four church-related colleges. By a five to four vote the Court approved on the basis of the *Tilton* precedent. Even though the colleges had mandatory theology classes and expenditures under the grants were to be audited annually by the state, Justice Blackmun found no excessive entanglement of church and state. Brennan, Marshall, Stewart, and Stevens dissented.

The Court had not, by 1976, passed on the provisions of Title I of the 1965 Education Act, which provide for federal funding of special programs for educationally deprived children in both public and private schools. The closest it had come was in *Wheeler* v. *Barrera* (1974), a suit from Missouri instituted on behalf of parochial school students who were eligible for Title I benefits but who claimed that the public school authorities in their area had failed to provide adequate Title I programs for them as compared with those made available to public school children. Recognizing that an important constitutional issue was present, the Court concluded it was not ripe for review. But Justice White read the Court's action as inferring that there were services the state could supply under Title I to nonpublic schools without violating the First Amendment.[34]

<hr/>

[34] A valuable study of all the important court decisions on church-state issues from 1951 to 1971, including consideration of the community contexts in which the cases developed and the strategies and goals of the persons or groups bringing the suits, is Frank J. Sorauf, *The Wall of Separation: The Constitutional Politics of Church and State* (Princeton, N.J.: Princeton University Press, 1976).

For the complete briefs and lower court proceedings in the Karen Quinlan case, see *In the Matter of Karen Quinlan* (Arlington, Va.: University Publications, 1975). The New Jersey supreme court in 1976 authorized termination of her life supports if the physicians and hospital officials agreed there was "no reasonable possibility" she could recover. *The New York Times, April 1, 1976.*

Chapter 25

Procedural Due Process

The concept of due process, introduced into the Constitution in the Fifth Amendment as a limitation on Congress and repeated in the Fourteenth Amendment as a limitation on the states, is perhaps the most expansive and adaptable of the Constitution's many broad phrases. As Justice Frankfurter has eloquently said:

> "Due process," unlike some legal rules, is not a technical conception with a fixed content unrelated to time, place and circumstances. Expressing as it does in its ultimate analysis respect enforced by law for that feeling of just treatment which has been evolved through centuries of Anglo-American constitutional history and civilization, "due process" cannot be imprisoned within the treacherous limits of any formula. Representing a profound attitude of fairness between man and man, and more particularly between the individual and government, "due process" is compounded of history, reason, the past course of decisions, and stout confidence in the strength of the democratic faith which we profess. Due process is not a mechanical instrument. It is not a yardstick. It is a process.[1]

The due process concept does not depend for its constitutional foundation

---

[1] *Joint Anti-Facist Refugee Committee* v. *McGrath* (1951).

solely on the two clauses of the Fifth and Fourteenth Amendments. All of the amendments from the Fourth through the Eighth embody important due process rights, mostly concerned with protection against abuses in criminal prosecutions. The existence in the Constitution of both general and specific due process provisions has presented the Supreme Court with some interesting and difficult issues of interpretation. In this chapter we will be concerned, first, with the Court's enunciation of the procedural rights of persons in their adverse relationships to the state under the general due process clauses and, second, with the Court's initial efforts to reconcile the general with the more specific procedural protections in the Fourth through Eighth Amendments.

DUE PROCESS AND LEGISLATION

The due process clause of the Fifth Amendment, as pointed out in Chapter 19, is generally traced to the Magna Carta of 1215, in one chapter of which the king promised: "No freeman shall be arrested, or imprisoned, or disseized, or outlawed, or exiled, or in any way molested; nor will we proceed against him, unless by the lawful judgment of his peers or by the law of the land." In England it was thus the king who was limited by due process. By contrast, anything Parliament enacted was "the law of the land" and not subject to judicial check. But in one of its first opinions interpreting the due process clause, *Murray's Lessee* v. *Hoboken Land & Improvement Co.* (1856), the Supreme Court held that in America due process was a limitation on the legislature as well as on the executive and the judiciary.

The problem in the *Murray* case was whether legislation providing for distress warrant levies on the property of federal tax collectors found to be indebted to the United States amounted to constitutional procedure. The Court said:

> That the warrant now in question is legal process, is not denied. It was issued in conformity with an act of Congress. But is it "due process of law"? The Constitution contains no description of those processes which it was intended to allow or forbid. It does not even declare what principles are to be applied to ascertain whether it be due process. It is manifest that it was not left to the legislative power to enact any process which might be devised. The article is a restraint on the legislative as well as on the executive and judicial powers of the government, and cannot be construed as to leave Congress free to make any process "due process of law" by its mere will.

A second contribution of the *Murray* decision, written by Justice Curtis, was its effort to ascertain and state the principles upon which the Court would rely in deciding whether a particular process was "due" process. Curtis thought there were two tests that should be used. First, "we must examine the constitution itself, to see whether this process be in conflict with any of its provisions." He did not say where he would look in the Constitution, but obviously he must have been thinking of the specific "process" guarantees found primarily in the Bill of Rights. If this search turned up a conflict, then of course the process was not "due process," and that would be the end of it.

In the *Murray* situation, however, no such conflict was found, and so Curtis went on to announce a second test—"those settled usages and modes of proceeding existing in the common and statute law of England, before the emigration of our ancestors, and which are shown not to have been unsuited to their civil and political condition by having been acted on by them after the settlement of this country." This was a test based on English and early American practice. A process otherwise unforbidden by the Constitution might still turn out to be contrary to Anglo-Saxon traditions, and if so it would not be due process of law. For the purposes of the *Murray* case Curtis conducted a search which showed that a summary method for the recovery of debts due the government had been provided for "by the common and statute law of England prior to the emigration of our ancestors, and by the laws of many of the States at the time of the adoption of this amendment," and consequently the statute "cannot be denied to be due process of law."

By the *Murray* decision, then, Congress was brought under the purview of the due process clause, and a standard for determining whether legislative action constituted due process was stated. The adoption of the Fourteenth Amendment meant that state legislatures were placed in a similar position. Thus the Supreme Court became responsible for testing the procedures stipulated by both federal and state statutes, so far as they affected life, liberty, or property, on due process grounds.

DUE PROCESS IN JUDICIAL AND ADMINISTRATIVE PROCEEDINGS

Due process in judicial proceedings, the Supreme Court said in *Pennoyer* v. *Neff* (1877), required principally that litigants have the benefit of a full and fair trial in the courts and that their rights be measured not by laws made to affect them individually but by general provisions applicable to all those in like condition. Judicial procedures might vary according to circumstances, but they would be *due* procedures if they followed the established forms of law or if, adapting old forms to new problems, they preserved the principles of liberty and justice.

Jurisdiction

Of the basic components in judicial due process, perhaps the most fundamental is jurisdiction. Jurisdiction has been defined as the power to create legal interests. We saw in Chapter 7 that the jurisdiction of the federal courts is conferred on them and defined by acts of Congress. Without jurisdiction, they cannot act. As the Supreme Court said in *Ex parte McCardle* (1869):

> Jurisdiction is power to declare the law, and when it ceases to exist, the only function remaining to the court is that of announcing the fact and dismissing the case.

The jurisdiction of state courts, however it may be defined by their constitutions and legislatures, is necessarily limited by their geography. Legal interests cannot be created if they cannot be enforced. The state must have actual physical power over persons or things if its courts are to render effective decrees concerning them. A state has jurisdiction over a person (such proceedings are called *in personam* actions) if he or she is physically present within the state, or is domiciled in the state but is temporarily absent, or has consented to the exercise of jurisdiction.

Corporations, being fictitious persons, can manifest their presence in states outside their state of origin only by activities carried on in their behalf. In general, such activities must be "continuous and systematic" in order to meet the "presence" test.[2] However, in some situations occasional acts of a corporate agent may be deemed sufficient to render the corporation liable to suit.[3]

Jurisdiction over things, usually exerted by actions *in rem,* may be exercised over property within the state, even though the owner is not within the state and control over him is never obtained. Thus a state can permit attachment of property within its borders owned by a nonresident, for the purpose of satisfying a debt owed by him to a citizen of the state, or in settlement of a claim for damages by the citizen against the nonresident.

Notice and Hearing

Jurisdiction, though potentially possessed, may not be exercised in a judicial proceeding until it has been perfected by appropriate notice which acquaints all parties of the institution of proceedings calculated to affect their rights. It is contrary to due process for a person to be deprived of property rights by a decree in a proceeding in which he does not appear, or is not served with process or effectively made a party to the case. The standard method of giving notice is by personal service, i.e., summons delivered to the defendant personally. However, various forms of substituted service, as by mail or newspaper publication, may meet the legal requirements. In general, due process requires the best notice that is possible under the circumstances.[4]

Due process requires that a party to judicial proceedings be afforded an opportunity to be heard at some stage before final judgment is entered. This includes the right to present such arguments, testimony, or evidence as may be pertinent to the case before a fair and impartial tribunal.

Illustrative of the notice and hearing requirement are two recent Supreme Court decisions involving actions for garnishment (seizure of wages for debt) and replevin (recovery of property, typically by creditors to repossess tangible goods purchased under installment sales contracts).[5] Statutes authorizing such actions have historically provided for summary procedures. In *Sniadach* v. *Family Finance Corp.* (1969), service on the garnishee had the effect of freezing the wage-earner's salary prior to opportunity to be heard or to tender a defense. *Fuentes* v. *Shevin*

---

[2] See *International Shoe Co.* v. *Washington* (1945).

[3] See *Travelers Health Assn.* v. *Virginia* (1950). In the case of *New York Times Co.* v. *Sullivan* (1964), the Alabama courts asserted jurisdiction over a libel suit against the newspaper because 394 copies containing the alleged libel out of an edition of 650,000 had been circulated in Alabama, 35 of them in Montgomery County where the suit arose. *The New York Times* contended that this was an inadequate basis for jurisdiction, but entered a general appearance in the action; the Supreme Court ruled that under Alabama law this amounted to waiving the jurisdictional objection.

[4] See *Mullane* v. *Central Hanover Bank & Trust Co.* (1950); *Walker* v. *Hutchinson* (1956); *Armstrong* v. *Manzo* (1965).

[5] See S. N. Subrin and A. R. Dykstra, "Notice and the Right to Be Heard," 9 HARVARD CIVIL RIGHTS–CIVIL LIBERTIES LAW REVIEW 449 (1974).

(1972) involved a replevin statute authorizing a seizure of property on the ex parte application to a court clerk and the filing of a security bond by the person claiming the right to possession of the property. In both instances the Court held that the absence of notice and hearing prior to seizure violated due process.[6]

Administrative agencies and officers often have considerable authority to take action affecting the rights of property and of person. Where they are given such powers, the obligations of due process also become applicable to them. This means that the requirements of jurisdiction, notice, hearing, and general fairness of procedure must be observed in administrative actions, though administrative procedures typically do not afford all the protections that would apply in a court proceeding. In the Administrative Procedure Act of 1946, Congress undertook to codify and standardize the procedural protections to be observed in federal actions affecting persons and property.[7]

Some significant recent Supreme Court decisions have brought new types of administrative decisions within the ambit of due process. *Goldberg* v. *Kelly* (1970) held that before welfare payments could be discontinued, there had to be an evidentiary hearing at which the recipient could appear personally to present evidence.[8] *Goss* v. *Lopez* (1975) invalidated the suspension of students from the public school system without a hearing. *Perry* v. *Sinderman* (1972) ruled that a state college teacher who was fired after ten years was entitled to a hearing. *Baker* v. *Owen* (1975) let stand a lower court decision allowing corporal punishment in disciplining students, but with certain due process safeguards.

THE INCORPORATION CONTROVERSY

The general due process requirements of jurisdiction, notice, and fair hearing apply to civil proceedings in all American courts, both federal and state. For criminal proceedings, however, the situation is more complicated. Federal courts must observe all the process provisions of the Fourth through Eighth Amendments. State courts, however, have only the general due process language of the Fourteenth Amendment as their guide. This difference in the constitutional situation of the two sets of courts has generated one of the most celebrated controversies in American constitutional law.

The Supreme Court's initial position was that in criminal proceedings state courts were obliged to observe only the general concept of due process and its historical requirements. Due process did not require the states to adopt specific measures of procedure or doctrines of law. Its effect was negative—to keep state

[6] While *Fuentes* was apparently undermined by *Mitchell* v. *W. T. Grant Co.* (1974), it was reconfirmed in *North Georgia Finishing, Inc.* v. *Di-Chem, Inc.* (1975). The *Sniadach* case was relied on in *Stanley* v. *Illinois* (1972), where an unwed father's children, on the mother's death, were declared state wards and placed in guardianship. The Supreme Court held that the father was entitled to a hearing on his fitness as a parent before his children were taken away from him.

[7] See Kenneth C. Davis, *Administrative Law and Government* (St. Paul, Minn.: West Publishing Company, 1975).

[8] See Robert M. O'Neil, "Of Justice Delayed and Justice Denied: The Welfare Prior Hearing Cases," in Philip B. Kurland (ed.), *The Supreme Court Review, 1970* (Chicago: University of Chicago Press, 1970), pp. 161–214. But *Mathews* v. *Eldridge* (1976) ruled that the Social Security Administration was not required to hold a full-dress hearing before cutting off disability insurance benefits.

courts within broad bounds—rather than positively to enforce certain mandatory procedures. The Court summed up this position in *Snyder* v. *Massachusetts* (1934) when it said that a state was "free to regulate the procedure of its courts in accordance with its own conception of policy and fairness unless in so doing it offends some principle of justice so rooted in the traditions and conscience of our people as to be ranked as fundamental."

The Court did not encounter this problem immediately on adoption of the Fourteenth Amendment, for at first litigation centered on the privileges and immunities clause, which was thought to be more promising in its protective potentialities than the due process clause. But in the *Slaughter-House Cases* (1873) the Court confined the privileges and immunities clause to the narrow protection of those rights peculiar to national citizenship, making it inapplicable to property rights and trials in the state courts.

Attention then turned to the due process clause of the Fourteenth Amendment, which got its first significant examination in *Hurtado* v. *California* (1884). Instead of being indicted by a grand jury, Hurtado had been brought to trial for murder on information after examination and commitment by a magistrate, as permitted by the California constitution. Thus the question before the Supreme Court was whether such departure from grand jury indictment violated due process of law.

On the basis of Justice Curtis's first test in the *Murray* case, due process had clearly been violated, for the Fifth Amendment makes indictment by grand jury mandatory for all capital or otherwise infamous crimes. However, Justice Matthews made the *Murray* rule seem to approve the *Hurtado* result. The "real syllabus" of the Curtis holding, Matthews said, is "that a process of law, which is not otherwise forbidden, must be taken to be due process of law, if it can show the sanction of settled usage both in England and in this country; but it by no means follows that nothing else can be due process of law." Then, having recognized Curtis's first test by the clause, "which is not otherwise forbidden," he proceeded to ignore it and to work from the last thought in the sentence, which is substantially Curtis's second test—the test of historical practice.

Matthews was able to show that grand jury indictment was not even known at the time of Magna Carta, or for centuries thereafter. In fact, some of the early practices had been so barbarous that he suggested "it is better not to go too far back into antiquity for the best securities for our 'ancient liberties.' " In any case, it would not be wise for the states to be bound to any fixed set of procedures in criminal cases.

> It is more consonant to the true philosophy of our historical legal institutions to say that the spirit of personal liberty and individual right, which they embodied, was preserved and developed by a progressive growth and wise adaptation to new circumstances and situations of the forms and processes found fit to give, from time to time, new expression and greater effect to modern ideas of self-government.

For those who might find this liberal philosophy unconvincing, Matthews had a more pedantic argument. Since the Fifth Amendment contains both the guarantee of due process and of indictment by grand jury, and since it must be assumed that no part of the Constitution is superfluous, it follows that due process as used in the

Fifth Amendment does not include indictment by grand jury. When the same phrase is repeated in the Fourteenth Amendment, it must be given the same meaning. Thus Matthews emerged with the remarkable conclusion, directly opposed to that of Curtis, that the due process clauses in both the Fifth and Fourteenth Amendments must be interpreted to *exclude* any rights specified elsewhere in the Constitution.

Justice Harlan was the only dissenter in the *Hurtado* case; he was an incorporationist. To him the Fourteenth Amendment evinced "a purpose to impose upon the States the same restrictions, in respect of proceedings involving life, liberty and property, which had been imposed upon the general government." Again, in *Maxwell* v. *Dow* (1900), he dissented in the most extensive examination the Fourteenth Amendment had received up to that time. He was thoroughly aroused by the fact that the development of substantive due process had made it possible for the Court to protect property rights against state legislative action, while procedural rights in state courts remained unprotected, and he commented bitterly:

> If then the "due process of law" required by the Fourteenth Amendment does not allow a State to take private property without just compensation, but does allow the life or liberty of the citizen to be taken in a mode that is repugnant to the settled usages and the modes of proceeding authorized at the time the Constitution was adopted and which was expressly forbidden in the National Bill of Rights, it would seem that the protection of private property is of more consequence than the protection of the life and liberty of the citizen.

This entire argument was resumed in *Twining* v. *New Jersey* (1908). The state practice under fire in *Twining* was self-incrimination; the jury, under state law, had been instructed that they might draw an unfavorable inference from the defendant's failure to testify in denial of evidence offered against him. Justice Moody for the Court upheld the law, but recognizing the weakness of the *Hurtado* decision, announced that the Court preferred to rest its decision "on broader grounds" than were there stated. The important thing was whether exemption from self-incrimination was "a fundamental principle of liberty and justice which inheres in the very idea of free government and is the inalienable right of a citizen of such a government."

How can judges proceed to answer such a question? One way, Moody asserted, was "to inquire how the right was rated during the time when the meaning of due process was in a formative state and before it was incorporated in American constitutional law." He found that it was omitted from the great declarations of English liberty, and that in fact English courts and Parliaments dealt with the exemption "as they would have dealt with any other rule of evidence." Moreover, only four of the thirteen original states insisted that this rule should be included in the Constitution, and two of these states did not have it in their own constitutions at the time. Thus the historical evidence demonstrated that "the privilege was not conceived to be inherent in due process of law, but on the other hand a right separate, independent, and outside of due process." Moody went on to note that the exemption was unknown outside the common-law countries, and was not observed "among our own people in the search for truth outside the administration of the law." So, "salutary as the principle may seem to the great majority, it cannot be ranked with the right to hearing before condemnation, the immunity from arbitrary power not acting by general laws, and the inviolability of private property."

After the *Twining* decision the incorporation controversy was relatively quiescent at the Supreme Court level for three decades. Then in 1937 *Palko* v. *Connecticut* offered an opportunity for reexamining the issue. In the interim the incorporation theory had achieved a very great success in another area. As already noted, *Gitlow* v. *New York* (1925) had admitted that the "liberty" protected by the Fourteenth Amendment against deprivation without due process included the freedoms of speech and press guaranteed by the First Amendment. If the First Amendment was incorporated into the Fourteenth, why were not the other guarantees in the Bill of Rights similarly situated?

It fell to Justice Cardozo to answer this question in the *Palko* case. The defendant had been convicted of second-degree murder and given a life sentence, but the state appealed the conviction, as was authorized by state law, and the state supreme court, finding there had been error in the trial to the prejudice of the state, ordered a new trial. The second time the defendant was convicted of murder in the first degree and sentenced to death. The question was whether the effect of the second trial was to place the defendant twice in jeopardy for the same offense.

Cardozo began by once more flatly rejecting the incorporation thesis. To the extent that some of the first eight amendments had been made effective against the states, that was not because they were incorporated into the Fourteenth Amendment when it was adopted, but because they had been found by the Supreme Court "to be implicit in the concept of ordered liberty." Cardozo admitted that when one looked at the line drawn by the Court between rights which meet this test and those which do not, it might seem "wavering and broken." But "reflection and analysis" would disclose a "rationalizing principle."

> The right to trial by jury and the immunity from prosecution except as the result of an indictment may have value and importance. Even so, they are not of the very essence of a scheme of ordered liberty. To abolish them is not to violate a "principle of justice so rooted in the traditions and conscience of our people as to be ranked as fundamental." . . . Few would be so narrow or provincial as to maintain that a fair and enlightened system of justice would be impossible without them. What is true of jury trials and indictments is true also . . . of the immunity from compulsory self-incrimination. . . . This too might be lost, and justice still be done.

On the other hand, freedom of thought and speech, as guaranteed by the First Amendment, is on "a different plane of social and moral values. . . . Of that freedom one may say that it is the matrix, the indispensable condition, of nearly every other form of freedom." So these freedoms have been "absorbed" into the Fourteenth Amendment, for "neither liberty nor justice would exist if they were sacrificed."

With this groundwork, it remained only for Cardozo to conclude that double jeopardy of the type presented in this case was not a value on the high plane represented by the First Amendment. All the state was asking was that the case against the defendant go on "until there shall be a trial free from the corrosion of substantial legal error." If there had been an error adverse to the accused, admittedly he could get another trial. To give the state a reciprocal privilege was "no seismic innovation. The edifice of justice stands, its symmetry, to many, greater than before."

Justice Black was in his first term on the Court when the *Palko* decision was made, and he did not dissent, though Butler did. This is interesting, for ten years later Black, in *Adamson* v. *California* (1947), led an assault on this entire line of cases which lacked only one vote of achieving success. The issue was again self-incrimination, this time as presented by a state statute permitting the failure of a defendant to explain or to deny evidence against him to be commented on by the court and by counsel and to be considered by the judge and the jury. For the defendant with a previous criminal record, the problem posed by this rule is that if he chooses to go on the witness stand to explain or deny evidence, he is then subject to cross-examination which can bring out his prior convictions. If he fails to take the stand, the assumption is that he cannot refute the evidence or has something to hide.

By a five to four vote, the Court held this statutory provision not contrary to due process. Justice Reed for the majority stood by the *Palko* rejection of the incorporation argument. The only question was whether a state statute permitting comment on the refusal of a defendant to take the stand met the Supreme Court's notions as to allowable procedure. Reed made practically no effort to answer by reference to standards outside the value systems of the individual justices, such as historical practice. Instead, he said very frankly, "We see no reason why comment should not be made upon his silence. . . . When evidence is before a jury that threatens conviction, it does not seem unfair to require him to choose between leaving the adverse evidence unexplained and subjecting himself to impeachment through disclosure of former crimes."

Black's dissent, which spoke for Douglas, Murphy, and Rutledge as well, was a powerful defense of the incorporation theory. In a lengthy appendix to his opinion, he marshaled the historical data favorable to the incorporation view, such as the speeches of Bingham and Howard already referred to, and concluded: "My study of the historical events that culminated in the Fourteenth Amendment . . . persuades me that one of the chief objects that the provisions of the Amendment's first section, separately, and as a whole, were intended to accomplish was to make the Bill of Rights, applicable to the states." The Court, he went on, had repeatedly declined to appraise this historical evidence. Instead, it had reiterated a "natural law" formula under which it had substituted "its own concepts of decency and fundamental justice for the language of the Bill of Rights. . . . I would follow what I believe was the original purpose of the Fourteenth Amendment—to extend to all the people of the nation the complete protection of the Bill of Rights."

Justice Frankfurter, concurring in the Court's majority opinion, devoted himself to answering Black and to ridiculing the "notion that the Fourteenth Amendment was a covert way of imposing upon the States all the rules which it seemed important to Eighteenth Century statesmen to write into the Federal Amendments." Actually, substantial victory for the incorporation position was only a decade away. The story of those developments, however, must await the more detailed examination of due process requirements for criminal prosecutions which is the subject of the following chapter.

Criminal Prosecutions

One of the Supreme Court's most important functions is to maintain constitutional standards for the criminal prosecutions conducted in both federal and state courts. The significance which the Constitution attaches to such protection is indicated by the fact that five of the ten amendments comprising the Bill of Rights are largely devoted to specifying the standards and procedures to be observed in criminal prosecutions. These amendments contain not only the broad guarantee of due process of law, but numerous specific procedural protections such as indictment by grand jury and speedy and public trial, as well as safeguards against self-incrimination, unreasonable searches and seizures, double jeopardy, and cruel and unusual punishments. In addition to enforcing these constitutional provisions, the Supreme Court has the general responsibility over administration of justice in the federal courts which comes from its position at the apex of the judicial hierarchy. This supervisory authority, the Court has said, "implies the duty of establishing and maintaining civilized standards of procedure and evidence."[1]

[1] *McNabb* v. *United States* (1943). In *Yates* v. *United States* (1958) the Court made a highly unusual use of its supervisory power by itself reducing a sentence for contempt of court after the district judge who imposed the original sentence had failed to respond to the Supreme Court's "gentle intimations" that the sentence should be reduced.

CRIMES AGAINST THE UNITED STATES

There are four principal references to federal crimes in the Constitution: "counterfeiting the securities and current coin of the United States," "piracies and felonies committed on the high seas," and "offences against the law of nations," all found in Article I, section 8; and "treason against the United States," which is defined in Article III, section 3. Obviously these four crimes do not account for the content of the United States Criminal Code, and there is no federal common law of crimes.[2] All the other multitudinous crimes on the federal statute books have been defined and made punishable by congressional exercise of implied power. Any law which Congress has the power to adopt, it also has the power to enforce by making violation a crime. Thus the power "to establish post offices and post roads" clearly implies the power to punish theft from the mails. Of the crimes which achieve the distinction of constitutional mention, only one, treason, has a history and a constitutional significance justifying consideration here.

The constitutional provision on treason is short. "Treason against the United States shall consist only in levying war against them, or in adhering to their enemies, giving them aid and comfort. No person shall be convicted of treason unless on the testimony of two witnesses to the same overt act, or on confession in open court." The intent of the framers in these words is well known: they were seeking to make convictions for treason very difficult to obtain. The members of the Convention "almost to a man had themselves been guilty of treason under any interpretation of British law."[3] They had been "taught by experience and by history to fear abuse of the treason charge almost as much as they feared treason itself." They believed that a government had to deserve the loyalty of its citizens, and that opposition to the abuses of a tyrannical government was justified and should not be punished as treason.

Consequently the Convention wrote into the Constitution every limitation on treason convictions "that the practice of governments had evolved or that politico-legal philosophy to that time had advanced." The result of this restrictive approach has been to render treason litigation comparatively unimportant in American constitutional development. The Supreme Court never had occasion to review a treason conviction until the case of *Cramer* v. *United States* in 1945. In the brief for that case, all previous proceedings in which construction of the treason clause had been involved were collected, and they totaled nineteen. As Justice Jackson said in his *Cramer* decision: "We have managed to do without treason prosecutions to a degree that probably would be impossible except while a people was singularly confident of external security and internal stability."

The treason provision has, however, been invoked often enough to demonstrate its problems of interpretation. The Aaron Burr conspiracy led to two treason rulings by Chief Justice Marshall. In *Ex parte Bollman* (1807) he warned that "the crime of treason should not be extended by construction to doubtful cases." He confined the meaning of levying war to the actual waging of war or the actual assembling of men

---

[2] *United States* v. *Hudson and Goodwin* (1812).
[3] This quotation and those immediately following are from *Cramer* v. *United States* (1945).

for that purpose. In presiding over the trial of Burr,[4] Marshall ruled that Burr, not having been present at the actual assemblage of men, could be convicted of procuring or levying of war only upon the testimony of two witnesses to his having procured the assemblage. The result was practically to limit convictions for "levying war" to actual participants in armed hostilities.

In more recent times treason charges have usually been based not on the "levying war" clause, but on the offense of "adhering" to the nation's enemies, "giving them aid and comfort." In *Cramer* v. *United States* (1945) the Supreme Cout divided five to four in applying this constitutional provision. Cramer had befriended two of the German saboteurs who were landed in the United States by submarine in 1942 for the purpose of sabotaging the American war effort. He met and lunched with them in public places, and took a large sum of money from one for safekeeping. The only overt acts established by two witnesses were the public meetings. The Court majority concluded that Cramer's eating and drinking in a public place "was no part of the saboteurs' mission and did not advance it."

Two years later the Supreme Court for the first time in its history sustained a treason conviction. *Haupt* v. *United States* (1947) grew out of the same incident of the German saboteurs, the defendant being the father of one of them. When the son turned up in Chicago on his mission, the father took him into his house, accompanied him when he sought employment in a plant manufacturing bomb sights, and purchased an automobile for him. This time the Court held the constitutional standard of treason had been met. The "harboring and sheltering" which Haupt had provided his son, an overt act established by two witnesses, was of direct value to his traitorous enterprise, in a way that Cramer's public meetings with the saboteurs had not been.

Since 1947 only one additional treason case has reached the Supreme Court, and it added little to the law.[5] Following the Korean War the Defense Department referred over two hundred cases of possible treason arising out of that conflict to the Department of Justice, but actual prosecutions were few. They seem likely to continue to be few.

In fact, to a considerable degree prosecutions under various antisubversive and espionage laws, which do not present such difficult problems of proof, have substituted for treason prosecutions. In the famous case of the Rosenbergs, who were executed in 1952 after conviction under the Espionage Act for giving aid to a country, not an enemy, the offense was held to be distinct from treason, so that neither the two-witness rule nor the overt act requirement was applicable.[6]

CRIMINAL PROCEDURE IN THE ORIGINAL CONSTITUTION

For the most part the original Constitution did not concern itself with spelling out the procedural protections in federal prosecutions, but there were four exceptions. One, the prohibition on suspension of the writ of habeas corpus, has been discussed

---

[4] *United States* v. *Burr* (1807).

[5] *Kawakita* v. *United States* (1952).

[6] *United States* v. *Rosenberg* (1952). On the general subject, see James Willard Hurst, "Treason in the United States," 58 HARVARD LAW REVIEW 226, 395, 806 (1944–1945), and *The Law of Treason in the United States: Collected Essays* (Westport, Conn.: Greenwood Press, 1971).

in Chapter 17. A second, the jury trial provisions of Article III, was quickly superseded by the Sixth Amendment. Only the prohibitions on bills of attainder and ex post facto laws need be examined here.

Bills of Attainder

Both Congress and the states were forbidden by Article I, sections 9 and 10, to pass any "bill of attainder." These provisions were adopted to outlaw the practice of legislative punishment common in England, where individuals could be condemned to death by special act of Parliament called a bill of attainder. Legislative acts inflicting lesser punishments were designated "bills of pains and penalties." As interpreted by the Supreme Court, the bill of attainder provisions forbid all legislative acts, "no matter what their form, that apply either to named individuals or to easily ascertainable members of a group in such a way as to inflict punishment on them without a judicial trial."[7]

The bill of attainder provisions were first applied after the Civil War. A congressional act requiring attorneys practicing in the federal courts to take an oath that they had never given aid to persons engaged in hostility to the United States was held unconstitutional in *Ex parte Garland* (1867). In *Cummings* v. *Missouri* (1867) a state constitutional provision seeking to exclude persons who had aided the Confederacy from following certain professions—a minister was involved in this case—was invalidated on similar grounds.

No other legislation was held to constitute a bill of attainder until 1946, when in *United States* v. *Lovett* the Court voided an act of Congress which had prohibited the payment of compensation to three named government employees who had been charged with subversive activities by the House Un-American Activities Committee. In *Communist Party* v. *SACB* (1961) Justice Black, dissenting, contended that the Internal Security Act of 1950 was a "classical bill of attainder" because it constituted a legislative finding of guilt against members of the Communist Party. The majority said, in rebuttal: "The Act is not a bill of attainder. It attaches not to specified organizations but to described activities in which an organization may or may not engage."

However, Black's view became that of the Court majority in *United States* v. *Brown* (1965) where, as already reported, a 1959 statute making it a crime for a member of the Communist Party to serve as an officer or employee of a labor union was held unconstitutional. It would be legitimate, said Chief Justice Warren, for Congress to adopt a generally applicable rule decreeing that any person who commits certain acts or possesses certain characteristics should not hold union office, leaving to courts and juries the task of deciding what persons fell in those categories. But this act designated the persons who possessed the feared characteristics—members of the Communist Party—and this made the act a bill of attainder.

Ex Post Facto Laws

The passage of ex post facto laws is also forbidden to both Congress and the states. An ex post facto law is "a law made after the doing of the thing to which it relates,

---

[7] *United States* v. *Lovett* (1946). See John Hart Ely, "*United States* v. *Lovett:* Litigating the Separation of Powers," 10 Harvard Civil Rights–Civil Liberties Law Review 1 (1975).

and retroacting upon it." The reason for inserting such sweeping prohibitions in the Constitution was apparently to be found in the freedom with which state legislatures in that era had passed paper money or legal tender laws setting aside existing contracts, so that what had been lent in gold and silver could be repaid in paper. However, in *Calder* v. *Bull* (1798) the Supreme Court construed the ex post facto clauses as covering only penal and criminal laws.

Every law that makes criminal an act done before the passage of such law that was innocent when done, or that aggravates a crime or makes it greater than when it was committed, or that changes the punishment and inflicts a greater penalty than the law annexed to the crime when committed, or that alters the rules of evidence, permitting less or different evidence to convict a person of an offense committed prior to its passage, or that operates in any way to the disadvantage of one accused of a crime committed prior to the enactment of the law is an ex post facto law. The clause is directed against legislative action only. It does not reach erroneous or inconsistent decisions of the courts.

A law cannot be held to be ex post facto unless it imposes punishment in the legal sense for past acts. A deportation law authorizing the Secretary of Labor to expel aliens for criminal acts committed before its passage was held not ex post facto, since deportation is not classified as punishment, but as a discretionary exercise of sovereign power.[8] Similarly, a statute terminating payment of social security benefits to an alien following deportation for Communist affiliation was declared not ex post facto on the ground that it was not a penalty.[9]

The right to practice a business or profession may be denied to one who was convicted of an offense before the statute was enacted, if the offense can reasonably be regarded as a continuing disqualification. Thus *DeVeau* v. *Braisted* (1960) upheld a statute excluding convicted felons from offices in New York waterfront unions, unless pardoned or holding a parole board's good conduct certificate. But the Civil War test oaths invalidated as bills of attainder in *Garland* and *Cummings* were also held to be ex post facto, on the assumption that they bore no reasonable relation to fitness to perform professional duties.

UNREASONABLE SEARCHES AND SEIZURES

The Fourth Amendment is the most specific recognition of the right of privacy in the Constitution. It reflects the strong resentment felt by the American colonists against the "general warrants" or "writs of assistance" that the British had employed to search private homes and other premises in enforcement of their tax laws and commercial regulations. Such searches were not permitted at common law. To be sure, English law did recognize broad powers of arrest; even private citizens could make arrests, and all felony arrests could be made without warrant. In fact, arrest warrants were accepted only reluctantly and primarily for the purpose of protecting those making arrests from tort liability. But the common law, with its

---

[8] *Mahler* v. *Eby* (1924).
[9] *Flemming* v. *Nestor* (1960).

strong bias toward property rights, did not grant any right to search the premises of suspected offenders on the grounds of "reasonable suspicion." English insistence that a man's home is his castle has been forever memoralized in Willam Pitt's speech on the Excise Bill:

> The poorest man may in his cottage bid defiance to all the force of the Crown. It may be frail; its roof may shake; the wind may blow through it; the storms may enter, the rain may enter,—but the King of England cannot enter; all his forces dare not cross the threshold of the ruined tenement.

The provisions in the Bill of Rights, as we know, apply only to the federal government unless they are extended to the states by the Fourteenth Amendment. Chapter 25 traced the developments in the early period of the "incorporation" controversy, as the Court rejected various efforts to make the criminal prosecution provisions of the Bill of Rights applicable to the states. The Supreme Court had no occasion to consider the relationship of the Fourth Amendment to the states until 1949, when it decided *Wolf* v. *Colorado.* Then the justices readily agreed, in an opinion by Justice Frankfurter, that freedom from unreasonable search and seizure was an essential element in the concept of "ordered liberty."

> The security of one's privacy against arbitrary intrusion by the police—which is at the core of the Fourth Amendment—is basic to a free society. . . . The knock at the door, whether by day or by night, as a prelude to a search, without authority of law but solely on the authority of the police, did not need the commentary of recent history to be condemned as inconsistent with the conception of human rights enshrined in the history and the basic constitutional documents of English-speaking peoples.

Another preliminary comment should be made concerning the coverage of the Amendment. It applies in arrests and searches of individuals' persons, their living quarters, offices, or the hotel rooms they are occupying, and even their automobiles. The basic elements bringing search and seizure protection into effect have historically been two—there must be a physical invasion of or trespass on a constitutionally protected area and there must be a seizure of a physical object. But, as we shall see, there have now been substantial modifications in both these standards.

Arrests and Probable Cause

Because of the close connection between searches and arrests, a few words are in order concerning the power to arrest. The Fourth Amendment recognizes warrants of arrest, which can be issued only on "probable cause." However, the amendment does not mean that warrants are required for an arrest. That would be completely impractical, because it would preclude officers from making arrests for offenses committed in their presence or where immediate action was necessary to apprehend a law violator. In *United States* v. *Watson* (1976) the Court even upheld a warrantless arrest in a public place on probable cause, although the officer had had time to secure a warrant and no exigency justified his failure to do so. As we shall see, a search would not have been valid under these conditions.

Probable cause for arrest exists where facts and circumstances within the officer's knowledge or of which he has "reasonably trustworthy information [are] sufficient in themselves to warrant a man of reasonable caution in the belief that an offense has been or is being committed."[10] In *Terry* v. *Ohio* (1968), the Court said that it had consistently refused to sanction arrests "based on nothing more substantial than inarticulate hunches." In *Papachristou* v. *City of Jacksonville* (1972), Douglas wrote, "Arresting a person on suspicion, like arresting a person for investigation, is foreign to our system." But in *Draper* v. *United States* (1959), an arrest by federal narcotics agents was ruled valid where the agents had only a tip that a man arriving on a certain train, dressed in a certain way, walking fast, and carrying a tan bag would be transporting narcotics.

An arrest occurs not only when the traditional forms are followed but, according to *Terry,* "whenever a police officer accosts an individual and restrains his freedom to walk away." Similarly, in *Henry* v. *United States* (1959), the Court held that an arrest had occurred when two FBI agents stopped a suspect's car, though the formal arrest did not take place until two hours later, after the suspect had been taken to their office and cartons he had been transporting had been found to contain stolen radios.

The Search Warrant

As the test of reasonableness in a search, the Fourth Amendment relies primarily upon the requirement of a search warrant, issued "upon probable cause, supported by oath or affirmation, and particularly describing the place to be searched, and the persons or things to be seized." Warrants are issued by judicial officers, who are brought into the procedure to exert a neutral or at least modifying influence upon the police. As Justice Murphy said, "In their understandable zeal to ferret out crime and in the excitement of the capture of a suspected person, officers are less likely [than judges] to possess the detachment and neutrality with which the constitutional rights of the suspect must be viewed."[11]

A judicial officer has probable cause for issuance of a warrant if presented with an affidavit setting forth apparent facts that would lead a reasonably discreet and prudent person to believe that the offense charged had been committed.[12] Accord-

---

[10] *Brinegar* v. *United States* (1949). A Florida procedure whereby a person arrested without a warrant and charged by information may be jailed without an opportunity for probable cause determination is unconstitutional; *Gerstein* v. *Pugh* (1975).

[11] *Trupiano* v. *United States* (1948). See also *Johnson* v. *United States* (1948). In *Coolidge* v. *New Hampshire* (1971), a warrant for search of an automobile in a murder case was issued by the chief law enforcement officer of the state—the attorney general—who acted in his capacity as a justice of the peace at the same time that he personally directed police investigation of the murder; later he was chief prosecutor at the trial. The Court held he was not a "neutral and detached magistrate." *Shadwick* v. *Tampa* (1972) held that municipal court clerks are "neutral and detached magistrates" for Fourth Amendment purposes.

[12] There was probable cause for issuance of a search warrant when officers had seen large amounts of sugar and five-gallon cans being taken into a house and had smelled fermenting mash when walking past the house; *United States* v. *Ventresca* (1965). Generally, the fact that evidence is available to officers which would justify issuance of a search warrant does not relieve them of the necessity to secure such a warrant. In *Jones* v. *United States* (1958), the Court held that protracted observation by federal agents of mash flowing from a house did not justify search and seizure of contraband distilling equipment without

ing to *Jones* v. *United States* (1960) and *Aguilar* v. *Texas* (1964), an affidavit resting on hearsay—that is, one which relies on the observations of an informer rather than an officer—meets the probable cause test if the informer has previously given correct information and if there is corroboration from other sources, or if the magistrate is informed of some of the underlying circumstances on which the informant's conclusions were based and from which the officer determined that the information was reliable.

In *Spinelli* v. *United States* (1969), the Warren Court held that an anonymous tip was not acceptable as probable cause even though it had been corroborated by a detailed FBI affidavit.[13] But the Burger Court, by a five to four decision in *United States* v. *Harris* (1971), undermined *Spinelli* by eliminating the requirement that the police must demonstrate the credibility of an anonymous informer, and it authorized the magistrate to rely on an officer's assertion about a suspect's reputation, which comes close to holding that a person with a bad reputation does not have any Fourth Amendment rights.[14]

Whatever the Supreme Court's standards may be, it is unfortunately true that many magistrates issue search warrants either automatically or after only the most perfunctory inquiry.

Search without a Warrant

Most constitutional issues as to search and seizure arise, however, not out of failure to observe the requirements in securing warrants but out of failure to secure any search warrants at all. Such failure does not necessarily void a search or seizure. It depends upon the circumstances.

Search without a warrant may be made in connection with a valid arrest. An officer making an arrest with a warrant of arrest, or on the basis of trustworthy information, or for a crime committed in the officer's presence may search the person of the suspect for weapons and seize any evidence of crime in plain sight within the immediate area of the arrest.

The "plain sight" and the "immediate area" rules have been the subject of intense controversy. In *Harris* v. *United States* (1947) the Court by a five to four vote upheld a search of a four-room apartment with only an arrest warrant. But the following year, in *Trupiano* v. *United States* the Court, again divided five to four, invalidated a seizure without a warrant of a still on a New Jersey farm where the illegal equipment was in plain sight, the reason being that the agents had had plenty of time to secure a warrant and seemed to have willfully disregarded the warrant requirement.

Then, in *United States* v. *Rabinowitz* (1950) the Court swung back toward the *Harris* position. A stamp dealer had been arrested on a warrant in his one-room office for selling stamps fraudulently overprinted to give them a higher value for

---

a warrant. Similarly, in *Johnson* v. *United States* (1948), the odor of burning opium coming from a hotel room was held insufficient to justify entry without a warrant.

[13] See also *Whiteley* v. *Warden* (1971).

[14] See Michael A. Rebell, "The Undisclosed Informant and the Fourth Amendment," 81 YALE LAW JOURNAL 703 (1972).

philatelists. A search was then made of the office for additional fraudulent stamps, over five hundred of which were found. Although the officers had thought to bring experts along to identify the stamps, they had not thought to secure a search warrant. The Court, by a five to three vote, held that the search was nevertheless reasonable, since the office was open to the public, small, and under the immediate control of the occupant. *Trupiano* was overruled, to the extent that it required "a search warrant solely upon the basis of the practicability of procuring it rather than upon the reasonableness of the search after a lawful arrest."

But both *Harris* and *Rabinowitz* were overruled by *Chimel* v. *California* (1969). Here the officers, with an arrest warrant but no search warrant, had nevertheless searched an entire three-bedroom house. The Court returned to a more literal interpretation of the rule that on an arrest warrant the officers can conduct only "a search of the person arrested and the area within his reach."

In *Coolidge* v. *New Hampshire* (1971), an arrest inside a house was held not to justify a search of the arrestee's automobile outside on the driveway (which was not in fact searched until two days later, after it had been seized and taken to the police station). *Vale* v. *Louisiana* (1970) ruled that arrest of a man outside his house did not justify search of the home.[15]

A ten-hour delay between arrest and search was held not to be fatal in *United States* v. *Edwards* (1974); the arrestee had been jailed about midnight but his clothing had not been taken away in a search for incriminating evidence until the next morning. With no arrest or search warrants but with probable cause to arrest one Hill, police arrested a man who looked like Hill, but who was not Hill, in Hill's apartment, and seized guns and stolen property that were in plain view. In *Hill* v. *California* (1971), the Court held that good faith arrest of the wrong man did not invalidate the search or Hill's conviction.

A search can be made without a warrant with the consent of the occupant of the quarters searched, who is thereby considered to have waived his or her Fourth Amendment rights. In *United States* v. *Matlock* (1974), an arrest was made in the front yard of a home. The officers were then admitted to the house by a woman living there and with her consent searched the bedroom which she told them was occupied jointly by the arrestee and herself. The Supreme Court held that this was adequate consent for the search.[16]

A suspect who is asked to consent to a search need not be told that there is a right to refuse; so the Court ruled in *Schneckloth* v. *Bustamonte* (1973) and *United States* v. *Watson* (1976). Justice Brennan, dissenting in *Schneckloth*, wrote, "It wholly escapes me how our citizens can meaningfully be said to have waived something as precious as a constitutional guarantee without ever being aware of its existence."

Conviction for murder by strangulation in *Cupp* v. *Murphy* (1973) rested on

---

[15] *United States* v. *Santana* (1976) held that a suspect sighted in a doorway in public view could be pursued into the house without a warrant.

[16] In *Chapman* v. *United States* (1961), the Court held unconstitutional seizure of a still in a rented house by officers acting without a warrant but with the permission of the landlord, who in fact had discovered the still when he entered the house in the absence of the tenant. Since the tenant was not there when the officers arrived either, the search could not be justified as incident to an arrest.

scrapings from under the suspect's fingernails taken in spite of his protests when he went voluntarily to the police station for questioning. The Court held there was probable cause for this search, though the police had neither an arrest nor search warrant.

The Fourth Amendment can be violated by guileful as well as forcible or stealthy intrusions into a constitutionally protected area. In *Gouled* v. *United States* (1921) a business acquaintance, acting under orders of federal officers, obtained entry into Gouled's office by falsely purporting only to pay a social visit. In Gouled's absence, the intruder ransacked the office and seized certain private papers of an incriminating nature. The Court held this an unconstitutional search and seizure.[17]

This precedent did not help James Hoffa, who was convicted in 1964 of jury tampering on the basis of evidence provided by one of his associates, Partin, who had been a frequent visitor to Hoffa's hotel room but who was secretly an informer for the government. Hoffa contended that Partin's role vitiated the consent Hoffa had given for Partin's repeated entries into the suite, and that by listening to Hoffa's statements Partin had conducted an illegal search for verbal evidence.

The Supreme Court, however, in *Hoffa* v. *United States* (1966), held that the security of his hotel room on which Hoffa was entitled to rely had not been breached. Partin was present by invitation, and Hoffa's revelations were voluntary. What Hoffa had relied on was "his misplaced confidence that Partin would not reveal his wrongdoing." Similarly, the Court held in *Lewis* v. *United States* (1966) that a drug pusher who had invited an undercover agent into his home and sold him narcotics there could not contend that there had been an unconstitutional invasion of the "sanctity" of his home.

Stop and Frisk

The common police practice of stopping and frisking suspicious persons without a warrant or probable cause was upheld in *Terry* v. *Ohio* (1968), though within certain limits. Many considerations may arouse an officer's suspicion but fall short of establishing probable cause for an arrest. In *Terry,* a veteran police officer patrolling in downtown Cleveland noted two men who were intently and repeatedly looking into a particular store window. Convinced that they were "casing" the store for a robbery and might be armed, he stopped them, grabbed one man, patted the outside of his clothing, and felt a gun in the overcoat pocket. Chief Justice Warren approved such a search by an officer provided it was limited to "outer clothing . . . in an attempt to discover weapons which might be used to assault him."[18] But in *Sibron* v. *New York* (1968), decided the same day, the Court refused to approve a stop and

---

[17] The Court also ruled in *Gouled* that even in a lawful search the police could seize only illegal articles, such as narcotics, weapons, or fruits of a crime, and not "mere evidence" of crime such as articles of clothing. In 1967 the Court overruled the "mere evidence" rule in *Warden* v. *Hayden,* holding that the principal object of the Fourth Amendment is the protection of privacy rather than the protection of property.

[18] In a companion case, *Peters* v. *New York* (1968), the Court upheld a stop and frisk where an officer had found burglar's tools when he frisked for a weapon after grabbing a furtive suspect who tried to flee from him.

frisk where the officer had no reason to believe the drug suspect he stopped was armed or dangerous. The officer had thrust his hand into the suspect's pocket searching for drugs, which he found. But, noted Warren, "the police officer is not entitled to seize and search every person whom he sees on the street."

A Burger Court ruling, *Adams* v. *Williams* (1972), approved a stop and frisk even though it was not based on the officer's personal observation. An informant had advised the officer that a man sitting in a nearby car was carrying narcotics and had a gun at his waist. The officer went to the vehicle and, when the occupant rolled down the window rather than complying with the officer's request to open the door, reached in and seized a loaded gun from the occupant's waistband. Douglas, Brennan, and Marshall dissented.

Entry

Even though armed with a warrant, officers have generally been required to announce and identify themselves before demanding entry into a house.[19] However, they can enter in "hot pursuit" of a suspect and search the house for the felon, the felon's weapons, and the fruits of the crime.[20]

In *Wong Sun* v. *United States* (1963) an agent, on the basis of information too vague to sustain a request for an arrest warrant, sought entry to a Chinese laundry at 6:00 A.M. by pretending he had some laundry there; after being refused admission he identified himself, broke open the door, and seized the fleeing suspect. The Court by a five to four vote held this to be an unlawful entry and an unauthorized arrest.

By contrast, in *Ker* v. *California* (1963), officers without warrants but with probable cause to suspect narcotics violations entered an apartment quietly and without announcement, using a passkey supplied by the building manager, because they feared the narcotics would be destroyed if they knocked and demanded entry. By another five to four vote, and apparently because these were state rather than federal officers, this justification for a no-knock intrusion was accepted.[21]

In a "law and order" mood, Congress in 1970 included no-knock provisions in the District of Columbia Court Reform Act and also in the Drug Abuse Prevention and Control Act. After several horrifying incidents in which agents broke into the wrong houses and terrorized occupants, Congress repealed the provision in the drug abuse act.

Entry by Other than Police Officers

Search warrants must be secured by city officials seeking to inspect private premises for possible violations of fire, health, and building regulations, but the warrants do not need to meet the same "probable cause" tests required in a criminal investigation. The Court so held in two 1967 cases, *Camara* v. *Municipal Court,* where a city public health inspector without a warrant had been refused entrance to an apartment, and *See* v. *Seattle,* involving an effort to inspect a commercial warehouse

---

[19] *Miller* v. *United States* (1958).
[20] *Warden* v. *Hayden* (1967). "Hot pursuit" was an issue in *United States* v. *Santana* (1976).
[21] In 1973 the Supreme Court of California ruled that California judges could not issue no-knock search warrants; *Parsley* v. *Superior Court of Riverside County* (1973).

under the fire code. In these opinions, decided by a vote of six to three, the Court overruled the earlier five to four holding in *Frank* v. *Maryland* (1959).[22]

In a controversial opinion, *Wyman* v. *James* (1971), the Court held by a vote of six to three that mandatory caseworker visits into homes receiving welfare assistance are rehabilitative, not investigative searches in the traditional criminal law sense, and so the Fourth Amendment does not apply. The visits were made during regular daytime working hours, and forcible entry and snooping were prohibited by law. Justice Marshall, dissenting, said: "A paternalistic notion that a complaining citizen's rights can be violated so long as the State is somehow helping him is alien to our Nation's philosophy."

Automobile Arrests and Searches

The interests of an automobile driver who is stopped and whose car is subjected to a search are three: mobility, which is restrained; control over personal property, which is invaded; and expectations of privacy for the contents of the car, which are breached.[23] Consequently, the Fourth Amendment does apply to automobiles, as the Supreme Court recognized in the leading case of *Carroll* v. *United States* (1925). However, because the mobility of autos would normally make it impossible to secure search warrants, the Court in *Carroll* upheld stopping and searching without a warrant where there is probable cause to believe that the car will yield contraband or evidence useful for prosecution of crime. In *Carroll* the search was for liquor in enforcement of the national prohibition laws.[24]

The search preceded the arrest in *Carroll*. When occupants of a car are placed under arrest before a search is made, the case for a warrantless search is weaker, for the car no longer has free mobility. Thus in *Preston* v. *United States* (1964), after arresting a man in his car for vagrancy, the police took custody of the car because they did not want to leave it on the street. The Court held that this gave them no right to search the car.[25] However, *Chambers* v. *Maroney* (1970) validated an automobile search after the driver's arrest, while the car was in police custody, Justice White claiming that "the mobility of the car . . . still obtained in the station house."

In *Cooper* v. *California* (1967), the car of a man arrested on narcotics charges was held as evidence pending forfeiture proceedings as required by statute. After holding the car for one week, during which time a warrant could have been obtained, the police searched the car without a warrant. The Supreme Court by a five to four vote ruled that police may search a car, with or without probable cause, if they have a continuing right to possess it.

After an accident, an off-duty Chicago policemen was arrested in Wisconsin for drunken driving, and his car was towed to a private garage. Assuming that as a policeman he was required to carry a gun, officers searched the car for it and

---

[22] *Air Pollution Variance Board* v. *Western Alfalfa Corp.* (1974) ruled that a government inspector did not need a search warrant to go onto the outdoor property of a manufacturing plant to observe smoke plumes emitted from chimneys.

[23] See "Warrantless Searches and Seizures of Automobiles," 87 HARVARD LAW REVIEW 835 (1974).

[24] See also *Brinegar* v. *United States* (1949).

[25] See also *Whiteley* v. *Warden* (1971). But *South Dakota* v. *Opperman* (1976) approved a warrantless search of a glove compartment in a car impounded for parking violations.

instead found evidence of a murder. The Court in *Cady* v. *Dombrowski* (1973) upheld the search, since its purpose had been benign and not aimed at discovering
criminal evidence. A warrantless examination of the exterior of an auto and a taking
of exterior paint samples while the car was in a public parking lot was upheld in
Cardwell v. *Lewis* (1974). No expectation of privacy was thereby violated.

Autos stopped for routine traffic inspections, where there is no probable cause
for arrest, can be subjected to search and seizure only if weapons or evidence of
crime are in plain view inside the car. But two 1973 decisions, *United States* v.
Robinson and *Gustafson* v. *Florida,* opened up alarming possibilities for searching the
persons of automobile drivers arrested for minor traffic offenses. A police officer in
the District of Columbia made a full custody arrest of an auto driver whom he knew
to be driving without a license. The officer frisked the arrestee and pulled from one
pocket a cigarette pack, which he opened and found to contain heroin. The *Robinson* decision held this to be a lawful search incident to a lawful arrest. In *Gustafson,* a driver arrested for not having his driver's license in his possession was subjected to a full search which yielded marijuana. The doctrine of these cases, according
to Justice Powell, is that "an individual lawfully subjected to a custodial arrest
retains no significant Fourth Amendment interest in the privacy of his person."[26]

Border and Airline Passenger Searches

Border searches have never been considered subject to the Fourth Amendment.
Since 1789, customs officials have been authorized to search, without warrant or
demonstration of probable cause, anyone entering the United States. In *Boyd* v.
United States (1886), the Court reasoned that since the statute was passed by the
same Congress that proposed the Bill of Rights, border searches were never intended to come within the scope of the Fourth Amendment.

The U.S. Border Patrol, finding it impossible to control illegal Mexican immigration by border searches, has regularly conducted roving patrols and maintained
fixed inspection checkpoints miles inside California and other border states. *Almeida-Sanchez* v. *United States* (1973) held, five to four, that the Fourth Amendment
prohibits the search of vehicles by roving patrols, without a warrant or probable
cause.[27] *United States* v. *Brignoni-Ponce* (1975) extended this ruling to forbid roving
patrols to stop autos for questioning of occupants unless there was reasonable suspicion that they were aliens. *United States* v. *Ortiz* (1975) applied the same rule to
stopping and questioning at fixed checkpoints. Closed by *Ortiz*, the checkpoints

---

[26] These decisions were widely condemned. The Massachusetts legislature passed a statute nullifying their impact and restoring the law in that state as it had been previously understood, permitting
warrantless searches only to remove weapons and to seize evidence of the crime for which the arrest had
been made. See Stephen Arons and Ethan Kutsh, "Reclaiming the Fourth Amendment in Massachusetts," 2 CIVIL LIBERTIES REVIEW 82 (Winter, 1975). In 1975 the California supreme court ruled that
police could not conduct full body searches of persons arrested for minor offenses and explicitly rejected
the *Robinson* rule, contending that the California constitution gave its citizens greater protection against
unreasonable searches and seizures than the federal Constitution. *Los Angeles Times,* August 8, 1975. For
analyses of the *Robinson* case, see Wayne R. La Fave, " 'Case-by-Case Adjudication' versus 'Standardized Procedures': The Robinson Dilemma," and James B. White, "The Fourth Amendment as a Way of
Talking about People: A Study of Robinson and Matlock," in Philip B. Kurland (ed.), *The Supreme
Court Review, 1974* (Chicago: University of Chicago Press, 1974), pp. 127–232.

[27] "Area Search Warrants in Border Zones: *Almeida-Sanchez* and *Camara,*" 84 *Yale Law Journal*
355 (1974).

were reopened when the Court reversed *Ortiz* in *United States* v. *Martinez-Fuerte* and *Sifuentes* v. *United States* (1976), which upheld the constitutionality of stopping autos at fixed checkpoints for brief questioning of occupants regarding citizenship, without warrants or reason to suspect the occupants of a particular car. The Court also said it was constitutional for officers to refer some of the motorists stopped to a secondary inspection area for further questioning, "even if it be assumed that such referrals are made largely on the basis of apparent Mexican ancestry."

The requirement that airline passengers submit to a search of their luggage and their persons is an obvious challenge to the rule of probable cause. The issue had not come to the Supreme Court by 1975, but searches had generally been upheld by lower courts.[28] It can be argued that prevention of hijacking is a compelling interest of such magnitude as to justify the searches. A more difficult problem is whether weapons or evidence of crime secured by such a search can be used in criminal prosecutions.

The Exclusionary Rule

The principal sanction against unconstitutional search and seizure is the "exclusionary rule" that forbids evidence secured in violation of the Fourth Amendment from being used against the defendant in court. The rule has been the subject of intense controversy. There is disagreement as to its justification and its purpose. One theory is that it is intended to act as a deterrent to police misconduct. A second argument is that it preserves the integrity of the courts, for accepting unconstitutionally secured evidence would make them partners in the illegality. Still a third position is that the rule gives effect to a personal constitutional right which the government cannot infringe, and that the rule needs no other justification.[29]

There has been much respectable criticism of the rule. The English do not accept it. The outstanding American authority on evidence, John Wigmore, argues against it. Justice Cardozo thought it unacceptable that "the criminal should go free because the constable has blundered."

The exclusionary rule was first stated by the Supreme Court in a federal case, *Weeks* v. *United States* (1914). The impression has prevailed that the Court promulgated it there only as a rule of evidence in federal courts, not as a requirement derived from the Fourth Amendment. But in fact Justice Day's opinion for a unanimous Court said explicitly that the refusal to repress illegally seized evidence was "a denial of the constitutional rights of the accused."

Originally this exclusionary rule applied only if federal agents were the guilty parties in procuring the evidence. If the evidence was illegally secured by state police or stolen by private parties and then turned over to federal officers on a "silver platter," it could be employed in a federal trial. But in *Elkins* v. *United States*

---

[28] See "The Constitutionality of Airport Searches," 72 MICHIGAN LAW REVIEW 128 (1973).
[29] For an eloquent defense of this third position, see Thomas S. Schrock and Robert C. Welsh, "Up from Calandra: The Exclusionary Rule as a Constitutional Requirement," 59 MINNESOTA LAW REVIEW 251 (1974). See also Anthony Amsterdam, "Perspectives on the Fourth Amendment," 58 MINNESOTA LAW REVIEW 349 (1974); John Kaplan, "The Limits of the Exclusionary Rule," 26 STANFORD LAW REVIEW 1027 (1974).

(1960) the Supreme Court by a vote of five to four abandoned the "silver platter" doctrine.[30]

The Supreme Court did not consider whether the exclusionary rule applied in state courts until *Wolf* v. *Colorado* (1949). As already noted, the Fourth Amendment was there held binding on the states, but six members of the Court voted not to embody the exclusionary rule in the Fourteenth Amendment. Justice Frankfurter, after a survey of practice on this point, concluded that "most of the English-speaking world does not regard as vital . . . the exclusion of evidence thus [illegally] obtained." Accordingly the Court "must hesitate to treat this remedy as an essential ingredient of the right." The sanctions suggested by Frankfurter, if evidence secured by illegal invasion of privacy was nonetheless used in court, were "the remedies of private action and such protection as the internal discipline of the police, under the eyes of an alert public opinion, may afford."

A strong dissent came from Justices Murphy, Rutledge, and Douglas. Justice Holmes had once said that without the exclusion of evidence as a sanction, the Fourth Amendment "might as well be stricken from the Constitution." Now the Court was reversing that view with a "bland citation of 'other remedies.'" Murphy proceeded to demonstrate that these other remedies were either unavailable or unrealistic, and he summed up: "The conclusion is inescapable that but one remedy exists to deter violations of the search and seizure clause. That is the rule which excludes illegally obtained evidence."

The Court's subsequent dilemmas in applying the *Wolf* rule may be illustrated by three decisions. The first, *Rochin* v. *California* (1952), was a prosecution for illegal possession of narcotics. Having information that Rochin was selling dope, three deputy sheriffs entered his house and forced open his bedroom door. Rochin was sitting on the bed partly dressed, and his common-law wife was in bed. There were two capsules on the night stand, which Rochin seized and put in his mouth. The deputies jumped on him and tried to extricate the capsules. This failing, they handcuffed him and took him to a hospital, where at the direction of the officers a doctor pumped his stomach and produced the capsules, which contained morphine. The capsules were the chief evidence on which he was convicted.

Justice Frankfurter for a unanimous Court invalidated the conviction. The *Wolf* rule would have admitted evidence secured illegally, but the conduct here went beyond any acceptable bounds.

> It is conduct that shocks the conscience. Illegally breaking into the privacy of the petitioner, the struggle to open his mouth and remove what was there, the forcible extraction of his stomach's contents—this course of proceeding by agents of government to obtain evidence is bound to offend even hardened sensibilities. They are methods too close to the rack and the screw to permit of constitutional differentiation.

Next came *Irvine* v. *California* (1954), where official conduct was also shocking, but not too shocking to permit application of the *Wolf* rule. The police suspected

---

[30] But *United States* v. *Janis* (1976) held that evidence illegally seized by state officials could be turned over to federal agents and used against the owner in a civil tax proceeding.

Irvine of illegal bookmaking. In his absence from home, they had a locksmith go there and make a door key. Two days later they entered the house with his key and installed a concealed microphone, boring a hole in the roof through which wires were strung to a neighboring garage, where officers were posted with listening devices. Subsequently they twice reentered the house to move the microphone into better positions. At the trial, the officers were allowed to testify to conversations heard by this method.

The Court majority, Justice Jackson writing the opinion, said that this was "trespass, and probably a burglary," but according to *Wolf* there was no basis for denying the state's right to get a conviction by use of such methods. "We adhere to *Wolf* as stating the law of search-and-seizure cases."

Four justices thought the *Irvine* procedure was unconstitutional regardless of the *Wolf* rule, and Frankfurter, author of *Wolf,* was included in the four. He contended that the *Wolf* ruling did not affect the decision on exclusion of the evidence in this case, because here there was "additional aggravating conduct which the Court finds repulsive," as there had also been in the *Rochin* case. There had been no direct physical violence in *Irvine,* as there had been in *Rochin,* but there had been "a more powerful and offensive control over the Irvines' life," a control which enabled police to hear every word said in a private home for an entire month.

The third case was *Breithaupt* v. *Abram* (1957). A truck driven by Breithaupt in New Mexico collided with another car and three persons were killed. An almost empty whisky bottle was found in the truck. Breithaupt, seriously injured, was taken to a hospital unconscious. When liquor was detected on his breath, the police directed a doctor to secure a sample of his blood by use of a hypodermic needle. Testimony regarding the blood test was admitted in evidence at the trial, and an expert gave his opinion that the amount of alcohol found in the blood was sufficient to induce intoxication.

By a six to three vote the Court distinguished these circumstances from those in the *Rochin* case and upheld the conviction. Justice Clark pointed out that blood tests are "routine"; they do not shock the conscience or offend the sense of justice; there is nothing brutal or offensive about them. Intoxication is one of the reasons for the "increasing slaughter on our highways," and the interests of society in reducing these hazards outweigh "so slight an intrusion" on the person.

The Court's effort to distinguish the *Rochin* case was unconvincing, as the three dissenters (Warren, Black, and Douglas) pointed out. In each case the operation was performed by a doctor in a hospital. In each case body fluids were extracted. Both operations are common, "scientific," and cause no lasting ill effects. In both cases evidence which had been obtained from a man on an involuntary basis was used to convict him.

The *Wolf* rule on evidence had apparently emerged unscathed from this series of encounters, but actually its days were numbered. In *Mapp* v. *Ohio* (1961), the Court by a five to three vote overruled *Wolf.* Cleveland police officers, suspecting that a law violator was hiding in a certain house, broke in the door, manhandled a woman resident, searched the entire premises, and discovered some obscene materials in a trunk. The woman was convicted of possession of these materials. The state court, pointing out that the objects had not been taken from the defendant's person by brutal or offensive physical force (as in *Rochin*), permitted their use in evidence on the basis of *Wolf*. But the Supreme Court disposed of *Wolf*, Justice Clark saying:

> The ignoble shortcut to conviction left open to the State [by *Wolf*] tends to destroy the entire system of constitutional restraints on which the liberties of the people rest. Having once recognized that the right to privacy embodied in the Fourth Amendment is enforceable against the States, and that the right to be secure against rude invasions of privacy by state officers is, therefore, constitutional in origin, we can no longer permit that right to remain an empty promise.

When a new constitutional standard is laid down by the Court, it is generally given retroactive effect. But in *Linkletter* v. *Walker* (1965) the Court ruled that the *Mapp* doctrine would not be applied to invalidate state criminal convictions which had become final before the decision was rendered. The existence of the *Wolf* rule prior to *Mapp* had had consequences which could not be ignored. "The past cannot always be erased by a new judicial declaration."[31]

The exclusionary rule has continued to be controversial. The general public undoubtedly sees it as one of the "technicalities" of the law which handcuffs police and lets criminals go free. But scholars and judges also join in the criticism. In a major article, Dallin H. Oaks concluded that the rule did not deter police misconduct and that it had the negative effects of fostering false testimony by law enforcement officers, seriously delaying and overloading criminal proceedings and diverting attention from the search for truth on the guilt or innocence of the defendant. But in spite of these weaknesses and disadvantages, Oaks would not abolish the rule "until there is something to take its place. . . . It would be intolerable if the guarantee against unreasonable search and seizure could be violated without practical consequence."[32]

Oaks would replace the exclusionary rule "by an effective tort remedy against the offending officer or his employer. . . . A tort remedy could break free of the narrow compass of the exclusionary rule, and provide a viable remedy with direct deterrent effect upon the police whether the injured party was prosecuted or not." In *Bivens* v. *Six Unknown Named Agents* (1971), Chief Justice Burger took the same position. Opposing the exclusionary rule, he likewise agreed that it could not be abandoned "until some meaningful alternative can be developed." He recommended that "Congress should develop an administrative or quasijudicial remedy against the government itself to afford compensation and restitution for persons whose Fourth Amendment rights have been violated."

---

[31] See discussions of the retroactivity issue by G. Gregory Fahlund, "Retroactivity and the Warren Court," 35 JOURNAL OF POLITICS 570 (1973); Ralph A. Rossum, "New Rights and Old Wrongs: The Supreme Court and the Problem of Retroactivity," 23 EMORY LAW JOURNAL 381 (1974); and Paul J. Mishkin, "The High Court, the Great Writ, and the Due Process of Time and Law," 79 HARVARD LAW REVIEW 56 (1965).

[32] "Studying the Exclusionary Rule in Search and Seizure," 37 UNIVERSITY OF CHICAGO LAW REVIEW 665 (1970).

There are two problems with these recommendations. The first is the practical one of drafting and funding a feasible plan of tort remedies, which would present great difficulties. The second is the moral problem of permitting individuals to be convicted of crime by the use of evidence secured in violation of their constitutional rights.

In the meantime, even though no discernible progress was being made toward providing a suitable tort remedy, the Burger Court began to dismantle the exclusionary rule piecemeal. In *United States* v. *Calandra* (1974), the Court held that the rule did not apply to grand juries and that witnesses could not refuse to answer questions merely because they were prompted by illegally obtained evidence. Justice Brennan, dissenting, had the "uneasy feeling that today's decision may signal that a majority of my colleagues have positioned themselves to . . . abandon altogether the exclusionary rule," and he repeated this concern in *United States* v. *Peltier* (1975). However, the rule survived a severe test in *Stone* v. *Powell* and *Wolff* v. *Rice* (1976), in spite of Justice Powell's expressed doubt that it had much deterrent effect on police and Burger's open opposition.

Wiretapping and Electronic Surveillance

When the Supreme Court first confronted the wiretapping problem in *Olmstead* v. *United States* (1928), it concluded that the Fourth Amendment was not applicable because there had been no trespass on a constitutionally protected area and no physical object had been seized. Federal prohibition agents had secured evidence against a gang of rumrunners by tapping their telephones and recording the conversations, and convictions were secured on the basis of this evidence. The Court majority determined that there had been no actual search and seizure in this case. The agents had never entered the quarters of the suspects, but had done the tapping in the basements of apartment buildings. "The evidence was secured by the use of the sense of hearing and that only."

Justice Holmes, dissenting, noted that wiretapping was a crime in the state of Washington, where these acts occurred, and said that the United States should have no part in such a "dirty business." Justice Brandeis, also dissenting, felt that the conception of a "search" should not be confined to actual physical entry.

> The progress of science in furnishing the Government with means of espionage is not likely to stop with wire-tapping. Ways may some day be developed by which the Government, without removing papers from secret drawers, can reproduce them in court . . . . Advances in the psychic and related sciences may bring means of exploring unexpressed beliefs, thoughts and emotions. . . . Can it be that the Constitution affords no protection against such invasions of individual security?

The Court did, however, point out in *Olmstead* that Congress had power to adopt "controlling legislation" in this field, and in the 1934 Communications Act Congress followed this suggestion by providing that "no person not being authorized by the sender shall intercept any communication and divulge or publish the . . . contents . . . of such intercepted communication to any person." Subsequently the Court in *Nardone* v. *United States* (1937) held that this law rendered inadmissible in federal trials evidence as to an interstate communication secured by wire tapping. Later the Court extended this interpretation to apply also to intrastate communications and to indirect or derivative use of evidence secured in this fashion.[33]

It might have been expected that the Roosevelt Court, which was so largely guided by the views of Holmes and Brandeis, would have taken the first opportunity to adopt their dissenting position in *Olmstead*. But when the occasion presented itself in *Goldman* v. *United States* (1942), only Frankfurter, Stone, and Murphy were prepared to do so. Douglas confessed ten years later, in *On Lee* v. *United States,* that his failure to join them had been an error. Black supported *Olmstead* because of his literalist interpretation of the Fourth Amendment as applying only to tangible objects.

In the *Goldman* case the Court for the first time encountered the practice of electronic eavesdropping or "bugging." No use is made of telephone lines; instead, bugs are planted in locations permitting conversations to be overheard at a distance. In *Goldman* government agents had used a detectaphone sensitive enough to pick up conversations in an adjoining office, the words being heard through the wall with no physical intrusion into the adjacent office. Since *Olmstead* had ruled that words are not protected against seizure, and since there had been no search involving physical trespass, the Court majority held that the Fourth Amendment had not been violated.[34]

The Communications Act did not stop wiretapping. In fact, the Department of Justice, relying on an interpretation of the act by Attorney General Jackson, contended it was not a criminal violation to intercept conversations by wiretapping so long as the results were not used in court. Consequently federal agencies carried on wiretapping on a large scale, though supposedly only with the express consent of the Attorney General and principally in cases of national security or where life was in danger.

Continuous efforts were made in Congress to pass legislation authorizing wiretapping, but they all failed. A number of states, however, passed laws permitting wiretapping if authorized in advance by a judge, judicial consent serving as the functional equivalent of a search warrant. But the Supreme Court in *Berger* v. *New York* (1967) declared a law of this type unconstitutional by a vote of five to four. The wiretapping, each instance of which could continue for two months, was condemned as the equivalent of a series of intrusions pursuant to a single showing of probable cause, and with no notice to those overheard. The broad sweep of the Court's language left it uncertain whether any practical wiretap law could be adopted.

[33] *Weiss* v. *United States* (1939) and *Nardone* v. *United States* (1939). See also *Rathbun* v. *United States* (1957); *Benanti* v. *United States* (1957).

[34] If trespass does occur during a bugging operation, then of course it becomes an unconstitutional search and seizure under the *Olmstead-Goldman* doctrine. In *Silverman* v. *United States* (1961), police officers in the District of Columbia had occupied a vacant house and driven a "spike mike" through the party wall of an adjoining row house. The spike made contact with the heating duct of the house, and all conversations in the house were audible to the officers next door. The Supreme Court held that the projection of the spike into the adjoining house, "by even a fraction of an inch," amounted to an unauthorized physical penetration of a constitutionally protected area.

The Court quickly reconsidered, however. *Katz* v. *United States* (1967) outlined a procedure by which wiretapping could be constitutionally employed, namely, prior judicial authorization justified by investigation and a showing of probable cause and for a strictly limited law enforcement purpose.[35] Equally important, *Katz* finally overruled *Olmstead* and *Goldman,* and abandoned the conception that the Fourth Amendment forbids only physical invasions and physical seizures. What the Fourth Amendment actually protects, said Justice Stewart, is "people, not places. What a person knowingly exposes to the public, even in his own home or office, is not a subject of Fourth Amendment protection. But what he seeks to preserve as private, even in an area accessible to the public, may be constitutionally protected."

In *Katz,* government agents had eavesdropped on a gambler by bugging a public telephone booth that he habitually used to place bets. But the fact that he was in a glass-enclosed booth where he could be readily seen was irrelevant. He was constitutionally entitled to make a private telephone call which would not be broadcast to government agents by a bug on top of the phone booth. The fact that there was no physical penetration of the agents into the phone booth was also irrelevant. The Court, Stewart said, has departed from the "narrow view" of the *Olmstead* case that property interests or technical notions of trespass control the right of the government to search and seize. "The Government's activities in electronically listening to and recording the petitioner's words violated the privacy upon which he justifiably relied while using the telephone booth and thus constituted a 'search and seizure' within the meaning of the Fourth Amendment."

With the support of the *Katz* decision, Congress in the Crime Control Act of 1968 provided for a system of judicially approved wiretapping for certain classes of crime on the request of the Attorney General. The provisions were carefully drawn to meet the requirements of *Berger* and *Katz*; applications for consent to wiretap or bug had to be detailed and particularized, and conditions for use of the order were carefully circumscribed.[36] Applications had to be signed by the Attorney General or an Assistant Attorney General specially designated by him for this purpose. However, Attorney General John Mitchell permitted his executive assistant to sign applications, a procedure the Supreme Court held illegal in *United States* v. *Giordano* (1974), thereby nullifying the prosecution of over six hundred defendants.

Attorney General Mitchell contended that the requirements of the 1968 act did not apply to wiretapping in "national security" investigations, citing a provision in the statute that nothing contained therein should "be deemed to limit the constitutional power of the President" to protect the United States. However, in *United States* v. *United States District Court* (1972), the Supreme Court unanimously held that this language was not a grant of power, and that so far as domestic security

[35] The Court referred for support to its favorable decision in *Osborn* v. *United States* (1966), where on the basis of a sworn statement that one of James Hoffa's attorneys had endeavored to bribe a prospective juror, the two federal judges in the district where the trial was being conducted had authorized the use of a tape recorder for the specific and limited purpose of ascertaining the truth of the allegation.

[36] In *United States* v. *Kahn* (1974), a court-approved wiretap on the phone of a man suspected of gambling yielded information about his wife, who had not been named in the application or suspected of complicity. The Court held that information concerning her was nonetheless validly obtained.

measures were concerned, the prior judicial warrant procedures had to be followed. Whether the same rules apply to wiretapping for foreign intelligence purposes within the United States was left unclear when the Court failed to decide the case of *Ivanov* v. *United States* in 1974.

In fact, the Department of Justice did construe its national security authority to cover wiretapping of domestic organizations with foreign contacts. In 1974, some 148 warrantless wiretaps were authorized by the Department. However, in a 1975 case involving taps on the Jewish Defense League, the Court of Appeals for the District of Columbia held that a warrant must be obtained before a tap was installed on a domestic organization that was neither an agent of nor acting in collaboration with a foreign power. The court went on to say that "absent exigent circumstances, no wiretapping in the area of foreign affairs should be exempt from prior judicial scrutiny." President Ford directed the Department of Justice to abide by this decision.[37] The Supreme Court denied review (*Barrett* v. *Zweibon* [1976]).

Third-Party Bugging

In *On Lee* v. *United States* (1952), the Court held admissible statements made by the accused to a supposed friend on his own premises which, through a transmitter concealed on the person of the "friend," were broadcast to a federal agent outside. The Court majority regarded this as simply "eavesdropping on a conversation, with the connivance of one of the parties"; but Justice Frankfurter thought that, like *Olmstead,* it was "dirty business." However, the *On Lee* ruling, to which four justices dissented, was reaffirmed in *Lopez* v. *United States* (1963). Here a federal agent investigating possible evasion of excise taxes by a restaurant owner was offered a bribe to call off the investigation. The agent returned with a pocket wire recorder on his person and secured a recording which was used at the trial. The Court majority denied this was eavesdropping. The agent was lawfully on the premises, and the recording was simply corroborating evidence of what he had heard with his own ears.

After the new notions of privacy enunciated in *Berger* and *Katz,* it seemed reasonable to conclude that *On Lee* and *Lopez* could not survive. But in *United States* v. *White* (1971), the Court accomplished the feat of reconciling *On Lee* with *Katz,* over the protests of Douglas, Harlan, Brennan and Marshall. Again, a government informant had carried a transmitter on his person which broadcast incriminating statements of the suspect to concealed agents. The Court majority approved this method of supplying "relevant and probative evidence which is also accurate and reliable," but Harlan condemned third-party bugging as violating the general principle that "official investigatory action that impinges on privacy must typically, in order to be constitutionally permissible, be subjected to the warrant requirement."

---

[37] *The New York Times,* June 24, 1975. A superb but critical analysis of the Supreme Court's Fourth Amendment decisions from 1969 to 1973 is found in Leonard W. Levy, *Against the Law: The Nixon Court and Criminal Justice* (New York: Harper & Row, Publishers, Incorporated, 1974), chap. 2. See, more generally, Jacob W. Landynski, *Search and Seizure and the Supreme Court* (Baltimore: The Johns Hopkins Press, 1966).

Private Papers and Records

In *Boyd* v. *United States* (1886), a proceeding for nonpayment of customs duties, a court order required the production of invoices covering the goods. The Supreme Court declared the statute authorizing this order unconstitutional on the ground that "any forcible and compulsory extortion of a man's . . . private papers . . . to convict him of crime" was a violation of both the Fourth and Fifth Amendments. But under *Andresen* v. *Maryland* (1976) the Fifth Amendment no longer protects private papers. Moreover, when personal papers are out of the possession of their owner and in the hands of another person who is ordered to surrender them by subpoena, there is no Fourth Amendment protection. Provisions of the Bank Secrecy Act requiring banks to keep records and make reports on transactions of their clients were held in *California Bankers Association* v. *Schultz* (1974) not to violate the Fourth Amendment, for the government could get access to these records only "by existing legal process." But this turned out to be quite easy. *United States* v. *Miller* (1976) upheld the government's right to demand from the banks microfilmed copies of checks and deposit slips, for a customer has "no legitimate expectation of privacy when he does business with a bank."

SELF-INCRIMINATION

The Fifth Amendment provides that no one "shall be compelled in any criminal case to be a witness against himself."[38] There has been much diversity of opinion concerning the privilege against self-incrimination. On the one hand, it has been regarded as "one of the great landmarks in man's struggle to make himself civilized."[39] Justice Field said: "The essential and inherent cruelty of compelling a man to expose his own guilt is obvious to everyone."[40] On the other hand, the privilege was subjected to a classic attack by Jeremy Bentham, and Charles Evans Hughes recommended serious consideration of its abolition.

The first, and most obvious, effect of the Fifth Amendment is that the defendant in a criminal trial cannot be required to take the witness stand. It is improper for opposing counsel or the judge to call attention to failure of a defendant to take the stand in his own defense, and by federal statute a jury must be instructed that the defendant's failure to testify creates no presumption against him.[41] If he does take the stand, then he lays himself open to cross-examination which may bring out evidence damaging to his cause.

Before a grand jury, congressional committee, or administrative tribunal, the situation is different. Since there has been no indictment for crime, a person from whom evidence is sought cannot refuse to be a witness, but once he has gone on the witness stand, he can decline to answer particular questions on the ground of self-incrimination. It is normally very difficult to challenge a witness who refuses to testify on Fifth Amendment grounds without forcing him to reveal the conduct which the Constitution entitles him to conceal. It is agreed that a witness may refuse

[38] See generally Leonard W. Levy, *Origins of the Fifth Amendment* (New York: Oxford University Press, 1968).

[39] Erwin N. Griswold, *The Fifth Amendment Today* (Cambridge, Mass.: Harvard University Press, 1955), p. 7.

[40] *Brown* v. *Walker* (1896).

[41] *Bruno* v. *United States* (1939); see also *Griffin* v. *California* (1965).

to give not only answers which constitute an admission of guilt but also those which merely furnish evidence of guilt or supply leads to obtaining such evidence. However, he may not refuse to talk when the danger of incrimination is "of an imaginary and unsubstantial character, having reference to some extraordinary and barely possible contingency, so improbable that no reasonable man would suffer it to influence his conduct."[42]

The Fifth Amendment does not justify a person in refusing to testify about matters which would merely impair his reputation or tend to disgrace him.[43] A divided Court has held that where a witness or defendant has voluntarily answered some questions, he may not refuse to answer related questions on the ground of self-incrimination.[44]

An individual who has acquired income in an illegal manner cannot refuse on self-incrimination grounds to make out an income tax return, but he could refuse to answer incriminating questions concerning it.[45] Even though criminal conduct would be disclosed by the answers, a person may not refuse to testify if the conduct is no longer punishable because the statute of limitations has run or because he has been granted immunity from prosecution by statute.

Grant of Immunity

Compatibly with the Fifth Amendment, there is a method of compelling witnesses to testify against themselves. Under appropriate statutory authority, the state can grant immunity from prosecution to persons for any incriminating evidence they may give under compulsion. Immunity is granted by court order on application of prosecuting officials, and if witnesses refuse to testify after being granted immunity, they can be jailed for contempt.[46] Immunity is typically sought for minor criminal suspects whose evidence will help to convict major malefactors.

The first federal immunity statute was upheld by a five to four vote of the Supreme Court in *Brown* v. *Walker* (1896). The majority admitted that, interpreted literally, the self-incrimination clause authorizes a witness "to refuse to disclose any fact which might tend to incriminate, disgrace or expose him to unfavorable comments," and as so interpreted would render the immunity act unconstitutional. But the Fifth Amendment could also be read as having for its object only "to secure the witness against a criminal prosecution, which might be aided directly or indirectly by his disclosure." The Court regarded this second interpretation as yielding a better balance between private right and public welfare. "If [a witness] secure legal immunity from prosecution, the possible impairment of his good name is a penalty which it is reasonable he should be compelled to pay for the common good."

The frequent blockage of government inquiries into subversion by claims of the privilege against self-incrimination led the Eisenhower administration to propose, and Congress to adopt, the Immunity Act of 1954, under which witnesses can be

---

[42] Quoted in *Emspak* v. *United States* (1955) from an 1861 decision by the Court of Queen's Bench, *The Queen* v. *Boyes*, 1 B. & S. 311.

[43] *Hale* v. *Henkel* (1906).

[44] *Rogers* v. *United States* (1951); *Brown* v. *United States* (1958).

[45] *United States* v. *Sullivan* (1927).

[46] See *United States* v. *Wilson* (1975).

compelled to testify before courts, grand juries, or congressional committees in national security cases by granting them immunity from prosecution for any criminal activities they may confess. The act was upheld in *Ullmann* v. *United States* (1956) on the authority of *Brown* v. *Walker*. Justice Douglas, dissenting with Black, thought that *Brown* v. *Walker* should be overruled. Under its doctrine, the constitutionally guaranteed privilege of silence was being traded away "for a partial, undefined, vague immunity." The 1954 statute protected individuals from criminal punishment but exposed them to the punishment of infamy and disgrace. "My view is that the Framers put it beyond the power of Congress to *compel* anyone to confess his crimes. The evil to the guarded against was partly self-accusation under legal compulsion. But that was only part of the evil. The conscience and dignity of man were also involved."

Until 1970 all immunity statutes granted "transactional immunity"—that is, they entirely barred subsequent prosecution for any "transaction, matter or thing" to which the witness testified. However, the Organized Crime Control Act of 1970 provided for a more limited form of immunity, called "use" or "testimonial" immunity, which only bars use of the witnesses' testimony (or any information derived directly or indirectly from such testimony) in any criminal case. If evidence of crime can be secured independently from the compelled testimony, the witness is not protected from prosecution.

Such partial, as compared with complete, immunity was held not to violate the Fifth Amendment in *Kastigar* v. *United States* (1972). The Court thought that the witness given use immunity was sufficiently protected because in any subsequent prosecution the state would have to assume "the affirmative duty to prove that the evidence it proposes to use is derived from a legitimate source wholly independent of the compelled testimony." But, as Levy says, these admissions, though technically not incriminating, "are an open invitation for the state to conduct its own investigation against him, secure in the knowledge that he is implicated, if not guilty, by his own admission."[47] Justice Douglas, dissenting in *Kastigar,* said: "Government acts in an ignoble way when it stoops to the end which we authorize today."

Self-Incrimination in State Courts

We have already seen that the Fifth Amendment was long regarded as inapplicable to state prosecutions. Two major decisions, *Twining* v. *New Jersey* (1908) and *Adamson* v. *California* (1947), upheld state statutes permitting the drawing of unfavorable inferences from the defendant's failure to take the witness stand. To similar effect was *Feldman* v. *United States* (1944), where by a four to three vote the Court held that the Fifth Amendment did not protect a person in refusing to give testimony in a hearing before a state body that might lead to a federal prosecution.

Cohen v. *Hurley* (1961) by a five to four margin held that New York could disbar an attorney who invoked the privilege and refused to testify before a judicially established committee of inquiry looking into "ambulance chasing." The majority held that the attorney's disbarment was based not on the exercise of the self-incrimi-

---

[47] Leonard W. Levy, *op. cit.,* p. 184, and Chap. 3 generally.

nation privilege but on his refusal to discharge obligations which as a lawyer he owed the court.

But only two months after *Cohen,* the *Mapp* decision began a constitutional revolution which eventually dethroned the "ordered liberty" test and absorbed the major protections of the Bill of Rights into the Fourteenth Amendment. In due course *Malloy* v. *Hogan* (1964), by another five to four vote, overruled the long-established doctrine of *Twining* and *Adamson.* Justice Brennan for the majority wrote: "The Twining view of the privilege has been eroded. . . . It would be incongruous to have different standards determine the validity of a claim of privilege . . . depending on whether the claim was asserted in a state or federal court."

Justice Harlan, one of the dissenters, agreed that principles of justice inherent in due process should forbid a state to imprison a person solely because he refused to give evidence which might incriminate him. But he objected to the majority's "wholesale incorporation" of federal requirements into the Fourteenth Amendment, for this would make applicable to the states the entire body of federal law that had grown up in this field, in inevitable "disregard of all relevant differences which may exist between state and federal criminal law and its enforcement."

On the same day that *Malloy* was decided, the Court overruled *Feldman* and held in *Murphy* v. *Waterfront Commission of New York Harbor* (1964) that evidence which a person was compelled to give before a state tribunal under guarantee of immunity from state prosecution could not be used against him in a federal prosecution. The basis for the *Feldman* decision, questionable enough when it was handed down in 1944, had been completely undercut by the *Elkins* ruling that evidence illegally seized by state officials could not be used in federal courts.

One week after *Malloy* and *Murphy,* the Warren Court handed down its famous decision in *Escobedo* v. *Illinois* (1964). While *Escobedo* and its even more famous twin, *Miranda* v. *Arizona* (1966), have a bearing on self-incrimination, they are more appropriately discussed in connection with the right to counsel. The *Malloy-Murphy* holdings were given effect in a number of later Warren Court cases. Self-incrimination was one of the protections extended to juvenile court proceedings in *In re Gault* (1967). *Spevack* v. *Klein* (1967) overruled *Cohen* v. *Hurley,* holding that lawyers were as much entitled to protection against self-incrimination as other persons, and should not have to suffer "the dishonor of disbarment and the deprivation of a livelihood as a price for asserting it."[48]

Self-Incrimination and the Burger Court

The Burger Court brought an abrupt change in attitudes toward self-incrimination. Leonard Levy noted that in the first two terms after Burger's appointment, the Court decided fourteen self-incrimination cases, and in all but one the right claimed under the Fifth Amendment lost.

A few examples will be given. *Williams* v. *Florida* (1970) held that the privilege was not violated by a requirement that the defendant give notice before trial if an alibi defense was going to be offered and disclose his alibi witnesses. *California* v.

---

[48] In *Garrity* v. *New Jersey* (1967), a companion case to *Spevack* v. *Klein,* the Court ruled that where police officers were given the choice of incriminating themselves or forfeiting their jobs and pension rights, and they chose to make confessions, the confessions were not voluntary and could not be used in subsequent criminal prosecutions in state courts.

Byers (1971) concluded that a state hit-and-run law requiring a motorist involved in an accident to stop at the scene and give his or her name and address did not compel self-incrimination. The state supreme court upheld the requirement to stop but, recognizing the self-incrimination issue, ruled that no prosecutorial use could be made of the required disclosures. The state could still prosecute if it could produce independent evidence of guilt. But four members of the Supreme Court, led by Burger, thought that the information required to be given was not "testimonial" in character and did not necessarily incriminate the driver. Harlan said the information was clearly incriminating, but he voted with the Burger group on the ground that the regulatory objectives of the statute outweighed in importance the constitutional right claimed.[49]

United States v. *Dionisio* (1973) ruled that the Fifth Amendment does not protect a person from a court order to make a voice recording to be played before a federal grand jury seeking to identify a criminal by the sound of a voice on a legally intercepted phone conversation. Here the Burger Court was continuing a line of Warren Court decisions dealing with identification through physical characteristics of suspects. *Schmerber* v. *California* (1966) had upheld compulsory blood tests for drunken drivers involved in accidents. *United States* v. *Wade* (1967) had compelled a suspect in a lineup to speak before witnesses to a bank robbery the words used by the robber. *Gilbert* v. *California* (1967) had approved the requirement that another suspected bank robber submit a handwriting sample for comparison with a note given during the robbery to a bank teller.

In all these cases the suspect was required to give evidence that might be incriminating, but their rationale was that the Fifth Amendment by its reference to "witness" was intending to cover only "testimonial" evidence, that is, communication of information based on one's own knowledge. It did not prevent the taking of evidence as to physical characteristics of suspects.[50]

Private Papers and Records

Boyd v. *United States* (1886) held that "the seizure of a man's private books and papers to be used against him is [not] substantially different from compelling him to be a witness against himself."[51] But subsequent decisions have undermined *Boyd* and made it clear that only personal compulsion of the accused is forbidden.[52] Moreover, the Fifth Amendment does not prevent the government from violating an accused's claims of privacy for books or papers in the possession of another person. Thus *Couch* v. *United States* (1973) held that a taxpayer who regularly turned her

---

[49] *Haynes* v. *United States* (1968) had held self-incriminatory a section of the National Firearms Act which made it unlawful to possess an unregistered firearm. The problem was a rather technical one having to do with the registration requirement, and after Congress amended the statute to limit the use of registration information as evidence in a criminal proceeding, the Court unanimously upheld the act in *United States* v. *Freed* (1971). For an analysis of the *Byers* case, see Bernard D. Meltzer, "Privileges Against Self-Incrimination and the Hit-and-Run Opinions," in Philip B. Kurland (ed.), *The Supreme Court Review, 1971* (Chicago: University of Chicago Press, 1971), pp. 1–30.

[50] This distinction traced back to a statement by Justice Holmes in *Holt* v. *United States* (1910) that the Fifth Amendment prohibited "the use of physical or moral compulsion to extort communication . . . not an exclusion of [the] body as evidence when it would be material." For a criticism of this distinction, see Levy, *op. cit.*, pp. 190–196.

[51] With respect to the production of records, *Boyd* held that the Fourth and Fifth Amendments "run almost into each other."

business and tax records over to an independent accountant had divested herself of control of the records to such a degree that she could not resist a government subpoena to the accountant for production of the records in a tax investigation. Similarly, *Fisher* v. *United States* (1976) upheld an Internal Revenue Service subpoena requiring an attorney to surrender records prepared by the taxpayer's accountant. The Fifth Amendment, said Justice White, "protects a person only against being incriminated by his own compelled testimonial communications," and he alleged that *Boyd* had "not stood the test of time." *Andresen* v. *Maryland* (1976) held there is no self-incrimination if a person's handwritten notes and business records are secured by a search warrant rather than by a subpoena.

Hale v. *Henkel* (1906) held that a corporation cannot resist a subpoena on Fifth Amendment grounds, though it may do so on the basis of the Fourth Amendment. Nor can a custodian of corporate or labor union books withhold them on the ground of possible personal incrimination by their production.[53] Similarly public documents must be produced by the official in possession even though they tend to incriminate him.[54]

COERCED CONFESSIONS

The Fifth Amendment forbids the use in federal courts of confessions secured under conditions of physical or mental coercion, for in such cases the defendant would obviously have been under compulsion to testify against himself.[55] In recent years additional limitations have been placed by the Supreme Court upon the use of confessions in federal prosecutions.

Federal statutes require suspects on apprehension to be taken before the nearest judicial officer "without unnecessary delay" for hearing, commitment, or release on bail. When suspects are taken before a committing magistrate, the law officers must show probable cause for the arrests, and the suspects must be informed of their right to remain silent and to have counsel. The motive of the police in delaying this process is usually to attempt to secure a confession before the suspect learns of his rights.[56]

In *McNabb* v. *United States* (1943) two men suspected of shooting a revenue officer were taken into custody by federal officials and questioned over a period of two days, without the presence of friends or counsel, until a confession was secured. The Supreme Court voided the conviction, not on the ground that the confession was coerced, but because of violation of the "without unnecessary delay" provision.

There was considerable criticism of the *McNabb* rule as placing a substantial

---

[52] *Hale* v. *Henkel* (1906); *Johnson* v. *United States* (1913); *Perlman* v. *United States* (1918).

[53] *Wilson* v. *United States* (1911); *United States* v. *White* (1944).

[54] *Shapiro* v. *United States* (1948). But see *Marchetti* v. *United States* (1968), which struck down a statute that required gamblers to register and to submit monthly detailed information concerning their wagering activities.

[55] *Bram* v. *United States* (1897).

[56] Since the *Escobedo* and *Miranda* decisions, of course, suspects must be informed of these rights as soon as they are arrested or subjected to interrogation.

impediment in the path of law enforcement, but the Court reaffirmed it in *Mallory* v. *United States* (1957). This decision, which voided a death sentence for rape in the District of Columbia, set off a concerted effort in Congress to revise the *McNabb* rule by new legislation providing that a confession or other evidence otherwise admissible should not be excluded solely because of delay in the arraignment. These initial efforts failed, but in 1967 Congress passed an act revising the *McNabb-Mallory* rule by permitting police in the District of Columbia to detain suspects for up to three hours of interrogation before having them arraigned.

Coerced Confessions in State Courts

Confessions extorted by force and violence are contrary to the most elemental notions of due process and any convictions based on them are void. The Supreme Court was first confronted with such a situation in *Brown* v. *Mississippi* (1936). The facts of brutality and torture by state officers were uncontroverted, and no evidence other than the coerced confessions of murder was presented at the trial. The state's defense was the *Twining* argument that immunity from self-incrimination was not an essential element in due process of law. Chief Justice Hughes replied for a unanimous Court that *Twining* simply gave a state some freedom to experiment with the procedures of criminal prosecution. But that freedom is "the freedom of constitutional government and is limited by the requirement of due process of law. Because a State may dispense with a jury trial, it does not follow that it may substitute trial by ordeal. The rack and torture chamber may not be substituted for the witness stand."

More difficult questions arise where confessions are secured by coercion which is mental rather than physical. At first the Court was reluctant to move against psychological coercion.[57] But in *Ashcraft* v. *Tennessee* (1944) a Court majority adopted the rule of "inherent coerciveness." Ashcraft had been convicted of murder on a confession elicited by thirty-six hours of continuous questioning under electric lights by relays of officers, investigators, and lawyers. Such a situation was held to be "so inherently coercive that its very existence is irreconcilable with the possession of mental freedom by a lone suspect against whom the full coercive force is brought to bear."

This stand against psychological coercion was generally maintained in subsequent decisions, though usually by a divided Court.[58] To give only one example, *Fikes* v. *Alabama* (1957) involved a black of low mentality who had been kept incommunicado for a week, had not been arraigned, and had been questioned intermittently. Justice Frankfurter's conclusion for the Court was that none of these circumstances standing alone would justify a reversal, but that "in combination they bring the result below the Plimsoll line of 'due process.' "

Whether a confession was voluntary or coerced must be decided without reference to its probable truth. The Court briefly departed from this rule in *Stein* v. *New*

---

[57] *Lisenba* v. *California* (1941).

[58] *Malinski* v. *New York* (1945), *Haley* v. *Ohio* (1948), *Watts* v. *Indiana* (1949), *Turner* v. *Pennsylvania* (1949), *Harris* v. *South Carolina* (1949), and *Leyra* v. *Denno* (1953) were all decided by five to four votes.

York (1953), which assumed that involuntary confessions are excluded solely because they are untrustworthy and that if there is independent evidence of the reliability of a confession it need not be rejected because it was involuntary. However, the Court rejected this view in *Rogers* v. *Richmond* (1961), and overruled *Stein* in *Jackson* v. *Denno* (1964). The latter decision held that the voluntariness of a decision must be determined prior to its admission into evidence before the jury.[59]

As the *Fikes* case indicated, the Court at that time, contrary to the *McNabb-Mallory* rule in the federal courts, did not regard confessions secured while a suspect was illegally detained by the police as unconstitutional for that reason alone. A divided Court upheld confessions secured between arrest and arraignment in *Gallegos* v. *Nebraska* (1951), *Stroble* v. *California* (1952), and *Brown* v. *Allen* (1953). In the latter case a preliminary hearing was not given until eighteen days after the arrest.

In 1958 the question was first raised as to whether a confession would be regarded as coerced which was secured after a suspect had been denied the opportunity to consult a lawyer during his questioning by the police. In *Crooker* v. *California* (1958) and *Cicenia* v. *La Gay* (1958), the Court treated this as a denial of counsel rather than as a coercion issue, and by votes of five to four and five to three in the two cases held that denial of access to counsel did not automatically invalidate the confessions. These decisions were reversed in *Escobedo* v. *Illinois* (1964), which along with the related case of *Miranda* v. *Arizona* (1966) will be discussed in the following section.

THE RIGHT TO COUNSEL

In establishing an accused person's right to have "the assistance of counsel for his defense," the Sixth Amendment represented an important advance over common-law practices. The actual wording of the amendment implies that the assistance of counsel is a privilege of which the accused has a right to avail himself, but not a mandatory feature of all criminal trials. In the Federal Crimes Act of 1790, Congress imposed a statutory duty on the courts to assign counsel to represent the defendant in capital cases, from which it could be logically implied that there was no such obligation in other types of cases. Up until 1938 it was the general understanding that where a person desired counsel, but for lack of funds or any other reason was not able to obtain counsel, the court was under no obligation in a noncapital case to secure counsel for him.

The Supreme Court abruptly and decisively changed this rule in *Johnson* v. *Zerbst* (1938), a counterfeiting prosecution in which it held that "the Sixth Amendment withholds from federal courts, in all criminal proceedings, the power and authority to deprive an accused of his life or liberty unless he has or waives the assistance of counsel." The Court justified this new interpretation of the amendment by adding that the "right to be heard would be, in many cases, of little avail if it did not comprehend the right to be heard by counsel." The right to counsel can be

---

[59] See also *Sims* v. *Georgia* (1967). In *Lego* v. *Twomey* (1972), the Court held that the voluntariness of a confession may be determined by the preponderance of evidence; it need not be established by the stricter standard of proof beyond a reasonable doubt.

waived, but the waiver must be intelligent and understanding, and judicial determination on this point depends "upon the particular facts and circumstances . . . including the background, experience, and conduct of the accused."[60]

Right to Counsel in State Trials

The Supreme Court first considered the issue of right to counsel in state court trials in the famous First Scottsboro case, *Powell* v. *Alabama* (1932).[61] The case involved seven black youths, ignorant and illiterate, who were charged with the rape of two white girls in an open gondola car of a freight train passing through Alabama. They were taken from the train near Scottsboro and jailed there. Public excitement was high, and they were guarded by state militia at all stages of the proceedings. At the arraignment they pleaded not guilty. They were not asked whether they had, or were able to employ, counsel, or wished to have counsel appointed. The presiding judge did appoint "all the members of the bar" as counsel for the purpose of arraigning the defendants, but this "expansive gesture" produced no results.

The first case came to trial with no counsel for the defense. As the trial began an out-of-state lawyer said some people had asked him to come down, and that he would be willing to appear along with local counsel that the court might appoint. A member of the local bar then agreed that he would help the out-of-state lawyer. As the Supreme Court subsequently noted:

> With this dubious understanding, the trials immediately proceeded. The defendants, young, ignorant, illiterate, surrounded by hostile sentiment, haled back and forth under guard of soldiers, charged with an atrocious crime regarded with especial horror in the community where they were to be tried, were thus put in peril of their lives within a few moments after counsel for the first time charged with any degree of responsibility began to represent them.

The state supreme court ruled that this arrangement met the requirements of the state constitution. The Supreme Court, however, said that did not decide the matter under the Fourteenth Amendment. "The right to the aid of counsel," wrote Justice Sutherland, is of a "fundamental character." In this country, "historically and in practice," a hearing has always included "the right to the aid of counsel when desired and provided by the party asserting the right." The Court went on to indicate why this should be so:

> The right to be heard would be, in many cases, of little avail if it did not comprehend the right to be heard by counsel. Even the intelligent and educated layman has small and sometimes no skill in the science of law. If charged with crime, he is incapable, generally, of determining for himself whether the indictment is good or bad. He is unfamiliar with the rules of evidence. Left without the aid of counsel he may be put on trial without

[60] See *Von Moltke* v. *Gillies* (1948). In *Faretta* v. *California* (1975), the Court held that a competent person accused of crime has a constitutional right to reject free, court-appointed legal assistance and conduct his own defense. *Middendorf* v. *Henry* (1976) held that persons in the armed services have no right to counsel at a summary court-martial.

[61] See Dan T. Carter, *Scottsboro: A Tragedy of the American South* (Baton Rouge, La.: Louisiana State University Press, 1969).

a proper charge, and convicted upon incompetent evidence, or evidence irrelevant to the issue or otherwise inadmissible. He lacks both the skill and knowledge adequately to prepare his defense, even though he have a perfect one. He requires the guiding hand of counsel at every step in the proceedings against him. Without it, though he be not guilty, he faces the danger of conviction because he does not know how to establish his innocence.

All these factors would operate even with intelligent defendants. Considering all the additional prejudicial circumstances in this case, the Court was clear that "the failure of the trial court to give . . . reasonable time and opportunity to secure counsel was a clear denial of due process."

But the Court did not stop there. If these defendants were unable to get counsel, even though opportunity were offered, then the due process clause required the trial court "to make an effective appointment of counsel." This was new law, and so it was natural that the Court should state careful limits for the new principle:

> Whether this would be so in other criminal prosecutions, or under other circumstances, we need not determine. All that it is necessary now to decide, as we do decide, is that in a capital case, where the defendant is unable to employ counsel, and is incapable adequately of making his own defense because of ignorance, feeble-mindedness, illiteracy, or the like, it is the duty of the court, whether requested or not, to assign counsel for him as a necessary requisite of due process of law; and that duty is not discharged by an assignment at such a time or under such circumstances as to preclude the giving of effective aid in the preparation and trial of the case.

To an unusual degree the principle of the *Powell* case was tied to the individual circumstances of that case. In *Betts* v. *Brady* (1942), the circumstances were different and the Court's holding was different. Betts, under indictment for robbery in Maryland, requested the court to appoint counsel for him, since he was financially unable to secure legal aid. The judge refused, on the ground that it was not the practice in that county to appoint counsel for indigent defendants except in murder and rape prosecutions. The trial proceeded before the judge, acting without a jury.

Betts's contention was that the *Powell* case required appointment of counsel in all state criminal cases. Justice Roberts, who spoke for the Supreme Court, admitted there was some ground for such a conclusion in the *Powell* opinion, but pointed out that the actual holding in the case had been limited to its specific facts. The question whether the *Powell* rule applied to all criminal cases was therefore a new one. "Is the furnishing of counsel in all cases whatever dictated by natural, inherent, and fundamental principles of fairness?"

The Court then proceeded to make the same kind of examination of the constitutions and statutes of the original states which, as applied in *Powell*, had resulted in the conclusion that aid of counsel "when desired and provided by the party asserting the right" was a fundamental requirement of a fair hearing. However, the Court's conclusion as to the mandatory *furnishing* of counsel was that "in the great majority of the States, it has been the considered judgment of the people, their representatives and their courts that appointment of counsel is not a fundamental right, essential to a fair trial. On the contrary, the matter has generally been deemed one of legislative policy." Whereas in *Powell* the Court had pointed out the great disadvantages any layman would encounter without legal guidance in a court of law, here Roberts said the defendant was "of ordinary intelligence and ability to take care of his own interests on the trial of [a] narrow issue." Therefore no constitutional error had been made.

Justice Black was joined by Douglas and Murphy in a vigorous dissent against this holding. Black of course believed that the Sixth Amendment was incorporated in the Fourteenth, but he was willing to argue the matter on the ground of fundamental fairness chosen by the majority, saying: "A practice cannot be reconciled with 'common and fundamental ideas of fairness and right,' which subjects innocent men to increased dangers of conviction merely because of their poverty." The majority opinion had admitted that in eighteen states the statutes required the courts to appoint in all cases where defendants were unable to procure counsel, and "any other practice seems to me to defeat the promise of our democratic society to provide equal justice under the law."

State counsel cases continued to come to the Court in unusual numbers, well over twenty in the decade following *Betts* v. *Brady*. The Court under the *Betts* rule had to consider the "special circumstances" in each case to determine whether the denial of counsel had amounted to a constitutional defect in the trial.[62] In several instances absence of counsel was held unobjectionable even though the possibility of serious unfairness seemed to exist.[63] But in most cases the Court did find that the circumstances required the furnishing of counsel. This was generally true, for example, where the offense was a capital one;[64] where the conduct of the trial judge appeared to be questionable;[65] where the defendant was young or ignorant or otherwise handicapped;[66] or where the points of law involved were too technical for a layman to grasp.[67] In fact, after 1950 the Supreme Court never affirmed a state criminal conviction where denial of counsel was claimed.

Clearly the Court was moving toward a firmer position on the necessity for counsel in state trials. Finally, in the celebrated case of *Gideon* v. *Wainwright* (1963), the Court overruled *Betts* v. *Brady* and held that representation by counsel is a constitutional necessity in all state criminal trials.[68] Justice Black wrote the opinion in *Gideon*, and thus had the opportunity to turn his *Betts* dissent into the law of the Constitution. Gideon was an uneducated ne'er-do-well who, convicted of a minor crime in Florida without the assistance of counsel, stubbornly and unaided from his prison cell drafted a petition printed painfully with pencil on lined paper to the

---

[62] For an interesting analysis of the factors considered by the Court in making these decisions, see Fred Kort, "Predicting Supreme Court Decisions Mathematically: A Quantitative Analysis of the Right to Counsel Cases," 51 AMERICAN POLITICAL SCIENCE REVIEW 1 (1957).

[63] See *Canizio* v. *New York* (1946); *Bute* v. *Illinois* (1948).

[64] See *Tomkins* v. *Missouri* (1945).

[65] See *Townsend* v. *Burke* (1948) and *White* v. *Ragen* (1945).

[66] See *De Meerleer* v. *Michigan* (1947); *Marino* v. *Ragen* (1947); *Moore* v. *Michigan* (1957).

[67] See *Rice* v. *Olson* (1945).

[68] This decision is the subject of a fascinating book by Anthony Lewis, *Gideon's Trumpet* (New York: Random House, Inc., 1964).

454

Supreme Court. The Court agreed to hear his claim and appointed a member of a leading Washington law firm, Abe Fortas, who in 1965 was himself to be appointed to the Court, to represent Gideon.

The Court was unanimous in concluding that the right to counsel was fundamental and essential to a fair trial. In fact, twenty-two states had filed briefs as friends of the Court arguing for this position, while only two states had come forward to support Florida's position. Even Justice Harlan agreed that the "special circumstances" rule had been "substantially and steadily eroded" and that *Betts* should be overruled; he only objected that it was entitled to "a more respectful burial" than Justice Black had given it.[69] The decision was generally well received in the legal profession, and programs for supplying counsel to indigent defendants were promptly inaugurated or existing programs improved throughout most of the states.

Escobedo and Miranda

The issue in the famous case of *Escobedo* v. *Illinois* (1964) had to do with the right to counsel in the pretrial period,[70] but the concerns expressed by the Court in *Escobedo* about abuses of police investigatory methods led to a full-fledged examination of that problem in *Miranda* v. *Arizona* (1966). These two decisions have had a major impact on subsequent thinking about criminal procedure.

As already noted, the Court denied in two 1958 cases, *Crooker* v. *California* and *Cicenia* v. *La Gay,* the right of suspects to consult counsel during police interrogation "irrespective" of the particular circumstances involved. An "inflexible rule" of this sort, the Court said in *Cicenia,* would be inconsistent with the latitude the states needed in administering their systems of criminal justice.

The "special circumstances" rule, however, was to suffer the same fate here as in *Gideon.* The process began in *Spano* v. *New York* (1959), where the Court ruled that counsel could not be denied a defendant after indictment.[71] But the major decision came five years later. Escobedo, under suspicion of murder, was questioned intensively by police officers who repeatedly denied his request to see his attorney and likewise rebuffed the persistent attempts of the attorney to see his client. Escobedo was not informed of his right to refuse to answer police questions, and eventually he made a confession.

The Supreme Court, having already agreed in *Spano* that counsel could not be denied after indictment, now concluded by a vote of five to four that no "mean-

---

[69] See Jerold H. Israel, "Gideon v. Wainwright: The 'Art' of Overruling," in Philip B. Kurland (ed.), *The Supreme Court Review: 1963* (Chicago: The University of Chicago Press, 1963), pp. 211–272. The decision was given retroactive effect because, as later explained in *Linkletter* v. *Walker* (1965), the principle applied in *Gideon* "went to the fairness of the trial—the very integrity of the fact-finding process," and there could be no assurance that a defendant convicted without the aid of counsel had received a fair trial.

[70] Though Justice Stewart, in *Kirby* v. *Illinois* (1972), contended that the doctrine of *Escobedo* was not to vindicate the right to counsel as such, but rather to guarantee full effectuation of the privilege against self-incrimination.

[71] *Massiah* v. *United States* (1964), a federal narcotics case, followed *Spano* in holding that the securing of incriminating statements from a defendant under indictment, by a ruse of government agents which involved electronic eavesdropping, was a denial of the right to counsel under the Sixth Amendment.

ingful distinction" could be drawn between interrogation before and after formal indictment. Justice Goldberg spoke for the Court majority:

> We hold, therefore, that where, as here, the investigation is no longer a general inquiry into an unsolved crime but has begun to focus on a particular suspect, the suspect has been taken into police custody, the police carry out a process of interrogations that lends itself to eliciting incriminating statements, the suspect has requested and been denied an opportunity to consult with his lawyer, and the police have not effectively warned him of his absolute constitutional right to remain silent, the accused has been denied 'the assistance of counsel' in violation of the Sixth Amendment to the Constitution as 'made obligatory upon the States by the Fourteenth Amendment,' *Gideon* v. *Wainwright* . . . and that no statement elicited by the police during the interrogation may be used against him at a criminal trial.

Justice Goldberg took account of objections that this rule would greatly reduce the number of confessions secured because, as Justice Jackson had once said, "any lawyer worth his salt will tell the suspect in no uncertain terms to make no statement to police under any circumstances." Goldberg replied that "no system worth preserving" should have to fear that an accused would be made aware of his constitutional rights. Moreover, officers could still gather evidence from witnesses and undertake other "proper investigative efforts." The Court's holding was only that "when the process shifts from investigatory to accusatory—when its focus is on the accused and its purpose is to elicit a confession—our adversary system begins to operate, and, under the circumstances here, the accused must be permitted to consult with his lawyer."

The *Escobedo* ruling was clear evidence of the Supreme Court's great concern about police abuses in interrogating suspects and its belief in the virtues of the adversary process, the protections of which it was extending from the trial to the pretrial period. *Escobedo* also represented an effort to substitute an objective test for the constitutionality of interrogation in place of the subjective, balancing, case-by-case examination of circumstances which the Court had been forced into in its previous decisions.

But *Escobedo* left many questions unanswered. When did warning of their rights have to be given to suspects? Did *Escobedo* preclude any questioning at all in the absence of counsel? Must counsel be supplied for indigents or others unable to secure counsel? And did *Escobedo* operate retroactively to invalidate every prior prosecution where conviction had been secured in violation of its standards? *Escobedo* quickly became the focus of a nationwide debate on law enforcement and the whipping boy of all who blamed the increase in crime on the "coddling of criminals" by such Court decisions.

The Supreme Court took an important step toward clarifying its standards and stepping up its war on police abuses in *Miranda* v. *Arizona* (1966) and three companion cases, all involving the use of confessions obtained by police interrogation without informing the suspects of their right to remain silent and to see counsel. The Court reversed the convictions in all these cases by a vote of five to four, on the ground that incommunicado police detention is inherently coercive. In the process it laid down a stiff code of conduct for police interrogation, including the following:

1 A person held in custody for interrogation must first be informed in clear and unequivocal terms that he has the right to remain silent.

2 He must be warned that anything he says can and will be used against him in court.

3 He must be given the right to consult with counsel prior to questioning and to have counsel present during questioning if he desires.

4 Failure to request counsel does not constitute a waiver of the right to have counsel.

5 If the accused is unable to secure a lawyer, one must be appointed for him.

The *Miranda* decision added new fuel to the flames started by *Escobedo*. Many law-enforcement officers contended that the new rules would make it impossible any longer to solve crimes by securing confessions. On the other hand, it was argued that police now concentrate on confessions because that is easier than going out to look for evidence, and that *Miranda* would force them to do a more creative job. Also, several studies purported to show that confessions are not presently involved in the great majority of convictions.

Some commentators who shared the Court's goals were nonetheless critical of the *Miranda* decision, on the ground that the Court had undertaken the essentially legislative task of adopting a complete code of law-enforcement procedures, a responsibility which belongs to legislatures, and on which substantial progress was being made in some areas. But the Supreme Court obviously felt that police malpractices were so widespread that the normal procedure of criticizing past abuses in individual cases was inadequate to correct them, and that consequently it must spell out in detail a code of constitutional conduct for the police. Chief Justice Warren gave assurance that the decision was not intended to hamper the traditional function of police officers in investigating crime; persons not under restraint could be questioned; any statements freely and voluntarily given would be admissible in evidence. He also suggested that the role of confessions in securing convictions had been overplayed; in all four of these cases there was very good evidence against the suspects besides the confessions. Finally, he encouraged "Congress and the States to continue their laudable search for increasingly effective ways of protecting the rights of the individual while promoting efficient enforcement of our criminal laws."

One week after *Miranda,* the Court held in *Johnson* v. *New Jersey* (1966) that neither the *Escobedo* nor the *Miranda* decision was to be applied retroactively. Law-enforcement agencies had fairly relied on prior cases in obtaining incriminating statements during the years preceding these two cases, and retroactivity in their application would seriously disrupt administration of the criminal laws, the Court held; but they would apply to prosecutions begun after the cases were announced. For persons whose trials were already completed, the case law on coerced confessions would still be available as a basis for appeals.[72]

In subsequent cases the Warren Court, in spite of violent criticism from many

---

[72] See comments on the decision by Yale Kamisar, "A Dissent from the *Miranda* Dissents," 65

quarters, stood by the position taken in *Escobedo* and *Miranda* and even extended it. As already noted, *United States* v. *Wade* (1967) and *Gilbert* v. *California* (1967) held that a defendant must have counsel present if required to take part in a police lineup for identification before trial. *Mempa* v. *Rhay* (1967) ruled that a probationer was entitled to be represented by appointed counsel at a combined probation revocation and sentencing hearing. But *Morrissey* v. *Brewer* (1972) and *Gagnon* v. *Scarpelli* (1973) avoided decision as to whether counsel was required in hearings on revocation of parole and probation.

Mathis v. *United States* (1968) held that a defendant who was questioned by an internal revenue agent while imprisoned in a state jail was entitled to *Miranda*-type warnings and to presence of counsel. *Coleman* v. *Alabama* (1970) ruled that a preliminary court hearing to determine whether there was sufficient evidence to warrant presenting the case to the grand jury was a critical stage of the criminal process, where those accused were entitled to counsel.[73]

Attacks on *Miranda* peaked during the 1968 "law and order" political campaign. Congress in the 1968 Crime Control Act undertook to restore to judges the right to decide on the admissibility of confessions on the basis of the "totality of circumstances" rather than on adherence to the *Miranda* rules. Specifically, the statute provided that confessions were admissible in federal courts if the trial judge found them "voluntary" (limiting *Miranda*) and despite delay in arraignment (repealing *Mallory*); it made eyewitness testimony admissible even if the defendant did not have counsel during a police lineup (reversing *Wade*).

The Burger Court was by no means hostile to the right to counsel.[74] In fact, in *Argersinger* v. *Hamlin* (1972), the Court unanimously extended *Escobedo* to require counsel in misdemeanors and petty offenses if imprisonment for any length of time was possible. But the Burger Court did deny a right to counsel claim in several instances. Thus, in *Kirby* v. *Illinois* (1972), counsel was held not to be required in an identification lineup conducted before indictment; *Wade* was distinguished because there the lineup was after indictment. *United States* v. *Ash* (1973) more directly attacked *Wade* by ruling that counsel was not required when the prosecution, after indictment, conducted a photographic display containing the defendant's picture to determine whether witnesses to the crime could identify him.

As for *Miranda*, the Crime Control Act covered only federal courts and the District of Columbia, leaving it fully applicable to the states.[75] But in *Harris* v. *New York* (1971), the Court by a five to four vote made a substantial inroad on *Miranda*

Michigan Law Review 59 (1966); Neil T. Romans, "The Role of State Supreme Courts in Judicial Policy Making: *Escobedo, Miranda* and the Use of Judicial Impact Analysis," 27 *Western Political Quarterly* 38 (1974).

[73] But a magistrate's determination of probable cause to charge a person arrested without a warrant is not a critical stage requiring appointed counsel; *Gerstein* v. *Pugh* (1975).

[74] See Levy, *op. cit.,* chap. 4.

[75] This assumes the act is constitutional. It had not by 1975 been passed on directly by the Supreme Court. See "Title II of the Omnibus Crime Control and Safe Streets Act of 1968," 82 Harvard Law Review 1392 (1969).

by holding that a statement inadmissible in the prosecution's case, because no *Miranda* warning had been given, was nonetheless usable for impeachment of the defendant's testimony should he take the witness stand.[76]

Continuing this trend, in *Michigan* v. *Tucker* (1974) a suspect's statements made without full *Miranda* warning were not admitted at the trial, but a witness discovered as a result of the statements was permitted to testify. Justice Rehnquist contended that the police action was an "inadvertent disregard" of procedural safeguards, quite unrelated to historic self-incrimination abuses, and he added: "The law does not require that a defendant receive a perfect trial, only a fair one."

Again, *Michigan* v. *Mosley* (1975) upheld the action of police who, after a two-hour interval, resumed interrogation of a suspect who had earlier exercised his right to remain silent. *United States* v. *Mandujano* (1976) held that the *Miranda* rules did not extend to witnesses before grand juries, even though they were criminal suspects. But *Doyle* v. *Ohio* (1976) ruled that where suspects had claimed their *Miranda* right to remain silent during police questioning at the time of arrest, their silence could not be used to discredit their testimony on the witness stand.

Plea Bargaining and Effective Representation by Counsel

Plea bargaining is the practice under which, by agreement between prosecutor and defendant's counsel, the defendant enters a plea of guilty to a lesser charge than the one originally made. The state's interest is in avoiding a long and expensive trial. If all criminal charges had to proceed to trial, the court system would be hopelessly overloaded. The defendant's interest in a reduced sentence may seem obvious, but the price is great. He or she forfeits the Fifth Amendment right against self-incrimination; the Sixth Amendment rights to public trial, confrontation, and presentation of witnesses; and possibly the Fourth Amendment right to have unlawfully seized evidence excluded. Pressures brought on the defendant by threat of a heavier sentence, and often by the defendant's counsel, raise questions about the voluntary character of the confession.

Nevertheless, the Supreme Court has ruled that plea bargaining is constitutional. In *Brady* v. *United States* (1970), Justice White spoke of the "mutuality of advantage" in the system. For the state, there is "the more promptly imposed punishment" and the conservation of "scarce judicial and prosecutorial resources." For the defendant, "his exposure is reduced, the correctional processes can begin immediately, and the practical burdens of a trial are eliminated." So it was not unconstitutional "for the State to extend a benefit to a defendant who in turn extends a substantial benefit to the State."[77]

In agreeing to a plea bargain, the defendant of course has the advice of counsel, but this is not necessarily to his or her benefit. In the first place, counsel in many

---

[76] In *Oregon* v. *Hass* (1975), the Court permitted the use for impeachment purposes of statements made to police by a suspect in custody, after he had asked for a lawyer but before the lawyer was present.

[77] *Santobello* v. *New York* (1971) held that where the state, due to a change in prosecutors, had broken its bargain with a defendant, the principle of due process had been violated and the bargain must be honored or the guilty plea allowed to be withdrawn.

such instances are court-appointed or overworked public defenders who find a guilty plea the most expeditious solution. Second, the fact that the guilty plea is made on advice of counsel makes it very difficult to challenge in a later proceeding. In *McMann* v. *Richardson* (1970), three defendants alleged that their confessions were secured by coercion and that their court-appointed counsel had incompetently represented them. But the Supreme Court ruled that a plea of guilty made by defendants who were represented by "reasonably competent" counsel could not be subsequently attacked. Defendants must accept the risk of "ordinary error" by their attorneys in their assessment of the law and facts. Only "serious derelictions" by counsel would vitiate a plea of guilty as not "a knowing and intelligent act."[78]

The reluctance of the Court to accept charges of incompetence of counsel is demonstrated in another plea bargaining case, *Tollett* v. *Henderson* (1973). Here the defendant had not been informed of the constitutional rights with respect to the composition of the grand jury or the possibility of challenging the indictment. But the Court rejected the contention that the counsel was incompetent, saying that a counseled plea of guilty could not be vacated "because the defendant was not advised of every conceivable constitutional plea in abatement he might have to the charge."[79]

INDICTMENT BY GRAND JURY

English practices with respect to indictment by grand jury and trial by jury, which were still in process of transition in the period of colonization, were not transferred bodily to the New World. There was initially a period of pronounced hostility toward the legal profession and its methods, and the law was applied in a rude and nontechnical fashion. There thus arose "the great difference between the limits of the jury trial in different States" that Alexander Hamilton commented on in *The Federalist,* No. 83, with the result that "no general rule could have been fixed upon by the Convention which would have corresponded with the circumstances of all the States." Consequently in its provisions for federal criminal prosecutions the Constitution made no mention of the grand jury whatever. The Fifth Amendment filled in this gap by the provision that "no person shall be held to answer for a capital or otherwise infamous crime, unless on a presentment or indictment of a grand jury."

The purpose of the grand jury provision is to require prosecuting officers to prove to a body of laymen that there is a prima facie case of criminal violation so that citizens will not be subjected to the expense and indignity of a criminal trial without reasonable cause. If the grand jury finds the evidence sufficiently strong, it votes an indictment or a "true bill."

This is one area where the states are not required to follow federal standards. In some twenty-eight states the grand jury had been abolished, and a prosecuting

---

[78] See also *Brady* v. *United States* (1970) and *Parker* v. *North Carolina* (1970).
[79] Contrary to *Powell* v. *Alabama* (1932) and *Hawk* v. *Olsen* (1945), *Chambers* v. *Maroney* (1970) rejected a claim of ineffective representation by counsel who had had no adequate opportunity to confer with defendant prior to trial. But *Henderson* v. *Morgan* (1976) set aside a conviction of a defendant who had pleaded guilty to second-degree murder without being fully informed of the consequences of the plea.

officer may bring a person to trial by filing an "information" against him. The Supreme Court upheld this practice in *Hurtado* v. *California* (1884), and has never reversed this decision.

A grand jury generally consists of from twelve to twenty-three members; the jurors are selected by lot from the voting rolls or are chosen by judges or other local officials. The district attorney meets with the grand jury, whose sessions are secret. It has the power to inquire into any alleged offense called to its attention by the judge's charge to the jury, but the usual practice is for the group to confine its attention to issues presented by the district attorney, and that official is often accused of dominating the grand jury.[80]

TRIAL BY JURY

Jury trial came to America with the English colonists. Though now used in perhaps only 1 percent of English criminal prosecutions, it remains a vital instrument of American justice in both civil and criminal cases. The justification is not primarily that untrained lay jurors are reliable fact finders, although the principal empirical study of the jury system concluded that judges agreed with jury findings in over three-fourths of the jury trial cases studied.[81] Rather, the case for the jury, as eloquently stated by Justice White in *Duncan* v. *Louisiana* (1968), is that "jury trial is granted to criminal defendants in order to prevent oppression by the Government . . . an inestimable safeguard against the corrupt or overzealous prosecutor and against the compliant, biased, or eccentric judge."[82] Another important consideration is that juries temper the application or enforcement of unpopular, outdated, or overstrict laws.

Jury Trial in Federal Courts

The Constitution provides for jury trials in criminal cases by the Sixth Amendment (and also by Article III, section 2, of the original Constitution), and in civil cases "where the value in controversy shall exceed twenty dollars" by the Seventh Amendment. Since the Sixth Amendment merely says that the accused "shall enjoy the right" to a trial by jury, jury trial in federal courts is not an institutional requirement, but only a "valuable privilege" which a person accused of crime may forego at his election. However, "before any waiver can become effective, the consent of government counsel and the sanction of the court must be had, in addition to the express and intelligent consent of the defendant."[83]

---

[80] See Roger T. Brice, "Grand Jury Proceedings: The Prosecutor, the Trial Judge, and Undue Influence," 39 UNIVERSITY OF CHICAGO LAW REVIEW 761 (1972); David J. Fine, "Federal Grand Jury Investigation of Political Dissidents," 7 HARVARD CIVIL RIGHTS–CIVIL LIBERTIES LAW REVIEW 432 (1972); Charles E. Goodell, "Where Did the Grand Jury Go?" 246 HARPERS 14 (May 1973).

[81] Harry Kalven Jr. and Hans Zeisel, *The American Jury* (Boston: Little, Brown and Company, 1966).

[82] See Justice Harlan's rebuttal in the same case.

[83] *Patton* v. *United States* (1930). See also *Singer* v. *United States* (1965). The death penalty provision of the Federal Kidnapping Act, which stated that defendant shall be punished by death if the kidnapped person has not been liberated unharmed and if the verdict of the jury shall so recommend, was held unconstitutional in *United States* v. *Jackson* (1968) as tending to deter exercise of the right to

The right to trial by jury in federal criminal cases has been held to be limited to those who, under the Fifth Amendment, are subject to indictment or presentment by grand jury. This means that there is a class of petty crimes for which jury trial cannot be claimed.[84] *Cheff* v. *Schnackenberg* (1966) was somewhat tentative in drawing the line between serious and petty crimes, saying: "The prevailing opinion today suggests that a jury is required where the sentence imposed exceeds six months but not when it is less than that period." Other situations in which jury trial may not be claimed include charges of criminal contempt of court[85] and petitions for the writ of habeas corpus; deportation proceedings for aliens and disbarment proceedings for attorneys, which are civil, not criminal; and extradition proceedings, which are administrative, not judicial. Moreover, trials by courts-martial are not affected by the Sixth Amendment, the provision of the Fifth Amendment waiving the grand jury requirement "in the land or naval forces" having been also read into the Sixth.[86]

Jury Trial in State Courts

The laws of every state require a right to jury trial in serious criminal cases, but the Supreme Court until 1968 had declined to hold that jury trial in state courts was a federal constitutional right. In fact, in *Maxwell* v. *Dow* (1900), the Court said by way of dictum: "Trial by jury has never been affirmed to be a necessary requisite of due process of law." This position was reiterated in *Palko* v. *Connecticut* (1937). However, in *Duncan* v. *Louisiana* (1968), after so many other provisions of the Bill of Rights had been absorbed into the Fourteenth Amendment, the Court concluded that the right to jury trial in criminal cases was also "fundamental to the American scheme of justice." Consequently, *Duncan* ruled that "the Fourteenth Amendment guarantees a right of jury trial in all criminal cases which—were they to be tried in a federal court—would come within the Sixth Amendment's guarantee."[87] Only Harlan and Stewart dissented.[88]

Adoption of the federal court rule meant that petty crimes would be exempt from the state jury trial requirement. In *Baldwin* v. *New York* (1970), the Court confirmed that petty crimes were those punishable by no more than six months in prison.

Jury Selection

The jury, according to the Sixth Amendment, must be "impartial." This raises the whole question of jury composition and method of selection. Bias, although difficult to guard against, may be thought of (1) as being simply a matter of opinion, or (2) as growing out of or being associated with social or economic status of jurors. Bias in the first sense is protected against by the right to challenge prospective jurors for

---

demand a jury trial as well as to discourage assertion of the Fifth Amendment right not to plead guilty.

[84] *Callan* v. *Wilson* (1888).

[85] But see the conditions under which jury trials may be required in criminal contempt cases, in *United States* v. *Barnett* (1964) and *Cheff* v. *Schnackenberg* (1966).

[86] *Ex parte Milligan* (1866).

[87] But *Ludwig* v. *Massachusetts* (1976) held that a defendant may be denied a jury in his initial trial provided the state allows through appeal a second trial in which there is a jury.

[88] *De Stefano* v. *Woods* (1968) held that *Duncan* did not apply retroactively.

cause. At the Aaron Burr trial for treason, his attorney argued that a juror to be selected must have a mind "perfectly indifferent and free from prejudice," but Chief Justice Marshall said this was too stringent a standard. A closed mind would be objectionable, but casual opinions on the subject should not disqualify a venireman. Obviously the challenged bias must have some direct relation to the issues of the case. In capital cases, the general practice was to exclude persons with constitutional scruples against the death penalty from the jury. But *Witherspoon* v. *Illinois* (1968) declared this practice unconstitutional. A jury drawn only from that minority that has no doubts about imposing capital punishment would not be impartial, the Court thought. Indeed, it would be a "hanging jury," said Justice Stewart.

In Chapter 21 we discussed the situation where an entire community is so inflamed by publicity about a crime that securing an impartial jury seems impossible. A change of venue is required in those circumstances. *Groppi* v. *Wisconsin* (1971) held that a statute prohibiting change of venue for a criminal jury trial in any misdemeanor case, regardless of the extent of local prejudice against the defendant, violated the right to trial by an impartial jury.

The main protection against bias resulting from a juror's race or employment or class status is the "cross-section" principle that forbids any systematic exclusion of identifiable segments of the community from jury panels or from the juries ultimately drawn from these panels.[89] In *Smith* v. *Texas* (1940), the Court said: "it is part of the established tradition in the use of juries as instruments of public justice that the jury be a body truly representative of the community"; and in *Taylor* v. *Louisiana* (1975), the Court reaffirmed "the fair cross section requirement as fundamental to the jury trial guaranteed by the Sixth Amendment." This principle was incorporated in the Federal Jury Selection and Service Act of 1968, which requires random selection from "a fair cross section of the community," and bars discrimination on account of race, color, religion, sex, national origin, or economic status.[90]

Prior to 1968, each federal district court followed its own methods in jury selection; these were not always in accord with the cross-section principle. One was the "key man" system, under which outstanding citizens recommended the veniremen. Or the venire might be drawn from lists of telephone subscribers, property owners, even church members—not sources that would provide a representative cross section. The 1949 Smith Act prosecution of Communists in New York was bogged down for seven weeks by unsuccessful defense efforts to establish that poor people were deliberately excluded from federal jury panels in New York.

Both the due process clause and the equal protection clause of the Fourteenth Amendment require the Supreme Court to review state jury selection practices

---

[89] The Supreme Court struck down some restrictive jury practices even when their purpose was benign. In *Thiel* v. *Southern Pacific Co.* (1946) the practice invalidated was that of automatically excusing from jury service all persons working for a daily wage, since the fee for jurors was inadequate to compensate them for loss of wages. In *Glasser* v. *United States* (1942) the Court indicated that intentional selection of jurors from among women who had taken League of Women Voters "jury classes" would not be approved.

[90] *Test* v. *United States* (1975) held that under this act the defendant has a right to inspect jury lists to determine whether a disproportionate number of people with Spanish surnames, students, and blacks have been systematically excluded.

where charges of discrimination are made. The chief problems, both in the selection of grand and trial juries, have resulted from discrimination against blacks. As early as 1880, a Virginia judge charged with excluding blacks from jury lists because of their race and color was found guilty of denying equal protection.[91] In the same year, a West Virginia statute requiring juries to be composed exclusively of white male citizens was likewise held unconstitutional.[92] However, where a state statute made no discrimination against blacks, the fact that no blacks had sat on the grand and trial juries in a murder case was not a constitutional objection to conviction. Petitioners had no right to have blacks on the jury, the Court said.[93] Thus, so long as open discrimination against blacks was avoided, it was possible for the Southern states to follow a successful exclusion policy based on practice and custom.

This system operated undisturbed by the Supreme Court until 1935, when it was challenged in *Norris* v. *Alabama,* known as the *Second Scottsboro* case. Following the Supreme Court's reversal in the first case on grounds of denial of counsel, a second trial had been held in another county and the defendants again convicted. This second conviction was attacked on the ground that blacks were systematically excluded from the grand jury in the county where the indictment was found, and from the trial jury in the county where the trial was held. The Supreme Court unanimously sustained this contention, finding that in each of the two counties no blacks had ever been called for jury service within the memory of the oldest inhabitants or any officer of the courts. This was in spite of the fact that there were black citizens in each county well able to render jury service, and that black citizens had been called on to serve on federal juries in that district. "For this long-continued, unvarying, and wholesale exclusion of Negroes from jury service," Chief Justice Hughes concluded, "we find no justification consistent with the constitutional mandate." The great advance of the *Norris* decision was that it permitted discriminatory practices to be inferred from the facts showing the actuality of unequal treatment.

The *Norris* rule was a fairly clear one, and for a time it took care of the situation.[94] Soon, however, things got more complicated as techniques were developed for evading the spirit of the Court's rulings. In the case of *Akins* v. *Texas* (1945) the jury commissioners had carefully placed one black on the grand jury. The commissioners freely admitted that the limitation of black representation to one juror was intentional, but the Supreme Court was unable to find any loophole in this technical compliance with constitutional requirements. Mathematical exactitude or proportional representation of races or groups, the Court said, was not required to meet the equal protection guarantee. But *Cassell* v. *Texas* (1950) held a grand jury panel illegal because in twenty-one consecutive grand jury panels there had never been more than one black.

The Court found discrimination to exist in *Avery* v. *Georgia* (1952), where the names of prospective black jurors were placed in the jury box on yellow tickets, and in *Whitus* v. *Georgia* (1967), where the names of prospective jurors were selected

---

[91] *Ex parte Virginia* (1880).
[92] *Strauder* v. *West Virginia* (1880).
[93] *Virginia* v. *Rives* (1880).
[94] See *Smith* v. *Texas* (1940); *Hill* v. *Texas* (1942); *Eubanks* v. *Louisiana* (1958).

from the books of the county tax receiver, which were maintained on a racially segregated basis. But in *Brown* v. *Allen* (1953), the Court approved selection of jurors from taxpayers' lists. Blacks amounted to 33 percent of the county population but only 16 percent of the taxpayers. The Court majority thought this was a "good faith effort to secure competent juries."

In *Swain* v. *Alabama* (1965), an average of six or seven blacks was placed on trial jury venires, but no black had actually served since 1950, every one apparently having been eliminated by the prosecutor on peremptory challenges. The Court held that this record did not make out a prima facie case of invidious discrimination; there had not been "total exclusion" of a racial group.

Carter v. *Jury Commission of Greene County* (1970) was the first case to reach the Supreme Court in which an attack on alleged racial discrimination in choosing juries was made by plaintiffs seeking affirmative relief rather than by defendants challenging judgments of criminal conviction. The district court, finding invalid racial discrimination, had enjoined the jury commissioners from systematically excluding blacks from the jury rolls; it ordered prompt action to compile lawful jury lists. The district judge, however, had declined to enjoin the enforcement of Alabama jury selection laws or to order the governor to appoint blacks to the jury commission. The Supreme Court affirmed on all points.

In *Hernandez* v. *Texas* (1954), the Court found that persons of Mexican descent had been systematically excluded from jury service; this was the first time the rule against racial discrimination had been extended to a group other than blacks.

The issue of racial bias was considered in *Ham* v. *South Carolina* (1973), where the Court ruled that the trial judge had erred in refusing to examine jurors as to possible prejudice arising from the fact that the defendant was black. But in *Ristaino* v. *Ross* (1976), the Court retreated from *Ham,* holding that questions about potential racial bias were constitutionally required only if there were "a significant likelihood" that racial prejudice might infect the trial.

Fay v. *New York* (1947) upheld the constitutionality of New York's "blue ribbon" juries, which were allegedly chosen from "the upper economic and social stratum" to the exclusion of manual workers. Noting that proportional representation was not required on juries, even for racial groups, the Court said: "how much more imprudent would it be to require proportional representation of economic classes."[95]

Following the common-law practice, women were originally ineligible for jury service in all states. *Strauder* v. *West Virginia* (1880) explicitly held that a state could constitutionally confine jury service to males. Utah was the first state to break the barrier in 1898, and eventually all other states followed. However, access of women to the jury box was often qualified. They could claim automatic exemption in many states. Florida law provided that women were not to be included on jury lists unless they registered their desire to serve with the court clerk. In *Hoyt* v. *Florida* (1961),

---

[95] The contention that government employees should be excluded from jury service in the District of Columbia because they would be biased in favor of the government was rejected in *Dennis* v. *United States* (1950).

the Court upheld this law as based on a reasonable classification. Since "woman is still regarded as the center of home and family life," she should have the right to determine whether jury service was compatible with her "special responsibilities." But only fourteen years later, in *Taylor* v. *Louisiana* (1975), the Court recognized "the current judgment of the country" and declared unconstitutional a comparable Louisiana statute, saying: "the exclusion of women from jury venires deprives a criminal defendant of his Sixth Amendment right to trial by an impartial jury drawn from a fair cross section of the community."[96]

Jury Size

The common-law jury was composed of twelve persons, and in *Thompson* v. *Utah* (1898), the Supreme Court held that the Sixth Amendment jury was a jury "constituted, as it was at common law, of twelve persons, neither more nor less."[97] After *Duncan* was decided in 1968, holding that jury trial in state courts was a fundamental constitutional right, it seemed logical to assume that state juries would have to conform to the rules for federal juries. In fact, the Court did take this position in *Williams* v. *Florida* (1970), but not in the way anticipated.

Florida had adopted a statute in 1967 providing that "six men" should constitute the jury to try all criminal cases except for capital crimes, for which the twelve-member jury was retained. By a vote of six to two, the Court came to the surprising conclusion that the Sixth Amendment did *not* require twelve-member federal criminal juries, and so obviously the states were under no obligation to continue using them. Justice White thought there was no firm evidence that the framers intended "to equate the constitutional and common law characteristics of the jury." Perhaps "the usual expectation was that the jury would consist of 12," but that number was an "historical accident." The important thing was to preserve the essential function that the framers expected the jury to perform, and that

> obviously lies in the interposition between the accused and his accuser of the common-sense judgment of a group of laymen, and in the community participation and shared responsibility which results from that group's determination of guilt or innocence. The performance of this role is not a function of the particular number of the body which makes up the jury. To be sure, the number should probably be large enough to promote group deliberation, free from outside attempts at intimidation, and to provide a fair possibility for obtaining a representative cross section of the community. But we find little reason to think that these goals are in any meaningful sense less likely to be achieved when the jury numbers six, than when it numbers twelve. . . .[98]

White dealt to his satisfaction with arguments that fewer jurors would be more likely to convict and reduce the number of viewpoints represented in a randomly

[96] From 1789 until the passage of the Civil Rights Act of 1957, women were eligible to sit on federal juries only if they were qualified for jury duty in the state where the federal court sat. *Ballard* v. *United States* (1946) held that in states where women were eligible, they must also be included on federal juries.

[97] This ruling was reaffirmed in *Maxwell* v. *Dow* (1900), *Rasmussen* v. *United States* (1905), and *Patton* v. *United States* (1930).

[98] See the demonstration to the contrary by Hans Zeisel, ". . . And Then There Were None: The Diminution of the Federal Jury," 38 UNIVERSITY OF CHICAGO LAW REVIEW 710 (1971).

selected jury. But his basic position was that jury size was "incidental to the real purpose of the [Sixth] Amendment."

Black and Douglas concurred in this result, but Harlan was appalled at such cavalier overruling of precedents and dismissal of the common-law tradition in favor of a "functional" analysis. "History," he said, "continues to be a wellspring of constitutional interpretation." Once the umbilical cord is cut, what controls? "For if 12 jurors are not essential, why are six?" Why not three? Marshall agreed with Harlan, and Blackmun did not participate.

While White's stripping of the twelve-member requirement from the Sixth Amendment was an essential step in upholding the six-member Florida jury, it was dictum in that no federal jury issue was before the Court. Moreover, no subsequent move has been made toward reducing the size of federal criminal juries. But well before the *Williams* decision, six-judge *civil* juries had been authorized in a number of federal district courts, and by 1973 no less than fifty-six had done so for at least some civil cases.

The Supreme Court gave its approval in *Colgrove* v. *Battin* (1973). It might seem that *Williams* had settled this issue, but in fact the Court had recognized in the *Williams* opinion that the federal civil jury problem might be complicated by the specific recognition in the Seventh Amendment of the right to jury trial in suits at "common law" where the value in controversy exceeds $20. But in a five to four decision, Justice Brennan proved no less adept than White in extricating the Court from history and its precedents. He held that the Seventh Amendment had not meant to freeze the common-law jury into the Constitution. It only meant to protect the principle of civil juries.

The rather odd assortment of Douglas, Marshall, Stewart, and Powell dissented. Marshall picked up the torch of the fallen Harlan and in a powerful opinion protested this "wholesale abolition" of the civil jury and its replacement by a "six-man mutation. . . a different institution which functions differently, produces different results, and was wholly unknown to the Framers of the Seventh Amendment."

The Unanimity Rule

Since at least 1367, the unanimous jury verdict has been considered an established and integral part of common-law criminal procedure. It was recognized as an indispensable feature of federal jury trials in an unbroken line of cases, virtually without dissent, the latest being *Patton* v. *United States* (1930). So far as state courts were concerned, there were dicta in two earlier cases, *Maxwell* v. *Dow* (1900) and *Jordan* v. *Massachusetts* (1912), holding that the unanimity requirement was not obligatory; but of course these decisions came long before the Court held in *Duncan* that jury trial in state courts was a fundamental constitutional right.

We have just seen what a surprising impact the implementation of *Duncan* had on jury size in *Williams* v. *Florida*. Two years later, in *Johnson* v. *Louisiana* (1972) and *Apodaco* v. *Oregon* (1972), Justice White sought to complete the dismantling of the Sixth Amendment that he had begun in *Williams*. The legislatures of both Louisiana and Oregon had authorized dispensing with the unanimity requirement in criminal cases. In the Louisiana case the jury vote on conviction for armed robbery was nine to three. In the Oregon case the two defendants were found guilty by votes of eleven to one and ten to two. The Court upheld these verdicts as against charges of denial of due process and equal protection.

Justice White repeated the antihistorical and jury-functional arguments he had originated in *Williams*. In that opinion he had foreseen that his case against the twelve-member jury could just as readily apply to the unanimity rule, but in a *Williams* footnote he had expressly reserved that question:

> We intimate no view whether or not the requirement of unanamity is an indispensable element of the Sixth Amendment. While much of the above historical discussion applies as well to the unanimity as to the 12-man requirement, the former, unlike the latter, may well serve an important role in the jury function, for example, as a device for insuring that the Government bear the heavier burden of proof.

But two years later, in *Johnson* and *Apodaco*, this virtue of unanimity was no longer compelling for White. Unanimity might not be a historical accident, like size, but it was to be judged on its contemporary function, not its history. Was unanimity necessary to give effect to the "reasonable doubt" standard which criminal convictions must satisfy? No. If nine jurors found guilt beyond a reasonable doubt, it was the three dissenting jurors who should consider whether their doubts were reasonable. Would not majority jurors, once they had achieved their nine or ten votes, refuse to listen to counterarguments and simply terminate the deliberations? No. "Appellant offers no evidence that majority jurors simply ignore the reasonable doubts of their colleagues or otherwise act irresponsibly in casting their votes in favor of conviction." Is not unanimity a necessary precondition for effective application of the cross-section principle, making it impossible for convictions to occur without the acquiescence of minority elements in the community? No. Every distinct voice in the community does not have "a right to be represented on every jury and a right to prevent conviction of a defendant in any case."

Justice Stewart, one of the four dissenters, rejected these assurances as completely "impervious to reality." He thought it more likely that "under today's judgment, nine jurors can simply ignore the view of their fellow panel members of a different race or class." Unanimity "provides the simple and effective method endorsed by centuries of experience and history to combat the injuries to the fair administration of justice that can be inflicted by community passion and prejudice."[99]

---

[99] In 1973 unanimity in criminal cases was still required in the courts of most states. In addition to Louisiana and Oregon, four other states permitted less than unanimous decisions, but in all four such verdicts could be rendered only in trials for offenses less than a felony. One of these states, Montana, permitted conviction by vote of two-thirds of the jurors. Justice Blackmun, concurring in *Johnson* and its acceptance of a nine to three vote, said he would find it difficult to approve a seven to five conviction, though it is difficult to see what the distinguishing principle is between the two majorities.

A 1967 English statute authorized ten to two verdicts in criminal cases but required the jury to deliberate for at least two hours, or longer if required by the court. Scotland allows convictions by a bare majority (eight to seven), but rules of evidence there are much stricter than in the United States, making the burden of proof about twice as great.

While White spoke for the five-judge majority in eliminating the unanimity requirement for state criminal juries, he failed to convince one of the five, Justice Powell, that the Sixth Amendment did not require unanimity on federal juries. Unanimity in the federal courts, Powell contended, was "mandated by history." Consequently the principle of unanimity on federal criminal juries was narrowly preserved.

OTHER SIXTH AMENDMENT PROTECTIONS

The Sixth Amendment spells out certain other protections of trial procedure. An accused is entitled to a "speedy and public trial." Of necessity speed is a relative concept, subordinate to the broader protections of the amendment. The federal Speedy Trial Act of 1974, adopted over opposition of the Department of Justice, requires that a person arrested be charged within thirty days of the arrest and arraigned within ten days of being charged and that trial begin within sixty days of the arraignment. The act provides for some circumstances under which elapsed time would not be counted toward the 100-day period. Charges would be dismissed against any defendant who moved for dismissal after the speedy trial period had elapsed and trial had not begun.[100] *Klopfer* v. *North Carolina* (1967) held that the speedy trial provision is also applicable to the states.

The requirement of the Sixth Amendment that "the accused shall enjoy the right . . . to be informed of the nature and cause of the accusation" is intended to make it possible for the defendant to prepare his defense adequately. Failure to meet this standard may be the result of either the statute defining the crime or the indictment charging it. However, vagueness in the statute is more properly attacked on the basis of the due process clause of the Fifth Amendment, thus limiting the purview of the Sixth Amendment to the indictment process.

The right to be informed of the nature and cause of the accusation also has some relevance to the Supreme Court's insistence that criminal statutes must be sufficiently specific in their terms to define and give adequate notice of the kind of conduct which they forbid. This is the familiar rule that criminal statutes may be held "void for vagueness." The applicable principle has been stated by the Supreme Court:

> That the terms of a penal statute creating a new offense must be sufficiently explicit to inform those who are subject to it what conduct on their part will render them liable to its penalties, is a well-recognized requirement, consonant alike with ordinary notions of fair play and the settled rules of law. And a statute which either forbids or requires the doing of an act in terms so vague that men of common intelligence must necessarily guess at its meaning and differ as to its application, violates the first essential of due process of law.[101]

---

[100] The Speedy Trial Act was in part a response to the Supreme Court's decision in *Barker* v. *Wingo* (1972). In defining the right to a speedy trial, the time period to be considered is the period between trial and either arrest or indictment, whichever comes first; *Dillingham* v. *United States* (1975).

[101] *Connally* v. *General Construction Co.* (1926). For illustrative decisions, see *Lanzetta* v. *New Jersey* (1939) and *Winters* v. *New York* (1948). In *Rose* v. *Locke* (1975), the Court reversed a lower court ruling that Tennessee's "crimes against nature" statute did not give adequate notice that it applied to the act of cunnilingus.

The Sixth Amendment right of a defendant "to be confronted with the witnesses against him" was held in *Pointer* v. *Texas* (1965) to be a "fundamental right" obligatory on the states. Here the transcript of testimony given by a witness at the preliminary hearing was introduced at the trial because the witness had left the state and was unavailable to testify. The Supreme Court ruled that this denied the defendant's right to confront the witness and cross-examine him by counsel.[102]

In *Turner* v. *Louisiana* (1965) the jury during a three-day period of sequestration in a murder trial was in the charge of two deputy sheriffs who were also witnesses for the state. The Court held that this close association undermined the basic guarantees of trial by jury, including confrontation and cross-examination.

The Immigration and Nationality Act of 1952 automatically, without prior judicial or administrative proceedings, imposed the penalty of forfeiture of citizenship on persons who, in time of war or emergency, leave or remain outside the United States to evade military service. In *Kennedy* v. *Mendoza-Martinez* (1963) the Court held this provision void as withholding a cluster of rights guaranteed by the Fifth and Sixth Amendments, namely, notice, confrontation, trial by jury, compulsory process for obtaining witnesses, and aid of counsel.

The unique "one-man grand jury" system of Michigan was held by the Court in *In re Oliver* (1948) to deny several Sixth Amendment trial rights. The case arose when a Michigan judge, sitting as a grand jury, concluded that a witness testifying before him in a secret session was not telling the truth. He thereupon assumed his role as judge, and with no break in the proceedings, charged the witness with contempt, immediately convicted him, and sentenced him to sixty days in jail. The only other persons present during this weird procedure were two other judges who sat as advisers, plus the court staff. The trial had, of course, proceeded without counsel, but there had also been a failure to give the accused anything definite as to the nature and cause of the accusation against him—the charge was that his story did not "jell." Moreover, although this charge was based in part on testimony of another witness before the judge–grand jury the same day, the accused was denied any opportunity to be confronted with the witnesses against him. On all these points the Supreme Court held the proceeding unconstitutional.[103]

Finally, the Sixth Amendment right of a defendant to have compulsory process for obtaining witnesses in his favor was held in *Washington* v. *Texas* (1967) to be incorporated into the due process clause and made binding on the states. *Webb* v. *Texas* (1972) ruled that a judge who badgered the defendant's principal witness and effectively drove him off the witness stand had denied the defendant his Sixth Amendment right to offer witnesses.

DUE PROCESS, FAIR TRIAL, AND EQUAL PROTECTION

Both federal and state trials are subject to requirements of fairness which may be grounded in general conceptions of due process or equal protection rather than in

---

[102] See also *Douglas* v. *Alabama* (1965), *Brookhart* v. *Janis* (1966), *Smith* v. *Illinois* (1968), and *Chambers* v. *Mississippi* (1973).

[103] See Robert G. Scigliano, *The Michigan One-Man Grand Jury* (East Lansing, Mich.: Governmental Research Bureau, Michigan State University, 1957).

the more specific procedural language of the Bill of Rights. It is a denial of due process if a prosecutor knowingly offers false evidence or suppresses evidence favorable to a defendant.[104] In *Miller* v. *Pate* (1967) a sex-murder conviction was reversed because the prosecutor had deliberately misrepresented paint on a pair of men's shorts as blood.

A conviction based on insufficient evidence, or totally devoid of evidentiary support, is a denial of due process. In *Thompson* v. *Louisville* (1960) a conviction for loitering and disorderly conduct, in *Garner* v. *Louisiana* (1961) a conviction for disturbing the peace by a civil rights sit-in, and in *Gregory* v. *Chicago* (1969) a conviction for disorderly conduct in a march around Mayor Daley's home, were all held completely devoid of support in the evidence. Moreover, due process limits the power of Congress or state legislatures to make the proof of one fact or group of facts evidence of the ultimate fact on which guilt is predicated.[105]

Tumey v. *Ohio* (1927) held invalid an arrangement under which city mayors tried bootlegging cases and received compensation for their "costs" only when defendants were convicted. The Supreme Court thought this gave the mayor-judge "a direct, personal, substantial, pecuniary interest" in convictions. The *Tumey* principle was applied in *Ward* v. *Village of Monroeville, Ohio* (1972), where the revenue produced by fines in the mayor's court provided a substantial part of the municipality's revenues.

A more complex problem of Supreme Court supervision over state criminal justice arises when the charge of unfairness in the trial is based on allegations that the verdict was affected by outside pressures not apparent on the record. There was a slogan on the frontier, "Give him a fair trial and then hang him." Is a lynching transformed into a fair trial when the requisite forms of legal action are gone through? In *Frank* v. *Mangum* (1915), the Court, over the protest of Holmes and Hughes, refused to review a conviction in a case of anti-Semitism from Georgia. But in *Moore* v. *Dempsey* (1923), growing out of race riots and a mob-dominated trial of blacks in Arkansas, Holmes had a chance to assert for the Court its responsibility for guaranteeing a fair trial:

> . . . if the case is that the whole proceeding is a mask—that counsel, jury and judge were swept to the fatal end by an irresistible wave of public passion, and that the State Courts failed to correct the wrong, neither perfection in the machinery for correction nor the possibility that the trial court and counsel saw no other way of avoiding an immediate outbreak of the mob can prevent this Court from securing to the petitioners their constitutional rights.

North v. *Russell* (1976) held that it does not deny due process for criminal cases

---

[104] *Mooney* v. *Holohan* (1935). But *Imbler* v. *Pachtman* (1976) threw out a damage suit against a public prosecutor for allegedly using perjured testimony in a murder trial, on the ground that prosecutors must have absolute immunity from suit if they are to carry out their duties vigorously and courageously.

[105] *Tot* v. *United States* (1943). *United States* v. *Romano* (1965) held unconstitutional a federal statute providing that the mere presence of a person at an illegal still should be deemed sufficient evidence to authorize conviction for possession and custody of the still, unless the defendant explained such presence to the satisfaction of the jury.

to be tried by judges without legal training, provided the defendant through appeal can get a second trial before a judge who is a lawyer.

Constitutional Rights of Indigents

A fairly recent concern of the Supreme Court has been to assure that indigents will not be denied due process and equal protection because of their inability to pay for justice. The leading case is *Griffin* v. *Illinois* (1956), which held it unconstitutional discrimination for a state to furnish free stenographic transcripts of trials only for review of constitutional questions and to indigent defendants under death sentence. This restriction prevented other defendants, unable to purchase a transcript, from exercising their right to appellate review.[106]

In *Douglas* v. *California* (1963) the Court for similar reasons struck down a state criminal procedure under which appellate courts could deny an indigent's request for appointment of counsel if they believed the appointment would be valueless.[107] *Swenson* v. *Bosler* (1967) held that poor defendants must be provided with lawyers when they appeal to higher state courts, even if they do not specifically request such aid. But *Ross* v. *Moffitt* (1974) ruled that, after the first appeal as of right, counsel did not have to be supplied for further discretionary state appeals or for application for review in the Supreme Court. And *Fuller* v. *Oregon* (1974) upheld a state recoupment statute requiring indigent criminal defendants who had been provided counsel to reimburse the state for the cost of counsel if they subsequently acquired the means to do so.

Williams v. *Illinois* (1970) ruled that indigents cannot be held in jail because of their inability to pay their fines beyond the maximum period of confinement fixed by statute. *Tate* v. *Short* (1971) held that fines for traffic offenses which an indigent was unable to pay could not be converted into a jail sentence.

In *Boddie* v. *Connecticut* (1971), the Court held that indigents could not be denied access to the divorce courts because of inability to pay the various fees involved. Justice Harlan concluded that "given the basic position of the marriage relationship in this society's hierarchy of values and the concomitant monopolization of the means for legally dissolving this relationship, due process does prohibit the State from denying, solely because of inability to pay, access to its courts to individuals who seek judicial dissolution of their marriages." But *United States* v. *Kras* (1973) held that the payment of filing fees for access to federal bankruptcy court had a rational basis and did not deny indigents equal protection of the laws. Justice Stewart, dissenting, said, "The Court today holds that Congress may say that some of the poor are too poor even to go bankrupt." *Ortwein* v. *Schwab* (1973) followed *Kras* in upholding Oregon's $25 appellate court filing fee.

Due Process in Juvenile Courts

The general conception of juvenile courts has been that the state is acting through them as *parens patriae* and not as adversary, and that the proceedings against juve-

---

[106] See also *Burns* v. *Ohio* (1959), *Douglas* v. *Green* (1960), and *Rinaldi* v. *Yeager* (1966). But *United States* v. *MacCollom* (1976) denied free trial transcripts in a habeas corpus proceeding.

[107] See also *Draper* v. *Washington* (1963); *Lane* v. *Brown* (1963); *Anders* v. *California* (1967); *Entsminger* v. *Iowa* (1967).

niles are civil and not criminal. Consequently it has been the usual practice that the child is not entitled to the constitutional rights of adult offenders, such as bail, indictment, public or jury trial, immunity against self-incrimination, or counsel. He can claim only the fundamental due process right to fair treatment.

In the case of *In re Gault* (1967), a fifteen-year-old boy who had made a lewd telephone call was committed to the state industrial school as a delinquent, with the possibility of remaining there until the age of twenty-one. For an adult, the maximum punishment for such an offense would have been a fine of $50 or imprisonment for not more than two months. The boy's parents brought a habeas corpus action, alleging that they had been given inadequate notice of the charges, that the complainant had not testified, that they had not been offered the assistance of counsel, that the boy had not been warned his testimony could be used against him, that no transcript had been made of the trial, and that Arizona law did not permit appeal of a juvenile court decision.

Justice Fortas, though recognizing the benign purposes which the informal procedures of juvenile courts had been intended to achieve, felt that the intelligent enforcement of due process standards would not compel the states to displace the substantive benefits of the juvenile process and would correct such grievous disregard of procedural protections as was demonstrated by this case. "Under our Constitution," said Fortas, "the condition of being a boy does not justify a kangaroo court." Specifically, he held that in a juvenile proceeding there must be notice of charges; notice of right to be represented by counsel and appointment of counsel if the parents are unable to afford counsel; the right to confront and cross-examine complainants and other witnesses; and adequate warning of the privilege against self-incrimination and the right to remain silent.[108]

Subsequently the Court ruled in *In re Winship* (1970) that juvenile courts must apply the same standard of proof for guilt as that governing criminal proceedings, namely, the rule of guilt "beyond a reasonable doubt." *Breed* v. *Jones* (1975) applied the prohibition against double jeopardy to juvenile courts. However, *McKeiver* v. *Pennsylvania* (1971) decided that the right to trial by jury is not constitutionally required in juvenile courts.[109]

Legal Incompetence

The conviction of an accused person while he is legally incompetent violates due process,[110] and state procedures must be adequate to protect this right.[111] The first formulation of an insanity test for judging criminal responsibility was the "rightwrong" criterion promulgated in *M'Naghten's Case* (1843), namely, that "at the time of the committing of the act, the party accused was labouring under such a defect of reason, from disease of the mind, as not to know the nature and quality of the act he was doing; or, if he did know it, that he did not know he was doing what was wrong." The federal courts adopted the *M'Naghten* rule, and then supplemented it

---

[108] See also *Kent* v. *United States* (1966).

[109] For a disturbing account of juvenile court practices, see Patrick T. Murphy, *Our Kindly Parent . . . The State: The Juvenile Justice System and How It Works* (New York: The Viking Press, Inc., 1973).

[110] *Bishop* v. *United States* (1956).

[111] *Pate* v. *Robinson* (1966).

with the "irresistible impulse" test after this modification had been approved by the Supreme Court in *Davis* v. *United States* (1895).

This remained the basis for judging criminal responsibility in all the federal courts until 1954, when the District of Columbia Court of Appeals adopted a new test for insanity in *Durham* v. *United States*. This rule was "simply that an accused is not criminally responsible if the unlawful act was the product of mental disease or mental defect." The *Durham* rule set off a vigorous debate, but was not adopted by other courts and was expressly repudiated by three federal circuits. *Durham* was criticized because of the inherent vagueness in its terms, its overemphasis on the causal relationship between "disease" and "product," and its lack of utility for juries, which must make a social judgment, not a medical analysis.

In 1962 the American Law Institute proposed another test which strikes a balance between the more restrictive *M'Naghten* and irresistible impulse rules and the *Durham* test. It provides:

> A person is not responsible for criminal conduct if at the time of such conduct as a result of mental disease or defect he lacks substantial capacity either to appreciate the criminality [wrongfulness] of his conduct or to conform his conduct to the requirements of law.[112]

Apart from its approval in the 1895 *Davis* case of jury instructions embodying the irresistible impulse test, the Supreme Court had not by 1975 found any of these four standards to be constitutionally required or preferred over the others.[113] However, a heightened national concern over commitment practices[114] and scandalous treatment of the inmates of state mental hospitals led to a unanimous Supreme Court decision in *O'Connor* v. *Donaldson* (1975) that mental patients who were not dangerous to others could not be confined in institutions against their will if they did not receive therapy and if they could survive in the outside world with the aid of relatives or friends.

Constitutional Rights of Prisoners

The treatment of prison inmates was historically regarded as strictly a matter for correctional administrators, and courts followed a "hands-off" policy. In 1871 a Virginia judge said in *Ruffin* v. *Commonwealth* that a convict is "for the time being the slave of the state." As late as 1954 the Court of Appeals for the Tenth Circuit held that "courts are without power to supervise prison administration or to interfere with the ordinary prison rules or regulations."[115]

But the situation began to change in the 1960s, first in the lower courts without notable leadership from the Supreme Court. In 1965 an Arkansas district judge held that persons convicted of crime were covered by the due process and equal protection clauses,[116] and in 1966 the Court of Appeals for the Fourth Circuit guaranteed

[112] This standard was adopted by the Ninth Circuit Court of Appeals in *Wade* v. *United States* (1970).

[113] For a general discussion, see Abraham S. Goldstein, *The Insanity Defense* (New Haven, Conn.: Yale University Press, 1967); Herbert Fingarette, *The Meaning of Criminal Insanity* (Berkeley: University of California Press, 1972).

[114] See the comprehensive analysis, "Civil Commitment of the Mentally Ill," 87 HARVARD LAW REVIEW 1190–1406 (1974); *Specht* v. *Patterson* (1967).

[115] *Banning* v. *Looney* (1954).

[116] *Talley* v. *Stephens* (1965).

474

inmates access to courts[117] and to medical care.[118] In *Holt* v. *Sarver* (1970), an Arkansas district judge held that barbaric conditions in the state's prisons violated the ban on cruel and unusual punishment and ordered prison authorities to submit a plan for bringing the system within constitutional standards.[119] In 1976 Judge Frank Johnson held that Alabama's prisons were "unfit for human habitation" and threatened to close them unless a long list of minimum constitutional standards was met.

The Supreme Court did, of course, have an established interest in protecting the right of convicted prisoners to pursue postconviction remedies by way of habeas corpus. In *Smith* v. *Bennett* (1961), the Court held that states could not refuse the writ to prisoners unable to pay the filing fee, and *Johnson* v. *Avery* (1969) struck down a prison regulation barring inmates from assisting other prisoners in preparation of petitions for postconviction relief. But at the same time the Court began to be concerned not merely with how inmates might get out of prison but also with their life and constitutional rights while in prison.

Among the first to raise these issues were the Black Muslims, who were almost invariably denied access to religious reading material and ministers of their faith. In *Cooper* v. *Pate* (1963), the Supreme Court ruled that the courts must hear their complaints. In *Cruz* v. *Beto* (1972) the Court held that a Buddhist who was denied a reasonable opportunity of pursuing his faith in prison comparable to that provided for adherents of the conventional religions had a valid civil rights complaint.

Censorship of prisoners' mail under California prison regulations was considered in *Procunier* v. *Martinez* (1974). The Court's ruling was that such censorship must be no greater than required to protect security interests and agreed with the district court that the California regulations were unconstitutional under the First Amendment. While granting that prisoners retained those First Amendment rights not inconsistent with legitimate penological objectives, *Pell* v. *Procunier* (1974) denied that these included the right to demand face-to-face interviews with news media representatives.

Wolff v. *McDonnell* (1974) held that prison misconduct proceedings, which could cause the loss of "good-time" credits, must observe certain minimal due process requirements. But *Montayne* v. *Haymes* (1976) and *Meachum* v. *Fano* (1976) held that prison inmates do not have a constitutional right to a hearing before a transfer to a maximum security penitentiary, whether or not the transfer was punitive.

DOUBLE JEOPARDY

The Fifth Amendment in archaic language forbids the government to put any person twice "in jeopardy of life or limb" for the same offense. The underlying idea, as Justice Black has said, "is that the State with all its resources and power should not be allowed to make repeated attempts to convict an individual for an alleged of-

117 *Coleman* v. *Peyton* (1966).
118 *Edwards* v. *Duncan* (1966).
119 See Case Note, 84 HARVARD LAW REVIEW 456 (1970).

fense, thereby subjecting him to embarrassment, expense and ordeal and compelling him to live in a continuing state of anxiety and insecurity, as well as enhancing the possibility that even though innocent he may be found guilty."[120]

Palko v. *Connecticut* held in 1937 that the states were not bound by the double jeopardy rule, on the ground that it was not essential to a scheme of "ordered liberty." But, like most of the other "ordered liberty" decisions, *Palko* was overruled during the "incorporationist" tide of the 1960s. In *Benton* v. *Maryland* (1969), the Warren Court asserted that the ban on double jeopardy "represents a fundamental ideal in our constitutional heritage" and was consequently binding on the states through the Fourteenth Amendment.[121]

Enforcement of the double jeopardy provision depends upon the views taken as to what constitutes "jeopardy" in a legal proceeding and what constitutes "sameness" in an offense. On the first question, an accused person has of course been placed in jeopardy when he has been tried by a court of competent jurisdiction and either acquitted or convicted. The government may not appeal such a verdict or institute a second prosecution for the same offense.[122] It is not even necessary for a trial to have reached the stage of a verdict to bring the jeopardy rule into operation; otherwise a prosecutor or judge would be able to stop a trial when it began to appear that the jury might not convict, in order to leave the way open for a second trial.[123] On the other hand, when a jury fails to agree on a verdict and is discharged by the judge, a second trial is permissible, the theory being that it is merely a continuation of the first.[124] And trial by a court which is subsequently found to lack jurisdiction cannot place the defendant in jeopardy, no matter how far the proceedings are carried.

The accused may waive his constitutional immunity against double jeopardy. He does this when he requests a new trial, or appeals from a verdict of guilty. If a conviction is set aside on appeal, the defendant may be tried a second time for the same offense,[125] and the accused assumes the risk of receiving a heavier penalty than in the first trial, but only if justified by some "identifiable conduct" occurring after the original sentencing.[126] But according to *Green* v. *United States* (1957), he cannot be subjected to the risk of being convicted on a more serious charge than in the first trial.[127] However, he may be tried on a different theory in the second trial;

---

[120] *Green* v. *United States* (1957). Courts-martial are governed by the double jeopardy provision; see *Wade* v. *Hunter* (1949).

[121] The *Benton* decision was given retroactive effect in *North Carolina* v. *Pearce* (1969).

[122] When a federal trial judge directs acquittal of a defendant, even though he acts on erroneous grounds, the double jeopardy clause precludes a second trial: *Fong Foo* v. *United States* (1962). *Breed* v. *Jones* (1975) involved a person who had been tried in juvenile court and found unfit for treatment as a juvenile; subsequent prosecution as an adult on the same charges was double jeopardy. But see *United States* v. *Wilson* (1975).

[123] See *United States* v. *Jorn* (1971). But when a judge declared a mistrial because of a defective indictment, before any evidence was presented, a subsequent trial did not constitute double jeopardy; *Illinois* v. *Somerville* (1973).

[124] *United States* v. *Perez* (1824).

[125] *United States* v. *Ball* (1896).

[126] *North Carolina* v. *Pearce* (1969).

[127] *Price* v. *Georgia* (1970) repeated this holding.

in *Forman* v. *United States* (1960) a defendant was convicted of a subsidiary conspiracy after the statute of limitations had run on the main conspiracy involved in the first trial.

The "same offense" provision means the identical offense as defined by the same governmental jurisdiction. The test of identity of offenses is whether the same evidence is required to prove them. If not, the fact that two charges grow out of one transaction does not make a single offense where two or more are defined by the statutes.[128] Thus Congress may provide for both civil and criminal prosecution for the same act or failure to act, or it may separate a conspiracy to commit a substantive offense from the actual commission of the offense, and attach a different penalty to each. A person who refused to testify before a Senate committee was not subjected to double jeopardy by being punished for contempt of the Senate and also indicted for a misdemeanor for such refusal.[129]

The Narcotic Drugs Act, as amended, provides for three separate offenses in connection with the vending of illicit drugs. In *Gore* v. *United States* (1958) a defendant was convicted of a single sale on each of two separate days under all three provisions, a total of six counts, and was given a separate sentence on each count. The Court held this was not double jeopardy.

The "same evidence" rule makes it possible to file multiple charges arising out of a single transaction (or, in Chief Justice Burger's phrase in *Ashe* v. *Swenson,* "one frolic"). In *Hoag* v. *New Jersey* (1958), a man who was alleged to have robbed five tavern patrons was tried for the robbery of three of them and was acquitted because of the unexpected failure of four of the state's witnesses to identify the defendant. The state then tried Hoag for robbery of a fourth patron, who was the only witness at the first trial to identify the defendant, and this time the jury convicted. By a five to three vote the Supreme Court upheld the state's action on the ground that, while a single trial would have been "preferable practice," the Fourteenth Amendment did not lay down an inflexible rule making multiple trials unconstitutional, and the circumstances of this case did not result in "fundamental unfairness." Chief Justice Warren, dissenting, thought that the state had relitigated "the same issue on the same evidence before two different juries."

Ciucci v. *Illinois* involved a man accused of killing his wife and three children. The initial prosecution for one of the murders brought conviction and a twenty-year sentence. Dissatisfied with this outcome, the prosecutor instituted a second trial for another of the murders, which yielded a forty-five-year sentence. The state then made a third effort, and was finally rewarded by a death sentence. The Court upheld these tactics by a five to four vote in 1958.

Comparable prosecution methods were finally declared unconstitutional by the Court in *Ashe* v. *Swenson* (1970) by reading the technical doctrine of "collateral estoppel" into the double jeopardy provision.[130] But three justices, speaking through

---

128 *Morgan* v. *Devine* (1915); *United States* v. *Ewell* (1966).

129 *In re Chapman* (1897).

130 Collateral estoppel "means simply that when an issue of ultimate fact has once been determined by a valid and final judgment, that issue cannot again be litigated between the same parties in any future lawsuit," said Justice Stewart in *Ashe* v. *Swenson.*

Brennan, directly attacked the "same evidence" rule. They favored the "same transaction" rule, requiring the prosecution "to join at one trial all the charges against a defendant which grow out of a single criminal act, occurrence, episode, or transaction." Potential prosecutorial abuses in bringing multiple trials under the same evidence rule were "simply intolerable."

Where both federal and state governments make the same act an offense, the Supreme Court has held that it is not double jeopardy for each government to prosecute and punish. This rule provoked considerable dissatisfaction during the era of national prohibition, but the Court justified dual prosecution in *United States* v. *Lanza* (1922) as resulting from our system of "two sovereignties, deriving power from different sources, capable of dealing with the same subject-matter within the same territory. . . . It follows that an act denounced as a crime by both national and state sovereignties is an offense against the peace and dignity of both."

This principle was developed further in two 1959 decisions. In *Abbate* v. *United States* several individuals who conspired in Illinois to blow up telephone properties in Mississippi were convicted on a conspiracy charge in Illinois, and were subsequently found guilty of the same acts by a federal court in Mississippi. In *Bartkus* v. *Illinois* a man was tried by a federal court for robbery of an Illinois bank and acquitted. He was then indicted for the same crime by an Illinois grand jury, convicted, and sentenced to life imprisonment.

The Supreme Court, by a divided vote, denied that the double jeopardy standard had been violated in either case. However, the Attorney General announced shortly thereafter, as reported in *Petite* v. *United States* (1960), that it would not be the general policy of the government to make several offenses arising from a single transaction the basis of multiple prosecutions.

Waller v. *Florida* (1970) held that a defendant who had been convicted in municipal court for violation of city ordinances could not be tried by the state on a charge of grand larceny based on the same acts.

A bizarre form of double jeopardy problem came to the Court's attention in *Louisiana ex rel. Francis* v. *Resweber* (1947). Francis had been duly convicted of murder and sentenced to death. He was placed in the electric chair, but because of some mechanical difficulty, it did not operate, and the prisoner was returned to his cell. Redress was then sought in the courts on the ground that a second trip to the electric chair would constitute double jeopardy contrary to the Fifth Amendment and cruel and unusual punishment in violation of the Eighth Amendment. The Court rejected both claims by a vote of five to four.

EXCESSIVE BAIL

"Excessive bail shall not be required," the Eighth Amendment says, copying a similar provision in the English Bill of Rights of 1689. Bail is the pledge of money or property by an accused person or his sureties in order to guarantee his appearance for trial. Admission to bail provides a means whereby an individual may obtain his freedom while awaiting trial. Apart from humanitarian considerations and the presumption that a person is innocent until proved guilty, it provides the accused with a better opportunity to prepare his defense. The constitutional provision has been construed as a limitation both on Congress, in adopting statutes governing admission to bail, and on federal courts, in fixing bail in individual cases.

Bail is excessive, the Supreme Court has said, when it is set "at a figure higher than an amount reasonably calculated" to fulfill the purpose of assuring the presence of the accused at the trial.[131] The Federal Rules of Criminal Procedure itemize the factors to be considered by the court in fixing bail as follows: "The nature and circumstances of the offense charged, the weight of the evidence against him, the financial ability of the defendant to give bail and the character of the defendant."

The Supreme Court applied the excessive bail provision in *Stack* v. *Boyle* (1951). Twelve "second-string" Communist leaders had been taken into custody in Los Angeles on Smith Act indictments, and bail of $50,000 fixed for each defendant. The government's reason for asking such high bail was that four Communist leaders convicted a few months earlier in New York had vanished and forfeited their bail. The Supreme Court unanimously held that in the circumstances bail in such amount was excessive.[132]

Widespread concern about abuses of the bail system led Congress in 1966 to pass the Bail Reform Act, which requires the release on personal recognizance or on unsecured bond of persons charged with noncapital federal offenses unless a judicial officer finds that release would "not reasonably assure" appearance as required. Bail reform in the states is also underway.

CRUEL AND UNUSUAL PUNISHMENT

The Eighth Amendment's ban on "cruel and unusual punishment" has raised some very difficult moral issues. Prior to the landmark capital punishment decision, *Furman* v. *Georgia*, in 1972, the Supreme Court had applied various standards in interpreting the provision. First, punishment considered grossly disproportionate to the offense was considered cruel and unusual in several cases. In *Weems* v. *United States* (1910), a Philippine law providing for a punishment of twelve years in chains at hard labor was held greatly excessive for the crime of falsifying an official document. In *Trop* v. *Dulles* (1958), the Court ruled that imposing loss of citizenship on a member of the Armed Forces convicted by court-martial of wartime desertion was cruel and unusual. Chief Justice Warren said this was "a form of punishment more primitive than torture," for it involved "the total destruction of the individual's status in organized society."

Again, a California law making it a crime to be a drug addict was held in *Robinson* v. *California* (1962) to be cruel and unusual punishment. The statute did not require any proof that the defendant bought or used drugs or had any in his possession. The mere status of being an addict, which could be established by needle marks in the arm, was sufficient. The Court regarded addiction as an illness rather than a crime and thought that ninety days in jail for being ill was cruel and

---

131 *Stack* v. *Boyle* (1951).
132 But see *Carlson* v. *Landon* (1951).

unusual punishment.[133] However, in *Powell* v. *Texas* (1968) the Court by a vote of five to four declined to rule that criminal conviction of chronic alcoholism was cruel and unusual. The majority thought that knowledge about alcoholism and the record in this case were inadequate for a "wide-ranging new constitutional principle."

Second, the Court has considered whether punishment is cruel and unusual because barbaric in some absolute sense.[134] Clearly death by torture or various forms of lingering death are forbidden. But the Court has accepted more "humane" forms of capital punishment. In *Wilkerson* v. *Utah* (1878), public execution by musketry was upheld. *In re Kemmler* (1890) approved the new method of electrocution as apparently instantaneous and painless. The second trip to the electric chair in the *Francis* case was regarded as acceptable by the Court majority in part because it was the result of an "unforseeable accident" and not any intentional cruelty.

Concerted legal attacks on the constitutionality of capital punishment began in the 1960s, stimulated in part by the fact that those receiving death sentences were disproportionately blacks. One result was the *Witherspoon* decision already noted. But other challenges to court procedures in capital cases were less successful. In *McGautha* v. *California* (1971) and *Crampton* v. *Ohio* (1971), the practice under which state statutes left the death verdict to the absolute discretion of the jury, with no standards of any sort to guide them, was held not to violate due process. Justice Harlan thought it would be impossible to draft statutory standards for this purpose:

> To identify before the fact those characteristics of criminal homicides and their perpetrators which call for the death penalty, and to express these characteristics in language which can be fairly understood and applied by the sentencing authority, appear to be tasks which are beyond present human ability.

California law called for a two-stage trial, one to determine guilt and the second to hear evidence and argument on the issue of punishment. In Ohio guilt and punishment were determined at a single trial. The bifurcated procedure might well be preferable, the Court said in *Crampton,* but it was not constitutionally required.

These decisions gave little warning of the ruling that was to come a year later in *Furman* v. *Georgia* (1972), where by a vote of five to four the Court held that the imposition of the death penalty in three cases, one for murder and two for rape, constituted cruel and unusual punishment in violation of the Eighth and Fourteenth Amendments.[135] The Court issued a brief per curiam opinion, which was followed by substantial statements by every member of the Court.

[133] See Herbert Fingarette, "Addiction and Criminal Responsibility," 84 YALE LAW JOURNAL 413 (1975), and "The Perils of Powell: In Search of a Factual Foundation for the 'Disease Concept of Alcoholism,'" 83 HARVARD LAW REVIEW 793 (1970).

[134] See Hugo Adam Bedau (ed.), *The Death Penalty in America* (New York: Doubleday & Company, Inc., 1967); Michael Meltsner, *Cruel and Unusual: The Supreme Court and Capital Punishment* (New York: Random House, Inc., 1973); Arthur J. Goldberg and Alan M. Dershowitz, "Declaring the Death Penalty Unconstitutional," 83 HARVARD LAW REVIEW 1773 (1970).

[135] See Daniel D. Polsby, "The Death of Capital Punishment? Furman v. Georgia," in Philip B. Kurland (ed.), *The Supreme Court Review, 1972* (Chicago: University of Chicago Press, 1972), pp. 1–40. The California supreme court had declared capital punishment unconstitutional under that state's constitution four months earlier; *People* v. *Anderson* (1972).

The five justices who made up the majority were divided into two groups. Douglas, Stewart, and White took an analytic and empirical approach, appraising the practice under the Eighth Amendment in the light of due process and equal protection. Their concern was whether the death penalty was evenly applied, and of course they found that it was not. Stewart's comment is quotable:

> These death sentences are cruel and unusual in the same way that being struck by lightning is cruel and unusual. For, of all the people convicted of rapes and murders in 1967 and 1968, many just as reprehensible as these, the petitioners are among a capriciously selected random handful upon whom the sentence of death has in fact been imposed.

Douglas contended that the death penalty was cruel and unusual because applied irregularly and "selectively to minorities whose members are few, who are outcasts of society, and who are unpopular, but whom society is willing to see suffer though it would not countenance general application of the same penalty across the boards."

White conceded that the death penalty, while cruel in "the dictionary sense," would nevertheless be justified if it served "social ends." But he did not believe "that society's need for specific deterrence justifies death for so few when for so many in like circumstances life imprisonment or shorter prison terms are judged sufficient, or that community values are measurably reenforced by authorizing a penalty so rarely invoked."

The other two majority justices, Brennan and Marshall, took a normative approach. For them, the Eighth Amendment posed a core question of values; they were concerned less with fairness and equality and more with mercy and charity. For them, capital punishment, no matter how often or how infrequently applied, was uncivilized, excessive, unacceptable. For Brennan, "the primary principle . . . is that a punishment must not by its severity be degrading to human dignity." Marshall, in by far the longest opinion of the day, not only made what he called "a long and tedious journey" through history and the precedents but also reviewed a great number of studies and reports bearing upon the "six purposes conceivably served by capital punishment: retribution, deterrence, prevention of repetitive criminal acts, encouragement of guilty pleas and confessions, eugenics, and economy." His impassioned conclusion was that ending the death sentence would recognize "the humanity of our fellow beings" and achieve "a major milestone in the long road up from barbarism."

Powell wrote the major opinion in dissent, and it was basically a plea for judicial restraint in this enormously difficult area. Stressing the "enormity of the step taken by the Court today," he said: "Not only does it invalidate hundreds of state and federal laws, it deprives those jurisdictions of the power to legislate with respect to capital punishment in the future, except in a manner consistent with the cloudily outlined views of those Justices who do not purport to undertake total abolition." This was "a classic case for the exercise of our oft-announced allegiance to judicial restraint."

After *Furman*, it was widely assumed that the Court had not declared capital punishment unconstitutional per se, but only its unpredictable and fortuitous use. Consequently the legislatures of 35 states acted to tighten the laws under which the death penalty was to be inflicted. They took two different approaches. Some states, including Georgia, Florida, and Texas, established new procedures for capital cases, requiring sentencing judges and juries to consider certain specified aggravating or mitigating circumstances of the crime and the offender. Courts of appeal were given broader authority to decide whether the death penalty was fair in the light of the sentences for similar offenses. These laws were intended to reduce the arbitrariness and possible racial prejudice denounced in *Furman*.

But ten other states, including North Carolina, Louisiana, and Oklahoma, sought to meet the *Furman* objections by removing all flexibility from the sentencing process, though limiting the offenses for which the death sentence could be imposed. Anyone found guilty of the specified offenses was to be sentenced to death automatically. There would be no more unpredictable lightning bolts.

On July 2, 1976, by which time there were some 600 persons on death rows under the new laws, the Supreme Court made the judgment it had postponed a year earlier. By a vote of seven to two in *Gregg* v. *Georgia* it ruled that the death penalty was not inherently cruel and unusual. Justice Stewart's opinion relied heavily on "society's endorsement of the death penalty for murder" as evidenced by action of the 35 state legislatures; "a heavy burden rests on those who would attack the judgment of the representatives of the people." The Georgia law, moreover, had met and remedied the *Furman* objections. "No longer can a jury wantonly and freakishly impose the death sentence; it is always circumscribed by the legislative guidelines." The Texas and Florida statutes were upheld by the same reasoning.[136]

However, the "automatic" statutes of North Carolina, Louisiana, and Oklahoma were held unconstitutional by votes of five to four.[137] Brennan and Marshall, who had dissented in the Georgia, Texas, and Florida decisions, now joined Stewart, Powell, and Stevens in striking down mandatory death sentences for specified crimes as "unduly harsh and unworkably rigid," incompatible with "contemporary values." These statutes simply "papered over the problem of unguided and unchecked jury discretion" and provided no way for appellate courts to check arbitrary and capricious exercises of discretion.[138] They treated "all persons convicted of a designated offense not as uniquely individual human beings, but as members of a faceless, undifferentiated mass to be subjected to the blind infliction of the penalty of death." Consequently, death sentences from these three states were vacated.

White, Burger, Blackmun, and Rehnquist were the dissenters in the mandatory sentence cases and, while voting to make up the majority in *Gregg*, they were sharply critical of Stewart's "muddled reasoning" in all the cases. White contended that legislatures should have the right to decide that mandatory death sentences would deter crime and that "the commission of certain crimes conclusively establishes that the criminal's character is such that he deserves death." By refusing to honor these

---

[136] *Jurek* v. *Texas; Proffitt* v. Florida.

[137] *Woodson* v. *North Carolina; Roberts* v. *Louisiana; Green* v. *Oklahoma.*

[138] On the impossibility of eliminating prosecutory or jury discretion by automatic death sentences, see Charles L. Black, Jr., *Capital Punishment: The Inevitability of Caprice and Mistake* (New York: W. W. Norton & Company, Inc., 1974).

legislative judgments, White thought the Court had "again surrendered to the temptation to make policy for and to attempt to govern the country through a misuse of [its] powers. . . ."

CONCLUSION

The Warren Court was responsible for a dramatic rethinking and strengthening of the constitutional rights of defendants in federal criminal trials. As for state courts, an inexorable process, whether called "incorporation" or "absorption," made binding most of the provisions of the Fourth through the Eighth Amendments. The new, stricter federal standards were thus given nationwide application; through such decisions as *Escobedo* and *Miranda,* they reached down into every police station in the nation. The line of decisions from *Mapp* to *Furman* clearly ranks as one of the major assertions of judicial power in the Court's long history.

This experience also vividly demonstrates the political limits on the Court's authority. While Congress sometimes shared the Court's concern for improving the standards of ciminal justice, as in adoption of the Bail Reform Act of 1966, the Jury Selection and Service Act of 1968, and the Speedy Trial Act of 1974, more often it was attacking the Court for "coddling criminals." The Crime Control and Safe Streets Act of 1968 and the no-knock provisions of the 1970 statutes reflect this attitude.

In 1968 a man who was to appoint a Chief Justice and three Associate Justices campaigned for the presidency on an anti-Court platform. Inevitably, the Burger Court subjected Warren Court criminal justice decisions to reconsideration. While the spirit of the new Court majority was considerably more hostile to constitutional claims, it cannot be said that there was a wholesale overruling of precedents. In fact, right to counsel was extended in *Argersinger.* The *Miranda* rules were preserved, though limited in application. The exclusionary rule of *Mapp* likewise survived, though not intact, in spite of the opposition of the Chief Justice. While accepting the constitutionality of capital punishment, the Court narrowly preserved a basis for judicial control of its imposition.

In other areas there was substantial erosion of Warren Court standards, the most significant being the limiting of federal habeas corpus review of state criminal convictions. *Stone* v. *Powell* and *Wolff* v. *Rice* (1976), discussed in Chapter 7, substantially closed the federal courts to claims of Fourth Amendment violations in state convictions, the Burger Court preferring to leave enforcement of these constitutional rights to state courts. Actually, in some states defendants and judges have found it preferable to rely on state constitutional provisions rather than on the Bill of Rights as interpreted by the Burger Court.[139]

It is well to remember, as Justice Frankfurter said in *Stein* v. *New York* (1953), that constitutional guarantees for criminal defendants are provided "not out of tenderness for the accused but because we have reached a certain stage of civilization"—a civilization, Justice Douglas added, which "by respecting the dignity even of the least worthy citizen, raises the stature of all of us."

[139] Donald W. Wilkes, Jr., "The New Federalism: State Court Evasion of the Burger Court," 62 *Kentucky Law Journal* 421 (1974); Ronald Blubaugh, "The State Supreme Court's Declaration of Independence," 7 *California Journal* 153 (1976); Linda Mathews and Philip Hager, *Los Angeles Times,* May 10, 1976.

Equal Protection: Racial

"Equal protection of the laws" is a phrase born with the Fourteenth Amendment, the first specific recognition of the doctrine of equality in the Constitution. The dictum of the Declaration of Independence that "all men are created equal," which was effectively used in the antislavery campaign, had a somewhat different import. Charles Sumner came closer to the equal protection notion with his phrase "equality before the law," which he developed in 1849 in contending before the Massachusetts supreme court that separate public schools for black children would be unconstitutional. Later he sought to get the principle of equal rights into the Constitution by way of the Thirteenth Amendment, his suggestion being: "All persons are equal before the law, so that no person can hold another as a slave."

But it was Representative Bingham who gave final form to the idea. In December, 1865, he proposed a constitutional amendment authorizing Congress "to secure to all persons in every State of the Union equal protection in their rights, life, liberty, and property." Within the same month Senators Wilson and Trumbull introduced the bill which became the Civil Rights Act of 1866, in which all inhabitants were guaranteed "full and equal benefit of all laws and proceedings for the security of person and estate." When Bingham came to prepare his draft of the Fourteenth Amendment, "equal protection in their rights" and "equal benefit of all laws" were merged to produce "equal protection of the laws."

THE ORIGINAL UNDERSTANDING

Obviously Congress was thinking primarily of the newly freed blacks when it drafted the Fourteenth Amendment. Their problems were of two sorts. The first was political. How could they be guaranteed the right to vote and to full political participation in the Southern states? Congress sought to include some formula for this purpose in the Fourteenth Amendment, but ultimately all it was able to produce was the provision in section 2 of the amendment reducing representation in the House for any state which denied the vote to qualified citizens.

The second problem was guaranteeing the civil, as distinct from the political, rights of the freedmen. This was the area that equal protection was meant to cover— but what fields, and how fully? There can be no doubt that the equal protection clause was meant to end discrimination enforced upon blacks by the "Black Codes" of certain states which limited their right to hold property, specified criminal offenses for blacks only, and hampered their access to the courts in a variety of ways. In 1862 Congress had repealed the Black Codes in the District of Columbia and prohibited exclusion of witnesses on account of color in court cases there. The Civil Rights Act of 1866, passed just prior to congressional adoption of the Fourteenth Amendment, spelled out clearly the purpose to guarantee blacks equality in courts and commerce, by giving

> . . . citizens, of every race and color . . . the same right, in every State and Territory . . . to make and enforce contracts, to sue, be parties, and give evidence, to inherit, purchase, lease, sell, hold, and convey real and personal property, and to full and equal benefit of all laws and proceedings for the security of person and property, as is enjoyed by white citizens, and shall be subject to like punishment, pains, and penalties, and to none other.

Congressional intent in other areas of discrimination is less clear. The impact which equal protection was intended to have on segregation is certainly open to doubt. The problem of segregation was never squarely faced during the incubation period of the amendment. There was a widespread assumption of a dichotomy between "civil" equality and "social" equality. The former was a matter which the law must control, but the latter was a matter of taste, with which the law had nothing to do. Just where the dividing line was between the two areas was not too clear, however.

Geographical segregation—that is, governmental restriction of blacks to certain sections of a city or their exclusion from areas by limiting their right to buy or live on particular pieces of property—was clearly forbidden under congressional interpretations of that period. Segregation in transportation, it would seem, was almost equally condemned by congressional attitudes of the time, which held that transportation companies had a common-law duty to take all comers, and that making any distinctions in the operation of this duty because of color denied an equal right to contract for transportation.

Concerning hotels and theaters, there was substantially more disagreement. Hotels were generally thought, like railroads, to have a common-law obligation to serve all comers, but there were problems of location as to rooms and at dining tables where preferences in tastes could legitimately be indulged. Theaters were scarcely in the same public utility category as railroads and hotels, but they were nevertheless subject to extensive regulation of various sorts.

On segregation in education, the situation was the most confused of all. At the close of the Civil War, blacks were generally excluded from education altogether in both North and South. The primary problem was to get any kind of education at all for blacks, not whether the schools were to be separate or mixed. In the District of Columbia, separate schools for blacks were established as they were freed during the war, so that a pattern of segregation was established before Congress could take a position on the subject. Several abortive efforts were made subsequently to legislate against school segregation, but the main battle was in connection with the Civil Rights Act of 1875. On May 22, 1874, an amendment permitting separate but equal schools was defeated in the Senate, twenty-six to twenty-one, and the next day the Senate passed the bill forbidding school segregation by a vote of twenty-nine to sixteen. However, when the House considered the measure a year later, it deleted the school clause, and it remained out of the final statute.[1]

The Civil Rights Act of 1875, then, forbade racial separation or discrimination in public conveyances, hotels, and theaters, and also required equality in jury service. The constitutional basis for the statute cited in the congressional debates was primarily the equal protection clause, with privileges and immunities as a subordinate support. There are two matters of major significance to note about this act. The first is that, apart from the jury provisions, it was directed at discriminatory actions not primarily of public officials, but of private individuals operating services traditionally subject to public regulation.

Second, the Civil Rights Act was based on an unquestioned assumption that Congress had plenary legislative power to enforce the protections of the Fourteenth Amendment, that its authority was as broad as was necessary to correct abuses which might be found, and that it could be invoked to punish acts of omission or failure to enforce the law, as well as affirmative discriminatory acts. There was this significant difference in the two situations. When a state discriminated by affirmative state action, redress simply required the negating of that action. But where the discrimination arose out of actions by private individuals which the state failed to prevent or punish, then redress necessarily required the assertion of power to coerce state officials into a positive program of law enforcement. Thus the latter situation involved substantially greater congressional control over state and local government than the former.

Nevertheless, both in the act of 1875 and in the earlier Ku Klux (Second Enforcement) Act of 1871, Congress asserted its power to legislate affirmatively in behalf of a racial group which states might neglect to protect from the actions of private persons. There can be no doubt that a large majority in Congress at this time

[1] See John P. Frank and Robert F. Munro, "The Original Understanding of 'Equal Protection of the Laws'," 50 *Columbia Law Review* 131 (1950); Alexander M. Bickel, "The Original Understanding and the Segregation Decision," 69 *Harvard Law Review* 1 (1955).

shared the view that Congress could enforce the Fourteenth Amendment on the states by affirmative legislation, and that a state denied equal protection when it tolerated widespread abuses against a class of citizens because of their color without seriously attempting to protect them by enforcing the law.

Within a decade the Supreme Court decided that Congress had been completely wrong on both these points. There is scarcely a more striking instance in American constitutional history of outright judicial disregard of congressional intent. In the *Civil Rights Cases* of 1883, the Supreme Court concluded that the Congress which had drafted the Fourteenth Amendment and which had provided for its enforcement by major enactments in 1871 and 1875 had not understood the amendment or congressional powers under it. By means of what Justice Harlan in his dissenting opinion called "a subtle and ingenious verbal criticism," the Court proceeded to sacrifice "the substance and spirit" of the amendment.

Justice Bradley's opinion is indeed a masterpiece of ingenuity. He started by giving literal effect to the language that "no state" shall deny equal protection, saying: "It is State action of a particular character that is prohibited. Individual invasion of individual rights is not the subject-matter of the amendment." The congressmen who had drafted and interpreted this language apparently had no such understanding of its meaning, but only one Supreme Court justice, Harlan, agreed with them. Railroads, he said, might be owned by private companies, but they were "none the less public highways," and the state may regulate their entire management. With railroads, and also with inns, "no matter who is the agent, or what is the agency, the function performed is *that of the State.*" As to places of public amusement, "the authority to establish and maintain them comes from the public," and "a license from the public . . . imports, in law, equality of right, at such places, among all the members of that public."

The defeat of the Harlan position meant that Congress was stripped of any power to correct or to punish individual discriminatory action. Only *state* action was subject to the amendment. Bradley then undertook a second exercise in strict construction, this time operating on section 5 of the amendment. What did that section give Congress power to do? Why, "to enforce the prohibition" on state legislation or "State action of every kind" denying equal protection of the laws; further,

> . . . to adopt appropriate legislation for correcting the effects of such prohibited State laws and State acts, and thus to render them effectually null, void, and innocuous. This is the legislative power conferred upon Congress, and this is the whole of it. It does not invest Congress with power to legislate upon subjects which are within the domain of State legislation; but to provide modes of relief against State legislation, or State action, of the kind referred to. It does not authorize Congress to create a code of municipal law for the regulation of private rights; but to provide modes of redress against the operation of State laws, and the action of State officers . . . when these are subversive of the fundamental rights specified in the amendment.

In other words, Congress was limited to the *correcting* of *affirmative* state action. "Until some State law has been passed, or some State action through its officers or agents has been taken, adverse to the rights of citizens sought to be protected by the Fourteenth Amendment, no legislation of the United States under said amendment, nor any proceeding under such legislation, can be called into activity." The Civil Rights Act was not corrective legislation. It was "primary and direct." It was a code of conduct which ignored state legislation, and assumed "that the matter is one that belongs to the domain of national regulation." Since the law was thus based on a misconstruction of the Fourteenth Amendment, and since it was not regarded by the Court as having any demonstrable relationship with the Thirteenth Amendment, it was unconstitutional.

RACIAL EQUALITY IN COMMERCE

An early use of the equal protection clause against racial discrimination occurred in *Yick Wo* v. *Hopkins* (1886). A San Francisco ordinance made it unlawful to operate a laundry, except in a brick or stone building, without securing the consent of the board of supervisors. Masquerading as a safety measure, this ordinance in actual use discriminated against Chinese laundry operators. The fact of discrimination was demonstrated to the satisfaction of the Supreme Court, which determined that there had been a "practical denial" of equal protection of the laws.

> Though the law itself be fair on its face and impartial in appearance, yet, if it is applied and administered by public authority with an evil eye and an unequal hand, so as practically to make unjust and illegal discrimination between persons in similar circumstances, material to their rights, the denial of equal justice is . . . within the prohibition of the Constitution.

In *Truax* v. *Raich* (1915), the discrimination resulting from operation of an Arizona law was against aliens, rather than on a strictly racial basis. The statute required that if a company or person employed more than five workers, 80 per cent of them must be native-born citizens of the United States or qualified electors. The Supreme Court held that the police power of the states, while broad, did not

> . . . go so far as to make it possible for the State to deny to lawful inhabitants, because of their race or nationality, the ordinary means of earning a livelihood. It requires no argument to show that the right to work for a living in the common occupations of the community is of the very essence of the personal freedom and opportunity that it was the purpose of the [Fourteenth] Amendment to secure.

California's discrimination against Japanese by a law forbidding aliens ineligible for American citizenship to acquire agricultural land was initially accepted by the Supreme Court.[2] In *Oyama* v. *California* (1948), the Court still assumed, though "for purposes of argument only," that the law was constitutional, but it was invalidated on the ground that the means chosen to enforce it exceeded constitutional limits. But a few months later *Takahashi* v. *Fish and Game Commission* (1948) declared unconstitutional the state's attempt to ban Japanese from commercial fishing which had used the same statutory test of ineligibility to citizenship.

[2] *Terrace* v. *Thompson* (1923); *Cockrill* v. *California* (1925).

RACIAL SEGREGATION IN HOUSING

The equal protection clause, we have seen, was clearly intended to protect equal rights in buying or disposing of property. After the *Civil Rights Cases* (1883), this protection would still be effective against state action which violated equal rights in property ownership, and the Supreme Court so held when cases came up for review. Baltimore, in 1910, was apparently the first city to adopt a municipal segregation ordinance. Shortly afterward, the same procedure was followed by other Southern cities. The Louisville ordinance came before the Supreme Court in *Buchanan* v. *Warley* (1917) and was invalidated on the ground that it was an unconstitutional interference with the right of a property owner to dispose of his real estate. Attempts to circumvent the *Buchanan* decision were defeated in both state and federal courts, and by 1930 the unconstitutionality of municipal segregation ordinances was firmly established.[3]

The field was thus left to a second protective device—restrictive covenants entered into by property owners binding themselves not to sell or lease their property to blacks or certain other social, national, or religious groups. Because this type of agreement results from action by private persons, not by the state, it was at first generally successful in meeting constitutional tests.

The first restrictive covenant case to reach the Supreme Court, *Corrigan* v. *Buckley* (1926), was dismissed on grounds of lack of jurisdiction, but Justice Sanford for the Court did hold that such private covenants were not contrary to the Constitution or to public policy. Not until 1948 did the Supreme Court reconsider this position. Then it handed down two unanimous decisions upholding the validity of restrictive covenants but denying them judicial enforcement. The first decision, *Shelley* v. *Kraemer*, concerned actions brought to enforce restrictive covenants in the states of Missouri and Michigan. Chief Justice Vinson found it relatively easy to reconcile the Court's new view with its previous decisions. *Corrigan* v. *Buckley*, he pointed out, had concerned only the right of private individuals to enter into such covenants, and he here reiterated the conclusion of the *Corrigan* case that "restrictive agreements standing alone cannot be regarded as violative of any rights guaranteed . . . by the Fourteenth Amendment."

But in *Shelley* v. *Kraemer* the Court was willing to push beyond this point and to consider the status of action by state courts to enforce these covenants. "It cannot be doubted," said the Chief Justice, "that among the civil rights intended to be protected from discriminatory state action by the Fourteenth Amendment are the rights to acquire, enjoy, own and dispose of property." The question, then, was whether judicial enforcement of restrictive covenants amounted to "state action." The Court answered:

We have no doubt that there has been state action in these cases in the full and complete sense of the phrase. The undisputed facts disclose that petitioners were willing purchasers of properties upon which they desired to establish homes. The owners of the proper-

[3] See *Harmon* v. *Tyler* (1927); *City of Richmond* v. *Deans* (1930); *City of Birmingham* v. *Monk* (1951).

ties were willing sellers; and contracts of sale were accordingly consummated. It is clear that but for the active intervention of the state courts, supported by the full panoply of state power, petitioners would have been free to occupy the properties in question without restraint.

The fact that "the particular pattern of discrimination, which the State has enforced, was defined initially by the terms of a private agreement" made no difference. "State action, as that phrase is understood for the purposes of the Fourteenth Amendment, refers to exertions of state power in all forms."

The second decision, *Hurd* v. *Hodge* (1948), involved two cases arising in the District of Columbia, where the equal protection clause could not be invoked. Consequently, it was contended that judicial enforcement was forbidden by the due process clause of the Fifth Amendment. The Court, speaking again through the Chief Justice, found it unnecessary to base its decision upon constitutional grounds at all. Primary reliance was placed upon section 1 of the Civil Rights Act of 1866, which guarantees to "all citizens" the same rights as white citizens "to inherit, purchase, lease, sell, hold, and convey real and personal property." The Court held that judicial enforcement of restrictive covenants would be a violation of this section. Even in the absence of the statute, however, the Court indicated that judicial enforcement would be contrary to the public policy of the United States, which the Supreme Court would have power to enforce in the exercise of its supervisory powers over the courts of the District of Columbia.

Since these two decisions left restrictive covenants legal, even though unenforceable, the question soon arose as to whether a signer of a covenant who breached its provisions could be sued for damages by other participants in the covenant. In *Barrows* v. *Jackson* (1953) a California property owner who had failed to live up to the conditions of a covenant was sued by three neighbors on the ground that the value of their property had dropped sharply since blacks moved in. But six justices thought that the Supreme Court should not permit or require California to coerce a property owner to pay damages for failure to observe a covenant that California had no right to incorporate in a statute or enforce in equity and which federal courts could not enforce because contrary to public policy.[4]

SEGREGATION IN PUBLIC TRANSPORTATION

Separate accommodations for blacks on public transportation were the rule in the Southern states at the time the Fourteenth Amendment was adopted. After the Civil War, Congress took several steps against this practice, culminating in the Civil Rights Act of 1875. One of the *Civil Rights Cases* (1883) arose out of the exclusion of a black woman from the ladies' car of an interstate train. But, as we have already seen, the Supreme Court held the Fourteenth Amendment applicable only against state action, and ruled that the actions of a railroad or its employees did not fall into this category.

This decision at least left open the possibility that *state* action *enforcing* segrega-

[4] But see *Leeper* v. *Charlotte Park Commission* (1956).

tion would be contrary to the equal protection clause. But this defense fell in the famous case of *Plessy* v. *Ferguson* (1896). Here a Louisiana statute *requiring* segregation of the two races on public carriers was held by the Supreme Court not to violate the Fourteenth Amendment. Said Justice Brown: "The object of the amendment was undoubtedly to enforce the absolute equality of the two races before the law, but in the nature of things it could not have been intended to abolish distinctions based upon color, or to enforce social, as distinguished from political equality, or a commingling of the two races upon terms unsatisfactory to either."

The Court denied that the enforced separation of the two races stamped the colored race with a "badge of inferiority." "If this be so, it is not by reason of anything found in the act, but solely because the colored race chooses to put that construction upon it." Thus *Plessy* v. *Ferguson* gave the Supreme Court's blessing to the view that segregation was compatible with equality. "Separate but equal" was the formula for reconciling the protection of the Fourteenth Amendment with a system of state-enforced segregation. Justice Harlan dissented, protesting that "our Constitution is color-blind, and neither knows nor tolerates classes among citizens."

Elimination of the equal protection clause still left the federal commerce power as a possible barrier to segregated transportation facilities. The Civil Rights Act of 1875 did not attempt to rely on the commerce power, but the Interstate Commerce Act of 1887 did contain in section 3(1) a ban on "undue or unreasonable prejudice or disadvantage" in service rendered in interstate commerce. This provision was almost immediately invoked to test segregated facilities, but the Interstate Commerce Commission ruled against the claim.

A second alternative under the commerce clause was to attack state laws pertaining to segregated transportation in the courts as an unconstitutional burden on commerce. This was done successfully in *Hall* v. *DeCuir* (1878), but the catch was that the state law voided there was an 1869 Louisiana Reconstruction statute *prohibiting* discrimination on account of race or color. The Court regarded this matter as one on which uniformity of practice was required, and consequently only Congress could adopt regulations on the subject.

It was not until 1890 that the Supreme Court encountered the opposite kind of statutory situation. An 1888 Mississippi statute required all railways carrying passengers in the state to provide "equal but separate" accommodations for white and black passengers. It seemed obvious that the Supreme Court, which in *DeCuir* had declared a state statute *prohibiting* segregation an unconstitutional burden on interstate commerce, would have to make a similar holding against a state statute *requiring* discrimination. By a seven to two vote, however, the Court avoided the simple but honest logic of this position by acceptance of Mississippi's contention that the act applied solely to commerce within the state, and so raised no interstate commerce question.[5]

Hall v. *DeCuir* had not been overruled, however; it had merely been distinguished. So efforts to challenge segregation on commerce grounds continued to be made. The Court avoided the issue in a variety of ways. For example, in *McCabe* v.

---

[5] *Louisville, New Orleans & Texas R. Co.* v. *Mississippi* (1890).

Atchison, Topeka & Santa Fe (1914), where an injunction was sought against the Oklahoma "separate coach" law of 1907, the Court denied that a case for relief in equity had been made out. However, the decision insisted that the separate but equal standard in the Interstate Commerce Act demanded "substantial equality of treatment of persons traveling under like conditions," and the failure to supply first-class accommodations for blacks because there was less demand for them was rebuked by Justice Hughes.

Finally, in *Mitchell* v. *United States* (1941) the Court squarely upheld a charge of denial of equal treatment brought by a black congressman from Illinois who had been refused Pullman accommodations in Arkansas. The ruling, however, did not challenge the constitutionality of segregation in interstate commerce. It merely insisted that accommodations must be "substantially equal" to meet the constitutional test, and from this point of view went no further than the *McCabe* decision.

There was evident, however, a changed temper on the Court, which needed merely the appropriate occasion to become manifest. The opportunity came in 1946, when *Morgan* v. *Virginia* was decided. This case arose out of the prosecution of a black woman who was making an interstate bus trip from Virginia to Baltimore and who refused to move to the back of the bus on the request of the driver so that her seat would be available for white passengers. The Supreme Court found the state law to be a burden on commerce in a matter where uniformity was necessary.

The Court, having thus willingly rediscovered the relationship of the commerce clause to segregation, in its very next case was embarrassed to find that the commerce clause could be relied on to protect as well as to condemn discrimination. In *Bob-Lo Excursion Co.* v. *Michigan* (1948), as already noted, the Court upheld a conviction under the Michigan Civil Rights Act of a Detroit amusement park company which refused to transport a black girl on its boat to an island on the Canadian side of the Detroit River. Although this was technically foreign commerce, to which the state law could not apply, the Court majority held that it was actually "highly local." The *DeCuir* and *Morgan* cases were distinguished on the ground that they did not involve such "locally insulated" situations. Moreover, in neither of those cases had complete exclusion from transportation facilities been attempted. Justice Jackson, dissenting, rejoined: "The Court admits that the commerce involved in this case is foreign commerce, but subjects it to the state police power on the ground that it is not very foreign."

Bob-Lo highlighted the Court's problem in attempting to achieve equalitarian goals through the cold-blooded and clumsy constitutional concept of commerce.[6] Justice Douglas gave expression to this feeling in his concurring opinion; he would have preferred to base the decision upon the more appealing foundation of the equal protection clause. Ultimately, in 1956, the Court did just that by affirming a lower court ruling that an Alabama statute and a Montgomery ordinance requiring segregation of races on intrastate buses violated both the equal protection and due process clauses.[7]

---

[6] See also *Henderson* v. *United States* (1950).
[7] *Gayle* v. *Browder* (1956). In the preceding year the Interstate Commerce Commission had re-

SEGREGATION IN EDUCATION

The fraudulent character of the protection afforded by the "separate but equal" rule was perhaps most obvious in the field of education. By any test which might be applied, black schools in states where segregation was the rule were markedly inferior to white schools. For many years, however, the Supreme Court persistently avoided getting itself into situations where it would have to recognize this fact.

The story starts in 1899, with *Cumming* v. *Richmond County Board of Education.* This case arose out of the decision of a Georgia school board to discontinue the existing black high school in order to use the building and facilities for black elementary education. No new high school for blacks was established, though the existing white high schools were continued. Black taxpayers sought to restrain the school board from using money to support white high schools until equal facilities for black students were provided. The unanimous Supreme Court decision avoided discussion of the segregation issue. It denied that discontinuance of the black high school was a violation of equal protection of the laws, but laid more stress on the conclusion that an injunction which would close the white high schools was not the proper legal remedy and would not help the black children. Justice Harlan concluded with a reminder that the management of schools was a state matter in which the federal government could intervene only in the case of a "clear and unmistakable disregard" of constitutional rights.

A Kentucky law requiring segregation of white and black students in all educational institutions, private and public, was upheld as applied to a private institution in *Berea College* v. *Kentucky* (1908). Again the Court found a way to avoid passing on the segregation issue. It argued that this was merely a matter between Kentucky and a corporation which it had created, and that the state could withhold privileges from one of its corporations which it could not constitutionally withhold from an individual.

Having successfully avoided the issue twice, the Court then felt able to act as though established practice had foreclosed discussion of the question. *Gong Lum* v. *Rice* (1927) concerned a child of Chinese descent who was required to attend a black school in Mississippi under the state constitutional obligation that separate schools be maintained for children of "the white and colored races." As to the equal protection problem posed by this arrangement, Chief Justice Taft said for the Court: "Were this a new question, it would call for very full argument and consideration, but we think that it is the same question which has been many times decided to be within the constitutional power of the state legislature to settle without intervention of the federal courts under the Federal Constitution." The fifteen state and lower federal court decisions cited by the Chief Justice to support this conclusion, however, could not hide the fact that there had been no Supreme Court ruling directly on the issue of segregation in educational institutions and that there had never been "full argument and consideration" by that body.

---

versed its 1887 decision and ruled that the Interstate Commerce Act forbade racial segregation on interstate trains and buses.

As in the transportation field, the pattern of segregation in education thus achieved a solid constitutional foundation. The more liberally oriented Court of the later 1930s was able, however, again as in the transportation area, to effect a substantial change of direction within the confines of the doctrine by stressing the need for *equality* in segregation. Missouri refused to admit blacks to its state law school, providing instead that the state would pay tuition fees for any of its black citizens who could obtain admission to law schools in neighboring states where segregation was not enforced. In *Missouri ex rel. Gaines* v. *Canada* (1938) the Court ruled that Missouri could not shift its responsibility for providing equal education to another state.[8]

Missouri met this ruling by setting up a separate, and inferior, law school for blacks, and other Southern states adopted the same device. How far was the Supreme Court prepared to go in insisting upon equality of facilities? The test came in 1950. *McLaurin* v. *Oklahoma State Regents* involved a black who sought admission to the state university as a Ph.D. candidate in education. The Legislature, under pressure of the *Gaines* ruling, had amended the state law to permit the admission of blacks to institutions of higher learning in cases where such institutions offered courses not available in the black schools. However, the program of instruction for such black students was to be given "upon a segregated basis." Accordingly, McLaurin was admitted to the University of Oklahoma graduate school but was subjected to certain segregation practices in classrooms, library, and cafeteria. These separations, which the state defended as "merely nominal," were declared unconstitutional by a unanimous Court. Such restrictions on McLaurin, Chief Justice Vinson wrote, "impair and inhibit his ability to study, to engage in discussions and exchange views with other students, and, in general, to learn his profession."

Sweatt v. *Painter* (1950) involved the petition of a black, who had refused to attend the separate law school for blacks that Texas had set up, for admission to the University of Texas Law School. The Texas courts, denying his petition, had claimed that the "privileges, advantages, and opportunities for the study of law" at the black law school were "substantially equivalent" to those available at the university law school.

The Supreme Court disagreed. Chief Justice Vinson's opinion contrasted the faculty, the student body, the library, the alumni, and the other facilities of the two institutions. In comparison with the University of Texas Law School, judged by the Court to be "one of the nation's ranking law schools," was the black law school with five full-time professors, a student body of twenty-three, a library of 16,500 volumes, and one alumnus who had become a member of the Texas bar. "It is difficult to believe that one who had a free choice between these law schools would consider the question close." Above all, the Court considered that a law school limited to blacks, a minority of the Texas population, could not be an effective "proving ground for legal learning and practice."

By this time the pressure against segregation was shifting from university and graduate professional education, where the breaking-down of segregation barriers

[8] See also *Sipuel* v. *Board of Regents of the University of Oklahoma* (1948).

presented a lesser problem because of the comparatively few black students involved, to public education at the primary and secondary levels. In December, 1952, the Court held hearings on five appeals in such cases, in all of which the lower courts had upheld segregation laws but demanded that educational facilities be made equal. On June 8, 1953, the Court announced the cases would be reargued on October 12 and set out a series of five questions to which counsel were requested to address themselves. Two of the five questions related to the intent of the Congress and the state legislatures which drafted and ratified the Fourteenth Amendment and whether they understood that it would abolish segregation in public schools.

Brown v. *Board of Education of Topeka* and the other school segregation cases[9] were finally decided on May 17, 1954. The vote was unanimous, an unexpected development which was immediately hailed as a diplomatic triumph for Chief Justice Warren, who wrote the opinion. It was a surprisingly brief statement of thirteen paragraphs. First, Warren noted that the historical background and the circumstances surrounding the adoption of the Fourteenth Amendment were at best "inconclusive" as to the intention of the drafters. But in any case the Court could not "turn the clock back to 1868 when the Amendment was adopted, or even to 1896 when *Plessy* v. *Ferguson* was written." The decision had to consider public education "in the light of its full development and its present place in American life throughout the Nation." Warren continued:

> Today, education is perhaps the most important function of state and local governments. Compulsory school attendance laws and the great expenditures for education both demonstrate our recognition of the importance of education to our democratic society. It is required in the performance of our most basic public responsibilities, even service in the armed forces. It is the very foundation of good citizenship. Today it is a principal instrument in awakening the child to cultural values, in preparing him for later professional training, and in helping him to adjust normally to his environment. In these days, it is doubtful that any child may reasonably be expected to succeed in life if he is denied the opportunity of an education. Such an opportunity, where the state has undertaken to provide it, is a right which must be made available to all on equal terms.

Thus the Court finally came to grips with the constitutionality of the "separate but equal" doctrine, which it had avoided in six preceding public education cases. "Does segregation of children in public schools solely on the basis of race, even though the physical facilities and other 'tangible' factors may be equal, deprive the children of the minority group of equal educational opportunities? We believe that it does." For this precedent-shattering conclusion, the Court's justification was surprisingly brief and simple. "To separate [children in grade and high schools] from others of similar age and qualifications solely because of their race generates a feeling of inferiority as to their status in the community that may affect their hearts and minds in a way unlikely ever to be undone." Consequently, "separate educational facilities are inherently unequal."[10]

[9] *Briggs* v. *Elliott; Davis* v. *County School Board of Prince Edward County; Gebhart* v. *Belton; Bolling* v. *Sharpe.*

[10] As evidence that this conclusion was "amply supported by modern authority," Warren cited in the famous footnote 11 Gunnar Myrdal's *An American Dilemma* and six psychological and sociological

Bolling v. *Sharpe* was handled in a separate decision from the other four cases, since it arose in the District of Columbia where the equal protection clause was not applicable. In a brief opinion, Warren held that the due process clause of the Fifth Amendment required the same result. It would be "unthinkable" that the Constitution imposed a lesser duty on the federal government than on the states. Equal protection is a more specific safeguard than due process, to be sure, and the concepts are not "interchangeable." But the liberty protected by the due process clause includes "the full range of conduct which the individual is free to pursue, and it cannot be restricted except for a proper governmental objective. Segregation in public education is not reasonably related to any proper governmental objective, and thus it imposes on Negro children of the District of Columbia a burden that constitutes an arbitrary deprivation of their liberty in violation of the Due Process Clause."

These holdings still left the problem of putting this potentially explosive doctrine into effect. Further hearings were held in April, 1955, and on May 31 the Supreme Court announced its plan of action. The cases would be remanded to the courts where they had originated, which would fashion decrees of enforcement on equitable principles and with regard for "varied local school problems." The local courts would consider whether the actions or proposals of the various school authorities constituted "good faith implementation of the governing constitutional principles." They would require "a prompt and reasonable start toward full compliance" with the 1954 ruling, but once such a start had been made, the courts might find that additional time was necessary to carry out the ruling in an effective manner. Such delays, however, would have to be proved "necessary in the public interest and . . . consistent with good faith compliance at the earliest practicable date." During this period of transition to full compliance, the courts where the cases originated would retain jurisdiction of them under obligation to take such proceedings "as are necessary and proper to admit to public schools on a racially nondiscriminatory basis with all deliberate speed the parties to these cases." Thus the Supreme Court committed its prestige to an experiment in judicially enforced revision of human behavior patterns without precedent in American experience.

ENFORCEMENT OF THE *BROWN* DECISION

At first it seemed that the prestige of the Court might substantially temper the expected resistance to the *Brown* decree. The Court may have expected that it would receive some support from Congress and the President in winning acceptance for the ruling, but no such aid was forthcoming. On the contrary, ninety-six Southern congressmen signed a manifesto in 1956 challenging the legality of the Court's decision, and President Eisenhower, while declaring that he would enforce the law, persistently declined to attempt any organization of support for the ruling.

After the 1955 mandate, the Court endeavored to give the lower courts the maximum opportunity and the maximum responsibility for pressing toward the constitutional goal of integration, not only for the schools but for other public

---

studies, which led to charges that the opinion was based on sociology rather than law. See Herbert Garfinkel, "Social Science Evidence and the School Segregation Cases," 21 *Journal of Politics* 37 (1959).

facilities. The desegregation requirement was extended to bus transportation, public parks and golf courses, swimming pools, public auditoriums, courtroom seating, and airport restaurants by Supreme Court rulings which merely reversed or affirmed lower court decisions by *per curiam* opinions or without any opinion. [11] Since the *Brown* opinion had been limited to demonstrating why segregation in education was unconstitutional, there were some who felt that the Court was neglecting its responsibility to spell out constitutional principles by failing to provide a reasoned argument against segregation in other areas of public activity.[12]

In the states of the "Old South" the legislatures, led by Virginia, promptly adopted complete batteries of new laws aimed to frustrate efforts to achieve integration. In many instances these laws were recognized even by their sponsors to be unconstitutional, but they were gestures of defiance and testing them in court would take time.

In addition to legal barriers to desegregation, delay was occasioned by threatened or actual violence. Major incidents occurred at Clinton, Tennessee, in 1956; at Little Rock, Arkansas, in 1957; at New Orleans in 1960; and at the University of Mississippi in 1962. In *Cooper* v. *Aaron* (1958) the Supreme Court held that the violent resistance to the Little Rock school board's desegregation plan was "directly traceable" to the Governor and state Legislature and warned that the constitutional rights of children not to be discriminated against in school admission because of race "can neither be nullified openly and directly by state legislators or state executive or judicial officers, nor nullified indirectly by them through evasive schemes for segregation."

Achieving desegregation of the public schools by lawsuits was inevitably a slow and difficult process. In the first place, the issue of segregation had to be raised in each individual school district by persons or groups who would take the responsibility, run the risks, and incur the costs of filing a suit. Usually this task had to be assumed by organized black groups, typically the NAACP. In some sections of the South reprisals against those active in the NAACP were so severe and effective that no one would initiate action against school segregation.

Second, the local school boards, acting either on their own initiative or under the compulsion of a federal district court order, had to prepare a desegregation plan. School boards, even when they were willing to act, usually preferred to wait for a court mandate in order to justify themselves to the segregationists in the community.

Third, the federal district judges had to order the desegregation plans into effect. At the time enforcement of the *Brown* decision got under way there were forty-eight federal district judges in the eleven Southern states. They were nearly all native Southerners, sharing the views of the white Southern establishment, subject

[11] *Mayor of Baltimore* v. *Dawson* (1955), public recreation; *Holmes* v. *City of Atlanta* (1955), municipal golf courses; *Gayle* v. *Browder* (1956), buses; *New Orleans City Park Improvement Assn.* v. *Detiege* (1958), public parks; *State Athletic Cmsn.* v. *Dorsey* (1959), athletic contests; *Turner* v. *Memphis* (1962), airport restaurants; *Johnson* v. *Virginia* (1963), courtroom seating; *Schiro* v. *Bynum* (1964), auditoriums; *Lee* v. *Washington* (1968), jails.
[12] See Herbert Wechsler, "Toward Neutral Principles of Constitutional Law," 73 HARVARD LAW REVIEW 1, 22 (1959).

to the social pressures of their communities, personally unsympathetic to the *Brown* ruling. It is not surprising that they tended to move very slowly, and in some cases not at all, in implementing school desegregation plans.

Fourth, the Federal Courts of Appeals for the Fourth and Fifth Circuits, located in Richmond and New Orleans, composed of ten judges, had the responsibility of reviewing the decisions of the district judges. Generally the appellate court judges, somewhat further removed from the pressures of local situations than the district judges, took a conscientious view of their obligations to enforce the Supreme Court's ruling, and they overturned many of the district court decisions.[13]

The Positive Duty to Desegregate

The *Brown* mandate could be interpreted to mean only that school districts must stop using discriminatory practices, not that they had a positive duty to undertake desegregation plans. This interpretation found support in *Shuttlesworth* v. *Birmingham Board of Education* (1958), which upheld a pupil placement plan that purported to assign students to schools on various bases, with race carefully excluded. In fact, transfers out of black schools were administratively impossible, but the Supreme Court upheld a lower court's "presumption" that the law was not being used to discriminate against black pupils.

Prince Edward County, Virginia, one of the parties covered by the *Brown* decision, undertook to meet its obligation not to discriminate by simply closing all public schools in the county and providing tuition grants for pupils attending private schools.[14] The county maintained it had no constitutional obligation to operate a public school system, but in *Griffin* v. *County School Board of Prince Edward County* (1964), the Court ruled that the decision not to operate a public school system had a clearly unconstitutional object.

Another "nondiscriminatory" technique was freedom of choice, under which each pupil was supposed to be free to choose the school to be attended. *Green* v. *County School Board of New Kent County* (1968) found that under this plan very little transfer out of a black school had occurred; but, more important, the Court took the occasion to announce that school boards had a positive duty to formulate plans promising prompt conversion to a desegregated system. The goal was complete integration, achievement of a "unitary, nonracial system of public education."

In a Mississippi case the following year, *Alexander* v. *Holmes County Board of Education* (1969), the Court was even more brusque, warning that the standard of "all deliberate speed" was "no longer constitutionally permissible" and demanding that every district "terminate dual school systems at once and . . . operate now and hereafter only unitary schools."

These decisions left no escape from the obligation to adopt positive desegrega-

---

[13] See the excellent study by J. W. Peltason, *Fifty-eight Lonely Men* (New York: Harcourt, Brace & World, Inc., 1961). The most complete account of the desegregation effort is Richard Kluger, *Simple Justice* (New York: Alfred A. Knopf, 1975).

[14] In *Runyon* v. *McCrary* (1976) the Supreme Court held that refusal of private schools to admit qualified black children was a violation of the Civil Rights Act of 1866 which guarantees to "citizens of every race and color . . . the same right . . . to make and enforce contracts . . . as is enjoyed by white citizens. . . ." This ruling relied on an interpretation of the Civil Rights Act announced in *Jones* v. *Alfred H. Mayer Co.* (1968), discussed *infra* at p. 508. See also *Norwood* v. *Harrison* (1973).

tion plans. In Montgomery, Alabama, Judge Frank M. Johnson had been supervising the progress of desegregation since 1964. In 1968 he added to his earlier orders the desegregation of school faculties by imposing racial quotas, requiring, for example, that in schools with twelve or more teachers, the race of at least one of every six faculty and staff members must be different from the race of the majority at the school. In *United States* v. *Montgomery County Board of Education* (1969), this provision was upheld as a reasonable step toward desegregation.

Swann v. *Charlotte-Mecklenburg Board of Education* (1971), in an opinion by Chief Justice Burger, went much further in providing guidelines for the lower courts.[15] First, the Supreme Court held that where one-race schools existed in a system with a history of segregation, there was a presumption that this was the result of present or past discriminatory action. Second, the Court made clear that the "neighborhood school" might have to be partially sacrificed to achieve desegregation.

> All things being equal, with no history of discrimination it might well be desirable to assign pupils to schools nearest their homes. But all things are not equal in a system that has been deliberately constructed and maintained to enforce racial segregation.

Third, the Court recognized the need for massive busing to achieve integration. "Desegregation plans cannot be limited to the walk-in school." Fourth, the Court reiterated its acceptance of teacher assignment by race to achieve faculty desegregation. Finally, to avoid any misunderstanding, Chief Justice Burger firmly announced that the Court's goal was not racial balance. "The constitutional command does not mean that every school in every community must always reflect the racial composition of the school system as a whole." Mathematical ratios were to be only an instrument in the process of shaping a remedy for segregation. The constitutional goal was to abolish dual school systems, not to achieve racial balance.

Up to this date all the Court's school segregation decisions had been unanimous, even after the first two Nixon appointments. But in 1972 the Nixon justices, by then four, broke away from the majority in *Wright* v. *Council of City of Emporia* (1972). The city of Emporia, Virginia, had been part of the county school system which operated segregated schools. After the *Green* decision, integration of the county schools was ordered. Emporia, where there were fewer blacks than in the surrounding county, then sought to withdraw from the county system and set up its own separate schools. The Court majority held that such a realignment of school districts in an area with a history of state-enforced segregation would impede the process of dismantling the segregated system and could not be allowed. The four-judge minority contended that Emporia had a lawful right to provide for the education of its own children and charged that the Court was pursuing a "racial balancing" approach.[16]

---

[15] See Robert I. Richter, "School Desegregation After *Swann*," 39 UNIVERSITY OF CHICAGO LAW REVIEW 421 (1972).

[16] In *United States* v. *Scotland Neck City Board of Education* (1972), decided the same day, and

The reverse situation—city-county consolidation—proved even more controversial. In 1972 Judge Robert R. Merhige ordered the Richmond school system, which was about 70 percent black, merged with those of the two surrounding counties, which were about 90 percent white. The Court of Appeals rejected this plan, and the Supreme Court, with Justice Powell, a Virginian, not participating, divided four to four, thereby leaving the appellate rejection of the merger in effect.[17]

The same issue returned to the Court the next year, this time from Detroit. In *Milliken* v. *Bradley* (1974), consolidation was rejected by a vote of five to four, with Stewart joining the four Nixon justices. A federal district judge had found the Detroit board of education guilty of creating and perpetuating school segregation. Concluding that a Detroit-only plan was inadequate to accomplish desegregation, the judge created an area composed of Detroit plus fifty-three suburban school districts, within which a massive busing program would operate. Chief Justice Burger for the majority held that bringing the outlying districts into the plan was unjustified because there had been no showing of significant violations by them and no evidence of any interdistrict violations. Nor was there any claim that the district boundary lines had been established to foster racial segregation. It would, Burger said, violate the deeply rooted tradition of local control of education for school district lines to be casually ignored or treated as mere administrative conveniences.

Justice White for the dissenters in *Milliken* warned that the ability of the federal judiciary to achieve school desegregation would be crippled if remedies must stop at the school district line unless and until some sort of "interdistrict" violation had been proved. The Court's ruling, he said, meant that "deliberate acts of segregation and their consequences will go unremedied."[18]

The Detroit case was one of the Court's first to come from a northern city. While a deliberate policy to segregate had been found to exist there, in most northern cities segregation was pricipally caused by neighborhood schools within segregated housing patterns. In legal terms, this was de facto rather than de jure—i.e., state-enforced—segregation. The Court had never decided whether de facto segregation was unconstitutional. The issue was raised but evaded in *Keyes* v. *School District No. 1, Denver* (1973). Justice Powell, who as a Virginian was particularly sensitive to the anomaly that the nation's most segregated schools were now in the North, argued that the de facto–de jure distinction had "long since . . . outlived its time" and should be replaced by "constitutional principles of national rather than merely regional application." The Court, however, found that there had been "*de jure* segregation in a meaningful portion of the [Denver] school system," and so there was no need to consider the de facto rule.

Boston schools were a classic case of deliberate, long-standing de jure segregation. In 1974 Judge Arthur Garrity issued detailed findings to that effect, and in

---

involving the same kind of effort by a city to withdraw from the county system, the Court was unanimous in voiding the plan, which would have left the county schools 89 percent black.

[17] *School Board of Richmond* v. *State Board of Education* (1973).

[18] However, in *Buchanan* v. *Evans* (1975), the Court affirmed a lower federal court decision that called for the overwhelmingly black school system of Wilmington, Delaware, to integrate with white schools in the surrounding county.

1975 ordered a remedial program which included busing for a fewer number of children with a lesser average travel time than in the program the Supreme Court had unanimously approved for Charlotte in the *Swann* case. The Boston reaction was violent, but the Garrity order was upheld by the court of appeals and in 1976 the Supreme Court denied review (*White* v. *Morgan, Doherty* v. *Morgan, Boston Home and School Assn.* v. *Morgan*). But the Court did review a district court desegregation order from Pasadena, and in *Pasadena City Board of Education* v. *Spangler* (1976) held that, once the affirmative duty to desegregate had been accomplished, school authorities could not be required to readjust attendance zones each year to keep up with population shifts. A similar position was taken in *Board of Education of Chattanooga* v. *Mapp* (1976), where because of "white flight" two racially mixed schools had become almost all black.

Congressional and Presidential Action

The first substantial congressional support of school integration came with the adoption of the Civil Rights Act of 1964. Title IV of that act authorized the Attorney General to bring school desegregation suits in the name of the United States, and Title VI prohibited racial discrimination in any local or state program receiving federal financial assistance. This sanction became of particular importance when in the Education Act of 1965 Congress adopted President Johnson's plan for federal financial assistance to elementary and secondary schools. To become eligible for these grants, all public schools had to certify that they were integrated or file acceptable plans for achieving complete integration. The federal Office of Education promptly issued guidelines for judging progress toward integration in terms of quotas and percentages, which were upheld by the Supreme Court.[19] However, under the Nixon administration, pressure for enforcement of the standards was relaxed, and there was an almost complete failure to use the fund-cutoff sanction.

Most judicially imposed integration plans involved busing, which had been approved by the Supreme Court in *Swann*. Opposition to busing was very strong and emotionally charged, however, as much so in the North as it had earlier been in the South. President Nixon took a firm antibusing position in 1972. He asked Congress to pass legislation providing for a moratorium of one year on court-ordered busing and imposing a variety of restrictions and prohibitions on future busing. Such legislative interference with constitutional decrees issued to enforce constitutional rights was regarded by many legislators as unconstitutional,[20] and Congress passed a more limited measure simply halting for eighteen months any school desegregation ordered by federal courts until all appeals had been exhausted. Nixon's plan to seek a constitutional amendment forbidding the assignment of any pupil to a school on the basis of race or color was aborted by Watergate.

In 1974 and 1975 Congress adopted some limits on busing, but they did not attempt to control court action if required to enforce constitutional rights. President

---

[19] *Caddo Parish School Board* v. *United States* (1967).
[20] See the analysis in "The Nixon Busing Bills," 81 YALE LAW JOURNAL 1542 (1972).

Ford took a strong anti-busing stance. In 1976 he encouraged the Department of Justice to file a friend of the court brief with the Supreme Court in the Boston case, but Attorney General Levi ultimately decided against it. Ford then proposed legislation which would clearly limit busing to elimination of racial concentrations in schools caused by proven acts of unlawful discrimination, rather than housing patterns, zoning laws, or economic conditions. The legislation would also place a five-year limit on busing orders if the affected school or district complied with them substantially and in good faith.

Two decades after *Brown,* the federal courts were still heavily involved in managing the process of school desegregation in many areas of the country, with little assistance from the Department of Justice or HEW and against an undiminished opposition to busing. The Supreme Court was badly divided on further steps toward integration, and its *Milliken* decision had reduced the options available to federal district judges for desegregation plans. Most significantly, the educational and social value of integrated schools was being seriously questioned, even by some blacks. Under the circumstances it appeared likely that further integration of the schools would be a slow and painful process.

AFFIRMATIVE ACTION

The Supreme Court's insistence in the school segregation cases that state neutrality was not enough, and that positive action must be taken to terminate racial segregation, raises the difficult constitutional question as to whether racial classifications can be employed for benign and ameliorative purposes. We have just seen that the Court did approve racial quotas for teaching staffs in the *Montgomery County* case. In American higher education and in professional schools such as law and medicine, the 1960s saw the inauguration of programs for recruiting minority students by special financial aid and preferential admissions policies.

The concern of the federal government to implement the antidiscrimination provisions of Title VI of the Civil Rights Act of 1964 was expressed in President Johnson's 1965 Executive Order No. 11246 and led in 1967 to the Department of Labor's development of preferential hiring requirements on the basis of race and sex in the construction industry and later for the entire business community. Enforcement of the Department of Labor's order in federal dealings with colleges and universities was delegated to the Department of Health, Education and Welfare. By 1970 HEW began to issue "guidelines" for nondiscriminatory faculty and staff employment, with the threat of withdrawal of federal financial grants if hiring goals were not met.

The practical justification offered for preferential admissions or employment was that the consequences of century-old discrimination could be remedied only by deliberate discrimination in the opposite direction. The constitutional justification offered was generally that racial classifications are prohibited only when they are invidious and used to stigmatize, and that *Brown* did not reject racial classifications per se, only their improper use. The opposing view holds that race can never be used as a basis for classification, even with worthy motives, and that the case for compensatory justice must always be made on the basis of individual circumstances, not on class status.[21]

The constitutionality of affirmative action was squarely presented to the Supreme Court in the case of *DeFunis* v. *Odegaard* (1974). The law school of the University of Washington had decided that the only way to secure a reasonable representation of minorities in its student body was to modify admission requirements and procedures to give certain advantages to minority applicants. DeFunis, a white, was denied admission in 1971, while less qualified blacks, he contended, were admitted. A state superior court held that DeFunis had been denied equal protection and ordered his admission. Though the state supreme court reversed and upheld the law school procedures, DeFunis was permitted to continue in school pending his appeal to the Supreme Court.

By the time the Court dealt with his case in the spring of 1974, DeFunis was in his last semester of law school and assured of graduation. By a five to four vote, the Supreme Court took advantage of this situation to declare the case moot. Justice Douglas nevertheless felt it important to discuss the merits of the case. His position was that it is unconstitutional for any racial preference to be extended. "The Equal Protection Clause commands the elimination of racial barriers, not their creation in order to satisfy our theory as to how society ought to be organized." This meant that all applications for law school had to be considered in a "racially neutral way." But he recognized that some applicants would be less able, because of past discrimination, to prove their capacities and potentials (on the culture-bound Law School Admissions Test, for example), and consequently he would approve separate treatment of minorities as a class "to make more certain that racial factors do not militate against an applicant or on his behalf." He would have remanded the case for a new trial to determine whether the selection procedures employed had met this test of racial neutrality.[22]

RACIAL DISCRIMINATION IN EMPLOYMENT

Title VII of the Civil Rights Act of 1964 makes it unlawful for employers to deprive any individual of employment opportunities "because of such individual's race, color, religion, sex, or national origin." The act excluded from its coverage many

---

[21] For representative discussions, see Frank Askin and Carl Cohen, "Preferential Admission in Higher Education," 2 THE CIVIL LIBERTIES REVIEW 95 (1975); Richard A. Posner, "The DeFunis Case and the Constitutionality of Preferential Treatment of Racial Minorities," in Philip B. Kurland (ed.), *The Supreme Court Review: 1974* (Chicago: The University of Chicago Press, 1974), pp. 1–32; John Hart Ely, "The Constitutionality of Reverse Racial Discrimination," 41 UNIVERSITY OF CHICAGO LAW REVIEW 723 (1974); Steven Nisenbaum, "Race Quotas," 8 HARVARD CIVIL RIGHTS–CIVIL LIBERTIES LAW REVIEW 128 (1973); Robert M. O'Neil, "Preferential Admissions," 80 YALE LAW JOURNAL 699 (1971); Ronald Dworkin, "The DeFunis Case," 23 *New York Review of Books* 29 (Feb. 5, 1976).

[22] While the Court thus left the constitutionality of remedial racial preference programs undecided, *McDonald* v. *Santa Fe Trail Transportation Co.* (1976) held that the Civil Rights Acts of 1866 and 1964 forbade all race-based discrimination against either whites or blacks. But *Franks* v. *Bowman Transportation Co.* (1976) ruled that blacks denied jobs because of their race should be granted special seniority rights and moved ahead of white workers hired in place of them. See also *Lau* v. *Nichols* (1974) and *Contractors Assn.* v. *Schultz* (1971).

employers and imposed strict procedural requirements. Thus a charge of discrimination had to be filed first with a state or local fair employment practices agency, if one existed, for sixty days, and subsequently with the federal Equal Employment Opportunities Commission (EEOC, which was created by the act) for another sixty days. The EEOC was given no enforcement power, only the role of conciliating job bias problems.[23]

If conciliation failed, complainants were authorized to bring class actions for enforcement of the act. In the leading case of *Griggs* v. *Duke Power Co.* (1971), the employer had required a high school education or the passing of a standardized general intelligence test as a condition of employment in or transfer to jobs. These standards, challenged by thirteen blacks, were found unlawful by the Court as not significantly related to job performance and operating to disqualify blacks at a substantially higher rate than white applicants. The general principle was that practices nondiscriminatory on their face but which have a disparate impact on blacks were unlawful unless the employer could show "business necessity."[24]

STATE MISCEGENATION LAWS

In many states interracial marriage has been a criminal offense. The Supreme Court had never passed on the constitutionality of such laws, although in *Pace* v. *Alabama* (1882) it upheld an Alabama statute whose penalties for fornication between a white person and a black were more severe than those provided in the general fornication statute.

After the *Brown* decision, an encounter with state miscegenation laws seemed inevitable. In 1955 the Virginia supreme court in *Naim* v. *Naim* upheld that state's law. Distinguishing the *Brown* ruling, the state court reasoned that intermarriage, unlike education, was not a foundation of good citizenship or a right which must be available to all on equal terms. The Fourteenth Amendment, the court said, did not foreclose the states from preserving the "racial integrity" of their citizens or preventing a "mongrel breed." The Supreme Court twice, in transparently evasive maneuvers, avoided review of this ruling.

Presumably the Supreme Court felt that the *Brown* decision had created enough problems for one decade without adding the issue of mixed marriages. But by 1964 it was ready to move cautiously. In *McLaughlin* v. *Florida* the Court unanimously declared unconstitutional a statute which made it a crime for a white person and a black, not married to each other, to habitually live in and occupy the same room at night. The state court had upheld the law on authority of the *Pace* decision, but the Supreme Court now ruled that *Pace* had embodied too narrow a view of the equal protection clause. Any classification based solely on race, said Justice White for the Court, must bear a heavy burden of justification. He found no such justification here, but his opinion seemed to assume that a justification might conceivably be

---

[23] In 1972 Congress amended the act to authorize the EEOC to take cases that could not be settled through conciliation to federal district courts for a finding of discrimination.

[24] But in *Washington* v. *Davis* (1976) a District of Columbia police examination which blacks failed in higher proportion than whites, challenged on due process rather than Title VII grounds, was upheld because there had been no "racially discriminatory purpose."

possible. Justice Stewart thought this was too cautious; he would not admit that under any circumstances a state law could make "the color of a person's skin the test of whether his conduct is a criminal offense."

Florida also had a law against mixed marriages, but the Court in *McLaughlin* was careful to avoid expressing any opinion on its validity. However, this issue was squarely raised by a 1966 Virginia supreme court decision, and in *Loving* v. *Virginia* (1967) the Supreme Court unanimously declared the Virginia antimiscegenation law unconstitutional. Holding that marriage is one of the "basic civil rights of man," Chief Justice Warren said: "To deny this fundamental freedom on so unsupportable a basis as . . . racial classifications . . . so directly subversive of the principle of equality at the heart of the Fourteenth Amendment, is surely to deprive all the state's citizens of liberty without due process of law."

STATE ACTION

An important factor in the expanding effectiveness of the equal protection clause against racial discrimination has been the Supreme Court's recent interpretation of the "state action" requirement of the Fourteenth Amendment. The Court's initial statement on state action in the *Civil Rights Cases* (1883) was that the Fourteenth Amendment forbade only those denials of due process or equal protection "sanctioned in some way by the state" or "done under state authority." But whether an act falls within these categories is not always easy to determine.

Actions of State Officials

Normally there is no doubt that actions by state or local officials in their official capacity constitute state action. This is obvious when they act under authorization of a specific state law, but it is also generally true when they take discriminatory action without authorization of law or even contrary to law. An early holding of the Supreme Court was in *Ex parte Virginia* (1880), where a county judge had been indicted for excluding blacks from jury service. The Court said: "Whoever . . . acts in the name and for the State, and is clothed with the State's power, his act is that of the State."

The Civil Rights Act of 1866, passed before adoption of the Fourteenth Amendment, made punishable racial discrimination by persons acting "under color of any law." This phrase has since been rather generally employed in civil rights statutes, and it has come to be accepted as one of the tests of state action. The Supreme Court in *United States* v. *Classic* (1941) applied the statute to officials guilty of election fraud, saying: "Misuse of power, possessed by virtue of state law and made possible only because the wrongdoer is clothed with the authority of state law, is action taken 'under color of' state law."

In the gruesome case of *Screws* v. *United States* (1945), where a sheriff had beaten a black prisoner to death in his jail, the defense against a federal civil rights prosecution was that the sheriff, having acted in abuse of his official capacity, could not be regarded as having acted under color of law. The Court majority rejected this view, Justice Rutledge contending that the sheriff had acted with the "power of official place," but Justice Roberts, dissenting, could not see how conduct "in flagrant defiance of State law, may be attributed to the State."

In *Palmer* v. *Thompson* (1971) the Court upheld the closing of all municipal swimming pools in Jackson, Mississippi, after a court order to desegregate them, on the ground that all persons, black and white, were equally affected. In *Gilmore* v. *City of Montgomery* (1974) the city, after a court order to desegregate its parks, turned them over to all-white private schools for their exclusive use. The Supreme Court upheld an injunction against this action, but did rule that city permission for nonexclusive use of the parks by segregated private schools did not constitute "state action." *Evans* v. *Abney* (1970) ruled that a property which had been willed in trust to the city of Macon, Georgia, for a public park for white people only, had been lawfully reclaimed by the heirs after a court order had desegregated the park.

Inaction of State Officials

A somewhat different question arises when injury is done to a person's civil rights as a result of official failure to act. Can official inaction be treated as "state action"? *Lynch* v. *United States* (1951) involved review of the conviction of a Georgia sheriff who had allowed black prisoners in his custody to be kidnapped and beaten by a Ku Klux mob. A Georgia federal court jury found him guilty of having acted under color of law to deprive a citizen of his protected rights, and the court of appeals agreed that official inaction, where designed to injure, may be punished. "There was a time when the denial of equal protection of the laws was confined to affirmative acts, but the law now is that culpable official inaction may also constitute a denial of equal protection."

In *Terry* v. *Adams* (1953), a group of private citizens regularly conducted an unofficial primary prior to the regular Democratic primary to select candidates for office in a Texas county who would then be entered in the regular primary. The theory of this pre-primary was that it was private action from which blacks could be constitutionally excluded, but the Supreme Court ruled that the pre-primary had become "an integral part" of the election process. Both Justices Black and Frankfurter emphasized that state inaction was the root of the offense. According to Black, the state had permitted "circumvention" to produce the equivalent of a discriminatory election, and Frankfurter referred to the state's "abdication."

Discrimination in Public Accommodations

The *Civil Rights Cases* (1883), as we have seen, held that the Fourteenth Amendment did not prevent discrimination in such privately owned public accommodations as hotels and theaters. Although that decision has never been overruled, the situation of public accommodations has been drastically changed by judicial interpretation and by state and federal statutes.

In the first place, any significant relationship between the state and the enterprise may be interpreted as transferring to the latter the constitutional obligations of the state. The leading case is *Burton* v. *Wilmington Parking Authority* (1961), involving a parking facility owned and operated by an agency of the state of Delaware. To help finance the building some of the space was leased to commercial operations.

This case arose when a restaurant located on the premises refused service to a black. The Supreme Court majority held that its location in, and relationship to, the parking facility had cost the restaurant its "purely private" character. By its inaction in failing to require the restaurant to serve all comers, the state had made itself a party to the refusal of service.

The sit-in cases of the early 1960s furnish additional illustrations of how public accommodations may come under the state action rule. In *Peterson* v. *Greenville* (1963), restaurant discrimination was held to be state action because a city ordinance required separation of the races. In *Lombard* v. *Louisiana* (1963), there was no ordinance, but the Court held that city officials had coerced the restaurant manager to operate a segregated facility, which made it state action. *Griffin* v. *Maryland* (1964) held that an amusement park's exclusion of blacks was state action because, to enforce this policy, the park employed a deputy sheriff who, though working on his off-duty hours, wore his badge and purported to exercise the powers of a deputy sheriff at the park.

However, there must be some link of this kind between the state and the enterprise, however tenuous or indirect, to justify treating the discriminatory action of public accommodations as state action under the Fourteenth Amendment. The Supreme Court has stopped short of a holding that public accommodations are by the very nature of their service public agencies governed by the equal protection clause. This was the position taken by the first Justice Harlan in his dissent to the *Civil Rights Cases,* and it was revived in the sit-in cases by Douglas and Goldberg.[25]

In the Civil Rights Act of 1964, also called the Public Accommodations Act, Congress took over from the Supreme Court the responsibility of determining what rights of access there should be to the most important types of public accommodations. Under the statute full and equal access without discrimination or segregation is guaranteed with respect to hotels and motels, restaurants, and catering establishments of all kinds, places of entertainment and sports exhibitions, gasoline stations, and such bars and barber shops as are physically within the premises of a covered establishment. Boarding houses with not more than five rooms for rent are not covered, nor are private clubs or other establishments not in fact open to the public.

This statute, as already noted in Chapter 12, invoked the commerce clause as authority for its enactment, and it was on this basis that the Supreme Court promptly upheld the act in *Heart of Atlanta Motel* v. *United States* (1964). But Congress also relied on the Fourteenth Amendment by defining the applicability of the act to cover discrimination and segregation required by action of the state or carried on "under color of any law" or "any custom or usage required or enforced by officials of the State." In the *Heart of Atlanta* case the Supreme Court found it unnecessary to consider this second basis for congressional action, since the commerce power alone was sufficient for the decision. This ruling relieved the Court from the necessity of reconsidering the *Civil Rights Cases* of 1883, the decision in which was held here to be "inapposite, and without precedential value."[26]

---

[25] See *Garner* v. *Louisiana* (1961) and *Bell* v. *Maryland* (1964).
[26] The act was applied in *Daniel* v. *Paul* (1969).

Private Discrimination and State Action

The state action rule of the Fourteenth Amendment leaves individuals free to discriminate for any reason in their personal relationships, in granting access to their homes, or in the operation of private associations. As Justice Goldberg said in his *Bell* opinion, "Rights pertaining to privacy and private association are themselves constitutionally protected liberties," and courts will safeguard the privilege of every person "to close his home or club to any person . . . on the basis of personal prejudices including race."

In *Moose Lodge No. 107* v. *Irvis* (1972), a black was denied food and beverage service as a guest of a member of a private club. The contention was made—and supported by Douglas, Brennan, and Marshall, in dissent—that by granting the club a liquor license the state had become an "active participant" in its operation. But the majority held that the liquor license did not derogate from the private character of the club. There was here "nothing approaching the symbiotic relationship" between the restaurant and the public parking author.ty in the *Burton* case.[27]

How far beyond the home or the club does this guarantee of the right to discriminate extend? The principal problems have concerned the buying, selling, and renting of property. "Open occupancy" laws making illegal refusal to sell or to rent to persons because of their race or color have generally met state constitutional tests. The experience of California is instructive. State statutes barred racial discrimination in the sale or rental of any private dwelling of more than four units, and the State Fair Employment Practice Commission was empowered to prevent violations. In 1964 California voters, by a margin of almost two to one, approved an amendment to the state constitution which nullified the effect of these acts and provided that property owners had "absolute discretion" to sell or rent to persons of their choice.

In 1966 the California supreme court by a vote of five to two in *Mulkey* v. *Reitman* declared the amendment unconstitutional as state action in violation of the equal protection clause. By adopting the amendment, the court said, the state had become "at least a partner in the . . . act of discrimination," adding that when "the electorate assumes to exercise the law-making function," it is "as much a state agency as any of its elected officials." In *Reitman* v. *Mulkey* (1967) the Supreme Court upheld this position by a vote of five to four, Justice White for the majority ruling that the amendment made the right to discriminate "one of the basic policies of the state." After the amendment was passed, "the right to discriminate, including the right to discriminate on racial grounds, was embodied in the state's basic charter, immune from legislative, executive or judicial regulation at any level of the state government. Those practicing racial discriminations need no longer rely on their personal choice. They could now evoke express constitutional authority." Under this ruling racial discrimination by private persons violates the Fourteenth Amendment if the state takes any action encouraging such discrimination.[28]

---

[27] In *Runyon* v. *McCrary* (1976), which held that refusal of private schools to admit black children violated the Civil Rights Act of 1866, the Court's opinion specifically left open the issue of validity of racially exclusive social clubs and organizations, as well as the legality of schools that limit enrolment to members of one sex or religious faith.

[28] See the extensive discussion by Charles L. Black, Jr., " 'State Action,' Equal Protection, and

In 1968, following the assassination of Martin Luther King, Jr., Congress for the first time passed a civil rights act containing comprehensive open-housing provisions applicable to a broad range of discriminatory practices. A few weeks later, the Supreme Court, in *Jones* v. *Alfred H. Mayer Co.,* ruled that the provision in the Civil Rights Act of 1866 giving all citizens the same right as white citizens "to inherit, purchase, lease, sell, hold, and convey real and personal property," although never previously so interpreted, was to be given its literal meaning and had made illegal every racially motivated refusal by property owners to rent or sell.[29]

A surprising feature of Justice Stewart's opinion for the Court was his broad reading of the Thirteenth Amendment, which he interpreted to forbid not only slavery but also "the badges and the incidents of slavery." He wrote:

> At the very least, the freedom that Congress is empowered to secure under the Thirteenth Amendment includes the freedom to buy whatever a white man can buy, the right to live wherever a white man can live. If Congress cannot say that being a free man means at least this much, then the Thirteenth Amendment made a promise the Nation cannot keep.

The dissenters, Harlan and White, thought that Stewart's history was "almost surely wrong"[30] and believed that the Court should not have revived an 1866 statute by questionable interpretation when Congress had just adopted a more appropriate fair-housing act.

Hunter v. *Erickson* (1969) involved a provision of the Akron city charter that prevented the city council from adopting any ordinance dealing with racial, religious, or ancestral discrimination in housing that had not first been submitted to and approved by the voters of the city. The Court ruled that the Civil Rights Acts of 1866 and 1968 did not preempt city housing legislation, but it struck down the charter provisions as placing a special burden on racial minorities within the governmental process.

FEDERAL PROTECTION OF CIVIL RIGHTS

Since 1957 Congress has adopted at least six major laws providing federal protection for civil rights. The Civil Rights Act of 1957, dealing largely and rather ineffectively with the guarantee of voting rights, also created the Civil Rights Commission, which through its hearings and reports has done much to focus attention on civil rights abuses.[31] The Civil Rights Act of 1960 was also concerned primarily with voting rights. The Civil Rights Act of 1964 was a major statute guaranteeing equal access

---

California's Proposition 14," 81 HARVARD LAW REVIEW 69–109 (1967).

[29] The *Jones* decision was followed in *Sullivan* v. *Little Hunting Park* (1969); also in *Tillman* v. *Wheaton-Haven Recreation Assn.* (1973), where a swimming pool association was denied status as a private club.

[30] The same conclusion is reached in the extended analysis by Gerhard Casper, "Jones v. Mayer: Clio, Bemused and Confused Muse," in Philip B. Kurland (ed.), *The Supreme Court Review: 1968* (Chicago: The University of Chicago Press, 1968), pp. 89–132.

[31] See Foster Rhea Dulles, *The Civil Rights Commission: 1957–1965* (East Lansing, Mich.: Michigan State University Press, 1968).

to public accommodations and barring discrimination in public programs receiving federal financial assistance and in private employment. The Voting Rights Act of 1965, renewed in 1975, finally found a formula for effectively breaking down the barriers to black voting. The Civil Rights Act of 1968 was a fair housing statute. The Equal Employment Opportunities Act of 1972 strengthened Title VII of the 1964 act.

This flurry of legislative activity was comparable to, but much more successful than, the civil rights laws enacted after the Civil War, between 1866 and 1875. In fact, those statutes proved largely valueless. With a hostile Supreme Court and an apathetic public, much of the legislative product of Radical Reconstruction was declared unconstitutional or repealed by later Congresses. What was left was largely ignored and unused by enforcement authorities.

A few provisions of the Reconstruction statutes did survive, however, and have played an important role in recent civil rights litigation. Section 241 of Title 18 of the U.S. Code, which had its origin in the Enforcement Act of 1870, provides a fine of up to $5,000 and imprisonment of up to ten years for a conspiracy by two or more persons to "injure, oppress, threaten, or intimidate any citizen" from exercising, or because he has exercised, any right or privilege "secured" to him by the Constitution or laws of the United States. Section 242, dating from the Civil Rights Act of 1866, provides a fine of $1,000 or one year in prison, or both, for any person who, acting "under color of any law, statute, ordinance, regulation, or custom," willfully deprives any inhabitant of the United States of any of the rights, privileges, or immunities "secured or protected" by the Constitution or laws of the United States. This second section is broader than the conspiracy statute in that its shield covers all "inhabitants," not merely "citizens." Moreover, section 242 refers to substantive acts and not just to conspiracies, and therefore can be used against a single individual who commits unlawful acts providing he is acting "under color of" law.

Another difference between the two sections is that 241 covers "secured" rights, while 242 covers both "secured" and "protected" rights. Initially 241 was given a limited reading as the equivalent of rights of national citizenship, such as the right to vote in national elections or to petition Congress for redress of grievances, and was held not available to enforce Fourteenth Amendment guarantees of equal protection and due process.

The combined use of the two statutes was declared constitutional in the election fraud case of *United States* v. *Classic* (1941). The Civil Rights Section of the Department of Justice, created by Attorney General Frank Murphy in 1939, relied on section 242 in the police brutality case of *Screws* v. *United States* (1945). While the statute was held constitutional, the conviction was reversed and a new trial ordered because the judge had not charged the jury that the deprivation of civil rights must be "willful." A conviction under 242 in another police brutality case was upheld in *Williams* v. *United States* (1951), but the conspiracy conviction under section 241, obtained on the same facts, was reversed by the Court in *United States* v. *Williams* (1951) because of the narrow interpretation of "secured" rights.

Violence against civil rights workers and blacks in the South during the 1960s led to widespread demands for more effective intervention by the federal government, and the Department of Justice made renewed efforts to use 241 and 242, which were successful in the cases of *United States* v. *Price* (1966) and *United States* v. *Guest* (1966).[32] The *Price* case was an aftermath of the murder of three young civil rights workers near Philadelphia, Mississippi, in 1964. A federal indictment against eighteen suspects under 241 was dismissed by the federal district judge in reliance on *United States* v. *Williams,* but the Supreme Court unanimously overruled the district judge, and in the process broadened the interpretation of 241 to cover not only rights of national citizenship but also Fourteenth Amendment rights. This ruling in the *Price* case made possible the trial of Price and six associates in 1967. Their conviction was the first for a civil rights slaying in Mississippi.

Two statutes generally paralleling the criminal sanctions just discussed allow damage suits against state officers and private persons who violate constitutional rights. The more important is section 1983 of Title 42 of the U.S. Code, which provides for civil suit against any person acting under "color of any statute, ordinance, regulation, custom, or usage" who deprives a citizen of his constitutional rights. This statute can be used in combination with other provisions of the Code to obtain an injunction or declaratory judgment against the enforcement of unconstitutional laws or policies. In this manner the white primary was invalidated, as was segregation in public schools, buses, and parks.[33]

Section 1983 is also available to secure money damages from officials who exceed legal bounds. In the leading case of *Monroe* v. *Pape* (1961), the Supreme Court held that police brutality constituted state action within the meaning of the statute. This decision unloosed a flood of private civil rights damage actions in the federal courts, an increase from 270 in 1961 to 7,294 in 1974.[34]

---

[32] The *Guest* decision was important for its construction of the right to travel and also for its holding that section 241 is not limited by a "state action" requirement but authorizes the punishment of "entirely private conspiracies to interfere with the exercise of Fourteenth Amendment rights."

[33] The second statute under which civil suits may be brought is section 1985 of Title 42; it was construed in *Collins* v. *Hardyman* (1951). See generally Robert K. Carr, *Federal Protection of Civil Rights* (Ithaca, N.Y.: Cornell University Press, 1947).

[34] See Note, "Limiting the Section 1983 Action in the Wake of Monroe v. Pape," 82 HARVARD LAW REVIEW 1486 (1969); Paul Chevigny, "Section 1983 Jurisdiction: A Reply," 83 HARVARD LAW REVIEW 1352 (1970). In *Preiser* v. *Rodriguez* (1973), section 1983 relief was held unavailable where prisoners did not seek damages but a ruling that they were entitled to release from prison.

In *Rizzo* v. *Goode* (1976) a federal district court, having found a "pattern" of police violation of the civil rights of blacks in Philadelphia and "official indifference" as to doing anything about it, granted an injunction against the mayor and police officials. By a five to three vote the Supreme Court, narrowly interpreting section 1983, held that "principles of federalism" forbade federal judicial interference in the internal disciplinary affairs of the police department.

Paul v. *Davis* (1976) also exemplified the tendency of the Burger Court to cut off access to federal courts for persons complaining of civil rights violations by state and local officials. Here the Court ruled against a claimant in a civil rights damage suit who had been listed by the Louisville police as an "active shoplifter" in a flyer distributed to city merchants. In fact he had been arrested once for shoplifting, but was never tried and the charges were dropped. The Supreme Court held that there is no constitutionally guaranteed right to a good reputation, and so no basis for a federal civil rights damage suit. Redress should be sought in state courts; Rehnquist noted that the complaint "would appear to state a classical claim for defamation actionable in the courts of virtually every state." This decision seemed contrary to *Wisconsin* v. *Constantineau* (1971), where the Court had invoked the federal Constitution against a state law which allowed police without notice to post in liquor stores the names of persons who drank too much and should not be sold liquor. But Rehnquist argued that in *Constantineau* the right to drink liquor,

To give only one example of these civil rights actions, the Ohio National Guardsmen who killed four students at Kent State University in 1970 were prosecuted under section 242 for depriving the students of their civil rights but were acquitted because of failure to prove "willful" intent. Representatives of the estates of three of the students then brought suit under section 1983 against the Governor of Ohio and officers of the National Guard and university. The trial court dismissed the suit on grounds of state immunity, but the Supreme Court, in *Scheuer* v. *Rhodes* (1974), held that state officers are not protected by state immunity if in fact they acted under state law in a manner violative of the Constitution. The trial proceedings were then reinstituted, but the jury found in favor of the defendants.

A statute of 1866, codified as section 1443, Title 28, authorized the removal of civil rights cases under certain circumstances from state to federal courts. Denial of removal petitions was not subject to appeal to the Supreme Court until so provided by the Civil Rights Act of 1964. In *Georgia* v. *Rachel* (1966) the Court held that the federal district court involved must grant a hearing to determine whether defendants under prosecution in state courts for a restaurant sit-in had been ordered to leave the restaurant solely for racial reasons. If so, their rights of free access to public accommodations under the 1964 Civil Rights Act would have been challenged, and they would be entitled to removal of the case to federal court.

However, in another case decided the same day, *City of Greenwood* v. *Peacock* (1966), the Court by a five to four vote held that removal would not be ordered on allegations that the defendants had been arrested and charged solely because they were blacks or were engaged in helping blacks to assert their civil rights. The majority asserted that the removal statute was not intended "to work a wholesale dislocation of the historic relationship between the state and the federal courts in the administration of the criminal law." If the defendants really were being prosecuted because they were blacks, Justice Stewart said, there were other possible remedies in the federal courts by way of injunction, habeas corpus, and appeal.[35]

Justice Douglas for the dissenters in *Peacock* contended that "the federal regime was designed from the beginning to afford some protection against local passions and prejudices by the important pretrial federal remedy of removal." He added:

> These defendants' federal civil rights may, of course, ultimately be vindicated if they persevere, live long enough, and have the patience and the funds to carry their cases for some years through the state courts to this Court. But it was precisely that burden that Congress undertook to take off the backs of this persecuted minority and all who espouse the cause of their equality.

---

not merely loss of reputation, was at stake.

[35] The *Peacock* decision was determinative for the Burger Court in *Johnson* v. *Mississippi* (1975), where a group of blacks in Vicksburg who were conducting a boycott of businesses that were alleged to discriminate in employment were prosecuted for conspiracy and unsuccessfully sought removal of the case to federal court.

Chapter 28

Property Rights and Substantive Due Process

In the original Constitution, the only specific protection of property rights was the provision forbidding the states to impair the obligation of contracts. The Fifth Amendment forbade the deprivation of property without due process of law or the taking of property without just compensation, both of which were limitations on the federal government. With the Fourteenth Amendment, the pregnant due process formula was extended to the states.

THE PROTECTION OF CONTRACTS

Article I, section 10, forbids any state to "pass any . . . law impairing the obligation of contracts." The fact that this language has comparatively little present-day significance should not be permitted to minimize the outstanding role which it played in an earlier period. In the absence of a due process requirement applicable to the states, the contract clause was invoked against state legislation early and often. As Benjamin F. Wright has noted in his definitive study, up to 1889 the contract clause had been considered by the Court in almost 40 percent of all cases involving the validity of state legislation.[1] During that period it was the constitutional justification for seventy-five decisions in which state laws were held unconstitutional, almost half

---

[1] Benjamin F. Wright, *The Contract Clause of the Constitution* (Cambridge, Mass.: Harvard University Press, 1938), p. 95.

of all those in which legislation was declared invalid by the Supreme Court. But after adoption of the Fourteenth Amendment, there was less and less occasion to invoke the contract clause.

Marshall's contribution to the development of doctrine in this field was preeminent. His four great contract decisions, written between 1810 and 1819—*Fletcher* v. *Peck* (1810), *New Jersey* v. *Wilson* (1812), *Sturges* v. *Crowninshield* (1819), and *Dartmouth College* v. *Woodward* (1819)—are among the most significant decisions that the Supreme Court has ever handed down. By employing a far broader conception of contract than had prevailed in 1787 and by combining this conception with the principles of eighteenth-century natural law, Marshall was able to make of the contract clause a powerful instrument for the protection of the vested rights of private property.

The original understanding as to the meaning of the contract clause is almost impossible to determine. The general assumption has been that the clause was desired by propertied interests who wanted to protect themselves against the kind of state legislation favoring debtors that had been passed during the hard times of the 1780s—issuance of paper money which was given legal tender status in payment of private debts, granting debtors postponements beyond the contract date for payment of debts, or permitting them to pay debts in installments or in commodities.

Public Contracts

It is almost certainly true that the clause was intended to affect only private contracts, that is, contracts between individuals. Yet in the series of important contract cases decided by the Marshall Court, practically all dealt with public contracts. In the first and most notorious case, *Fletcher* v. *Peck* (1810), Marshall ruled that a huge land grant secured by bribing the Georgia Legislature could not be revoked because the legislative action constituted a contract.[2] Apparently uncertain about the validity of this claim, he also invoked in a rather vague way the ex post facto and bill of attainder provisions, though *Calder* v. *Bull* (1798) had already held the ex post facto clause to be confined to criminal cases. In addition, and almost in the same breath, he suggested that the limits on the Georgia Legislature came not from the Constitution, but from "the nature of society and of government." In his concluding paragraph, he could do no better than say that the rescinding act was invalidated "either by general principles, which are common to our free institutions, or by the particular provisions of the constitution of the United States."

This sorry performance inflamed public opinion, which was already antagonistic to the nationalistic trends of the Marshall Court on states' rights grounds. Nevertheless, the doctrine that the contract clause covered public contracts remained firmly established. Marshall himself quickly conquered the doubts he had exhibited in *Fletcher* v. *Peck,* and in *New Jersey* v. *Wilson* (1812) applied the contract clause to prevent a state from exercising one of its most fundamental powers, taxation. Tax exemption which had been granted by the colonial New Jersey Legislature to an

---

[2] See C. Peter Magrath, *Yazoo: The Case of Fletcher v. Peck* (New York: W. W. Norton & Company, Inc., 1967).

Indian tribe for the land on which they lived was held to be a contract still valid after the Indians had sold the land.

Next came *Dartmouth College* v. *Woodward* (1819), which held that a charter of incorporation was a contract protected against subsequent legislative infringement.[3] Though this case concerned a college, it was largely business corporations that were to benefit from the decision.

These three decisions raised a truly alarming specter of a venal or unwise legislature giving away the public birthright or even divesting the government of its essential taxing power—actions which would be irremediable under the contract clause. It is hardly surprising that a doctrine so potentially dangerous tended to generate its own correctives, which can be summarized under three headings.

First, the Dartmouth College decision itself recognized that the state may insert as a condition in the corporate charter the right to "amend, alter, and repeal" the same. This reservation is then part of the contract, and exercise of the power does not impair the contractual obligation. Again, the reservation may be not in the contract itself, but in general legislation which has the effect of incorporating the reservation in all charters of subsequent date. Especially after the Dartmouth ruling, such reservations were commonly provided, both by statutory and constitutional provisions.

Second, there is the rule of strict construction of public contracts or grants, which stems from Chief Justice Taney's famous decision in *Charles River Bridge* v. *Warren Bridge* (1837). The Charles River Bridge, a privately owned toll structure, was incorporated in 1785, and its franchise was extended in 1792. In 1828 Massachusetts incorporated the Warren Bridge and authorized it to build and operate a toll bridge near the other bridge. After a short period the Warren Bridge was to become free and part of the public highway; this would of course be fatal to the toll bridge. Taney, speaking for the Court, ruled that the state had not given the Charles River Bridge an exclusive charter. There was no express language in the contract that another bridge would not be established nearby. Public grants or franchises are to be strictly construed, and nothing passes to the grantee by implication. Taney added: "While the rights of private property are sacredly guarded, we must not forget that the community also have rights, and that the happiness and well being of every citizen depends on their faithful preservation."

Third, contractual grants are subordinate to the power of eminent domain and the police power. In *Stone* v. *Mississippi* (1880), a lottery franchise had been granted for a definite term of years, but two years later a new constitution was adopted which forbade lotteries. The unanimous Court ruled that "the power of governing is a trust committed by the people to the government, no part of which can be granted away."

Private Contracts

Only about 10 percent of the Supreme Court's contract cases have involved private contracts, but in that number are cases of considerable interest and importance. Again we go back to the Marshall Court for the beginning of the story. *Sturges* v.

---

[3] Francis N. Stites, *Private Interest and Public Gain: The Dartmouth College Case, 1819* (Amherst, Mass.: University of Massachusetts Press, 1972).

Crowninshield (1819) involved the validity of a New York bankruptcy act as applied to a contract of debt made *before* the law was passed. Marshall declared the law in violation of the contract clause, which he contended protected all contracts from legislative regulation. The sole exception he was willing to make was for laws abolishing imprisonment for debt.

Although Marshall carried the Court for this extreme view in *Sturges,* he was unable to do so in *Ogden* v. *Saunders* (1827), where the bankruptcy law being questioned was in force *before* the contract was made. Marshall would have declared this law unconstitutional also, but for the only time in his thirty-four years as Chief Justice he was in the minority on a constitutional issue. The majority held that the *Sturges* decision had to be limited to contracts already made. A statute in effect at the time a contract is entered into is a part of the contract, and therefore cannot be held to impair its obligation. The true meaning of the contract clause, said Justice Johnson, was to protect against "arbitrary and tyrannical legislation over existing right." Bankruptcy legislation was no more in this category than laws regulating usurious contracts or the collection of gaming debts. This view of insolvency laws has been consistently maintained since.

State authority to modify contractual remedies is derived from the police power, and we have already seen that the police power cannot be frustrated by public contracts. Even less should private contracts be permitted to override public policy. Thus a state prohibition act is not invalid because it nullifies contracts for the sale of beer,[4] and contracts of employment may legitimately be modified by later workmen's compensation laws.[5] As the Supreme Court said in 1905, "Parties by entering into contracts may not estop the legislature from enacting laws intended for the public good."[6]

There may be real difficulty in determining how far a legislature may reasonably go when the "public good" sought under the police power is such a controversial problem as the relief of debtors. The most famous debtor relief case of recent times is *Home Building and Loan Assn.* v. *Blaisdell* (1934), where the Court by a five to four vote upheld depression legislation passed by Minnesota to prevent the wholesale loss of mortgaged properties by debtors unable to meet their obligations. On application from the mortgagor, state courts could extend the existing one-year period of redemption from foreclosure sales for an additional limited time. During this period in which the mortgagor was allowed to retain possession, he was obliged to apply the income or reasonable rental value to the payment of taxes, interest, insurance, and the mortgage indebtedness.

In upholding the law, Chief Justice Hughes stressed the government's emergency powers. "While emergency does not create power," he said, "emergency may furnish the occasion for the exercise of power." The states have a reserved power to protect the interests of their citizens in time of emergency. They also have an obligation not to impair contracts. These two powers "must be construed in harmony with each other." One must not be used to destroy the other. Certainly "state power exists to give temporary relief from the enforcement of contracts in the presence of

[4] *Boston Beer Co.* v. *Massachusetts* (1878).
[5] *New York Central R. Co.* v. *White* (1917).
[6] *Manigault* v. *Springs* (1905).

disasters due to physical causes such as fire, flood or earthquake." The same power must exist "when the urgent public need demanding such relief is produced by other and economic causes." Hughes concluded: "The question is no longer merely that of one party to a contract as against another, but of the use of reasonable means to safeguard the economic structure upon which the good of all depends. . . . The principle of this development is . . . that the reservation of the reasonable exercise of the protective power of the State is read into all contracts."

Shortly thereafter, less carefully drawn moratorium legislation in two other states was invalidated by the Court,[7] but these decisions do not detract from the authority of the *Blaisdell* opinion. In 1945 Justice Frankfurter for a unanimous Court said that the Hughes opinion had left "hardly any open spaces of controversy concerning the constitutional restrictions of the Contract Clause upon moratory legislation." The *Blaisdell* principle was restated by Frankfurter to say that

> When a widely diffused public interest has become enmeshed in a network of multitudinous private arrangements, the authority of the State "to safeguard the vital interests of its people" . . . is not to be gainsaid by abstracting one such arrangement from its public context and treating it as though it were an isolated private contract constitutionally immune from impairment.[8]

EMINENT DOMAIN

Eminent domain is the power of government to take private property when it is needed for a public purpose. Since such authority is an incident of sovereignty, it requires no explicit constitutional recognition. The Fifth Amendment assumes the existence of this power in the national government when it imposes the requirement of "just compensation." While there is no comparable language in the Fourteenth Amendment, the significant constitutional questions applying to the exercise of eminent domain power by both the states and the federal government are largely the same, namely: What is a public purpose? What is a taking of property? and What is just compensation?

Public Purpose

Where a public agency itself proposes to use land for a public building, highway, park, or other facility for general public use, the public character of the taking is obvious. But the taking need not be for a use to which all the public will have access. Condemnation of property for public housing projects, in which only a small percentage of the population can live, is now thoroughly established. The "access" test is not relevant here; rather, public purpose results from the contribution of public housing to slum clearance, reduction of crime and disease, lowering of police and fire costs, and general community improvement.[9]

Eminent domain power is customarily granted to public utility corporations,

---

[7] *Worthen Co.* v. *Thomas* (1934); *Worthen Co.* v. *Kavanaugh* (1935).
[8] *East New York Savings Bank* v. *Hahn* (1945). The *Blaisdell* opinion was relied on in *City of El Paso* v. *Simmons* (1965).
[9] *City of Cleveland* v. *United States* (1945).

which have no difficulty in meeting the public use test. Even private corporations or individuals may be considered to qualify under sufficiently pressing circumstances, as in connection with access to water for irrigation in the arid West or the damming of streams for the operation of mills.[10]

The Supreme Court gives great weight to legislative determinations as to what is a public use. In *United States ex rel. TVA* v. *Welch* (1946) Justice Black said in the opinion for the Court: "We think that it is the function of Congress to decide what type of taking is for a public use." Justice Douglas added, in *Berman* v. *Parker* (1954): "Subject to specific constitutional limitations, when the legislature has spoken, the public interest has been declared in terms well-nigh conclusive." So far as state cases are concerned, the Supreme Court has tended to follow the decisions of the state courts.

The Taking of Property

Property need not be literally or fully "taken" in order to establish a basis for claiming compensation. An individual may remain in possession of his property, and still find that by reason of governmental action his use or enjoyment of the property has been seriously impaired. Property is taken within the meaning of the Constitution "when inroads are made upon an owner's use of it to an extent that, as between private parties, a servitude has been acquired either by agreement or in course of time."[11]

For example, *United States* v. *Causby* (1946) concerned a chicken farm which adjoined an airport leased by the United States. Bombing planes roared over the farm day and night on a glide path carrying them only 83 feet above the farm. The chicken business had to be abandoned because as many as ten chickens a day were killed by flying into walls in their fright. The Supreme Court ruled that the government action constituted a taking of the property, saying: "The flight of airplanes, which skim the surface but do not touch it, is as much an appropriation of the use of the land as a more conventional entry upon it." But jet aircraft operations which disturb residents adjacent to airports but do not make their homes uninhabitable do not constitute a taking of an interest for which compensation must be paid.[12]

Acts done in the proper exercise of governmental power and not encroaching on private property, though their consequences may impair its use or reduce its value, are not generally regarded as a taking of property. Thus, changes in grade level of a street do not require compensation to owners whose access to their property is impaired, nor does the government have to compensate a riparian owner for cutting off his access to navigable waters by changing the course of a stream to improve navigation.[13] Congress may lower the tariff or cheapen the currency without having to compensate those who suffer losses as a result. Restrictions on use of

[10] *Clark* v. *Nash* (1905); *Otis Co.* v. *Ludlow Mfg. Co.* (1906).

[11] *United States* v. *Dickinson* (1947).

[12] *Batten* v. *United States* (1963). The California supreme court ruled in 1972 that, though the property of residents near airports had not been "taken," they could seek damages on grounds of nuisance, negligence, and zoning violations. *Nestle* v. *City of Santa Monica* (1972).

[13] *United States* v. *Commodore Park, Inc.* (1945).

property in wartime have been held not to constitute a taking of property, even when they extend to a complete ban on its use, as in the *Wartime Prohibition Cases* (1919).[14]

Just Compensation

So far as state takings are concerned, the Supreme Court has pretty well kept out of disputes over the adequacy of compensation. Unless a state court has, by its rulings of law, prevented an owner from receiving substantially any compensation at all, the Court will not intervene. "All that is essential is that in some appropriate way, before some properly constituted tribunal, inquiry shall be made as to the amount of compensation, and when this has been provided there is that due process of law which is required by the Federal Constitution."[15]

In federal takings, however, the Supreme Court has been more concerned with the standards applied. An owner of land to be condemned is entitled to "market value fairly determined."[16] That value may reflect not only the use to which the property is presently devoted but also that to which it may be readily converted. But a reasonable probability of the land's being devoted to a more profitable purpose must be shown if it is to affect the compensation awarded.[17]

THE INVENTION OF SUBSTANTIVE DUE PROCESS

Substantive due process is defined by Edward S. Corwin as the judicial doctrine that "every species of State legislation, whether dealing with procedural or substantive rights, [is] subject to the scrutiny of the [Supreme] Court when the question of its essential justice is raised."[18] The transformation of the due process clause from a guarantee of fair procedures into an activist judicial warrant for passing judgment on the substantive policies of legislative regulations must rate as one of the Supreme Court's most significant creative efforts.

Corwin traces the idea to a New York State court decision, *Wynehamer* v. *New York* (1856), which declared unconstitutional a very drastic prohibition statute making liquor a nuisance that owners must destroy on pain of criminal prosecution. The court concluded that the harsh operation of the statute on liquors lawfully owned at the time the act went into effect amounted to an act of destruction not within the power of government to perform, "even by the forms which belong to 'due process of law.'"

The next year Taney invoked the Fifth Amendment due process clause as a defense of property against substantive legislative power in his *Dred Scott* opinion. In 1870 *Hepburn* v. *Griswold* set aside the Legal Tender Act of 1862 on the ground,

14 See also *United States* v. *Central Eureka Mining Company* (1958).

15 *Backus* v. *Fort Street Union Depot Co.* (1898).

16 For problems of determining fair value under wartime price ceilings or dislocations of the market, see *United States* v. *Commodities Trading Corp.* (1950), *United States* v. *Felin & Co.* (1948), and *United States* v. *Cors* (1949).

17 See *United States ex rel. TVA* v. *Powelson* (1943).

18 Edward S. Corwin, *Liberty against Government: The Rise, Flowering and Decline of a Famous Juridical Concept* (Baton Rouge, La.: Louisiana State University Press, 1948), pp. 135–136.

among others, that retroactive application of the law deprived creditors of property without due process of law.

The initial effort to protect property rights under the Fourteenth Amendment was made in the *Slaughter-House Cases* (1873). Counsel for the New Orleans butchers who were attacking the slaughterhouse monopoly granted by state statute was John A. Campbell, former justice of the Supreme Court. He argued that the Fourteenth Amendment had not been intended merely to guarantee the rights of the newly freed blacks. This purpose was only incidental to the Amendment's broader goal of protecting "laissez-faire individualism." The colonists who settled this continent were seeking "freedom, free action, free enterprise." A monopolistic charter such as was here involved abridged "privileges and immunities," denied "equal protection of the laws," and was a deprivation of "liberty."

Justice Miller's majority opinion was largely confined to the privileges and immunities point. As for due process and equal protection, Miller observed that they had "not been much pressed" by counsel, and he felt that it was "sufficient to say that under no construction" of the due process clause "that we have ever seen, or any that we deem admissible" could the Louisiana law be held "a deprivation of property." There were four dissenters. Justice Field took his stand primarily on the privileges and immunities clause, but Justice Bradley dissented squarely on due process grounds:

> [The] right to choose one's calling is an essential part of that liberty which it is the object of government to protect; and a calling, when chosen, is a man's property and right. Liberty and property are not protected where these rights are arbitrarily assailed. . . . In my view, a law which prohibits a large class of citizens from adopting a lawful employment, or from following a lawful employment previously adopted, does deprive them of liberty as well as property, without due process of law.

Four years later, in *Munn* v. *Illinois* (1877), the Court again refused to interfere with a regulatory statute, but by this time all members of the Court had accepted the obligation to appraise the legislation on substantive due process grounds. The state law involved fixed the maximum charges for storage of grain in warehouses and elevators and had been attacked as taking property without due process. Chief Justice Waite for the majority upheld the fixing of rates only after recognizing that a judicial case needed to be made for it on due process grounds. This he did by discovering that grain elevators were in a category of "businesses affected with a public interest" which, like ferries, inns, and gristmills, the common law had recognized as subject to regulation "for the common good." Whether a business fell within this category was primarily for the legislature to determine. Judicial intervention would be permissible only in cases where the Court was able to say of its own knowledge that no "state of facts could exist" which would justify the legislative conclusion. As for the rates and charges fixed by a legislature for businesses affected with a public interest, they were not subject to judicial review. "For protection against abuses by legislatures the people must resort to the polls, not to the courts."

This ruling failed to discourage efforts to involve the courts in reviewing regulatory statutes. In *Davidson* v. *New Orleans* (1878), Justice Miller was led to comment:

. . . the docket of this court is crowded with cases in which we are asked to hold that State courts and State legislatures have deprived their own citizens of life, liberty, or property without due process of law. There is here abundant evidence that there exists some strange misconception of the scope of this provision as found in the Fourteenth Amendment. In fact, it would seem, from the character of many of the cases before us, and the arguments made in them, that the clause under consideration is looked upon as a means of bringing to the test of the decision of this court the abstract opinions of every unsuccessful litigant in a State court of the justice of the decision against him, and of the merits of the legislation on which such a decision may be founded.

But Miller was no more successful than Canute in holding back the tides. Within a decade the Court was openly considering the "merits" of state legislation. A good statement of the Court's new position was given by Justice Harlan in *Mugler* v. *Kansas* (1887), where the constitutionality of a state prohibition act was being challenged. The Court had to review the law, Harlan said, because

. . . not . . . every statute enacted ostensibly for the promotion of [the public welfare] is to be accepted as a legitimate exertion of the police powers of the State. There are, of necessity, limits beyond which legislation cannot rightfully go. . . . The courts are not bound by mere forms, nor are they to be misled by mere pretences. They are at liberty—indeed, are under a solemn duty—to look at the substance of things, whenever they enter upon the inquiry whether the legislature has transcended the limits of its authority. If, therefore, a statute purporting to have been enacted to protect the public health, the public morals, or the public safety, has no real or substantial relation to those objects, or is a palpable invasion of rights secured by the fundamental law, it is the duty of the courts to so adjudge, and thereby give effect to the Constitution.

HEALTH, WELFARE, AND MORALS LEGISLATION

Just because judges felt obliged to appraise the "substance" of statutes did not mean, of course, that they were always, or even usually, going to reach unfavorable conclusions as to their validity. Even in the heyday of substantive due process, the great bulk of all regulatory legislation never encountered any problems with judicial review. In spite of the searching inquiry into the "real" purpose of such laws promised by Harlan, the Court's approach tended to be what Corwin calls "presumed validity."[19] Consider the case of *Powell* v. *Pennsylvania* (1888), where an antioleomargarine statute was accepted as a health measure, in spite of justifiable doubts that this was the major purpose of the enactment. Justice Harlan, in an orgy of double negatives, ruled that the Court

. . . cannot adjudge that the defendants' rights of liberty and property . . . have been infringed by the statute of Pennsylvania, without holding that, although it may have been enacted in good faith for the objects expressed in its title, namely, to protect the public health and to prevent the adulteration of dairy products and fraud in the sale thereof, it has, in fact, no real or substantial relation to those objects. . . . The Court is unable to affirm that this legislation has no real or substantial relation to such objects.

[19] *Op. cit.,* p. 143.

In its subsequent experience the Court generally presumed the validity of statutes enacted for the declared purpose of furthering the public health, welfare, or morals. Regulation of professions or occupations with a close relationship to public health, such as doctors, dentists, druggists,[20] nurses, beauticians, barbers, plumbers, and the like, have been readily accepted. Such regulation, moreover, may extend beyond the basic considerations of health to cover activities only tangentially related. Thus *Semler* v. *Oregon State Board of Dental Examiners* (1935) upheld a statute that forbade dentists to advertise in any competitive or spectacular manner.

Jacobson v. *Massachusetts* (1905), upholding a state requirement of vaccination against smallpox, excellently exemplifies the presumption of validity that almost automatically attached to legislation for health purposes. Jacobson offered to prove that vaccination was ineffective or dangerous, but the Court refused to credit his evidence. Justice Harlan was quite willing to believe that there were those, some of them perhaps even doctors, who attached little or no value to vaccination. But

> . . . what everybody knows the court must know, and therefore the state court judicially knew, as this court knows, that an opposite theory accords with the common belief and is maintained by high medical authority. We must assume that when the statute in question was passed, the legislature of Massachusetts was not unaware of these opposing theories, and was compelled, of necessity, to choose between them. It was not compelled to commit a matter involving the public health and safety to the final decision of a court or jury. It is no part of the function of a court or a jury to determine which one of two modes was likely to be the most effective for the protection of the public against disease. That was for the legislative department to determine in the light of all the information it had or could obtain.

Similarly, legislation aimed at the prevention and punishment of activities generally regarded in the society as offensive to moral standards is unlikely to generate constitutional objections. But it is only too well known that fanatics and bigots often seek on allegedly moral grounds the passage of legislation which amounts to serious invasions of privacy and coercion of individuals with different standards of morality.

The most striking example was the adoption of prohibition of intoxicating liquor in the United States and in many of the states. Substantive due process was never invoked against prohibition legislation. In *Mugler* v. *Kansas,* Justice Harlan wrote:

> There is no justification for holding that the State, under the guise merely of police regulation, is here aiming to deprive the citizen of his constitutional rights; for we cannot shut out of view the fact, within the knowledge of all, that the public health, the public morals, and the public safety, may be endangered by the general use of intoxicating drinks; nor the fact, established by statistics accessible to everyone, that the idleness, disorder, pauperism, and crime existing in the country are, in some degree at least, traceable to this evil.

[20] One of the few decisions declaring such a statute unconstitutional, *Liggett Co.* v. *Baldridge* (1926), involving a law requiring all stockholders of a corporation owning drugstores to be licensed pharmacists, was overruled in *North Dakota State Board of Pharmacy* v. *Snyder's Drug Stores* (1973).

The Supreme Court recognized in the *Mugler* case that the effect of the statute would be to render practically worthless property invested in the liquor business at a time when it was a perfectly legal occupation, but this was not contrary to due process.[21] Moreover, the *Mugler* decision even held it was permissible for the legislature to prohibit individuals from manufacturing intoxicating liquors for their own use, on the ground that such a loophole might cause the prohibitory plan to fail. Along the same line, a subsequent decision held that the mere possession of intoxicating liquor might be prohibited.[22] Indeed, a state might prohibit the sale of *nonintoxicating* malt liquors in order to make effective its prohibition against the sale of intoxicants.[23]

As for federal action, the so-called Wartime Prohibition Act, passed ten days after the Armistice in 1918, was upheld on the basis of the government's war powers in 1919.[24] The adoption of the Eighteenth Amendment of course wrote prohibition into the Constitution.

Long before scientific proof of the dangers of cigarette smoking became available, some states sought to prohibit cigarettes on both health and morals grounds. A Tennessee statute of this sort was sustained by the Supreme Court in *Austin* v. *Tennessee* (1900). In 1932 a Utah statute which forbade billboard or streetcar advertising of tobacco was upheld by the Supreme Court, Justice Brandeis saying: "The law deals confessedly with a subject within the scope of the police power. No facts are brought to our attention which establish either that the evil aimed at does not exist or that the statutory remedy is inappropriate."[25]

The public welfare which states can promote by use of the police power has on occasion been defined in terms broader than the traditional categories of health, morals, and safety. Increasingly the Supreme Court has accepted promotion of public convenience or prosperity, or even aesthetic purposes, as justifying legislative interference with liberty or property.

Euclid v. *Ambler Realty Co.* (1926), upholding the constitutionality of zoning, was a landmark case in the development of a broader judicial attitude toward police power regulation. Zoning ordinances typically divide a city into various classes of residential, commercial, and manufacturing districts, and buildings and land use within each area must conform to the regulations for this district. Such restrictions of course constitute a serious limitation on freedom of the owner to employ his property as he sees fit, and the Supreme Court held two hearings in the *Euclid* case before it approved the zoning regulations by a five to four vote.

Many of the purposes which zoning seeks to achieve—limits on heights of buildings and billboards, exclusion of offensive trades from residential districts, and so on—had, it is true, already been judicially approved.[26] But the exclusion of all

---

[21] See also *Boston Beer Co.* v. *Massachusetts* (1878).

[22] *Crane* v. *Campbell* (1917).

[23] *Purity Extract & Tonic Co.* v. *Lynch* (1912).

[24] *Hamilton* v. *Kentucky Distilleries and Warehouse Co.* (1919).

[25] *Packer Corp.* v. *Utah* (1932).

[26] See *Welch* v. *Swasey* (1909); *Cusack* v. *Chicago* (1917). More recently, some zoning regulations have been attacked as "restrictive" or "exclusionary" under the equal protection clause. See Chap. 29.

businesses and trades, including hotels and apartment houses, from residential districts was a more extreme control than any the Court had approved in the past. To support such restriction, Justice Sutherland rehearsed the findings and the philosophy of the zoning experts as set forth in numerous reports which, he concluded, were "sufficiently cogent to prelude us from saying, as it must be said before an ordinance can be declared unconstitutional, that such provisions are clearly arbitrary and unreasonable, having no substantial relation to the public health, safety, morals, or general welfare."

The *Euclid* decision established the constitutionality of new and far-reaching controls on use of property, but it is significant that Sutherland's defense was based primarily on the old concept of nuisances. It was not until the decision in *Berman* v. *Parker* (1954), involving the constitutionality under the Fifth Amendment of a slum-clearance and redevelopment program in the District of Columbia, that Justice Douglas for a unanimous Court accepted aesthetics as a proper public purpose in its own right.

> The concept of the public welfare is broad and inclusive. . . . The values it represents are spiritual as well as physical, aesthetic as well as monetary. It is within the power of the legislature to determine that the community should be beautiful as well as healthy, spacious as well as clean, well-balanced as well as carefully patrolled.

ECONOMIC REGULATION

It is only when we come to consider legislation regulating economic activities that we see the full potentialities of the doctrine of substantive due process. Judges who were willing to accept state intervention to protect the public health and developed reasons for justifying it tended to be much less ready to accept state intervention in the economy and much more likely to produce rationalizations for striking down state action.[27] As early as 1897, in *Allgeyer* v. *Louisiana,* the Supreme Court announced the principle that the right to make contracts was a part of the liberty guaranteed by the due process clause, and stated the doctrine of freedom of contract in a most forthright fashion:

> The "liberty" mentioned in [the Fourteenth] Amendment means not only the right of the citizen to be free from the mere physical restraint of his person, as by incarceration, but the term is deemed to embrace the right of the citizen to be free in the enjoyment of all his faculties; to be free to use them in all lawful ways; to live and work where he will; to earn his livelihood by any lawful calling; to pursue any livelihood or avocation, and for that purpose to enter into all contracts which may be proper, necessary and essential to his carrying out to a successful conclusion the purposes above mentioned.

The immediate beneficiaries of this judicial antagonism toward economic regulation were customarily business corporations. A word should be said about how corporations came within the protection accorded to "persons" under the due pro-

---

[27] *Chicago, M. & St. P. R. Co.* v. *Minnesota* (1890) was the first case to strike down state ecomomic regulation on substantive due process grounds, holding that the reasonableness of railroad rates was a question for ultimate judicial decision.

cess clause. It is rather anomalous that the Fourteenth Amendment for a half century after its adoption should have been of very little value to the blacks in whose
behalf it was primarily adopted, while it should so quickly have been accepted by
the Court as a protector of corporate rights. Some have argued that this was not an
accident. The "conspiracy theory" of the Fourteenth Amendment presents it as a
deliberate Trojan horse which, purporting merely to protect Negro rights, smuggled
into the Constitution the principle of judicial review over state legislation affecting
corporate property interests. Supporting this contention is the argument made before the Supreme Court in 1885 by Roscoe Conkling, a member of the joint congressional committee which drafted the amendment, that the committee had purposely
inserted the term "person" rather than "citizen" in the due process and equal protection clauses in order to cover corporations.[28]

Actually it requires no such theory, which in any event is now rather thoroughly discredited, to explain the development of judicial concern for corporate rights. A
knowledge of the temper of the times is sufficient. In *Santa Clara County* v. *Southern
Pacific Rr. Co.* (1886) the Court was unanimous in asserting that the Fourteenth
Amendment covered corporations, Chief Justice Waite saying: "The Court does not
wish to hear argument on the question." No dissent was expressed until 1938, when
Justice Black sought to repeal a half century of holdings by denying that the amendment had been intended to apply to corporations.[29] Again in 1949 Douglas joined
Black in reasserting this view, but at the same time they admitted that "history has
gone the other way."[30]

Judicial Acceptance of Economic Regulation

Many types of economic regulation encountered little opposition from the courts.
Economic legislation was often presented as based on health considerations, and
where courts were convinced that the health rationale was valid they would usually
concede constitutionality. This was generally true, for example, of laws regulating
hours of work in industrial employment. In *Holden* v. *Hardy* (1898) the Supreme
Court, with only two dissents (Brewer and Peckham), upheld a Utah statute providing for an eight-hour day in mines and smelters. This law was clearly tied in with the
protection of life and health. It affected workers in only two occupations which the
legislature had judged to be dangerous when too long pursued. Since there were
reasonable grounds for holding this conclusion to be true, the Court would not
review the legislative decision.

More importantly, the Court went on to challenge the whole freedom of contract idea by pointing out that the workers and owners were not on an equal bargaining basis. Consequently the self-interest of the workers was not a safe guide, and
in the interests of the public health the legislature could impose its authority to

---

[28] *San Mateo County* v. *Southern Pacific Rr. Co.* (1885). See Howard Jay Graham, "The 'Conspiracy
Theory' of the Fourteenth Amendment," 47 *Yale Law Journal* 371–403 (1938), 48 *ibid.* 171–194 (1938).
[29] *Connecticut General Life Ins. Co.* v. *Johnson* (1938).
[30] *Wheeling Steel Corp.* v. *Glander* (1949). Considering the importance of groups in a liberal democratic society, it would be a dubious and even illiberal policy to guarantee rights to individuals while
denying them to organized groups. See the defense of group rights in *Joint Anti-Fascist Refugee Committee* v. *McGrath* (1951).

protect one party to the contract against himself. This case was brought by the employer, who argued solicitously that the law interfered with the right of his employees to contract freely. "The argument," the Court rejoined, "would certainly come with better grace and greater cogency from the latter class."

Muller v. *Oregon* (1908) unanimously upheld a ten-hour law applying to women in industry. Taking "judicial cognizance" of factors which make women the weaker sex, the Court held that "she is properly placed in a class by herself, and legislation designed for her protection could be sustained, even when like legislation is not necessary for men and could not be sustained." The Court acknowledged its debt to "the brief filed by Mr. Louis D. Brandeis," which gathered an enormous amount of information on foreign and state laws limiting hours for women, and official reports stressing the dangers to women from long hours of labor. Such laws and opinions "may not be, techically speaking, authorities," the Court said, but "they are significant of a widespread belief that woman's physical structure, and the functions she performs in consequence thereof, justify special legislation restricting or qualifying the conditions under which she should be permitted to toil."

So health considerations provided the Court with police power justification for some hours legislation. For a time it also appeared that health arguments would legitimize regulation of wages, even though the connection with health was more indirect here and the assault on freedom of contract was more painful to employers. An Oregon minimum wage law came up to the Supreme Court in 1917. The Oregon supreme court had upheld the law on the strength of the *Muller* principle, finding it a protection for women's health and also for their morals. In *Stettler* v. *O'Hara,* the Supreme Court split four to four, with Brandeis abstaining, and thus the state court decision was left in effect. Within the next six years three more state supreme courts upheld minimum wages for women, relying upon the *Stettler* case.

Even the regulation of prices, a still more direct incursion on the principles of laissez faire, was initially approved in the case of *Munn* v. *Illinois* (1877) where, as already noted, the Court upheld the fixing of rates for Chicago grain elevators on the ground that they fell within a category of businesses recognized by the common law as "affected with a public interest."

In later decisions the Court added such business operations as insurance companies,[31] stockyards,[32] and tobacco warehouses[33] to the category of businesses affected with a public interest and so subject to regulation of rates and charges. The *Munn* principle was also applied in *Davidson* v. *New Orleans* (1878) to hold that businesses subject to control of rates were not entitled under the due process clause to judicial review of the question of just compensation.

In the early part of the twentieth century, state legislatures began to feel that industrial accidents should be recognized as a cost of production and compensated for by the employer. Laws of various types aiming at this goal were passed. In 1917 the Supreme Court upheld the New York law, saying that although it no doubt

---

[31] *German Alliance Insurance Co.* v. *Lewis* (1914).
[32] *Cotting* v. *Godard* (1901).
[33] *Townsend* v. *Yeomans* (1937).

limited freedom of contract to some extent, this was a legitimate exercise of the police power for protection of the health, safety, and welfare of an important group of individuals.[34]

Judicial Rejection of Economic Regulation

Although these illustrations of judicial acceptance of economic regulation are significant, they are not fully representative of the Supreme Court's position for the first third of the twentieth century. During this period the Court grew steadily more critical of legislative efforts to deal with what were widely regarded as economic abuses and more inflexible in its interpretation of the due process clause.

Lochner v. *New York* (1905) sounded the Court's call to battle against welfare economics. This case involved a state law which forbade bakery employees to work for more than ten hours a day or sixty hours a week. In spite of the fact that the Court had upheld a ten-hour law for miners in *Holden* v. *Hardy* (1898), it now declared the New York statute unconstitutional, by a five to four vote.

The law, said Justice Peckham for the majority, could be upheld only as a measure "pertaining to the health of the individual engaged in the occupation of a baker." Did the health of bakers need protection? Peckham did not think so, and he gave two reasons. First, "to the common understanding the trade of a baker has never been regarded as an unhealthy one." Second, statistics regarding trades and occupations show that although "the trade of a baker does not appear to be as healthy as some other trades, [it] is also vastly more healthy than still others." Since there were no special health hazards about baking, then to permit bakers' hours to be regulated would be to permit general legislative control of hours in industry. This was so unthinkable to Peckham that it clinched his argument.

The majority opinion did not bother to hide its distaste for such legislative interference. "Statutes of the nature of that under review, limiting the hours in which grown and intelligent men may labor to earn their living, are mere meddlesome interferences with the rights of the individual." Unless the Court called a halt, we would all be "at the mercy of legislative majorities." The Court must pierce through legislative pretenses when laws purporting to protect the public health or welfare were "in reality, passed from other motives."

There was nothing in Peckham's opinion to suggest that it would come with better grace if employee freedom of contract were defended by employees rather than employers. There was nothing about any inequality of bargaining power on the part of employees. In fact, Peckham inferred that such notions were an insult to red-blooded American workingmen. "There is no contention that bakers as a class are not equal in intelligence and capacity to men in other trades or manual occupations, or that they are not able to assert their rights and care for themselves without the protecting arm of the State, interfering with their independence of judgment and of action. They are in no sense wards of the State."

The Peckham opinion, which has long been a museum piece, called forth some of Justice Holmes's best-known phrases.

[34] *New York Central Ry. Co.* v. *White* (1917).

> This case is decided upon an economic theory which a large part of the country does not entertain. . . . The Fourteenth Amendment does not enact Mr. Herbert Spencer's Social Statics. . . . I think that the word liberty in the Fourteenth Amendment is perverted when it is held to prevent the natural outcome of a dominant opinion, unless it can be said that a rational and fair man necessarily would admit that the statute proposed would infringe fundamental principles as they have been understood by the traditions of our people and our law.

In this instance, Holmes thought that it did not need "research to show that no such sweeping condemnation can be passed upon the statute before us."

Of course Holmes was right in saying that *Lochner* was decided "upon an economic theory." But it is also true that it was decided on a legal theory—that use of the police power was limited to grounds of health, morals, and safety. Holmes concluded that a "reasonable man" might think the New York law "a proper measure on the score of health." But actually it was not a health law. It was, as Peckham charged, a labor law. Holmes knew this, too, and was ready to approve it as a labor law, because "men whom I certainly could not pronounce unreasonable would uphold it is a first instalment of a general regulation of the hours of work." But the Court majority was not willing to follow Holmes's "reasonable man" so far or so fast.

Eighteen years later the *Lochner* ruling was invoked in *Adkins* v. *Children's Hospital* (1923) to strike down a District of Columbia minimum wage law for women. It had been widely thought that *Lochner* had lost much of its authority, for in the interim the Court had upheld the Oregon ten-hour law for women, and in *Bunting* v. *Oregon* (1917) it had approved a ten-hour law for both men and women in industry without ever mentioning the *Lochner* decision. Consequently, as Chief Justice Taft said in his *Adkins* dissent, there was reason to assume that the *Lochner* case had been "overruled *sub silentio.*" But for the five-judge majority in *Adkins, Lochner* was still the law.

The *Adkins* opinion, written by Justice Sutherland, was a paean to freedom of contract in its purest form, with no nonsense about the special needs of women or inequality of bargaining position. The Court saw the statute as

> . . . simply and exclusively a price-fixing law, confined to adult women . . . who are legally as capable of contracting for themselves as men. It forbids two parties having lawful capacity . . . to freely contract with one another in respect of the price for which one shall render service to the other in a purely private employment where both are willing, perhaps anxious, to agree, even though the consequence may be to oblige one to surrender a desirable engagement and the other to dispense with the services of a desirable employee.

Sutherland had two main reasons why this was unconstitutional. First, the standards set up by statute to guide the administering board in fixing minimum wages were too vague and fatally uncertain. The sum necessary to maintain a woman worker in good health and protect her morals is not precise or unvarying. It will depend on her temperament, her habits, her moral standards, her independent resources, and so on. It cannot be determined "by a general formula prescribed by a statutory bureau." Second, the law was invalid because it took account "of the necessities of only one party to the contract," compelling the employer to pay the minimum wage whether or not the employee was worth that much to him.

Chief Justice Taft, dissenting, thought that the *Adkins* case was controlled by the *Muller* decision, and he could see no difference in principle between regulating maximum hours and minimum wages. Holmes agreed.

> The bargain is equally affected whichever half you regulate. *Muller* v. *Oregon,* I take it, is as good law today as it was in 1908. It will need more than the Nineteenth Amendment to convince me that there are no differences between men and women, or that legislation cannot take those differences into account. I should not hesitate to take them into account if I thought it necessary to sustain this act. . . . But after *Bunting* v. *Oregon* . . . I had supposed that it was not necessary, and that *Lochner* v. *New York* . . . would be allowed a deserved repose.

Holmes went on to admit that he personally had doubts about this statute, but they were irrelevant according to his standard of judicial review. "When so many intelligent persons, who have studied the matter more than any of us can, have thought that the means are effective and are worth the price, it seems to me impossible to deny that the belief reasonably may be held by reasonable men."

Following the *Adkins* decision, many states assumed that a minimum wage law which *did* take into account the value-of-service-rendered principle would be constitutional, and passed statutes including such provisions. A New York law of this type came before the Supreme Court in *Morehead* v. *Tipaldo* (1936), in the midst of the Court's furious battle against the New Deal. The four surviving members of the *Adkins* majority—Sutherland, Butler, Van Devanter, and McReynolds—joined with Justice Roberts to invalidate the New York law.[35] The value-of-service feature in the New York law was held insufficient to meet the *Adkins* objection, which was dogmatically restated in these words: "The State is without power by any form of legislation to prohibit, change or nullify contracts between employers and adult women workers as to the amount of wages to be paid."

This bland reiteration in 1936 of a conclusion which had had little enough support in the palmy days of 1923 was one of the great mistakes of Supreme Court history, and did more to destroy the country's confidence in the Court as then constituted than some of its more publicized anti-New Deal decisions. The ruling earned the dissent of as distinguished a foursome as ever sat on the high court— Chief Justice Hughes and Justices Brandeis, Cardozo, and Stone. The Chief Justice wrote a long dissent which was a devastating refutation of Butler's majority view, but for present purposes it may be preferable to note Stone's effort to point out to the majority some of the facts of life in 1936.

---

[35] For an explanation of Justice Roberts's vote, see Felix Frankfurter, "Mr. Justice Roberts," 104 UNIVERSITY OF PENNSYLVANIA LAW REVIEW 311 (1955).

In the years which have intervened since the *Adkins* case we have had opportunity to learn that a wage is not always the resultant of free bargaining between employers and employee; that it may be one forced upon employees by their economic necessities and upon employers by the most ruthless of their competitors. We have had opportunity to perceive more clearly that a wage insufficient to support the worker does not visit its consequences upon him alone; that it may affect profoundly the entire economic structure of society and, in any case, that it casts on every taxpaper, and on government itself, the burden of solving the problems of poverty, subsistence, health and morals of large numbers in the community. Because of their nature and extent these are public problems. A generation ago they were for the individual to solve; today they are the burden of the nation.

Here for the first time in an economic regulation case a Supreme Court justice burst out of the traditional health and morals boundaries on state police power and asserted—what was shortly to become axiomatic for the Court—that public power is as broad as is necessary to meet urgent public problems.

During this period the Court also struck out at legislative efforts to protect the organization of labor unions. Congress in 1898 adopted legislation outlawing the so-called "yellow-dog" contract, an agreement not to join a labor union which many employers forced workers to sign as a condition of employment. Discharging an employee of an interstate railroad on grounds of his membership in a labor organization was made a criminal offense against the United States. This statute was declared unconstitutional by the Supreme Court in the 1908 case of *Adair* v. *United States,* on familiar freedom of contract grounds.[36] Reminiscent of Anatole France, who spoke of the majestic equality of the law which forbids both rich and poor to steal bread, beg in the streets, or sleep under bridges, Harlan concluded: "In all such particulars the employer and the employee have equality of right, and any legislation that disturbs that equality is an arbitrary interference with the liberty of contract which no government can legally justify in a free land."

In the area of legislative rate and price fixing, the Court's initial favorable attitude as manifested in *Munn* v. *Illinois* was reversed by significant decisions in the 1920s. In *Tyson & Brother* v. *Banton* (1927) a New York law forbidding the resale of theater tickets at more than a 50-cent markup was declared unconstitutional by a five to four vote. Theaters, said Justice Sutherland, are not public utilities or affected with a public interest.

The following year the Court by a six to three vote in *Ribnik* v. *McBride* (1928) held unconstitutional New Jersey's effort to regulate the fees charged by employment agencies. Such businesses are "essentially private," and there is no more justification for fixing their rates than for setting the prices for food or housing or fuel.

Legislative efforts at business regulation were not confined to price fixing, of course.[37] In 1920 a Kansas statute declared that food, clothing, fuel, and transportation industries were affected with a public interest, and endeavored to subject them

[36] The Supreme Court struck down a comparable state statute in *Coppage* v.*Kansas* (1915).

[37] *Adams* v. *Tanner* (1917) declared invalid a law prohibiting the taking of fees from persons seeking employment.

to compulsory arbitration and fixing of wages and working conditions by an industrial relations court. The Supreme Court ruled that a packing company was a "private" concern which could not be constitutionally subjected to such controls.[38] Nebraska in 1921 established maximum weight for loaves of bread, and provided penalties for selling or making bread in other weights. The Court invalidated this measure, which was presented as one to protect consumers from fraud, calling it arbitrary interference with a private business.[39] However, the Court later upheld a statute of the same sort with somewhat modified enforcement standards.[40]

Oklahoma had varying experiences in undertaking to regulate by the licensing power businesses which it conceived to fall within the public interest. In 1929 the Court upheld a state law declaring the business of operating a cotton gin to be one having a public interest, and requiring a showing of public necessity before it could be undertaken.[41] But in the famous case of *New State Ice Co.* v. *Liebmann* (1932), the Court refused to grant such status to the ice business, holding that it was "as essentially private in its nature as the business of the grocer, the dairyman, the butcher. . . . [It] bears no such relation to the public as to warrant its inclusion in the category of businesses charged with a public use."

Finally, the Court's earlier reluctance to undertake judicial review of public utility rate fixing disappeared. *Smyth* v. *Ames* (1898) held that due process required the courts not merely to review the reasonableness of rates but also to determine whether the rates permitted a fair return on a fair valuation of property devoted to public use. *Smyth* v. *Ames* opened up over forty years of confusion, as regulatory commissions tried to guess what standards reviewing courts would employ and the methods they would require to be used in determining fair value of utility property.

The Abandonment of Economic Due Process

The structure of substantive due process which the Supreme Court built in these economic cases was probably its most original intellectual achievement during the first third of the twentieth century. Edward S. Corwin referred to substantive due process as "the most important field of American constitutional law."[42] These were the cases for which the Court was best known up to 1933; these were the decisions which primarily gave the Court its reputation as the bastion of conservatism, the protector of property rights, "the sheet anchor of the Republic."[43]

Then, within a few years, the Court completely abandoned economic due process. This striking reversal began with *Nebbia* v. *New York* (1934), as the Court by a five to four vote accepted the validity of a depression-born law regulating milk prices. A New York State statute had established a milk control board with power to fix minimum and maximum retail prices, and in this case the objective had been to prevent ruinous price cutting by fixing minimum prices. Justice Roberts spoke for the majority, which included also Hughes, Brandeis, Stone, and Cardozo.

[38] *Wolff Packing Co.* v. *Court of Industrial Relations* (1923); see also *Dorchy* v. *Kansas* (1924).
[39] *Burns Baking Co.* v. *Bryan* (1924).
[40] *Petersen Baking Co.* v. *Bryan* (1934).
[41] *Frost* v.*Corporation Commission (1929).*
[42] *Op. cit.,* p. 64.
[43] See Arthur S. Miller, *The Supreme Court and American Capitalism* (New York: The Free Press, 1968).

Roberts began by admitting that the milk industry had never been regarded as affected with a public interest and had none of the characteristics relied on in the past in attributing such status—no public grant or franchise, no monopoly, no obligation to serve all comers, no devotion of property to a use which the public might itself appropriately undertake. But that made no difference. It was a misconception to think that the power to regulate depended upon holding a franchise or enjoying a monopoly. Munn had no franchise nor anything that could "fairly be called a monopoly." Nor was there any mystical power in the standard, "affected with a public interest." This phrase, rightly understood, "is the equivalent of 'subject to the exercise of the police power' . . . nothing more was intended by the expression." Then came the heart of the *Nebbia* decision.

> It is clear that there is no closed class or category of businesses affected with a public interest, and the function of courts in the application of the Fifth and Fourteenth Amendments is to determine in each case whether circumstances vindicate the challenged regulation as a reasonable exertion of governmental authority or condemn it as arbitrary or discriminatory. . . . The phrase "affected with a public interest" can, in the nature of things, mean no more than that an industry, for adequate reason, is subject to control for the public good.

The *Nebbia* decision was followed by others supporting state and federal price fixing in a variety of fields.[44] However, the contrary decisions of the 1920s had not been specifically overruled, and when a Nebraska statute fixing rates which private employment agencies might charge an applicant for employment came before that state's supreme court in 1940, the court rather unimaginatively declared the law unconstitutional on the authority of *Ribnik* v. *McBride*. The Supreme Court unanimously reversed the state court in *Olsen* v. *Nebraska* (1941). "The drift away from *Ribnik* v. *McBride*," said Justice Douglas, "has been so great that it can no longer be deemed a controlling authority." In *Gold* v. *DiCarlo* (1965) the Court without opinion upheld a New York law limiting theater-ticket-broker surcharges, in effect overruling the 1927 *Tyson* decision.

In 1937 the Court upheld minimum wage laws for women in *West Coast Hotel Co.* v. *Parrish*. This case arose under the Washington state minimum wage law which, be it noted, had been passed in 1913 and enforced continuously thereafter, quite irrespective of the *Adkins* ruling. The act, like that of the District of Columbia, contained no value-of-service standard, and so seemed more in defiance of the *Adkins* decision than the New York law had been. But Chief Justice Hughes upheld the Washington law, constructing his majority opinion out of quotations from Taft and Holmes, and asking such questions as "What can be closer to the public interest than the health of women and their protection from unscrupulous and overreaching employers?" More important, he wrote the principles of Stone's *Morehead* dissent into the law of the land, thereby finally releasing the police power from dependence

---

[44] *Townsend* v. *Yeomans* (1937), upholding a Georgia statute fixing maximum warehouse charges for the handling and selling of leaf tobacco; *United States* v. *Rock Royal Co-Operative, Inc.* (1939), upholding the power of Congress to fix minimum prices for milk under the commerce clause; *Sunshine Anthracite Coal Co.* v. *Adkins* (1940), upholding the price-fixing provisions of the federal Bituminous Coal Act of 1937.

on health and morals considerations. The opinion concluded with a direct overruling of the *Adkins* decision. Nothing was said about *Lochner,* but this time we can be sure, with Taft, that it had been overruled *sub silentio.*

In 1941 the Court upheld the minimum wage and maximum hours regulations of the Fair Labor Standards Act, passed in 1938. The validity of this statute under the commerce clause, as determined in *United States* v. *Darby Lumber Co.* (1941), has already been discussed. Due process objections to the statute were disposed of in one short paragraph which cited *Holden, Muller,* and *Bunting* on hours, and *West Coast Hotel* on wages. The federal act covered men as well as women, so that *West Coast Hotel* was no precedent at all on minimum wages for men. But the sexual distinction, which as late as 1937 had been absolutely vital in establishing constitutional power, was by 1941 completely unimportant to the Court.

In *Federal Power Commission* v. *Hope Natural Gas Co.* (1944) the Court definitely repudiated the judicial control over rate making which it had assumed in *Smyth* v. *Ames.* The *Adair* and *Coppage* doctrine on labor organization was gradually outflanked, but the two decisions were not specifically repudiated until 1949 in *Lincoln Federal Labor Union* v. *Northwestern Iron & Metal Co.* Involved were a North Carolina statute and a Nebraska constitutional amendment outlawing the closed shop. No person was to be denied an opportunity to work in the two states either because he was or because he was not a member of a labor organization. The Supreme Court unanimously upheld these laws against free speech, equal protection, and due process charges.

It is not the mere reversal of position in these economic due process cases which is surprising. That was bound to happen. The Court could not continue to live in the nineteenth century. But the Court did not merely retreat to the test of reasonableness which it employed in *Jacobson* v. *Massachusetts.* As Robert McCloskey so well pointed out, the Court appeared to say that it would no longer subject economic legislation to *any* constitutional test.[45] It would abandon any responsibility for reviewing legislative decisions on economic problems and, returning to the spirit of *Munn,* tell plaintiffs to carry their objections to the legislature, not the courts.

Thus in *Olsen* v. *Nebraska* Justice Douglas for a unanimous Court stated that differences of opinion on the needfulness or appropriateness of a law "suggest a choice which 'should be left where . . . it was left by the Constitution—to the states and to Congress.' " Again, *Day-Brite Lighting* v. *Missouri* (1952) involved a state law which provided that employees could absent themselves from their jobs for four hours on election days, and forbade employers to deduct wages for their absence. The Court majority admitted that the social policy embodied in the law was debatable, but said: "Our recent decisions make plain that we do not sit as a superlegislature to weigh the wisdom of legislation nor to decide whether the policy it expresses offends the public welfare."[46]

[45] "Economic Due Process and the Supreme Court," in Philip B. Kurland (ed.), *The Supreme Court Review: 1962* (Chicago: The University of Chicago Press, 1962), pp. 34–62.

[46] *Dean* v. *Gadsden Times Publishing Corp.* (1973) upheld up a state law requiring employers to compensate employees when absent on jury duty, the Court saying: "If our recent cases mean anything,

Williamson v. *Lee Optical of Oklahoma* (1955) asked the Court to review a statute which was the product of an interest group struggle in the Oklahoma legislature, and represented a victory for the ophthalmologists and optometrists of the state over the opticians. It forbade any person not in the first two categories from fitting lenses to the face or duplicating or replacing lenses into frames, except on the prescription of an ophthalmologist or optometrist.

The trial court held that there was no sound health or welfare reason why opticians should not be able to fit old glasses into new frames or to duplicate lenses without a prescription. The Supreme Court agreed that this might be "a needless, wasteful requirement in many cases," but said:

> It is for the legislature, not the courts, to balance the advantages and disadvantages of the new requirement. . . . The day is gone when this Court uses the Due Process Clause of the Fourteenth Amendment to strike down state laws, regulatory of business and industrial conditions, because they may be unwise, improvident, or out of harmony with a particular school of thought.

Finally, in *Ferguson* v. *Skrupa* (1963) the Court upheld a Kansas statute prohibiting anyone except lawyers from engaging in the business of "debt adjustment," overruling *Adams* v. *Tanner* (1917) in the process. Black, condemning again the *Lochner-Coppage-Adkins-Burns* line of cases, repeated that "it is up to legislatures, not courts, to decide on the wisdom and utility of legislation." Justice Harlan registered the sole protest against judicial abdication; insisting that the Court could not shirk the responsibility to judge even in this field, he assumed that task and concurred in upholding the statute as bearing "a rational relation to a constitutionally permissible objective."

But McCloskey's question remains a good one. Why is "liberty of economic choice . . . less indispensable to the 'openness' of a society than freedom of expression?" Why should the Court give legislatures unreviewable power in the field of economic legislation, refusing to subject it even to the time-honored test of rationality? Even for a Court convinced that personal rights are on a higher plane than property rights, how clear is it that these are actually distinguishable categories?

In *Barsky* v. *Board of Regents* (1954), a New York physician who had organized a committee to aid refugees in the Spanish civil war refused to give his committee's records to the House Committee on Un-American Activities and was convicted of contempt. His license to practice medicine was then revoked because of his criminal record. The Court majority upheld this action as within the state's legitimate power to regulate professions and businesses, but it was too much for Black and Douglas. The latter said: "the right to work, I had assumed, was the most precious liberty that man possesses. Man has indeed as much right to work as he has to live, to be free, to own property." In a 1957 bar-admission case, Black declared for the Court that

---

they leave debatable issues as respects business, economic, and social affairs to legislative decision. We could strike down this law only if we returned to the philosophy of the *Lochner, Coppage,* and *Adkins* cases." See also *New Orleans* v. *Dukes* (1976).

state-imposed qualifications "must have a rational connection with the applicant's fitness or capacity" to practice the profession.[47]

It is significant that Justice Douglas, having read the Court out of the picture in *Olsen* v. *Nebraska, Day-Brite Lighting* v. *Missouri,* and *Williamson* v. *Lee Optical,* found it necessary to read it at least partially back in again in *Poe* v. *Ullman* (1961):

> The error of the old Court, as I see it, was not in entertaining inquiries concerning the constitutionality of social legislation but in applying the standards that it did. . . . Social legislation dealing with business and economic matters touches no particularized prohibition of the Constitution, unless it be the provision of the Fifth Amendment that private property should not be taken for public use without just compensation. If it is free of the latter guarantee, it has a wide scope for application. Some go so far as to suggest that whatever the majority in the legislature says goes . . . that there is no other standard of constitutionality. That reduces the legislative power to sheer voting strength and the judicial function to a matter of statistics. . . . While the legislative judgment on economic and business matters is "well-nigh conclusive," . . . it is not beyond judicial inquiry.

In the following chapter we will see how "judicial inquiry" has inevitably led even a "strict constructionist" Court back into the activist tradition of the substantive due process philosophy.[48]

---

[47] *Schware* v. *New Mexico Board of Bar Examiners* (1957).

[48] See Richard Funston, "The Double Standard of Constitutional Protection in the Era of the Welfare State," 90 POLITICAL SCIENCE QUARTERLY 261 (1975).

The New Due Process– Equal Protection

Due process and equal protection, discussed in the two preceding chapters, rank along with the First Amendment as the most fundamental tenets of the American Constitution. They outrank the First Amendment in breadth and expansive capability. Racial equality is only the most obvious of the demands of the equal protection clause, and freedom of contract, though the first to be discovered by the Supreme Court, is only one of the many substantive meanings that can be read into the due process clause.

The due process and equal protection concepts are closely related. We have already seen that in the District of Columbia school segregation case, *Bolling* v. *Sharpe,* where the Fifth Amendment rather than the Fourteenth applied, the Court held that due process performed the same function in the District that equal protection did in the states. For Justice Jackson the difference between the two standards was largely a matter of tactics.

The burden should rest heavily upon one who would persuade us to use the due process clause to strike down a substantive law or ordinance. Even its prudent use . . . frequently disables all government . . . from dealing with the conduct in question . . . leav[ing] ungoverned and ungovernable conduct which many people find objectionable. Invocation of the equal protection clause, on the other hand, does not disable any governmental body from dealing with the subject at hand. It merely means that the prohibition or regulation must have a broader impact. I regard it as a salutary doctrine that cities, states and the Federal Government must exercise their powers so as not to discriminate between their inhabitants, except upon some reasonable differentiation fairly related to the object of regulation. . . . There is no more effective practical guaranty against arbitrary and unreasonable government than to require that the principles of law which officials would impose upon a minority must be imposed generally.[1]

Following the adoption of the Fourteenth Amendment, it did not take the Supreme Court long to realize the expansionist potentialities in the concepts of equal protection and due process. In 1873 Justice Miller supposed in the *Slaughter-House Cases* that the equal protection clause would never be used except in racial discrimination situations, yet for over half a century it was corporations that were the principal beneficiaries of this standard. The development of the due process clause was even more portentous. As a limit on substantive legislation, it developed into a freewheeling, open-ended doctrine which judges used to "circumscribe legislative choices in the name of newly articulated values that lacked clear support in constitutional text and history."[2]

The bad reputation that substantive due process earned was due to the unwise uses to which this creative judicial urge was put in the first third of the twentieth century. Only the fundamentalist Hugo Black really believed that all the values which American society needed were clearly articulated in the constitutional document. With few exceptions American judges have been convinced that the judicial role is not only interpretation but also extrapolation, not only discovery but also invention. The battle of strict construction was fought and lost in *McCulloch* v. *Maryland* (1819).

The battle for judicial activism was fought and won even earlier, in *Marbury* v. *Madison* (1803). Perhaps the best modern defense of the activist role is to be found in Justice Stone's famous *Carolene Products Co.* footnote, quoted in Chapter 19, which defined three situations in which judges should curb their normal deference toward legislatures and subject legislative action to a "more searching judicial inquiry." Those three situations, it will be recalled, were (1) when legislation appears on its face to violate a specific prohibition of the Constitution, such as those of the Bill of Rights; (2) where legislation restricts those political processess that ordinarily can be relied on to prevent undesirable legislation; and (3) where "prejudice against discrete and insular minorities . . . tends seriously to curtail the operation of those political processes ordinarily to be relied upon to protect minorities."

We have already seen how Stone's prescription for judicial positivism fortified the Court for its defense of the First Amendment and the rights of criminal defendants and minorities. But there is lacking in the footnote any suggestion that the Court may need to use its imagination in defense of claims newly achieving legiti-

---

[1] *Railway Express Agency* v. *New York* (1949).
[2] Gerald Gunther, "In Search of Evolving Doctrine on a Changing Court: A Model for a Newer Equal Protection," 86 HARVARD LAW REVIEW 1, 8 (1972).

macy yet lacking support in explicit constitutional language or established constitutional interpretation.

Significantly, Justice Murphy did see this need. When Black was making the literal incorporation argument in his *Adamson* dissent, Murphy, with Rutledge concurring, was careful to reserve the right, not merely to incorporate but, where appropriate, to expand the Bill of Rights. "Occasion may arise where a proceeding falls so far short of conforming to fundamental standards of procedure as to warrant constitutional condemnation in terms of a lack of due process despite the absence of a specific provision in the Bill of Rights," he wrote. In this chapter we deal with significant new personal due process or equal protection rights which the Supreme Court has recognized or is considering for recognition.[3]

FUNDAMENTAL RIGHTS

The idea of "fundamental rights" as a justification for protective judicial activism can be traced to *Skinner* v. *Oklahoma* (1942). The case involved a state habitual-criminal sterilization act, under which persons convicted two or more times of felonies involving moral turpitude could be rendered sexually sterile.

This statute appeared to have constitutional support in *Buck* v. *Bell* (1927), where the Court with only one dissent had upheld a Virginia statute under which persons affected with hereditary insanity, idiocy, imbecility, feeblemindedness, or epilepsy could be subjected to compulsory sexual sterilization. This operation could be performed only on inmates of state institutions, and adequate provisions were made by the statute for notice, hearing, and judicial review before such operations were performed. In this particular case the law was applied to Carrie Buck, a seventeen-year-old "feeble-minded" female inmate of a state institution whose mother was also a "feeble-minded" inmate of the same institution, and who had given birth to an allegedly mentally defective child just before admission to the institution. The contention was that if she were rendered incapable of childbearing, she could be released from the institution and become self-supporting. In the judicial proceedings held to authorize the operation there was presented, in addition to evidence concerning the mental and social status of Carrie Buck, testimony in support of the statute by eugenicists to the effect that feeblemindedness was hereditary and incurable.

Justice Holmes's opinion supporting the sterilization order, and accepting without question the scientific justification for the statute, was very brief. This is the heart of it.

---

[3] See generally Gunther, *supra* note 2; Wallace Mendelson, "From Warren to Burger: The Rise and Decline of Substantive Equal Protection," 66 AMERICAN POLITICAL SCIENCE REVIEW 1226 (1972); Laurence H. Tribe, "Toward a Model of Roles in the Due Process of Life and Law," 87 HARVARD LAW REVIEW 1 (1973); Richard Fielding, "Fundamental Personal Rights: Another Approach to Equal Protection," 40 UNIVERSITY OF CHICAGO LAW REVIEW 807 (1973); Henry P. Monaghan, "Foreword: Constitutional Common Law," 89 *Harvard Law Review* 1 (1975).

We have seen more than once that the public welfare may call upon the best citizens for their lives. It would be strange if it could not call upon those who already sap the strength of the State for these lesser sacrifices, often not felt to be such by those concerned, in order to prevent our being swamped with incompetence. It is better for all the world, if instead of waiting to execute degenerate offspring for crime, or to let them starve for their imbecility, society can prevent those who are manifestly unfit from continuing their kind. The principle that sustains compulsory vaccination is broad enough to cover cutting the Fallopian tubes. . . . Three generations of imbeciles are enough.

Seldom has so much questionable doctrine been compressed into five sentences of a Supreme Court opinion. The first two sentences state a completely unacceptable standard for measuring legislative action. If it were true that, because the state can demand the supreme sacrifice of life itself, it is thereby justified in demanding any lesser sacrifice, then every constitutional protection could be disregarded at will. Because the government can require a man to lay down his life in battle, it does not follow that he can be deprived of freedom of speech or the right to trial by jury. Moreover, it is a rather perverse view which sees the *Jacobson* decision as a precedent broad enough to cover Carrie Buck. As Walter Berns has said: "It is a broad principle indeed that sustains a needle's prick in the arm and an abdominal incision, if only in terms of the equipment used. It becomes something else again in terms of the results obtained: no smallpox in the one case and no children in the other."[4]

By 1942 the Court had become aware of the moral shortcomings of *Buck* v. *Bell*. Douglas, writing for the Court in *Skinner*, said: "We are dealing here with legislation which involves one of the basic civil rights of man. Marriage and procreation are fundamental to the very existence and survival of the race." An individual proceeded against under this act "is forever deprived of a basic liberty." Where Douglas invoked equal protection in striking down the act, Stone used due process for the same end. But Jackson more clearly than either based his rejection not on these constitutional provisions but rather on a natural law kind of argument, saying, "There are limits to the extent to which a legislatively represented majority may conduct biological experiments at the expense of the dignity and personality and natural powers of a minority."

The doctrine of the *Skinner* case, then, is that when "fundamental rights" are involved, the judicial task is not simply to presume the validity of legislative interference or to apply the minimal rationality test. It is rather to press that "more searching judicial inquiry" of which Stone spoke, even though it requires constitutional extrapolation. In short, protection of fundamental rights requires the rebirth of substantive due process and the invention of substantive equal protection.

EQUAL PROTECTION: THE OLD AND THE NEW

Equal protection, like substantive due process, was originally employed principally in the service of economic claims.[5] Economic equal protection, however, was never

---

4 "Buck v. Bell: Due Process of Law?" 6 *Western Political Quarterly* 764 (1953).

5 Robert J. Harris reports that, out of 554 decisions of the Supreme Court up to 1960 in which the equal protection clause was involved, 426 (77 percent) dealt with legislation affecting economic interests,

carried to the extremes that characterized economic due process, and it produced no such parade of horribles as the *Lochner-Coppage-Adair* line of due process cases that Black inveighed against so often. The old equal protection presumed the validity of challenged legislation and subjected it to only a minimal test of rationality. Seldom is legislation so irrational that it cannot be justified by some state of facts, real or hypothetical.[6]

The Supreme Court generally understood that legislatures, in dealing with the regulation of economic life, must classify and make distinctions based on differences in degree.[7] The decided cases are full of warnings against judicial interference with legislative classifications. The differences between persons or things on which the classification is based need not be scientific or marked, so long as there are some practical distinctions.[8] A classification must be clearly and actually arbitrary to be held invalid, and not merely possibly so.[9] Every presumption as to facts which could conceivably justify the legislative classification will be assumed.[10] The state may do what it can to prevent what it deems an evil, and stop short of those cases in which the harm to the few concerned is thought less important than the harm to the public that would result if the rules laid down were made mathematically exact.[11] Legislative reform may take one step at a time, addressing itself to the phase of the problem which seems most acute to the legislative mind.[12] The legislature may select one phase of one field and apply a remedy there, neglecting the others.[13]

In spite of the permissive character of the rationality test, economic regulatory statutes were occasionally snagged on the equal protection hook by the pre-New Deal conservative Court.[14] But when the Roosevelt Court took over, equal protection, which Justice Holmes had once referred to as the "usual last refuge of constitutional arguments,"[15] was abandoned almost as completely as substantive due process. No effort was spared to find "rational" justifications for legislative classifications. *Goesaert* v. *Cleary* (1948) upheld a state statute forbidding women to tend bar unless they were wives or daughters of the proprietor. *Railway Express Agency* v. *New York* (1949) approved a city traffic regulation forbidding the carrying of display advertising for hire on the sides of the agency's trucks.

Kotch v. *Board of River Port Pilot Commissioners* (1947) upheld a Louisiana statutory plan of licensing pilots for the port of New Orleans. Members of the licensing board were themselves pilots, and they operated the certification process

---

while only 78 (14 percent) concerned state laws alleged to impose racial discrimination or acts of Congress designed to stop it: *The Quest for Equality* (Baton Rouge, La.: Louisiana State University Press, 1960), p. 59.

[6] For an attack on the entire rationality principle, see "Legislative Purpose, Rationality, and Equal Protection," 82 *Yale Law Journal* 123 (1972).

[7] *Barbier* v. *Connolly* (1885).

[8] *Orient Ins. Co.* v. *Daggs* (1899).

[9] *Bachtel* v. *Wilson* (1907)

[10] *Crescent Cotton Oil Co.* v. *Mississippi* (1921).

[11] *Dominion Hotel* v. *Arizona* (1919).

[12] *Semler* v. *Oregon State Board of Dental Examiners* (1935).

[13] *A.F. of L.* v. *American Sash Co.* (1949).

[14] *Smith* v. *Cahoon* (1931); *Mayflower Farms* v. *Ten Eyck* (1936); *Hartford Steam Boiler Inspection and Ins. Co.* v. *Harrison* (1937).

[15] *Buck* v. *Bell* (1927).

so that only selected relatives and friends of present pilots could secure licenses. Justice Black ruled that the Court should not interfere with "the right and power of a state to select its own agents and officers." In *Williamson* v. *Lee Optical of Oklahoma* (1955), legislative regulation of opticians in fitting and replacing lenses completely exempted sellers of "ready-to-wear" glasses from control. The Court was ready with a supporting hypothesis: "For all this record shows, the ready-to-wear branch of the business may not loom large in Oklahoma or may present problems of regulation distinct from the other branches."

On only one occasion after 1937 did the Court fail to defer to the legislature on an economic classification issue, and that was in *Morey* v. *Doud* (1957), where an Illinois statute had exempted American Express Company money orders from a requirement that any firm issuing money orders in the state must secure a license and submit to state regulation. The state argued that the worldwide operations and unquestioned solvency of this company made the exemption reasonable, but the Court disagreed.

In contrast to the permissiveness of the old equal protection, the new equal protection imposes much more rigorous tests on legislative classifications in those areas where fundamental rights are involved. Rationality is no longer enough. As in the new due process, a compelling state interest must be established by rigid scrutiny to justify a challenged classification affecting fundamental rights. Moreover, certain classifications are "suspect" on their face and almost automatically invalid.

Race was the original suspect classification, but it was explicitly made so by the Fifteenth Amendment and implicitly by the Fourteenth Amendment. Classifications based on national origin were added by *Korematsu* v. *United States* (1944), where Black wrote that "all legal restrictions which curtail the civil rights of a single racial group are immediately suspect."[16]

Aliens, as the Supreme Court said in *Graham* v. *Richardson* (1971), "are a prime example of a 'discrete and insular' minority . . . for whom . . . heightened judicial solicitude is appropriate." Thus in *Takahashi* v. *Fish and Game Commission* (1948), the Court ruled that the power of a state to apply its laws exclusively to its alien inhabitants was confined within narrow limits, and *Graham* held that denial of welfare to lawfully admitted resident aliens was a denial of equal protection.

Voting was accepted as a fundamental right entitled to equal protection in the Reapportionment Cases, and any infringement on the rule of one person, one vote was inherently suspect. The right to travel interstate, as noted in Chapter 5, was confirmed in *Shapiro* v. *Thompson* (1969) without attributing it to any particular constitutional provision.[17] But the new equal protection, along with a revived substantive due process, has been challenging old inequalities in several other areas which require more extended comment.

[16] In this case the Court nevertheless found no ground for challenging executive action in expelling persons of Japanese ancestry from the West Coast after Pearl Harbor. And note that *United States* v. *Martinez-Fuerte* (1976) permitted the Border Patrol to stop autos at fixed checkpoints within California and question occupants, even though those questioned were selected "on the basis of apparent Mexican ancestry."

[17] But *Sosna* v. *Iowa* (1975) upheld a state law requiring residence in the state for one year before beginning divorce proceedings against objections that it interfered with the right to travel.

PRIVACY AND THE ABORTION CASES

The foremost example of the new substantive due process was the Court's pronouncement of privacy as a broad constitutional value in *Griswold* v. *Connecticut* (1965). At issue was a state law forbidding the use of contraceptives or advice as to their use, for violation of which the medical and executive directors of a New Haven planned-parenthood center were convicted. Justice Douglas, speaking for the Court, held that this law interfered with "a right of privacy older than the Bill of Rights." Admittedly this zone of privacy is not specified in the Constitution, but he found it within the "penumbra" of several fundamental constitutional guarantees. There is the right of association in the penumbra of the First Amendment. There is the recognition of the privacy of the home in the Third and Fourth Amendments, as well as the zone of personal privacy derived from the self-incrimination clause of the Fifth Amendment. Finally, there is the Ninth Amendment's warning that the enumeration of certain rights in the Constitution does not mean that there are not others "retained by the people."

Douglas did not go on to the Fourteenth Amendment to invoke the due process clause, presumably because he was sensitive about charges that he would be exhuming substantive due process. Justices Harlan and White, never having rejected substantive due process, had no hesitation in saying that due process was more to the point than vague "penumbras" of the Bill of Rights. For Black also this was substantive due process, and he would have none of it. The Court's reasoning, for him, came straight out of *Lochner* and *Adkins*. This was the same "natural law due process philosophy" which he thought the Court had abandoned and which he charged was "no less dangerous when used to enforce this Court's views about personal rights than those about economic rights." He reiterated his willingness "to hold laws unconstitutional where they are forbidden by the Federal Constitution." But where the Court had no guide as specific as the First Amendment, then he denied that the Court had power "to sit as a supervisory agency over acts of duly constituted legislative bodies and set aside their laws because of the Court's belief that the legislative policies adopted are unreasonable, unwise, arbitrary, capricious or irrational."

Of course Black was right. The Court had created a value out of the whole cloth of the Constitution and used it to superimpose its own views of wise social policy on those of the legislature. It was, as John Hart Ely put it, "Lochnering."[18] But that does not condemn *Griswold*. *Lochner* was bad because it was wrong to conclude that long working hours had no rational relation to health and safety. *Griswold* was right because it struck down a statute which prohibited the use of contraceptives by married couples, a ridiculous law ("uncommonly silly" was Stewart's description) which could have been enforced only by putting policemen in bedrooms. Harlan had condemned the statute four years earlier in his dissent to *Poe* v. *Ullman* (1961) without ever invoking the test of privacy. He held it repugnant to the old *Palko* test, violative of basic values "implicit in the concept of ordered liberty."[19]

---

[18] "The Wages of Crying Wolf," 82 YALE LAW JOURNAL 920, 944 (1973).

[19] In the *Poe* case, an attack on the constitutionality of the Connecticut statute had been rejected by the Court by a five-to-four vote on the ground that the parties bringing the suit lacked standing.

Once enshrined as a constitutional value, privacy demonstrated the power of an idea whose time has come and was freed from any limitations associated with its origin in *Griswold.* The right asserted there was the privacy of married couples in their bedrooms. *Eisenstadt* v. *Baird* (1972) brought to the Court a Massachusetts statute that made it illegal for single persons, but not for married persons, to obtain contraceptives in order to prevent pregnancy. The Court held that the statute was neither a health measure nor intended as a deterrent to premarital sexual relations but simply a prohibition on contraception resting on a moral judgment. So considered, it was unnecessary for the Court to invoke due process. It was a violation of equal protection for the state "to legislate that different treatment be accorded to persons placed by a statute into different classes on the basis of criteria wholly unrelated to the objective of the statute." Brennan continued: "If the right of privacy means anything, it is the right of the *individual,* married or single, to be free from unwarranted governmental intrusion into matters so fundamentally affecting a person as the decision whether to bear or beget a child."

Eisenstadt provided the momentum for the abortion decisions in the following year.[20] *Roe* v. *Wade* (1973) held unconstitutional a strict Texas criminal statute which prohibited abortions at any stage of pregnancy except to save the life of the mother. *Doe* v. *Bolton* (1973) similarly condemned a Georgia statute that required abortions to be conducted in hospitals, required the interposition of a hospital abortion committee and confirmation by other physicians, and limited abortions to Georgia residents. The opinions in both cases were written by Justice Blackmun, who prior to appointment to the Supreme Court had been a member of the board of the Mayo Clinic, and he prefaced his discussion of the constitutional issues with a "history of abortion, for such insight as that history may afford us."

Blackmun's constitutional position was that the right of privacy, whether a Fourteenth Amendment due process right (as he contended) or a right reserved to the people by the Ninth Amendment, was "broad enough to encompass a woman's decision whether or not to terminate her pregnancy." But this is not an absolute right; Blackmun cited *Jacobson* v. *Massachusetts* (1905) to reject the position "that one has an unlimited right to do with one's body as one pleases." It is, however, a "fundamental" right, and consequently its regulation can be justified only by a compelling state interest, and through legislation "narrowly drawn to express only the legitimate state interests at stake."

Texas contended that safeguarding the life of the unborn child was such a compelling state interest, but Blackmun held that a fetus is not a person whose right to life is guaranteed by the Fourteenth Amendment and that the state, by adopting the position that a fetus is a living person, cannot override the rights of the pregnant woman. He did concede that the state had two legitimate interests justifying intervention—to preserve and protect the health of the pregnant woman and to protect

    [20] For comments and critique, see Harry H. Wellington, "Common Law Rules and Constitutional Double Standards," 83 YALE LAW JOURNAL 221 (1973); Richard A. Epstein, "Substantive Due Process by Any Other Name: The Abortion Cases," in Philip B. Kurland (ed.), *The Supreme Court Review: 1973* (Chicago: University of Chicago Press, 1973), pp. 159–186; Ely, *supra* note 18.

the *potentiality* of human life. Each of these interests "grows in substantiality as the woman approaches term and, at a point during pregnancy, each becomes 'compelling.'"

This stress on time sequence was essential to Blackmun's solution of the constitutional problem of state interest. For the first trimester of pregnancy, during which mortality in abortion is less than mortality in normal childbirth, state interest is minimal, and the abortion decision and its effectuation must be left to the woman and her physician, free from interference by the state. Following the third month, the state may regulate the abortion procedure to the extent reasonably necessary to the preservation and protection of maternal health, including such matters as the qualification and licensing of the person performing the abortion and the facility in which it is performed. Finally, after the fetus becomes viable, roughly at the end of the second trimester, the state interest in protecting life may go so far as to proscribe abortion except when necessary to preserve the life and health of the mother.

Justice Stewart, concurring, wanted it clearly understood that *Roe* was a substantive due process decision, despite the fact that obsequies had been conducted so often for substantive due process, most recently in *Ferguson* v. *Skrupa* (1963). Justice Rehnquist, dissenting, also wanted it understood that this was substantive due process in the *Lochner* tradition of passing on the wisdom of legislative policies and that breaking up pregnancies into three trimesters with varying permissible restrictions was pure "judicial legislation." White also dissented.[21]

Privacy as a constitutional value, of course, extends far beyond the abortion issue, and beyond the possibility of adequate discussion here.[22] Douglas's concurring opinion in *Doe* v. *Bolton* seemed to equate the right of privacy with a right of personal autonomy, including "control over the development and expression of one's intellect, interests, tastes, and personality." Some lower courts have interpreted the right of privacy recognized in *Griswold* as extending to any kind of private sexual activity between consenting adults,[23] but the Supreme Court rejected this contention in *Doe* v. *Commonwealth's Attorney* (1976), by affirming without opinion a lower court ruling upholding a Virginia law prohibiting consensual sodomy.

A principal privacy concern has been the collection of personal information by credit agencies, the police, and various government agencies and its instant availability and potential misuse through storage in computers and data banks.[24] The Fair Credit Reporting Act of 1971 took a first step toward assuring the accuracy and

---

[21] The abortion decisions aroused tremendous opposition, particularly among Catholics, and various "right to life" constitutional amendments were proposed in Congress. In *Planned Parenthood of Central Missouri* v. *Danforth* (1976) the Court ruled that states could not force a married woman to obtain her husband's consent before securing an abortion, and that parents could not exercise an absolute veto over abortions for unmarried daughters under 18. A Massachusetts parental consent statute was referred back to the state courts for interpretation; *Bellotti* v. *Baird* (1976). The Court declined review in *Greco* v. *Orange Memorial Hospital Corp.* (1975) and *Taylor* v. *St. Vincent's Hospital* (1976).

[22] See generally Alan F. Westin, *Privacy and Freedom* (New York: Atheneum Publishers, 1967).

[23] "The Constitutionality of Laws Forbidding Private Homosexual Conduct," 72 MICHIGAN LAW REVIEW 1616 (1974).

[24] Arthur R. Miller, *The Assault on Privacy: Computers, Data Banks, and Dossiers* (Ann Arbor, Mich.: University of Michigan Press, 1971).

limiting the use of credit reports.[25] The Privacy Act of 1974 permitted individuals to inspect information about themselves contained in government agency files and to challenge or correct the material.

The misnamed Bank Secrecy Act of 1970 actually authorizes the invasion of privacy of bank customers by the government. Enacted because of the difficulty of securing foreign and domestic bank records of customers suspected of illegal activities, the act required banks to make microfilm copies of checks and to report currency transactions over $5,000 into or out of the country. The Court upheld this statute and the administrative regulations issued under it in *California Bankers Association* v. *Shultz* (1974), a case which saw an unusual joinder of bankers and the American Civil Liberties Union in an unsuccessful defense of privacy.[26]

The Supreme Court also denied a privacy claim in *Paul* v. *Davis* (1976), ruling against a claimant in a civil rights damage suit who had been listed by the Louisville police as an "active shoplifter" in a flyer distributed to city merchants. In fact he had been arrested once for shoplifting, but was never tried and the charges were dropped. The Court held that there is no constitutionally guaranteed right to a good reputation, and so no basis for a federal civil rights damage suit. The police had not invaded any area traditionally regarded as private, said Justice Rehnquist, such as "matters related to marriage, procreation, contraception, family relationships and child rearing and education." The due process clause protected only liberty and property, not reputation and good name.

WEALTH AS A SUSPECT CLASSIFICATION

The general rule in capitalist society is that access to goods and services is controlled by the market. Ability to pay, not need, is the criterion. One gets what one can afford to purchase. But even Adam Smith conceded that certain services must be supplied by the community without being rationed through the market, and the modern welfare state has accepted in greater or lesser degree the theory of "just wants"—namely, that certain commodities are so basic that a just society must ensure them to each of its members regardless of their ability to pay for them. Decisions as to what will be recognized as "just wants" are among the most difficult policy choices on the current political agenda and are essentially legislative. However, the equal protection clause justifies judicial participation in this process.[27]

We have already seen in Chapter 26 what steps the Supreme Court has taken in attempting to ensure that justice will not be denied in the courts for those unable to pay for it. Black's eloquent opinion in *Griffin* v. *Illinois* (1956) said: "In criminal

---

[25] "Protecting the Subjects of Credit Reports." 81 YALE LAW JOURNAL 1035 (1971).

[26] "Government Access to Bank Records," 83 YALE LAW JOURNAL 1439 (1974). In *United States* v. *Bisceglia* (1975), the Court upheld the power of the Internal Revenue Service to use a "John Doe" civil summons to obtain from a bank general records which the IRS believed might lead to the identity of a person who had not paid proper federal taxes. See also *United States* v. *Miller* (1976).

[27] See Frank I. Michelman, "On Protecting the Poor through the Fourteenth Amendment," 83 HARVARD LAW REVIEW 7 (1969); Ralph K. Winter, Jr., "Poverty, Economic Equality, and the Equal Protection Clause," in Philip B. Kurland (ed.), *The Supreme Court Review: 1972* (Chicago: University of Chicago Press, 1972), pp. 41–102.

trials a State can no more discriminate on account of poverty than on account of religion, race, or color." While no one would contend that money has been neutralized so far as court access and representation are concerned, substantial progress has been made through public defenders' offices, public interest law firms, and the federal legal services corporation.[28]

As we shall see in Chapter 30, the Court has endeavored to prevent wealth from being a factor in terms of access to the ballot. In the poll tax case, *Harper* v. *Virginia State Board of Elections* (1966), Douglas wrote, "Voter qualifications have no relation to wealth nor to paying or not paying this or any other tax." Candidates' filing fees, Burger held in *Bullock* v. *Carter* (1972), could not be judged on the basis of the old rationality test; under the *Harper* doctrine they must be "closely scrutinized" and sustained only if necessary to accomplish a legitimate state objective.

If access to the courts and to the ballot are fundamental rights, limitations on which are subject to rigid scrutiny and the compelling state interest test, why is not access to equal public education a fundamental right? This issue came to the Court in *San Antonio Independent School District* v. *Rodriguez* (1973). With the exception of Hawaii, public schools in all states have been financed primarily by the local property tax, though state and federal contributions are increasing. The result is that the level of school finance varies greatly, depending upon the property tax base in the school district. This issue had been taken to the California supreme court in 1971, in the case of *Serrano* v. *Priest,* and by a vote of six to one that court had ruled that education was a fundamental interest and that discrimination in financing education on the basis of school district wealth was a violation of equal protection.[29]

The U.S. Supreme Court rejected this reasoning. Justice Powell's opinion held, first, that education, no matter how important, is not a fundamental constitutional right.

> It is not the province of this Court to create substantive constitutional rights in the name of guaranteeing equal protection of the laws. Thus the key to discovering whether education is "fundamental" is not to be found in comparisons of the relative societal significance of education as opposed to subsistence or housing. . . . Rather, the answer lies in assessing whether there is a right to education explicitly or implicitly guaranteed by the Constitution.

The second issue was whether the property tax system of financing public education operated to the disadvantage of some suspect class. Powell held that it did not. There was here no identifiable class of disadvantaged "poor," no "indigents" as in the criminal justice cases. In fact, it was not even evident that the poorest people necessarily clustered in the poorest property districts. Often the poor lived around commercial and industrial areas which provided substantial property tax income for

---

[28] See "The New Public Interest Lawyers," 79 YALE LAW JOURNAL 1069 (1970).

[29] The issues are discussed in David A. J. Richards, "Equal Opportunity and School Financing," 41 UNIVERSITY OF CHICAGO LAW REVIEW 32 (1973); Robert L. Graham and Jason H. Kravitt, "The Evolution of Equal Protection—Education, Municipal Services, and Wealth," 7 HARVARD CIVIL RIGHTS–CIVIL LIBERTIES LAW REVIEW 105 (1972); "Educational Financing, Equal Protection of the Laws, and the Supreme Court," 70 MICHIGAN LAW REVIEW 1324 (1972).

schools. Moreover, any discrimination which there might be against the poor was relative, not absolute. No one was being denied public education; the charge was simply that poor school districts were supplying a poorer quality of education, and Powell did not think that the equal protection clause required "absolute equality or precisely equal advantages."

Rodriguez was a five to four decision, with White, Douglas, Brennan, and Marshall dissenting. White held that the Texas statutory scheme was devoid of a rational basis. Both Brennan and Marshall protested Powell's assertion that the only fundamental rights were those explicitly or implicitly guaranteed in the Constitution. Where, said Marshall, does the Constitution "guarantee the right to procreate . . . or the right to vote in state elections . . . or the right to appeal from a criminal conviction," all of which the Court had previously held to be fundamental rights? Marshall also rejected the defense that mere inequality of education would not deny equal protection so long as there was not complete denial of education.

The reluctance of the Court to order a new basis for school finance is an indication of the limited area within which judges are likely to move in alleviating societal inequalities based on wealth. Substantial reforms in the system of distributive justice are obviously beyond the power of the courts to effect. Justice Harlan did not think it was a task for judges even to open up access for indigents to the appeals courts, but his dissent in *Douglas* v. *California* (1963) did accurately suggest the limits on judicial activism in neutralizing the consequences of poverty.

> Every financial exaction which the State imposes on a uniform basis is more easily satisfied by the well-to-do than by the indigent. . . . The Equal Protection Clause does not impose on the States "an affirmative duty to lift the handicaps flowing from differences in economic circumstances." To so construe it would be to read into the Constitution a philosophy of leveling that would be foreign to many of our basic concepts of the proper relations between government and society. The State may have a moral obligation to eliminate the evils of poverty, but it is not required by the Equal Protection Clause to give to some whatever others can afford.

SEX AS A SUSPECT CLASSIFICATION

The Supreme Court was very slow in recognizing discrimination based on sex as a constitutional problem. In 1873 the Court upheld an Illinois law denying women the right to practice law, and in 1875 it ruled that women had no constitutional right to vote.[30] Even after the adoption of the Nineteenth Amendment in 1920, it took another fifty years to begin to question whether sex might not be a suspect classification. This was one area where Congress was ahead of the Court. The Equal Pay Act of 1963 added to the Fair Labor Standards Act the principle of equal pay for equal work regardless of sex.[31] Title VII of the Civil Rights Act of 1964 prohibited discrimination on the ground of sex by employers, labor organizations, and employment agencies.

---

[30] *Bradwell* v. *State* (1873); *Minor* v. *Happersett* (1975)
[31] The Equal Pay Act was applied in *Corning Glass Works* v. *Brennan* (1974). The Civil Rights Act was interpreted in *Phillips* v. *Martin Marietta Corp.* (1971).

The Court finally moved in *Reed* v. *Reed* (1971), where it declared unconstitutional an Idaho statute which provided that as between persons equally qualified to administer estates, males must be preferred to females. The Chief Justice did not hold sex to be a suspect classification, however. He applied the rationality test, found that the sex criterion was wholly unrelated to the objective of the statute, and so was an arbitrary legislative choice forbidden by the equal protection clause. A similarly based ruling in *Stanton* v. *Stanton* (1975) held that there was nothing rational in a statute specifying eighteen as the age of majority for females but twenty-one for males.[32]

The issue as to whether sex was a suspect classification was first explicitly discussed in *Frontiero* v. *Richardson* (1973), which grew out of a federal statute denying to male dependents of female members of the Armed Forces the allowances and benefits that would be available to female dependents of male soldiers. Brennan wrote the opinion, and he deduced from the unanimous decision in *Reed* v. *Reed* that the Court had now held that "classifications based on sex, like classifications based upon race, alienage, or national origin, are inherently suspect." But while the Court was unanimous in *Frontiero* in condemning the statute, five justices rejected Brennan's claim that sex was a suspect classification, Powell asserting that it would be "premature" for the Court to take that position while the ratification of the Equal Rights Amendment—which, if adopted, would settle the issue definitively—was pending.

Frontiero was followed by another unanimous decision in *Weinberger* v. *Wiesenfeld* (1975), striking down a provision of the Social Security Act which provided benefits for mothers who survived their husbands but not for surviving fathers. Brennan avoided another debate over the suspect classification issue, merely holding that the statute unjustifiably discriminated against women wage earners required to pay social security taxes by affording them less protection for their survivors than was provided for male wage earners. Equal protection was here derived, it should be noted, from the due process clause of the Fifth Amendment.[33]

Cleveland Board of Education v. *LaFleur* (1974) held unconstitutional mandatory maternity leave regulations which required pregnant teachers to quit their jobs without pay beginning five months before the expected birth. With a sly reference to the singularly inappropriate language of the *Skinner* case about "the basic civil rights of man," Stewart held that these maternity rules violated due process "because of the use of unwarranted conclusive presumptions that seriously burden the exercise of protected constitutional liberty."[34]

That sex was not yet regarded as a suspect classification by the Court majority was made clear in *Kahn* v. *Shevin* (1974), where the Court upheld a Florida law

---

[32] As already noted, *Taylor* v. *Louisiana* (1975) held that a separate classification of women in relation to jury service violated the Sixth Amendment. See also *Stanley* v. *Illinois* (1972).

[33] See Julius G. Getman, "The Emerging Constitutional Principle of Sexual Equality," in Philip B. Kurland (ed.), *The Supreme Court Review: 1972* (Chicago: University of Chicago Press, 1972), pp. 157–180.

[34] Similarly, *Turner* v. *Department of Employment Security* (1975) struck down a Utah law automatically denying unemployment compensation to pregnant women for twelve weeks before childbirth and six weeks after.

granting widows, but not widowers, an annual $500 property tax exemption. Unlike *Frontiero,* Douglas found here a legitimate legislative purpose of "cushioning the financial impact of spousal loss upon the sex for whom that loss imposes a dispro-portionately heavy burden." Brennan, one of three dissenters, held that equal pro-tection had been denied because the state had not shown the goal could not be achieved by a more precisely tailored statute or less drastic means.[35]

WELFARE AND MEDICAL CARE AS FUNDAMENTAL RIGHTS

Welfare and medical care are among the newest claimants for the status of funda-mental rights and rigid judicial scrutiny. In *Shapiro* v. *Thompson,* as we know, it was the right to interstate travel, not the right to welfare, that was upheld by the Court. When the welfare issue was presented directly, in *Dandridge* v. *Williams* (1970), the fundamental right claim was denied. Maryland had placed an absolute limit of $250 per month on the amount of a grant under the aid to dependent children social security program, regardless of family size or actual need. For the six-judge majori-ty, Stewart held that this was a "regulation in the social and economic field, not affecting freedoms guaranteed by the Bill of Rights" and consequently subject to review under the old equal protection standard of rationality. He confessed that public welfare assistance, involving "the most basic economic needs of impover-ished human beings," was hardly comparable to the regulations of business and industry for which the test of minimal rationality had been developed. But this "dramatically real factual difference" justified no difference in constitutional stan-dards. The Court would not second-guess state views of wise social or economic policy.

Marshall, dissenting along with Douglas and Brennan, vehemently protested this emasculation of equal protection in the area of social welfare administration on the theory that it was economic policy that was involved. "Appellees are not a gas company or an optical dispenser; they are needy dependent children" who are discriminated against by the state "on the wholly arbitrary basis that they happen to be members of large families."[36]

---

[35] *Geduldig* v. *Aiello* (1974) upheld a California disability insurance system supplementary to workmen's compensation which excluded from its coverage certain disabilities resulting from pregnancy. The Court held that this legislative classification rationally promoted legitimate state interests in keeping the costs of the wholly contributory program as low as possible, but Brennan felt that *Reed* and *Frontiero* mandated a stricter standard of scrutiny.

Schlesinger v. *Ballard* (1975) likewise upheld a gender-based distinction. Male commissioned offi-cers in the Navy, if not promoted after nine years of active service, are subject to mandatory discharge, but female officers are allowed thirteen years. This discrimination was upheld as rational by a vote of five to four, on the ground that female officers are barred from combat and most sea duty and so require a longer period to demonstrate their proficiency. Brennan, dissenting, returned again to his claim that sex was a suspect classification and held that this discrimination served no compelling interest.

[36] In his dissent Marshall expressed dissatisfaction with "the abstract dichotomy between two dif-ferent approaches to equal protection problems which have been utilized by this Court." *Dandridge,* he felt, defied easy characterization either under the old "mere rationality" test (which the majority insisted on using) or the "fundamental right–compelling interest" test of the new equal protection. He wanted to break out of this dichotomy and concentrate "upon the character of the classification in question, the relative importance to individuals in the class discriminated against of the governmental benefits which

Subsequent decisions confirmed that the Court would apply the old equal protection rule in the welfare field. *Richardson* v. *Belcher* (1971) upheld, as rationally based and free from invidious discrimination, the federal law which reduced social security payments to reflect workmen's compensation awards. In *Jefferson* v. *Hackney* (1972), Texas, unable to fund all its welfare programs completely, placed a limit of 75 percent of the standard of need on recipients of aid to dependent children grants, who were 87 percent blacks and Chicanos, while funding aid to the aged and the blind, who were predominantly white, at 100 percent and 95 percent. The Court said it would not accept "naked statistical arguments" as proving racial discrimination, and there was no constitutional requirement that each relief category be treated exactly alike.[37]

United States Department of Agriculture v. *Moreno* (1973) dealt with a provision of the Federal Food Stamp Act that limited food stamps to related people living in one household. The Court held that the distinction between related and unrelated households (which was aimed at "hippie communes") was invalid under traditional equal protection analysis, though Douglas spoke of failure to demonstrate a "compelling interest."

Medical care received a certain amount of recognition as a constitutional right in *Memorial Hospital* v. *Maricopa County* (1974). An Arizona statute required one year's residence in a county as a condition to receiving nonemergency hospitalization or medical care at county expense. The Court, invoking the *Shapiro* ruling, held that this durational residency requirement was an invidious classification impinging on the right of interstate travel. Douglas thought the issue was invidious discrimination against the poor, not the right to travel interstate.

HOUSING, EXCLUSIONARY ZONING, AND NO-GROWTH

The Supreme Court's two most important housing decisions, *Reitman* v. *Mulkey* (1967) and *Jones* v. *Alfred H. Mayer Co.* (1968), have already been discussed in Chapter 27; both grew out of racial discrimination. *Hunter* v. *Erickson* (1969), involving a requirement that any city ordinance regulating real estate on the basis of race, religion, or national origin must be approved in a city referendum, was also invalidated as based on a racial classification. *Hills* v. *Gautreaux* (1976) ordered the government to subsidize low-income housing in white Chicago suburbs to relieve racial segregation in inner-city public housing, thereby promoting a metropolitan area approach to housing desegregation which *Milliken* v. *Bradley* (1974) had denied for school desegregation.

Without a racial component, the Court found no basis for applying the new equal protection to housing legislation. In *James* v. *Valtierra* (1971), a California

---

they do not receive, and the asserted state interests in support of the classification." Using this realistic analysis rather than the formalism of the two-tiered approach, the issue in *Dandridge* would be seen as "support to needy dependent children provid[ing] the stuff which sustains those children's lives: food, clothing, shelter." Marshall repeated this position in *San Antonio Independent School District* v. *Rodriguez* and is supported in "The Supreme Court, 1972 Term," 87 HARVARD LAW REVIEW 56, 113 (1973).

[37] See also *Weinberger* v. *Salfi* (1975).

constitutional provision required that low-rent housing projects be approved by majority vote in a community election. For a five judge majority, Black accepted this arrangement as conforming with a California tradition of local participation in expenditure decisions.

Housing as a constitutional right was explicitly rejected in *Lindsey* v. *Normet* (1972), which upheld Oregon's judicial procedure for eviction of tenants after non-payment of rent. The appellants argued that the need for decent shelter was a fundamental interest which required the statute to pass the compelling state interest test, but White rejected the contention, saying, "We do not denigrate the importance of decent, safe and sanitary housing. But the Constitution does not provide judicial remedies for every social and economic ill."

The constitutionality of zoning has been accepted ever since *Euclid* v. *Ambler Realty Co.* was decided in 1926, but more recently it has been subject to attack as an exclusionary device for fencing off the suburbs and excluding low-income families and minorities from access to housing and jobs outside the central city ghettoes. Zoning is exclusionary when it seriously impedes or prevents the construction of lower-cost housing by building codes and lot size or square footage requirements. The legal argument against exclusionary zoning is that, to be a valid use of the police power, zoning must further the general welfare, and that where the effect of zoning laws is to discriminate against a racial minority or the poor, even though the laws may not have been originally discriminatory in motive or purpose, there is a denial of equal protection.[38]

In 1975 the New Jersey supreme court accepted this position in a unanimous decision, barring "the use of the zoning power to advance the parochial interests of the municipality at the expense of the surrounding region and to establish and perpetuate social and economic segregation."[39]

While declining to review the New Jersey decision, the United States Supreme Court had by 1976 taken no clear position against exclusionary zoning. In *Village of Belle Terre* v. *Boraas* (1974), the Court upheld an ordinance of a small village on Long Island which restricted land use to one-family dwellings, excluding lodging houses, fraternity houses, boardinghouses, and communes. Douglas held that the ordinance invaded none of the fundamental rights previously announced by the Court and that the values sought were legitimate. "A quiet place where yards are wide, people few, and motor vehicles restricted are legitimate guidelines in a land use project addressed to family needs."

---

[38] "Exclusionary Zoning and Equal Protection," 84 HARVARD LAW REVIEW 1645 (1971).

[39] *Southern Burlington County N.A.A.C.P.* v. *Township of Mount Laurel* (1975). The Supreme Court denied certiorari in the case for want of jurisdiction; *Township of Mount Laurel* v. *Southern Burlington County N.A.A.C.P.* (1975). The Court also denied review in *Maldini* v. *Ambro* (1975),leaving in effect a ruling by the New York Court of Appeals permitting communities to amend their zoning ordinances to authorize multiple-unit high-density housing for the elderly in areas previously restricted to single-family houses on plots of one acre or more. However, the Court did agree to review *Village of Arlington Heights* v. *Metropolitan Housing Development Corp.* (1975) in which the Court of Appeals for the Seventh Circuit held that an almost 100-percent white Chicago suburb had violated the Fourteenth Amendment when it refused to rezone a parcel of land to allow an integrated low- and moderate-income housing project.

The *Belle Terre* case did not present the exclusionary zoning issue squarely, but *Warth* v. *Seldin* (1975) did. Various organizations and individuals living in the Rochester metropolitan area brought suit against a Rochester suburb, claiming that its zoning regulations excluded persons of low and moderate income from living in the town. By a five to four vote, the Court avoided a decision on the merits by holding that none of the plaintiffs had a sufficiently personalized grievance to give them standing to bring the suit.

The "no-growth" movement of the 1970s led an increasing number of cities to adopt a variety of devices, from explicit population ceilings to limitations on building permits. The purposes stated were usually to prevent overload on public services and the desire to preserve environmental values. Already by 1976, a number of courts had passed on these limits. Perhaps the best-known example came from the city of Petaluma, California, which limited large building projects to 500 new residential units per year, though imposing no limit on the construction of single dwellings. The decision of a federal district court holding the law unconstitutional as infringing the right of interstate travel was reversed in 1975 by the Court of Appeals for the Ninth Circuit, which held: "the concept of the public welfare is sufficiently broad to uphold Petaluma's desire to preserve its small-town character, its open spaces and low density of population, and to grow at an orderly and deliberate pace." The Supreme Court declined to review this decision in 1976.[40] More positive approval for local control over growth was provided in *City of Eastlake* v. *Forest City Enterprises* (1976), where the Court upheld an ordinance requiring approval of land zoning changes by 55 percent of the voters in a referendum.

ILLEGITIMACY

In 1968 the Court began to consider whether state laws discriminating against illegitimate children were subject to the constitutional tests of due process and equal protection. Initially no claim was made that newly discovered "fundamental rights" were at stake or that rigid scrutiny of such laws was demanded. *Levy* v. *Louisiana* (1968) simply applied the old rationality test and concluded that a law denying to illegitimate children the right to recover damages for the wrongful death of their mother, on whom they were dependent, constituted invidious discrimination against them.

Black, Harlan, and Stewart dissented, however, and in the next case, *Labine* v. *Vincent* (1971), Black had the opportunity to implement his long-standing opposition to use of the "vague generalities" of the due process and equal protection clauses to nullify state legislation. The statute involved barred an illegitimate child from sharing equally with legitimates in the estate of their father, who had publicly acknowledged the child but had died without a will. In a bitter dissent, Brennan charged that the decision upholding this result "cannot even pretend to be a principled decision" and that this statute constituted invidious discrimination, supportable only by "moral prejudice."

[40] *Construction Industry Association of Sonoma County* v. *City of Petaluma* (1976). The Court also declined review of two other challenges to zoning regulations from California cities designed to limit growth which had been upheld by the California supreme-court—*San Diego Building Contractors Assn.* v. *City Council of San Diego* (1976) and *Building Assn. of Santa Clara–Santa Cruz Counties* v. *Superior Court of California* (1976).

Surprisingly, the 1972 Court, with Black and Harlan gone, took a much more sympathetic position. *Weber* v. *Aetna Casualty Co.* held that workmen's compensation statutes denying equal recovery rights to dependent, unacknowledged, illegitimate children denied equal protection. Powell now conceded that this was an area of "sensitive and fundamental personal rights" requiring "stricter scrutiny." He found that the statute served "no legitimate state interest, compelling or otherwise," and that it was a discriminatory law "relating to status of birth." Visiting society's condemnation of "irresponsible liaisons beyond the bonds of marriage . . . on the head of an infant is illogical and unjust."[41]

Rehnquist, dissenting in *Weber,* was left as the only defender of the Black-Harlan position against expanding the Fourteenth Amendment by the creation of new fundamental rights. To Powell's condemnation of the Louisiana law as "illogical and unjust," he rejoined: "A fair-minded man might regard it as both, but the Equal Protection Clause of the Fourteenth Amendment requires neither that state enactments be 'logical' nor does it require that they be 'just' in the common meaning of those terms."

It is significant that the Burger Court, no less than the Warren Court, found that "justice" requires the identification of new fundamental rights under the Fourteenth Amendment and their activist judicial defense.[42]

---

[41] *Jiminez* v. *Weinberger* (1974) followed *Weber* in invalidating certain discriminations against illegitimate children under the Social Security Act program of disability insurance benefits. See also *Trimble* v. *Gordon* (1976). But *Mathews* v. *Lucas* (1976) upheld against constitutional challenge the Social Security Act requirement that some illegitimate children must prove their dependence upon their deceased father to obtain survivor's benefits, whereas other children were presumed eligible.

[42] Classifications on the basis of age have also been challenged on equal protection grounds. In *Massachusetts Board of Retirement* v. *Murgia* (1976) the Court upheld a requirement that members of the uniformed branch of the state police must retire at age 50. Age, said the Court, unlike race or national origin, was not a "suspect classification," and so had only to meet the rational basis test. *Cannon* v. *Guste* (1976) upheld a Louisiana law requiring all state employees to retire at age 65. But in *Manson* v. *Edwards* (1972) a federal district court held unconstitutional a Detroit charter provision requiring candidates for the common council to be 25 years of age. However, see *Whitehead* v. *Westbrook* (1976).

Elections and the Franchise

The framers of the Constitution had to deal with the problem of the franchise only in connection with the selection of members of the House of Representatives, since senators were elected by the state legislatures and presidential electors were appointed in such manner as the state legislatures might direct. Eventually the responsibility for electing the President and members of both houses of Congress devolved upon this same national electorate. Although the states have the major responsibility under the Constitution of determing the standards for voting eligibility, in recent years Congress and the Supreme Court have become increasingly involved in regulating electoral processes.[1]

CONSTITUTIONAL FOUNDATION OF THE RIGHT TO VOTE

The basic provision in the Constitution governing the right to vote in federal elections is Article I, section 2, which provides that electors for members of the House in the several states "shall have the qualifications requisite for electors of the most

[1] See generally Richard Claude, *The Supreme Court and the Electoral Process* (Baltimore: The Johns Hopkins Press, 1970); "Developments in the Law—Elections," 88 HARVARD LAW REVIEW 1111–1339 (1975).

numerous branch of the state legislature." By this device the Constitution assured election of the House on a popular base but avoided creation of a national electorate separate from the state electorates, which were defined by legal provisions varying widely from state to state.

Second, there is the "times, places and manner" clause of Article I, section 4. As already noted, Congress first took action under this authority in 1842, when it required that members of the House should be elected by districts rather than on a general state ticket. An act of 1866 regulated the procedure of state legislatures in choosing senators. The first comprehensive federal statute on elections came in 1870, motivated by the political problems of the Reconstruction period. The Enforcement Act of 1870 and subsequent measures made federal offenses of false registration, bribery, voting without legal right, making false returns of votes cast, interference in any manner with officers of elections, or the neglect by any such officer of any duty required of him by state or federal law.

In addition to these two provisions of Article I, five of the amendments to the Constitution have a bearing on elections and the electorate. The equal protection clause of the Fourteenth Amendment has been applied, as we shall see, to forbid discriminatory practices by state election officials. The Fourteenth Amendment also contains the threat of reduction of representation for denial of the right to vote. When it appeared that this provision would not achieve its purpose of securing the suffrage for blacks, the Fifteenth Amendment was adopted in 1870, specifically guaranteeing that "the right of citizens of the United States to vote shall not be denied or abridged by the United States or by any state on account of race, color, or previous condition of servitude." The Nineteenth Amendment, adopted in 1920, uses the same formula to guarantee women the right to vote. The Fourteenth, Fifteenth, and Nineteenth Amendments all authorize Congress to enforce their provisions by appropriate legislation. The Twenty-fourth Amendment, adopted in 1964, provides that the right to vote in a federal election shall not be denied for failure to pay a poll tax or any other tax, and the Twenty-sixth Amendment extends the franchise to eighteen-year-olds.

In spite of the Fifteenth Amendment's use of the phrase "the right to vote," the Supreme Court was at first reluctant to give effect to such a right. Under Article I, section 2, participation in federal elections depends upon state laws prescribing the electorate, and so it is strictly true, as the Supreme Court held in the early case of *Minor* v. *Happersett* (1875), that "the Constitution of the United States does not confer the right of suffrage upon anyone." Mrs. Minor had sought to compel election officials in Missouri, where suffrage was limited to male citizens, to accept her vote on the ground that she had a right to vote as a citizen of the United States under the Fourteenth Amendment, but the Court decisively rejected this contention. The following year the Court took a similarly negative attitude toward the Fifteenth Amendment, contending that it did not confer the right to vote on anyone, but merely "invested the citizens of the United States with a new constitutional right which is . . . exemption from discrimination in the exercise of the elective franchise."[2]

---

[2] *United States* v. *Reese* (1876); *United States* v. *Cruikshank* (1876).

Within a decade, however, the Court had reconsidered this doctrine. *Ex parte Yarbrough* (1884) affirmed the conviction of several Klansmen for conspiring to prevent a black, by intimidation, from voting for a member of Congress. They were held to have violated the Enforcement Act of 1870, which provided punishment in cases of conspiracy to injure or intimidate a citizen in the exercise of any federal right. In spite of *Minor* v. *Happersett,* there was a *right* involved in this case. The earlier decision, explained the Court, merely meant that state law, not the federal Constitution, determined what classes of citizens could exercise the franchise. But once state law had determined who was eligible to vote by statutory provisions covering state elections, then the federal Constitution through Article I, section 2, stepped in to guarantee their *right* to vote for members of Congress.

STATE LIMITATIONS ON THE FRANCHISE

State regulation of the franchise thus proceeds under watchful congressional and constitutional supervision. Of all the state limitations on the franchise, only two have been noncontroversial. All states require that voters be citizens of the United States,[3] and persons who are idiots, insane, or under guardianship are specifically disqualified from voting in almost all states.

Residence

All states require a certain period of residence in the state and locality as a qualification for the franchise. This is understandable for participation in state and local elections, but it is irrelevant in voting for President,[4] and in the Voting Rights Act of 1970 Congress limited voting requirements in presidential elections to a thirty-day registration period.

Extended residence periods to qualify in state and local elections also came into question; in *Dunn* v. *Blumstein* (1972), the Supreme Court held that such requirements were unconstitutional restrictions on the right to vote and travel. Only bona fide residence and a minimal registration period were permissible residence limitations on the franchise, and Marshall suggested that "30 days appears to be an ample period of time for the State to complete whatever administrative tasks are necessary to prevent fraud." Certainly a year, or even three months, was "too much." But *Marston* v. *Lewis* (1973) and *Burns* v. *Fortson* (1973) accepted a fifty-day period.

In *Carrington* v. *Rash* (1965), the Supreme Court ruled that Texas had carried its residence restrictions too far when it provided that any member of the Armed Forces who moved to Texas during the course of his military duty was prohibited from voting in the state so long as he remained in the Armed Forces. The Court agreed that Texas had a right to require that voters be bona fide residents, but anyone who met that test could not be denied opportunity for equal political representation. " 'Fencing out' from the franchise a sector of the population because of the way they may vote is constitutionally impermissible."[5]

---

[3] In the past, however, aliens were permitted to vote in some states. Not until 1928 was there a presidential election in which no alien was eligible to vote.

[4] In 1968 an estimated 5 to 8 million otherwise qualified citizens were unable to vote for President because of durational residence requirements.

[5] *Evans* v. *Cornman* (1970) ruled that Maryland could not deny the right to vote in state elections

Age

In 1943 Georgia broke the traditional voting age barrier of twenty-one, reducing it to eighteen. In the Voting Rights Act of 1970, Congress, influenced by the slogan that if eighteen-year-olds were old enough to be sent to Vietnam they were old enough to vote, set the voting age at eighteen for all federal and state elections. A badly divided Court in *Oregon* v. *Mitchell* (1970) held that, while Congress could fix the voting age in federal elections, the Constitution guaranteed states the right to set voting "qualifications" for state and local elections. The vote on both issues was five to four, with Justice Black in the majority in each holding. Congress immediately adopted the Twenty-sixth Amendment to reverse the Court's ruling as to state and local elections, and it was promptly ratified.

Imprisonment or Conviction for Crime

Thousands of qualified voters are unable to vote at elections because, though they have not been convicted for crime, they are in prison awaiting trial on nonbailable offenses or because they are unable to post bail. They could, of course, vote by absentee ballot if state law so provided. But in *McDonald* v. *Board of Election Commissioners of Chicago* (1969), the Supreme Court held that the failure of Illinois to make such provision did not deny the constitutional right to vote.

It subsequently turned out, however, that this decision did not mean what it seemed to say. In *O'Brien* v. *Skinner* (1974), the Court explained that the *McDonald* decision was based only on deficiencies in the record which had failed to show that appellants were in fact absolutely prohibited from voting by the state. The New York law in *O'Brien* clearly denied absentee ballots or any alternative means of voting, to prisoners awaiting trial, and the Court said that this was a denial of equal protection.

State statutes generally deny the right to vote to persons who have been convicted of felonies, this disqualification continuing after they have served their sentences. The Supreme Court of California held in 1973 that this lifetime exclusion from the franchise served no compelling state interest; but in *Richardson* v. *Ramirez* (1974), the Supreme Court found a justification for the disqualification in the almost forgotten section 2 of the Fourteenth Amendment, which impliedly recognizes the right of states to deny the right to vote "for participation in rebellion or other crime." Rehnquist said that if current views about rehabilitating ex-felons stress their return to society in a fully participating role, this must be a legislative, not a judicial, decision.

The Grandfather Clause

A device for racial discrimination in voting was the so-called "grandfather clause," which the Supreme Court declared unconstitutional in *Guinn* v. *United States* (1915). An Oklahoma law imposed a literacy test for voting but gave exemption for persons whose ancestors had been entitled to vote in 1866. The Court held this provision to be a clear attempt to evade the Fifteenth Amendment. Oklahoma rejoined with a

to residents in a federal enclave, the National Institutes of Health.

new election registration law which permitted a twelve-day registration period but exempted from the registration requirement those who had voted in the 1914 election under the unconstitutional grandfather clause. The Court held this law also invalid in *Lane* v. *Wilson* (1939).

Poll Taxes

Poll (or head) taxes were once a familiar source of revenue but gradually fell into disuse. They were revived around 1900 by a number of states and made a condition of the franchise as a deliberate device to reduce the possibility of black voting. In practice the poll tax was a substantial bar to voting by poor whites as well. While the tax was only about $2, that was a large sum for many, and there was usually a provision that unpaid back taxes had to be paid if a person wanted to start voting. Moreover, the tax requirement was a source of corruption in elections, taxes often being paid by candidates in return for voting support.

On its face, however, the poll tax was not discriminatory, and in *Breedlove* v. *Suttles* (1937) the Supreme Court refused to hold that its use constituted a denial of equal protection or a violation of the Fifteenth Amendment. However, it was gradually abandoned, and by 1960 was maintained by only five states—Alabama, Arkansas, Mississippi, Texas, and Virginia.

Efforts in Congress to abolish the poll tax as a voting requirement date back to the early 1940s. Five times between 1942 and 1949, bills to ban the poll tax by statute passed the House but died in the Senate, three times as a result of Southern filibuster.

There was some uncertainty in Congress as to whether it would require a constitutional amendment rather than a statute to outlaw the poll tax. Finally, in 1962, the Senate acquiesced in an amendment banning the poll tax in federal elections, which was ratified in 1964 as the Twenty-fourth Amendment.

Recognizing that a broadened electorate would threaten its long-established power, the Byrd political organization in Virginia immediately put through the state legislature a law requiring voters in federal elections either to pay a poll tax or to file a certificate of residence at least six months prior to each election. The Supreme Court in *Harman* v. *Forssenius* (1965) held this law unconstitutional as an abridgement of the right to vote, because it imposed a material and burdensome requirement on persons who wished to exercise their constitutional right to vote in federal elections without paying a poll tax.

The poll tax after the Twenty-fourth Amendment remained as a restriction on the franchise in *state* elections in four states, Arkansas having abolished the requirement in 1964. But in 1966 the Supreme Court, in *Harper* v. *Virginia State Board of Elections*, declared the Virginia poll tax unconstitutional as an "invidious discrimination" and a denial of equal protection. "Voter qualifications have no relation to wealth nor to paying or not paying this or any other tax." The right to vote, the Court added, "is too precious, too fundamental to be so burdened or conditioned." The contrary decision in *Breedlove* v. *Suttles* was overruled. Justice Black, dissenting, had no doubt that Congress could have abolished the poll tax in state elections by legislation, but he thought that for the Court to take this step itself on the authority of the Fourteenth Amendment was to resort to natural-law reasoning and to usurp the power of amending the Constitution.

Literacy Tests

In 1960 over twenty states had a literacy requirement for voting. Such a test had been upheld by the Supreme Court in *Guinn* v. *United States* (1915) as so clearly within state power as to require no discussion. The Court unanimously adhered to this view in the North Carolina case of *Lassiter* v. *Northampton County Board of Elections* (1959), Justice Douglas saying: "Illiterate people may be intelligent voters. Yet in our society where newspapers, periodicals, books, and other printed matter canvass and debate campaign issues, a State might conclude that only those who are literate should exercise the franchise."

Though not charged in this case, the Court in *Lassiter* did recognize that a literacy test, fair on its face, might be used for discriminatory purposes. Since there was overwhelming evidence that the test was in fact used for this purpose in some Southern states, the Civil Rights Commission in its 1961 report on voting recommended that literacy be established by a method which would be objective and not subject to manipulation, namely, by accepting attainment of the sixth grade in school as fulfilling the literacy requirement. The New York literacy law had this provision.

A special problem was presented in New York, where the requirement of literacy in English excluded from the franchise those members of the large Puerto Rican community who were literate only in Spanish. This issue was raised in *Cardona* v. *Power* (1966) but was avoided by the Court majority; four justices who did express an opinion on the question were evenly divided as to whether the English requirement was a denial of equal protection to Spanish-speaking citizens.

Interpretation of the Constitution

Particularly in Southern states, literacy tests have been combined with a requirement to understand or interpret provisions of the state or federal constitutions. In *Williams* v. *Mississippi* (1898) the Supreme Court upheld such a law because on its face it did not discriminate against blacks. But a half century later, in *Davis* v. *Schnell* (1949), the Court affirmed a lower court ruling that an Alabama "understand and explain" law was invalid on its face because of its legislative setting and the great discretion it vested in the registrar.

This decision had little impact on the continued widespread use of such requirements for achieving disfranchisement on racial grounds. As concern about the denial of black voting rights escalated in the 1950s, it became increasingly clear that the "understanding" test was one of the principal techniques by which Southern registrars excluded blacks from the franchise. In their completely uncontrolled discretion they gave impossibly hard questions to black registrants and refused them registration because of technical or inconsequential errors.

This account of legal barriers to voting does not suggest adequately the fertility of Southern legislatures in devising additional hurdles for would-be black voters, nor of course does it take into account the use of intimidation and violence to prevent black registration or to punish those who voted or participated in voter-registration campaigns. The Civil Rights Commission summarized the situation in its 1961 voting report by pointing out that in at least one hundred twenty-nine counties in ten Southern states less than 10 percent of eligible blacks were registered. In seventeen representative "black belt" counties where blacks constituted a majority of the population, only about 3 percent were found to be registered.

THE VOTING RIGHTS ACTS

The Civil Rights Acts of 1957 and 1960 were intended to protect black voting rights, but they were largely ineffective. Both placed the burden of correcting voting discrimination on Southern federal district judges, who were usually unsympathetic with this goal. It was clear that further and more drastic federal action would be required if the blockade to black voting were to be broken. This action took the form of the Voting Rights Act of 1965, adopted by Congress under the authority granted by section 2 of the Fifteenth Amendment, to enforce by "appropriate" measures its ban on racial discrimination in voting.[6]

This historic act flatly declared that "no voting qualification or prerequisite to voting" was to be imposed to deny or abridge the right of any citizen to vote on account of race or color. The act concentrated on four types of "tests or devices": (1) literacy and understanding tests; (2) educational achievement or knowledge of any particular subject; (3) good moral character; and (4) proof of qualifications by voucher of registered voters. The use of such tests or devices, which had accounted for the great bulk of "legal" discrimination, was prohibited in any state or political subdivision where less than 50 percent of the persons of voting age were registered on November 1, 1964, or had voted in the presidential election of November, 1964.

The 50 percent test was of course a very rough index of voting discrimination. Its use made the statute applicable to six Southern states—Alabama, Georgia, Louisiana, Mississippi, South Carolina, and Virginia—but also to Alaska, twenty-six counties in North Carolina, and a few other scattered counties. It did not apply to Arkansas, Texas, and Florida, where in some sections there were large black populations but few black voters, because those states did not use literacy tests.

In states and counties covered by the act, voting qualifications of the above four types were suspended, and they could be restored only by a suit brought in the district court of the District of Columbia proving that such tests or devices had not been used for purposes of racial discrimination in the preceding five years.[7] Moreover, such states had to obtain the approval of the Attorney General or the District of Columbia district court before enacting any new voting-qualification laws.[8]

The 1965 statute also provided for appointment by the United States Civil

---

[6] See Charles V. Hamilton, *The Bench and the Ballot: Southern Federal Judges and Black Voters* (New York: Oxford University Press, 1973).

[7] Alaska won exemption from the 1965 act by this procedure in 1966, but a North Carolina county was denied release in *Gaston County* v. *United States* (1969).

[8] This requirement was enforced in *Allen* v. *State Board of Elections* (1969), *Perkins* v. *Matthews* (1971), *Georgia* v. *United States* (1973), and *Connor* v. *Waller* (1975). But see *Beer* v. *United States* (1976).

Service Commission of voting examiners in any political subdivision where the Attorney General certified that they were needed to enforce the Fifteenth Amendment. These examiners were to register all applicants meeting the voting requirements of state law, insofar as these requirements had not been suspended by the statute. The Attorney General acted promptly to place federal examiners in counties with the worst records of discrimination, and within six months the number of blacks registered in Alabama had doubled.

The Supreme Court upheld the constitutionality of the Voting Rights Act in *South Carolina* v. *Katzenbach* (1966). Admittedly the statute amounted to an unprecedented abridgement of the power to set voting qualifications for the states caught by the 50 percent test. They lost the right to enforce registration laws which could still be enforced in all other states. They had to get the consent of the District of Columbia federal court to resume enforcement of suspended statutes, and permission from the Attorney General to adopt new voting-qualification laws.

This was, as the Supreme Court recognized, an "inventive" use of congressional power to enforce the Fifteenth Amendment. But the Court also recognized that the provocation had been great. Congress had tried milder measures, and they had not worked. Now, in the 1965 act, Congress was manifesting a "firm intention" to rid the country of racial discrimination in voting, and the states had only themselves to blame for the drastic remedies adopted.

The Court stated the basic constitutional principle involved in these words: "As against the reserved powers of the States, Congress may use any rational means to effectuate the constitutional prohibition of racial discrimination in voting." The means here employed were rational, the Court held. South Carolina contended that the coverage formula was "awkwardly designed in a number of respects and that it disregards various local conditions which have nothing to do with racial discrimination," but the Court found the formula "rational in both practice and theory." Congress had learned that widespread and persistent discrimination in voting had typically entailed the misuse of tests and devices, and this was the evil for which the new remedies were specifically designed. The Court was unanimous, except that Justice Black regarded the provisions requiring review of state laws by the District of Columbia court and the Attorney General as unconstitutional.

New York was exempt from the effect of the 1965 statute, and consequently its requirement of literacy in English for voting would not have been affected. But at the urging of the state's two senators, Congress inserted a provision prohibiting the states from imposing an English-language literacy test, for the purpose of securing "the rights under the fourteenth amendment of persons educated in American-flag schools in which the predominant classroom language was other than English." Completion of the sixth grade in such a school was to be accepted as meeting the literacy requirement.

While this provision was regarded by many as of dubious constitutionality, the Supreme Court upheld it in *Katzenbach* v. *Morgan* (1966) as appropriate legislation under section 5 of the Fourteenth Amendment to enforce the equal protection clause. By prohibiting New York from denying the franchise to large segments of its

Puerto Rican community, Congress was helping that community gain nondiscriminatory treatment in public services through enhancement of its political power.

The 1965 statute had a dramatic effect. Between 1965 and 1972, black registration in the seven southern states covered by the act increased from 29.3 percent to 56.6 percent, according to the U.S. Civil Rights Commission. The difference between the proportion of white and black voting-age residents registered fell from 44.1 percent to 11.2 percent. There were 1,100 black elected officials in these states by 1974.

The 1965 act had a five-year limitation. It was extended for another five years by the Voting Rights Act of 1970, which made the suspension of literacy tests nationwide[9] and also revised the so-called "triggering" formula to bring more areas under the act's coverage. The statute was again extended in 1975, this time for seven years. The 1975 act made permanent the ban on literacy tests, but its most noteworthy feature was extension to cover areas in twenty-four states where Spanish, Asian languages, and Indian and Alaskan dialects are spoken by large numbers of voters. The act required that bilingual voting information and, in some cases, federal enforcement officers be provided in areas where less than 50 percent of those minorities registered to vote in 1972.

THE CONSTITUTIONAL STATUS OF PRIMARY ELECTIONS

Another device, which was successful for a time in achieving racial discrimination, was to bar blacks from primary elections. The authority of the Constitution and Congress over primaries was thrown into serious doubt by the decision in *Newberry* v. *United States* (1921). In the Corrupt Practices Act of 1910 Congress had restricted campaign expenditures in securing nomination as well as in the election, and Truman H. Newberry was convicted of violating this statute in his successful campaign for a Michigan Senate seat in 1918. The Supreme Court set aside his conviction, five justices holding that when the Constitution referred to election it meant the "final choice of an officer by the duly qualified electors," and that the primary was "in no real sense part of the manner of holding the election."

This ruling was weakened because one of the majority, Justice McKenna, thought that the constitutional situation would be different if Congress had passed the statute in question *after* the adoption of the Seventeenth Amendment providing for the direct election of senators.

In spite of the dubious majority in this case, Congress seemingly accepted this check on its powers and expressly excluded primary elections from the purview of the new Corrupt Practices Act passed in 1925. The Southern states also took the *Newberry* ruling as indicating that no constitutional protections covered primary elections, and so they set about discriminating against black voters in primaries in a perfectly open fashion. In 1923 the Texas Legislature flatly prohibited blacks from

---

[9] The nationwide suspension of literacy tests was upheld in *Oregon* v. *Mitchell* (1970) on the ground that discriminatory use of literacy tests had been nationwide. The Court mentioned as examples discrimination against Puerto Ricans in New York and against Spanish-Americans in Arizona.

voting in that state's Democratic primaries. When this statute was tested in *Nixon* v. *Herndon* (1927), the Supreme Court avoided a reconsideration of the constitutional status of primaries and their relationship to the Fifteenth Amendment. Instead it invalidated the statute on the ground that it was a "direct and obvious infringement" of the equal protection clause in the Fourteenth Amendment.

The Texas Legislature then came back with another law authorizing political parties in the state, through their state executive committees, to prescribe the qualifications for voting in their primaries. The theory of this statute was that what the state could not do directly because of the Fourteenth Amendment, it could authorize political parties to do. The Democratic state executive committee then excluded blacks from primary elections, but in *Nixon* v. *Condon* (1932) the Court held that the party committee had acted as the agent of the state, which made the action equivalent to that by the state itself, and so unconstitutional as an official denial of equal protection.

In neither of these decisions did the Court question the *Newberry* assertion that party primaries were outside the protection of the Constitution; it was only the fact that state legislation was the basis for party action in these cases which made the Fourteenth Amendment applicable. Taking advantage of this situation, the Texas Democratic party convention, immediately after the *Condon* decision, on its own authority and without any state legislation on the subject, adopted a resolution confining party membership to white citizens. By unanimous vote the Court concluded in *Grovey* v. *Townsend* (1935) that this action did not infringe the Fourteenth Amendment because it was taken by the party and not by the state.

The Supreme Court thus endorsed the view that political parties are private clubs uncontrolled by constitutional limitations on official action, and that the primaries they hold are constitutionally no part of the election process. Both of these propositions are so directly contrary to the obvious facts of party operation that they were bound to fall sooner or later of their own weight. The occasion for disposing of the *Newberry* doctrine came in 1941. *United States* v. *Classic* involved a prosecution brought by the Civil Rights Section of the U.S. Department of Justice against election officials in Louisiana who had tampered with the ballots in a primary where candidates for representative in Congress were chosen. The Court pointed out that Louisiana election laws made the primary "an integral part" of the process of electing congressmen, and that in fact the Democratic primary in Louisiana was "the only stage of the election procedure" where the voter's choice was of significance. The Court was thus taking a highly realistic view in its conclusion that the authority given Congress by Article I, section 4, "includes the authority to regulate primary elections when, as in this case, they are a step in the exercise by the people of their choice of representatives in Congress."

The *Classic* opinion did not even mention *Grovey* v. *Townsend,* but it clearly left the private club theory on very shaky legal ground. Consequently a new test case from Texas was begun, which resulted in a direct reversal of the *Grovey* decision by the Court in *Smith* v. *Allwright* (1944). The Court held that after the *Classic* ruling, party primaries could no longer be regarded as private affairs nor the parties conducting them as unaffected with public responsibilities. Noting that parties and party primaries in Texas were in fact regulated at many points by state statutes, the

Court reasoned that a party required to follow these directions was "an agency of the State," and if it practiced discrimination against blacks that was "state action within the meaning of the Fifteenth Amendment."[10]

In *Terry* v. *Adams* (1953) the Court, with only one justice dissenting, applied the principle of *Smith* v. *Allwright* to invalidate the unofficial primaries conducted in a Texas county by the Jaybird party, a Democratic political organization which excluded blacks. The winners in the Jaybird primaries then entered the regular Democratic party primaries, where over a sixty-year period they were never defeated for county office. In fact, other candidates seldom filed. The Court ruled that the "Jaybird primary has become an integral part, indeed the only effective part, of the elective process that determines who shall rule and govern in the county," and consequently that the Fifteenth Amendment was applicable and must be observed.

JUDICIAL SUPERVISION OF ELECTIONS

The Supreme Court's initial position was one of great reluctance to get involved in electoral problems other than those raised by racial discrimination. As we have seen, in the *Newberry* case the Court even denied that primaries were part of the election process, and *Colegrove* v. *Green* warned judges to stay out of the "political thicket" of legislative apportionment.

Party Access to the Ballot

This same attitude governed the Court's reaction in *MacDougall* v. *Green* (1948). An Illinois statute required that for new political parties to nominate candidates for general election, they must submit petitions signed by at least 25,000 qualified voters, including 200 from each of fifty counties. The Court upheld this law, which obviously handicapped political independents and new parties, as justified by a legislative concern "to assure a proper diffusion of political initiative as between . . . thinly populated counties and those having concentrated masses."

But after *Baker* v. *Carr, Harper* v. *Virginia State Board of Elections,* and other decisions of the 1960s, the Court was more willing to accept responsibility for judging the equity of electoral systems. *Moore* v. *Ogilvie* (1969) held the same Illinois statute unconstitutional and the *MacDougall* decision "out of line with our recent apportionment cases." This statutory discrimination against the populous counties in favor of the rural sections was rejected as "hostile to the one man–one vote basis of our representative government."

Laws with the similar purpose of making it difficult for new parties to get on the ballot were in effect in many other states. In spite of these hurdles, the George Wallace American Independent Party succeeded in meeting the requirements in forty-nine states for the 1968 election, but in Ohio it failed to obtain the huge total of 433,100 petition signatures required. Candidates of established parties were not required to secure any petition signatures. In *Williams* v. *Rhodes* (1968), the Court held that imposition of such a heavy and unequal burden on the right to associate and to vote denied equal protection.

[10] See *Rice* v. *Elmore* (1948) for an unsuccessful attempt to evade this ruling.

Ohio then revised its election code, one of the new provisions being a require-ment that political parties file a loyalty oath. The Court in *Socialist Labor Party* v. *Gilligan* (1972) dismissed the case on the ground that the minor party involved had not yet suffered any injury, though Douglas, dissenting, thought the statute was "plainly unconstitutional." The Court did reach that conclusion unanimously in *Communist Party of Indiana* v. *Whitcomb* (1974) in a strong freedom of association defense by Justice Brennan, but the four Nixon appointees concurred only because the two major parties had been certified without filing the oath.

In *American Party of Texas* v. *White* (1974), the Court upheld requirements that minor parties nominate candidates by convention rather than by primary election and that they gain access to the ballot by submitting up to 500 petition signatures. However, the Court invalidated the state failure to list minor parties on the absentee ballots.

The Right of Candidacy

It can be contended that the right to be a candidate and the right to vote are two aspects of the same general political right. Although the Court did not explicitly discuss the right to candidacy in *Williams* v. *Rhodes,* it recognized that the right to vote is functionally dependent upon the ability of candidates to place their names before the electorate. In *Turner* v. *Fouche* (1970), the Court invalidated a state requirement that all members of a Georgia county school board be freeholders, saying that there is "a federal constitutional right to be considered for public service without a burden of indiviously discriminatory disqualifications."

Exorbitant filing fees were declared an unconstitutional burden on the right to candidacy in *Bullock* v. *Carter* (1972).[11] Texas law imposed filing fees for local offices which ranged up to a maximum of $8,900, without alternative means of getting on the ballot. Such fees, the Court said, gave the election system a "patently exclusionary character," and other methods must be found of testing the seriousness of candidacies.

The California filing fees in *Lubin* v. *Panish* (1974) were more reasonable ($701.60 for Los Angeles county commissioner), but again there were no alternative methods of getting on the ballot; even a write-in candidate had to pay fees. The constitutional standard, said Chief Justice Burger, "is that ballot access must be genuinely open to all subject to reasonable requirements." The California system did not meet this test.

Storer v. *Brown* (1974) upheld a California law that denied a place on the ballot to independent candidates who had been registered members of recognized political parties within seventeen months prior to the election. The law was held to reflect a compelling state interest in protecting the electoral process from splintered parties and unrestrained factionalism.

The Closed Primary

Many states have a closed system of party primaries, whereby only enrolled mem-bers of a political party may vote in that party's primary. A related feature prevents

---

11 See "The Constitutionality of Candidate Filing Fees," 70 MICHIGAN LAW REVIEW 558 (1972).

voters from changing parties within specified time periods prior to elections.[12] The New York closed primary system was upheld in *Rosario* v. *Rockefeller* (1973). The law there required voters to enroll in the party of their choice at least thirty days before the general election in order to vote in the next party primary, a time span of from eight to eleven months. The Court thought that this restriction on changing parties served the legitimate state purpose of avoiding disruptive party raiding. But a more restrictive law was declared unconstitutional in *Kusper* v. *Pontikes* (1973). Illinois prohibited a person from voting in a primary if he or she had voted in the primary of another political party within the preceding twenty-three months. This unnecessarily burdened a constitutionally protected liberty, Stewart said. The *Rosario* formula showed that a "less drastic means" of achieving the state's purpose was available.

Party Conventions

In the opening stages of the 1972 Democratic national convention, the credentials committee recommended unseating certain delegates from Illinois and California in a contest between pro- and anti-McGovern factions. The losing delegates went to court, and the Court of Appeals for the District of Columbia held the decisions of the credentials committee invalid. The Supreme Court in *O'Brien* v. *Brown* (1972) promptly reversed the lower court, ruling that a federal court had no authority "to interject itself into the deliberative processes of a national political convention."[13]

A slate of anti-Daley delegates from Illinois was seated at the 1972 Democratic convention, in spite of an injunction issued by an Illinois judge barring them from acting as delegates. Following the convention, they were held in contempt of the court order; but the Supreme Court in *Cousins* v. *Wigoda* (1975) held that a national party convention served a "pervasive national interest" superior to that of any state and that the Illinois judge's order had abridged the associational rights of the party and the party's right to determine the composition of its national convention.[14]

State Election Problems

In *Fortson* v. *Morris* (1966), the Court declined by a vote of five to four to extend the one-man, one-vote rationale to the situation of a disputed election for governor in Georgia. The state constitution provided that in case no candidate received a majority in the gubernatorial election, the state legislature should make the choice from between the two highest candidates. This occurred in the 1966 election, and the legislature chose Lester Maddox, though he had fewer votes than his principal oppo-

---

[12] See Glen S. Lewy, "The Right to Vote and Restrictions on Crossover Primaries," 40 UNIVERSITY OF CHICAGO LAW REVIEW 636 (1973).

[13] But see "Judicial Intervention in National Political Conventions: An Idea Whose Time Has Come," 59 CORNELL LAW REVIEW 107 (1973); "Judicial Review of Credentials Contests," 42 GEORGE WASHINGTON LAW REVIEW 1 (1973).

[14] *Bode* v. *National Democratic Party* (1972) let stand a lower court's holding that delegates to the 1972 Democratic national convention need not be divided among the states on a strict basis on one Democrat, one vote. See "One Man, One Vote and Selection of Delegates to National Nominating Conventions," 37 UNIVERSITY OF CHICAGO LAW REVIEW 536 (1970). *Graham* v. *March Fong Eu* (1976) upheld without opinion the "winner-take-all" primary system used in California to select delegates to the Republican national convention. See also *Ripon Society, Inc.* v. *National Republican Party* (1976).

nent. The Court minority thought that legislative election of a governor violated the reasoning of the Georgia county unit case, *Gray* v. *Sanders,* but Justice Black for the majority ruled that *Gray* was only a "voting case" and had no relation to how a state could elect its governors.

Bond v. *Floyd* (1966) was a different matter. Julian Bond, a black activist, because of statements he had made in opposition to the war in Vietnam and the draft, was twice denied the seat to which he had been elected in the Georgia legislature. He was prepared to take the required oath to support the federal and state constitutions and he met the other stated qualifications, but the legislature excluded him on the ground that his remarks showed he could not take the oath "in good faith." The Supreme Court, relying primarily on the First Amendment, unanimously held that Bond was entitled to his seat. Warren said, "The manifest function of the First Amendment in a representative government requires that legislators be given the widest latitude to express their views on issues of policy."

In *Baker* v. *Carr* (1962) Justice Brennan wrote: "Of course the mere fact that [a] suit seeks protection of a political right does not mean it presents a [nonjusticiable] political question."[15] There are "political thickets" that courts will do well to avoid, but access to the franchise and fair election procedures present issues of constitutional rights fundamental to a practicing democracy.

[15] See the definitive study by Louis Henkin, "Is There a 'Political Question' Doctrine?" 85 *Yale Law Journal* 597 (1976).

Appendixes

Constitution of the United States of America

WE THE PEOPLE of the United States, in Order to form a more perfect Union, establish Justice, insure domestic Tranquility, provide for the common defence, promote the general Welfare, and secure the Blessings of Liberty to ourselves and our Posterity, do ordain and establish this CONSTITUTION for the United States of America.

Article I

Section 1   All legislative Powers herein granted shall be vested in a Congress of the United States, which shall consist of a Senate and House of Representatives.

Section 2   [1.] The House of Representatives shall be composed of Members chosen every second Year by the People of the several States, and the Electors in each State shall have the Qualifications requisite for Electors of the most numerous Branch of the State Legislature.

[2.] No Person shall be a Representative who shall not have attained to the Age of twenty five Years, and been seven Years a Citizen of the United States, and who shall not, when elected, be an Inhabitant of that State in which he shall be chosen.

[3.] Representatives and direct Taxes[1] shall be apportioned among the several States which may be included within this Union, according to their respective Numbers, which shall be determined by adding to the whole Number of free Persons, including those bound to Service for a Term of Years, and excluding Indians not taxed, three fifths of all other Persons.[2] The actual Enumeration shall be made within three Years after the first Meeting of the Congress of the United States, and

[1] Modified as to direct taxes by the Sixteenth Amendment.
[2] Replaced by the Fourteenth Amendment.

within every subsequent Term of ten Years, in such Manner as they shall by Law direct. The Number of Representatives shall not exceed one for every thirty Thousand, but each State shall have at Least one Representative; and until such enumeration shall be made, the State of New Hampshire shall be entitled to chuse three, Massachusetts eight, Rhode-Island and Providence Plantations one, Connecticut five, New-York six, New Jersey four, Pennsylvania eight, Delaware one, Maryland six, Virginia ten, North Carolina five, South Carolina five, and Georgia three.

[4.] When vacancies happen in the Representation from any State, the Executive Authority thereof shall issue Writs of Election to fill such Vacancies.

[5.] The House of Representatives shall chuse their Speaker and other Officers; and shall have the sole Power of Impeachment.

Section 3 [1.] The Senate of the United States shall be composed of two Senators from each State, chosen by the Legislature thereof,[3] for six Years; and each Senator shall have one Vote.

[2.] Immediately after they shall be assembled in Consequence of the first Election, they shall be divided as equally as may be into three Classes. The Seats of the Senators of the first Class shall be vacated at the Expiration of the second Year, of the second Class at the Expiration of the fourth Year, and of the third Class at the Expiration of the sixth Year, so that one third may be chosen every second Year; and if Vacancies happen by Resignation, or otherwise, during the Recess of the Legislature of any State, the Executive thereof may make temporary Appointments until the next Meeting of the Legislature, which shall then fill such Vacancies.

[3.] No Person shall be a Senator who shall not have attained to the Age of thirty Years, and been nine Years a Citizen of the United States, and who shall not, when elected, be an Inhabitant of that State for which he shall be chosen.

[4.] The Vice President of the United States shall be President of the Senate, but shall have no Vote, unless they be equally divided.

[5.] The Senate shall chuse their other Officers, and also a President pro tempore, in the Absence of the Vice President, or when he shall exercise the Office of President of the United States.

[6.] The Senate shall have the sole Power to try all Impeachments. When sitting for that Purpose, they shall be on Oath or Affirmation. When the President of the United States is tried, the Chief Justice shall preside: And no Person shall be convicted without the Concurrence of two thirds of the Members present.

[7.] Judgment in Cases of Impeachment shall not extend further than to removal from Office, and disqualification to hold and enjoy any Office of honor, Trust or Profit under the United States: but the Party convicted shall nevertheless be liable and subject to Indictment, Trial, Judgment and Punishment, according to Law.

Section 4 [1.] The Times, Places and Manner of holding Elections for Senators and Representatives, shall be prescribed in each State by the Legislature thereof; but the Congress may at any time by Law make or alter such Regulations, except as to the Places of chusing Senators.

[2.] The Congress shall assemble at least once in every Year, and such Meeting

---

[3] Modified by the Seventeenth Amendment.

shall be on the first Monday in December, unless they shall by Law appoint a different Day.[4]

Section 5   [1.] Each House shall be the Judge of the Elections, Returns and Qualifications of its own Members, and a Majority of each shall constitute a Quorum to do Business; but a smaller Number may adjourn from day to day, and may be authorized to compel the attendance of absent Members, in such Manner, and under such Penalties as each House may provide.

[2.] Each House may determine the Rules of its Proceedings, punish its Members for Disorderly Behaviour, and, with the Concurrence of two thirds, expel a Member.

[3.] Each House shall keep a Journal of its Proceedings, and from time to time publish the same, excepting such Parts as may in their Judgment require Secrecy; and the Yeas and Nays of the Members of either House on any question shall, at the Desire of one fifth of those Present, be entered on the Journal.

[4.] Neither House, during the Session of Congress, shall, without the Consent of the other, adjourn for more than three days, nor to any other Place than that in which the two Houses shall be sitting.

Section 6   [1.] The Senators and Representatives shall receive a Compensation for their Services, to be ascertained by Law, and paid out of the Treasury of the United States. They shall in all Cases, except Treason, Felony and Breach of the Peace, be privileged from Arrest during their Attendance at the Session of their respective Houses, and in going to and returning from the same; and for any Speech or Debate in either House, they shall not be questioned in any other Place.

[2.] No Senator or Representative shall, during the Time for which he was elected, be appointed to any civil Office under the Authority of the United States, which shall have been created, or the Emoluments whereof shall have been encreased during such time; and no Person holding any Office under the United States, shall be a member of either House during his Continuance in Office.

Section 7   [1.] All Bills for raising Revenue shall originate in the House of Representatives; but the Senate may propose or concur with Amendments as on other Bills.

[2.] Every Bill which shall have passed the House of Representatives and the Senate, shall, before it become a Law, be presented to the President of the United States; If he approve he shall sign it, but if not he shall return it, with his Objections to that House in which it shall have originated, who shall enter the Objections at large on their Journal, and proceed to reconsider it. If after such Reconsideration two thirds of that House shall agree to pass the Bill, it shall be sent, together with the Objections, to the other House, by which it shall likewise be reconsidered, and if approved by two thirds of that House, it shall become a Law. But in all such Cases the Votes of both Houses shall be determined by Yeas and Nays, and the Names of the Persons voting for and against the Bill shall be entered on the Journal of each House respectively. If any Bill shall not be returned by the President within ten Days (Sundays excepted) after it shall have been presented to him, the same shall be

---

[4] Modified by the Twentieth Amendment.

a Law, in like Manner as if he had signed it, unless the Congress by their Adjournment prevent its Return, in which Case it shall not be a Law.

[3.] Every Order, Resolution, or Vote to which the Concurrence of the Senate and House of Representatives may be necessary (except on a question of Adjournment) shall be presented to the President of the United States; and before the same shall take Effect, shall be approved by him, or being disapproved by him, shall be repassed by two thirds of the Senate and House of Representatives, according to the Rules and Limitations prescribed in the Case of a Bill.

Section 8   The Congress shall have Power [1.] To lay and collect Taxes, Duties, Imposts and Excises, to pay the Debts and provide for the common Defence and general Welfare of the United States; but all Duties, Imposts and Excises shall be uniform throughout the United States;

[2.] To borrow Money on the credit of the United States;

[3.] To regulate Commerce with foreign Nations, and among the several States, and with the Indian Tribes;

[4.] To establish an uniform Rule of Naturalization, and uniform Laws on the subject of Bankruptcies throughout the United States;

[5.] To coin Money, regulate the Value thereof, and of foreign Coin, and fix the Standard of Weights and Measures;

[6.] To provide for the Punishment of counterfeiting the Securities and current Coin of the United States;

[7.] To establish Post Offices and post Roads;

[8.] To promote the Progress of Science and useful Arts, by securing for limited Times to Authors and Inventors the exclusive Right to their respective Writings and Discoveries;

[9.] To constitute Tribunals inferior to the supreme Court;

[10.] To define and punish Piracies and Felonies committed on the High Seas, and Offences against the Law of Nations;

[11.] To declare War, grant Letters of Marque and Reprisal, and make Rules concerning Captures on Land and Water;

[12.] To raise and support Armies, but no Appropriation of Money to that Use shall be for a longer Term than two Years;

[13.] To provide and maintain a Navy;

[14.] To make Rules for the Government and Regulation of the land and naval Forces;

[15.] To provide for calling forth the Militia to execute the Laws of the Union, suppress Insurrections and repel Invasions;

[16.] To provide for organizing, arming, and disciplining, the Militia, and for governing such Part of them as may be employed in the Service of the United States, reserving to the States respectively, the Appointment of the Officers, and the Authority of training the Militia according to the discipline prescribed by Congress;

[17.] To exercise exclusive Legislation in all Cases whatsoever, over such District (not exceeding ten Miles square) as may, by Cession of particular States, and the Acceptance of Congress, become the Seat of the Government of the United States, and to exercise like Authority over all Places purchased by the Consent of the Legislature of the State in which the same be, for the Erection of Forts, Maga-zines, Arsenals, dock-Yards, and other needful Buildings;—And

[18.] To make all Laws which shall be necessary and proper for carrying into Execution the foregoing Powers, and all other Powers vested by this Constitution in the Government of the United States, or in any Department or Officer thereof.

Section 9 [1.] The Migration or Importation of such Persons as any of the States now existing shall think proper to admit, shall not be prohibited by the Congress prior to the Year one thousand eight hundred and eight, but a Tax or duty may be imposed on such Importation, not exceeding ten dollars for each Person.

[2.] The Privilege of the Writ of Habeas Corpus shall not be suspended, unless when in Cases of Rebellion or Invasion the public Safety may require it.

[3.] No Bill of Attainder or ex post facto Law shall be passed.

[4.] No Capitation, or other direct, Tax shall be laid, unless in Proportion to the Census or Enumeration herein before directed to be taken.[5]

[5.] No Tax or Duty shall be laid on Articles exported from any State.

[6.] No Preference shall be given by any Regulation of Commerce or Revenue to the Ports of one State over those of another: nor shall Vessels bound to, or from, one State, be obliged to enter, clear, or pay Duties in another.

[7.] No Money shall be drawn from the Treasury, but in Consequence of Ap-propriations made by Law; and a regular Statement and Account of the Receipts and Expenditures of all public Money shall be published from time to time.

[8.] No Title of Nobility shall be granted by the United States: And no Person holding any Office of Profit or Trust under them, shall, without the Consent of the Congress, accept of any present, Emolument, Office, or Title, of any kind whatever, from any King, Prince, or foreign State.

Section 10 [1.] No State shall enter into any Treaty, Alliance, or Confederation; grant Letters of Marque and Reprisal; coin Money; emit Bills of Credit; make any Thing but gold and silver Coin a Tender in Payment of Debts; pass any Bill of Attainder, ex post facto Law, or Law impairing the Obligation of Contracts, or grant any Title of Nobility.

[2.] No State shall, without the Consent of the Congress, lay any Imposts or Duties on Imports or Exports, except what may be absolutely necessary for execut-ing its inspection Laws: and the net Produce of all Duties and Imposts, laid by any State on Imports or Exports, shall be for the Use of the Treasury of the United States; and all such Laws shall be subject to the Revision and Controul of the Congress.

[3.] No State shall, without the Consent of Congress, lay any Duty of Tonnage, keep Troops, or Ships of War in time of Peace, enter into any Agreement or Com-pact with another State, or with a foreign Power, or engage in War, unless actually invaded, or in such imminent Danger as will not admit of delay.

Article II

Section 1 [1.] The executive Power shall be vested in a President of the United States of America. He shall hold his Office during the Term of four Years, and,

---

[5] Modified by the Sixteenth Amendment.

together with the Vice President, chosen for the same Term, be elected, as follows

[2.] Each State shall appoint, in such Manner as the Legislature thereof may direct, a Number of Electors, equal to the whole Number of Senators and Representatives to which the State may be entitled in the Congress: but no Senator or Representative, or Person holding an Office of Trust or Profit under the United States, shall be appointed an Elector.

[3.] The Electors shall meet in their respective States, and vote by Ballot for two Persons, of whom one at least shall not be an Inhabitant of the same State with themselves. And they shall make a List of all the Persons voted for, and of the Number of Votes for each; which List they shall sign and certify, and transmit sealed to the Seat of the Government of the United States, directed to the President of the Senate. The President of the Senate shall, in the Presence of the Senate and House of Representatives, open all the Certificates, and the Votes shall then be counted. The Person having the greatest Number of Votes shall be the President, if such Number be a Majority of the whole Number of Electors appointed; and if there be more than one who have such Majority, and have an equal Number of Votes, then the House of Representatives shall immediately chuse by Ballot one of them for President; and if no Person have a Majority, then from the five highest on the List the said House shall in like Manner chuse the President. But in chusing the President, the Votes shall be taken by States, the Representation from each State having one Vote; A quorum for this Purpose shall consist of a Member or Members from two thirds of the States, and a Majority of all the States shall be necessary to a Choice. In every Case, after the Choice of the President, the Person having the greatest Number of Votes of the Electors shall be the Vice President. But if there should remain two or more who have equal Votes, the Senate shall chuse from them by Ballot the Vice President.[6]

[4.] The Congress may determine the Time of chusing the Electors, and the Day on which they shall give their Votes; which Day shall be the same throughout the United States.

[5.] No Person except a natural born Citizen, or a Citizen of the United States, at the time of the Adoption of this Constitution, shall be eligible to the Office of President; neither shall any Person be eligible to that Office who shall not have attained to the Age of thirty five Years, and been fourteen Years a Resident within the United States.

[6.] In Case of the Removal of the President from Office, or of his Death, Resignation, or Inability to discharge the Powers and Duties of the said Office, the Same shall devolve on the Vice President, and the Congress may by Law provide for the Case of Removal, Death, Resignation, or Inability, both of the President and Vice President, declaring what Officer shall then act as President, and such Officer shall act accordingly, until the Disability be removed, or a President shall be elected.

[7.] The President shall, at stated Times, receive for his Services, a Compensation, which shall neither be increased nor diminished during the Period for which he shall have been elected, and he shall not receive within that Period any other Emolument from the United States, or any of them.

[6] This paragraph was replaced in 1804 by the Twelfth Amendment.

[8.] Before he enter on the Execution of his Office, he shall take the following Oath or Affirmation:—"I do solemnly swear (or affirm) that I will faithfully execute the Office of President of the United States, and will to the best of my Ability, preserve, protect and defend the Constitution of the United States."

Section 2   [1.] The President shall be Commander in Chief of the Army and Navy of the United States, and of the Militia of the several States, when called into the actual Service of the United States; he may require the Opinion, in writing, of the principal Officer in each of the executive Departments, upon any Subject relating to the Duties of their respective Offices, and he shall have Power to grant Reprieves and Pardons for Offences against the United States, except in Cases of Impeachment.

[2.] He shall have Power, by and with the Advice and Consent of the Senate, to make Treaties, provided two thirds of the Senators present concur; and he shall nominate, and by and with the Advice and Consent of the Senate, shall appoint Ambassadors, other public Ministers and Consuls, Judges of the supreme Court, and all other Officers of the United States, whose Appointments are not herein otherwise provided for, and which shall be established by Law: but the Congress may by Law vest the Appointment of such inferior Officers, as they think proper, in the President alone, in the Courts of Law, or in the Heads of Departments.

[3.] The President shall have Power to fill up all Vacancies that may happen during the Recess of the Senate, by granting Commissions which shall expire at the End of their next Session.

Section 3   He shall from time to time give to the Congress Information of the State of the Union, and recommend to their Consideration such Measures as he shall judge necessary and expedient; he may, on extraordinary Occasions, convene both Houses, or either of them, and in Case of Disagreement between them, with Respect to the Time of Adjournment, he may adjourn them to such Time as he shall think proper; he shall receive Ambassadors and other public Ministers; he shall take Care that the Laws be faithfully executed, and shall Commission all the Officers of the United States.

Section 4   The President, Vice President and all civil Officers of the United States, shall be removed from Office on Impeachment for, and Conviction of, Treason, Bribery, or other high Crimes and Misdemeanors.

Article III

Section 1   The judicial Power of the United States, shall be vested in one supreme Court, and in such inferior Courts as the Congress may from time to time ordain and establish. The Judges, both of the supreme and inferior Courts, shall hold their Offices during good Behaviour, and shall, at stated Times, receive for their Services, a Conpensation, which shall not be diminished during their Continuance in Office.

Section 2   [1.] The judicial Power shall extend to all Cases, in Law and Equity, arising under this Constitution, the Laws of the United States, and Treaties made, or which shall be made, under their Authority;—to all Cases affecting Ambassadors, other public Ministers and Consuls;—to all Cases of admiralty and maritime Jurisdiction;—to Controversies to which the United States shall be a Party;—to Controversies between two or more States;—between a State and Citizens of another State;[7]—between Citizens of different States;—between Citizens of the same State claiming Lands under Grants of different States, and between a State, or the Citizens thereof, and foreign States, Citizens or Subjects.

[2.] In all Cases affecting Ambassadors, other public Ministers and Consuls, and those in which a State shall be Party, the supreme Court shall have original Jurisdiction. In all the other Cases before mentioned, the supreme Court shall have appellate Jurisdiction, both as to Law and Fact, with such Exceptions, and under such Regulations as the Congress shall make.

[3.] The Trial of all Crimes, except in Cases of Impeachment, shall be by Jury; and such Trial shall be held in the State where the said Crimes shall have been committed; but when not committed within any State, the Trial shall be at such Place or Places as the Congress may by Law have directed.

Section 3 [1.] Treason against the United States, shall consist only in levying War against them, or in adhering to their Enemies, giving them Aid and Comfort. No Person shall be convicted of Treason unless on the Testimony of two Witnesses to the same overt Act, or on Confession in open Court.

[2.] The Congress shall have Power to declare the Punishment of Treason, but no Attainder of Treason shall work Corruption of Blood, or Forfeiture except during the Life of the Person attainted.

Article IV

Section 1 Full Faith and Credit shall be given in each State to the public Acts, Records, and judicial Proceedings of every other State. And the Congress may by general Laws prescribe the Manner in which such Acts, Records and Proceedings shall be proved, and the Effect thereof.

Section 2 [1.] The Citizens of each State shall be entitled to all Privileges and Immunities of Citizens in the several States.

[2.] A Person charged in any State with Treason, Felony, or other Crime, who shall flee from Justice, and be found in another State, shall on Demand of the executive Authority of the State from which he fled, be delivered up, to be removed to the State having Jurisdiction of the Crime.

[3.] No Person held to Service or Labour in one State, under the Laws thereof, escaping into another, shall, in Consequence of any Law or Regulation therein, be discharged from such Service or Labour, but shall be delivered up on Claim of the Party to whom such Service or Labour may be due.

Section 3 [1.] New States may be admitted by the Congress into this Union; but no new State shall be formed or erected within the Jurisdiction of any other State; nor any State be formed by the Junction of two or more States, or Parts of States, without the Consent of the Legislatures of the States concerned as well as of the Congress.

[2.] The Congress shall have Power to dispose of and make all needful Rules

[7] Restricted by the Eleventh Amendment.

and Regulations respecting the Territory or other Property belonging to the United States; and nothing in this Constitution shall be so construed as to Prejudice any Claims of the United States, or of any particular State.

Section 4 The United States shall guarantee to every State in this Union a Republican Form of Government, and shall protect each of them against Invasion; and on Application of the Legislature, or of the Executive (when the Legislature cannot be convened) against domestic Violence.

Article V

The Congress, whenever two thirds of both Houses shall deem it necessary, shall propose Amendments to this Constitution, or, on the Application of the Legislatures of two thirds of the several States, shall call a Convention for proposing Amendments, which, in either Case, shall be valid to all Intents and Purposes, as Part of this Constitution, when ratified by the Legislatures of three fourths of the several States, or by Conventions in three fourths thereof, as the one or the other Mode of Ratification may be proposed by the Congress; Provided that no Amendment which may be made prior to the Year One thousand eight hundred and eight shall in any Manner affect the first and fourth Clauses in the Ninth Section of the first Article; and that no State, without its Consent, shall be deprived of its equal Suffrage in the Senate.

Article VI

[1.] All Debts contracted and Engagements entered into, before the Adoption of this Constitution, shall be as valid against the United States under this Constitution, as under the Confederation.

[2.] This Constitution, and the Laws of the United States which shall be made in Pursuance thereof; and all Treaties made, or which shall be made, under the Authority of the United States, shall be the supreme Law of the Land; and the Judges in every State shall be bound thereby, any Thing in the Constitution or Laws of any State to the Contrary notwithstanding.

[3.] The Senators and Representatives before mentioned, and the Members of the several State Legislatures, and all executive and judicial Officers, both of the United States and of the several States, shall be bound by Oath or Affirmation, to support this Constitution; but no religious Test shall ever be required as a Qualification to any Office or public Trust under the United States.

Article VII

The Ratification of the Conventions of nine States, shall be sufficient for the Establishment of this Constitution between the States so ratifying the Same.

AMENDMENTS

Amendment I

Congress shall make no law respecting an establishment of religion, or prohibiting the free exercise thereof; or abridging the freedom of speech, or of the press; or the right of the people peaceably to assemble, and to petition the Government for a redress of grievances.

Amendment II

A well regulated Militia, being necessary to the security of a free State, the right of the people to keep and bear Arms, shall not be infringed.

Amendment III

No Soldier shall, in time of peace be quartered in any house, without the consent of the Owner, nor in time of war, but in a manner to be prescribed by law.

Amendment IV

The right of the people to be secure in their persons, houses, papers, and effects, against unreasonable searches and seizures, shall not be violated, and no Warrants shall issue, but upon probable cause, supported by Oath or affirmation, and particularly describing the place to be searched, and the persons or things to be seized.

Amendment V

No person shall be held to answer for a capital, or otherwise infamous crime, unless on a presentment or indictment of a Grand Jury, except in cases arising in the land or naval forces, or in the Militia, when in actual service in time of War or public danger; nor shall any person be subject for the same offence to be twice put in jeopardy of life or limb; nor shall be compelled in any criminal case to be a witness against himself, nor be deprived of life, liberty, or property, without due process of law; nor shall private property be taken for public use, without just compensation.

Amendment VI

In all criminal prosecutions the accused shall enjoy the right to a speedy and public trial, by an impartial jury of the State and district wherein the crime shall have been committed, which district shall have been previously ascertained by law, and to be informed of the nature and cause of the accusation; to be confronted with the witnesses against him; to have compulsory process for obtaining witnesses in his favor, and to have the Assistance of Counsel for his defence.

Amendment VII

In suits at common law, where the value in controversy shall exceed twenty dollars, the right of trial by jury shall be preserved, and no fact tried by a jury shall be otherwise re-examined in any Court of the United States, than according to the rules of the common law.

Amendment VIII

Excessive bail shall not be required, nor excessive fines imposed, nor cruel and unusual punishments inflicted.

Amendment IX

The enumeration in the Constitution, of certain rights, shall not be construed to deny or disparage others retained by the people.

Amendment X

The powers not delegated to the United States by the Constitution, nor prohibited by it to the States, are reserved to the States respectively, or to the people.

[The first ten Amendments were adopted in 1791.]

Amendment XI

The Judicial power of the United States shall not be construed to extend to any suit in law or equity, commenced or prosecuted against one of the United States by Citizens of another State, or by Citizens or Subjects of any Foreign State. [Adopted in 1798.]

Amendment XII

The Electors shall meet in their respective states, and vote by ballot for President and Vice-President, one of whom, at least, shall not be an inhabitant of the same state with themselves; they shall name in their ballots the person voted for as President, and in distinct ballots the person voted for as Vice-President, and they shall make distinct lists of all persons voted for as President, and of all persons voted for as Vice-President, and of the number of votes for each, which lists they shall sign and certify, and transmit sealed to the seat of the government of the United States, directed to the President of the senate;—The President of the Senate shall, in the presence of the Senate and House of Representatives, open all the certificates and the votes shall then be counted;—The person having the greatest number of votes for President, shall be the President, if such number be a majority of the whole number of Electors appointed; and if no person have such majority, then from the persons having the highest numbers not exceeding three on the list of those voted for as President, the House of Representatives shall choose immediately, by ballot, the President. But in choosing the President, the votes shall be taken by states, the representation from each state having one vote; a quorum for this purpose shall consist of a member or members from two-thirds of the states, and a majority of all the states shall be necessary to a choice. And if the House of Representatives shall not choose a President whenever the right of choice shall devolve upon them, before the fourth day of March next following, then the Vice-President, shall act as President, as in the case of the death or other constitutional disability of the President.— The person having the greatest number of votes as Vice-President, shall be the Vice-President, if such number be a majority of the whole number of Electors appointed, and if no person have a majority, then from the two highest numbers on the list, the Senate shall choose the Vice-President; a quorum for the purpose shall consist of two-thirds of the whole number of Senators, and a majority of the whole number shall be necessary to a choice. But no person constitutionally ineligible to the office of President shall be eligible to that of Vice-President of the United States. [Adopted in 1804.]

Amendment XIII

Section 1 Neither slavery nor involuntary servitude, except as a punishment for crime whereof the party shall have been duly convicted, shall exist within the United Sates, or any place subject to their jurisdiction.

Section 2   Congress shall have power to enforce this article by appropriate legislation. [Adopted in 1865.]

Amendment XIV

Section 1   All persons born or naturalized in the United States, and subject to the jurisdiction thereof, are citizens of the United States and of the State wherein they reside. No State shall make or enforce any law which shall abridge the privileges or immunities of citizens of the United States; nor shall any State deprive any person of life, liberty, or property, without due process of law; nor deny to any person within its jurisdiction the equal protection of the laws.

Section 2   Representatives shall be apportioned among the several States according to their respective numbers, counting the whole number of persons in each State. excluding Indians not taxed. But when the right to vote at any election for the choice of electors for President and Vice President of the United States, Representatives in Congress, the Executive and Judicial officers of a State. or the members of the Legislature thereof, is denied to any of the male inhabitants of such State, being twenty-one years of age, and citizens of the United States, or in any way abridged, except for participation in rebellion, or other crime, the basis of representation therein shall be reduced in the proportion which the number of such male citizens shall bear to the whole number of male citizens twenty-one years of age in such State.

Section 3   No person shall be a Senator or Representative in Congress, or elector of President and Vice President, or hold any office, civil or military, under the United States, or under any State, who, having previously taken an oath, as a member of Congress, or as an officer of the United States, or as a member of any State legislature, or as an executive or judicial officer of any State, to support the Constitution of the United States, shall have engaged in insurrection or rebellion against the same, or given aid or comfort to the enemies thereof. But Congress may by a vote of two-thirds of each House, remove such disability.

Section 4   The validity of the public debt of the United States. authorized by law, including debts incurred for payment of pensions and bounties for services in suppressing insurrection or rebellion, shall not be questioned. But neither the United States nor any State shall assume or pay any debt or obligation incurred in aid of insurrection or rebellion against the United States, or any claim for the loss or emancipation of any slave; but all such debts, obligations and claims shall be held illegal and void.

Section 5   The Congress shall have power to enforce, by appropriate legislation, the provisions of this article. [Adopted in 1868.]

Amendment XV

Section 1   The right of citizens of the United States to vote shall not be denied or abridged by the United States or by any State on account of race, color, or previous condition of servitude.

Section 2   The Congress shall have power to enforce this article by appropriate legislation. [Adopted in 1870.]

Amendment XVI

The Congress shall have the power to lay and collect taxes on incomes, from whatever source derived, without apportionment among the several States, and without regard to any census or enumeration. [Adopted in 1913.]

Amendment XVII

The Senate of the United States shall be composed of two Senators from each State, elected by the people thereof, for six years; and each Senator shall have one vote. The electors in each State shall have the qualifications requisite for electors of the most numerous branch of the State legislatures.

When vacancies happen in the representation of any State in the Senate, the executive authority of such State shall issue writs of election to fill such vacancies: *Provided,* That the legislature of any State may empower the executive thereof to make temporary appointments until the people fill the vacancies by election as the legislature may direct.

This amendment shall not be so construed as to affect the election or term of any Senator chosen before it becomes valid as part of the Constitution. [Adopted in 1913.]

Amendment XVIII

Section 1   After one year from the ratification of this article the manufacture, sale, or transportation of intoxicating liquors within, the importation thereof into, or the exportation thereof from the United States and all territory subject to the jurisdiction thereof for beverage purposes is hereby prohibited.

Section 2   The Congress and the several States shall have concurrent power to enforce this article by appropriate legislation.

Section 3   This article shall be inoperative unless it shall have been ratified as an amendment to the Constitution by the legislatures of the several States, as provided in the Constitution, within seven years from the date of the submission hereof to the States by the Congress. [Adopted in 1919.]

Amendment XIX

The right of citizens of the United States to vote shall not be denied or abridged by the United States or by any State on account of sex.

Congress shall have power to enforce this article by appropriate legislation. [Adopted in 1920.]

Amendment XX

Section 1   The terms of the President and Vice President shall end at noon on the 20th day of January, and the terms of Senators and Representatives at noon on the 3d day of January, of the years in which such terms would have ended if this article had not been ratified; and the terms of their successors shall then begin.

Section 2   The Congress shall assemble at least once in every year, and such meeting shall begin at noon on the 3d day of January, unless they shall by law appoint a different day.

Section 3   If, at the time fixed for the beginning of the term of the President, the President elect shall have died, the Vice President elect shall become President. If a President shall not have been chosen before the time fixed for the beginning of his term, or if the President elect shall have failed to qualify, then the Vice President elect shall act as President until a President shall have qualified; and the Congress may by law provide for the case wherein neither a President elect nor a Vice President elect shall have qualified, declaring who shall then act as President, or the manner in which one who is to act shall be selected, and such person shall act accordingly until a President or Vice President shall have qualified.

Section 4   The Congress may by law provide for the case of the death of any of the persons from whom the House of Representatives may choose a President whenever the right of choice shall have devolved upon them, and for the case of the death of any of the persons from whom the Senate may choose a Vice President whenever the right of choice shall have devolved upon them.

Section 5   Sections 1 and 2 shall take effect on the 15th day of October following the ratification of this article.

Section 6   This article shall be inoperative unless it shall have been ratified as an amendment to the Constitution by the legislatures of three-fourths of the several States within seven years from the date of its submission. [Adopted in 1933.]

Amendment XXI

Section 1   The eighteenth article of amendment to the Constitution of the United States is hereby repealed.

Section 2   The transportation or importation into any State, Territory, or possession of the United States for delivery or use therein of intoxicating liquors, in violation of the laws thereof, is hereby prohibited.

Section 3   This article shall be inoperative unless it shall have been ratified as an amendment to the Constitution by conventions in the several States, as provided in the Constitution, within seven years from the date of the submission hereof to the States by the Congress. [Adopted in 1933.]

Amendment XXII

Section 1   No person shall be elected to the office of the President more than twice, and no person who has held the office of President, or acted as President, for more than two years of a term to which some other person was elected President shall be elected to the office of the President more than once. But this Article shall not apply to any person holding the office of President when this Article was proposed by the Congress, and shall not prevent any person who may be holding the office of President, or acting as President, during the term within which this Article becomes operative from holding the office of President or acting as President during the remainder of such term.

Section 2   This Article shall be inoperative unless it shall have been ratified as an amendment to the Constitution by the legislatures of three-fourths of the several States within seven years from the date of its submission to the states by the Congress. [Adopted in 1951.]

Amendment XXIII

Section 1 The District constituting the seat of Government of the United States shall appoint in such manner as the Congress may direct:

A number of electors of President and Vice President equal to the whole number of Senators and Representatives in Congress to which the District would be entitled if it were a State, but in no event more than the least populous State; they shall be in addition to those appointed by the States, but they shall be considered, for the purposes of the election of President and Vice President, to be electors appointed by a State; and they shall meet in the District and perform such duties as provided by the twelfth article of amendment.

Section 2 The Congress shall have power to enforce this article by appropriate legislation. [Adopted in 1961.]

Amendment XXIV

Section 1 The right of citizens of the United States to vote in any primary or other election for President or Vice President, for electors for President or Vice President, or for Senator or Representative in Congress, shall not be denied or abridged by the United States or any State by reason of failure to pay any poll tax or other tax.

Section 2 The Congress shall have power to enforce this article by appropriate legislation. [Adopted in 1964.]

Amendment XXV

Section 1 In case of the removal of the President from office or of his death or resignation, the Vice President shall become President.

Section 2 Whenever there is a vacancy in the office of the Vice President, the President shall nominate a Vice President who shall take office upon confirmation by a majority vote of both Houses of Congress.

Section 3 Whenever the President transmits to the President pro tempore of the Senate and the Speaker of the House of Representatives his written declaration that he is unable to discharge the powers and duties of his office, and until he transmits to them a written declaration to the contrary, such powers and duties shall be discharged by the Vice President as Acting President.

Section 4 Whenever the Vice President and a majority of either the principal officers of the executive departments or of such other body as Congress may by law provide, transmit to the President pro tempore of the Senate and the Speaker of the House of Representatives their written declaration that the President is unable to discharge the powers and duties of his office, the Vice President shall immediately assume the powers and duties of the office as Acting President.

Thereafter, when the President transmits to the President pro tempore of the Senate and the Speaker of the House of Representatives his written declaration that no inability exists, he shall resume the powers and duties of his office unless the Vice President and a majority of either the principal officers of the executive departments or of such other body as Congress may by law provide, transmit within four days to the President pro tempore of the Senate and the Speaker of the House of Representatives their written declaration that the President is unable to discharge the powers and duties of his office. Thereupon Congress shall decide the issue, assembling within forty-eight hours for that purpose if not in session. If the Congress, within twenty-one days after receipt of the latter written declaration, or if Congress is not in session, within twenty-one days after Congress is required to assemble, determines by two-thirds vote in both Houses that the President is unable to discharge the powers and duties of his office, the Vice President shall continue to discharge the same as Acting President; otherwise, the President shall resume the powers and duties of his office. [Adopted in 1967.]

Amendment XXVI

Section 1 The rights of citizens of the United States, who are eighteen years of age or older, to vote shall not be denied or abridged by the United States or any state on account of age.

Section 2 The Congress shall have the power to enforce this article by appropriate legislation. [Adopted in 1971.]

Amendment XXVII (Proposed)

Section 1 Equality of rights under the law shall not be denied or abridged by the United States or by any state on account of sex.

Section 2 The Congress shall have the power to enforce, by appropriate legislation, the provisions of this article.

Section 3 This amendment shall take effect two years after the date of ratification. [Proposed by Congress on March 22, 1972.]

MEMBERS OF THE UNITED STATES SUPREME COURT 1789–1976

Chief Justices	State	Term	Appointed by	Life Span
John Jay	N.Y.	1789–1795	Washington	1745–1829
John Rutledge	S.C.	1795*	"	1739–1800
Oliver Ellsworth	Conn.	1796–1800	"	1745–1807
John Marshall	Va.	1801–1835	J. Adams	1755–1835
Roger B. Taney	Md.	1836–1864	Jackson	1777–1864
Salmon P. Chase	Ohio	1864–1873	Lincoln	1808–1873
Morrison R. Waite	Ohio	1874–1888	Grant	1816–1888
Melville W. Fuller	Ill.	1888–1910	Cleveland	1833–1910
Edward D. White	La.	1910–1921	Taft	1845–1921
William H. Taft	Conn.	1921–1930	Harding	1857–1930
Charles E. Hughes	N.Y.	1930–1941	Hoover	1862–1948
Harlan F. Stone	N.Y.	1941–1946	F. D. Roosevelt	1872–1946
Fred M. Vinson	Ky.	1946–1953	Truman	1890–1953
Earl Warren	Calif.	1953–1969	Eisenhower	1891–1974
Warren Earl Burger	Minn.	1969–	Nixon	1907–

Associate Justices	State	Term	Appointed by	Life Span
John Rutledge	S.C.	1789–1791	Washington	1739–1800
William Cushing	Mass.	1789–1810	"	1732–1810
James Wilson	Pa.	1789–1798	"	1742–1798
John Blair	Va.	1789–1796	"	1732–1800
James Iredell	N.C.	1790–1799	"	1751–1799
Thomas Johnson	Md.	1791–1793	"	1732–1819
William Paterson	N.J.	1793–1806	"	1745–1806
Samuel Chase	Md.	1796–1811	"	1741–1811
Bushrod Washington	Va.	1798–1829	J. Adams	1762–1829
Alfred Moore	N.C.	1799–1804	"	1755–1810
William Johnson	S.C.	1804–1834	Jefferson	1771–1834
Henry B. Livingston	N.Y.	1806–1823	"	1757–1823
Thomas Todd	Ky.	1807–1826	"	1765–1826
Joseph Story	Mass.	1811–1845	Madison	1779–1845
Gabriel Duval	Md.	1811–1835	"	1752–1844
Smith Thompson	N.Y.	1823–1843	Monroe	1768–1843
Robert Trimble	Ky.	1826–1828	J. Q. Adams	1777–1828
John McLean	Ohio	1829–1861	Jackson	1785–1861
Henry Baldwin	Pa.	1830–1844	"	1780–1844
James M. Wayne	Ga.	1835–1867	"	1790–1867
Philip P. Barbour	Va.	1836–1841	"	1783–1841
John Catron	Tenn.	1837–1865	"	1786–1865
John McKinley	Ala.	1837–1852	Van Buren	1780–1852
Peter V. Daniel	Va.	1841–1860	"	1784–1860

*Unconfirmed recess appointment.

Samuel Nelson	N.Y.	1845–1872	Tyler	1792–1873
Levi Woodbury	N.H.	1846–1851	Polk	1789–1851
Robert C. Grier	Pa.	1846–1870	Polk	1794–1870
Benjamin R. Curtis	Mass.	1851–1857	Fillmore	1809–1874
John A. Campbell	Ala.	1853–1861	Pierce	1811–1889
Nathan Clifford	Maine	1858–1881	Buchanan	1803–1881
Noah H. Swayne	Ohio	1862–1881	Lincoln	1804–1884
Samuel F. Miller	Iowa	1862–1890	"	1816–1890
David Davis	Ill.	1862–1877	"	1815–1886
Stephen J. Field	Calif.	1863–1897	"	1816–1899
William Strong	Pa.	1870–1880	Grant	1808–1895
Joseph P. Bradley	N.J.	1870–1892	"	1813–1892
Ward Hunt	N.Y.	1872–1882	"	1810–1886
John M. Harlan	Ky.	1877–1911	Hayes	1833–1911
William B. Woods	Ga.	1880–1887	"	1824–1887
Stanley Matthews	Ohio	1881–1889	Garfield	1824–1889
Horace Gray	Mass.	1881–1902	Arthur	1828–1902
Samuel Blatchford	N.Y.	1882–1893	"	1820–1893
Lucius Q. C. Lamar	Miss.	1888–1893	Cleveland	1825–1893
David J. Brewer	Kans.	1889–1910	B. Harrison	1837–1910
Henry B. Brown	Mich.	1890–1906	"	1836–1913
George Shiras, Jr.	Pa.	1892–1903	"	1832–1924
Howell E. Jackson	Tenn.	1893–1895	"	1832–1895
Edward D. White	La.	1894–1910	Cleveland	1845–1921
Rufus W. Peckham	N.Y.	1895–1909	"	1838–1909
Joseph McKenna	Calif.	1898–1925	McKinley	1843–1926
Oliver W. Holmes	Mass.	1902–1932	T. Roosevelt	1841–1935
William R. Day	Ohio	1903–1922	"	1849–1923
William H. Moody	Mass.	1906–1910	"	1853–1917
Horace H. Lurton	Tenn.	1909–1914	Taft	1844–1914
Charles E. Hughes	N.Y.	1910–1916	"	1862–1948
Willis Van Devanter	Wyo.	1910–1937	"	1859–1941
Joseph H. Lamar	Ga.	1910–1916	"	1857–1916
Mahlon Pitney	N.J.	1912–1922	"	1858–1924
James C. McReynolds	Tenn.	1914–1941	Wilson	1862–1946
Louis D. Brandeis	Mass.	1916–1939	"	1856–1941
John H. Clarke	Ohio	1916–1922	"	1857–1945
George Sutherland	Utah	1922–1938	Harding	1862–1942
Pierce Butler	Minn.	1922–1939	"	1866–1939
Edward T. Sanford	Tenn.	1923–1930	"	1865–1930
Harlan F. Stone	N.Y.	1925–1941	Coolidge	1872–1946
Owen J. Roberts	Pa.	1930–1945	Hoover	1875–1955
Benjamin N. Cardozo	N.Y.	1932–1938	"	1870–1938
Hugo L. Black	Ala.	1937–1971	F. D. Roosevelt	1886–1971
Stanley F. Reed	Ky.	1938–1957	"	1884–
Felix Frankfurter	Mass.	1939–1962	"	1882–1965
William O. Douglas	Conn.	1939–1975	"	1898–
Frank Murphy	Mich.	1940–1949	"	1890–1949
James F. Byrnes	S.C.	1941–1942	"	1879–1974

Robert H. Jackson	N.Y.	1941–1954	"	1892–1954
Wiley B. Rutledge	Iowa	1943–1949	"	1894–1949
Harold H. Burton	Ohio	1945–1958	Truman	1888–1964
Tom C. Clark	Tex.	1949–1967	"	1899–
Sherman Minton	Ind.	1949–1956	"	1890–1965
John M. Harlan	N.Y.	1955–1971	Eisenhower	1899–1971
William J. Brennan, Jr.	N.J.	1956–	"	1906–
Charles E. Whittaker	Mo.	1957–1962	"	1901–
Potter Stewart	Ohio	1958–	"	1915–
Byron R. White	Colo.	1962–	Kennedy	1917–
Arthur J. Goldberg	Ill.	1962–1965	"	1908–
Abe Fortas	Tenn.	1965–1969	Johnson	1910–
Thurgood Marshall	Md.	1967–	"	1908–
Harry A. Blackmun	Minn.	1970–	Nixon	1908–
Lewis F. Powell, Jr.	Va.	1971–	"	1907–
William H. Rehnquist	Ariz.	1971–	"	1924–
John Paul Stevens	Ill.	1975–	Ford	1920–

Index of Cases

Hirota v. *MacArthur,* 338 U.S. 197 (1948), 281

Hoag v. *New Jersey,* 356 U.S. 464 (1958), 476

Hoffa v. *United States,* 385 U.S. 293 (1966), 431

Hoke v. *United States,* 227 U.S. 308 (1913), 187

Holden v. *Hardy,* 169 U.S. 366 (1898), 524, 526, 532

Hollingsworth, v. *Virginia,* 3 Dall, 378 (1798), 27

Holmes v. *City of Atlanta,* 350 U.S. 879 (1955), 496

Holt v. *Sarver,* 309 F. Supp. 362 (1970), 474

Holt v. *United States,* 218 U.S. 245 (1910), 447

Holt v. *Virginia,* 379 U.S. 957 (1965), 85

Holtzman v. *Schlesinger,* 414 U.S. 1304 (1973), 272

Home Building and Loan Assn. v. *Blaisdell,* 290 U.S. 398 (1934), 515–516

Honda v. *Clark,* 386 U.S. 484 (1967), 284

Hood, H. P., & Sons v. *United States,* 307 U.S. 588 (1939), 154, 197

Hooven & Allison v. *Evatt,* 324 U.S. 652 (1945), 213

Hortonville Joint School Dist. v. *Hortonville Education Assn.,* 96 S. Ct. 2308 (1976), 331

Hospital Bldg. Co. v. *Trustees of Rex Hospital,* 96 S. Ct. 1848 (1976), 200

Hostetter v. *Idlewild Bon Voyage Liquor Corp.,* 377 U.S. 324 (1964), 214

Hoyt v. *Florida,* 368 U.S. 57 (1961), 464

Hudgens v. *NLRB,* 96 S. Ct. 1029 (1976), 321

Huffman v. *Pursue, Ltd.,* 420 U.S. 592 (1975), 119

Hughes v. *Superior Court of California,* 339 U.S. 460 (1950), 323

Humphrey's Executor v. *United States,* 295 U.S. 602 (1935), 247–248

Hunt v. *McNair,* 413 U.S. 734 (1973), 410

Hunter v. *Erickson,* 393 U.S. 385 (1969), 508, 549

Huntington v. *Attrill,* 146 U.S. 657 (1892), 76

Hurd v. *Hodge,* 334 U.S. 24 (1948), 489

Huron Portland Cement Co. v. *Detroit,* 362 U.S. 440 (1960), 212

Hurtado v. *California,* 110 U.S. 516 (1884), 417–418, 460

Hutcheson v. *United States,* 369 U.S. 599 (1962), 161

Hylton v. *United States,* 3 Dall. 171 (1796), 168

Hynes v. *Borough of Oradell,* 96 S. Ct. 1755 (1976), 322

Iannelli v. *United States,* 420 U.S. 770 (1975), 381

Illinois v. *Somerville,* 410 U.S. 458 (1973), 475

Imbler v. *Pachtman,* 96 S. Ct. 984 (1976), 106, 470

Income Tax Cases (see *Pollock* v. *Farmers Loan and Trust Co.*)

Indianapolis School Commissioners v. *Jacobs,* 410 U.S. 128 (1974), 331

Ingels v. *Morf,* 300 U.S. 290 (1937), 215

Insular Cases, The 182 U.S. 1, 222, 244 (1901), 68

International Brotherhood of Teamsters v. *Hanke,* 399 U.S. 470 (1950), 323

International Brotherhood of Teamsters, Local 695 v. *Vogt,* 354 U.S. 284 (1957), 323

International Shoe Company v. *Washington,* 326 U.S. 310 (1945), 415

International Textbook Co. v. *Pigg,* 217 U.S. 91 (1910),184

International Union v. *O'Brien,* 339 U.S. 454 (1950), 211

Interstate Commerce Commission v. *Brimson,* 154 U.S. 447 (1894), 186

Interstate Commerce Commission v. *Illinois Central R.R.*

Co., 215 U.S. 452 (1910), 153

Interstate Transit v. *Lindsey,* 283 U.S. 183 (1931), 215

Irvin v. *Dowd,* 366 U.S. 717 (1961), 121, 344

Irvine v. *California,* 347 U.S. 128 (1954), 436–437

Ivanov v. *United States,* 419 U.S. 881 (1974), 442

Jackson, Ex parte, 96 U.S. 727 (1878), 339

Jackson v. *Denno,* 378 U.S. 368 (1964), 450

Jacobellis v. *Ohio,* 378 U.S. 184 (1964), 355, 356

Jacobson v. *Massachusetts,* 197 U.S. 11 (1905), 393, 521, 532, 538, 542

James v. *Dravo Contracting Co.,* 302 U.S. 134 (1937), 174

James v. *Valtierra,* 402 U.S. 137 (1971), 549

Jamison v. *Texas,* 318 U.S. 413 (1943), 336

Jecker v. *Montgomery,* 13 How. 498 (1851), 274

Jefferson v. *Hackney,* 406 U.S. 535 (1972), 549

Jenison, In re, 125 N.W. 2d 588 (1963), 395

Jenkins v. *Georgia,* 418 U.S. 153 (1974), 360

Jiminez v. *Weinberger,* 417 U.S. 628 (1974), 552

John F. Kennedy Memorial Hospital v. *Heston,* 279 A. 2d 670 (1971), 400

Johnson v. *Avery,* 393 U.S. 483 (1969), 474

Johnson v. *Louisiana,* 406 U.S. 356 (1972), 466–467

Johnson v. *Mississippi,* 421 U.S. 213 (1975), 511

Johnson v. *New Jersey,* 384 U.S. 719 (1966), 456

Johnson v. *Robison,* 415 U.S. 361 (1974), 399

Johnson v. *United States,* 228 U.S. 457 (1913), 447

Johnson v. *United States,* 333 U.S. 10 (1948), 428, 429

Johnson v. *Virginia,* 373 U.S. 61 (1963), 496

Johnson v. *Zerbst,* 304 U.S. 458 (1938), 450

Joint Anti-Fascist Refugee Committee v. *McGrath,* 341 U.S. 123 (1951), 385, 412, 524

Jones v. *Alfred H. Mayer Co.,* 392 U.S. 409 (1968), 293, 497, 508, 549

Jones v. *Opelika,* 316 U.S. 584 (1942) 306–307, 396

Jones v. *United States,* 137 U.S. 202 (1890) 67

Jones v. *United States,* 357 U.S. 493 (1958), 428

Jones v. *United States,* 362 U.S. 257 (1960), 429

Jordan v. *Massachusetts,* 225 U.S. 167 (1912), 466

Joseph v. *Carter & Weekes Stevedoring Co.,* 330 U.S. 422 (1947), 215

Juilliard v. *Greenman,* 110 U.S. 421 (1884), 177

Jurek v. *Texas,* 96 S. Ct. 2950 (1976), 481

Kahn v. *Shevin,* 461 U.S. 351 (1974), 547–548

Kansas v. *Colorado,* 206 U.S. 46 (1907), 80, 152

Kastigar v. *United States,* 406 U.S. 441 (1972), 445

Katz v. *Tyler,* 386 U.S. 942 (1967), 271

Katz v. *United States,* 389 U.S. 347 (1967), 441, 442

Katzenbach v. *McClung,* 379 U.S. 294 (1964), 200–201

Katzenbach v. *Morgan,* 384 U.S. 641 (1966), 560

Kawakita v. *United States,* 343 U.S. 717 (1952), 424

Kedroff v. *St. Nicholas Cathedral of Russian Orthodox Church,* 344 U.S. 94 (1952), 400

Keifer & Keifer v. *Reconstruction Finance Corporation,* 306 U.S. 375 (1939), 111

Kemmler, In re, 136 U.S. 436 (1878), 479

Kennecott Copper Corp. v. *State Tax Commission,* 327 U.S. 573 (1946), 112

Kennedy v. *Mendoza-Martinez,* 372 U.S. 144 (1963), 469

Kennedy v. *Sampson,* 364 F. Supp. 1075 (1973), 511 F. 2d

Name and Subject Index